P9-DMD-263

The Decline of Laissez Faire

1897–1917

DISCARD

BETHANY
COLLEGE
LIBRARY

THE ECONOMIC HISTORY OF THE UNITED STATES

Edited by Henry David, Harold U. Faulkner, Louis M. Hacker,
Curtis P. Nettels, and Fred A. Shannon

THE DECLINE OF LAISSEZ FAIRE

1897—1917

By HAROLD U. FAULKNER

VOLUME VII

The Economic History of
the United States

M. E. SHARPE, INC.

Armonk, New York   London, England

Copyright 1951 by Harold U. Faulkner.

All rights reserved. No part of this book may be reproduced in any form without written permission from Holt, Rinehart and Winston, Inc.

This book was originally published as volume VII of The Economic History of the United States series by Holt, Rinehart and Winston in 1951. It is here reprinted by arrangement with Holt, Rinehart and Winston, Inc.

Library of Congress Cataloging-in-Publication Data

Faulkner, Harold Underwood, 1890-1968.
    The decline of laissez faire, 1897-1917.

    Reprint. Originally published: New York : Rinehart, c11951. (The economic history of the United States ; v. 7)
    Includes bibliographical references.
    1. United States—Commercial policy. 2. Tariff—United States—History. 3. Free trade—United States—History. 4. Protectionism—United States—History. 5. United States—Economic conditions—1865-1918. I. Title. II. Series: Economic history of the United States ; v. 7)
HF1455.F29   1989   330.973′091   89-10654
ISBN 0-87332-102-2

Printed in the United States of America

ED   10   9   8   7   6   5   4   3   2   1

Foreword

WHEN this series of nine volumes on the economic history of the United States was first conceived, the nation's economy had reached a critical stage in its development. Although the shock of the depression of 1929 had been partially absorbed, the sense of bewilderment which it produced had not yet vanished, and the suffering and the bitterness of its first years were being transformed into less substantial, though still anguished, memories. Reform measures, either in operation or proposed, were being actively debated, but with less sense of urgency than earlier.

To the Editors of this series a fresh consideration of America's economic history was justified by more than the experiences of the recent past or the obscurity of the future. Rich contributions to the literature of American history had been made through cooperative series dealing with the political, social, and cultural aspects of American life. Numerous single-volume surveys of the country's economic development have been written. But, as late as the end of the fourth decade of the twentieth century, the world's foremost economic power had not yet produced an integrated, full-length, and authoritative treatment of its own economic history.

Scholarly concern with American economic history has been constantly growing during the past half century, and chairs of economic history have been established in leading universities. A more profound understanding of the role of economic forces in the nation's history has not only been developed by historians and economists, but has also won some measure of popular acceptance. The earlier thin trickle of monographs has broadened in recent years into a flood of publications. At present, such specialized studies, the many collections of documentary materials, and the mountains of government reports on different facets of American economic life, are staggering in their richness and scope.

This series has been planned to utilize these available sources in the preparation of a full-scale, balanced, cooperative, and readable survey of the growth of American economy and of its transformation from one of primitive character to world pre-eminence in industry, trade, and finance. Clearly, in nine volumes all aspects of the nation's economic life cannot be treated fully. But such a series can point the way to new fields of study and treat authoritatively, if not definitively, the main lines of economic development. Further, the series is intended to fill a present need of those professionally concerned with American economic history, to supplement the economic materials now available in general school and college histories of the United States, and finally to provide the lay reader with the fruits of American scholarship. If these objectives are attained, then the efforts which have gone into the creation of this economic history of the United States will have been amply repaid.

Contributors to the series have been chosen who have already established their competence in the particular periods they are to survey here; and they are, of course, solely responsible for the points of view or points of departure they employ. It is not intended that the series represent a school of thought or any one philosophical or theoretical position.

The Decline of Laissez Faire, volume VII in *The Economic History of the United States,* offers an unusually rich and balanced account of the changes in American economic life between the turn of the present century and the First World War. Harold U. Faulkner's detailed treatment of a vast range of subjects rides no single thesis, but it develops with admirable coherence and clarity two central themes. One is the story of the growing size of the business unit in industry, transportation, public utilities, banking and finance, and other fields. The concentrations of economic power and the changes in the character and intensity of competition which accompanied the rise of the big enterprise and of consolidations and combinations provide a bridge to the second major theme. That may be expressed as the interventionist role of the government in the economy. Without forcing the argument, Professor Faulkner makes it quite clear that government promoted and encouraged, as well as regulated and controlled, activities in many segments of the economy to an extent which puts quite a different face upon the traditional picture of the so-called laissez-faire society of the first two decades of the twentieth century. Before the nineteenth century closed, the United States was the leading industrial nation in the world, but not the most industrialized.

Professor Faulkner gives proper weight to the place of agriculture in the country's economic life, and to the key developments affecting farm technology and holdings. Full attention is also paid to the place of the United States in the international economy, and such matters as foreign commerce and the import and export of capital are made an integral part of the economic changes at home. The institutional characteristics of finance capitalism and the role of the individuals who dominated its appearance are delineated sharply and without tendentious overtones. The complex story of population growth and of internal and external migration is related with a full sense of its wide-ranging economic implications.

Professor Faulkner's insistence that economic history deals with people and not with abstractions gives his narrative, as, for example, in the chapters dealing with the workers of the nation and the labor movement, a quality of reality and immediacy lacking in much of the literature in economic history.

THE EDITORS

Preface

AS with other volumes of this series, it has been impossible in the space allowed to cover every aspect of economic history. Even for a relatively full discussion, such as this, there must be some choice in emphasis, and that choice has rested chiefly on industry, labor, transportation, agriculture, finance, the movement of population, and foreign trade and investments. The development has been largely topical rather than chronological.

Acknowledgment of heavy indebtedness, particularly for statistical material, is made to the special studies of government agencies and of such research organizations as the National Bureau of Economic Research and the Brookings Institution. What value the book may have should be attributed in no small degree to the author's coeditors, whose varied interests did much to improve the presentation, integration, and interpretation of the enormous mass of data contained in the economic history of this period. The author has experienced a real satisfaction in doing this volume; these years have unusual significance in our history and have long held for him a particular interest.

HAROLD U. FAULKNER

Northampton, Massachusetts
March, 1951

Contents

Illustrations

Tables

The Decline of Laissez Faire
1897–1917

CHAPTER I

Economic America
at the End of the Century

A GLANCE AHEAD

AS the United States approached the end of the nineteenth century her capitalist economic society gave many indications that it had reached an advanced stage. In the thirty years after the Civil War the factory system, which had started in the years after the War of 1812, had developed as the cornerstone of an industrial revolution. As manufacturing shifted from the home to the factory and from the hand to the machine, the United States assumed the pattern of an urban industrialized nation. More than that, it took on the mold of later capitalist production. Following the depression of the middle nineties, industry pushed production to new and higher levels. It found wider markets at home and abroad; it gained from the increasing population, the abundance of immigrant labor, the advance of technology, and the application of science to production. Industry was also aided by a continued appearance of new products and improvements made in industrial technique and business management. If further stimulation was needed, it was provided by an abundance of capital, and an upward sweep of prices.[1]

As industrialization triumphed over an agricultural economy in a highly competitive environment, integration and concentration of industry followed. The "trust movement," which had its beginnings in earlier years, flowered at the end of the century with a new luxuriance. While small establishments grew into large ones, both large and

---

[1] Don D. Lescohier and Elizabeth Brandeis, *History of Labor in the United States* (New York: The Macmillan Company, 1935), p. 293.

3

small hastened to unite into great combinations. Big business was
aflame with the prospect of larger and easier profits which it believed
could be obtained by the simple formula of eliminating competition.
It was not long, however, before small business and the consumer
were again stricken with the same fear of the effects of this concentration of power which had aroused them in the 1880's.

The trends which dominated the industrial world were accompanied by a similar concentration in transportation, finance, and labor.
By the time the consolidation movement had reached its apex the
hundreds of little railroads, built during the previous half century,
had been combined into a few more or less permanent financial and
operating groups.[2] Nor had the financiers overlooked the possibilities
of uniting the transatlantic steamship lines, including the remnants of
what was once a prosperous American merchant marine.[3] Consolidation of industry and transportation by the very nature of its processes
was preceded or accompanied by an inevitable financial consolidation. At the same time it brought a shift in the control of production.
Industrial magnates relinquished the reins of industry to financiers
and bankers and the "age of finance capitalism" developed in
America.

Concentration of industry was followed by a similar but less
spectacular development of labor organizations. The labor movement
had its beginnings seventy-five years earlier and had reached considerable size and activity with the Knights of Labor, only to decline
in the years thereafter. Labor organization in 1897 was confined
almost entirely to the four railroad brotherhoods and the American
Federation of Labor, all together numbering 447,000 members. They
comprised not more than 4 per cent of the nonagricultural wage
earners. However, their influence and power, if one is to judge from
their subsequent rapid advance, were greater than their actual membership might indicate. The railroad brotherhoods, particularly, had
succeeded in keeping pace with the expanding railroad system and
in establishing a strong position. The American Federation of Labor,
on the other hand, had grown slowly during the first fifteen years of
its existence (1881–1896), but it had profited from the rough school
of experience and was now in a position to move forward rapidly

    [2] William Z. Ripley, *Railroads: Finance and Organization* (New York: Longmans,
Green and Co., 1915), p. 456.
    [3] Edward S. Mead, "The Capitalization of the International Mercantile Marine
Company," *Political Science Quarterly*, XIX, No. 1 (March, 1904), 50–65; reprinted
in William Z. Ripley, *Trusts, Pools and Corporations* (Boston: Ginn and Company,
1905), pp. 105–120.

during the next five years. It had superseded the Knights of Labor, and with the exception of the railway operating groups, now largely pre-empted the field of labor organization. "The year 1897," says Leo Wolman, "may conveniently be chosen as the beginning of the contemporary phase of the American labor movement." [4]

Agriculture as well as industry and labor was coming of age. Like industry, agriculture profited from an increasing population, an abundance of immigrant labor, and a widening market at home and abroad. Influenced by the end of the frontier, the findings of science, and the necessity for conservation, methods and viewpoints were changing. Notable influences included the impact of agricultural education and a beginning of the shift of farming technique from horse power to machine power. Agriculture from 1897 to 1917 achieved a relative stability and prosperity enjoyed but rarely in its history.[5]

No period has been more significant in transportation history or more pregnant with future possibilities than the first two decades of the twentieth century. In an expanding nation of vast distances concerned with long-haul movement of heavy commodities, the development of transportation facilities has been vital to progress. Americans had tackled this problem with energy and vision, and they had tried to solve it with turnpikes, river steamboats, canals, and steam railroads. The early decades of the new century saw the high point of the railroad and indications of its relative decline; the period also saw a revival of interest in internal waterways, both rivers and canals, and a renascence of road building. Of more significance, these years witnessed the invention of the practical automobile and airplane, presaging a significant revolution in transportation.

No aspect of the changing economic scene was more evident to the generation which saw the old century end than the advent of territorial expansion and economic imperialism. For almost three centuries America had been developed to no small extent through the influx of foreign capital. Tremendous industrial production, however, was piling up a surplus of capital wealth which might now be used for foreign investments. The United States began to follow the footsteps of older industrial nations in lending money abroad. This country, as will be seen,[6] continued to be a debtor nation until the First World War, but the pattern of her economic and political relations with the rest of the world had already rapidly changed.

[4] Leo Wolman, *The Growth of American Trade Unions* (New York: National Bureau of Economic Research, Inc., 1924), p. 29.
[5] Below, Chaps. XIII and XIV.
[6] Below, Chap. IV.

American economic history in the two decades preceding the First World War is not alone concerned with the growth of business consolidation, the rise of finance capitalism, the advent of economic imperialism, and significant developments in agriculture, transportation, and labor. It is also characterized by an effort to bring many of them under greater public control.[7] The country was disturbed by a restlessness, a discontent, and an eager desire to improve some of the worst aspects of its social and economic life. Americans during these years were in a mood to take stock of their resources, and to appraise the economic trends and their social effects. Many Americans refused any longer to accept without question the economic brigandage and ruthless exploitation which ushered in the new century. A wave of reform flowed over the country stronger than any which had occurred since the days of the Jacksonian democracy. This meant an extension of legislative control and government supervision. A history of the years after 1900 deals with the decline of laissez faire along with other momentous developments in the economic life. The years 1897 to 1917 marked an era both of expansion and of regulation.

THE TURN OF THE CENTURY

An attitude of confidence and buoyancy permeated America at the end of the century.[8] Forgotten by many were the lean years of the early eighties and the depression from 1893 to 1897. Pushed into the background for the moment were the bitter controversies over the tariff and railroad control which had raged in the eighties, and over the monetary system which had been almost continuous from the end of the Civil War to the campaign of 1896. Beginning in the last quarter of 1897, the nation began to work out of the five-year depression following the panic of 1893.

Excellent wheat, cotton, and corn crops, a reversal of the long downward trend of prices which had characterized the period since the Civil War, and a favorable balance of trade and exchange rates which reversed the outward flow of gold and safeguarded the gold standard—all these restored confidence and promoted an upward swing of the business cycle.[9] Along with this was the confidence en-

[7] Developed in detail in Harold U. Faulkner, *The Quest for Social Justice* (New York: The Macmillan Company, 1931).

[8] Frederick C. Mills, *Economic Tendencies in the United States* (New York: National Bureau of Economic Research, 1932), pp. 125–126.

[9] Willard L. Thorp, *Business Annals* (New York: National Bureau of Economic Research, 1926), pp. 136–138; O. M. W. Sprague, *History of Crises under the National Banking System* (Washington: Government Printing Office, 1910), pp. 191–195.

gendered among business leaders by the election of William Mc-Kinley in the epochal campaign of 1896. McKinley, long the political leader of the high-tariff interests, and now pledged to the maintenance of the gold standard, had been victorious over William Jennings Bryan, the nation's chief exponent of free and unlimited coinage of both gold and silver at a ratio of 16 to 1. In his defeat Bryan carried down with him the Populists who had indorsed him—the "wild radicals" of the West whose platform had called for government ownership of railroads, telegraphs, telephones, postal savings banks, a federal income tax, and direct election of senators as well as "free silver" and other forms of inflation.

Economic discontent, which had seethed continuously since the panic of 1873 and had found expression in the Greenback and Populist parties and in the Democratic uprising of 1896, seemed definitely quelled. Recovery would take place under the aegis of the Republican party pledged to a high tariff, the gold standard, and a close alliance with "big business." McKinley had been hailed during the campaign of 1896 as the "advance agent of prosperity." For once, hopes, prophecies, and promises were fulfilled and the presidency of McKinley was blessed with prosperity. Optimism spurred on the upswing of the business cycle. Stock and commodity prices pushed upward, wages increased, and business consolidation went merrily on. A short and easy war added a final impetus to economic prosperity. "In brief," said the *Commercial and Financial Chronicle* in 1897, "no one can study the industrial conditions of today in America without a feeling of elation." [10]

The optimism and confidence of the closing years of the century were reflected in the *Final Report* of the Industrial Commission.[11] Although the commission recognized many weak spots in the economic system, it took the position that the future would be better. Many of the difficulties, it believed, had been due to the tremendous changes which gave "too little time for ready accommodation to the new conditions" and which had resulted particularly in "suffering and disturbance to many employers and workmen alike." These, however, "were the 'growing pains' of the industrial system." The *Report* continued: "The prosperity of the average citizen has continually and rapidly improved through the whole period of transformation from the home and hand labor of earlier days to the factory

[10] *Commercial and Financial Chronicle*, LXV (December 4, 1897), 1046.
[11] *Final Report of the Industrial Commission*, Vol. XIX of the Commission's *Reports* (Washington: Government Printing Office, 1902).

and machine production of our own time, and the hardships caused to individuals and classes in some cases by sudden changes have been less than those which the entire community suffered before modern methods of production were introduced." The commission even rashly predicted that "the radical industrial changes of the nineteenth century and the crises and crashes which, at intervals of 10 to 20 years, have been their accompaniment, are likely to be less severe in the future." [12]

What did the nation look like at the end of the century? The population of continental United States, according to the Twelfth Census, was approximately 76,000,000, of which over three fifths lived in the North Atlantic and North Central divisions. Of this 76,000,000, slightly over 29,000,000 were listed as "breadwinners," distributed as follows: agricultural pursuits, 10,381,765; manufacturing and mechanical pursuits, 7,085,309; domestic and personal service, 5,580,657; trade and transportation, 4,766,964; professional service, 1,258,739.[13] Agricultural workers, operating over 5,700,000 farms remained the largest single group. Moreover, 59.8 per cent of the population still lived in areas of fewer than 2,500 inhabitants. These statistics, however, might easily obscure basic changes. By 1900 industry had assumed the leading role in American economy. The value of manufactured products in 1900, amounting to over $13,010,000,000, far surpassed the $4,717,000,000 estimated for agriculture.[14] Furthermore, urbanization was proceeding rapidly, as the surplus rural population migrated to industrial centers.[15] The movement toward the cities was not new; it was a phenomenon that had been continuous for a century.[16]

By 1900, commercial agriculture based on the productive facilities of the respective regions had become the pattern of American farming. Corn, hay, cotton and wheat, led the list of crops according to value, and to these basic commodities American farmers gave most of their attention. Rising prices of crops and farm land and increased domestic demand for cereals and meat products enabled farmers to participate in the prosperity and optimism so different from the dis-

[12] *Ibid.*, p. 537.

[13] U.S. Bureau of the Census, *Occupations of the Twelfth Census* (Washington: Government Printing Office, 1904). Also *Supplementary Analysis and Derivative Tables*, 1906, pp. 438–461.

[14] *Abstract of the Twelfth Census, 1900* (Washington: Government Printing Office, 1904), pp. 219, 300.

[15] Below, Chap. V.

[16] Arthur M. Schlesinger, *The Rise of the City, 1878–1898* (New York: The Macmillan Company, 1933), Chap. III.

couraging days of Populism. Travelers through the Middle and Trans-Mississippi West noted the signs of the growing prosperity in new buildings and equipment and in improved roads.[17] Machinery was reaching the farms in increasing amount and variety, but it was still almost exclusively horse-drawn equipment. Although this prosperity was widespread, it was not universal, if the depletion of certain rural areas is an indication. Two geographic sections, New England and the East North Central states, showed a decrease in rural population between 1900 and 1910, and this was again true of the East North Central states in the following decade.

Like agriculture, industry had pulled itself out of the doldrums following 1893 and was enjoying almost unprecedented peacetime prosperity. Industrial capital had increased by over three billion dollars since 1890 ($6,525,000,000 to $9,831,000,000) and value of products also by a like amount ($9,372,000,000 to $13,010,000,000). The number of establishments had grown almost 45 per cent in the decade.[18] All major sections of the country had shared in this growth, but the great center remained in the "manufacturing belt" running from New England and the Middle Atlantic states westward through the East North Central states. One development revealed by the Twelfth Census was significant—the growth of the metal industries. In 1860 the five most important manufactures ranked in value of their products were flour and meal, cotton goods, lumber planed and sawed, boots and shoes, and iron (cast, forged, rolled, and wrought); forty years later the most important five were iron and steel, slaughtering and meat packing, foundry and machine shop products, lumber and timber products, and flour and other gristmill products. In earlier decades American manufacturing was mainly concerned in the processing of the products of the farm and the forest. By 1900 the emphasis had shifted to products of the mines and efforts to service the machine age.

Agricultural and industrial production was supported by a foreign commerce which was active and prosperous in the late years of the nineteenth century. Exports of merchandise in 1900 amounted to over $1,394,000,000 and imports close to $850,000,000. This fat balance of trade, however, was partly equalized by large sums paid to Europeans for marine freight and insurance, dividends and interest paid to foreign stock and bond holders, and money sent home by immigrants and expended by American travelers. About 61 per cent

[17] Faulkner, *The Quest for Social Justice*, pp. 4–6.
[18] *Abstract of the Twelfth Census*, p. 300.

of exports were agricultural products (mainly cotton, wheat, and meat) and about 32 per cent were manufactured products. About three fourths of the exports went to Europe, chiefly foodstuffs and crude materials for use in manufacture.

Although foreign commerce was largely carried by British, German, French, and Scandinavian vessels, the vast structure of internal commerce was supported by 193,000 miles of railroads, an unsurpassed system of inland waterways, and almost 2,000,000 miles of wagon roads. But inland waterways, except on the Great Lakes, had declined in importance and relatively were little used. The great network of wagon roads was still limited in usefulness by the speed of the horse-and-buggy age. On city streets dray horses clumped heavily on brick, asphalt, or stone pavements of various types and in some cases drew the street cars along sunken rails. From the latter duty, however, they were being freed by electric trolley cars rapidly introduced on the streets of every city of any size.

In 1900, the wealth of the United States was estimated at about $88,500,000,000 (per capita about $1,165) and national income at $18,000,000,000.[19] The net ordinary government receipts approximated $669,595,000, of which over $233,000,000 came from tariffs and $295,000,000 from internal revenue.[20] The nation's business was carried through a somewhat confusing system of banking which included 3,732 national banks, over 4,000 state banks, about 1,000 savings banks, as well as private banks and loan and trust companies. Total deposits of all banks in 1900 were about $7,300,000,000. Some indication of the economic condition of the country may be seen from the fact that the savings banks had over 6,100,000 depositors with deposits amounting to about $2,300,000,000, an average of over $400 for each depositor.[21] Savings bank deposits, however, were distributed with extreme inequality, and were no true indication of a general prosperity.

THE ADVENT OF ECONOMIC IMPERIALISM

The revival of optimism and confidence which characterized the end of the century is best illustrated by the attitude of many Americans toward the rest of the world. They again began to talk of "mani-

[19] George W. Edwards, *The Evolution of Finance Capitalism* (New York: Longmans, Green and Co., 1938), p. 416; Willford I. King, *The Wealth and Income of the People of the United States* (New York: The Macmillan Company, 1923), pp. 13, 129.
[20] *Statistical Abstract of the United States*, 1901, p. 30.
[21] *Ibid.*, p. 68; *Statistical Abstract of the United States*, 1903, pp. 531–533.

fest destiny" and to exhibit a willingness for territorial expansion. This attitude helps to explain the Spanish-American War, the annexation of Hawaii, Puerto Rico, Guam, and the Philippines, the development of a sphere of influence in the Caribbean, and the formulation of a definite Far Eastern policy. Unlike the confident enthusiasm of the agrarian expansion of the 1840's which had taken the American people to the Pacific, the "manifest destiny" of 1898 was approached with caution and uncertainty. Behind it was the growth of a new philosophy and a decade of agitation, for the new imperialism meant extension of control beyond the continental boundaries and over alien races in distant lands. It meant annexation of new areas destined for defense and for economic exploitation rather than homes for an expanding population. It was an American expression of the new imperialism which had dominated western Europe since the 1870's.

Imperialist philosophy, as it developed in America, had many roots. Darwin's evolutionary thesis of the survival of the fittest had been picked up by the historian-philosopher John Fiske, by the Congregational clergyman Josiah Strong, by the political scientist John W. Burgess, and by many others who stressed the superiority of the Anglo-Saxon and the need to assume the "white man's burden." The Anglo-Saxon, asserted Strong, was "divinely commissioned to be in a peculiar sense, his brother's keeper." [22] It was only a step from Anglo-Saxon superiority and the "white man's burden" to overseas' expansion for national strength and economic power. Captain Alfred T. Mahan provided the argument. In his famous book, *The Influence of Sea Power upon History, 1660–1783,* and elsewhere, he expounded the theory that no nation without sea power could attain the greatest means of well-being or become important in world affairs. Sea power meant colonies with a merchant marine and a strong navy to protect them. [23] Mahan added little to the old mercantilist philosophy except his lessons from history drawn to prove his point, but his influence was great both in Europe and in America.

Henry Cabot Lodge and Theodore Roosevelt were, perhaps, his most persistent and influential followers, but there were many others. To what extent Mahan may have influenced President Harrison and his two Secretaries of State, James G. Blaine and John W. Foster, is unknown, but there is no doubt that they all worked harmoniously to promote American interests and sovereignty in the Caribbean and

[22] Josiah Strong, *Our Country: Its Possible Future and Its Present Crises* (New York: American Home Missionary Society, 1885), p. 161.

[23] Alfred T. Mahan, *The Interest of America in Sea Power, Present and Future* (Boston: Little, Brown & Company, 1897), pp. 4–27.

the Pacific. Moreover, the Republican party throughout the nineties veered consistently toward a stronger foreign policy, a policy that meant the expansion of American economic interests into foreign areas. In 1892 its platform pledged belief in "the achievement of the manifest destiny of the republic in its broadest sense." [24]

Nevertheless, it is doubtful if the rising consciousness of manifest destiny played a large part in the annexation of Hawaii. As McKinley remarked when he signed the joint resolution, July 7, 1898, which made Hawaii a territory of the United States, "Annexation is not change; it is consummation." Or, as Secretary of State John Sherman put it, it was the "destined culmination of the progressive policies and dependent associations of seventy years." [25] For more than half a century American traders and whalers had stopped at Hawaiian ports and American missionaries had labored on the Islands. By 1890 American sugar planters dominated its economic life. Hawaii's foreign trade in 1890 amounted to $20,104,000; three fourths of her imports came from the United States and she sent 99 per cent of her exports to the same country. In that year her exports to the United States were about $12,314,000 and her imports from the United States over $4,711,000. Her exports were mainly sugar, to be refined on the west coast by the Spreckels interests and consumed in that area. The close cultural and economic relations were recognized by a reciprocity treaty in 1875, which was renewed in 1887 with a clause giving the United States the exclusive right to use Pearl Harbor as a naval station. Hawaii by 1890 had become in fact "the fartherest extension of the American frontier." [26]

The close economic relationships had rested mainly on the export of sugar. This trade, made possible by the reciprocity treaties, had brought great prosperity to Hawaii. The favorable situation was suddenly upset by the McKinley Tariff of 1890, which not only put sugar on the free list, but provided a bounty of two cents a pound for American producers. There can be no doubt that the effect of the McKinley Tariff was disastrous. According to the United States minister, sugar prices in Honolulu fell from $100 to $60 a ton and property in the islands depreciated by at least $12,000,000. Moreover, exports to the United States decreased by more than one fourth between 1890

[24] Kirk H. Porter, *National Party Platforms* (New York: The Macmillan Company, 1924), p. 175.
[25] Albert K. Weinberg, *Manifest Destiny* (Baltimore: The Johns Hopkins Press, 1935), p. 261.
[26] Harold W. Bradley, "The American Frontier in Hawaii," Pacific Coast Branch of the American Historical Association, *Proceedings*, 1930, p. 150.

and 1892. One result of the McKinley Tariff was to encourage the movement for annexation. Nevertheless it would not be accurate to charge that the early movement for annexation was wholly a plot of the sugar magnates to obtain the two cents a pound bounty. Many of them, in fact, feared that annexation would end the contract system by means of which labor was obtained from the Far East to man their plantations. It was only after the revolt of 1893 that many of these planters were won over.[27]

Even without the problems of sugar, the economic drive was strong enough to explain the movement for annexation. American economic interests largely dominated the island and were growing restless under the autocratic and nationalistic rule of the native Queen Liliuokalani, who had assumed power in 1891. Hawaii's future seemed obviously linked with the United States and in January, 1893, certain white leaders of Hawaii, most of whom were Americans, organized a revolt with the encouragement of the American minister, John L. Stevens, and under the protection of American marines. "The Hawaiian pear," wrote Stevens to the State Department, "is now fully ripe and this is the golden hour for the United States to pluck it." [28]

Officially the Harrison administration had apparently done nothing to encourage the revolution, unless there was a secret understanding with Minister Stevens. Whether the latter existed or not, Harrison was now ready to pluck the pear, and a treaty of annexation between the successful revolutionary government and the United States was sent to the Senate. Before that deliberate body could act, the Harrison administration came to an end. The anti-imperialistic Cleveland withdrew the treaty, sent a special commissioner to investigate the situation in Hawaii, and, having received his report, sought to restore as far as practicable the *status quo* existing at the time of the *coup d'état*. Since this could be done only by force and in opposition to the general sentiment of the United States, Cleveland contented himself with turning the problem back to Congress, where both bodies passed resolutions of nonintervention.[29] In the next administration annexation was voted by joint resolution, but only after a treaty of annexation appeared doomed, and the Spanish-American War had intervened to speed action.

[27] Julius W. Pratt, *Expansionists of 1898* (Baltimore: The Johns Hopkins Press, 1930), pp. 155–160.

[28] *U.S. State Department, Foreign Relations,* 1894 (Washington: Government Printing Office, 1895), Appendix II, p. 402. Stevens to Foster. February 1, 1893.

[29] Allan Nevins, *Grover Cleveland* (New York: Dodd, Mead and Company, 1931), p. 552.

The debates on the new treaty and the joint resolution (approved July 7, 1898) developed nothing new in the way of arguments for annexation except the necessity for such action to aid in carrying on the war against Spain. The other arguments were those repeatedly used during the previous decade in behalf of expansion: commercial growth and supremacy in the Pacific depended on the possession of strategic coaling and supply depots; Hawaii was needed as a base to maintain a strong navy in the Pacific and protect the west coast; the annexation of Hawaii was part of the "manifest destiny" of the United States to extend its institutions into all corners of the earth. In any event, it was argued, the annexation of Hawaii was not a new policy, but simply the consummation of one that had been followed for many years.[30]

CUBA AND THE PHILIPPINES

The story of Cuba and the causes of America's declaration of war against Spain are more complicated. They, too, have economic causes, but they were more indirect than in the case of Hawaii and less important in bringing American entry into the Cuban civil war. As in the case of Hawaii, sugar provided the immediate background. By the 1890's Cuban economic life was based essentially on that commodity. The development in Europe of the beet sugar industry had forced Cuba to depend largely upon the American market for her outlet, and her prosperity rested mainly on the prices allowed by American tariffs and the American sugar trust. Under the McKinley Tariff, which removed all duties on raw sugar, and a reciprocity treaty of 1891, Cuba had prospered. The situation changed, however, in 1894 with the Wilson-Gorman Tariff, which restored the 40 per cent duty on raw sugar, automatically ended the reciprocity treaty, and plunged Cuba into a bitter depression. Depression brought low sugar prices, idle mills, unemployment, and a revolution in 1895. Under the circumstances, Cuban capital was won to the revolution and actively supported it.

By the nineties the United States had a very definite interest in Cuban economic life. Cuba was the chief source of her sugar supply, and in return took American foodstuffs and manufactured products. Trade between the United States and Cuba amounted in 1896 to

---

[30] Pratt, *Expansionists of 1898*, Chaps. V, VI. The most exhaustive study of Congressional attitudes and votes on Hawaiian annexation is in Barbara A. Morin, "The Reaction of Congress to the Annexation of Alaska and the Hawaiian Islands," a Smith College Master's Thesis, 1944.

about $100,000,000. Moreover, American capital investments in that island had grown to about $50,000,000, chiefly in sugar and tobacco plantations, and in iron mines. The Cuban revolution was disastrous to American property and complaints of property losses were continually at the forefront of negotiations between Spain and the United States. The "wholesale destruction of property on the Island," wrote Secretary of State Richard Olney to the Spanish minister in Washington in 1896, ". . . is utterly destroying American investments that should be of immense value, and is utterly impoverishing great numbers of American citizens." [31] Stewart L. Woodford, American Minister to Spain, later pointed out at Madrid that the United States raised only "one-tenth of the sugar we consume; that we are dependent upon other countries for nearly nine-tenths of the sugar we use; and that until the Cuban rebellion we obtained very much of our sugar from Cuba." The rebellion, he noted, had curtailed the market for "wheat, corn, meat and various manufactured articles with which we have hitherto supplied a large proportion of the wants of Cuba." [32] Cleveland, who prevented war during his own administration, was afraid that it might come eventually as the result of the activities of Americans in Cuba.[33] Although many Americans interested in Cuban sugar pressed the government to intervene to bring peace, there seems little evidence that they wanted more than this. None of them seemed to urge control, annexation, or strong imperialistic measures. Some even seemed afraid that intervention might lead to war and to conditions worse than those already existing.[34]

The point of view taken by certain economic historians that the United States went to war with Spain primarily for economic reasons seems not warranted by the evidence, unless the propaganda of the jingo press can be described as economic. This is said despite the fact that the United States had reached a stage of economic development in which economic expansion into foreign lands might presumably be a normal development in a capitalist economy, and despite the "manifest destiny" propaganda of Mahan and his followers. War spirit in America seems to have been largely stirred up by a jingoistic press, led by Joseph Pulitzer's New York World and William Randolph Hearst's New York Journal. Both of these exponents of "yellow journalism" used Spanish atrocities during the Cuban revolu-

[31] Olney to de Lome (April 4, 1896), Foreign Relations, 1897, p. 541.
[32] Woodford to Sherman (October 4, 1897), Foreign Relations, 1898, p. 572.
[33] Walter Millis, The Martial Spirit (Boston: Houghton Mifflin Company, 1931), p. 72.
[34] Pratt, Expansionists of 1898, pp. 248–252.

tion to increase circulation and whip up demand for intervention.[85] Hearst may never have sent instructions to the artist Remington, "You furnish the picture and I'll furnish the war," but he later boasted that he spent a million dollars to bring about the war.

Jingoism was popular not only with many newspaper owners, but with politicians of all the major parties and, as it turned out, with the people. Just what made the war so popular with the masses is difficult to say. In part it was undoubtedly an artificially stimulated sympathy for an oppressed people. It may have been a reaction from the long and grinding economic controversies of the eighties and nineties which found release in a crusade to free a persecuted people. Perhaps the end of the frontier had an influence in turning the eyes of Americans beyond their continental boundaries at a time when a series of gold rushes to Australia, South Africa, and the Klondike drew attention to distant adventure. The newspapers subtly channeled the restlessness into a demand for the war, and political pressure put it over.

Whatever the masses may have felt, American business as a whole opposed embarking on war. This can be seen in the attitude of such leaders as Mark Hanna,[36] and by the position taken by most financial and business journals.[37] So pronounced, in fact, was the antiwar attitude of Wall Street that it was charged with lack of patriotism. The reasons for this opposition seem to have been fear that war would endanger currency stability, interrupt trade, and threaten commerce. Years of depression were changing to prosperity in 1897; optimism pervaded the business world and no one wanted to reverse the trend. "It seems safe to conclude, from the evidence available," says Julius W. Pratt, "that the only important business interests (other than the business of sensational journalism) which clamored for intervention in Cuba were those directly or indirectly concerned in the Cuban sugar industry; that opposed to intervention were the influence of other parties (including at least one prominent sugar planter) whose business would suffer direct injury from war and also the overwhelming preponderance of general business opinion." [38]

Not only had most American businessmen reluctantly yielded to

[85] Millis, *The Martial Spirit*, Chaps. III, V; Marcus M. Wilkerson, *Public Opinion and the Spanish American War, a Study in War Propaganda* (Baton Rouge: University of Louisiana Press, 1932); and Joseph E. Wisan, *The Cuban Crisis as Reflected in the New York Press, 1895–1898* (New York: Columbia University Press, 1934), pp. 22–27.

[36] Herbert Croly, *Marcus Alonzo Hanna* (New York: The Macmillan Company, 1919), p. 278.

[37] Pratt, *Expansionists of 1898*, pp. 234 ff.

[38] *Ibid.*, p. 252.

a war with Spain, but in the months before the war they had shown little interest in acquiring colonies as markets for commodities or capital, or as sources for raw materials. The attitude seemed widespread that, if given a fair chance, American business could make its own way in the export market. This attitude, however, changed rather quickly with Dewey's spectacular victory at Manila Bay and with the encroachments of Japan and the European nations on the political integrity of China. Trade with China in 1897 was only 2 per cent of American foreign commerce, but even this might be curtailed unless steps were taken to foster it. Trade with the Philippine Islands was far less in that year: imports slightly less than $4,384,000 and exports $94,597. American business began to see the possibilities of trade expansion through foreign possessions and cooperated with imperialists in their propaganda for annexation of new territories.

By the end of the war the "large policy" was in the ascendant. The protocol (August 12) ensured the cession of Puerto Rico and an island in the Ladrones (eventually Guam) but left the future of the Philippines to be decided by the peace treaty. Although the Peace Commission which went to Paris in 1898 was weighted with expansionists, McKinley was by no means committed to annexation at that time. Nor was his final decision to insist on the entire archipelago motivated largely by economic imperialism. Probably the "white man's burden" argument was the principal influence that won him over.[39] But economic imperialism was certainly a leading objective of the "large policy" men, led by Lodge, Mahan, and Roosevelt, who kept up an unceasing pressure during the autumn of 1898.[40] The fateful decision was made on October 26, when Secretary John Hay cabled the commissioners that to leave any of the Philippines in Spanish hands could "not be justified on political, commercial, or humanitarian grounds. The cession must be the whole archipelago or none. The latter is wholly inadmissible and the former must therefore be required."[41]

The treaty of peace (signed December 10, 1898) reached the Senate on January 6. Although much of the discussion was behind closed doors, there was enough debate in open session to ascertain

[39] Charles S. Olcott, *William McKinley* (Boston: Houghton Mifflin Company, 2 vols., 1916), II, 108–111.

[40] On the peace treaty see Charles E. Hill, *Leading American Treaties* (New York: The Macmillan Company, 1922), pp. 314–346.

[41] U.S. State Department, *Papers Relating to the Treaty with Spain* (*Senate Document* No. 148, 56 Cong., 2 Sess., Washington: Government Printing Office, 1901), p. 35.

the arguments of both sides. Anti-imperialists attacked the annexation of the Philippines as unconstitutional, inexpedient, and dangerous. Some predicted only too accurately that it would embroil the United States in international difficulties in the Far East.[42] Others with similar accuracy challenged the economic value of a Far Eastern colony.[43] The Democrats saw a gloomier domestic future. Said their platform in 1900: "We assert that no nation can long endure half republic and half empire and we warn the American people that imperialism abroad will lead quickly and inevitably to despotism at home." Expansionists, on the other hand, chiefly stressed "manifest destiny," the hand of God, and the prospects of foreign trade.

Senators opposed to annexation, led by George Frisbie Hoar, Eugene Hale, Arthur Pue Gorman, and Richard F. Pettigrew, were by no means alone in their fight. Backing them was a strong Anti-Imperialist League, founded in Boston but soon nation-wide in its activities. Its membership included many of the most distinguished citizens of the nation—not alone reformers and "intellectuals," but politicians and business leaders. With adequate financial backing it maintained headquarters in Washington, circulated pamphlets and petitions opposing annexation, and maintained a ceaseless agitation. It drew support from the tobacco, beet, sugar, and other agricultural interests fearful of competition; from labor leaders like Samuel Gompers, who disliked many aspects of imperialism including the menace of cheap Oriental labor; from many who believed the whole expansionist experiment a dangerous thing; and from idealists who refused to abandon the Declaration of Independence and had no stomach for the forceful subjugation of the Islanders. As a whole the Democratic press and many independent papers, such as the *New York Evening Post,* the *Boston Herald,* the *Baltimore Sun,* and the *Springfield Republican,* opposed expansion. Nor should be forgotten the fact that both Democratic leaders, Cleveland and Bryan, were anti-imperialists.[44]

Despite a bitter battle, the treaty was ratified by the Senate on February 6; the vote was 57 to 27, a margin of one more than the required two-thirds majority. Amazingly enough, it was probably

[42] Pratt, *Expansionists of 1898,* p. 350.
[43] A. Whitney Griswold, *The Far Eastern Policy of the United States* (New York: Harcourt, Brace and Company, 1938), p. 33.
[44] Fred W. Harrington, "The Anti-Imperialist Movement in the United States, 1898–1900," *Mississippi Valley Historical Review,* XXII, No. 2 (September, 1935), 211–230, and "Literary Aspects of American Anti-Imperialism, 1898–1902," *New England Quarterly,* X, No. 4 (December, 1937), 650–667. American Federation of Labor, *Report of Proceedings,* 1898, pp. 26–27.

the anti-imperialist Bryan who was responsible for this narrow victory. During the midst of the fight he came to Washington to urge Democratic senators to vote for ratification. He believed the best policy was to make peace at once and later grant independence. Senator Hoar asserted that Bryan's purpose was to make imperialism the paramount issue in the campaign of 1900, but a more convincing explanation is that he hoped that the problem of imperialism (including Philippine independence) could be cleared away before the campaign and so make possible an emphasis on free silver.[45] The question still remains, of course, whether Bryan actually changed any votes.[46]

Undoubtedly all of the propaganda of "manifest destiny" played its part in the final decision. As Senator Albert J. Beveridge insisted later, we must "not renounce our part in the mission of our race, trustee, under God, of the civilization of the world." [47] The hope of economic advantage also counted heavily, for to many the Philippines would serve as "pickets of the Pacific, standing guard at the entrance of trade." [48] A more general explanation was the widespread feeling of nationalism arising from the patriotism and enthusiasm engendered by the war with Spain. Americans were inflamed by the thought of distant possessions and a world empire. To ardent expansionists the position of the anti-imperialists seemed negative rather than positive and idealistic rather than "practical." Expansionists won, in part because their opponents were never able to coalesce behind a single great political leader.[49]

Although imperialism triumphed in 1899, there is no certainty that the great majority of people favored it. The treaty was ardently backed by the administration, which gave it artificial strength. Like the annexation of Hawaii, it was a partisan measure, and this despite the fact that Republican senators took the leadership in opposing it.[50] It should be recalled that the Bacon resolution, which

[45] Merle Curti, "Bryan and World Peace," *Smith College Studies in History*, XVI, Nos. 3–4 (Northampton, Mass.: Smith College, April–June, 1931), 129–132.
[46] According to Erving Winslow, Secretary of the Anti-Imperialist League, "Senator Allen of Nebraska and Senator Jones of Nevada may have been gained to the Administration side by the 'tribune of the people,' though Senator Jones of Arkansas maintained to the last that Mr. Bryan had not caused the change of a vote." "The Anti-Imperialist League," *Independent*, LI, No. 2,633 (May 18, 1899), 1349.
[47] *Congressional Record*, January 9, 1900, 56 Cong., 1 Sess., Vol. XXXIII, Pt. 1, p. 704.
[48] Frank A. Vanderlip, "Facts about the Philippines," *Century Magazine*, LVI, No. 4 (August, 1898), 555.
[49] Harrington, "Anti-Imperialist Movement," p. 230.
[50] Pratt, *Expansionists of 1898*, pp. 357–358.

promised the Philippines their independence, failed by only one vote
—that of the Vice-President. Nor can much light be thrown on the
question by the campaign of 1900. There is little evidence in this
confusing election to show that imperialism was the burning and
paramount issue, as many historians have assumed, and that the
result was an endorsement of imperialism. True, Bryan started off
by denouncing colonialism, imperialism, and militarism, but when
he found his audiences apathetic, he shifted to trusts, plutocracy,
and special privilege. The mere fact that he held to his old platform
of "free silver" alone would have ruined any possible chance of success. Most of the voters were unresponsive and confused over the
numerous issues. For the moment the Philippine question was stale.
Issues were obscured by the Republican plea for a continuation of
prosperity, and this argument was the most powerful one used against
Bryan.[51]

THE DARKER SIDE OF THE DOMESTIC PICTURE

Optimism and confidence are normal attitudes in a prosperous
economy. What surprises the student without a full knowledge of
the background is the appearance within a few years of a wave of
criticism of existing conditions and widespread demands for reform.[52]
The dissatisfaction, however, had a background which gave validity
to the sudden attacks of the "muckrakers." The strong groups opposed
to territorial expansion were in themselves evidence of discontent
with dominant tendencies. Moreover, it was increasingly clear that
neither the Interstate Commerce Act of 1887 nor the Sherman Antitrust Act of 1890 had safeguarded the nation from the abuses of
monopolies and economic exploitation. Nor had the ethics of big
business improved greatly since the lush days of the "robber barons."
Organized labor was growing in size, but so also was the industrial
unit. Consolidation of business into great corporations, dominated
by opponents of organized labor, made it more difficult for labor to
organize the leading industries. The employer, profiting from the
influx of cheap labor from eastern and southern Europe, found himself in a strategic position to keep wages of unskilled labor low and
develop the various techniques of keeping the wage earner in sub-
jection. Hours were long and child labor persisted. One effect of

[51] Thomas A. Bailey, "Was the Presidential Election of 1900 a Mandate on Imperialism?" *Mississippi Valley Historical Review*, XXIV, No. 1 (June, 1937), 43–52.
[52] Below, Chap. XV.

consolidation, and with it the growth of absentee ownership, was to make the labor policies of corporations more harsh and impersonal.

America might be the land of opportunity and the over-all standard of living higher than in other nations, but conditions were far from satisfactory. Real wages, it is true, had increased during the years from the Civil War to the end of the century, but they were still low and were destined to improve little during the next decade.[53] Except for a minority of skilled workers, as will be seen later, few wage earners obtained an income beyond an existence level.[54] And there were millions below this level. Robert Hunter, after a careful study of the available data, concluded in 1904 that 10,000,000 persons (or roughly one eighth of the population) in the United States lived in poverty.[55]

Quite as sobering are the findings of students on the distribution of wealth. The per capita income and the per capita wealth were greater at this time in the United States than in Europe, but the distribution was not strikingly different. C. B. Spahr's careful study made in 1890 showed that seven eighths of the families held but one eighth of the wealth, and that 1 per cent of the families owned more than the remaining 99 per cent.[56] Studies made ten years later of estates probated in Wisconsin and Massachusetts revealed the same situation. Both point to the fact that fully 80 per cent of the people lived on the margin of existence while the wealth of the nation was owned by the remaining 20 per cent.[57]

In brief, all the abuses that followed the Civil War—monopoly conditions, irresponsible control of the economic life by big business, wasteful utilization of the nation's resources, exploitation of labor, all resulting in extremes of wealth and poverty—still persisted. To many, in fact, the prospects for the future looked darker than the past. The battle for economic and political reform waged in 1896 seemed lost and the nation committed to laissez faire and a continuation of older ideals and methods. By contrast, the first fifteen years of the new century developed a wave of reform which influenced every phase of American social and economic life.

[53] Paul H. Douglas, *Real Wages in the United States, 1890–1926* (Boston: Houghton Mifflin Company, 1930), pp. 389–400.

[54] Below, Chap. XI.

[55] Robert Hunter, *Poverty* (New York: The Macmillan Company, 1904), pp. 59–62.

[56] C. B. Spahr, *The Present Distribution of Wealth in the United States* (New York: Thomas Y. Crowell Company, 1896), p. 69.

[57] King, *The Wealth and Income of the People of the United States*, pp. 72–87, 90–115.

CHAPTER II

The Business Cycle and the
Rise of Finance Capitalism

THE UPSWING OF THE BUSINESS CYCLE OF 1897–1907

BY the end of 1897 the nation was definitely working out of the slough of an economic depression which had started with the panic of 1893 and reached its lowest point, except for agriculture, in 1894. "A retrospect of 1897," said the *Financial Review,* "is much more pleasing and encouraging than was the similar retrospect of 1896. The year was marked by a decisive recovery in business . . . and at the year's close we find the outlook more hopeful than for many years past." [1] The corner had been turned, and, with the exception of the so-called "rich-man's panic" of 1903, economic prosperity continued until 1907. National wealth estimated at $88,500,000,000 in 1900 expanded to $351,700,000,000 by 1917, while income increased from $18,000,000,000 to $51,300,000,000 (current dollars). [2]

Although the defeat of "free silver" in the election of 1896 and the subsequent passage of the Gold Standard Act of 1900 contributed to the restoration of confidence in the financial world, they were by no means the primary causes for the upswing of the business cycle. This is even more true of the Dingley Tariff of 1897, which raised the rates to unparalleled heights. In itself the new tariff neither solved at the moment the government's financial needs nor promoted industrial activity. Prosperity came in spite of the Dingley Tariff rather

[1] *The Financial Review, 1898,* p. 1. Published annually by the William B. Dana Company, publishers of the *Commercial and Financial Chronicle.*

[2] Willford I. King, *The Wealth and Income of the People of the United States* (New York: The Macmillan Company, 1923), pp. 13, 129, and *The National Income and Its Purchasing Power* (New York: National Bureau of Economic Research, 1930), p. 74.

than because of it.[3] It came, in fact, as a result of conditions over which Americans had virtually no control. The most important cause of the upward turn was the tremendous demand in Europe for American wheat. Drought in France, floods and storms in Austria, Russia, and the Balkans had reduced the European crop of 1897 some 30 per cent (350,000,000 bushels) under that of 1896. Fortunately for both Europe and America, the American harvest of 1897 was unusually large. About 150,000,000 bushels of wheat were exported in the twelve months after the harvest of 1897, an amount almost twice that of 1896, with a value at least $122,000,000 over the previous year. The increased export of wheat contributed chiefly during 1898 to an import of $120,000,000 in gold, "the first movement of the kind in this direction since the autumn of 1891." [4]

This turn of events brought important results; the flood of gold contributed to the success of the Gold Standard Act and it helped to revive the general trade, particularly in the grain-growing West. The gold standard was also aided by the doubling of the world's production of gold in the years after 1896, a development which brought inflation and aided agriculture. Nor should be forgotten an extensive national bank note inflation before 1897. Increased expenditures resulting from the Spanish-American War in 1898 also gave impetus to a revival which had already begun. One result of this revival of American economic activity was the increased investment of European capital in the United States. Although some liquidation occurred in 1898 and 1899, foreign investments in this country almost doubled between 1899 and 1908—from $3,145,000,000 to $6,000,-000,000. This was a more rapid increase than that of the national wealth of the country and more rapid than at any time except during the 1850's and 1860's. These investments moved closely with the expansion of American investment markets.[5]

America profited not only from the bad European wheat crop of 1897, but also from the fact that Europe's recovery from the panic of 1893 had preceded recovery in the United States. By 1897 Europe enjoyed such prosperity that her own factories could not keep up with the demand. American factories with their own production restricted through lack of a domestic market, but with an abundance of labor

[3] Alexander D. Noyes, Forty Years of American Finance (New York: G. P. Putnam's Sons, 1909), pp. 267–270.

[4] Ibid., pp. 271–272.

[5] Cleona Lewis, America's Stake in International Investments (Washington: The Brookings Institution, 1938), pp. 154–155, 523–531, 560. The estimates of 1899 are those of Nathaniel T. Bacon; those of 1908 were made by Sir George Paish.

and raw materials, quickly turned to foreign markets. The result was an increased exportation of many commodities which pushed the total export trade in 1897 over the billion-dollar mark for the first time. It reached $1,500,000,000 in 1901. This sudden expansion in export trade brought with it an excess of exports over imports which reached $286,000,000 in 1897 and $615,000,000 in 1898. Such an unusual balance of trade resulted in a pressure of domestic capital in the home investment markets and raised prices of American securities high enough to induce Europeans to sell back some of their American holdings. With an excess of free capital in the United States and with England engaged in a costly South African war, Americans actually purchased over $200,000,000 of the British war loans and bought at least $30,000,000 of other European government bonds. It appeared for a brief period that the direction of capital flow had been reversed and it was predicted that New York would displace London as the financial center of the world.[6]

One important effect of the favorable balance of trade and the flow of capital to the United States was the opportunity given for the financial and material reconstruction of the railroad system. The panic of 1893 had left almost one quarter of the country's railroad mileage bankrupt and much of the rest in a deteriorated condition.[7] But American railroad transportation had by no means reached the end of its expansive power. Moreover, it was necessary to keep in repair the 184,000 miles already built in 1897. Reorganization, re-capitalization, consolidation, and rehabilitation went on with great rapidity after 1896. In 1895, at least 169 railroads representing 37,856 miles of track and a capitalization of $2,439,000,000 were in the hands of receivers. By 1900 these figures had been reduced to 52 railroads, with a mileage of 4,178 and a capital of $251,000,000.[8] In 1898 railroads sold $67,000,000 worth of securities mainly for physical reconstruction, $199,000,000 worth in 1900, and $527,000,000 in 1902. This reconstruction was forced both by the deterioration after the panic of 1893 and by the rise in railroad traffic in 1897. Between 1895 and 1900 net earnings of American railroads increased 50 per cent and dividends doubled.[9]

[6] Noyes, *Forty Years of American Finance*, p. 283.

[7] Interstate Commerce Commission, *Seventh Annual Report of the Statistics of Railways in the United States*, 1894 (Washington: Government Printing Office, 1895), p. 10, and for 1895, pp. 10, 107–109.

[8] Interstate Commerce Commission, *Statistics of Railways in the United States*, 1900, p. 11.

[9] Noyes, *Forty Years of American Finance*, pp. 279, 290.

Although the rehabilitation of railroads helped many groups, the chief benefits went to the iron and steel industry. The introduction of larger cars and locomotives called for heavier rails, new bridges, and new terminal facilities.[10] Old railroads such as the Union Pacific were virtually rebuilt, and new mileage to the extent of 3,400 a year (1897–1902) was constructed. The iron industry profited not only from enlarged exports and railroad construction, but also from the introduction of the steel frame for large city buildings and the general progress of invention. Since iron and steel was the basic industry, its improvement stimulated the entire economic life of the nation.

These influences already noted, plus a resumption of large-scale immigration and increasing urbanization, explain American recovery. So rapid, thorough, and comprehensive was it that by 1900 the capital market was glutted with money for investment and speculation. Since real wages were barely holding their own, these funds were coming mainly from the upper middle and wealthy classes. Savings bank deposits, however, grew by 4.8 per cent annually, and insurance companies developed new methods of tapping the wage earner as well as other groups. Bank operations expanded more rapidly than other general fields of economic operations. The railroads took a good slice of these funds for rehabilitation, for reorganization, and for watered stock. Then into the industrial field came promoters of new companies, reorganizers of old ones, and consolidators of existing ones, often companies already quite prosperous and in no need of reorganization or consolidation. In 1897 there were 20 "trusts" or large consolidations, but the census of 1900 listed 185 manufacturing consolidations with a capitalization of $3,000,000,000, and Moody in 1904 reported 445 such trusts with a capitalization of over $20,000,-000,000.[11] The climax, as we shall see, came in 1901 with the formation of the billion-dollar steel trust and the battle between Harriman and Morgan over control of the Northern Pacific.

As the investing and speculating public with little discrimination gobbled up both good investments and watered stocks, it seemed clear by the late spring of 1901 that many purchasers had lost their heads in a mania of speculation and easy profits as they did again in the late 1920's. Daily sales on the stock exchange, which in the late

[10] Henry Clews, *Fifty Years in Wall Street* (New York: Irving Publishing Co., 1908), p. 773.
[11] John Moody, *The Truth about the Trusts* (New York: Moody Publishing Company, 1904), p. 488.

1890's had sometimes reached 400,000 a day, climbed by April 30, 1901, to 3,250,000. Total shares for the week rose to over 14,500,000.[12] This activity was obviously dominated by professional speculators, "big shot" financiers, and the new millionaires created by the current consolidations, but there is ample evidence that the little speculator and the general public were participating. "Our daily newspapers," said the *Commercial and Financial Chronicle*, "have for weeks been full of descriptions which we believe were not exaggerated, of the crowds of petty speculators who hang about the tape in the commission brokers' offices and in the 'bucket shop,' including in many instances, by all appearances, people who could not afford to lose and who were speculating only because they could not fail to win." Then it comments that "the presence of women in unusual numbers in these speculative gatherings has been one of the most extraordinary features of the episode." [13] All this, it should be remembered, developed in spite of dampening influences, such as the revival of the "free silver" issue in the McKinley-Bryan campaign of 1900, and the decline in export orders and the price of steel in that year.

This speculating mania reached its climax on May 9, 1901, when it was discovered that in the battle for control of the Northern Pacific, Edward H. Harriman and J. Pierpont Morgan had contracted for more stock than could be bought or borrowed. The market was cornered and the price of the stock jumped in an hour from 160 to 1,000. To save a panic, the giants called a truce and the market ferment subsided. There was plenty of speculation in the years that followed, but it was some time before it reached the buoyant optimism of 1901. In addition to the close call experienced in the Northern Pacific battle, a number of factors tended to dampen the ardor: the wiping out of the foreign credit balances, the flow of gold to Europe in the autumn of that year when it should have been coming to America, the failure of Amalgamated Copper to maintain an artificial price, and the poor corn crop.

Although business was generally good in 1902, the money market gradually tightened. That, combined with the growing distrust of investors in new consolidations, made it difficult to float new stock issues. Morgan called these unbought stocks "undigested securities," but James J. Hill, with more realism, called them "indigestible securities." It was already evident that consolidation alone did not assure

---

[12] Noyes, *Forty Years of American Finance*, p. 301; *Commercial and Financial Chronicle*, LXXII (May 4, 1901), 842.

[13] *Commercial and Financial Chronicle*, LXXII (May 11, 1901), 903.

higher profits; in most cases the effect had been quite the contrary.[14] The passing of dividends by the United States Steel Corporation in 1903, the inability to consummate important consolidations, and the failure of numerous concerns, including the United States Shipbuilding Corporation, one of the most fantastic of all the consolidations, led to the stock market panic of that year.[15] Fortunately the panic was largely confined to the stock market. It was, as it has often been described, a "rich men's panic." As a whole, economic conditions were fundamentally sound, and the nation quickly recovered, to press onward until overtaken by the more serious panic of 1907. The year 1903 was "merely an interlude in the cycle of prosperity." [16]

Many factors helped in the continued prosperity: resumption of gold production in South Africa at the end of the Boer War as well as increased production in Alaska and Australia, followed by higher prices and higher wages; excellent crops, particularly in 1905 and 1906; and increased foreign exports. They also helped to revive speculation on the stock exchange and elsewhere. Two other factors particularly encouraged the revival of speculation. The first was the large surplus reserves accumulated in the New York banks as a result of the slowing up of speculative activity after the panic of 1903, a huge reservoir which could be drawn on.[17] Another was the world-wide mania for speculation which encouraged that in America. The orgy of speculation from 1899 to 1903 was largely limited to the United States; that from 1904 to 1907 was world-wide.[18]

Events counteracting these bullish factors were the Russo-Japanese War, the dwindling of bank reserves and the tightening of money after late 1905, and the lagging of wages behind prices. There was also the dampening influence of much public disapprobation with the methods of big business which often led to state and federal investigations and new legislation. By 1907 the "muckrakers" were actively attacking big business, Congress had passed the Hepburn Act to strengthen railroad control, and the New York legislature had investigated life insurance companies and passed laws to remedy some of the worst practices. All this may have been one reason why the hectic speculation which preceded the panic of 1907 was largely limited to professionals and to the wealthy, and why general partici-

[14] Arthur S. Dewing, *Financial Policy of Corporations* (New York: The Ronald Press Company, 1934), pp. 746–775.

[15] Clews, *Fifty Years in Wall Street*, Chaps. LXVIII–LXIX.

[16] Noyes, *Forty Years of American Finance*, p. 312.

[17] Clews, *Fifty Years in Wall Street*, pp. 774–775.

[18] Noyes, *Forty Years of American Finance*, pp. 323–329; Willard L. Thorp, *Business Annals* (New York: National Bureau of Economic Research, 1926), pp. 139–140.

pation was limited. A more likely reason for the decline of wider participation was the immense amount of economic activity throughout the nation—more than enough to absorb the funds of the smaller businessman without his entering the stock exchange.

Like the panic of 1903, that of 1907 was also to a large extent a rich men's panic, but its effects were more severe, and it continued longer. By late 1906 stock market speculation was again beginning to get out of bounds. It was stimulated by upward of $500,000,000 obtained from Europe, by heavy capital movements from the interior banks to New York, and by the heavy purchases of Union Pacific and of other railroad stocks after the Union Pacific had unexpectedly increased its dividends from 6 to 10 per cent. By fall, however, credit was strained. New York banks in September reported a deficit in reserves and only aid from the United States Treasury and the importation of gold from England kept the structure from tottering. Railroads committed to expansive improvement programs, and unable to obtain funds from the banks, began large-scale selling of stocks in March of 1907. There was also evidence that important financiers were liquidating their investments.

Many straws in the wind pointed toward trouble. England admitted a serious credit stringency late in 1906. Panics in Egypt in April, 1907, in Japan in May, and in Germany in October made it clear that economic difficulties were world-wide. Tightening money and bankruptcies in the late spring as well as the inability of New York City twice during the summer to float a loan offered for public subscription showed that credit had been strained to a breaking point. This was also made clear by the failure in early autumn of the $52,000,000 New York street railway combination and shortly after by that of the $34,000,000 Westinghouse Electric Company.[19]

More than a year after the crash, the leading financial journal undoubtedly gave voice to the feelings of many a Wall Street financier when it emphasized the "antecedent loss of confidence." Said the *Commercial and Financial Chronicle:* "Adverse legislation, national and State, directed against railroads primarily, but also against corporations generally; political attacks against men of wealth and men of capital; the serious advocacy of political and economic doctrines which would completely change the theory of our Government and revolutionize social relations—these and kindred matters had threatened the security and stability of investment values."[20] One shrewd

[19] Noyes, *Forty Years of American Finance*, pp. 364–365.
[20] *Commercial and Financial Chronicle*, LXXXVIII (January 2, 1909), 5.

broker, who had spent a lifetime on Wall Street, found causes that were closer to the truth. He noted that stocks had reached too high a price relative to interest rates on money, that capital was moving into real estate and other fixed forms, thereby losing its liquid quality, that big operators, realizing that prices were abnormally high, had dumped $800,000,000 worth on the market, and that the Knickerbocker Trust Company had failed because of injudicious loans. He mentioned the San Francisco earthquake with losses amounting to $350,000,000 and the shock to public confidence through disclosures in the life insurance investigations and in the investigations of the Metropolitan Street Railroad and the Chicago and Alton manipulation.[21] These and other factors doubtless had a more profound influence in halting the upward swing of the business cycle than adverse legislation and political attacks.

Tight money and declining confidence were primary causes, but there can be no doubt that it was the extraordinary strain on the credit facilities of the New York banks and trust companies that gave the immediate impetus to the panic and depression.[22] By 1907 a number of the New York banks of second rank had come under the control of F. Augustus Heinze, Charles W. Morse, and other financiers who were using their resources largely for speculative purposes. One of them, the Mercantile National of New York City, controlled by Heinze, encountered heavy withdrawals, when the market for the United Copper Company (of which Heinze was president) collapsed, dragging to failure two stock exchange houses. The Mercantile National applied on October 16 to the other banks of the clearinghouse for aid. A committee investigated, found that the bank's trouble was due to copper share speculation, but offered to help on condition that the directors resign.[23] As news ᴐ: this leaked out, worried depositors began a run on other banks, particularly the Knickerbocker Trust Company, whose president, Charles T. Barney, had resigned on October 21. The trust companies, as will be seen, were in a particularly vulnerable position and least able to weather the storm.

The Knickerbocker Trust Company was forced to close its doors on October 22 and the next day almost every trust company in the

[21] Clews, *Fifty Years in Wall Street*, p. 799.

[22] This is emphasized in William C. Schluter, *The Pre-War Business Cycle, 1907–1914* (*Columbia University Studies in History, Economics and Public Law*, CVIII, No. 1 (New York: Columbia University Press, 1923), 13–14.

[23] Clews, *Fifty Years in Wall Street*, pp. 790–791; Wesley C. Mitchell, *Business Cycles and Their Causes* (Berkeley: University of California Press, new ed., 1941), pp. 74–77.

city was besieged by panic-stricken depositors. J. Pierpont Morgan and a committee of the clearinghouse stepped in to lend their aid to solvent banks. Secretary of the Treasury George B. Cortelyou deposited $35,000,000 of the government surplus with the national banks and every possible means was used to increase the gold supply and other monetary mediums, notably by Clearing House Loan Certificates.[24] The New York City banks were not the only ones under pressure from local panic-stricken depositors; moreover, they held $470,000,000 owed to other institutions, mostly out of town. About a dozen of the smaller banks and trust companies in New York failed, but heroic efforts managed to save two of the largest, the Lincoln Trust Company and the Trust Company of America. Savings banks survived by taking advantage of the sixty and ninety days' time allowed for the payment of deposits after notice.

THE PREWAR BUSINESS DECLINE

The depression following the banking panic of 1907 was acute. Iron production during the first half of 1908 was 50 per cent less than in 1907, and railroad traffic receipts for the full year 1908 were over 11 per cent less. Foreign trade declined; prices of commodities, both raw materials and finished goods, slumped; prices on the stock market dropped one third; bankruptcies and unemployment increased. Both money earnings and real earnings of labor declined in 1908. The acute state of the depression, however, was relatively brief. By the middle of 1908, liquidation had largely run its course, the downward trend of prices had halted, and the banks, now supplied with increased reserves, were offering cheap credit. Inflated security prices, worthless paper, weak banks, and overstocked inventories had been eliminated. Good crops, improved railroad earnings, and increased construction helped the upward movement. Financiers and speculators, refusing to believe that a long depression had started, were back in the market offering new securities and playing stocks for a rise.[25] Throughout 1909 many of the indications of a sound recovery were in evidence, and this despite the fact that Europe offered little encouragement.[26]

The upswing of 1909 was of brief duration. It was followed by a

[24] Mitchell, *Business Cycles and Their Causes*, pp. 77–83; Abram P. Andrew, "Substitutes for Cash in the Panic of 1907," *Quarterly Journal of Economics*, XXII (August, 1908), 497–516.
[25] Schluter, *The Pre-War Business Cycle*, pp. 13–34.
[26] *Ibid.*, p. 54.

depression in 1910–1911, a second upswing in 1912, and a relapse in 1913. The upset of 1907 had proved more fundamental than had been supposed. From that year until America felt the impact of war prosperity in 1915, American economic history was largely one of brief spurts and recessions. To find one's way through the maze of conflicting causes and effects is not easy. The most detailed study made of these minor fluctuations lays the primary cause upon the "inefficient and inelastic nature of our credit system." [27] The American banking structure proved without question of doubt its inadequacy to deal with the problems of a modern industrial society, particularly one which was expanding rapidly and which normally needed an increased volume of credit.

An inefficient and inelastic credit system, however, was by no means the only cause for the unstable condition of American economic life between 1907 and 1914. High finance had overloaded railroads and other corporations with fantastic capital structures; industrial "trusts," as in the case of United States Steel after the panic of 1907, were reluctant to adjust prices to decreasing demand. Wages were barely keeping up with the increased cost of living, whereas unemployment in manufacturing and transportation amounted to 12 per cent or over in 1908, 1914, and 1915. One series of alleged causes for these constant economic fluctuations, causes upon which Wall Street and the financial interests laid so much weight, has been largely discounted by economists. Exposures of muckrakers, government investigations, antitrust prosecutions, and even federal and state legislation seem to have had little or no effect. [28] If regulatory legislation sporadically worried business magnates and stock market speculators, it also inspired greater confidence on the part of disillusioned investors both here and abroad. Antitrust suits apparently had practically no effect on the earnings of corporations. The Hepburn Act actually aroused such confidence on the part of European investors that millions poured in for railroad securities, exciting Morgan, Hill, and Harriman to vaster schemes of consolidation and extension. [29]

Whatever the causes for these minor advances and recessions, the year 1912 was one of prosperity. With its large crops, increased exports of agricultural commodities and manufactured goods, unprecedented iron production, and large imports of gold, most economic

[27] *Ibid.*, pp. 103, 173.
[28] *Ibid.*, pp. 33, 126.
[29] Noyes, *Forty Years of American Finance*, pp. 353–354.

signs pointed to "genuine industrial recovery." [30] Instead, there came a relapse into business uncertainty and financial discouragement. Wall Street ascribed it to the reductions in the Underwood Tariff of 1913, to the refusal of the Interstate Commerce Commission to grant higher freight rates to the railroads, to uncertainty over the proposed banking bill, and generally to the "radical tendencies" evident (so they claimed) in Washington. Added to this was the Democratic victory of Wilson in November, 1912. Alexander Noyes, on the other hand, believed that a "far more convincing explanation" was the outbreak of the Balkan War in 1912, its effect upon the financial markets of Europe, and the reaction of this upon America.[31]

In Europe, the Balkan War had the usual effect upon the money market: an increase in discount rates, sale of securities, withdrawal of gold, and importation of it from the United States. In America, however, there appeared to be little or no effect. When the conflict ended late in 1913, even the European financial world showed little appreciation of the fact that this might be a curtain raiser to a greater war. Confidence quickly returned, money eased, discount rates were lowered by the great banks of Europe and America; demand loans on the New York Stock Exchange commanded only 2 per cent five days before the First World War broke out. A vigorous speculative advance was evident even in the early months of 1914 on both the London and New York stock exchanges. This favorable financial picture, however, was not duplicated in the commercial and industrial world, particularly in America. The world saw no revival in trade and industry. In the United States the recession of 1913 sank into a depression in 1914 with an increase in gold exports, a decline in foreign trade, a weakening of commodity prices, and an increase in unemployment.[32]

ECONOMIC RESULTS OF THE EUROPEAN WAR

Germany's ultimatum to France and Russia on July 31 and Britain's declaration of war on August 5 deepened the American depression. The first effect was temporarily to ruin the export trade. With a wheat crop 21 per cent higher than in any previous year, exports dropped sharply. Instead of the traditional rise in wheat prices at the opening of war, cash prices at Chicago dropped from 95 1/2 cents

[30] Alexander D. Noyes, *War Period of American Finance, 1908–1925* (New York: G. P. Putnam's Sons, 1926), p. 16.
[31] *Ibid.*, pp. 17–20.
[32] Thorp, *Business Annals*, pp. 141–142.

a bushel on July 30 to 85 1/4 by August 30. The situation for cotton looked even worse. Although the United States at that time exported about one fifth of its wheat crop, it exported three fifths of its cotton. Half of the cotton exports went to England, France, Belgium, and Russia; another quarter went to Germany. Within two months after the war began, cotton exports virtually ceased. In a similar manner the exports of such industrial products as copper, steel, meat, and oil declined. United States Steel, which produced over 90 per cent of capacity at the end of 1912, now operated at barely 30 per cent. The copper market was completely demoralized. American railroads experienced a serious decline in gross earnings every month of the year except March. At the same time the United States was cut off from important foreign metals and German dyes.[33]

To the financial world the declaration of war brought a demoralization quite as complete as that in commerce and industry. European governments declared moratoria on debts, prohibited the exportation of gold, and resorted to paper money. Stock exchanges all over the world closed their doors, even the London Stock Exchange, which had never before suspended business. Fearing that the full force of the selling market would converge on New York, wipe out values, and bring catastrophe, the New York Stock Exchange followed the example of London on July 31. The selling of bonds and a restricted business in stocks were finally resumed on November 28 and December 15. Not until April, 1915, however, was the exchange opened to unrestricted trading in stocks. Nevertheless, several hundred million dollars worth of American securities held abroad were sold on the New York Stock Exchange before it closed.

Undoubtedly the closing of the stock exchange contributed materially to the strengthening of the position of the American banks by preventing the evaporation of stock values used as collateral. The banks, however, faced serious problems. The first was the danger that frightened depositors, as in 1907, might start wholesale withdrawals. The drain was indeed large, but the banks met the problem in two ways. As in earlier panics, the banks issued clearinghouse certificates by which balances owed by one bank to another might be discharged with certificates of debt rather than with cash. These certificates amounted in New York at the end of September to over $109,000,000, a sum larger than in 1907. In the second place the bankers took advantage of the Aldrich-Vreeland Emergency Currency Act (1908), passed as the result of the panic of 1907. This act, which was to

[33] *Financial Review, 1915,* pp. 7–12.

terminate June 30, 1914, had fortunately been renewed for another year. A tide-over measure until the Federal Reserve System could be organized, it made available $500,000,000 in currency to national banks organized as "national currency associations" upon deposit of United States bonds or other qualified securities or commercial paper. Quite similar to the later Federal Reserve notes, this currency met the emergency, and $363,632,080 were outstanding in October, 1914.[34] As depositors discovered that money was available, the "runs" subsided and the hoarding of money ceased.

A second problem faced by the banks was that of meeting gold obligations. Europe was demanding payment of obligations in gold despite the fact that sterling exchange had reached seven dollars a pound and shipments at the beginning of the war were almost physically impossible. Since the belligerent nations of Europe put moratoria on their own debts, many bankers urged that the United States do the same. Payment of immediately maturing gold obligations would be very difficult in any event, amounting as they did to more than half the gold reserve of all the national banks. Determined to maintain the credit of the United States, a syndicate of New York bankers raised a fund of $52,000,000 ($35,000,000 in gold and $17,000,000 in available exchange) and, with the help of the Secretary of the Treasury and the newly organized Federal Reserve Board, raised $100,000,000 from the out-of-town banks. Before October ended and before more than $10,000,000 of this fund had been exported to the Bank of London's branch in Ottawa, sterling rates began to decline and the pressure on the dollar was relieved.

This courageous decision of the New York banks to meet their obligations had important effects on the nation's future. "The promptness of the decision," says Alexander Noyes, "the clear-cut distinctness with which the American banking community pledged its resources to the task of standing single-handed against the expected requisitions of the whole outside world, had as much to do with the subsequent amazing financial strength and prestige of the United States as did the turn in Europe's conduct of the war which eventually . . . created an abnormally large foreign demand on our productive resources." [35] With the United States the only nation maintaining gold payments, this policy went far to make New York almost overnight the banking center of the world. Neutral as well

[34] Following the provisions of the Emergency Currency Act, the Treasury had printed the $500,000,000 in currency, but had never expected to use it.
[35] Noyes, *War Period of American Finance*, pp. 87–88.

as belligerent nations kept their working balances in New York. By November 12, sterling exchange had reached par and before the end of the year was favorable to the United States. By that time the trend of gold was toward the United States as Europeans cashed their American securities and belligerent nations placed war orders for American agricultural and manufactured products. It was the liquidation by Europeans of some $3,000,000,000 in American investments, as well as subsequent loans, that turned the United States from a debtor to a creditor nation and shifted the center of world finance from London to New York.

Early in 1915, the war reversed the downward trend and started the nation on the upgrade of a new period of prosperity. The year which opened in doubt and pessimism ended in a flush of economic optimism. Many precedents to the contrary, few at the beginning of the year could see the stimulating effects of the war upon the economic life of the neutral nations.[36] About the only hopeful sign discerned by the editors of the leading financial weekly was that the people were finally beginning to react against government interference with business.[37] The future, however, turned out to be much like that experienced by the United States during the wars of the French Revolution and Napoleon. Just as the increased demands of wartime Europe from 1792 to 1812 had enlarged American foreign trade and brought prosperity, so the increased demand for American products during the First World War changed the whole economic picture. The chief difference was that during the earlier period American exports were mainly foodstuffs and other agricultural products, whereas from 1914 to 1918 they included both agricultural and industrial commodities. Important among the latter were metals and other raw materials for munitions.

RISE OF FINANCE CAPITALISM

In following the yearly variations in the business cycle one may easily miss the fundamental economic revolution which took place during these years. This was no less than a shift in the control of American economic life from industrial to financial capitalists. Unregulated and virtually unhindered, finance capitalists achieved a power hitherto unknown in American history and probably never reached again even in the lush years of the 1920's. This power had

[36] *Ibid.*, pp. 92–96.
[37] *Commercial and Financial Chronicle,* C (January 2, 1915), 2.

not appeared overnight, but had been the result of long development. From the settlement of Jamestown to the end of the nineteenth century, wealth had accumulated in America, but it was largely in fixed form. When America during these three centuries needed large amounts of liquid capital it had sought them in Europe. Such great European firms as Baring of London, Hottinguer of Paris, and Hope of Amsterdam had floated American securities and kept in close touch with the American money market through their agents in this country.[38]

In the meantime surplus liquid capital increased in America, coming mainly from the profits of the wealthy and the savings of the prosperous middle class. National wealth increased from $88,500,000,000 in 1900 to $351,700,000,000 in 1917, and national income from $18,000,000,000 to $51,300,000,000. Assets of financial institutions including national banks, savings banks, private banks, loan and trust companies, and life insurance companies rose from $9,156,000,000 in 1897 to $27,795,000,000 in 1911. There can be no doubt that the volume of individual savings grew rapidly in the early years of the present century. When to individual savings were added foreign investments, undistributed business earnings, and the expansion of bank credits, it is clear that the sources of income both from capital expansion and from the purchase of securities were expanding. Foreign investments, which had remained at a low level during the early nineties, increased rapidly in the intense industrial expansion after 1897. Moreover, the percentage of banking funds invested in securities rose from 18.0 in 1890 to 27.7 in 1910. During the nineteenth century most of the surplus capital had gone into the westward movement and into transportation facilities. After 1897 large amounts continued to go into railroads, but the investment market now widened to include public utilities, industrial enterprises, foreign properties, and the bonds of local and state governments and those of the federal government.[39]

By the 1890's there were sufficient investment funds to promote business for large American investment houses, and American as well as European money was drawn upon heavily for industrial and transportation projects. Such concerns, primarily interested in the early

---

[38] Margaret G. Myers and Others, *The New York Money Market* (New York: Columbia University Press, 4 vols., 1931–1932), Vol. I, Chaps. II, IV.

[39] Harold G. Moulton, George W. Edwards, James D. Magee, and Cleona Lewis, *Capital Expansion, Employment, and Economic Stability* (Washington: The Brookings Institution, 1940), pp. 4–30; George W. Edwards, *The Evolution of Finance Capitalism* (New York: Longmans, Green and Co., 1938), pp. 183–184, 416, 422.

years in the sale of securities, included J. P. Morgan & Co., Kuhn, Loeb & Co., J. and W. Seligman & Co., Speyer, and Brown Brothers of New York; Kidder, Peabody & Co., and Lee, Higginson & Co. of Boston; and Drexel & Co. (a Morgan affiliate) of Philadelphia. Although American capital increased, European money continued to flow to America, and these investment houses were concerned with both sources. As this capital found its way into an increasing number of stocks and bonds, facilities for the ready purchase and sale of such securities expanded. The number of stocks listed on the New York Stock Exchange increased from 143 in 1870 to 426 in 1910, and the number of bonds from 200 to 1,013.[40] A million-share day was reached in December, 1886, and on April 30, 1913, the volume rose to 3,281,226 shares, a record to that date.

The shift of power from the industrial to the finance capitalist came when the expansion of industry reached a size beyond the resources of individual entrepreneurs or banks, and when the movement for consolidation reached a stage where the services of a central investment house became necessary to handle the finances involved. The technique was worked out by J. P. Morgan, who entered railroads in the 1880's to salvage various lines that had been wrecked by high financing and the speculative wars of Drew, Fiske, Gould, and other "robber barons." Morgan's first great success was in 1879, when he saved control of the New York Central for William Vanderbilt by selling 250,000 shares of New York Central stock in Great Britain without breaking the market. Morgan's reward was $3,000,000 and a representation on the board of directors. Thereafter he was the banker for that railroad.[41]

Refinancing and reorganization accompanied by rich rewards and a share in the future management were the usual steps to power taken by finance capitalists. Along with this were the profits, prestige, and power which came from organizing "trusts" during the great period of consolidation. Note will be taken later of the large returns which went to the Morgan firm for underwriting the United States Steel Corporation and other consolidations. From the time that it organized United States Steel, J. P. Morgan & Company dominated the corporation. When it is remembered that in these three years—1899, 1901, and 1902—79 great trusts were formed with a total capitalization of more than $4,000,000,000, the almost unlimited possibilities

---

[40] Edwards, *The Evolution of Finance Capitalism*, p. 167.
[41] Lewis Corey, *The House of Morgan* (New York: G. Howard Watt, 1930), pp. 141–146.

opened to finance capitalists are apparent. It should be noted that in the development of finance capitalism, bankers and investment houses worked closely together.

These investment bankers, as Louis Brandeis points out, were not content merely to deal in securities:

They desired to manufacture them also. They became promoters, or allied themselves with promoters. Thus it was that J. P. Morgan & Company formed the Steel Trust, the Harvester Trust and the Shipping Trust. And, adding the duties of undertaker to those of midwife, the investment bankers became, in times of corporate disaster, members of security holders' "Protective Committees"; then they participated as "Reorganization Managers" in the reincarnation of the unsuccessful corporations and ultimately became directors. It was in this way that the Morgan associates acquired their hold upon the Southern Railway, the Northern Pacific, the Reading, the Erie, the Père Marquette, the Chicago and Great Western, the Cincinnati, Hamilton and Dayton. Often they insured the continuance of such control by the device of the voting trust; but even where no voting trust was created, a secure hold was acquired upon reorganization. It was in this way also that Kuhn, Loeb & Co. became potent in the Union Pacific and in the Baltimore and Ohio.[42]

And when a banker once entered a board of directors, "his grip proves tenacious and his influence usually supreme; for he controls the supply of new money." [43] The imperious Morgan represented this power at its greatest extent. "Wherever Morgan sits on a board is the head of the table even if he has but one share," said a railroad president in 1905.[44] Charles S. Mellen, president of the New York, New Haven and Hartford Railroad, testifying before the Interstate Commerce Commission, admitted that the board "used to vote as a rule pretty near where Mr. Morgan voted. . . . There were strong men on the New Haven Board other than Mr. Morgan, but I do not recall anything where Mr. Morgan was determined, emphatic, insistent— I recall no case in which he did not have his way." [45] Morgan's way incidentally brought financial ruin to the [New Haven] railroad.

The extension of investment banker control into industry by the technique just described was not wholly new. What was significant was the speed with which it was accomplished and the extent to which it was practiced. What made the latter possible was a simultaneous penetration into the nation's sources of credit. Although J. P.

[42] Louis D. Brandeis, *Other People's Money and How the Bankers Use It* (New York: Frederick A. Stokes Company, 1913, new ed., 1932), pp. 9–10.
[43] *Ibid.*, p. 11.
[44] Quoted by Frederick Allen, *The Lords of Creation* (New York: Harper & Brothers, 1935), p. 81.
[45] New York *Times*, May 20, 1914, p. 4.

Morgan & Co. operated its own private bank with sizable resources, the extent of its operations was so great that it quickly stretched out to gain control of many of the leading banks of New York City and thus control of larger resources. Morgan first acquired direct control of the National Bank of Commerce, then purchased part ownership in the First National Bank. These two banks, in cooperation with the House of Morgan and by means of stock ownership and interlocking directorates, then secured control of the Liberty, Chase, Hanover, and Astor National Banks. Since the trust companies could operate under the state law more freely than the national banks under federal law, Morgan interests organized the Bankers Trust Company and by 1903 were in control of five others. Morgan himself was a large stockholder in the First National Bank of Chicago and his associates were directors in other important out-of-town banks.[46] It looked for a time as if the new era of finance capitalism would be largely centered in the hands of J. P. Morgan and his close associates, the most powerful of whom were George F. Baker, president of the First National Bank, James J. Hill, president of the Great Northern, and John A. McCall, president of the New York Life Insurance Company.

The House of Morgan, however, did not go unchallenged. By the 1890's the huge surpluses of the Standard Oil had piled so high that there was no need for much of them in the oil business itself. In the skillful hands of William Rockefeller, Henry H. Rogers, Oliver H. Payne, William C. Whitney, and others, this wealth began to penetrate into railroads, mining, public utilities, and investment banking. Closely allied with the investment banking house of Kuhn, Loeb & Co. and with James Stillman's National City Bank, the Rockefeller interests controlled the Second National Bank, the Farmers' Loan and Trust Company, and others. The resources of Standard Oil were already so vast that it was virtually independent of the banks, but it nevertheless found them a convenience. "While the House of Morgan," said Lewis Corey, "represented finance penetrating industry, Standard Oil represented the transformation of industrial capitalists into financial capitalists." [47] And this transformation was far-reaching. A banker returning from a tour of the country remarked that "wherever he went he found by scratching beneath the surface a Standard Oil connection with some leading bank in the locality." [48] Said one New York banker in despair: "With them [the Standard Oil group]

[46] Corey, *The House of Morgan*, pp. 255–258.
[47] *Ibid.*, p. 259.
[48] Sereno S. Pratt, "Who Owns the United States?" *World's Work*, VII, No. 2 (December, 1903), 4264–4265.

manipulation has ceased to be speculation. Their resources are so vast that they need only to concentrate on any given property in order to do with it what they please. . . . There is an utter absence of chance that is terrible to contemplate." [49]

John Moody, who was thoroughly conversant with Wall Street, was convinced in 1904 that the economic power of the nation rested in the financial hands of Morgan and Rockefeller. Even these two powers, he believed, would eventually combine. Around the Morgan-Rockefeller interests, wrote Moody

. . . or what must ultimately become one greater group, all other smaller groups of capitalists congregate. They are all allied and intertwined by their various mutual interests. . . . Viewed as a whole, we find the dominating influence in the Trust to be made up of an intricate network of large and small capitalists, many allied to one another by ties of more or less importance, but all being appendages to or parts of the greater groups, which are themselves dependent on and allied with the two mammoth, or Rockefeller and Morgan groups. These two mammoth groups jointly . . . constitute the heart of the business and commercial life of the nation.[50]

One more important step was still to be taken in the development of finance capital and its domination of the nation's economic life—the integration of the great insurance companies with the investment bankers. Through the payments of millions of small policy holders, the life insurance companies provided a never-failing reservoir of capital; the three largest, the New York Life, the Mutual of New York, and the Equitable, had aggregate bond investments of over $1,019,153,000 on January 1, 1913, and at least $70,000,000 in new money to invest every year. Although other investment bankers had maintained close relations with the insurance companies, and had drawn heavily upon them, it was J. P. Morgan & Co. which eventually got control of the big three. For Mutual and the New York Life, interlocking directorates or an exchange of officers and partners provided the means. A notable case was that of George W. Perkins, vice-president of New York Life, who became a partner of Morgan. While Perkins held both positions, New York Life bought from J. P. Morgan in four years $38,805,000 in securities. Testifying before an Armstrong Legislative Committee investigating the life insurance scandals, Perkins insisted that in one of these transactions he had secured a bargain. "Did you bargain with any person other than yourself?" in-

[49] Clews, *Fifty Years in Wall Street*, p. 746.
[50] Moody, *The Truth about the Trusts*, p. 493; Corey, *The House of Morgan*, pp. 258–261.

quired Charles E. Hughes, the lawyer of the committee. Answered Perkins, "I think I did it with myself, probably." [51]

Controlling stock in the Equitable was owned for some years by Thomas F. Ryan, an active promoter and speculator. Some of it he had sold to Harriman, and this had been purchased by Morgan after Harriman's death (1909). Morgan now forced Ryan to sell the rest to him, paying $3,000,000 for stock which had a par value of $51,000. Since dividends were limited, the stock had a yield of one eighth of 1 per cent on the purchase price. Although Morgan later refused to admit anything to the Pujo Committee, it was clear enough that he, like Ryan, was interested in control, not immediate financial return. Three years later Equitable owned $48,000,000 of securities issued by J. P. Morgan & Co.

A further link between the insurance companies and the investment bankers was disclosed by the Armstrong investigation. Although the purchase of stock by life insurance companies was closely restricted, they were allowed to invest in bank stock. Large purchases of stock in national banks and trust companies brought insurance directors and investment bankers together in the ownership and management of banks, and allowed insurance companies to profit indirectly from financial operations and speculations which they might not carry on directly. The insurance companies in this manner entered the business of banking and speculation as well as insurance. After the Armstrong investigation the New York legislature enacted a law ordering the insurance companies to sell their holdings in bank and trust companies within five years, but later extended the time. A few years later the Pujo Committee discovered that the stocks had been sold to the investment bankers who controlled or were closely associated with the insurance companies.[52]

As finance capitalists became more powerful and gradually took over control of the banks, the center of banking interest shifted increasingly from commercial to investment banking. The banks themselves became more interested in buying bonds for their own portfolios and they naturally bought them from the investment brokers

---

[51] State of New York, *Report of the Joint Committee of the Senate and Assembly of the State of New York Appointed to Investigate the Affairs of Life Insurance Companies* (Albany: 1907), *Testimony*, p. 1218. See also Burton J. Hendrick, "The Story of Life Insurance," *McClure's Magazine*, XXVII, No. 1 (May, 1906), 36–49, and following numbers; and Edwards, *The Evolution of Finance Capitalism*, pp. 171–195.

[52] Brandeis, *Other People's Money*, pp. 16–17; *Report of the Committee Pursuant to House Resolutions 429 and 504 to Investigate the Concentration of Control of Money and Credit*, House Report No. 1,593, 62 Cong., 3 Sess., p. 135, generally referred to as the report of the "Money Trust Investigation" or the "Report of the Pujo Committee."

who owned the banks. Likewise, loans to brokers and to individual investors and speculators became an increasingly important part of the banking business. Only one step remained to enter completely into investment banking—the selling of securities themselves. This began in 1908, when the First National Bank, the "keystone of the Morgan system of commercial banks," initiated the First Securities Corporation by declaring a dividend in the form of stock in the new company. Technically separated, they were bound together by an organization agreement between George F. Baker on behalf of the trustees and J. P. Morgan acting for the stockholders.[53] Two years later the National City Bank formed the National City Company by declaring a 40 per cent dividend to provide $10,000,000 of stock for the new company.

These security affiliates, of course, were organized to allow commercial banks to conduct a business denied to them by the banking laws. This technique of conducting business illegal in spirit if not in fact by the organization of a security affiliate, one writer has described as "a masterpiece of legal humor." [54] It may have been humorous to lawyers and bankers, but it led to abuses so intolerable, particularly in the 1920's, that Congress in the Banking Act of 1933 ordered all banks in the Federal Reserve System and all insuring with the Federal Deposit Insurance Corporation to relinquish their security affiliates and limit themselves to a strictly banking business.

During the great period of industrial consolidation it was not difficult to see what was happening and to sense the danger to the small businessman and the consumer. The consolidation and integration of finance, which proceeded simultaneously with that of industry, was not so obvious. In retrospect it is clear that two important financial developments were taking place during the early years of the twentieth century. The first was a rapid and tremendous concentration of capital; the second was a shift of power from industrialists to financiers and banking houses. The former was soon sensed and resulted in the famous investigation of the "money trust" by the Pujo Committee of the House in 1913. The second, which meant a shift in the control of economic life from farmers, merchants, and manufacturers to bankers, was a logical outcome of the concentration of capital and marked a new era in American economic history.

[53] Edwards, *The Evolution of Finance Capitalism*, p. 171; House Banking and Currency Committee, *Investigation of the Financial and Monetary Conditions in the United States*, 62 Cong., 3 Sess. (Washington: Government Printing Office, 29 pts., 1913), Pt. 20, p. 1423
[54] Allen, *The Lords of Creation*, p. 174.

The investigation by the Pujo Committee was skillfully done and its work carefully evaluated. The result was a clear picture of the concentration of control of money and credit and how it had developed.[55] It had been effected, said the committee, chiefly through the consolidation of competitive or partially competitive banks and trust companies; through interlocking directorates and stockholdings; through the influence of the powerful investment houses, banks, and trust companies brought to bear upon insurance companies, railroads, and industries; and, finally, through partnership arrangements between a few of the banking houses in the purchase of security issues, which had the effect of virtually destroying competition. The committee named J. P. Morgan & Co., the First National Bank of New York, and the National City Bank as the most powerful banking units, placing their combined assets in New York City, including seven subsidiary banks controlled by them, at over $2,000,000,000. In addition to the interests named, the committee believed that Lee, Higginson & Co., Kidder, Peabody & Co., and Kuhn, Loeb & Co. were the principal banking agencies through which the corporate enterprise of the United States obtained capital for their operations. Four allied financial institutions in New York City, it affirmed, held 341 directorships in 112 banks, transportation, public-utility, and insurance companies, whose aggregate resources were $22,245,000,000.[56]

Summarizing the committee's findings, the *Report* asserted:

If by a "money trust" is meant an established and well defined identity and community of interest between a few leaders of finance which has been created and is held together through stock holdings, interlocking directorates, and other forms of domination over banks, trust companies, railroads, public service, and industrial corporations, and which has resulted in a vast and growing concentration of control of money and credit in the hands of a comparatively few men—your committee has no hesitation in asserting as a result of its investigation that this condition, largely developed within the past five years, exists in this country today.[57]

The Pujo Committee may not have proved without cavil the existence of an absolute money trust, but it did prove a tremendous concentration and control of capital, so great and far-reaching as virtually to dictate the obtaining of large amounts of money and the terms upon which such funds would be granted. Moreover, this con-

[55] Louis Brandeis, *Other People's Money,* is based on the Pujo Report.
[56] "Money Trust Investigation," pp. 55–56, 87–88, 89–90; reprinted in H. U. Faulkner and Felix Flügel, *Readings in the Economic and Social History of the United States* (New York: Harper & Brothers, 1929), pp. 597–700.
[57] "Money Trust Investigation," p. 130.

centration was much greater in 1913 than it had been a few years earlier. The Rockefeller capitalists, more interested in industrial expansion than in financial domination, engaged in no open battle with Morgan after the Northern Pacific struggle, and they gradually disintegrated as a united group. After 1906 Standard Oil devoted its resources chiefly to developing the mid-continent oil fields. Harriman's death in 1909 removed the most active challenger to Morgan's control. Stillman's National City Bank, the instrument of the Harriman and Rockefeller groups, gradually drifted into the Morgan orbit. Lesser rivals in New York had been weakened or destroyed in the panic of 1907. There existed strong financial groups in the economic provinces, notably the Mellon interests of Pittsburg, but they avoided conflict with the Morgan power. Bankers in Boston and Chicago generally cooperated with Morgan & Co. At the time of his death in 1913 Morgan was the acknowledged financial dictator of the century.[58]

Concentration of control over credit and with it the penetration of banker control over industry marked the dominance of finance capitalism. Whether this domination conferred any economic benefit on the nation is hard to say. Morgan undoubtedly believed that he was contributing to the "rationalization" and "stabilization" of business. In a sense monopolization is a stabilizing factor. On the other hand, as Brandeis points out, the control of credit made it possible for the "banker-barons" to levy "through their excessive exactions, a heavy toll upon the whole community; upon owners of money for leave to invest it; upon railroads, public service and industrial companies, for leave to use this money of other people; and, through these corporations, upon consumers." [59] More serious was the fact that the money trust was able to suppress competition. Efforts to break or prevent private monopolies had little chance of succeeding with the control of credit as concentrated as it had become in the United States. In effect it was a supermonopoly of money dominating other monopolies in industry, transportation, utilities, and almost every economic activity of the nation.

Outside and beyond the problem and effects of financial monopoly was the significance of banker control of the nation's economic life. American economic history shows but little aid or encouragement given by bankers to the initiation or early development of great economic projects. Inventors and individual capitalists have gener-

[58] Corey, *The House of Morgan*, pp. 349–354.
[59] Brandeis, *Other People's Money*, pp. 46–50.

ally started them. Only after success was proved have the bankers entered to participate and often to gain control. The process of taking over control was often accompanied by overcapitalization of assets, deterioration in the quality of the securities based on these assets, impoverishment of the property for the benefit of bankers, and a disregard of the welfare of stockholders and the community.

Having gained control, banker management has frequently tended to be inefficient, unimaginative, and often ruinous.[60] At its best, banker control meant domination by men usually unacquainted with the business they were directing. At its worst, it resulted in the ruination of a property. The classic example of the latter was Morgan's use of the assets of the New Haven to build a transportation monopoly in New England which resulted finally in the financial collapse of the railroad.[61] Except for its function of sometimes saving a concern from bankruptcy and providing funds for rehabilitation, finance capitalism had little to contribute.

BANKING REFORM

The upward swing of the business cycle, as already noted, ended with the panic of 1907. Economists up to that time had given little intensive study to the business cycle and the reasons for the advances and recessions of economic life. One fact, however, was clear both to economists and to businessmen—the intensity and devastation of this particular crash was to no small extent the result of an inadequate banking system. To many who looked with concern upon the increasing concentration of capital, a development made unquestionably clear by the Pujo Committee, a much greater control of the banks by the government seemed necessary.

Until the panic of 1907 demonstrated without question the serious weakness of the American banking system as it operated under the National Banking Act, there were many who believed that it was adequate and in many ways superior to any in the world, at least for American needs. It had, indeed, certain merits. The national banks were reasonably safe; they were adaptable to the local needs of different types of communities; and they had perfected a check and clearing system to an extent hardly achieved in any other country.[62]

---

[60] *Ibid.*, Chaps. IX–X.
[61] *Ibid.*, pp. 189–208.
[62] E. W. Kemmerer, *The ABC of the Federal Reserve System* (Princeton: Princeton University Press, 10th ed., 1936), p. 2.

But the system had serious defects, and many of them were clear to objective students long before 1907.

One characteristic of the American banking system, and also one of its chief defects, was its unusual decentralization in an era of developing economic integration and concentration. The United States in 1914 had approximately 26,765 banks, of which 7,525 were national banks. This was a larger number than in any other nation. Generally they were locally owned, independent units acting alone except for the loose association of banks in the clearinghouses of the principal cities. This local independence and individualism scattered the resources widely and also rendered them immobile. Reserves of these banks were chiefly of three types: money deposited on call in other banks, capital invested in securities, and call loans and cash. In actual practice only the last named were quickly available in times of crises. Their effectiveness was also handicapped by the lack of any central coordinating body which could quickly concentrate the cash reserves where needed.

An even stronger criticism of the national banking system was the inelasticity of its currency and credit facilities. The amount of the principal paper currency, that is, bank notes, was dependent upon the amount of federal bonds purchased by the banks. The Gold Standard Act of 1900 had extended the issue of bank notes from 90 per cent to the full face value of the bonds, but in times of emergency this did not provide enough currency. Worse than that, it was during periods of prosperity, when a greater amount of currency was needed, that the government was in a position to liquidate its own bonds, a practice which automatically reduced the currency in circulation. Only the fact that the banks as well as the government bought bonds at this time mitigated the situation. In practice, bank notes expanded when expansion was not needed and contracted when the nation needed expansion. Moreover, it was extremely difficult to expand the currency when money was badly needed, particularly during crop-moving periods, and almost impossible during times of crises. Decentralization of bank reserves, coupled with credit inelasticity, was the chief cause of the frequent and wide fluctuations in the interest rates on call and short-time loans so characteristic of the American money market. It was also a cause for the alternating periods of excessive speculation brought on by redundant credit and those of stringency resulting from a scarcity of credit.[63] The result was higher interest rates for both farmer and businessman. Other criticisms included the

[63] *Ibid.*, pp. 18, 20–27.

cumbersome and expensive exchange and transfer systems and the defective relationship between the United States Treasury and the national banks which handled part of the general funds of the Treasury.

Many of these defects had already become clear, at least to some bankers, by the late 1890's. An Indianapolis Currency Convention of 1897 appointed a Monetary Commission whose report in 1898 anticipated certain of the reforms later included in the Federal Reserve Act. Notable was its recommendation for an issue of bank note currency based upon commercial assets and guaranteed by the banks which joined in issuing it. Nothing came of the "Indianapolis Movement" at the time, but Congress in the Gold Standard Act of 1900 made efforts to improve the banking situation. It lowered the minimum capitalization of national banks from $50,000 to $25,000 to make possible a larger number of rural banks, and it tried to provide for a more abundant currency by refunding outstanding government bonds into new issues bearing only 2 per cent interest on the theory that this rate was so low that the bonds would be unattractive for any purpose except for supporting currency. Instead of improving the situation, says Henry P. Willis, these changes simply "emphasized those features of the National Banking Act which had been adjudged undesirable on the basis of nearly forty years' experience and they very materially tended to weaken the banking system, as the numerous failures among the small banks afterwards abundantly demonstrated." [64]

Although the need for banking reform grew with the expanding economic life of the nation, Congress, dominated by Nelson W. Aldrich and other conservative senators, did nothing. It was not until the panic of 1907 made some reform mandatory that Aldrich reluctantly allowed temporary legislation, known as the Aldrich-Vreeland Act of 1908. This act provided for an expanded currency by allowing national banks to deposit with the Secretary of the Treasury bonds of states, cities, towns, and counties and to receive direct issues of currency based upon them. It also allowed the issue by national currency associations of currency based upon commercial paper, but all of the new currency was subject to high taxation to force its retirement as rapidly as possible. The act also provided for a national monetary commission of senators and representatives to investigate the problem of currency and banking and report to Congress recommenda-

[64] Henry P. Willis, *The Federal Reserve System* (New York: The Ronald Press, 1923), pp. 15–16.

tions for further action. The Aldrich-Vreeland Act was a step in the right direction, but it was unsatisfactory and recognized as inadequate. It expired by limitation in 1914 but was continued until June 30, 1915, to bridge the gap until the Federal Reserve Act could go into operation.

Although the National Monetary Commission (Aldrich Commission) itself contained few specialists in banking, it employed many experts whose monographs on conditions in the United States and abroad contributed a mass of valuable information on the history and conditions of world currency. The commission finally made its report in 1912. After listing twenty-seven principal defects of the existing system it offered a bill to incorporate a national reserve association which it believed would remedy these defects.[65] The great reforms which were needed, it held, were, first, a currency based upon gold and commercial paper endorsed by the banks, which would be responsive to the needs of business; and, second, a mobilization of a part of the cash reserves in the hands of a central organization, where it could be used instantly and in overwhelming amounts wherever needed.[66]

The plan presented by the National Monetary Commission was given slight attention by Congress, partly because its sponsor was regarded as the conservative spokesman of Wall Street. More important was the fact that the Republicans had lost control of the House in the elections of 1910 and of the Senate and the executive branch in 1912. Both of the major parties had promised banking reform, and the Democrats now assumed the responsibility for it. Hammered out by the House Committee on Banking and Currency headed by Carter Glass (whose "expert" and most influential person was the economist Henry Parker Willis), and the Senate Committee headed by Robert L. Owen, the Federal Reserve Act became law on December 23, 1913. Although many of the banking operations and other fundamental features of the Federal Reserve System are similar to those of the Aldrich plan, the organization of the new system was different. The Aldrich plan proposed to keep government influence at a minimum by providing that members of the central supervisory body be elected by the participating banks; the plan of the Demo-

---

[65] *Report of the National Monetary Commission* (Washington: Government Printing Office, 1912).

[66] The background history of the Federal Reserve Act is given in detail in Willis, *The Federal Reserve System*, Chaps. I–XXI and more briefly in Henry P. Willis, *The Federal Reserve* (Garden City, New York: Doubleday, Page & Company, 1915), pp. 25–84.

crats provided for appointment of members of the Federal Reserve Board by the President. The Aldrich plan would have had one central reserve association or bank; the Democrats, respecting the long-standing prejudice against a central bank and hoping to counteract the further development of a "money trust," divided the country into twelve reserve districts.

Under the Federal Reserve Act of 1913 the nation was divided into twelve regions with a federal reserve bank established in a leading city of each district. All national banks were required, and other banks encouraged, to become members of the federal reserve bank of their district by subscribing to the capital stock of the reserve bank an amount equal to 6 per cent of their own capital stock and surplus. In this manner each of the twelve federal reserve banks was to be owned by the member banks of the district and the bank of each district was to be governed by a board of nine members, six chosen by the member banks and three by the Federal Reserve Board at Washington. The Federal Reserve Board, which had supervisory powers and determined larger questions of policy, consisted of seven members including the Secretary of the Treasury, the Controller of the Currency, and five others (a sixth was added in 1922) appointed by the President. A Federal Advisory Council, composed of one representative from each federal reserve bank, was established to consult with the Federal Reserve Board and help it in unifying and carrying out the policies decided upon.

The federal reserve banks were not created to do direct banking with individuals or business houses. They are simply bankers' banks, central agents for the member banks, which rediscount commercial paper for the member banks of the district, purchase or sell bills of exchange, grant loans to member banks on government securities as collateral, and carry on similar banking operations. They were also to act as fiscal agents of the government. One of the most important functions of the federal reserve banks was to supervise the transition of the old national bank notes into federal reserve bank notes and the creation of a new type of paper money, the federal reserve bank notes. The federal reserve bank notes, like the national bank notes, were to be issued upon the deposit of government bonds (also commercial paper after 1933), and were expected eventually to supplant the older notes. The federal reserve notes, on the other hand, were created to expand and contract as needed, and the reserve banks were empowered to issue them on the security of short-term commercial (three months) and agricultural (six months) paper. When the paper matured, the federal reserve bank, the ultimate holder, was paid largely with federal reserve notes, and the volume of these notes thus corresponded with the volume of commercial paper and the needs of business. These new notes are obligations of the United States, receivable for taxes, customs, and all public dues, and until 1933 were redeemable in gold.

To safeguard the system, member banks were required (after 1917) to maintain with the district reserve bank 3 per cent of their time deposits and from 7 to 13 per cent of their demand deposits, depending on the population of the city. The federal reserve banks in turn were required to carry a 40 per cent reserve of gold (since 1933, gold certificates) against federal reserve notes outstanding, and a 35 per cent reserve of lawful money against deposits. One check on inflation was the requirement that no federal reserve bank might pay out the notes of another reserve bank, but must return them to the issuing bank for retirement.

By the time the Federal Reserve System was established in August, 1914, the First World War had begun. Its early development, therefore, was far from normal. Its contribution, however, in the financing of the war was so great that its value was proved almost immediately in at least one sphere. Other objectives for which the system had been established were also accomplished. It brought greater coordination of the nation's credit under government control, improved the facilities for banking over large areas, created a general discount market for commercial paper, economized the use of gold and reserve money, and created a new and elastic but unquestionably sound currency. It also liberalized certain checks under the old systems, for example, the new authorization for member banks to make five-year loans on real estate up to one quarter of their capital, and to accept drafts and bills drawn against them on foreign transactions based upon commodity imports and exports. When the federal reserve banks later took over the functions of the subtreasuries, they proved of great service to the government. Although the Federal Reserve System has never included a majority of the banks of the country, its proportion of the banking resources of the nation grew from less than one half in 1915 to more than four fifths by the late 1920's.

Certainly the Federal Reserve System wrought a great improvement in the American banking structure, even if it did not create a perfect system. Writing ten years after its establishment, H. Parker Willis, a leading contributor to the new design, pointed out that "its faults have been found in the acceptance of political dictation, a consequent inability to apply discount rate control of credit, a disposition to permit undue centralization to occur in some of the Reserve banks, a failure to furnish the right kind of leadership in domestic credit and in foreign trade, and generally a lack of constructive ability, so far as the fundamental ideas involved in the application of central banking was concerned." [67]

Certainly the new system, with its Reserve Board, its twelve reserve banks, its member banks, and its new method of creating currency, was a great improvement over the old. Nevertheless, the Reserve Board and its Open Market Committee, as Willis suggested, often failed to use their power effectively to stabilize the credit structure through changes in the discount rate, open-market operations, and other devices. This was evident in the late 1920's when it failed to control the disastrous tendencies leading to the crash of 1929. The fact that only a part of the nation's banks belongs to the Federal Reserve System has handicapped it, and the large amount of individualism still existing in the American banking structure has contributed to the thousands of bank failures which occurred in the years after the establishment of the Federal Reserve System. With all its improvements, the new system did not apparently in its early years make American banks much safer for the depositors, contribute particularly to the control of the business cycle, or stay the hand of the "money trust." The Pujo Committee had found many things wrong with the banks in 1913 and had offered legislation to correct them. Some of its best suggestions were ignored. Among them were prohibitions against security-holding companies being adjuncts to banks and against the underwriting, sale, or promotion of securities by banks.[68] It took the country twenty years to get around to these reforms in the 1930's and to methods to bolster the strength of the banks and the safety of the depositor. A decade of operation under the latter legislation has proved its usefulness.[69]

[67] H. Parker Willis and George W. Edwards, *Banking and Business* (New York: Harper & Brothers, 1925), pp. 459–460.
[68] "Money Trust Investigation," pp. 162–170. The committee's recommendation to prevent interlocking directorates in banks was introduced with the Clayton Antitrust Act.
[69] Broadus Mitchell, *Depression Decade*, pp. 154–178, Vol. IX in this series, discusses this legislation.

CHAPTER III

The Problems of Foreign Trade

FOREIGN TRADE 1897–1914

WHILE finance capitalists were taking over the control of American money markets, equally significant changes occurred in the international economic relations of the United States. The changes were evident both in the content and direction of foreign trade and in the development of American investments in the outside world. Regardless of wars, depressions, changing policies of government, or the rise and decline of the merchant marine, American foreign trade has been characterized by rapid expansion. It doubled, in fact, every twenty years from 1830 to 1910. Although this expansion occurred both in exports and in imports, it was greater and more rapid during the nineteenth century in exports. Richly endowed with most of the important raw materials for industry and possessing a growing industrial equipment, the United States had less need of imports than most nations. After 1889 there was but one year (1893) without an excess of exports over imports. Expanding wheat farms and cotton plantations were chiefly responsible for this excess in earlier years. It was not until the twentieth century that industrial products began to play an important part in the export trade. As a new country not yet fully developed, the United States rested heavily upon this active export commerce and a favorable balance of trade. It made possible, among other things, the large importation of foreign capital needed for internal economic development.

Rapid as was the increase in foreign commerce during the nineteenth century, the acceleration was speeded during the first two decades of the twentieth. Annual exports of merchandise, for example, increased in value from $1,394,483,000 in 1900 to $2,465,884,-

000 in 1913, and imports from $849,941,000 to $1,813,008,000. This was an advance of 76 per cent in exports and 113 per cent in imports. These increases are measured, of course, in terms of prices and not volume of commodities. Since price levels rose during these twelve years somewhere between 17 and 27 per cent, the growth in export trade was not so great as the value increase might seem to indicate.[1] The fact should also be noted that, after 1900, imports increased more rapidly than exports, a reversal of the situation during the previous years. This expansion of the import trade was due primarily to the development of American manufacturing and to the need of certain raw materials from abroad. Between 1901 and 1913 the value of imports increased at the rate of 6 per cent a year and exports at the rate of 4.8 a year, while American domestic production (measured in dollars) increased about 5 per cent.[2]

Whether measured in dollar values or in physical terms, the increase of world trade not only for the United States but for other nations as well was extraordinary. The fact that a similar rapid expansion had occurred in the decade 1850–1860 led some economists to explain the growth in terms of gold production and expanding prices. This theory, however, is based on little more than precedent. More probably, says Taussig, "the main explanation is to be found in the accumulated effects of improvements in transportation by land and by ocean, such as were made on so great a scale in the second quarter of the nineteenth century, and were again made in its last quarter, combined with the opening of new sources of supply for those raw materials and foodstuffs for which cheapened transportation signifies most."[3] As far as the United States was concerned, it bore a close relation to overseas expansion, to the rapid development of domestic industry, and to a definite start in the field of foreign investment.

Despite the general increase in world trade, the expansion of American commerce was a remarkable achievement, for it had been accomplished in the face of many difficulties. Up to this time American foodstuffs and raw materials had been welcomed by the more industrially advanced nations of Europe, and the United States in turn had purchased many finished products from Europe. It was a normal trade satisfactory to both sides. When American exporters,

[1] E. R. Johnson, T. W. Van Metre, G. G. Huebner, and D. S. Hanchett, *History of Foreign and Domestic Commerce of the United States* (Washington: Carnegie Institution, 2 vols., 1915), II, 86–87.

[2] Frederick C. Mills, *Economic Tendencies in the United States* (New York: National Bureau of Economic Research, 1932), pp. 161–164.

[3] Frank W. Taussig, *International Trade* (New York: The Macmillan Company, 1927), pp. 292–293.

however, pushed the sale of American manufactured goods, they immediately encountered stiff opposition from Europeans on every continent of the globe. In this competition the Europeans had many advantages. Years earlier they had obtained footholds and had learned the habits and needs of other nations; they had adjusted the art of doing business according to local customs; and they had established banks and invested money. Favored by superior steamship service and banking facilities, they were often in a position to dominate the market. In such areas as Australia, New Zealand, and the Argentine, American exporters found it difficult to sell their goods, because there was little, except wool, that the United States could buy in exchange. These areas, moreover, had already established economic contacts with Europe. The Asiatic market had also been pre-empted by Europe and Japan, and the entry of Americans into it was stubbornly opposed.

In spite of these handicaps Americans made progress, particularly the large corporations with wealth to establish exporting organizations and branch houses, and to promote advertising campaigns. Large manufacturers were in a position to cater to foreign needs and, if necessary, as in the case of the United Fruit Company, to build and operate their own ships. Furthermore, there was always the possibility of government aid, and the finest theories of laissez faire generally broke down in the face of such a possibility. Since 1789, manufacturers had received tariff help of one kind or another in exploiting the domestic market. Now they were eager for aid in penetrating foreign areas. Such aid, as will be noted, was extended in various ways.

Diplomatic and military aid to commerce, of course, was by no means new. America's traditional stand for "freedom of the seas" and her part in the opening of China and Japan to foreign commerce are cases in point.[4] Blaine's efforts in the 1880's and 1890's to promote Pan-Americanism were primarily motivated by the desire for commercial expansion. This interest took on new activity about 1900 not only in the United States but in Germany, Japan, and other nations where the industrial revolution had progressed sufficiently to bring them in competition with Great Britain. Such activity was noted by the Industrial Commission as well as the need for a greater extension of it in the United States.[5]

[4] Benjamin H. Williams, *Economic Foreign Policy of the United States* (New York: McGraw-Hill Book Company, 1929), Chap. XIII.
[5] Industrial Commission, *Final Report* (Washington: Government Printing Office, 1902), XIX, 572–576.

Increase of government interest was evidenced in 1897 by the establishment in the State Department of a Bureau of Foreign Commerce. As late as 1902 this bureau had a meager force of six clerks; yet it managed to issue an annual report on the *Commercial Relations of the United States,* and a monthly publication, *Consular Reports.* Advance sheets of the latter were given out to the newspapers almost daily. Recognizing the "promptness and energy with which several consuls have taken hold of the promotion of the foreign commerce of the United States," the Industrial Commission favored legislation for the improvement and reorganization of the consular service.[6] It also noted and approved of the widespread desire for a department of commerce and industry in the cabinet. Bills to accomplish this were introduced in the Fifty-sixth and Fifty-seventh Congresses and resulted in the Department of Commerce and Labor (1903). Commerce and Labor were separated in 1913 into two departments, with the problem of foreign trade given to the Bureau of Foreign and Domestic Commerce (created in 1912) in the Department of Commerce.

The shift from agriculture to manufactured products in the export trade, a shift already discernible in the 1890's, was more accentuated in foodstuffs than in other agricultural products and more evident in breadstuffs than in provisions. Despite rising prices, food exports declined from $545,474,000 in 1900 to $502,094,000 in 1913 and from 39.8 per cent of total exports to 20.7. Wheat exports dropped from 102,000,000 bushels in 1900 to 46,680,000 in 1910; flour exports from 18,699,000 barrels to 9,041,000. By 1913 breadstuffs were no longer a principal group of American exports; they were then surpassed by cotton, iron and steel manufactures, and provisions. Although the number of cattle shipped abroad had declined from 397,000 in 1900 to less than 25,000 in 1913, the recession in exportation of provisions as a whole had not been so great as that of breadstuffs.[7]

While foodstuffs declined, manufactured commodities moved steadily upward. Iron and steel products comprised the most important category by 1913, when they led all American exports in value except raw cotton. Following iron and steel manufactures were refined copper and copper products; refined mineral oils; lumber, timber, and wood manufactures; cars, carriages, and automobiles;

[6] *Ibid.,* p. 574.
[7] Johnson and Others, *History of Foreign and Domestic Commerce in the United States,* II, 89–90, and Mills, *Economic Tendencies of the United States,* p. 163. American export trade in agricultural products is discussed more fully in Chap. XIII.

cotton goods; and agricultural implements. Exported manufactures as a whole (except manufactured foodstuffs) increased from 35.31 per cent of the total in 1900 to 48.80 per cent in 1913. Next to manufactured commodities, the largest group of exports during these years was crude materials for further use in manufacturing. Notable in this group were cotton and tobacco. Undoubtedly the most significant trend in exports between 1900 and the First World War was the shift from agricultural to manufactured products. In 1900 over 60 per cent of exports were agricultural; thirteen years later, the products of agriculture and industry were about the same.

The relative decline of agricultural exports and the increase in manufactured products are not difficult to explain. First of all, domestic consumption of food increased at a more rapid rate than production. The increase in wheat, for example, hardly kept up with

PERCENTAGE DISTRIBUTION OF UNITED STATES EXPORTS BY ECONOMIC CLASSES, 1896–1917

(*Yearly Average or Year*)

Year	Crude Materials	Crude Foodstuffs	Manufactured Foodstuffs	Semi-manufactures	Finished Manufactures
1896–1900 ..	26.11	18.90	24.01	9.64	21.23
1901–1905 ..	30.27	12.19	22.16	11.30	24.07
1906–1910 ..	31.68	8.90	18.12	14.23	27.07
1911–1915 ..	30.74	8.83	14.32	15.41	30.70
1916	15.04	7.76	11.95	16.82	48.43
1917	13.50	8.28	13.08	21.39	43.77

Source: *Statistical Abstract of the United States,* 1942, p. 551.

the domestic demand for flour. At the same time the number of beef cattle in the country steadily declined after 1907.[8] America was using a larger proportion of her own foodstuffs. Simultaneously Europe had turned to rebuilding her own agriculture and was protecting it through higher tariffs.[9] Exportation of manufactured goods from the United States was stimulated by the tremendous growth of factory production, which had expanded beyond the domestic market and was aggressively searching for foreign buyers.

These and other influences obviously had an effect upon the marketing areas. In 1900 Europe took three fourths of American exports; by the time the United States entered the First World War this amount had declined to about two thirds, and it receded to 40 per

[8] Johnson and Others, *History of Domestic and Foreign Commerce of the United States,* II, 88–89.
[9] Below, Chap. XIII.

cent in the postwar years. On the other hand, the proportion of exports going to Canada and Asia had doubled. The decline of the European market was largely caused by the dwindling purchase of foodstuffs. Europe continued to buy other agricultural products such as cotton and tobacco; crude materials for further manufacturing, such as lumber, copper, leather, and mineral oils; and certain manufactured products; but as a whole she was definitely not interested in American manufactures. Anxious to exclude competitive products, fearful of an invasion of American goods, and resentful of the high rates of the Dingley Tariff, most of the nations of Europe, with the exception of Great Britain and the Netherlands, raised their tariffs in the two decades after 1890. Some efforts were made to halt this trend by reciprocity agreements, but as a whole they accomplished little.

PERCENTAGE OF EXPORT DISTRIBUTION, 1896–1917

(*Yearly Average or Year*)

Year	North America		South America	Europe	Asia	Oceania	Africa
	Northern	Southern					
1896–1900 ...	6.9	5.6	3.1	76.7	3.9	2.3	1.5
1901–1905 ...	8.6	6.7	3.2	72.3	5.3	2.0	1.9
1906–1910 ...	10.2	8.7	4.6	68.2	5.5	1.8	1.0
1911–1915 ...	14.2	7.7	5.2	64.0	5.6	2.2	1.1
1916	11.2	5.7	4.0	69.6	7.1	1.5	1.0
1917	13.5	6.8	5.0	65.2	7.5	1.2	0.8

Source: *Statistical Abstract of the United States*, 1942, p. 560.

Rapid increase and diversification of American manufacturing influenced the nature of American imports as well as exports. The proportion of raw and semiraw materials for use in factories and mills, such as rubber, hides, raw silk, wool, leaf tobacco, fibers, and long staple cotton increased tremendously. Likewise, the proportion of crude materials and semimanufactured goods, such as uncut diamonds, lumber, cabinet woods, tin, and chemicals advanced. At the same time the proportion of manufactured goods and foodstuffs, although increasing in amount, declined in proportion to the total. The relative decline of important manufactured products was caused not alone by the ability of American industries to supply the domestic market, but also by the high American tariffs which existed until the Underwood Act of 1913. Sugar continued to be the leading import, but its increase in value was small.

Because of the abnormal situation produced by the First World

War, the discussion of foreign trade in this chapter has emphasized the period before 1914. The effect of the war is particularly noticeable upon the geographic distribution of imports. The sources re-

PERCENTAGE DISTRIBUTION OF UNITED STATES IMPORTS
BY ECONOMIC CLASSES 1896-1917
(*Yearly Average or Year*)

Year	Crude Materials	Crude Foodstuffs	Manufactured Foodstuffs	Semi-manufactured	Finished Manufactured
1896–1900 ..	29.47	15.08	15.93	13.35	26.17
1901–1905 ..	33.38	12.92	12.36	16.65	24.69
1906–1910 ..	34.56	10.98	11.80	17.82	24.84
1911–1915 ..	34.91	12.80	12.56	17.37	22.36
1916	43.04	10.88	14.16	17.47	14.45
1917	43.56	13.07	11.90	18.18	13.28

Source: Statistical Abstract of the United States, 1942, p. 551.

mained relatively stable from 1900 to 1913. There was, it is true, some increase in the proportion of imports coming from Canada and the southern areas of North America, but elsewhere the changes were slight. The proportion from Europe, the chief source, shifted only from 51.8 per cent in 1900 to 49.2 in 1913. This maintenance of the strong position of Europe was not due to any particular progress made by Europeans in selling manufactured goods to the United States, but rather to their superior facilities for collecting goods from all over the world. With colonial possessions, superior transportation services, and mercantile and investment connections, they acted as broker nations in the import trade of the United States. As one student of foreign trade pointed out, "More india-rubber came to the United States from Europe than from South America or Africa, more wool than from Australia, more mahogany than from Central America, Mexico, and Africa, and practically all the diamonds received from the diamond fields of South Africa came by way of European countries." [10]

This situation obscured the fact that the American import trade was gradually shifting from the European orbit. The war revealed it, however, with sudden clarity. The war, of course, cut off the chemicals, the high-grade textiles, and other manufactured commodities that the United States had been accustomed to buy from Europe, some of which trade was restored at the end of the conflict. But it also forced the United States to build her own merchant marine and

[10] J. J. Huebner, in Johnson and Others, *History of Foreign and Domestic Commerce of the United States*, II, 93.

to import her foodstuffs and raw materials more directly than she had before. The statistics of 1917 gave a much truer picture of the future trends of direct commerce than those of 1913.

PERCENTAGE OF IMPORT DISTRIBUTION 1896–1917
(*Yearly Average or Year*)

Year	North America		South America	Europe	Asia	Oceania	Africa
	Northern	Southern					
1896–1900 ...	5.0	10.3	13.2	52.6	14.6	3.1	1.3
1901–1905 ...	5.4	13.3	12.5	51.3	15.4	0.9	1.1
1906–1910 ...	5.9	13.4	11.7	51.3	15.2	1.2	1.2
1911–1915 ...	7.7	14.5	12.8	46.6	15.8	1.1	1.4
1916	10.0	17.5	17.9	26.5	23.0	2.5	2.6
1917	14.2	15.3	20.3	18.7	27.8	1.2	2.5

Source: *Statistical Abstract of the United States,* 1942, p. 560.

THE TARIFF 1897–1913

McKinley had hoped to fight the campaign of 1896 on the tariff, but there was little interest in it, and the issue played no important part. Indeed, there appeared at the time no great demand for a revision of the rates. The Wilson-Gorman Act had been high enough for most protectionists, and the nation had easily adjusted itself to the new rates. McKinley, nevertheless, had no sooner taken office than he called an extra session of Congress to deal solely with the tariff. No possible excuse for this could be advanced, except a Treasury deficit during the previous four years. Theoretical high protectionists like McKinley, and others seeking special favors, however, had prepared the way. With the previous Congress (the Fifty-fourth, 1895–1897) under Republican control, a new tariff had been drawn up which was now pushed through, becoming law on July 24, 1897.

The Dingley Tariff was the highest in American history to that time. Its most significant item was the removal of raw wool from the free list. This action, taken over the opposition of woolen manufacturers, involved a complicated system of compensating duties upon manufactured woolens. Even the wool growers, who had adjusted themselves to the lack of protection, showed little interest. The move was largely political. The Republican party, having opposed western farmers on currency in the campaign of 1896, felt the need of reaffirming its loyalty to agriculture. Duties on wool, however, did not benefit agriculture as a whole; they aided mainly a small number of sheep farmers in the thinly populated trans-Missouri region. Whatever the effect upon sheep raisers, the restoration of the tariffs on raw wool and the retention of those on manufactured woolen goods left woolens in a position not shared by silk or cotton, commodities with no duties on the raw materials. It allowed the woolen industry to expand and broaden under a protection so high as to perpetuate its dependency on the tariff. It also kept the price artificially high for the ultimate consumer.[11]

Duties on hides were also restored, and here the political aspect was again dominant. Hides had been on the free list since 1872 and were still there when the bill reached the Senate, but 15 per cent was then tacked on to please senators from the ranching states. On cottons the duties of 1897 were slightly lower than those of 1890. But for the plain goods and products of medium quality, which constituted the bulk of the output of American mills, the high duties maintained until 1913 made but little difference. Superiority to Europe in the effectiveness of labor and machinery made tariffs unnecessary on this type of cotton goods. On the other hand, because of the superiority of high-grade English cottons, the tariff kept their price high in the United States without developing similar quality here.[12] On silks and linens, the duties were raised. It is doubtful, however, if the higher duties had much effect on the consumer of the staple varieties of silk. Silk was one important industry that the tariff had helped to develop. Specialties continued to be imported, but America could produce many lines as cheaply as other nations.

On the other hand, the metal schedules of the former tariff were largely retained except for some advances on finished products. There seemed little point in this since the iron and steel industry by 1897 had reached the stage where, even under the protectionist theory, it needed no help. By that date, steel rails, for example, were often manufactured more cheaply in the United States than abroad. Copper, which by the wildest stretch of the imagination, needed no protection, remained on the free list. The duties on lead, however, were increased. The Dingley Tariff of 1897 is chiefly significant in reversing —and without any general demand from the nation as a whole—the downward trend revealed in the Wilson-Gorman Act of 1894.[13] This

---

[11] Frank W. Taussig, *Some Aspects of the Tariff Question* (Cambridge: Harvard University Press, 1915), pp. 342–365; Arthur H. Cole, *The American Wool Industry* (Cambridge: Harvard University Press, 2 vols., 1926), II, 32–38.

[12] Taussig, *Some Aspects of the Tariff Question*, pp. 279–295.

[13] Frank W. Taussig, *Tariff History of the United States* (New York: G. P. Putnam's Sons, 7th ed., 1923), pp. 284–320; Edward Stanwood, *American Tariff Controversies in the Twentieth Century* (Boston: Houghton Mifflin Company, 2 vols., 1903), II, 360–394.

reversal had little to commend it. The United States had already become a great manufacturing nation and was destined to continue to be one. Lower tariffs would have promoted, not hindered, this trend. The great increase in foreign trade in the decade after 1897 came in spite of the tariff.

Although the Dingley Act was under continued attack, it remained on the statute books for twelve years. Its long life can be explained chiefly by the continued control of the federal government by the Republican party, by the economic prosperity which proponents of protection attributed to the tariff, and by the fact that the attention of Congress was turned during much of the time to other problems, primarily that of consolidation and monopoly. The problem of monopoly, however, was to some extent tied with the tariff, and the two were never far apart in those years. Henry O. Havemeyer's pronouncement that the tariff was the mother of trusts applied to the sugar, tin plate, and steel rail industries in their early years, but otherwise was greatly exaggerated.[14] But the tariffs did benefit trusts and in some cases contributed to their establishment. Another factor in the discontent over the tariff was the rising cost of living which characterized the first two decades of the century. That the tariff kept the cost of certain commodities higher in the United States than elsewhere was clear, but it was also obvious that the world-wide rise in the cost of living was not a result of the American tariff.[15] It may be added that the muckrakers had by no means neglected the iniquities of the tariff and that western progressives were demanding a downward revision.[16]

By 1908 the nation was ready for a change. This Roosevelt knew, but it was easier to follow conservative advice and evade a politically dangerous issue. Taft and his party, however, could no longer escape it. During the election of 1908 Taft promised "revision," which the average voter interpreted as meaning a reduction of rates. Even the Republican platform had gone so far as to proclaim: "In all protective legislation the true principle of protection is best maintained by the imposition of such duties as will equal the difference between the cost of production at home and abroad, together with a reasonable profit to American industries."

When the Payne-Aldrich Tariff finally passed (1909), it followed

[14] Taussig, *Some Aspects of the Tariff Question*, pp. 104, 189.
[15] Taussig, *Tariff History of the United States*, pp. 410–411.
[16] Kenneth W. Hechler, *Insurgency* (New York: Columbia University Press, 1940), pp. 92, 96.

neither the "true principle" according to Republican theory, nor real revision downward. Although cluttered with the usual unnecessary concessions to individuals and regions, it nevertheless indicated, when introduced in the House by Chairman Sereno Payne of the Ways and Means Committee, a disposition toward a downward revision. This trend was strengthened by the Republican insurgents, who succeeded, except in lumber, in preventing increases in the schedules. In the Senate, its history was different. Under the leadership of the unflinching protectionist, Nelson W. Aldrich, 847 amendments were made to the House bill, at least half of them of substantial importance and tending upward. Senators Jonathan P. Dolliver, Albert J. Beveridge, Albert B. Cummins, Robert M. La Follette, and other western progressive Republicans, put up a stiff fight, but failed to change the general course.[17]

The final result showed that the wool and sugar schedules remained virtually the same as those of 1897, whereas the rates on the finer grades of cotton and silk were advanced. One substantial victory for a lower tariff was the restoration of hides to the free list, where they had been before 1897. This was accompanied by lower duties on shoes. President Taft asserted in his Winona speech of December 7, 1909, that 1,150 items in the Dingley Act were left unchanged and 874 were changed, of which 654 were decreases and 220 increases. Something new was introduced in this tariff by describing the rates as "minimum" and instructing the President to increase them by 25 per cent of the value of the imported articles after March 31, 1910, unless he was satisfied that there was "no undue discrimination" against the United States. Taft never applied the maximum tariff.

The Payne-Aldrich Tariff brought no essential changes in the tariff system, certainly none which were likely to bring any important economic reactions. The best that can be said for it was that "it was less aggressively protectionist than the previous Republican measures." [18] The worst was said by Republican Senator Joseph L. Bristow in a letter to a friend:

If you had been here the last six weeks that I have been and observed the insatiable greed with which men pursue Senators and committees in behalf of a tariff, sometimes for protection, but usually for as much profit as can be extracted, you would conclude, as I sometimes do, that the policy of protection, which has done so much for the American people

[17] Hechler, *Insurgency*, pp. 96–145.
[18] Taussig, *Tariff History of the United States*, p. 408.

and which is sacred to old-line Republicans, like you and I, is being contorted into a synonym for graft and plunder.[19]

This spectacle of "logrolling" and plunder thinly disguised as protection was not lost upon the public. Possibly for this reason the act had authorized the creation of a tariff board to gather information on the tariff. In any event the board was not taken seriously, and the Democratic House in 1912 ended its existence by withdrawing appropriations for its support.[20] Failure to lower the tariff and the resulting split in the Republican party contributed greatly to the Democratic victory in the Congressional elections of 1910 and the presidential campaign of 1912. Just as in 1890 the tariff had been virtually the only issue between the two major parties, so it was in 1910. After the election the Democratic House proceeded to pass various bills reducing the rates. Three of them, with the help of insurgent Republicans, finally passed the Senate—a farmers' free list which promised admission duty-free of about a hundred articles, a drastic downward revision of the rates on wool (Schedule K), and a reduction of the cotton rates. Taft vetoed all three on the ground that Congress should wait until the Tariff Board had reported. The veto was expected; hence the so-called "popgun" bills were essentially political moves in preparation for the coming election rather than serious efforts to reduce the tariff.

Since the tariff had played an important part in splitting the Republican party and was bound to an important issue in 1912, the voters scanned the tariff planks with particular interest. The Republicans reaffirmed their faith in protection and promised to continue the Tariff Board. The Progressives asserted their belief "in a protective tariff which shall realize conditions of competition between the United States and foreign countries," a position esentially the same as the Republican plank in 1908. The Democrats held, as in 1892, that any tariff except for revenue was unconstitutional, but assured the country that downward revision would be gradual to allow ample time for adjustment.[21] The Democrats talked much of a "competitive tariff," but when reduced to careful scrutiny the principle behind it seemed not very different from that of equalizing the cost of pro-

---

[19] Quoted by Hechler, *Insurgency*, p. 100.

[20] During its life the Tariff Board made three useful reports: on the "Pulp and Newsprint Industry" (1911); on "Wool and the Manufactures of Wool" (4 vols., 1912); and on "Cotton Manufacture" (2 vols., 1912).

[21] Kirk H. Porter, *National Party Platform* (New York: The Macmillan Company, 1924), pp. 320–321, 335, 354–355.

duction offered by the Republicans in 1908 and the Progressives in 1912.

Almost immediately after inauguration Wilson called a special session of the Sixty-third Congress to deal with the tariff. Here a bill was already virtually completed under the direction of Oscar W. Underwood, and it quickly passed the House with slight alteration. As the Senate began debate and the lobbyists flocked to Washington, Wilson succeeded in checkmating their influence by a public denunciation of their activities. As a result, the Underwood Act of 1913 was relatively free from the excessive lobbying which had ruined the previous Democratic effort at tariff revision in 1894. The new tariff, although essentially protective, was an honest effort to reduce the rates. When it became law in October it revealed 958 reductions, 86 increases, chiefly in the chemical section, with 307 rates left unchanged. The act put raw iron, steel, raw wool, sugar (in 1916), and certain agricultural products on the free list and made large reductions on manufactured iron goods and on woolen goods.

Although the tariff of 1913 marked an important reversal in general policy, the reductions of duty made in that act were unlikely to affect American industry or the prices of commodities to any extent. As Taussig puts it, the changes "seemed to lower duties that had been prohibitive and to abolish duties that had been nominal." [22] In any event, the abnormal conditions in international trade resulting from the First World War prevented a full appraisement of the results of a lower tariff. Although there was great temptation to raise the rates to help meet the tremendous costs of the war, the administration refused to sanction this policy.

EFFORTS TO PROMOTE RECIPROCITY

From the Civil War to the 1930's the American tariff policy was essentially protective. Nevertheless, efforts were made at one time or another to promote commerce by means of tariff-bargaining laws, reciprocity treaties, and most-favored-nation clauses. A penalty clause in the McKinley Tariff of 1890, for example, provided that if the President believed that any nation exporting certain specified commodities was imposing duties on American products which appeared reciprocally unequal, he could remove the foreign products from the free list and impose specified duties. Under this provision, agreements

[22] Taussig, *Tariff History of the United States,* p. 446.

were made with ten nations, but all were virtually abrogated by the Wilson-Gorman Act of 1894.[23]

Despite much high-tariff sentiment in the late nineties, the Dingley Tariff of 1897 revived a penalty clause similar to but weaker than that of 1890. Intended mainly for France and Germany, it allowed the President, in section 3 of the act, to negotiate reciprocity agreements by reducing the tariffs on argols (crude tartar), wines, brandies, spirits, paintings, and statuary, and on a few commodities in the Latin-American trade. It also permitted the President within two years to negotiate treaties under section 4 reducing tariffs not more than 20 per cent on any commodity in return for concessions to American exports, but only upon approval of Congress. He could also increase tariffs if he found discrimination. Between 1898 and 1900 a number of agreements were made under section 3 with France, Germany, Portugal, Italy, and Switzerland, and between 1906 and 1909 with Great Britain, Bulgaria, Spain, and the Netherlands, as well as supplementary agreements with several of the powers already named. Since the Paine-Aldrich Tariff of 1909 ended the agreements, the effect of the so-called "argol agreements" was slight, except for temporarily removing certain discriminations against American exports and obtaining minor remissions or reductions of duties. Only in one case, that of Brazil, did the threat of penalties lead to an important concession. American flour millers and other exporters were eager to break through Brazil's tariff walls but had encountered stiff opposition. Since Brazil sold 50 per cent of her coffee in the American market, the threat of penalty duties was serious and a way was soon found to mitigate the Brazilian tariff.

Most of the negotiations for the early group of agreements under Section 3 of the Dingley Act of 1897 were conducted by Special Commissioner John A. Kasson.[24] He also negotiated eleven treaties under section 4 of the act, but not one was ever ratified. Nevertheless, one significant reciprocity treaty was consummated. By a special enabling act in 1903 Congress made provision for such a treaty with Cuba. Doubtless the hope of binding Cuba more closely to the United States stimulated this action, but the influence of American sugar importers, American investors in Cuban sugar plantations, and Cuban leaders played a part. It was opposed by sugar producers in the United States,

[23] Johnson and Others, *History of Foreign and Domestic Commerce of the United States,* II, 342–345; Williams, *Economic Foreign Policy of the United States,* pp. 269–271; Taussig, *Tariff History of the United States,* pp. 352–355.

[24] John Bell Osborne, "The Work of the Reciprocity Commission," *Forum,* XXX (December, 1900), 394–411.

Hawaii, and Puerto Rico and by American tobacco growers. At the time the treaty was passed the United States was already absorbing 80 per cent of Cuban exports, but Cuba purchased only 40 per cent of her imports from the United States.

By the treaty the United States agreed to admit all dutiable products of Cuba at a reduction of 20 per cent from the general tariff rates. Cuba in turn agreed to admit American products (except tobacco and manufactured tobacco) at reductions of 20, 25, and 40 per cent. Goods on the free list of either country at the time were to remain there. Concessions were understood to be preferential and not to be extended to other countries. This agreement was highly advantageous to both nations, and the exports of each nation to the other tripled during the first ten years of the treaty. By the opening of the First World War the United States bought almost 90 per cent of Cuban exports and sent to Cuba 50 per cent of her imports. The most successful and longest lived of reciprocity treaties, that with Cuba lasted until superseded by the Trade Agreement of 1934.[25]

Taft as well as his predecessors followed the theory of promoting commerce through reciprocity arrangements. As it worked out in practice, Republican politicians passed high tariffs and Republican executives sought to promote trade by mitigating some of the worst effects of the tariffs. In a few cases, but not many, Congress responded to the leadership. The last important effort at reciprocity previous to the trade agreements of the Franklin D. Roosevelt administration was the treaty with Canada in 1911. Canada had gained much from an earlier reciprocity treaty (1853–1864) and many in that country were eager to stimulate the exports of raw materials by this means. American manufacturers at this point, particularly food processors, were anxious to obtain cheap raw materials. American newspapers, in search of cheap wood pulp and paper, strongly supported the idea. Taft, who had earlier signed the high Payne-Aldrich Tariff, initiated the treaty and sponsored it in Congress.

Even a casual examination of the Canadian reciprocity rates makes it clear that it favored American manufacturers at the expense of American food farmers. On the free list of both countries were livestock, grains, and many other agricultural products along with fish, lumber, gypsum, and pulp and print paper. Equalization of rates was provided or promised on many manufactured goods, particularly

---

[25] Johnson and Others, *History of Foreign and Domestic Commerce of the United States*, II, 344–346; Williams, *Economic Foreign Policy of the United States*, pp. 283–285; Percy W. Bidwell, *Tariff Policy of the United States* (New York: Council on Foreign Relations, 1933), pp. 24–37.

processed foods. On the grounds that farmers would have to meet the competition of freely imported agricultural products while they paid inflated prices for protected domestic manufactured commodities, representatives from the farm states opposed the treaty in Congress. The tariff bill passed the House easily enough, 221–93, with scores of Republicans abstaining from voting, but in the Senate the fight was strong. Senators La Follette, Bristow, Asle J. Gronna, and other insurgents from the West had no difficulty in showing how the tariff helped eastern manufacturers to the detriment of western farmers, but the measure passed 55–27.[26]

In Canada the results were quite different. Although the treaty was highly advantageous to that country, it was opposed by strong nationalists, who considered it a preliminary step to domination, if not annexation, by the United States. The Liberal Prime Minister, Sir Wilfrid Laurier, dissolved Parliament and appealed to the country. His defeat ended for the time being any hope of reciprocity, and it also concluded a long period of Liberal government in Canada. The immediate effects of the reciprocity efforts were chiefly political. Canada reverted to nationalism and conservatism. In the United States, says Hechler, "it is not an exaggeration to say that no issue disorganized the Republican Party so much as the Canadian reciprocity agreement of 1911, which never went into effect. . . ."[27]

[26] Hechler, *Insurgency*, pp. 178–186.
[27] *Ibid.*, p. 186. The story is told in detail in Lewis E. Ellis, *Reciprocity, 1911* (New Haven: Yale University Press, 1939).

CHAPTER IV

The Development of Economic Imperialism

BACKGROUND OF EXPANSION

IN the field of foreign relations the two decades 1897–1917 marked a new era in American history. These were years when American capital began to move aggressively outside the continental boundary lines, and the United States shifted from the status of a debtor nation to that of a creditor. This export of capital was consistently encouraged by the government in the Caribbean and the Far East, but in Mexico and Canada, the two chief outlets, the movement was quite voluntary and received little or no official backing. Although the Spanish-American War gave great impetus to the export of capital, particularly in the Caribbean, the war was not promoted by business interests. The real background of American imperialism seems to rest essentially on three factors: the economic development of the United States, the fact that the federal government from 1897 to 1913 was controlled by groups who favored expansion into foreign areas, and the belief that the United States must exercise control over the Caribbean area to build and defend a canal.

By 1897 the economic development of the country had reached a stage where the domestic market was being supplied with manufactured as well as agricultural goods, and surpluses of commodities were seeking foreign markets. A certain proportion of American capital also found reasons for seeking foreign investment. Moreover, there were certain commodities which this country did not have in sufficient quantities, and which tempted capitalists to move elsewhere to obtain them. The frontier of good agricultural land had been occupied, industrial equipment created, and a transportation system largely built. Already the United States had become the greatest manufacturing nation in the world, equipped with the largest railroad mileage and producing the largest amount of agricultural products. By 1898 it was the richest and economically the most powerful nation in the world. Although foreign capital continued to seek investment in America, the United States itself had reached a position in the economic world in which she could normally break from the position of a continental country concerned almost entirely with internal problems to one possessing foreign colonies and interested in the exploitation of foreign resources.

The United States may have been economically ready for expansion into foreign markets, but there can be no doubt that the process was also speeded by the attitude and policies of federal officials. McKinley generally stressed the altruistic rather than the economic causes, but he nevertheless made the decisions which brought the war with Spain and the annexation of the Philippines. Said McKinley in 1899: "The Philippines, like Cuba and Porto Rico, were entrusted to our hands by the war, and to that great trust, under the providence of God and in the name of human progress and civilization, we are committed. . . . We could not discharge the responsibilities upon us until these colonies became ours, either by conquest or treaty. Our concern was not for conquest or trade or empire, but for the people whose interests and destiny, without our willing it, had been put in our hands." [1] To many this moralistic overtone justified annexation and the conquest of an unwilling people.

McKinley's wartime Secretary of State, William R. Day, was merely a mild expansionist, but his successor, John Hay, who became Secretary in 1898, "served as the suave escort of American imperial expansion." [2] Hay favored annexation of the Philippines, attempted in vain to purchase the Virgin Islands, prepared the way in the Hay-Pauncefote Treaty for building the Panama Canal, helped formulate the Caribbean policy, and promulgated the "open-door" doctrine. The American Caribbean policy, in fact, was largely formulated by the McKinley administration.[3] McKinley's successor, Theodore Roosevelt, like Hay, had been one of the ardent expansionists of 1898.

[1] Speech in Boston, February 16, 1899, Boston *Herald*, February 17, 1899, pp. 2–3.
[2] Frederick L. Schuman in *Encyclopedia of the Social Sciences* (New York: The Macmillan Company, 15 vols., 1930–1934), VII, 284. See also Julius W. Pratt, "The Large Policy of 1898," *Mississippi Valley Historical Review*, XIX, No. 2 (September, 1932), 219–242.
[3] Tyler Dennett, *John Hay* (New York: Dodd, Mead & Company, 1933), pp. 212–275.

Roosevelt kept Hay as his Secretary of State until the latter's death, and together they continued the McKinley foreign policy. Roosevelt used a revolution in Panama to speed construction of the canal and during his term of office reduced the republics of Cuba, Panama, and Santo Domingo to protectorates of the United States. The Roosevelt Corollary to the Monroe Doctrine, which established the United States as the policeman of the Caribbean, along with his handling of the Dominican debt, widened the pattern of American Caribbean policy.

When Theodore Roosevelt opened the way for American bankers in Santo Domingo in 1905, he used the policy of "dollar diplomacy" so ardently followed by William Howard Taft and the latter's Secretary of State, Philander C. Knox. "This policy," said Taft, "has been characterized as substituting dollars for bullets. It is one that appeals alike to idealistic sentiments, to the dictates of sound policy and strategy, and to legitimate commercial aims." [4] In the name of "dollar diplomacy" Nicaragua was virtually reduced to a dependency and the first measures were taken to penetrate Haiti. Efforts to promote investments in the Far East were pushed harder under Taft than under any other president.

Woodrow Wilson began his administration by refusing to follow Taft's dollar diplomacy in China, but by 1918 he was proposing a four-power consortium to make all public loans to China. During Wilson's administration, American forces landed in Haiti and Santo Domingo and completed the domination of those countries, while the Bryan-Chamorro Treaty gave the United States permission to build a canal through Nicaragua, a ninety-nine-year lease on the Great Corn and Little Corn Islands, and the right to establish a naval base on the Gulf of Fonseca. Although American investors suffered great loss during the Mexican revolution, Wilson desired to keep hands off. In the end he interfered to oust Victoriano Huerta, sent an expedition into Mexico to capture the revolutionary leader and bandit Francisco Villa, and ordered naval forces to occupy Vera Cruz. In 1917 the United States purchased the Virgin Islands.

Fortuitously for investors, the whole Caribbean area became involved in American strategy of naval and military defense. The decision to build the Panama Canal necessitated immediate control of naval bases, and it also made imperative the elimination of interference by other nations in the Caribbean region. Such interference was a constant danger in an area cursed by unstable governments,

[4] Message to Congress, December 3, 1912.

frequent political upheavals, and repudiation of debts. With this situation as a background, the United States evolved a Caribbean policy which included the maintenance of the Monroe Doctrine, opposition to forcible collection of debts by European nations, and a recognition of the duty of the nations in that area to pay their just debts. Finally, it included the obligation of the United States, if necessary, to maintain peace and stability. It must be emphasized that, as far as the United States government was concerned, canal strategy was the dominant interest. The expansion of American economic interests was promoted and perhaps was inevitable, but it was incidental to the larger policy.

As this policy developed, the United States worked out a technique so well known that it can be passed over briefly. Puerto Rico was annexed by conquest at the end of the Spanish-American War; the Virgin Islands were purchased from Denmark (1917) for $25,000,000, and Cuba became a protectorate through the Platt Amendment, which she was forced to add to her constitution in 1901.[5] She agreed not to enter into any treaty with a foreign power which would impair her independence, not to alienate any of her land, nor to contract any public debt beyond her capacity to repay. She agreed to sell or lease to the United States coaling or naval stations and to allow American intervention for the protection of life, property, and individual liberty. Subsequently, American investors largely financed Cuban development, and American troops landed in 1906, 1912, and 1917 to preserve order.

The protectorate over Santo Domingo came in a somewhat different way. In that country backruptcy along with political and economic chaos led Roosevelt to make an executive arrangement in 1904 (later modified and passed in treaty form in 1907) with the Dominican government to allow the United States to take over control of the customs, paying the Dominican government 45 per cent and foreign creditors 55 per cent. To get rid of European bondholders, Kuhn, Loeb & Co. of New York refunded the Dominican debt of $20,000,000 under a treaty by which a representative of the United States was to collect the customs until the debt was paid, and the debt was not to be increased without the consent of the United States. Political interference began in 1912, when Taft forced the resignation of a Dominican president and it culminated with the invasion of United

[5] *Treaties, Conventions, International Acts, Protocols and Agreements between the United States and Other Powers* (Washington: Government Printing Office, 4 vols., 1910–1938), I, 362–364. The Platt Amendment was abrogated by treaty in 1934.

States marines in 1916.[6] The main features of this agreement were the elimination of European creditors, the consolidation of the public debt in the hands of American bankers, and the methods of ensuring its payment. The contracts between the Caribbean republics and the bond houses were remarkable in the security given to the bondholders.

Penetration of Haiti began in 1910, when Knox made an opportunity for American capital to purchase shares in the National Bank of Haiti. Thereafter American control of Haitian economic life progressed rapidly. A revolution in 1915, combined with fears of German designs on the island, gave excuse for occupation by the marines and a treaty which reduced Haiti to a protectorate. The treaty of 1915 imposed conditions much like those applied to Santo Domingo: a financial adviser appointed by the President of the United States, no increase in public debt without American consent, and no alienation of land to a foreign power. The United States insisted on the right to intervene for the protection of life, property, and individual liberty. A Haitian constabulary, officered at the beginning by Americans, was established. Under the coercion of marines and naval guns, a government amenable to American wishes ruled Haiti for nineteen years.

Even more than in the Caribbean islands, American diplomacy in Central America was dominated by the canal problem. The success of the revolution in Panama was assured by sending American naval units to prevent the landing of Colombian troops. The United States made possible the existence of the newly established Republic of Panama by recognition and the signing of a treaty granting a perpetual lease of land for a canal across the Isthmus. The treaty also gave the United States the use, occupation, and control of any other lands and waters outside the Canal Zone necessary for the construction, maintenance, operation, sanitation, and protection of the Canal. Created by the grace of the United States, Panama's economic and political life has been largely dominated by the owner of the Canal. Roosevelt cut to the truth of a long and complicated story when he stated in 1911, "I took the Canal Zone." [7]

Dollar diplomacy became vigorous in Nicaragua in 1910, when the United States supported a revolution against the government of

[6] The story is told in detail in Melvin M. Knight, *The Americans in Santo Domingo* (New York: The Vanguard Press, 1928).

[7] Howard C. Hill, *Roosevelt and the Caribbean* (Chicago: The University of Chicago Press, 1927), Chap. III; Dwight C. Miner, *The Fight for the Panama Route* (New York: Columbia University Press, 1940).

José Zelaya. Actual occupation by marines occurred two years later and continued with a brief interruption until 1933. In the meantime the Knox-Castrillo Convention (1911) providing for a Nicaraguan loan and American control of customs was signed, but failed to pass the United States Senate. Private New York financiers, however, stepped in and under the benign eye of the State Department, secured control of the National Bank and arranged for a loan to be secured by a customs lien, the latter to be collected by an American nominated by the lending banks and approved by the State Department. With this as a beginning, it was not long before American bankers tightened their grip not only on the customs, but on the internal taxes, the national bank, and the railways. The main objective, as far as the American government was concerned, was achieved in 1916, when the Bryan-Chamorro Treaty gave the United States, for the sum of $3,000,000, the right to construct a canal.[8] American investments, as will be seen, also penetrated other Central American nations, and American economic relations with them have been important. As a whole, however, they have escaped financial domination.

GROWTH OF AMERICAN INVESTMENTS: WESTERN HEMISPHERE

That the expansion of American foreign investments between 1897 and 1914 was large is amply demonstrated by the fact that direct investments more than quadrupled from $634,500,000 to $2,652,500,-000. During these same years portfolio investments jumped from $50,000,000 to $861,500,000. Both types were to keep on expanding until the depression of 1929. How these investments were geographically distributed follows:

A glance at the table shows that the chief areas of American foreign investment up to 1914 were Mexico and Canada. Mexico had the largest total in 1897, and Canada in 1914. After that, Canada maintained the lead until temporarily surpassed by Europe during World War I and the 1920's. Before 1897 the movement of American capital into Canada had been gradual and on a relatively small scale, but after 1897 it developed with increased acceleration. About 5 per cent of American-owned or -controlled industrial plants in Canada were established before 1900, 11 per cent from 1900 to 1909, 22 per cent from 1910 to 1919, 36 per cent from 1920 to 1929, and 26 per

[8] *Foreign Relations of the United States, 1916* (Washington: Government Printing Office, 1925), pp. 849–852.

cent from 1930 to 1934.[9] The causes were chiefly three: the desire
to exploit the Canadian market, to obtain raw materials needed in
the United States, and to escape Dominion tariffs on commodities
that could be as easily or as cheaply manufactured there as in the
United States. That Canadian tariffs played an important part in
stimulating this migration can be seen by the acceleration of capital
movements subsequent to the increases in the Canadian tariff after
1906 and the relative decline during periods of quiescence in tariff
making.[10] Preference given in later years by Canada to Empire goods
also had an influence in the migration of capital. One estimate of
American investments in Canada in 1899 places $25,000,000 in rail-
roads, $25,000,000 in timber lands and loans, and $100,000,000 in
mining and smelting, with no estimates at all on manufacturing.[11]

DIRECT AND PORTFOLIO INVESTMENTS BY GEOGRAPHIC AREAS
(*In millions of dollars*)

Areas	1897	1908	1914	1919	1924	1929	1935
Europe	$151.0	$489.2	$691.8	$1,986.8	$2,652.8	$4,600.5	$3,026.0
Canada and New-foundland	189.7	697.2	867.2	1,542.8	2,631.7	3,660.2	3,657.6
Cuba and other West Indies	49.0	225.5	336.3	606.2	1,101.3	1,153.9	871.7
Mexico	200.2	672.0	853.5	908.9	1,005.1	975.2	912.9
Central America	21.2	41.0	93.2	114.8	155.3	286.3	192.0
South America	37.9	129.7	365.7	776.2	1,411.2	3,013.8	2,574.4
Africa	1.0	5.0	13.2	31.2	58.7	119.2	125.8
Asia	23.0	235.2	245.9	309.5	671.8	1,040.4	915.3
Oceania	1.5	10.0	17.0	54.2	140.7	403.0	413.1
International, including banking	10.0	20.0	30.0	125.0	125.0	140.1	151.9
Total: Long-term credits	$684.5	$2,524.8	$3,513.8	$6,455.6	$9,953.6	$15,392.6	$12,840.7
Short-term credits	.....	....	....	$500.0	$800.0	$1,617.0	$853.0
All foreign investments	$684.5	$2,524.8	$3,513.8	$6,955.6	$10,753.6	$17,009.6	$13,693.7

Source: Cleona Lewis, *America's Stake in International Investments* (Washington:
The Brookings Institution, 1938), p. 606. Reprinted by permission of The Brookings Institution.

Short-term credits are omitted here. Likewise the portfolio investments (those in
the stocks and bonds of foreign corporations or the bonds of foreign governments) do
not include debts payable to the United States government.

Since then American capital has penetrated almost every type
of Canadian economic life, concentrating in the manufacture of auto-

[9] Herbert Marshall, Frank A. Southard, Jr., and Kenneth W. Taylor, *Canadian
American Industry* (New Haven: Yale University Press, 1936), p. 19.
[10] *Ibid.*, pp. 20–21.
[11] Nathaniel T. Bacon, "American International Indebtedness," *Yale Review*, IX
(November, 1900), 265–285. Also given by Lewis, *America's Stake in International Investments*, pp. 607–608.

motive goods, rubber, electrical equipment, machinery, metals, chemicals, and pulp, paper, and lumber. By the early 1930's, Americans controlled more than a third of the mining output, a third of the electric power, two thirds of the natural gas, and at least one fourth of the manufacturing. Canadians, on the other hand, remained dominant in railways, telegraphs, telephones, airlines, radio, financial services, and merchandising, as well as in food processing and textiles, and in smelting, rolling, and forging.[12]

American millers entered Canada in 1910 and other food processors followed in succeeding years. The United States Rubber Company moved across the border in 1906 and Goodyear in 1910. The International Paper and Power Company, greatest of the American pulp and paper companies, entered Canada in 1905. In 1909 Canada supplied less than 4 per cent of the newsprint used in the United States; by 1916 she sent 25 per cent, and in 1934 about 62 per cent. General Electric organized its Canadian subsidiary in 1892; Westinghouse, in 1896; the International Harvester Company, in 1903; Ford, in 1904; and Buick, in 1910. Besides these dates, many others could be given to show the movement of American capital up to 1914. American investors were generally the owners of American firms which set up branches in Canada, rather than individuals investing in Canadian firms. It may be added that American investments in Canada in 1914 were much less than half those of British interests; by the early 1920's they considerably surpassed those of Great Britain.[13]

Almost equal to Canada was Mexico as a field for American investments. Encouraged by the government of Porfirio Diaz and favored by the peace of a dictator, American money flowed into Mexico between 1897 and 1914 at the rate of $40,000,000 a year. Total investments increased from $200,000,000 in 1897 to $853,500,000 in 1914.[14] This was almost three times that of British investments, which ranked second among foreign commitments. This rich market for

[12] Marshall and Others, *Canadian American Industry*, pp. 173–174.

[13] Robert W. Dunn, *American Foreign Investments* (New York: B. W. Huebsch and The Viking Press, 1926), pp. 57–61.

[14] The chief items of American investments in Mexico, as estimated (millions of dollars) by Lewis, *America's Stake in International Investments*, pp. 578–604, follows:

	1897	1914	1919
Selling organizations,	$1.5	$4.0	$5.0
Mining and smelting (precious metals and stones)	50.0	140.0	100.0
Mining and smelting (industrial minerals)	18.0	162.0	122.0
Oil	1.5	85.0	200.0
Agriculture	12.0	37.0	48.0
Railroads	110.6	110.4	122.9
Public utilities	5.6	33.2	31.7
Manufacturing	....	10.0	8.0

American capital, however, was suddenly curtailed by the revolution led by Francisco Madero in 1911. A decade of turmoil and civil war followed, involving heavy losses to American investors and the temporary or permanent closing of many enterprises. The revolution itself was primarily an uprising of an exploited and landless peasantry against the large landowners, and the opposition of middle-class liberals to the autocratic rule of a handful of financiers, large landowners, and government officials.[15] But the revolution also encompassed a nationalist resentment against the Diaz regime, which had transferred much of Mexico's potential wealth to foreign investors. Before the turmoil subsided, Mexico had gone far to reduce the power of foreign capital and had written many of her nationalist and economic objectives into her new constitution of 1917.

In 1897 more than half of American investments in Mexico were in Mexican railroads, 80 per cent of which had been built by American capital. When the railroads were once built, however, Mexico became fearful of "Yankee influence" and nationalized a large part of them in 1906–1908. This nationalization came in part because of the desire of Diaz to forestall Harriman's schemes to unite the Mexican Central and the Mexican National railroads. This nationalization changed American railroad investments from "direct" to "portfolio," but with the extension of the Southern Pacific to Mexico City, American direct investments in Mexican railroads by 1914 again reached the earlier figure of 1897.[16]

American mining interests, especially in the precious metals, were well established by 1897. Although investments in the precious metals doubled by 1917, capital in the mining and smelting of industrial minerals, notably lead and copper, increased ninefold. Driven by the high duties on imported lead in the tariff of 1890, the Guggenheim interests in the following year moved south of the border. This was the first of the vast chain of Guggenheim foreign properties (American Smelting and Refining Company) which were to expand in the next few years from Alaska to Chile. Copper exploitation began in earnest when William C. Greene, backed by Wall Street money, began to open up Mexican copper. His interests operated through the Greene Cananea Copper Company, which took the leadership in Mexican copper mining, and eventually came under control of the

15 Graham H. Stuart, *Latin America and the United States* (New York: Appleton–Century-Crofts, Inc., 4th ed., 1943), pp. 149–150.
16 Edgar Turlington, *Mexico and Her Foreign Creditors* (New York: Columbia University Press, 1930), pp. 237–240; Lewis, *America's Stake in International Investments*, pp. 316–317, 320.

Anaconda Copper Company. Its chief competitor became the Moctezuma Copper Company, organized in 1895 as a subsidiary of the Phelps Dodge Corporation. American mining enterprises suffered severely during the revolutionary period. One student who examined the records of 110 American mining companies of all kinds found only 14 in operation between 1914 and 1919. At least two thirds of American capital invested in mining was idle during this period.[17]

Although investments in mining headed the list of American interests, the most spectacular development was in oil production and refining. Moreover, it increased between 1914 and 1919, whereas investments in mining declined. In 1897 the only oil interest of the United States in Mexico was the Waters-Pierce Oil Company, a refining and distributing company and a subsidiary of Standard Oil. All this changed quickly when Edward L. Doheny and his American associates (Mexican Petroleum Company) purchased concessions in 1901 and began production. Mexican oil fields turned out to be fabulously productive, and soon other American oil interests were scrambling for Mexican concessions. The first official returns show a production of 220,650 barrels in 1904; production in 1913 was 25,902,439.

Domestic policies, international rivalry, economic competition, and fantastic profits provide the confused background of the story of Mexican oil. Testimony is often conflicting; facts are difficult to obtain. By 1910, under the liberal policy of Diaz, American oilmen had obtained control of 70 per cent of Mexican production. Most of the rest was controlled by the Anglo-Dutch interests. Then Diaz, worried over the extent of American interests, began to encourage British oil groups, headed by the Royal-Dutch Shell, and to play off one group against another. American oilmen, irritated over the encouragement of the British, apparently helped to finance the overdue revolution of Madero. Madero's government, however, was overthrown by the conservatives under Victoriano Huerta and Madero was assassinated. Huerta's counterrevolution was aided by British interests, and he in turn supported them. President Wilson, shocked by the murder of Madero and by Huerta's extralegal methods of obtaining power, and convinced that he was a puppet of British oil interests, refused to recognize his government and eventually drove him from office. Venustiano Carranza, backed by Wilson and aided by American oilmen, succeeded to power in 1914. Throughout these years of revolution, American oilmen, by paying for protection, man-

[17] Lewis, *America's Stake in International Investments*, pp. 201–207, 234–237, 249–250, 585.

aged to escape much of the destruction and loss suffered by other economic interests. Governments and revolutionary operations had to be supported, and the oil business provided the easiest source of revenue.[18]

In addition to railroads, mining, and oil, American investors had also placed considerable sums in agricultural properties and public utilities. By 1914 Americans owned several million acres of agricultural land in chicle, sisal, sugar, tobacco, and fruit plantations, and in ranches and timberland. In earlier years Americans also experimented with rubber production. Perhaps the largest interests were those of the American Chicle Corporation and the Hearst estate. Mexican lands owned by Americans were valued for tax purposes in 1923 at $42,000,000.[19] Around the turn of the century, Americans, who had taken the leadership in the practical application of electricity, aggressively entered the world-wide boom in the building of electric light and power plants, electric railways, and telephone systems. American engineers and investors provided many of the facilities built in Mexico during these years, as they did in the Caribbean islands and Central America.[20]

As late as 1914, American investments in Mexico were as large as those in the West Indies and the rest of Latin America combined. But the great era of capital movement into Mexico was about over, whereas that into the West Indies and South America was on the verge of a great expansion. Between 1897 and 1919 American investments in the West Indies increased from $50,000,000 to $600,000,000, not counting the almost complete domination of Puerto Rico. Except for Mexico, it was Cuba, the "Pearl of the Antilles," that turned out to be the greatest single capital market in Latin America. The $50,000,000 in 1897 grew to $200,000,000 in 1914 and much more rapidly after that.[21] The 1914 figure may not seem large, but it represented over half of all foreign investments in the island. The Platt Amendment gave protection to able entrepreneurs, such as Frank Steinhart, who found ever-increasing opportunities. Up to 1914,

[18] Ibid., pp. 220–223; Scott Nearing and Joseph Freeman, Dollar Diplomacy (New York: The Viking Press, 1925), pp. 84–120; Dunn, American Foreign Investments, pp. 89–107.
[19] Frank Tannenbaum, The Mexican Agrarian Revolution (New York: The Macmillan Company, 1929), p. 365; Dunn, American Foreign Investments, pp. 105–106; Lewis, America's Stake in International Investments, pp. 282–284, 288.
[20] Lewis, America's Stake in International Investments, pp. 324–325.
[21] Leland H. Jenks, Our Cuban Colony (New York: The Vanguard Press, 1928), pp. 33–37, 160–166; Lewis, America's Stake in International Investments, pp. 615–616; Foreign Relations of the United States, 1896, p. lxxxv.

Americans shared Cuba with other nations, but by the 1920's the United States had largely monopolized the market and dominated virtually every phase of Cuban economic life. In the meantime American capital moved into Haiti and Santo Domingo through government-sponsored loans, and through purchase of bank shares and investments in plantations of various kinds.

Of the $21,000,000 of American investments in Central America in 1897, three fourths were in railroads; the rest was in the production of bananas and the mining of precious metals. The amount changed rapidly after 1899, when the Boston Fruit Company merged with Minor C. Keith's Costa Rican railroads to form the United Fruit Company. American investments in 1914 (direct and portfolio) have been estimated at $93,200,000, of which $37,900,000 were in railroads; $36,500,000 in fruit, almost entirely in bananas in Costa Rica and Guatemala under the virtual monopoly of United Fruit; and $10,200,-000 in the mining of precious stones. A few million in government loans, public utilities, and other enterprises made up the remainder.[22]

References to the table at the beginning of this section (page 74) will show that the total (direct and portfolio) investment in all South America in 1897 ($37,900,000) was less than that in the island of Cuba, and, in 1914, less than half the investment in Mexico. Although the amount had increased to $365,700,000 by the latter date, it was still not much above that in the West Indies. Of these South American investments, approximately two thirds were in mining, of which $23,000,000 were in the precious metals and stones and $197,-800,000 in industrial metals, almost entirely copper. More than half of the precious metals came from Peru and were taken out chiefly by an American company, the Cerro de Pasco Copper Corporation and its subsidiaries. South American copper, largely produced in Chile, has been exploited almost entirely by American capital through the Kennecott Copper Corporation and the Anaconda Copper Company, both under Guggenheim control. American interest in Chilean copper began in 1903, when William Braden began exploring for low-cost ore which could be profitably produced through large-scale operations. With the organization of the Braden Copper Company in 1914 (controlled by Kennecott) Americans poured millions into Chilean copper mining until that country became the second largest copper-producing area in the world.

[22] Lewis, *America's Stake in International Investments*, pp. 279–281, 578–607; Charles D. Kepner and Jay H. Soothill, *The Banana Empire* (New York: The Vanguard Press, 1935), pp. 25–42.

United States oil companies began to take a cautious interest in Venezuelan and Colombian oil during the first decade of the century, but little was produced until after 1916. In the next ten years, however, oil expanded rapidly and soon challenged copper as the leading outlet for United States capital in South America. Compared to metals and oil, American investments in 1914 in railroads, public utilities, and manufacturing were comparatively trivial, but some $20,000,000 were tied up in selling organizations and a similar amount was in oil distribution.[23]

THE FAR EAST

Big business and finance, as already noted, were in general by no means eager to go to war with Spain. It was only after the war was over and the problem of territorial expansion presented itself that business joined with imperialist politicians to urge the annexation of the Philippines. But it was as a steppingstone to new markets rather than as a field for direct investments that American business contemplated the Philippines. Whitelaw Reid, one of the members of the Peace Commission and owner of the New York *Tribune,* waxed lyrical over the prospects:

The Pacific Ocean . . . is in our hands now. Practically we own more than half the coast on this side, dominate the rest, and have midway stations in the Sandwich and Aleutian Islands. To extend now the authority of the United States over the great Philippine Archipelago is to fence in the China Sea and secure an almost equally commanding position on the other side of the Pacific—doubling our control of it and of the fabulous trade the Twentieth Century will see it bear. Rightly used, it enables the United States to convert the Pacific Ocean into an American lake.[24]

As it turned out, the Far East, including the Philippines, never fulfilled the roseate dreams of the early imperialists. "China's illimitable markets," as Senator Beveridge described them,[25] proved relatively small. American exports to all Asia in 1897 were valued at $39,274,905 or 3.74 per cent of our total export trade. Twenty years later we exported $380,249,708 or 6.05 per cent. Of this about $37,150,000 went to China. Except for raw silk from Japan and rubber

[23] Lewis, *America's Stake in International Investments,* pp. 213–215, 223–228, 237–240; Dunn, *American Foreign Investments,* pp. 71–74.
[24] Whitelaw Reid, *Problems of Expansion* (New York: The Century Company, 1900), p. 42. Reprinted by permission of Appleton-Century-Crofts, Inc.
[25] *Congressional Record,* January 9, 1900, 56 Cong., 1 Sess., Vol. XXXIII, Pt. 1, p. 704.

from the East Indies, the Far East had little of importance to offer. The small total of American exports was largely due to the severe competition offered by European countries already established in the Far East and to the poverty of the mass of Orientals. The United States eventually also had to meet the aggressive competition of the rising Japanese Empire.

The story was much the same in capital investments. Total American investments (direct and portfolio) in Asia in 1897 have been placed at $23,000,000, of which $14,000,000 were in oil distributing organizations and $6,000,000 in other trading companies and sales corporations. By 1914 direct investments in Asia, including the Philippines, amounted to only $119,500,000 and total investments to $235,200,000. The increase in portfolio investments is accounted for chiefly by loans to the Japanese government. Investments in the West Indies alone were considerably greater than in all Asia. The largest single item of direct investments in 1914 continued to be oil distribution ($40,000,000).[26]

The failure of the Far East to develop as a market for trade or for capital was not due to lack of government encouragement. "What we want," said McKinley, "is new markets, and as trade follows the flag, it looks very much as if we were going to have new markets." [27] His Secretary of State, John Hay, did his best to secure these markets when he restated an old American Far Eastern policy in the "open-door" notes and expanded it in 1900 to include the territorial and political integrity of China.[28] Time and again Roosevelt urged American investments in China; Taft and Secretary Knox were even more aggressive. Said Taft in his inaugural address in 1909: "In the international controversies that are likely to arise in the Orient growing out of the question of the open door and other issues the United States can maintain her interests intact and can secure respect for her just demands. She will not be able to do so, however, if it is understood that she never intends to back up her assertion of right and her defense of her interest by anything but mere verbal protest and diplomatic notes."

Such protests were made, but in the long run they did not secure the objectives at which they were aimed.[29] The reasons were mainly two. Efforts of the United States to win economic concessions or to

[26] Lewis, *America's Stake in International Investments*, pp. 577–606.
[27] Williams, *Economic Foreign Policy of the United States*, p. 323.
[28] A. Whitney Griswold, *The Far Eastern Policy of the United States* (New York: Harcourt, Brace and Company, 1939), pp. 36–86, 122–132.
[29] *Foreign Relations*, 1909, pp. 144–178.

participate in Chinese loans were checkmated by Japan, and by Russia and other European nations interested in the exploitation of China. Invariably Great Britain backed her ally Japan in opposing American economic expansion. In the second place, American financiers as a whole were lukewarm or indifferent to the possibilities of the Far East. Opportunities at home were greater and the risks less; the domestic market was as yet not satiated, whereas the profits of consolidation were immense. "Active imperialism," says Lewis Corey, "limited itself to the Caribbean and the Philippines, although issuing a challenge to Europe in China and preparing for the future. Instead of making New York the world's money market, American finance, under the leadership of the House of Morgan, proceeded to consolidate, combine and recapitalize industry, establishing more firmly the foundations of industrial concentration and financial control." [30]

Nevertheless, some efforts were made, chiefly at the behest of the State Department, toward the establishment of American economic interests in China. As early as 1897 the State Department instructed Charles Denby, United States Minister to China, to "employ all proper methods for the extension of American commercial interests in China, while refraining from advocating the projects of any one firm to the exclusion of others." After 1895 most of the interests of governments and investors were concentrated upon an effort to participate in the feverish Chinese efforts to build railroads. During the years when various powers were scrambling for concessions in China, the American China Development Company obtained in 1900 a concession to build the southern portion of a railroad from Hankow to Canton. Rivalry between Belgian and American interests delayed the project, and the Belgians bought control of the American concern. Later J. P. Morgan bought back enough stock to secure control. In the meantime the Chinese government determined to cancel the entire contract. At first the American government opposed, but finally withdrew its objections and Morgan sold out at a large profit in 1905. Thus ended the first effort of America to enter Chinese railroad financing, and it must be admitted that, as far as private investors were concerned, there was no great interest in the project. [31]

Despite the fact that Russia and Japan, the two nations most vitally interested in Chinese territory, were engaged in bitter rivalry over control of Manchuria, it was this area that Americans picked as

[30] Lewis Corey, *The House of Morgan* (New York: G. Howard Watt, 1930), p. 230.
[31] *Ibid.*, pp. 328–331; Herbert Croly, *Willard Straight* (New York: The Macmillan Company, 1925), pp. 286–288; Charles F. Remer, *Foreign Investments in China* (New York: The Macmillan Company, 1933), pp. 257–259.

their major field of operations. Early trade connections and Harriman's grandiose railroad plans, as well as minerals and other products, seem to account for this interest. Britain's premier trading position elsewhere in China may also have played a part. Shortly after Morgan sold out the American China Development Company contracts, Harriman took up his plans to obtain a Manchurian railroad as a link in his round-the-world transportation system. Kuhn, Loeb & Co., financiers for Harriman, had recently headed the syndicate which had raised $130,000,000 in war loans for Japan. Using the prestige of his Kuhn, Loeb connection, Harriman secured an agreement from Japan for joint ownership of the South Manchurian Railroad after Russia had relinquished it.

At the end of the war, however, both Russian and Japanese opposition killed the project. Japan no longer needed American financial help and a growing hostility toward the United States was evident among the Japanese people. The renewal of the Anglo-Japanese alliance strengthened her hand. Nevertheless, Harriman persisted. With the aid of Willard Straight, then American Consul at Mukden, an agreement was concluded with the Chinese Governor of Manchuria for the establishment of a bank of $20,000,000 to stabilize Manchurian currency and promote railway and industrial enterprises. Kuhn, Loeb & Co. agreed to raise the money and the State Department gave the plan its blessing. However, the death of the Chinese Emperor and a shift in internal politics ended the project. Undiscouraged, Harriman sought to purchase the Chinese Eastern Railway from Russia. This he intended to use as a lever to force Japan to sell the connecting South Manchurian Railway. Russia seemed willing, if Japan would sell the South Manchurian Railway to American interests. Japan refused.[32]

The impending failure of these negotiations had led Harriman to plan the building of a rival railway from Chinchow on the south to Aigun on the Siberian border. His death in 1909 did not hold up the plans, for Straight succeeded in the same year in negotiating a preliminary agreement with the Manchurian provincial government for the financing of such a railroad by an American group consisting of the Morgan and the Kuhn, Loeb interests. At this point the State Department entered the picture, and Secretary Knox urged upon the European powers and Japan the neutralization of the Manchurian

[32] Nearing and Freeman, *Dollar Diplomacy*, pp. 40–42; Croly, *Willard Straight*, pp. 286–338; Griswold, *The Far Eastern Policy of the United States*, pp. 141–142, 152–153.

railways through a large loan to the Chinese government and the supervision of the railroads by an international body. His objective was obviously to prevent the exclusive economic domination and exploitation of Manchuria by Russia or Japan and to open the area to the rest of the world. Russia, backed by her ally France, refused, as did Japan, supported by Great Britain. The project of neutralization collapsed, and along with it the newly planned railroad. Instead of opening Manchuria to American investors, these maneuvers only drove Japan and Russia together in the agreements of 1907, 1910, and 1912 to keep other nations out of northern China.[33]

In the meantime Taft had taken office and was prepared to push dollar diplomacy vigorously in the Far East. Learning that China had signed a contract with British, French, and German bankers in May, 1909, for a loan to construct the Hukuang Railway running west and south from Hankow, he applied for the admission of an American group. When no action was forthcoming, Taft appealed personally to the Chinese regent and virtually forced the entry of America into the consortium over the stiff opposition of Great Britain. "I have an intense personal interest," wrote Taft, "in making the use of American capital an instrument for the promotion of the welfare of China, and an increase in her material prosperity without entanglements or creating embarrassments affecting the growth of her independent political power and the preservation of her territorial integrity." [34] Despite the excitement about the Hukuang loan, finally signed in 1911, it was not until 1913 that any actual construction started. Up to 1927 the United States had done no construction on her share of the road. The total amount of the loan was a mere £6,000,000, divided between the four nations. The American share was a little over $7,000,000, the total holding of Americans in Chinese government securities.[35]

Once again America, under the influence of Straight's enthusiasm and State Department pressure, attempted to enter Manchuria through an agreement in 1910 to finance a currency loan of $50,000,-000 to stabilize the currency of China proper and develop Manchurian industries. Knox invited British, French, and German participation, and the loan was widened to include all four powers (1911). The agreement provided that in future loans demanding foreign

---

[33] The diplomatic background of the economic rivalry in the Far East and America's frustration is clearly and objectively told in Griswold, *The Far Eastern Policy of the United States*, pp. 133–175.

[34] *Foreign Relations*, 1909, p. 178.

[35] Griswold, *The Far Eastern Policy of the United States*, pp. 161–164; Remer, *Foreign Investments in China*, pp. 268–272; Croly, *Willard Straight*, pp. 281 ff.

capital "the contracting banks shall first be invited so to participate." [36] "Dollar diplomacy is justified at last," wrote Willard Straight,
the guiding hand in the negotiations. At this point, however, a
Chinese revolution headed by Yuan Shih-kai broke out. Two years
later, after the Chinese Republic had been established, Yuan asked
the Four-Power Consortium for a loan. Russia and Japan demanded
admission and the other powers reluctantly agreed. The American
syndicate, headed by Morgan and by Kuhn, Loeb, consented to
participate in this new Six-Power loan of $125,000,000 only if re-
quested by the new Wilson administration and actually supported
by it.

This support was not forthcoming. Wilson, at least for the time
being, refused to follow the Taft policy in the Far East. "The conditions of the loan," said he, "seem to us to touch very nearly the administrative independence of China itself; and this administration
does not feel that it ought, even by implication, to be a party to those
conditions." [37] The American bankers immediately withdrew, but six
years later Wilson returned to the Taft policies by urging the bankers
to re-enter a consortium to finance China's needs. In the meantime
the American International Corporation, a Morgan subsidiary organized in 1915 to promote foreign business, obtained in 1916 a contract
to loan the Chinese government $3,000,000 to improve the Grand
Canal in Shantung Province. Likewise, a Chicago firm (Siems and
Carey) obtained a concession for building a railroad in Hunan
Province. These and a few other relatively small loans represented
the obligations of the Chinese government to American bankers. If
anything is clear about this story of American economic penetration,
it is the fact that generally it was government officials and not the
private bankers who were most interested and who took the initiative.[38]

More than a decade of government backing had brought by 1914
an investment of only $7,299,000 in Chinese railroads. This was not
as much as the $10,000,000 which Americans had already put into
mission property. Direct business investments, mainly in the sale and
distribution of American products such as oil, amounted to $42,000,-
000. Total investments in 1914 amounted to about $59,299,000, a
relatively trivial amount. Japan, on the other hand, offered far greater

[36] Croly, *Willard Straight*, p. 402.
[37] Both Wilson's statement and that of the bankers are given in the *American Journal of International Law*, VII, No. 2 (April, 1913), 335-341.
[38] Details are in Croly, *Willard Straight;* pp. 366-454, and in Griswold, *The Far Eastern Policy of the United States*, pp. 133-175.

opportunities. As against the $7,299,000 Chinese government bonds purchased by Americans, Japan had sold $183,800,000. Direct investments in Japan were about the same as in China, primarily in selling organizations, oil refineries, utilities, and the manufacture of electric equipment, but they were to grow with far greater rapidity in the 1920's.[39] Japan also offered far greater opportunities for commerce. While exports to China tripled between 1897 and 1917, those to Japan multiplied ten times. Imports from China to the United States increased fivefold; those from Japan about ninefold.[40] The reasons are obvious—greater political stability and higher economic productivity.

FROM A DEBTOR TO A CREDITOR NATION

The brief discussion just given of the movement of American capital abroad during the years 1897–1914 points to a significant shift in the international credit position of the United States. From the beginning of American history until the First World War the United States had been a debtor nation. Until the panic of 1873 these debts were incurred chiefly to finance the excess of imports over exports. By that time America had developed as a manufacturing nation sufficiently to supply her own needs. Borrowing, from that time on, was chiefly to pay interest rates on foreign investments, which continued to accumulate in the United States. These net debts, which had amounted to about $75,000,000 in 1803, had risen to $1,500,000,000 in 1869, $2,710,000,000 in 1897, and $3,686,000,000 in 1914. This growth of net liabilities occurred despite the increase in America's own foreign investments. As estimated by Cleona Lewis, the international balance sheet for the period of America's first great financial expansion follows on the next page.

Whereas American foreign investments had largely concentrated in Canada, Mexico, and the West Indies, foreign investments in the United States had come almost entirely from Europe, considerably over half coming from Great Britain. The five leading investors in the United States in 1914 in the order named were Great Britain, Germany, the Netherlands, France, and Canada.[41] Although Europeans

[39] Lewis, *America's Stake in International Investments*, p. 347; Remer, *American Investments in China*, pp. 260–264.

[40] Domestic exports (merchandise) to China in 1897 were valued at $11,916,888; in 1917 they were $36,547,229. Imports for the two years were $20,403,862 and $105,-915,531. Exports to Japan for 1897 were $13,233,970; for 1917 they were $130,427,061. Imports for the two years were $24,009,756 and $208,127,478.—*Statistical Abstract of the United States*, 1911, p. 381 and in the *Statistical Abstract*, 1918, p. 406.

[41] Foreign investments in the United States, estimated at par (July 1, 1914) were:

had invested in almost every type of economic enterprise, over half of the total was in railroads.[42] As against about $6,750,000,000 invested by Europeans in the United States on July 1, 1914 (with common stock at the market), American total investments (direct and portfolio) in Europe were only $691,800,000. Much of this was distributed among manufacturing, trading, sales and distributing organizations, and portfolio loans.[43] For a short period around 1900 it looked as if New York might become a source for European borrowing. Germany in 1899 floated a $20,000,000 loan through Kuhn, Loeb & Co.; and Sweden, $10,000,000 through the National Park Bank. England borrowed $223,000,000, one fifth of the cost of the Boer War,

AMERICA'S INTERNATIONAL BALANCE SHEET

(*In millions of dollars*)

Items	1897 (December 31)	1908 (December 31)	1914 (July 1)
Assets:			
Securities	$ 50	$ 886	$ 862
Direct investments	635	1,639	2,652
Total assets	$685	$2,525	$3,514
Liabilities:			
Securities	} $3,145	} $6,000	$5,440
Direct investments			1,310
Short-term credits	250	400	450
Total liabilities	$3,395	$6,400	$7,200
Net liabilities	$2,710	$3,875	$3,686

Source: Cleona Lewis, *America's Stake in International Investments* (Washington: The Brookings Institution, 1938), p. 445.

through J. P. Morgan & Co. New York's sudden prominence as a buyer of Europe's securities was brief; England resumed her former position as the world's investment banker at the end of the South African war.

The First World War, however, not only shifted the position of the United States to that of a creditor, but made New York rather than London the financial center of the world. The change came from the heavy purchases in America by the Allied nations of raw materials, semimanufactured goods, foodstuffs, and munitions. For the

Great Britain, $4,250,000,000; Germany, $950,000,000; the Netherlands, $635,000,000; France, $410,000,000; Canada, $275,000,000; all others, $570,000,000.—Lewis, *America's Stake in International Investments*, p. 546.

[42] *Ibid.*, pp. 546, 562–567, and Chap. II.

[43] Lewis estimates the leading American investments in Europe in 1914 as: manufacturing, $200,000,000; portfolio, $118,500,000; oil distribution, $130,000,000; selling organizations, $85,000,000.—*Ibid.*, pp. 578–579, 595, 606.

first time in history, exports from the United States in 1915 exceeded imports by $1,000,000,000; in 1916 and in 1917 the excess was $3,000,-000,000. The warring nations paid in part for the excess by the resale to America up to 1917 of over $3,000,000,000 worth of American securities owned in Europe. Some of this was done through the British and French governments, which induced their citizens to lend their securities or exchange them for domestic bonds. As a result, a large share of American securities held in Europe were eventually repatriated to the United States.[44]

Of equal significance were the loans made to foreign governments, both neutral and belligerent, during these years. The *Journal of Commerce* places the total loaned to the Allied nations from August, 1914 to April 1, 1917, at $2,263,400,000, of which $2,145,000,000 were for war purposes. Of the total loans for war purposes, Great Britain obtained $1,150,000,000; France, $685,000,000; Russia, $160,000,000; Italy, $25,000,000; Canada, $120,000,000, and China, $5,000,000. In addition were loans to Germany of approximately $45,000,000 and to neutral powers (to January 1, 1917) of $365,500,000. The final total is $2,567,500,000.[45] Another estimate puts the total dollar loans to all Allied borrowers from January 1, 1915, to April 5, 1917, at $2,581,-300,000.[46]

By the middle 1930's many Americans were convinced that the heavy American financial stake in Allied victory had been a fundamental cause for American entry into the war, a position taken by a Senate committee investigating the munitions industry. The war had just begun when the Allied governments raised the question of establishing credits in the United States to purchase American commodities. J. P. Morgan & Co., later the purchasing agent of the Allied governments and their chief agent for securing loans, referred the problem to the State Department. Secretary William Jennings Bryan opposed such a policy, arguing that "money is the worst of all contrabands because it commands everything else." [47] Backed apparently

---

[44] Charles J. Bullock, John H. Williams, and Rufus S. Tucker, "The Balance of Trade of the United States," *Review of Economic Statistics*, I (July, 1919), 245–246; and Lewis, *America's Stake in International Investments*, pp. 114–130.

[45] *Journal of Commerce and Commercial Bulletin*, January 2, 1917, and January 2, 1918, reproduced in Charles C. Tansill, *America Goes to War* (Boston: Little, Brown & Company, 1938), Appendix B. Estimates of the Secretary of the Treasury made January 27, 1920, and based upon unofficial sources, place loans to the Allied Powers up to April 1, 1917, at $2,506,591,377, but a portion of this amount had been liquidated by that time. Given in *Senate Document* No. 191, 66 Cong., 2 Sess., Serial No. 7,670; also in Tansill, *America Goes to War*, Appendix A.

[46] Lewis, *America's Stake in International Investments*, p. 355.

[47] *Special Committee Investigating the Munitions Industry, Senate Resolution No.*

by President Wilson, he wrote to J. P. Morgan & Co. on August 15, 1914, that it was the judgment of this government "that loans by American bankers to any foreign nation which is at war are inconsistent with the true spirit of neutrality." [48]

This clear-cut decision was modified a few weeks later when the National City Bank, in a letter to Robert Lansing, counselor of the State Department, pointed out the necessity of facilitating Allied purchases by bank credits. According to Lansing, who consulted the President on October 23, Wilson then took the position that there was "a decided difference between an issue of government bonds, which are sold in the open market to investors, and an arrangement for easy exchange in meeting debts incurred in trade between a government and American merchants." [49] Bankers' credits and acceptances were used for a year to an extent that made the distinction between them and loans virtually fictitious.[50] In any event, they no longer sufficed. By the summer of 1915, Allied credit had approached exhaustion. Without a new source of credit in the United States, Allied purchases would be sharply curtailed.

At this point Wilson, under the pressure of Secretary of the Treasury William G. McAdoo, Robert Lansing (now Secretary of State), and others, reversed his stand and withdrew his opposition to loans. Immediately came the five-year Anglo-French loan for $500 million, to be followed by other loans already noted. This policy lasted until April 24, 1917, when the first Liberty Loan Act authorized the Secretary of the Treasury, with the approval of the President, to purchase obligations of foreign governments at war with enemies of the United States up to $10 billion. On the following day the Secretary of the Treasury handed to the British ambassador a check for $200 million. This was the first of many cash advances, which by the end of 1920 aggregated $9,581,000,000, reduced by repayment to $9,467,000,000. The amount outstanding in 1922 shortly before the debt agreement with Great Britain was $9,386,700,000. When the government took over the burden, private loans to Allied governments ceased.

The contention of the Nye Committee [51] that the United States

286, 73 Cong., 2 Sess. (40 pts., 1934–1943), *Report* No. 944, Pt. V (1936), Report on Existing Legislation, p. 60 and Appendix, Exhibit No. 55.

[48] *Ibid.*, p. 60.

[49] *Ibid.*, and Appendix, Exhibit No. 56.

[50] George W. Edwards, *The Evolution of Finance Capitalism* (New York: Longmans, Green and Co., 1938), pp. 206–207.

[51] Charles A. Beard, "Solving Domestic Crises by War," *New Republic*, LXXXVI, No. 1,101 (March 11, 1936), 127–129.

entered the war because of heavy economic interest in the victory of the Allies was not proved. Nor was the influence of Wall Street upon the decisions of the government, although the government eventually followed the private decisions regarding loan policies already taken by the bankers.[52] It would, moreover, be difficult to prove that business could be justly charged with "warmongering." A recent examination of thirty leading trade and financial papers between 1914 and 1917 "shows that the businessman was interested primarily in his own economic welfare, but it does not show that he was any more desirous of war than the majority of Americans." [53] Nor would it be possible to show that the President was influenced in the weeks immediately preceding American entry into the war by demands of "big business" that America intervene to save investments that might be imperiled by Allied defeat.[54]

More significant than loans to the Allies in the economic background which may have led to American entry into the war was the fact that the European conflict had pulled the nation out of the recession of 1913 and 1914. The tremendous growth in the export of foodstuffs, iron and steel, and raw materials of various kinds, which invigorated American economic life, had gone almost entirely to Allied markets rather than to those of the Central Powers. Britain's control of the sea and her restrictions on neutral commerce had made such a destination inevitable. That legal commerce with the belligerents had restored prosperity was as obvious to government officials as it was to business, and it could hardly be expected that the government would end it. On the contrary, the efforts to maintain neutral rights were designed to broaden this commerce. Whether protests to Great Britain over violations of neutral rights were less aggressive because she was America's chief customer is almost impossible to determine.

To place any substantial weight upon the influence of munitions makers in bringing on the war would be less realistic than placing the blame on bankers. Strictly speaking, munitions makers were few, and their best efforts could not even meet the feeble attempts at preparedness in the United States after 1915.[55] Producers of metal for export were paid as they sent their commodities abroad and were fully

[52] Summarized in Edwards, *The Evolution of Finance Capitalism*, pp. 205–213, and discussed in Tansill, *America Goes to War*, pp. 114–134.

[53] Harold C. Syrett, "The Business Press and American Neutrality, 1914–1917," *Mississippi Valley Historical Review*, XXXII, No. 2 (September, 1945), 215–230.

[54] Tansill, *America Goes to War*, p. 657.

[55] Newton D. Baker, "Why We Went to War," *Foreign Affairs*, XV, No. 1 (October, 1936), 61–69.

prosperous while America remained in a neutral status. The same was true of producers of foodstuffs. Economic interests may have played some part in the road to war, but they appear to be minor in comparison to Allied propaganda, the violation of neutral rights by Germany, and the widespread sympathy of the nation and its leaders to the Allied cause.

It is obvious, of course, that strong economic relations had developed through loans and commerce between the United States and the Allies from 1914 to 1917. But it should be remembered that Woodrow Wilson, who had to assume the final responsibility for American entry into the war, was essentially a political rather than an economic man. His advisers who urged the final step did not over-emphasize the economic, and it seems that Wilson himself did not give it undue attention.[56] Moreover, the influence of Wall Street bankers was not great in Washington during the Wilson administration. "The real reasons why America went to war," as Tansill well says, "cannot be found in any single set of circumstances. There was no clear-cut road to war that the President followed with certain steps that knew no hesitation. There were many dim trails of doubtful promise and one alone which he traveled with early misgivings and reluctant tread was that which led to American economic solidarity with the Allies." [57]

[56] Tansill, *America Goes to War*, pp. 131–134, 657.
[57] *Ibid.*, p. 134.

CHAPTER V

The Movement of Population

GROWTH AND INTERNAL MIGRATION

IT may be safely asserted that no period was more significant in the history of American demography and population movements than the twenty years after 1897. This can be said in spite of the fact that these years showed characteristics which had been evident before 1897 and which continued after 1917. These years reveal a decline in the rate of population growth and a persistence in the internal movement of population, particularly toward the West and toward the urban areas. They also show an acceleration of movement of the Negro migration to the North. There was a notable increase in immigration. At the same time, the shift in its origin, evident in the 1890's, persisted. Moreover, this deluge of the "new migration" developed for the first time a strong demand for restriction. What made these years so significant was the fact that certain earlier trends had become so strong as greatly to modify the distribution and the type of the American people.

Up to 1860 the population of the United States had increased by one third or more each decade. After that a decline in the percentage of increase set in. Nevertheless, the actual increase was large, averaging one and a third million each year for the 40 years 1880–1920. The unusual decline in the percentage of increase in the decade after 1910 was largely caused by the curtailment of immigration during the First World War.

The increase in population, of course, was due chiefly to a natural growth within the nation and to a tremendous wave of immigration which numerically reached a high watermark during the first decade of the century. A background for both was provided by the prosperity of the nation in the decade after 1897 and the expanding economic life of the country. Neither the economic expansion nor the growth of population, however, was uniform throughout the nation (see Appendix, p. 414).

Before a discussion of the relationship between population changes and the economic life of the nation, the migratory tendencies of Americans should be stressed. Since 1850, when such information was first collected, each census reported that over one fifth of the native Americans had migrated from the state of their birth.[1] In one respect, this migration followed a general pattern. The surplus of people who migrated to a state over the number who left it reached a maximum about three decades after the first settlement. After three more decades of declining surplus a deficit appeared. This pattern

POPULATION INCREASE

Year	Population	Decennial Increase	Per Cent of Increase Since Preceding Census
1890	62,947,714	12,791,931	25.5
1900	75,994,575	13,046,861	20.7
1910	91,972,266	15,977,691	21.0
1920	105,710,620	13,738,354	14.9

Source: William S. Rossiter, *Increase of Population in the United States 1910–1920* (U.S. Bureau of the Census, *Census Monograph I*, Washington: Government Printing Office, 1922), p. 21.

continued into the 1900's. By 1910 the deficit area extended westward across the Mississippi into Iowa and Missouri and by 1930 included Minnesota, Nebraska, and Kansas. These statistics, based on inter-state migration of native whites, illustrate, as will be noted later, a continuation of the dominant westward movement. The general trend was modified only by particularly strong counterinfluences, such as the growth of industry. Michigan, for example, has never showed a deficit, and New Jersey has had a surplus since 1890. Florida, for quite other reasons, experienced a continued surplus since 1850.[2] In addition there was much migration within states, particularly toward larger urban areas, but this movement has not been adequately tabulated. It is clear, however, that the migratory rate went up.

[1] Charles J. Galpin and Theodore B. Manny, *Interstate Migration among the Native White Population as Indicated by Differences between State of Birth and State of Residence* (U.S. Department of Agriculture, Bureau of Agricultural Economics, Washington: Government Printing Office, 1934), pp. 6–7.

[2] C. Warren Thornthwaite, assisted by Helen I. Slentz, *Internal Migration in the United States* (Philadelphia: University of Pennsylvania Press, 1934), pp. 5–23.

As in earlier decades the motivation of population movements was chiefly economic. One recent authority insists that until 1910 internal migration, as far as it was interstate, was primarily agricultural.[3] There is ample evidence, however, that as industry developed, its influence became increasingly important. Census studies show close correlation between population growth and industrial development, and this increase in population in industrial areas was the result both of interstate and of intrastate migration. One government expert, studying the period from 1910 to 1920, found that increases in population, in value added by manufactures, and in persons engaged in manufactures have a high positive correlation.[4] His findings indicate that manufacturing, certainly after 1910, rather than agriculture was the determining factor in marked population changes in the period under consideration.

In any event, a detailed examination of population shifts and increases in the decade 1900–1910 shows the influence of both industry and agriculture.[5] During this decade a growth of the lumber industry in northern Maine, New Hampshire, Michigan, and Wisconsin and in southern Mississippi, Alabama, and Georgia accounts for a movement of people into those areas. In similar manner a mining development in southwestern Pennsylvania, West Virginia, Kentucky, and Tennessee provides the background for added population. Developing industry was responsible for the rapidly growing areas around Chicago and Milwaukee and the prosperous lake ports of Detroit, Toledo, and Buffalo.

On the other hand, the most spectacular movement of population toward the end of the century was influenced by agriculture—the heavy flow into Oklahoma in the three decades after 1889. Along with the Oklahoma development was a large migration from the Old South into Texas, as well as a lesser movement into Arizona and New Mexico. Missouri, Arkansas, and Mississippi gained some population from improvements in the levee systems of the Mississippi. Conversely, a deficiency of rainfall and other water resources was doubtless the main cause for the population decline in certain areas of South Dakota, Nebraska, and Kansas. The only state to report an absolute

[3] *Ibid.*, pp. 16–17.

[4] William S. Rossiter, *Increase of Population in the United States, 1910–1920* (U.S. Bureau of the Census, *Census Monograph* I, Washington: Government Printing Office, 1922), pp. 155–170. See also Frederic B. Garner, Francis M. Boddy and Alvar J. Nixon, *The Location of Manufactures in the United States, 1899–1929* (Minneapolis: University of Minnesota Press, 1933).

[5] Walter F. Wilcox, *A Discussion of Increase of Population* (U.S. Census Office, *Bulletin* No. 4, Washington: Government Printing Office, 1903), p. 25.

loss in the decade 1900–1910 was Iowa. In 1910–1920, losses were registered in Vermont, Mississippi, and Nevada.

Important in the migration of the decade was that into California, which came largely from the corn and wheat belts. The proportion of California's population born outside the state was greater in 1910 than in any preceding census back to and including 1870. There was also a strong agricultural migration into the Pacific Northwest. Three states, Washington, Oklahoma, and Idaho, more than doubled their population during the decade; six others, Nevada, North Dakota, New Mexico, Arizona, California, and Oregon, increased it by more than 60 per cent. Only the populous industrial states of New York and Pennsylvania showed a larger actual increase than Oklahoma and California. East of the Mississippi only the important industrial states exhibited notable increases in population, except Florida, which had begun to profit from its salubrious winter climate. In brief, most of the increase and shift of population west of the Mississippi had its economic background in agriculture; that east of the river, in industry.

Internal migration in the decade 1910–1920 shows an accelerated migration to California from the Middle West and from the Southwest. On the other hand, there was a virtual cessation of migration into Washington and Oregon as well as a great decline in the movement into Oklahoma and Texas. One of the most important migration trends of the decade was the movement into Michigan, Ohio, and Indiana from all directions, in part as a result of the wartime stimulation of industry and the rapid growth of automotive manufacture. In this later migration Negroes as well as whites participated.[6]

Despite the fact that the frontier had officially ended in 1890, it was clear that the westward movement had continued. The movement of native population from the region east of the Mississippi to the area west of the river showed a net gain in the decade 1910–1920 of over 4,000,000 as against the eastward migration from the West. Nevertheless, the relative strength of the westward movement was declining. Between 1910 and 1920 every state west of the Mississippi registered a decline in the percentage of increase over the figure of the previous decade, with Nevada, as noted above, showing an actual loss. At the same time, both the industrial and the agricultural areas in the East were holding their own far better than during 1900–1910. In some eastern states the percentage of increase was higher than in the previous decade. The trans-Mississippi West had begun to give back

[6] Thornthwaite, *Internal Migration in the United States*, pp. 12–13 and Plate VI.

to the East some part of its population—over a million from 1910 to 1920, or almost twice that of the previous decade.[7] The corn and wheat belts, which had contributed so lavishly to the building of the Pacific states, were now also contributing population to the industrial areas east of the Mississippi. At the same time a migration of mountain whites from the border states was moving north, as was an even heavier migration of Negroes.

FROM COUNTRY TO CITY

The tendency toward urbanization in the United States, which had been evident since the First Census was taken in 1790, is so well known that it hardly needs elaboration. It was quite as pronounced during the years under study as at any time in American history. In

INCREASE OF RURAL AND URBAN POPULATION: 1900–1920

	Rural		Urban		Per Cent Increase	
Year	Total	Increase	Total	Increase	Rural	Urban
1900	45,614,142	....	30,380,433	....	...	....
1910	49,806,146	4,192,004	42,166,120	11,785,687	9.2	38.8
1920	51,406,017	1,599,871	54,304,603	12,138,483	3.2	28.8

Source: Rossiter, *Increase of Population in the United States, 1910–1920*, p. 75.

fact, one authority on population movement, writing in 1934, insists that "at no time or place in the world's history has the phenomenon of city development been so rapid as in the United States during the last half century." [8] Some idea of the predominance of urban growth may be seen in the above table.

Urbanization continued to be greatest in the regions where it had early developed; long before 1900, New England, the Middle Atlantic, and the East North Central states, all industrial areas, had become predominantly urban. In these regions the rural population was stationary between 1900 and 1910 and increased but slightly from 1910 to 1920. Although a large part of the urban increase of the nation was in these areas, the tendency was almost universal. The West North Central states, for the most part agricultural, showed small increases in rural population but large urban growth. In the Pacific states the urban element predominated by 1910 and continued to grow faster than the rural. Even in the South, an essentially rural area in 1900, urbanization was clearly in evidence. Here the increase in

[7] *Fourteenth Census: Population*, II, 613; also I, 17.
[8] Thornthwaite, *Internal Migration in the United States*, p. 2.

rural population, 1910–1920, was approximately 1,400,000 but the urban increase was nearly 2,300,000.

Although the South remained a rural area, a rapid trend toward urbanization was evident after 1900 both in the Southeast and in the Southwest. Since the South had not developed great metropolises, this urbanization was reflected in the growth of a number of small cities. In 1900 there were only three cities in the Southeast with 100,000 inhabitants and none in the Southwest; in 1930 there were eight in the Southeast and four in the Southwest. The growth of all these cities was substantial; in the case of Tulsa, Oklahoma City, Dallas, and Miami, it was spectacular.

Many causes contributed to the development of urbanization in the South, but none were more important than the growth of industry. The cities of the Old South were originally almost exclusively commercial, though some of the small "ubiquitous" industries existed. As collecting, wholesaling, and financial centers, many continued to grow, and commercial life also played a strong part in the development of many of the newer cities. Nevertheless, predominantly industrial cities developed after 1900—Birmingham (iron and steel), Greenville and Gastonia (textiles), Durham and Winston-Salem (tobacco). Iron and coal in the Appalachian mountain ranges are responsible for Birmingham; water-power developments along the eastern fall line as well as raw cotton explain the string of textile cities in the Carolinas and Georgia. No city of any size in the South is without industries.[9] This is true of the Southwest as well as of the Southeast. Tulsa and Oklahoma City have a background of oil, Houston and Dallas process many of the products of a rapidly growing agricultural and industrial area.

Taking the nation as a whole, the proportion of urban population to the entire population increased from 5 to 6 per cent each decade, 1900 to 1920. The population living in communities of 2,500 or more was 40 per cent in 1900, 45.8 in 1910, and 51.4 in 1920. As for the cities of various sizes, those from 50,000 to 1,000,000 developed more rapidly than either the very largest or the very smallest.[10] Many of the large cities showed a remarkable capacity to expand, but it seems evident that suburban and satellite communities often grew more rapidly than the city proper or the central portions of the metropolitan areas.

[9] The discussion of the eastern South is based largely on Walter J. Metherly, "The Urban Development on the South," *Southern Economic Journal*, I, No. 4 (February, 1935), 3–26.

[10] *Fifteenth Census: Population*, 1931, I, 14.

About 70 per cent of the new population of the cities came from foreign immigrants or migrants from rural sections or small towns. Job opportunities chiefly explain the immigrant movement, whereas the exodus from farms was caused by reduced opportunities or the desire to exchange the loneliness, isolation, and drudgery for the excitements and challenge of the city. Mechanization of agriculture released much labor from the farm and the competition of richer lands to the west eliminated marginal farms. A study of the new urban population 1900–1910 (11,826,000 persons) indicates that 41 per cent were alien immigrants, 29.8 rural migrants, 21.6 a natural increase, and 7.6 the result of incorporation of new territories.[11]

NEGRO MIGRATION

One of the most important movements of population during the two decades 1897–1917 was the northward migration of Negroes, particularly after the opening of the First World War. This migration was not a new phenomenon, for Negroes, like the white population, have sought new homes and opportunities. What was new about the movement were its predominating direction, its acceleration, and its size. From the days of the "Underground Railroad," Negroes have moved toward the North but never before had this been the predominating direction.[12] Up until the decade 1910–1920 the direction had generally been toward the West or the Southwest, where new areas had been opened adaptable to Southern crops.

Another trend was also obvious. Up to this time Negro migration was almost entirely local, that is, from one state to the next. About half of those who had moved across Mason and Dixon's line and the Ohio River had come from Virginia and Kentucky. Now the migration began to come from the cotton belt states of Georgia, Alabama, Mississippi, Louisiana, and Texas. And it was a straight-line movement "roughly along meridians of longitude." [13]

[11] John M. Gillette and George R. Davies, "Measure of Rural Migration and Other Factors of Urban Increase in the United States," *Publications of the American Statistical Association*, XIV (September, 1915), 642–653. Earle Clarke, "Contributions to Urban Growth," *Publications of the American Statistical Association*, XIV (September, 1915), pp. 654–670, comes to virtually the same conclusions.

[12] Louise V. Kennedy, *The Negro Peasant Turns Cityward* (New York: Columbia University Press, 1930), pp. 23–27, 37.

[13] Carter Goodrich and Others, *Migration and Economic Opportunity* (Philadelphia: University of Pennsylvania Press, 1936), pp. 680–681; Thornthwaite, *Internal Migration in the United States*, p. 12; Emmet J. Scott, *Negro Migration During the War* (New York: Carnegie Endowment for International Peace, Oxford University Press, 1920), pp. 59–71.

The sudden acceleration of the northward migration of Negroes aroused great interest in the North and also produced exaggerated estimates of its size. Actually the Negro migration to the North had not been great between 1870 and 1910 except for the decade 1890–1900. From 1910 to 1920, the migration to the North and West showed a net gain of about 334,000.[14] Even so the percentage of Negroes born in the United States and living in a state other than that of birth increased only from 15.6 per cent in 1900 to 19.9 per cent in 1920. The second decade of the century was the great period of regional redistribution of Negro population as the following table shows.

GAIN OR LOSS OF NEGRO POPULATION THROUGH
INTERDIVISIONAL MIGRATION

Division	Gain or Loss	
	1920	1910
New England	+21,325	+20,310
Middle Atlantic	+296,664	+186,384
East North Central	+296,111	+119,649
West North Central	+68,222	+40,497
South Atlantic	−455,410	−392,827
East South Atlantic	−405,511	−200,876
West South Atlantic	+127,350	+194,658
Mountain	+20,085	+13,229
Pacific	+31,164	+18,976

Source: *Fourteenth Census: Population*, II, 616.

It was not only the acceleration of migration that emphasized the movement, but also the concentration of Negroes in the cities of the Middle Atlantic and East North Central states. Whether they came from the urban or rural districts in the South, the Negroes, when they reached the North, concentrated in the cities. Sixty per cent of the Negro population of Illinois lived in Chicago, 68 per cent of those in Michigan were in Detroit, and more than 75 per cent of the Negroes in New York State lived in New York City.[15] The per cent of urban Negroes in 1900 was 22.7; in 1920, it was 34.[16]

Many reasons account for the northward migration. Both contemporary observers and later students agree that the economic were the most important.[17] Negro students have also rightly emphasized

[14] Kennedy, *The Negro Peasant Turns Cityward*, p. 39.
[15] Kennedy, *The Negro Peasant Turns Cityward*, pp. 32–33.
[16] See graphs in Gunnar Myrdal and Others, *An American Dilemma* (New York: Harper & Brothers, 1944), I, 192.
[17] U.S. Department of Labor, *Negro Migration in 1916–1917* (Washington: Government Printing Office, 1919); Scott, *Negro Migration During the War*, p. 13; Kennedy, *The Negro Peasant Turns Cityward*, pp. 41–57.

the social disabilities under which the Negro suffered in the South.[18] The decline of European immigration after 1914, combined with increased production of war goods and, after America's entry into the war, the draft of workers into the army, created a labor shortage in the North. Rumors of high wages in munitions factories spread by advertisements and labor agents did much to start the movement. Low wages in the South, unsatisfactory tenant conditions, and economic exploitation everywhere, added to Mississippi floods and devastation wrought by the boll weevil, gave a push that helped turn the Negro toward the North. Wages in northern munitions factories were triple those in the South and were paid once a week in cash and not once a year in credit at the country store.

Other causes which in a greater or less degree influenced this migration include political disfranchisement, racial discrimination in education and in the carrying out of many civic laws and government services, segregation of all types, and lynchings. Increasingly the Negro resented the inferior and subservient position in which he was expected to remain. It might be added that Negroes, like the white population, were influenced by the restlessness of wartime and by the lure of the city.[19] A southern expert, observing the migration at close hand, covered the situation fairly well when he stated that "The causes may be grouped as *beckoning* and *driving*, the first group arising from conditions in the North and the second from conditions in the South." Among the beckoning influences in 1916–1917 were high wages, a shorter working day than on the farm, less political and social discrimination, and better educational facilities. Among the driving causes were the relatively low wages paid farm labor, an unsatisfactory tenant or crop-share system, the crop failures of 1916, lynching, disfranchisement, segregation, poor schools, and the monotony, isolation, and drudgery of farm life.[20]

Whatever the causes for this migration, the effects were significant. Only one, and that economic, will be noted here—the increasing participation of Negro wage earners in the industrial life of the nation. In 1900, agriculture and domestic and personal service, traditional Negro work, occupied 86.7 per cent of those gainfully employed; by 1920, the percentage of Negroes engaged in these two

[18] Carter G. Woodson, *A Century of Negro Migration* (Washington: Association for the Study of Negro Life and History, 1918), Chap. IX.

[19] Kennedy, *The Negro Peasant Turns Cityward*, pp. 41–57.

[20] William O. Scroggs, "Interstate Migration of Negro Population," *Journal of Political Economy*, XXV, No. 10 (December, 1917), 1040–1041. These and other reasons were also discovered by the historian Charles H. Wesley on interviewing Negro arrivals at the Union Station in Washington, *Negro Labor in the United States* (New York: The Vanguard Press, 1927), p. 292.

occupations had declined to 67.06. By 1920, about 1,506,000 Negroes, 31.2 per cent of those gainfully employed, were engaged in manufacturing, the mechanical industries, and trade and transportation. The developing participation of the Negro in industrial life was caused not alone by the migration to northern factories, but also by the movement of Negroes to southern cities where the increasing industrialization of the South was evident. It came also from a growing realization that Negroes, when given an opportunity to adapt themselves to new conditions, could render the same service as others.[21]

Most of these Negroes, it is true, went into the lower-paid unskilled or semiskilled jobs, notably in steel mills, automobile plants, foundries, and packing houses. Others went into road building and construction, or into transportation as Pullman porters. As with men, the percentage of female Negroes engaged in agriculture also declined notably. Their occupation shifted mainly from agriculture to domestic and personal service and to manufacturing. Lack of adequate training and opposition to Negro admittance by most unions, if any existed in industries employing Negroes, operated against both men and women to keep them in the lowest-income brackets.[22]

THE NEW IMMIGRATION

Two aspects of immigration during the two decades after 1897 immediately catch the attention of the student—its tremendous size and the continued shift in origin. In the entire history of American immigration only the decade 1840–1850 showed a larger inflow relative to the population already in the United States. In actual number of immigrants, however, the years 1900–1909 showed a higher total than any similar period. Beginning in 1900, the tide of immigrants passed the 400,000 mark; it did not fall under that figure again until 1915. During six of these years (1905, 1906, 1907, 1910, 1913, 1914) over 1,000,000 immigrants reached the United States. More than 8,000,000 came in the years 1900–1909 and another 5,000,000 in the period 1910–1914.[23]

A search for an explanation of this inundation reveals, first of all,

[21] Lorenzo J. Greene and Carter G. Woodson, *The Negro Wage Earner* (Washington: Association for the Study of Negro Life and History, 1930), pp. 340–344.

[22] Kennedy, *The Negro Peasant Turns Cityward*, pp. 71–134; Sterling D. Spero and Abram L. Harris, *The Black Worker* (New York: Columbia University Press, 1913), pp. 149–382.

[23] *Statistical Abstract of the United States*, 1919, p. 89; Niles Carpenter, *Immigrants and Their Children* (U.S. Bureau of the Census, *Census Monograph* VII, Washington: Government Printing Office, 1927), p. 45.

a culmination of causes which had operated for many years. Jews, Armenians, and others suffered religious persecution. Subject peoples, such as the Finns, Poles, and various groups of Slavs, were denied political equality. A low standard of living, accentuated by occasional crop failures, famines, plagues, depressions, and other misfortunes supplied a major reason. Money wages in southern and eastern Europe, from which more than 80 per cent of the "new immigration" came, were often not more than one third those in the United States.[24] A minor cause was dislike for compulsory military training. As always, the main driving impetus was economic.

Although older causes continued to operate, two particular reasons help to account for this unusual flood of aliens—the greater ease of getting to America and the prosperity enjoyed in the United States, at least up to 1907. The hardships and dangers of earlier years had been largely surmounted. Instead of weeks of weary travel and bitter hardship, any immigrant accessible to railroad and steamship could reach America in fourteen days. Immigrant ships had become mere ferryboats plying between the two continents. Not only was transportation more rapid than in earlier years but steerage accommodations were more comfortable. Moreover, millions of immigrants already in the United States were prepared to remit funds to bring their friends and relatives to America. By this time, also, there had appeared an intricate network of steamship agents to propagandize prospects, immigrant bankers to finance the journey, and labor contractors (*padrones*) to find jobs for the newly arrived immigrant. The American Consul General in Italy reported that "immigrants are generally well informed by foremen, contractor agents, and friends in the United States as to chances of obtaining work." [25]

Although artificially stimulated immigration has probably always existed, it is doubtful if the technique was as highly perfected as in the latter years of the nineteenth and early twentieth centuries. Professor Commons asserted that "the desire to get cheap labor, to take in passenger fares, and to sell land have probably brought more immigrants than the hard conditions of Europe, Asia, and Africa have sent." [26] Writing several years later, another careful student also believed that "much of our immigration since 1880 . . . has come in

[24] Jeremiah W. Jenks and W. Jett Lauck, *The Immigrant Problem* (New York: Funk & Wagnalls, 6th ed., 1926), pp. 12–13.

[25] Quoted by Frank J. Warne, *The Immigrant Invasion* (New York: Dodd, Mead & Company, 1913), p. 33.

[26] John R. Commons, *Race and Immigrants in America* (New York: The Macmillan Company, 1907), p. 108.

response to inducements of transportation companies and American employers operating through various methods and devices." [27]

Even without "induced immigration," the pull from America was exceedingly strong. The wave of prosperity which swept the nation after 1897, and only briefly halted by recessions in 1904, 1907, 1911, and 1913, provided expanding opportunities in factories, mines, and railroad construction and in almost every phase of economic life. The sensitivity of immigration and emigration to economic conditions and opportunities can hardly be questioned. Correlations of data pertaining to male immigration, pig iron production, and factory employment during these years reveal this clearly.[28] The influence of major cyclical changes in industrial conditions in the United States was usually apparent in immigration within less than half a year. Immigration increased with prosperity and declined with depression; and such conditions influenced emigration conversely. Moreover, immigration was closely related not only to employment opportunities, but also to the ability of friends and relatives to remit funds for the journey.

Immigration from central, southern, and eastern Europe began to increase rapidly after 1890; by the middle of the decade it surpassed that from northern and western Europe. Before 1883, northern and western Europe (the British Isles, Germany, the Scandinavian peninsula, and other neighboring countries) furnished 95 per cent of the immigrants. By 1907, over 80 per cent of the European immigrants came from Austria-Hungary, Italy, Russia, and the Balkan nations. In 1914, only 10 per cent of the entire immigration came from northern and western Europe. By that time any one of the three countries of Austria-Hungary, Italy, or Russia furnished more immigrants than all the northern European countries put together.[29]

According to the census of 1920 the "new immigration," as it was then called, comprised 46.4 per cent of the foreign-born white population, and the "old immigration" 40.2. A careful examination of immigration statistics, however, reveals the fact that this shift was neither so uniform nor so revolutionary in its effect on American population as many believed. The new immigration had been slowly increasing for some time, and that from certain areas of northern and

[27] Warne, *The Immigrant Invasion*, pp. 47–48.

[28] Harry Jerome, *Migration and Business Cycles* (New York: National Bureau of Economic Research, 1926), pp. 87–122.

[29] Jenks and Lauck, *The Immigration Problem*, pp. 25–26; *Reports of the Immigration Commission* (*Senate Reports*, 61 Cong., 2 and 3 Sess., Washington: Government Printing Office, 42 vols., 1911), I, 166–167.

western Europe declining. German immigration had been particularly large in the 1880's but had fallen off steadily after that. Nevertheless, as late as 1920, the largest number of foreign-born whites in the United States was from Germany. The Irish, on the other hand, had been losing their relative position among the foreign-born whites since 1860. While immigration from Germany and Ireland declined, that from England, Sweden, Holland, and other northeastern European nations held up fairly well. The first ten countries, according to their contribution to the foreign-born white population of the United States in 1920, were:

FOREIGN-BORN WHITE POPULATION IN 1920

Country	Number	Percentage of Total
Germany	1,686,102	12.3
Italy	1,610,109	11.7
Russia	1,400,489	10.2
Poland	1,139,978	8.3
Canada (French and "others")	1,117,878	8.1
Ireland	1,037,233	7.6
England	812,828	5.9
Sweden	625,580	4.6
Austria	575,625	4.2
Mexico	478,383	3.5

Source: Niles Carpenter, *Immigrants and Their Children* (U.S. Bureau of the Census, *Census Monograph* VII, Washington: Government Printing Office, 1927), p. 74.

If this table is compared with a similar one showing foreign white stock (foreign-born and native white stock of foreign or mixed parentage), the result is quite different. Such an enumeration would show that the white stock from Germany and Ireland alone comprised almost one third of the foreign stock and surpassed that of all from south central and eastern Europe.[30]

The new immigrants often differed markedly from the old in their tendency to consider America as a temporary abode with the expectation of returning to their home country. Until 1907, immigration records did not tabulate aliens leaving American ports. After that, however, the difference in this respect between the two types of immigrants was evident. Records from 1908 to 1910, for example, show that from every one hundred, 16 of the old immigration, and 38 of the new, returned. The typical immigrant who came to America simply to make a stake and return usually had less interest in learning the English language or American ways of living.[31] His economic aid

[30] Carpenter, *Immigrants and Their Children*, pp. 74, 88, 92–94.
[31] Jenks and Lauck, *The Immigrant Problem*, pp. 36–40; *Reports of the Immigration Commission*, I, 112–114.

might be great, but his cultural contribution was slight. At the same time he was more easily exploited by employer and *padrone*. The new immigration, as might be expected from its impermanent character, was predominantly male and single. During the decade 1899–1909, the percentage of females in the old immigration from Europe was 45.5; that of the new immigration, 27. The new immigration was also somewhat younger than the old. Of the new immigrants, about 83.5 per cent were in the age groups 14 to 44 years.

It was also clear that the new immigration as a whole represented a lower economic and cultural background. During the decade 1899–1909, the illiterates among the new immigration at the time of admission amounted to 35.8 per cent and that of the old, 2.7. From south Italy, where the largest group of illiterates originated, the percentage was 54.2 and the number 822,113.[32] This obviously meant an utter lack of formal education for over one third of the new immigrants and a greater difficulty in social assimilation. Since at least two thirds of the new arrivals could not speak English, the tendency to crowd into cities where they could live with their own kind was accentuated. Moreover, the problem of illiteracy soon played its part in the history of immigration restriction.

Large as was this inundation, it did not change to any degree the proportion of immigrants in the total population. In 1900, approximately 10,214,000 people representing 13.4 per cent of the population were foreign-born whites; in 1920, the number was 13,713,000 and the percentage 13. The mere size of this immigration did not increase its numerical importance in the American population. Actually there was a slight decline.[33] Likewise there were no major geographical shifts in the United States in the distribution of foreign born between 1900 and 1920. Minor shifts are noted in the West North Central states, where the foreign born declined from 14.8 per cent of the population to 11; and in the Mountain states, from 18 per cent to 14.[34] Older tendencies continued and were perhaps strengthened. The immigrant seemed to prefer the city to the country, employment in industry to employment in agriculture, large cities to small ones, large seaports to inland cities, and he did not seek to compete in an important way with the Negro, chiefly because of the low wages and standards of Negro employment.[35]

[32] Jenks and Lauck, *The Immigrant Problem*, pp. 33–36; *Reports of the Immigration Commission*, I, 98–100, 156–160.
[33] Carpenter, *Immigrants and Their Children*, 1920, p. 5.
[34] *Ibid.*, p. 14.
[35] *Ibid.*, p. 41. The preference of immigrants for the great cities on the Atlantic sea-

The tendency of immigrants to remain in urban areas is clear from the census studies. By 1920, at least 71.6 per cent of the entire foreign white stock (foreign born and natives of foreign or mixed parentage) lived in urban regions, and 28.4 per cent in rural. This group comprised 48 per cent of the urban population and 20.1 per cent of the rural. More than 70 per cent of the populations of New York, Boston, Chicago, and Milwaukee were foreign-born whites or native whites of foreign or mixed parentage. Cleveland had a similar population of 69 per cent, and seven other cities had over 60 per cent. It was the thickly populated industrial states of New York, Pennsylvania, and Massachusetts that showed the largest proportions of foreign born, and in general the correlation between the concentration of population and foreign born was close.

DISTRIBUTION OF FOREIGN BORN 1920

Geographic Division	Percentage of Foreign Born in Total Population, 1920	Percentage of Foreign White Stock in Total Population, 1920 (foreign born or of foreign or mixed parentage)
The Northeast		
New England	25.5	61.0
Middle Atlantic	22.3	54.0
The Far West		
Pacific	20.3	44.3
Mountain	14.0	36.3
The Middle West		
East North Central	15.1	42.6
West North Central	11.0	37.9
The Southwest		
West South Central	4.5	11.3
The South		
South Atlantic	2.4	6.2
East South Central	0.8	3.1

Source: Carpenter, *Immigrants and Their Children*, p. 16.

On the other hand, there was wide variation, as the accompanying table shows, in the percentage of foreign born and foreign white stock between the sections. New England showed the highest percentage in both categories after 1900, with the Middle Atlantic states second after 1910. The variation in the percentage of foreign born ranged in 1920 from 0.8 in the East South Central to 25.5 in New England. Individual states showed even wider differences. Only 0.3 per cent of the population of North Carolina was foreign born as against 29.0

---

board was earlier questioned by Walter F. Willcox, "The Distribution of Immigrants in the United States," *Quarterly Journal of Economics*, XX (August, 1906), 523–546.

in Rhode Island; the percentage of the entire foreign white stock of these two states was 0.7 and 69.6, respectively.

Urban concentration may have been accentuated by the fact that many immigrants clung to the large cities at the points of debarkation or on main-traveled roads where earlier colonies of immigrants had established themselves. They went where there were jobs and friends. The rapid occupation of western agricultural areas and the end of the frontier undoubtedly backed up the immigrants into the cities; many of them had come from rural areas in eastern Europe and might normally have sought labor on the farms. The urban trend of immigrants was also strengthened by the tendency of industry to follow the labor supply. This helps to explain the concentration of the clothing industry in certain cities, the labor for which was mainly supplied by Jewish immigrants.

Since the foreign born largely massed in urban areas, it is not surprising that the census of 1910 showed that of the 6,588,711 foreign born males having some occupation, five sixths were engaged in essentially urban pursuits. About one third of them were in manufacturing. These immigrants furnished 45.4 per cent of the labor in extracting minerals, 36.0 per cent of that in manufacturing, 27.3 of that in the building and hand trades, and 25.0 in transportation. Of the female foreign born workers in 1910 (1,222,791), about one half were engaged in domestic and personal service and more than one fourth in manufacturing. Although there were many skilled workers among the immigrants, the masses were likely to be engaged in the less skilled work. By 1910 more than half of the coal miners and two thirds of the copper and iron miners were foreign born. In transportation more than half of the longshoremen and laborers in the electric and steam railways were immigrants. In many of the great industries of the country, at least half of the wage earners were foreign born; in some, approximately two thirds or more were in this category. The latter industries included clothing manufacturing, construction work, copper mining and smelting, cotton manufacturing in the North Atlantic states, leather manufacturing, oil refining, and sugar refining.[36]

GROWTH OF IMMIGRATION RESTRICTION

Americans were by no means unaware of the size, change of origins, and the problems raised by the new immigration. Books and

[36] William M. Leiserson, *Adjusting Immigrant and Industry* (New York: Harper & Brothers, 1924), pp. 7–14. His statistics are drawn mainly from the Thirteenth Census, 1910, Vol. IV, Table 6, pp. 302–433.

magazine articles on various aspects began to appear in large numbers. An examination reveals that from 1900 to 1907 these studies
were primarily interested in the economic aspects and only second-
arily in the ethnic.[37] On the whole they showed an attitude favorable
to large-scale immigration. The new immigration was seldom regarded as a menace, nor was there any strong demand that the number be reduced. Those who urged restriction at all believed that it
might lessen pauperism and crime, purify American politics, and
preserve the democratic ideal. These writers urged a more careful
selection emphasizing good character, health, thrift, honesty, and
intelligence. The most persistent advocate of restriction was organized labor, which insisted that the continued deluge of cheap labor
kept American wages low and prevented a rise in the standard of
living. The annual convention of the American Federation of Labor
in 1910, for example, hoped that the flood of bills then before Congress would "result in the enactment of legislation which will protect
the workers from unfair competition resulting from indiscriminate
immigration." [38]

There was real substance to the complaints of organized labor.
The Immigration Commission, in fact, had studied with the greatest
care the influence of the new immigration upon labor conditions and
wages. It was, it said, "the most important and exhaustive feature
of the Commission's investigation." The commission was convinced
that the new immigrants had "almost completely monopolized unskilled labor activities in many of the most important industries." [39]
This mass of illiterate and untrained labor had not only monopolized
unskilled jobs in many industries; it contributed to keep wages low
and to drive out older immigrants and native labor. Although no
proof exists that the new immigration lowered wages, it seems clear
that it was important in preventing a rise in the real wages of unskilled labor during the first two decades of the century. Since this
group did not compete to any extent with skilled labor, apparently it
had little effect upon wages of the latter group.

That the inflow of large numbers of unskilled workers of various
foreign groups, often impermanent and unwilling to lose time through
strikes, delayed the advance of American labor unions, was a belief

[37] Thomas J. Woofter, Jr., *Races and Ethnic Groups in American Life* (New York:
McGraw-Hill Publishing Company, 1933), pp. 22–25.
[38] *Report of the Proceedings of the Thirtieth Annual Convention of the American
Federation of Labor* (Washington: The Law Reporter Publishing Company, 1910),
p. 312.
[39] *Reports of the Immigration Commission*, I, 38; Isaac A. Hourwich, *Immigration
and Labor* (New York: B. W. Huebsch, Inc., 1922), pp. 284–310.

held both by union officials and by students of the immigration problem.[40] It is true, of course, that the membership of organized labor increased rapidly from 1898 to 1904, but this new membership was largely in the skilled group and it was not until later years that it included many of the new unskilled immigrants. Another effect of the migration was the perpetuation of dangerous and unsanitary working conditions. It was, moreover, the opinion of the Immigration Commission that a saturation point had been reached in the employment of recent unskilled immigrants in basic industries.[41]

After 1907 the tone of the discussion gradually changed. Interest in the economic aspects continued, but the dominant concern was the racial and ethnic problems. Students now emphasized the different background of the new immigration, with its low economic and social standards. They pointed to the difficulties of assimilating millions of Jews, Italians, and various groups of Slavs. The influx of the new immigration was so large, they insisted, that the great American "melting pot" could no longer resolve these people into a homogeneous whole.[42] Against such an invasion, American ideals and Anglo-Saxon stock could not survive. Although older Americans complained that the new immigration could not be assimilated, they also feared that too much assimilation would "adulterate" Anglo-Saxon blood and ideals.

With the coming of war in 1914 immigration assumed a political aspect. It had long been pointed out that the new immigration had come to a large extent from nations autocratically ruled and ignorant of political democracy, and that this inundation would endanger political democracy in America. After the war had begun, the residence in America of millions of aliens whose official allegiance was to European governments strengthened the political arguments. This danger proved to be far less important than had been expected, but it gave strength to the demand for restriction. To a list that was already growing long were added the arguments of national safety and the demand that America have a right to solve its own national and international problems without the influence of millions of resident aliens.

Up to 1907 the preponderance of opinion on immigration policy favored selection rather than restriction, selection mainly by physical and literacy tests. In the years thereafter there was more talk of re-

[40] Jenks and Lauck, The Immigration Problem, pp. 202–204.
[41] Reports of the Immigration Commission, I, 47.
[42] Henry Pratt Fairchild, The Melting Pot Mistake (Boston: Little, Brown & Company, 1926), pp. 9–12.

striction with a growing demand to limit the number of immigrants. The chief method proposed was by a literacy test. If the nation had any national immigration policy in the nineteenth century, it was one of encouragement. It had shown little concern about immigration, and the slight amount of regulation, except for Asiatics, had been done by the customs-revenue service of the Treasury Department.[43] In 1882 the federal government passed a general immigration act and in 1891 a Superintendent of Immigration (Commissioner after 1895) was appointed and federal control completely established. The legislation of 1882 and 1891 had provided for a small head tax and for the exclusion of lunatics, persons suffering from loathsome or dangerous contagious diseases, convicts (except those convicted for political offenses), polygamists, and persons likely to become public charges. These laws, however, had had little effect and had debarred but a handful of aliens.

By the early nineties the indifference had ended. The Senate had appointed a standing committee on immigration, and the law of 1891 had been followed by the appointment of a joint committee of both houses to continue a study of the problem. A few years later the Industrial Commission also gave it serious attention, resulting in new legislation in 1903.[44] Following the eighteen recommendations of the commission, all previous legislation was precisely codified, the insanity clause was strengthened, and new undesirables were added to the list: epileptics, professional beggars, prostitutes, anarchists, and persons who believed in the overthrow of the government of the United States by force or violence. In line with the emphasis upon selectivity rather than numerical restriction, new groups of undesirables were added in 1907: tubercular persons, feeble-minded, those having mental or physical defects which might affect ability to earn a living, and unaccompanied children under sixteen. In 1917, Congress added alcoholics, stowaways, and persons of "constitutional psychopathic inferiority." [45]

These various acts extending from 1882 to 1917 would seem to include almost every type of undesirable and to give a fairly wide basis upon which to construct a system of selectivity. Nevertheless the demand for restriction increased. It was given added strength

[43] *Reports of the Immigration Commission*, II, 568–584. All federal immigration activities were transferred to the Department of Commerce and Labor when that department was established in 1903.

[44] Industrial Commission, *Final Report* (Washington: Government Printing Office, 1902), XIX, 1010–1030.

[45] Roy L. Garis, *Immigration Restriction* (New York: The Macmillan Company, 1927), pp. 104–116.

in 1910, when the Immigration Commission asserted that a slower industrial expansion was preferable to a rapid one if the latter resulted "in the immigration of laborers of low standards and efficiency, who imperil the American standards of wages and conditions of employment." It reported that a "majority of the Commission favor the reading and writing test as the most feasible single method of restricting undesirable immigration." [46] Rising nationalism inspired by the First World War and fear of an inundation of immigrants after the war added to the demand for restriction.

The Immigration Commission suggested not only a literacy test but also the limitation of the number of immigrants arriving annually at each port and the "limitation of the number of each race arriving each year to a certain percentage of the average of that race arriving during a given period of years." [47] This latter suggestion, which was finally tried after the war, was ignored at the moment in favor of a literacy test. Although many had pointed out that such a test might have little bearing on native intelligence, mental or physical health, or other factors upon which selectivity had been based, it had long seemed to many congressmen the simplest method of cutting down the size. President Cleveland had vetoed the test in 1897, but Congress returned to it in 1913, only to have it vetoed by Taft. Wilson also vetoed the literacy test in 1915 but Congress inserted such a provision in the Immigration Act of 1917 and overrode a second veto. The act of 1917, which is still part of the basic immigration law of the nation, repealed or reversed earlier laws and enlarged excluded classes. Its most important innovation was its provision, with certain exceptions, for the exclusion of "all aliens over sixteen years of age, physically capable of reading, who can not read the English language, or some other language or dialect, including Hebrew or Yiddish." [48] That Congress wanted the literacy test there could be no doubt; such a test had passed in one house or the other thirty-two times.

Despite the deluge of immigration during the first fifteen years of the century, it was the problem arising out of a few thousand Japanese on the Pacific Coast that occupied the major attention of the executive branch of the federal government. This was a recrudescence

[46] *Reports of the Immigration Commission,* I, 45, 48.

[47] *Ibid.,* p. 47.

[48] Jenks and Lauck, *The Immigration Problem,* 6th ed., reprints the Immigration Act of 1917 in Appendix A. The Congressional history is given in Henry P. Fairchild, "The Literacy Test and Its Making," *Quarterly Journal of Economics,* XXXI (May, 1917), 447–460.

of the old opposition to Oriental immigration which had been directed in the seventies and eighties against the Chinese. The essential background had been the economic competition between unskilled Chinese labor and that from Ireland and other countries. It had resulted in the exclusion of Chinese immigrants by legislation which had been re-enacted and made permanent in 1902 and 1904.[49] By the latter date legal Chinese immigration had ceased and the number of Chinese in the United States was declining. They numbered 106,701 in 1890 and 43,560 in 1920.

No sooner had the problem of Chinese immigration been solved to the satisfaction of the West Coast than that of the Japanese developed. Japanese aliens in 1890 numbered a bare 2,000. The number increased to 24,000 in 1900 and to 111,000 in 1910, of whom 70,000 resided in California. Although this was an infinitesimal percentage of the population of the nation and but 2 per cent of that of California, it developed a major issue between the United States and the Japanese government. Chiefly responsible for the migration were Emigration Societies in Japan and American employers seeking cheap labor. As with the Chinese, economic competition seems to have been the underlying influence behind the opposition. Japanese labor, as a whole, was cheaper than native and more industrious; moreover, it had no difficulty in competing with European or Mexican immigrants. Not important in industry, except in canning, the Japanese concentrated chiefly on agriculture. By 1919 they cultivated almost half a million acres, mainly in the areas of Sacramento, Fresno, Los Angeles, and El Centro, which were devoted chiefly to crops requiring intensive cultivation.[50] In certain irrigated regions, such as the counties of San Joaquin, Colusa, Placer, and Sacramento, the Japanese controlled from 50 to 75 per cent of the irrigated crops. Actual ownership, however, at its height in 1920 was but 74,769 acres, a tiny fraction of the 11,000,000 cultivated in the state.

If the Japanese had not been in competition with native laborers and farmers, and in some cases with small businessmen, and if they had been content to remain in segregated districts and in a subservient position, the anti-Japanese agitation might not have developed. As it was, an opposition reminiscent of the sand-lot agitation of the

[49] Garis, *Immigration Restriction*, pp. 296 and 304; Jenks and Lauck, *The Immigration Problem*, pp. 394–396.

[50] Map in Jenks and Lauck, *The Immigration Problem*, p. 248; Harry A. Millis, *The Japanese Problem in the United States* (New York: The Macmillan Company, 1915), pp. 79–151; Yamato Ichihashi, *The Japanese in the United States* (Stanford University: Stanford University Press, 1932), Chaps. XI–XII.

seventies appeared, born of economic competition, nurtured by race prejudice, and strengthened by talk of the yellow peril. The agitation was directed by the Asiatic Exclusion League, organized in 1905 and largely supported by labor organizations. It came to a head in an order of the San Francisco School Board in 1906 to establish separate schools for Chinese and Japanese children. The Japanese in San Francisco protested to the Japanese government, which in turn protested to the United States on the basis of the treaty of 1894. Roosevelt denounced the discrimination in a message to Congress and sent Secretary of Commerce and Labor Victor H. Metcalf to investigate the situation. On the basis of his report, the federal government filed suits in the federal circuit court and in the California state court to enforce the provisions of the treaty, which gave Japanese equal school privileges. The suits were never tried, for Roosevelt also invited the mayor and the school board to confer at Washington. On their return the order was rescinded.[51]

Out of this controversy came the "Gentlemen's Agreement" of 1907 between the two countries. Congress amended the immigration act, authorizing the President to refuse admission to any alien making use of passports to other countries to gain access to the United States. Roosevelt immediately took advantage of this provision and excluded Japanese laborers who had received passports for Mexico or Hawaii. Japan acceded to this and also agreed not to issue passports to continental United States to laborers except returning immigrants, and also to parents, wives, and to children under twenty years of age of emigrants already in the United States. Japan claimed to have abided by the "Gentlemen's Agreement" and during the fifteen years it was in force only 8,681 more Japanese arrived in continental United States than departed. The Japanese population, however, continued to increase, and the agitation in California continued. Californians particularly pointed to six thousand "picture brides" who came to that state between 1910 and 1920, women secured by marriage arrangements made through parents in Japan. So great was the protest in Canada as well as in the United States that Japan extended the "Gentlemen's Agreement" to include the "picture brides."

One result of the continuation of the anti-Japanese agitation was the introduction in the California legislature of a law rigidly restricting the holding of land either through purchase or through lease by

[51] Ichihashi, *The Japanese in the United States,* pp. 234 ff.; Thomas A. Bailey, *Theodore Roosevelt and the Japanese American Crises* (Stanford University: Stanford University Press, 1934), pp. 28–45, 123–149; Philip P. Jessup, *Elihu Root* (New York: Dodd, Mead & Company, 2 vols., 1938), II, 7–33.

aliens ineligible to citizenship under the naturalization laws. After a strong remonstrance by the Japanese government, President Wilson sent Secretary of State Bryan to California to explain the international situation and use his influence to prevent hostile legislation. Some gestures were made to prevent the bill from technically violating treaty obligations; it was then passed over protests of the Japanese government. It provided that aliens might lease agricultural land for three years only and that land already owned should not pass upon death to those ineligible to citizenship. The same limitation was placed upon corporations a majority of whose stock was owned by aliens not eligible to citizenship. The California act of 1913 was by no means the first discriminatory land legislation in this country and it was followed by other such acts, particularly in the western states.[52]

Any effort to summarize American demography in the twenty years after 1897 would show a population still growing rapidly but with the speed of growth declining. The old characteristic of mobility was evident, the general trend toward the West persisted, and the movement toward the cities continued with accelerated speed. Immigrants in unprecedented numbers sought American shores, but their origin had largely shifted from northwestern Europe to south, central, and eastern Europe. Unlike the "old immigration," which tended to take up western land, the "new immigration" sought industrial work in urban areas. The Negro population, increasing slowly but declining relatively to the size of the white population, was stirred as never before to move toward the North, a migration made possible by war jobs in the industrial areas and declining immigration from Europe. The flow of Oriental immigration, confined largely to the West Coast, had been largely halted by 1897 for the Chinese by exclusion laws, and for the Japanese before 1917 by the "Gentlemen's Agreement" and stringent land laws. By this time the nation had turned from an immigration policy of selection to one of restriction. The literacy test had been imposed and the quota plan was already being discussed.

[52] Millis, *The Japanese Problem in the United States*, Appendix B, reprints the California act of 1913, and Jenks and Lauck, *The Immigration Problem*, Appendix D, reprints a later act of 1920. See also Ichihashi, *The Japanese in the United States*, Chap. XVII; and Thomas A. Bailey, "California, Japan and the Alien Land Legislation of 1913," *Pacific Historical Review* (1932), I, 36–59.

(*Above*) Depositors gathered in front of one of the endangered New York banks during the Panic of 1907. (*Brown Brothers*)

(*Left*) Woodrow Wilson, President 1913–1921, taken about the time he assumed office. (*Culver Service*)

(*Below*) An optimistic cartoon appearing at the time of the adoption of the Federal Reserve banking system in 1913. (*Culver Service*)

(*Above left*) John D. Rockefeller, about 1908, founder of the Standard Oil Company, whose interests by 1900 were spreading into other industries and into transportation and banking. (*Above right*) J. Pierpont Morgan in 1902, financier and banker, who shared with the Rockefeller interests the domination of American economic life. (*Both pictures Culver Service*)

(*Below left*) William Rockefeller, brother of John D., a supersalesman, a commercial diplomat and audacious promoter. (*Below right*) Henry H. Rogers, who with William Rockefeller, operated a huge financial machine known to Wall Street as "Standard Oil." (*Both pictures Culver Service*)

(*Above*) Negroes working as ironers in a steam laundry in New York during the first great migration to the North. (*Below*) The first Negroes were moving into Harlem when this picture was taken during the First World War. (*Both pictures Brown Brothers*)

(*Above*) Immigrants from Eastern Europe arriving in New York about 1890. (*Below*) A Canadian asbestos mine operated by the Johns-Manville Company; an example of early economic expansion abroad. (*Both pictures Brown Brothers*)

(*Above*) Dropping the body on a Ford chassis, an early example of the development of the assembly line and mass production. (*Courtesy Ford Motor Company*) (*Insert*) Frederick Winslow Taylor, pioneer in improved machine tools and father of "scientific management." (*Brown Brothers*) (*Below*) Water used to provide power in this New England Power House of 1897. (*Bettmann Archive*)

(*Left*) A southern textile factory at the turn of the century. (*Brown Brothers*)

(*Below left*) Lee De Forest, a pioneer in wireless telegraphy and radio, in his laboratory. (*Culver Service*) (*Below right*) Elbert H. Gary, organizer of the United States Steel Corporation and J. P. Morgan's chief assistant. (*Both pictures Culver Service*)

(*Above*) Grand Central station in New York, completed in 1913. (*Courtesy New York Central Railroad*) (*Below left*) The Pennsylvania station, New York, opened in 1910. (*Culver Service*) (*Below right*) Edward H. Harriman (*top*) who dominated the central and southern routes to the Pacific, and (*bottom*) James J. Hill, who controlled the northern routes. (*Both pictures Culver Service*)

(*Above*) A Union Pacific engine of 1911. (*Courtesy Baldwin-Lima-Hamilton Corporation*) (*Below*) The Grand Central area in New York City before and after electrification of the New York entrance by the New York, New Haven and Hartford Railroad and the New York Central. (*Courtesy The New York, New Haven and Hartford Railroad*)

CHAPTER VI

The Technology of
American Manufactures

GROWTH AND CHARACTERISTICS

THE development of American manufacturing in the two decades after 1897 was impressive. During the years 1899 to 1919 the number of wage earners almost doubled, wages increased almost fivefold, and the value of products almost sixfold. Substantial as was this advance, it was not spectacular compared to that of certain other periods. The percentage of increase of wage earners, for example, large as it was in each of the first two decades of the century, was surpassed in the decades 1859–1869 and 1879–1889. The percentage of increase in wages was almost as great from 1879 to 1889 as in the decade 1909–1919, and it was not accompanied by a rampant inflation. Although the growth of industry, except in the war years 1914–1919, may not have been spectacular, it is clear that production had doubled in volume in the two decades. It had, in fact, increased twice as rapidly as population.[1]

In general most of the causes for this expansion were similar to those of earlier periods, with differences in detail or emphasis. As in every period since the birth of the factory system, technological improvements speeded the volume of production. This was particularly evident during the second decade of the century as increasing emphasis was placed on mass production and the assembly line. Although an expanding labor force was an important factor in in-

[1] Edmund E. Day and Woodlief Thomas, *The Growth of Manufactures 1899–1923* (U.S. Bureau of the Census, *Census Monograph* VIII, Washington: Government Printing Office, 1928), p. 35.

115

creasing production during the period as a whole, a study of the years 1899 to 1914 reveals the fact that the only notable gain in number of workers occurred during the expansion from 1904 to 1909. Except for those years the main agencies of increased production were "those elements of skill, mechanism and management which offset per capita output." [2] There was a speeding of factory production as it spread out to assume many of the functions performed in the home, a good example being the canning of fruits and vegetables. There were new industries, notably the manufacture of automobiles and electric appliances. Changes in foreign trade also influenced the character and amount of American manufactures. The nation was exporting smaller quantities of crude foodstuffs and importing more of them. At the same time the exportation of semimanufactured and finished goods increased rapidly.[3] Finally there was the stimulation of the First World War. The closing years of the nineteenth century witnessed an industrial expansion stimulated in part by the Spanish-American War; twenty years later the nation experienced a much greater war boom.

Unlike the growth in population, which tended to be relatively steady, that of manufacturing fluctuated under varying economic and other influences. Moreover, durable goods, as would be expected, fluctuated with wider variations than nondurable.[4] Conditions after 1899 were highly favorable, and rapid industrial expansion continued until the minor setback of 1903–1904. Despite this setback, the five years 1899–1904 showed a 22 per cent increase in volume of production. The next five-year period opened under unfavorable conditions and included the depression years 1907–1908, but demand picked up sufficiently by 1909 to show an increase in volume of 30 per cent. Industrial activity rose rapidly in 1909, but by 1913–1914 the nation had sunk into a recession, from which it was rescued by the First World War. Nevertheless, the volume of manufacturing increased by 6 per cent during the years 1909–1914. The next five years, which included the war, showed a new spurt in industrial production, which would have been even greater but for shortage of manpower and raw materials. Production increase for the period 1914–1919 was at least 26 per cent.[5] The Day and Thomas production index for these years follows:

[2] Frederick C. Mills, *Economic Tendencies in the United States* (New York: National Bureau of Economic Research, 1932), p. 29.
[3] *Ibid.*, p. 5.   [4] *Ibid.*, p. 25.
[5] Day and Thomas, *The Growth of Manufactures, 1899–1923*, p. 34.

Census Years	Production Index (1899 = 100)
1899	100
1904	122
1909	159
1914	169
1919	214

Source: Edmund E. Day and Woodlief Thomas, *The Growth of Manufactures, 1899–1923* (U.S. Bureau of the Census, *Census Monograph* VIII, Washington: Government Printing Office, 1928), pp. 32–33.

Other characteristics of this expanding production become evident upon close scrutiny. One is that the output of manufactured goods advanced at a rate almost double that of the production of raw materials.[6] The reasons seem generally to be the same as those already given to explain the increase in production of manufactured goods: advance in manufacturing outside the home, changes in the character of American foreign trade, and a rising standard of living. Relatively greater attention was given to the processing of raw materials than to their production. With regard to raw materials, these years saw an increasing use of nonagricultural products. It is evident that the "growth of production in the years preceding the World War was due largely to the development of mineral resources and the increasing volume of fabricated goods into which raw mineral products entered."[7] Industrial production was becoming increasingly dependent on minerals. In this connection it may be noted that the processing of food increased in volume more slowly than the processing of other raw materials.

Another important characteristic was the emphasis upon goods intended for use in capital equipment (machines, tools, and implements for further production) rather than for human consumption. In actual value the former probably amounted to not more than 20 per cent of the total production of the nation. Nevertheless, the volume of physical production of durable goods intended for capital equipment increased between 1901 and 1913 at an average annual rate of 5 per cent as against 2.6 per cent for goods intended for human consumption.[8] Mills's study shows that the average annual rate of increase of the physical volume of production (1901–1913) of nondurable goods (raw and processed) was 2.5 per cent, that of semidurable (mainly textile and leather) was 2.6, and that of durable, 4.6.[9] Among the groups showing the largest gains were the fabricat-

[6] Mills, *Economic Tendencies in the United States*, p. 4, gives the annual rate of increase of raw materials as 2.2 per cent and manufactured goods as 3.9.

[7] *Ibid.*, p. 13.   [8] *Ibid.*, p. 21.   [9] *Ibid.*, p. 23.

ing of iron and steel, the production of the nonferrous metals, and chemicals.

Fundamentally the increased production of durable goods was due to the movement toward industrialization. In the words of Day and Thomas, "We resort increasingly to the factory, and within the factory, increasingly to the machine. Inventions, technical improvements, new industrial processes make for continual change. Labor is displaced by machinery; old machines are rapidly replaced with new—all of which calls for larger and larger output of industrial materials and equipment." [10] In brief, this increased investment in machinery and the widening factory production of consumers' goods was a clear indication that the industrial life of the nation had advanced rapidly.

The list of leading industries in the Appendix (page 416) will give an idea of the relative importance of the first fifteen American industries rated by value of products. Although slaughtering and meat packing, judged by this criterion, was America's leading industry after 1904, it should be noted that by 1919 metal industries comprised three out of the first five. A clearer picture of the growing importance of minerals in American manufacture may be seen from a study of the growth of physical output. By industry groups, the following grew most rapidly in the order named between 1899 and 1909: iron and steel products, printing and publishing, paper products, petroleum and coal products, and chemical products. Between 1909 and 1919 the order was transportation equipment, petroleum and coal products, chemical products, tobacco products, and printing and publishing. During the second decade, there was a decline in forest products and beverages.[11] A more specific list is furnished by Mills, who gives the following as showing the greatest increase in physical volume for 1899–1914: automobiles, including bodies and parts, beet sugar, manufactured ice, manufactured gas, refining of petroleum, fertilizers, explosives, salt, canning and preserving, paper and wood pulp.[12]

TECHNOLOGICAL ASPECTS

Essential to any study of industry since the beginning of the Industrial Revolution is the history of mechanization. Virtually every

[10] Day and Thomas, *The Growth of Manufactures, 1899–1923,* pp. 90–91.
[11] Solomon Fabricant, *The Output of Manufacturing Industries* (New York: National Bureau of Economic Research, 1940), pp. 60–61.
[12] Mills, *Economic Tendencies in the United States,* p. 30.

type of measurement available shows that mechanization went on rapidly, and did so despite the deluge of cheap immigrant labor which entered the country until the opening of the First World War. The period of most rapid mechanization was from 1899 to 1909, and the period of slowest growth from 1909 to 1914. During the twenty years from 1899 to 1919, the horsepower capacity in manufacturing tripled, whereas the horsepower per wage earner increased from 2.11 to 3.24. Important as was the mechanization of manufacture, it should be noted in passing that between 1909 and 1919 the amount of horsepower per worker was greater and the percentage increase was more rapid for agriculture, mines and quarries, and steam railroads, than for manufactures.[13]

HORSEPOWER PER WAGE EARNER FOR INDUSTRIAL GROUPS, 1899–1919

	1899	1909	1919
Chemical and allied industries	2.34	3.84	4.78
Iron and steel and their products	2.94	4.44	5.10
Stone, clay, and glass products	2.30	2.62	5.20
Paper and printing	3.06	4.02	4.61
Rubber products	1.95	2.49	2.71
Food and kindred products	4.03	4.44	4.04
Nonferrous metals and their products	1.33	1.86	2.91
Lumber and its remanufactures	3.15	3.56	4.07
Vehicles, including railroad repair shops	0.79	1.29	1.51
Textiles and their products	1.36	1.58	2.03
Leather and its finished products	0.64	0.91	1.11
Tobacco manufactures	0.17	0.17	0.28
All industries	2.11	2.82	3.24

Source: Harry Jerome, *Mechanization in Industry* (New York: National Bureau of Economic Research, Inc., 1934), pp. 456–462.

This mechanization of industry was characterized by enlarging the capacity of the machine unit by increasing either its physical size or the speed at which it functioned. It was accompanied by an increase in the size of the establishment. And one result, of course, was to increase the productivity of the worker. The latter development may be illustrated by the fact that in 1900 the annual amount of finished steel produced by each wage earner in the industry was 85 tons; in 1920 it was 114 tons. What happened has been well summarized by Mills:

The record of the fifteen years from 1899 to 1914 indicates that the factors responsible for the great advance in the production of manufactured goods were an increasing number of workers, larger and better

[13] Harry Jerome, *Mechanization in Industry* (New York: National Bureau of Economic Research, 1934), pp. 216–225.

equipped establishments and steadily rising output per worker employed.
. . . The stream of manufactured goods produced in 1914, a stream
greater by 76 per cent in volume than that of 1899, was turned out by a
working force of wage earners only 36 per cent greater, and by a number
of establishments only 13 per cent greater. There are clear signs here of
the growing emphasis upon technical efficiency and enhanced productivity per unit as factors of increased production, an emphasis which has
been even more pronounced in recent years.[14]

Technology was improved not alone by the enlargement of machine capacity but also by the use of improved materials and all of
the management methods that concern the selection and training of
workers and their conditions of work.[15] Moreover, the years 1897–
1917 were productive of many inventions or improved processes.
Many lists of such inventions or discoveries have been offered. One
presented to the Temporary National Economic Committee suggests
twenty-four: 1898, radium (Curie); 1899, loading coil for long-
distance telegraphy and telephony (Pupin); 1900, high-speed tool
steel (Taylor and White); 1900, Nernst lamp; 1902, radical type of
airplane engine (Manly); 1902, hydrogenation of oils; 1903, first man-
lifting airplane (the Wrights); 1903, arc process nitrogen fixation
(Birkeland and Eyde); 1903, oil-burning steamer; 1903, tantalum
lamp (Von Bolton); 1903, flotation process for nonferrous metals;
1905, cyanimide process for nitrogen fixation (Rothe); 1905, domestic
electric washing machine; 1906, synthetic resins (Baekeland); 1906,
Audion tube (De Forest); 1907, automatic bottle machine (Owens);
1907, tungsten lamp; 1907, television photograph (Korn); 1907, multiple disk clutch; 1909, Duralumin (Wilm); 1910, gyrocompass
(Sperry); 1910, synthetic ammonia process for nitrogen fixation
(Haber); 1914, tungsten filament light (Coolidge); 1917, mechanical
refrigeration.[16]

At least half of these improvements or inventions were produced
in the United States. Moreover, a large proportion of them were in
the field of electricity or chemicals, and were of tremendous impor-

[14] Mills, *Economic Tendencies in the United States*, pp. 38–39. Reprinted by permission of National Bureau of Economic Research, Inc., publishers.

[15] Lewis L. Lorwin and John M. Blair, *Technology in Our Economy* (Temporary
National Economic Committee, *Monograph* No. 22, Washington: Government Printing
Office, 1941), pp. 89–123.

[16] *Transcript of Testimony of Dr. Theodore J. Kreps on Technology and the Organi-
zation of Economic Power, April 8, 1940* (Washington: The Bureau of International
Affairs), p. 28. The list is compiled from Lewis Mumford, *Technics and Civilization*
(New York: Harcourt, Brace and Company, 1934), pp. 445–446, and William P.
Ogburn and S. Colum Gilfillan, "The Influence of Invention and Discovery," in Report
of the President's Research Committee on Social Trends, *Recent Social Trends* (New
York: McGraw-Hill Book Company, 2 vols., 1933), I, 135–148.

tance in the development in America of both of these industries. Of the many influences during those years which speeded mechanization and factory production, two stand pre-eminent—the evolution of mass production and the widening application of electric power to factory production.

MASS PRODUCTION

"Mass production," according to Henry Ford, one of its chief exponents, "is the focussing upon a manufacturing project of the principles of power, accuracy, economy, system, continuity and speed. . . . And the normal result is a productive organization that delivers in quantities a useful commodity of standard material, workmanship and design at minimum cost." [17] Certainly such an objective was by no means new to American manufacturers. The fundamental idea upon which mass production rested—the standardization of parts and interchangeable mechanism—had been practically applied since Eli Whitney introduced it in the manufacture of guns in the 1790's. Many other factors and conditions were essential to the full evolution of mass production, and more than a century passed between Whitney's "interchangeable mechanism" and Henry Ford's assembly line.

Essential to mass production were the progress of technology and invention, the availability of adequate capital, and a national market big enough to absorb the product, for mass production was based upon mass consumption.[18] By 1900 these conditions had been met. Population had grown to 76,000,000, and the purchasing power of the people as a whole was relatively high. It was estimated in 1900 that the per capita consumption of manufactures in the United States was 50 per cent higher than that in Great Britain and twice as great as that in Germany and France. It seems also apparent that the development of mass production had been correlated with the growth in the size of the manufacturing plant and with the process of industrial integration and consolidation.[19]

By 1900, invention and technology had reached a stage where standardization and rapid production could join hands. This situation was based on the development of the machine-tool industry and

[17] Henry Ford, "Mass Production," in *Encyclopædia Britannica*, 13th ed. (New York: Encyclopædia Britannica, 13th ed., 28 vols., and 3 supp. vols., 1926), Supp. Vol. II, p. 821.
[18] Samuel Resnick, "Mass Production since the War between the States," in Harold F. Williamson, ed., *The Growth of American Economy* (New York: Prentice-Hall, 1944), pp. 497–501.
[19] *Ibid.*, p. 509.

the improvement of machine tools, that is, such machinery as lathes, grinders, boring mills, drill presses, planers, and milling machines. Although hundreds of new machine tools were invented and thousands of improvements perfected, the great advance was based on the development of a new high-speed carbon steel. Since machine tools are no better than their cutting edge, the improvement of steel was essential. The research for this was largely done by the great engineer, Frederick Winslow Taylor and his collaborator at the Bethlehem Steel Company, J. Maunsel White, and was climaxed by the publication in 1906 of the paper, "The Art of Cutting Metal." The Taylor-White high-speed carbon tool steel more than doubled the productivity of machine tools.

While Taylor was doing his revolutionary work on cutting metal, he was also agitating for improved management and a more scientific and efficient use of the workers' time. Taylor's ideas, which he called "scientific management," won many followers. Without scientific application of management and labor to production, mass production was hardly possible and "scientific management," says Samuel Resnick, became "a major contribution to the rapid development of mass production after 1910." [20] Such a contribution was bound to be particularly important in the era of industrial integration and consolidation, which opened in 1897, and which was generally followed by larger plant output.

With the groundwork laid before 1900, the development of mass production was stepped up during the following years. By that time the industries making machinery employed 414,000, or 8.8 per cent of all workers in the country. By 1919 the workers had grown to 998,000 and the percentage to 11.[21] Moreover, production of machinery had increased more rapidly than total manufacturing output. The machine-tool industry was now building new and complex machinery of automatic and multiple design. To the high-speed Taylor-White carbon tool steel were added, after 1910, molybdenum, tantalum, and tungsten-steel alloys. Finer cutting tools also allowed greater precision. To increase productivity came the application of the electric motor to machine tools, giving them greater power, speed, and flexibility at the same time that it gave the workers portable, power-driven hand tools. Electricity also made important contributions in the assembly of metal parts after electric welding had been invented in the 1880's.

Now that machine-tool improvement had reached a stage where

[20] *Ibid.*, p. 500. Scientific management will be discussed in Chapter XI.
[21] Jerome, *Mechanization in Industry*, pp. 232–235.

interchangeability of parts had become practical even for the most complicated machinery, industry was ready to concentrate on the last stage of mass production—the problem of assembly. The leadership here was taken by the Ford Motor Company, which by 1913 had a daily capacity of 1,000 cars and an annual production of more than 250,000, almost half the total output of the industry. Automobile manufacturing had already become one of the nation's great industries; during the 1920's it became the leading industry in the country in the value of its products. The automobile industry, and the Ford Motor Company in particular, was pre-eminently fitted for experimentation in assembly technique. The industry was growing rapidly and the demand for its products seemed insatiable as long as the cost of the product could be steadily reduced to meet the income of the middle class and the wage earner. Moreover, the automobile industry in its early years was largely a business of assembling parts made in various machine shops and collected at an assembly point. Whether parts were manufactured on the outside or within the plant, assembly was always a major operation. Not only was Ford the largest producer; from 1908 until 1927 he manufactured the same type of car without important modification. This standardized design offered great possibilities for specialized machinery and dies and for almost infinite subdivision of labor.

Ford began with the system developed in earlier years in the manufacture of watches, sewing machines, guns, and bicycles—that of "stationary assembly." Under this system all the component parts of an assembly were brought to the worker, who then put them together. At the Ford plant a hundred of these stations were set up for chassis assembly; at each station five workers served as assemblers while others brought up the necessary parts. In 1913 Ford began to experiment with the "moving assembly," a much more efficient method of delivering work to the men. Starting with smaller parts, Ford began in 1914 to apply the technique to the assembly of the chassis. At first the men drew the chassis with a rope and windlass. These soon gave way to belt-and-chain conveyors moved by motors. Other methods quickly followed, such as gravity chutes and monorail conveyers. All this was to deliver work at a predetermined speed sufficient to accomplish a small and specialized task. With assembly lines and subassembly lines and specialization by individuals and crews, mass production reached maturity.[22]

That the assembly line reduced time and labor cost was quickly

[22] Evan B. Alderfer and Herman E. Michl, *Economics of American Industry* (New York: McGraw-Hill Book Company, 1942), pp. 117–121.

demonstrated. Ford found that the new method reduced the assembly of the flywheel magneto from twenty minutes to five. Stationary assembly of the chassis had required twelve and one half hours; subdivision of the work and the assembly line finally cut the time to slightly over one hour and a half. Mass production based on the assembly line was mainly responsible for the reduction of the base price of the Model T from $950 to $290. At the same time Ford was increasing the pay of his workers to a minimum daily rate of $5 and decreasing the workday from nine to eight hours (1914). It is little wonder that American industry turned to the assembly line as the capstone of mass production.

THE USE OF ELECTRIC POWER

One of the most revolutionary aspects of American manufacturing history in the years 1897–1917 was the development of electric power and its rapid substitution for other forms. This revolution had by no means been completed at the latter date, but it had gone far enough to make clear the trend. In 1899, the amount of power purchased and applied through electric motors represented but 1.8 per cent of the industrial power machinery in the United States; in 1919, the percentage had grown to 31.7. After that it continued to increase rapidly, while most other forms of industrial power machinery declined both actually and relatively. At the same time the total primary factory power applied through electric motors increased from 5 per cent in 1899 to 55 per cent in 1919.[23] Six years later it was 73 per cent. The Department of Commerce estimated in 1930 that "practically all the increase in factory power equipment since 1914 has been in electric motors operated by current from central stations." [24]

Two causes account for this significant shift in power: first, the superiority of electric power in convenience and cost for many industrial producers; second, technical advances in electricity which made the whole change possible. It is obviously more convenient and usually less expensive for the manufacturer, particularly in the light industries, to obtain his power by simply turning a switch than to build and maintain his own power plant. Electricity is superior when

[23] Leon P. Alford, "Technical Changes in Manufacturing Industries," in report of the Committee on Recent Economic Changes of the President's Conference on Unemployment, Recent Economic Changes (New York: McGraw-Hill Book Company, 2 vols., 1929), I, 126.

[24] U.S. Department of Commerce, Bureau of Foreign and Domestic Commerce, Commerce Yearbook, 1930 (Washington: Government Printing Office, 2 vols., 1930), I, 268.

constant speed is required in order to turn out maximum amounts of a uniform product, as in the textile industry. It is also a superior power when constant adjustments of speed may be necessary or where portable machine tools are used. As the electrical industry reduced the cost of electric power and produced motors of noncorrosive structure, electric power proved superior for the chemical industry and for electrochemical processes.[25]

Technical convenience and superiority, however, were by no means the only reasons why industry turned to electric power. After electrical engineers had solved the problem of transporting power over long distances, industry was freed from the necessity of locating close to the source of power. Factories could be established almost anywhere. As graphically expressed in 1928 by Glenn Frank:

> In a machine civilization created by steam power, the worker must go to the power, but in a machine civilization created by electric power, the power can be taken to the worker; and that is a revolutionary fact which means that when we say "machine civilization" in terms of 1950, we may be dealing with a machine civilization that is as different as imagination can conceive from the machine civilization which began when James Watt first harnessed the expansive power of steam to the processes of production.[26]

Since the electrical industry was relatively new in the 1890's, its tremendous advance during the first two decades of the twentieth century encompasses fundamental advances in every phase of the industry. It was not until 1882, it will be remembered, that Thomas A. Edison built the first central station in New York to provide electric power for public use, and shortly after that George Westinghouse and William Stanley developed the principle of alternating current. It was as late as 1888 that Nikola Tesla invented a simple and reliable alternating current motor and thus made possible the wider use of electric power in industry.

Two events in the middle 1890's gave a tremendous boost to the use of electric power in industry. The first, in 1895, now universally recognized as an outstanding event of the electrical industry, was the building of a 5,000-horsepower alternating current generator, the first of three such generators to be driven by power derived directly from Niagara Falls. This was the basis of a hydroelectric de-

[25] L. A. Osborne, "The Electric Industry" in Herman T. Warshow, ed., *Representative Industries in the United States* (New York: Henry Holt and Company), pp. 313–315.

[26] Address delivered at the Midwest Power Conference, Chicago, February 14–17, 1928, quoted in *Recent Economic Changes*, I, 125.

velopment which reached 4,000,000 horsepower by 1912. Before this great development could take place, inventions were necessary which would lengthen the transportation of electric power from the few miles needed for the Niagara power in 1895 to the long distances used in succeeding years. Again it was Nikola Tesla who made this possible through his development of a high-potential magnifying transmitter.

Almost simultaneously with the development of hydroelectric power came a similar expansion in the production of electricity by steam power. In 1896 George Westinghouse purchased the American rights to the compound reaction steam engine known as the steam turbine, invented in 1884 by Charles Parsons in England. Westinghouse and others so quickly adapted the steam turbine to production of low-cost electricity that engines of the old type were quickly driven from the field. Before many years, steam-turbine electric generator units of 100,000-horsepower capacity were in operation, making the first hydroelectric generators at Niagara Falls look like pygmies. "Largely to the turbine," said Osborne in 1928, ". . . belongs the credit for the immense amount of low-cost electric power that is now being supplied to users throughout the United States." [27] The story is told of how seventeen 10,000-horsepower reciprocating engines were built in 1899 for the New York subway system then under construction. In the opinion of many engineers, these magnificent machines, towering forty feet above their massive concrete foundations, were not only the largest engines of their type ever built but were so well designed and constructed that they were capable of operating for a century with unimpaired efficiency. Three years later, high-speed compound turbines of one tenth their size had rendered them obsolete.

In surveying the history of the electrical industry during the period 1897–1917, the student finds it easy to assume that the fundamental inventions were made before 1897 and the great fruition of a century of research came after the First World War. The two decades under study appear to be chiefly a period of extension, application, and improvement. In a sense this is true. The first electric household appliance, the flat iron, made its appearance at the World's Fair in 1893. Numerous others were gradually invented, but it was not until the 1920's that the electrically equipped home became a reality. Edison had developed a practical light bulb long before 1900, but the full possibilities of a vacuum tube with its various applications and

[27] Osborne in Warshow, ed., *Representative Industries in the United States*, p. 310.

ramifications were hardly fulfilled until the days of radio after the First World War. The work of Wilhelm K. Roentgen in Germany and Michael I. Pupin in the United States brought epoch-making applications of electricity to medicine in the X ray by 1896, but it was not until 1913 that William D. Coolidge greatly improved the original machine when he produced a high-voltage tube in which X rays were created by a bombardment of electrons from the tungsten electrode.[28] The telephone had been invented in the 1870's and great technical improvements had been made after that date, but in 1915 Pupin and other scientists, by loading through coils and condensers, made it possible to carry on a conversation across the continent.

However these decades are characterized, no period in American history saw a greater galaxy of brilliant scientists working in the field of electricity. To the pioneering giants, Thomas A. Edison, George Westinghouse, and Elihu Thomson, who continued to work into the twentieth century, were added the brilliant immigrants Nikola Tesla (polyphase alternating current motor), Michael I. Pupin (loading telephone wires through circuits and coils), Charles P. Steinmetz (law of hysteresis and symbolic method of calculating alternating current phenomena), and E. F. W. Alexanderson (high-frequency alternator). Among the native born were Irving Langmuir (structure of atoms, "surface chemistry," gas-filled incandescent lamp, vacuum tube improvements), William D. Coolidge (tungsten and X ray), and Lee De Forest (wireless telegraphy and radio telephone). With these men as leaders in a rapidly developing science it is easy to understand how the number of establishments manufacturing electrical machinery, apparatus, and supplies should grow from 581 in 1899 to 1,404 in 1919, wage earners in the industry from 42,013 to 212,374, and capital from $83,660,000 to $857,855,000.[29] Exports of electrical machinery and appliances grew from $10,507,000 in 1904 to $79,719,000 in 1919.

INVENTIONS AND IMPROVEMENTS

Of the tens of thousands of mechanical inventions which helped to speed the development of industry in the twenty years after 1897, it is impossible to deal in detail with more than a few which stand

[28] John W. Hammond, *Men and Volts: The Story of General Electric* (Philadelphia: J. B. Lippincott Company, 1941), p. 355. On the work of these men see also Alfred B. Morgan, *The Pageant of Electricity* (New York: D. Appleton–Century Company, 1939).

[29] Warshow, ed., *Representative Industries in the United States*, p. 323.

out as mileposts in their industries. The introduction, about 1899, of the rotating kiln, which produced a standardized Portland cement at reasonable cost, inaugurated a great development in that industry. The old stationary kilns consumed less fuel, but the rotating kiln saved labor and also produced a uniform and standardized product. After 1900 the production of Portland cement skyrocketed and that of natural cement declined.

In similar manner, the glass-container industry, which was in an extremely backward state in 1900, was utterly revolutionized by Michael Owens, an Ohio glassmaker who patented in 1903 a method of drawing the glass from the furnace by mechanical means and then forming the bottle in the mold by compressed air. This invention was introduced slowly, but it eventually eliminated the skilled worker of earlier days who made his bottle with blowpipe and hand power. In the same industry, window glass in 1900 was also produced almost entirely by hand craftsmen, with five classes of skilled workers participating in the fashioning of molten glass into a sheet. In 1900 a cylinder machine and a mechanical glass blower took the place of the old method of blowing a cylindrical bubble of glass which, when cooled, was split open and flattened. Between that year and 1913–1914, when a better technique was introduced, the cylinder machine cut down by 56 per cent the window glass produced by hand power.[30]

The rotating cement kiln and the Owens bottle machine fundamentally changed two industries. Less revolutionary, but at the same time important effects were experienced by improvements in the metal industries. Significant in the technique of the basic iron and steel industry was the decline after 1905 of the production of steel by the Bessemer process and the rapid advance of the open-hearth method. The primary reasons were two: both low-phosphorous and high-phosphorous iron could be used in Bessemer converters, but medium-phosphorous iron, the type most common in the United States, could not; and the Bessemer container consumed only molten pig iron whereas the open-hearth furnace could take scrap metal. A minor development during these years was the production of steel by electric heat. Knowledge of European experiments was finally taken up in the United States about 1908. After that, electric steel increased rapidly, particularly after the outbreak of the First World War.[31] One of the outstanding developments in copper technology

[30] Lorwin and Blair, *Technology in Our Economy*, p. 141.
[31] Alderfer and Michl, *Economics of American Industry*, pp. 47–49.

occurred about 1914, when "froth flotation" was introduced in the "concentration" process to separate in a mixture of water and oil the pulverized ore from the gangue or refuse. This was a notable improvement in one of the world's oldest industries.

The first industry affected by the inventions of the industrial revolution was textile manufacturing, in which the fundamental inventions had been made within a half century after the introduction of Kay's fly shuttle. Not until 1895, when the Northrop loom was introduced, did the industry experience another epoch-making invention. This loom, invented and perfected by James H. Northrop and George A. Draper, contained two basic improvements: it saved the time of the worker by automatically ejecting empty bobbins from the shuttle and inserting fresh ones in the brief time (one twentieth of a second) the shuttle is at rest between trips across the loom; and it introduced a mechanism which automatically and instantly stopped the loom when even a single warp broke.[32] Northrop looms were rapidly introduced after the opening of the century. Within a decade the number of looms a weaver could tend had increased from eight to twenty-four.

The impression that the chemical industry had its first great American development after the First World War is far from correct. It is true that the defeat of Germany and the capture of 4,500 patents opened the way for a tremendous expansion of dyestuff manufacturing and that the manufacture of plastics and synthetics is comparatively recent. The United States, nevertheless, had made considerable progress in the heavy chemical industries before 1917, particularly in the manufacture of sulphuric acid, ammonia, and the alkalis. "It was the successful introduction of the Solvay process and the development of the electrolytic process in this country," says Victor Clark, "that promoted the American chemical industry from a local, comparatively unimportant and technically backward branch of manufacturing to a leading position in the chemical industry of the world." [33] Although the Solvay process was in use in the 1880's, its great expansion came in the 1890's; the electrolytic process awaited the development of large-scale electric power after 1900.

These two processes did much to promote the production of such alkalis as ammonia soda and caustic and bleaching powders. Domestic electrolytic chlorine was produced in the 1890's and became com-

---

[32] *Ibid.*, p. 305.
[33] Victor Clark, *History of Manufactures in the United States* (New York: McGraw-Hill Book Company, 3 vols., 1929), III, 287.

mon in subsequent years. The rapid substitution after 1903 of the superior Louisiana sulphur for that imported from Sicily was also a boon to the chemical industry. The plastic discoveries of Leo H. Baekeland in 1909 added a new subdivision to chemical manufacture, and Milton C. Whitaker's methods of producing absolute alcohol by distilling with benzene put America in the forefront in this product and made possible the production of many essential oils not hitherto economically practical. Nor should the fact be forgotten that the background was laid in the 1890's for the development of oxyacetylene welding and cutting.[34] These discoveries and improvements, along with scores of others, contributed to an impressive growth of the chemical industry after 1900; its aggregate product rose in value from $48,000,000 in 1899 to $158,000,000 in 1914.

During this period certain manufactures were established which may be fairly described as "new industries." Although their growth was usually rapid, none reached maturity until after the First World War. Four may be noted: the manufacture of automobiles, aluminum products, rayons, and airplanes. The most spectacular in its rise was the automobile, but no single invention and no single person accounts for it. When Charles E. Duryea, Ransom E. Olds, Elwood Haynes, Henry Ford, and other tinkering mechanics began playing with the idea of the "horseless carriage" in the early nineties, the fundamental inventions had been made. All of them were in a crude stage; all had to be refined, improved, and assembled to make the finished product a practical one. This was the business of early automobile manufacturing, and the job was done from the quality of the rubber in the tires to the perfection of the timing of the internal-combustion engine. Important for the manufacturer was the introduction in 1903 of a multiple press to work cylinder blocks and treads, and in the same year a machine to grind the cylinders, a lathe to turn camshafts, and a vertical turret lathe designed to turn fly shafts. For the consumer the most notable invention between 1900 and 1917 was the self-starter, which increased beyond measure the convenience of driving.[35]

Aluminum resembled the automobile in that the fundamental inventions were made before 1897. By that time chemists and metallurgists had conquered the basic problems for commercial produc-

---

[34] Henry Wigglesworth, in Warshow, ed., *Representative Industries in the United States*, pp. 130–182.

[35] The development of the automobile will also be described in Chap. X.

tion. After that the industry had to establish the importance and superiority of aluminum for kitchen utensils, automobiles, electrical equipment, and other commodities where a hard but light metal was needed. The aluminum industry came of age simultaneously with the automobile. Although the fundamental knowledge had been acquired before 1897, improvements in the process of concentration of bauxite and in the reduction of aluminum continued. None was more important than the Hoopes method for the refining of impure aluminum through an electrolytic process, an outstanding example of the application of electricity to industrial production.

Americans made important contributions in the fundamental discoveries that made possible the development of the aluminum industry. Unlike aluminum, "artificial silk," or "rayon"—as it came to be called after 1924—was based entirely on European discoveries. American production did not begin until 1911, but development in this country was exceedingly rapid after 1918, and from then on Americans made their contributions.

The fourth new industry mentioned above—the production of airplanes—unlike rayon, largely originated in America as the result of the epoch-making experiments of Samuel P. Langley, of Charles M. Manly, and of Orville and Wilbur Wright. But even the famous experiments of the Wright brothers involved little that was new. The heavier-than-air flying machine was a combination of the knowledge gradually accumulated by Otto Lilienthal, the Wrights, and other experimenters with gliders and the internal-combustion engines. Like the automobile, the airplane was a collection and assemblage of knowledge gleaned widely, but no person in the automobile industry occupies the same important position that the Wright brothers have in the history of airplanes. The patience, the persistence, and above all, the skill of these men, which amounted to genius, were necessary to produce the airplane.

As significant as the new industries was the development of older ones. This is notable in the electrical industry not alone in the improvement of power machinery, but in such fields as the transportation of sound and in home appliances. It can be seen in the production of oils and gases and in the improvement of rubber goods. Two American chemists discovered methods which opened a new day for the rubber industry. The first was Arthur Marks, who obtained in 1899 a patent for his alkali process of reclaiming rubber. The second was George Oenslager, who discovered new methods of rubber acceleration processes which speeded manufacture and improved the rubber.[36] One of the greatest revolutions in any single industry was the substitution of gasoline for kerosene as the main product of the petroleum industry. In 1896 gasoline was a waste product in the manufacture of kerosene; by the early 1920's it represented half the value of the total refined products of the industry. Industrial improvements were particularly noteworthy in photographic appliances, office equipment, and building materials, and in the combinations of photography and electricity which have produced the moving picture.

INDUSTRIAL RESEARCH

One of the outstanding aspects of the period from 1897 to 1917 was the transition of scientific research from the individual workshop or laboratory to the industrial laboratory financed by commercial concerns. The last quarter of the nineteenth century, represented by such men as Edison, marked the great day of the individual inventor, and his type carried over in the new century in the work of the Wright brothers. Large-scale organized research had developed in Europe before it became commonplace in the United States, and had proved its value. It had been held back in America partly because of the fact that much of American manufacturing was concerned with the simple processes of reducing raw materials to a form for the export market and for further use in manufacturing, all this giving little encouragement for elaborate organized research. Brilliant individual inventors, in fact, had managed to keep ahead of industrial entrepreneurs in providing possibilities for industrial expansion. Moreover, large and well-organized laboratories waited upon large-scale industry financially able to support them and upon business sufficiently organized and consolidated to appreciate research that was also organized.

By 1900 such conditions had developed. The principle of scientific management might now be applied to organized research as well as to organized production. Although Edison, Thomson, and other great inventors had assistants, it was the federal government that pioneered with the research laboratory, whose greatest contribution was in agriculture. The Hatch Act of 1887, which set up experiment stations, was as much a milestone in scientific research as the Morrill Act had

[36] Howard and Ralph Wolf, *Rubber: A Story of Glory and Greed* (New York: Covici, Friede, 1936), pp. 334–356.

been in vocational education. The bureaus of the Department of Agriculture, the Bureau of Mines of the Department of the Interior, the Federal Bureau of Standards (1901) and many other government bureaus, offices, and organizations, as well as the Smithsonian Institution, had already done significant research by the time private industry swung into line. Said a leading chemist in 1913: "It may be said without fear of contradiction that through the combined efforts of the Department of Agriculture, the Experiment Stations, the Agricultural Colleges, and our manufacturers of agricultural machinery, there is devoted to American agriculture a far greater amount of scientific research and effort than is at the service of any other business in the world." [37]

Not only were the agricultural colleges engaged in research of an immediate practical nature; technical schools and other colleges and universities were similarly occupied. Taking its cue from the government laboratories and those of the technical schools and universities, private industry began to realize the tremendous advantages and great ultimate profits in such type of work. Led by the Bell Telephone System, the Du Pont Company, the General Electric Company, and the Eastman Kodak Company, at least fifty concerns had set up important laboratories by 1913.[38] The expenditure of several of them was over $300,000 a year, the United States Steel Company alone spending that amount on a single project. As early as 1913 the Du Pont Company was employing 250 trained chemists. Between 1903 and 1918, said Frank B. Jewett, head of the research laboratories for the Western Electric Company, which then handled research for the Bell System, the work in the Bell laboratories grew from one or two back rooms to a half million feet of floor space and "from inventive experimentation and rule of thumb methods to one in which principles of research govern practically every course of action." [39] By that time these laboratories employed about one thousand men. Some of the more famous of the large group of scientists in the laboratory of the General Electric Company (founded in 1901) under the direction of Willis R. Whitney have already been mentioned.

Although industrial research advanced from 1900 to 1913, it was

[37] Arthur D. Little, *Industrial Research in America*. Presidential address before the American Chemical Society of Rochester, N.Y., September 9, 1913 (Boston: Arthur D. Little, Inc., 1913), p. 13.

[38] *Ibid.*, p. 18.

[39] Frank B. Jewett, *Industrial Research* (Washington: National Research Council, 1918), p. 2.

the First World War which gave it a real impetus. Spurred on by the war, the National Research Council was organized in 1916 by the National Academy of Sciences at the request of President Wilson. It acted as a clearinghouse of information, as an integrator of scientific information, and as a formulator of general policies. The war also brought an exodus of many research professors from the colleges and universities to industries. Industrial research, according to Jewett grew ten times between 1915 and 1918. In his opinion, this development was at a stiff price. It cut down the advance of theoretical science and destroyed for the moment the chance to develop new men to carry on investigations both in the universities and in industry.[40]

It was not until 1920 that the National Research Council made a survey of existing industrial research in the country. It contained the names of 300 laboratories which stated in direct correspondence with the Council that they were engaged in research. This study was revised in 1921, when about 250 new names were added.[41] These surveys clearly illustrate that industrial research at the end of the First World War was in its infancy in the United States. It had grown rapidly, but the majority of the laboratories had been established since 1914. Moreover, they were surprisingly small. The corporations noted above and a few others had large staffs, but most of the laboratories had less than ten workers. However, large concerns were already solving their own problems rather than turning them over to outside inventors or to machine-tool manufacturers. In another decade industry would reach the stage of "deliberately developed" inventions by the group rather than by the individual.[42]

[40] *Ibid.*, p. 2.
[41] Alfred D. Flinn, *Research Laboratories in Industrial Establishments of the United States of America* (Washington: National Research Council, 1920); and Alfred D. Flinn and Ruth Cobb, *Research Laboratories in Industrial Establishments of the United States* (Washington: National Research Council, 1921).
[42] Ralph C. Epstein, "Industrial Invention: Heroic or Systematic?" *Quarterly Journal of Economics,* VL (February, 1926), 254–255.

CHAPTER VII

The Movement of Industry

LOCALIZATION AND GEOGRAPHIC CHANGES

AMERICAN industry at the beginning of the century was centered in the Northeast, with New England and the Middle Atlantic states accounting for more than half the nation's manufacturing. If the East North Central states are added, at least three fourths of the manufacturing was concentrated in the region bounded by the Great Lakes and the St. Lawrence on the north, the Mississippi River on the west, and the Ohio River and the Mason and Dixon line on the south.[1] In area, this so-called "manufacturing belt" comprised only one seventh of the land area of the nation.

Despite a general movement of industry toward the west, accompanied by notable increases in the West South Central and Pacific states, the picture of concentration twenty years later had changed but slightly. Measured by the number of industrial wage earners, the manufacturing belt in 1919 still contained 72.8 per cent of that group. A glance at the table on page 136 will show that New England and the Middle Atlantic states declined somewhat in their relative position during the two decades. Nevertheless, the average number of manufacturing wage earners in each thousand of population increased in New England between 1899 and 1919 from 152 to 183 and in the Middle Atlantic states from 104 to 129.[2]

So striking was the concentration of industry in the United States, as well as the localization of specific industries in certain limited

---

[1] Besides New England, this area includes the states of New York, New Jersey, Pennsylvania, Ohio, Indiana, Illinois, Michigan, and Wisconsin.

[2] Harold D. Kube and Ralph H. Danhof, *Changes in Distribution of Manufacturing Wage Earners, 1899–1939* (U.S. Bureau of the Census and Bureau of Agricultural Economics, Washington: Government Printing Office, 1942), p. 30.

areas, that the Twelfth Census gave special attention to the subject.[3] Seven of the various causes giving rise to localization were emphasized: nearness to materials, nearness to markets, water power, a favorable climate, a supply of labor, available capital, and the momentum of an early start. The study noted in conclusion

that in proportion as a country develops industrially and upon a larger scale; in proportion, moreover, as there is a mobility of labor and freedom from the influence of inherited and over-conservative ideas, the localization of industries tends to be governed increasingly by purely economic considerations and less by the fortuitous considerations which accounted in many cases for localization in earlier years. . . . The system of uniform bookkeeping . . . enables managers to know accurately the comparative advantages of several localities for the industry in question, and to redistribute their production accordingly.[4]

Another study of this problem made thirty years later closes with the observation that "in the long run goods do tend to be produced where technical conditions are favorable and unit costs of manufacture are low." [5]

DISTRIBUTION OF MANUFACTURING WAGE EARNERS BY REGIONS, 1899–1919, AND PERCENTAGE INCREASE

Region	Percentage of U.S. Total		Percentage Increase in Manufacturing Wage Earners, 1899–1919
	1899	1919	
United States	100	100	93.0
New England	18.1	14.9	58.6
Middle Atlantic	34.1	31.6	79.0
East North Central	22.8	26.3	123.0
West North Central	5.6	5.5	87.8
South Atlantic	9.7	9.0	78.3
East South Central	3.8	3.6	85.8
West South Central	2.4	3.1	151.6
Mountain	0.9	1.2	145.4
Pacific	2.6	4.8	253.2

Source: Harold D. Kube and Ralph H. Danhof, *Changes in Distribution of Manufacturing Wage Earners, 1899–1939* (U.S. Bureau of the Census and Bureau of Agricultural Economics, Washington: Government Printing Office, 1942), pp. 25, 29.

If these two statements are valid, the concentration of manufacturing in New England, the Middle Atlantic, and the East North Central states and the continuation of that concentration must have

[3] Frederick S. Hall, "The Localization of Industries," *Twelfth Census; Manufactures*, VII, Pt. 1, pp. cxc–ccxvii.

[4] *Ibid.*, p. ccxiv.

[5] Frederic B. Garner, Francis M. Boddy, and Alvar J. Nixon, *The Location of Manufactures in the United States*, University of Minnesota *Bulletin* of the Employment Stabilization Institute (Minneapolis: University of Minnesota Press, 1933), Vol. II, No. 6, p. 105.

rested upon firm foundations. Such was the case. Since industrialized economy had been based primarily upon the production of iron and steel, basic industry was bound to concentrate in areas furnishing the raw materials—fuel, chemicals, and iron ore. This combination existed best until about 1914 in western Pennsylvania and there the center remained, gradually moving westward after that date.[6] Although innumerable other raw materials helped to hold industry to this section, the fundamental influence was the existence of iron ore and, in later years, the ease with which it could be imported from elsewhere.

Closely connected with the existence of raw materials is the presence of power. Whether considered in terms of coal, water power, or hydroelectric power, the manufacturing belt as defined above was abundantly supplied with all three. One of the most careful studies so far made on this subject asserts that the "location of manufacturing in general, excluding such ubiquitous industries as bread baking, is associated with the coal fields. This connection is becoming more apparent as time passes and the machine comes to play a more and more important role in production in general and in providing direct consumer services." [7] Perhaps coal played a more important role in this particular period than before or since. In the earlier years of the industrial revolution, water was the primary power, and the innumerable streams flowing from the Appalachians into the Atlantic helped to establish manufacturing in that area. Steam began to displace water power, especially where coal existed in abundance. During the third phase of hydroelectric power, this section continued to remain in a favorable position. Hydroelectric power was first developed in an important way in the United States about 1900 on the Niagara River. Scores of other sites soon provided new power for a rapidly expanding industry.

Although the factors which determine the location of industries are sometimes complex and vary with different industries, the influence of nearness to markets is important. Just as the concentration of manufactures and industrial wage earners remained about the same during the two decades 1899–1919, so did the proportion of the general population. The population of New England, the Middle Atlantic, and the East North Central states was 48.7 per cent of the nation in 1899 and 43.8 in 1919; approximately one half of the people

[6] Garner, Boddy, and Nixon, *The Location of Manufactures in the United States,* Chap. VII.
[7] *Ibid.,* p. 102.

lived in the area, where three fourths of the manufacturing was concentrated.[8] It is also clear that industry itself creates a larger local market. One study of 33 great industrial areas of the country notes that 27.6 per cent of the population and 55.9 per cent of the wage earners lived in them in 1899. Two decades later the percentage of population was 33 per cent and the wage earners 58.2.[9] Obviously the nearby market was increasing more rapidly than industrial wage earners and was caused by an influx of manufacturing activities.

WESTWARD MOVEMENT OF MANUFACTURING

Although the main area of manufacturing remained essentially the same during these two decades, there was a continuation of the long prevailing westward movement and there were internal shifts within the manufacturing belt. The accelerated industrial development of the western and southern states during the period 1899–1919, in fact, pulled the center of manufactures westward 71.9 miles and southward 9.6 miles, whereas the center of population moved westward but 48.7 miles and northward 0.9 mile.[10] The westward development was notable in the West South Central states and on the Pacific coast. The opening of new petroleum fields and the increased demand for petroleum products provided an important impetus in both areas. An acceleration of migration to California was the basis for a rapid development of the manufacturing of consumer goods and of railroad repair shops.[11] As early as 1900, food canning for export to other sections of the country had become important in California; by 1914 that state ranked first in the value of canned and preserved fruits and vegetables. Lumbering also increased, and during the First World War the shipbuilding industry grew to national importance in the San Francisco and Seattle areas.

By far the most important movement in industry in the two decades after 1899 was its expansion in the East North Central states. While the relative position of New England and the Middle Atlantic

[8] Tracy E. Thompson, *Location of Manufactures, 1899–1929* (U.S. Bureau of the Census, Washington: Government Printing Office, 1933), p. 9.

[9] Kube and Danhof, *Changes in Distribution of Manufacturing Wage Earners, 1899–1939*, p. 36.

[10] Thompson, *Location of Manufactures: 1899–1929*, p. 7. The center for 1919 was computed both from wage-job data and from gross value of products. The approximate center in 1919 was 0.7 miles north of Rushsylvania, Logan County, Ohio, as determined by value of products; and 2.4 miles southwest of Sparta, Morrow County, Ohio, as determined by number of wage-jobs.

[11] Garner, Boddy, and Nixon, *The Location of Manufactures in the United States*, p. 166.

states declined, that of the East North Central advanced. Only in this area were the gains of sufficient volume to challenge the long supremacy of the seaboard. Whether measured in increased number of wage earners, amount of horsepower used, or value of products, the development in this section was relatively greater than in New England and the Middle Atlantic states. Clearly there was a shift in manufacturing importance from the Atlantic coast to the Great Lakes district.[12] This growth was caused primarily by the expansion in the production of machinery and metal products, particularly in the automobile industry. The number of wage earners employed in the production of automobiles rose from 73,000 in 1909 to 343,000 in 1919, one of the greatest ten-year gains in employment for any single industry in American history.

Students of manufacturing locations in general are agreed that there is a tendency toward decentralization, at least in the sense that "manufacturing in general is slowly becoming dispersed over the country more nearly as population is dispersed." [13] Within metropolitan areas a certain amount of suburbanization of both population and manufacturing took place with the advent of electric street transportation and the automobile. Satellite manufacturing towns have grown up around great manufacturing centers such as St. Louis, Chicago, Cincinnati, and Pittsburgh. The general belief, however, that the concentration of American industry, so apparent during the first twenty years of the century, is being relieved by a trend toward decentralization is probably exaggerated. First of all, the spread of manufacturing, as revealed by the census, is in part accounted for by the wide development of certain "ubiquitous" manufactures, such as the making of ice cream and soft drinks, the baking of bread in commercial establishments, and printing and publishing.[14] New industries of this type naturally follow population and are not highly concentrated except where population is concentrated.

On the other hand, certain new industries which expanded rapidly after 1900, such as the manufacture of electric equipment and automobiles, were highly concentrated geographically as well as by population. Old industries seem to follow no definite pattern as a whole. Cotton textiles dispersed toward the south and west, and

[12] *Ibid.*, Chap. III.

[13] *Ibid.*, p. 102; Thompson, *Location of Manufactures, 1899–1929*, p. 47; Glenn E. McLaughlin, *Growth of American Manufacturing Areas* (Pittsburgh; Bureau of Business Research, University of Pittsburgh, 1938), pp. 219 ff.; Daniel B. Creamer, *Is Industry Decentralizing?* (Philadelphia: University of Pennsylvania Press, 1935), p. 15.

[14] Garner, Boddy, and Nixon, *The Location of Manufactures in the United States*, p. 234.

shoes toward the west, but woolens, worsteds, and rayons remained highly localized and concentrated, as did the manufacture of clothing. When decentralization occurred, specific influences in particular industries were responsible, rather than a tendency to follow a general pattern. In any event, the influences toward decentralization were undoubtedly stronger after 1917 than in the previous two decades. One cause was the more rapid production and wider distribution of electric power.

MOVEMENT OF SPECIFIC INDUSTRIES

When the movement of certain specific industries is examined, many of the influences already noted in the last two sections are more firmly established. The trend of the slaughtering and meat-packing industry was definitely toward the west, and this despite the fact that the ranks of the three leading states (Illinois, Kansas and Nebraska), measured by value of the product, were the same from 1899 to 1919. In 1890, the centers of packing ranked by value of product were Chicago, Kansas City (Kansas), New York, Philadelphia, and East St. Louis, all but one east of the Mississippi. Thirty years later, they were Chicago, Kansas City, South Omaha, East St. Louis, St. Paul, Fort Worth, Sioux City, St. Joseph, Denver, Wichita, Indianapolis, and Oklahoma City, most west of the Mississippi.[15] The development of refrigeration and the introduction of the refrigerator car before 1897 made possible the shipment of fresh meat, and as this became the main business of the packers the industry shifted closer to the source of supply. Refrigeration also made it easier for the industry to extend into the South and this fact, combined with the practice of fattening cattle on cottonseed meal, a by-product of cottonseed oil, led to the development of meat packing in Dallas and Fort Worth.

A similar general shift west and south can be seen in flour-mill products. Rated by value of products, the eight leading states in 1899 were Minnesota, New York, Ohio, Pennsylvania, Illinois, Indiana, Missouri, and Wisconsin. In 1919 the rank was Minnesota, Kansas, New York, Illinois, Missouri, Ohio, Washington, and Texas. The background for this shift was the extension, after the 1870's, of the area of hard, red winter wheat into Kansas, Oklahoma, Texas, and other

[15] *Twelfth Census,* VII, ccvii, ccxxxviii; *Fourteenth Census,* VIII, 217; Charles B. Kuhlmann, "Processing of Agricultural Products after 1860," in Harold F. Williamson, ed., *The Growth of American Economy* (New York: Prentice-Hall, 1944), p. 437.

states. By 1892, Kansas led all of the states in the production of wheat; by 1901, Kansas City had become an important rival of Minneapolis. As the area of hard, red winter wheat extended, new mills were set up at Wichita, Salina, Hutchinson, and Topeka in Kansas, at Dallas, Fort Worth, and San Antonio in Texas, and at Oklahoma City. Minneapolis and the Northwest were definitely declining in relative position.[16]

In the meantime there developed one important exception to this westward trend—the rehabilitation of Buffalo as a milling center. Buffalo had developed as a large milling city by 1885 but had declined in the next few years. In 1901, however, the railroads ended the practice of allowing western millers free storage for their flour at Buffalo. Freight rates on the Great Lakes more favorable to wheat than to flour, a development of cheap hydroelectric power on the Niagara River, and Buffalo's favorable position as a distributing point —all these factors also helped to revive the milling industry in Buffalo. Moreover, Buffalo was able to get not only northwestern wheat by lake steamer at low cost but also Canadian wheat. The latter could be imported in bond and the flour exported. The Washburn-Crosby Company built a mill in Buffalo in 1903 which became the largest flour mill in the world—and eventually all of the large Minneapolis millers established plants at that point. By 1930 Buffalo had passed Minneapolis as the largest milling center in the nation.[17]

Although canning is an industry widely distributed throughout the country, it also moved definitely westward. Moreover, it became after 1900 the most rapidly growing food-processing industry in the nation. During the eighties and nineties, important inventions in the process of canning and progress in chemical and bacteriological control provided the technical background for the swift advance. A rapidly growing urbanized population provided the market. As in the meat industry, improved transportation facilities greatly aided the expansion. Although the states on the West coast had already become important by 1900, their position, particularly that of California, was far stronger by 1920. By the latter date, California's canned fruit and vegetables were equal in value to those of almost all the rest of the country. The canned fish of California and Washington were worth more than that of all the remaining states.

Turning from food to clothing, we find that these decades showed

[16] Other reasons for this decline are given in Kuhlmann, "Processing of Agricultural Products after 1860," p. 444, and Victor G. Pickett and Roland S. Vaile, *The Decline of Northwestern Flour Milling* (Minneapolis: University of Minnesota Press, 1933), p. 19.

[17] Kuhlmann in Williamson, ed., *The Growth of American Economy*, pp. 443–444.

a trend of shoe manufacturing toward the West and of cotton textiles toward the South. In 1900, Massachusetts produced 40.3 per cent of the nation's shoes; New York, 11.1; Ohio, 9; New Hampshire, 8.5, and Missouri, 4.2. In 1919, the percentages were Massachusetts, 38; New York, 16.4; Missouri, 8.3; New Hampshire, 5.8, and Ohio, 6.7. New York and Missouri had gained at the expense of Massachusetts, New Hampshire, and Ohio. The cities which showed the greatest increase were St. Louis and New York; in almost every case the New England shoe towns showed a relative decline.[18]

New England's recession is attributed chiefly to distance from the interior market. The long period of concentration of shoe manufacturing in New England had led to specialization, whereas the rural and small town markets of the interior wanted a general line of shoes. At the same time there was an increasing emphasis after 1900 upon styles. This developing importance of fashion emphasized speed and nearness to market. "The manufacturer on the spot," says one student, "who could keep his ear to the ground and give quick and almost personal service, served a territory better than some far-away establishment whose shipments might arrive too late to catch the Saturday rush." [19] New England, moreover, had handled most of the export trade in shoes, largely centered in Latin America and South Africa. By 1919, this trade had largely declined. American manufacturers had aggressively pushed their products in foreign countries; these countries had now established their own shoe industries and were protecting them by high tariffs. Another important influence tended to decentralize the industry—the effort to escape higher labor costs due to labor organization. This checked the industry's growth in the more specialized centers and stimulated it in the satellite towns or in other nonunionized centers.[20] One other reason for the dispersal of the shoe industry should be mentioned—the fact that it required a relatively small amount of investment capital. Shoe machinery is leased, not sold, and local agencies encouraged new establishments by providing buildings and other facilities at low cost.

The most important migration ever experienced by a major branch of American industry took place during these years [21]—the shift of the cotton goods industry from the cities of New England to

[18] Edgar M. Hoover, Jr., "The Location of the Shoe Industry in the United States," *Quarterly Journal of Economics*, XLVII (February, 1933), 265 ff.

[19] *Ibid.*, p. 270.

[20] *Ibid.*, p. 270.

[21] Harold H. McCarty, *The Geographic Basis of American Economic Life* (New York: Harper & Brothers, 1940), p. 377.

the mill towns of the southern Piedmont. In 1890, southern mills consumed 538,000 bales of cotton, and New England mills, 1,502,000 bales; in 1920, the South consumed 3,714,000, and New England, 2,418,000. The over-all picture during these three decades shows a relative, not actual, decline in New England. New England cotton manufacturing continued to grow, but at a much slower speed than that of the South. The following table shows the distribution of cotton spindles measured in number of active mills.

COTTON SPINDLES IN NEW ENGLAND AND THE SOUTH

Year	Total United States	South	New England
1890	14,384,000	1,570,000	10,934,000
1900	19,472,000	4,368,000	13,171,000
1910	28,267,000	10,494,000	15,735,000
1920	35,481,000	15,231,000	18,287,000
1925	35,032,000	17,292,000	15,975,000

Source: Statistical Abstract of the United States, volumes for 1903–1931.

Before 1920, cotton manufacturing in the Piedmont of the Carolinas, Georgia, and Alabama was not established primarily because of migrating New England capital or mills. Although some New England mills moved to the South and others set up branches there, the development was largely locally sponsored. An investigation by the National Association of Cotton Manufacturers made in 1922 reported that 84 per cent of southern spindleage was owned or controlled by southern capital, 11 per cent by northern capital, 3 per cent by New England mills, and 2 per cent by western capital. The prosperity of the early southern mills attracted local capital, but Northerners, particularly commission houses, took stock in them in payment for machinery and services. The textile industry, moreover, continued to expand in New England until 1920, providing a nearby outlet for surplus capital.[22]

In competing with New England, the South profited in the earlier years from certain advantages. First of all, the small amount of legislative protection afforded adult workers and children made possible longer hours, lower wages, and child labor. Southern mills also profited from lower taxes and assessments, local exemptions, and inducements. Power costs were lower, as well as the costs of constructing factories and mill villages. The same was true of freight rates on raw materials and manufactured goods. The age and condition of the machinery was often better. There was no question that the costs of

[22] Herbert J. Lahne, The Cotton Mill Worker (New York: Farrar & Rinehart, 1944), p. 89.

manufacturing, including the freight on raw cotton, were cheaper.[23]

Although many of these advantages have persisted, they have in general declined in importance. Social legislation made some progress in that area and wages increased. In 1900, the percentage of cotton mill operators in New England under sixteen years of age was about 10.2; in the South it was 29.6. By 1920, the percentages were respectively 5.5 and 6.2. With rising costs in the South and increased efforts in New England to keep textile mills functioning, the tax differentials have been largely eliminated. Moreover, the cost advantage in freight has declined as southern factories have had to reach beyond local sources of cotton and into the better supplies of the Mississippi delta and the Southwest. Since the chief area for manufacturing clothing remains in New York, the New England mills save transportation costs in marketing their finished goods. Southern advantages in newer machinery and northern advantages in a supply of skilled labor have both declined.[24] The South continued to profit from the tremendous development of hydroelectric power on the Piedmont rivers and gained from the experience and increased skill of labor and management.

All of the differentials operating at one time or another played their part in promoting southern textiles. The one item of manufacturing cost which has been most important and which has remained permanent has been that of lower wage rates. True, the earnings of cotton mill workers in the country as a whole during this period were always below the average for all manufacturing workers, and their hourly earnings were invariably at the bottom of the scale. But wages in New England remained considerably above those in the South. From 1912 to 1914 they were 37 per cent above, and during the war period 55 per cent. However, explanations for this differential on the grounds that southern mills produced a lower grade of goods than New England mills and that the cost of living was lower in the South have no sound basis.[25]

As to the general pattern of production, it was clear by 1919 that the South was supreme by a wide margin in spinning lower-grade yarns, with medium grades divided between the two sections, and New England dominating the finer yarns. In woven goods the South by 1900 had passed New England in shirting, sheeting, duck, and

[23] *Ibid.*, p. 94; Ben F. Lemert, *The Cotton Textile Industry in the Southern Appalachian Piedmont* (Chapel Hill: University of North Carolina Press, 1933), pp. 38, 46–119.

[24] Lahne, *The Cotton Mill Worker,* pp. 94–100.

[25] *Ibid.*, pp. 164–172.

drill; by 1905, in ticks, denims, and stripes; and by 1919, in print cloth. Since then she has improved the higher-grade goods, but the quality has remained slightly below that of New England in all grades of this type.[26]

Unlike the manufacture of shoes and the spinning and weaving of textiles, the center of the clothing industry remained relatively stable during these years. In men's factory-produced clothing New York State turned out somewhat less than half of the total in 1900, with Illinois, Ohio, Pennsylvania, and Maryland following. In 1921, New York's proportion was still 43.2 per cent, but Pennsylvania and Ohio had changed places. In women's clothing, New York produced about 60 per cent in 1900, but almost 76 per cent in 1921. Following New York were Pennsylvania, Illinois, and Ohio in both years. Here the trend was definitely toward the East rather than the West.

This was the period in which both men and women largely shifted from custom-made to factory-made clothing. The increase of the latter was tremendous; the value of men's factory-made clothing increased during the twenty-one years almost eightfold and that for women twenty-one times. In men's clothing, New York City specialized in cheap and high-style types, Chicago and Rochester in higher-grade clothing. In women's clothing, New York City produced all grades from the cheapest to the most expensive. Since styles in men's clothing changed slowly, if at all, factory production was more stable than in women's, and the factories, particularly in Rochester and Chicago, were much larger. The larger Chicago factories are explained in part by the fact that they developed later than those in New York State and catered to the western rural trade that demanded four to six months' credit, which could be supplied only by large enterprises. The very nature of women's clothing, with its rapidly changing styles and innumerable types, tended to perpetuate thousands of small establishments and a continuous succession of factories and new entrepreneurs. The manufacture of men's and women's clothing was characterized, especially in New York City, by a large number of contract shops.

Why New York City remained the center of the industry, particularly in women's clothing, is not difficult to understand. The workers were mainly Jewish and Italian immigrants, who poured into that area after 1895. The city is close to the largest markets and is the center of the sales divisions of the textile manufacturers, both domestic and foreign. For women's clothing it profited from the nearness to

[26] *Ibid.*, pp. 93–94.

France, which, during these years, set the styles followed throughout the world.[27]

The old saying that "ore moves to the fuel" is generally true, but it is also true, as this period proved, that fuel moves in some cases to the ore, and sometimes there is a compromise. Moreover, as in the case of most commodities, the location of the iron and steel industry is influenced by the markets. All of these influences are discernible in the tendency of iron and steel production to move westward and particularly to the shores of the Great Lakes. One calculation illustrates the trend clearly.

IRON AND STEEL PRODUCTION BY MAJOR DISTRICTS
(Percentage of total)

District	Pig Iron		Steel	
	1904	1929	1904	1929
Eastern	13.8	12.2	25.7	17.0
Pittsburgh	63.8	56.4	53.5	52.5
Great Lakes	11.4	22.6	16.1	23.2
Southern	8.8	6.5	2.9	4.7
Western	2.2	2.3	1.8	2.6

Source: Evan B. Alderfer and Herman E. Michl, Economics of American Industry (New York: McGraw-Hill Book Company, 1942), p. 59. The percentage for the eastern district would have declined more but for the fact that the American Iron and Steel Institute includes Buffalo here rather than in the Great Lakes district, where economically and geographically it should be.

This trend toward the West was at the expense of the eastern and Pittsburgh districts. The southern region (mainly Alabama) had its chief development in the 1890's and in the early years of the twentieth century. Since then its rate of growth has been about equal to the rate of the country as a whole. In percentage of production of iron it declined; in that of steel it increased. The western area (chiefly Colorado) approximately held its own. The region which gained was that of the Great Lakes. The shift was illustrated in a dramatic way in 1900, when the Lackawanna Steel Company moved its $40,000,000 plant, which it had operated for sixty years, from Scranton to Buffalo, and in 1907, when the United States Steel Corporation erected a gigantic plant on the sand dunes of Lake Michigan and created the city of Gary, Indiana. Three years later the same corporation opened a modern plant at Duluth.

The main reason for this movement was the development of the Lake Superior ore deposits, particularly the Vermillion and Mesabi area in Minnesota in the 1890's and early years of the century. The

[27] Joel Seidman, The Needle Trades (New York: Farrar & Rinehart, 1942, pp. 16–28); Evan B. Alderfer and Herman E. Michl, Economics of American Industry (New York: McGraw-Hill Book Company, 1942), pp. 367–381.

Lake Superior iron was not only extremely rich but cheap to obtain. Some of the ore in the Mesabi range yielded from one half to two thirds pure iron. Moreover, it was soft and near the surface, and could be easily removed by the stripping and steam-shovel technique. By the opening of the First World War the Lake Superior district was producing more than half of the iron ore of the country, and most of this was from Minnesota.

In brief, cheap ore drew many iron and steel plants to the shores of the Great Lakes, where transportation costs were cheaper. These plants, which extended in a 900-mile area from Duluth to Buffalo, but mainly concentrated around Chicago and Cleveland, brought in their coal from the fields of southern Indiana and Illinois, or from those of western Pennsylvania and eastern Ohio. Even the plants in the Pittsburgh district generally used the Lake Superior ore despite the extra transportation costs caused by transshipment of ore from ship to train at the lake ports. What saved the Pittsburgh district was its nearness to the best coking coal. It actually cost more to produce pig iron in Chicago than in Pittsburgh and the costs for Pittsburgh and Cleveland were about the same. It was a fine balancing of the costs of producing and transporting ore as against coal. The cost of the limestone or "flux" was too small greatly to influence the location. The determining point in many cases was the nearness to market.

Copper mining, and along with it the smelting establishments, experienced a far more elastic relocation than iron and steel. Until the middle eighties Michigan had been the largest copper-producing state. Discoveries at Butte, Montana, and other regions in that state, however, pushed Montana into first place in 1887, where she remained until displaced by Arizona in 1907. In 1919, Arizona produced 46.5 per cent of the copper, with Michigan again in second place with 19 per cent, followed by Montana and Utah. While copper production in the United States was shifting to the Southwest, the Guggenheim interests began the exploitation of Alaskan copper. This waited upon the building of the Copper River and Northwestern Railroad in 1911 and the opening of the Kennecott and Mother Lode mines. Although mining and smelting moved westward, refining remained largely on the Atlantic seaboard to process imported copper and to prepare the domestic output for the fabricating industries of New England and the Middle Atlantic states.[28]

More spectacular than copper in its shift of location was the south-

---

[28] F. E. Richter, "The Copper Industry" in Herman T. Warshow, ed., *Representative Industries in the United States* (New York: Henry Holt and Company, 1928), pp. 224–230.

westward movement of petroleum. In 1900, the center of production was east of the Mississippi, with Ohio, West Virginia, Pennsylvania, Indiana, and California the chief producing states in the order named. By 1919, production had shifted largely to the middle of the continent, with Oklahoma, Texas, California, West Virginia, and Kansas as the leading states. This shift was speeded by the increased demand of the automobile industry and the greater supplies in the mid-continent area and California. Between these years Illinois had enjoyed a spectacular rise (1905–1908), only to experience a precipitous decline.[29] The period of discoveries, explorations, and early production in the new field was from about 1899 to 1904. The next decade completed the revolution in location. To some extent, refining followed production centers. Nevertheless, at least half of the gasoline supply came from refineries on deep water, to which the crude oil was shipped by tank or pipeline. In 1900 Illinois was the center. As the production area moved southwest, about 70 per cent of the total refining capacity centered in the five states of Texas, California, Pennsylvania, Oklahoma, and New Jersey.

Bituminous coal production also tended to move westward and southward, but the movement was slow. Some development took place in Colorado and in other trans-Mississippi states and much more in Alabama, stimulated by the Birmingham steel industry. But Pennsylvania remained the leading state in 1919, with production almost twice that of Western Virginia, her leading competitor. Throughout the period, however, there was a notable development of strip mining in southern Illinois to supply the industries of St. Louis and Chicago.

LOCATION OF NEW INDUSTRIES

Before leaving the subject of industrial location, note should be taken of several industries which had their first important development in these years. The first great period of the growth of aluminum came after 1898. The location of the industry was influenced mainly by raw material and power. Bauxite, the chief raw material, was obtained during these years chiefly in Arkansas, the concentration center being located at East St. Louis. The ore is reduced by hydroelectric power, and the industry followed this power to Niagara

[29] O. E. Kissling and Others, *Technology, Employment and Output per Man in Petroleum and Natural-Gas Production* (Philadelphia: Work Projects Administration, National Research Project, 1939), pp. 37–42.

Falls and Massena, New York, then to the Little Tennessee and Yadkin rivers, and later, as the industry grew, to new power developments in Canada, in the region of the Tennessee Valley Authority, and in the Northwest.

During its early years the manufacture of automobiles was by no means as concentrated as it later became. The fifty-seven establishments devoted entirely to the manufacture of automobiles in 1900 were widely scattered. The Locomobile Company, which in that year produced 95 per cent of all the steam carriages in the country, erected its plant on the Hudson just north of New York City.[30] The main plant of the largest concern manufacturing electrical vehicles, that founded by Albert Augustus Pope, the bicycle magnate, was located at Hartford, Connecticut. The small machine shops were mainly in the Northeast, as was the market in the early days of high-priced cars. For a brief period it appeared that the center of manufacturing would be along the Connecticut and Hudson rivers. Its future, however, was to be in the East North Central states. In Detroit two famous pioneers were experimenting with internal-combustion engines and gasoline-driven cars. Ransom E. Olds, with a model perfected in 1899, led the field for several years, and Henry Ford, after organizing his own concern in 1903, became a close rival. By 1907 he led all others in the number of cars sold. The market rapidly shifted to the gasoline car, and in 1905 Michigan took the leadership in the industry and kept it. Nearness to raw materials and specialization in the gasoline engine and the low-priced car (where the market was) gave Michigan the leadership.[31]

Two industries were particularly influenced by the developing production of automobiles—rubber and petroleum. The latter has already been mentioned. Although many influences account for the expansion of oil production from 51,000,000 barrels in 1899 to 378,500,000 in 1919, none was more important than the automobile. Rubber manufacturing before the automobile was largely limited to boots, shoes, raincoats, druggists' and surgical supplies, and bicycle tires. In 1900, imports amounted to 4,377,000 pounds of crude rubber; twenty years later, the amount jumped to 566,546,000, about 70 per cent being consumed in automobile tires, tubes, and accessories. The growth of automobile manufacturing and the growth of rubber manufacturing are closely parallel. The early rubber industry was largely

[30] Victor Clark, *History of Manufactures in the United States* (New York: McGraw-Hill Book Company, 3 vols., 1929), III, 160.
[31] Edward D. Kennedy, *The Automobile Industry* (New York: Reynal & Hitchcock, 1941), Chaps. I–II.

centered in New England. The sudden development of Akron as the rubber capital of the world seems to have been due chiefly to nearness to market—the automobile industry. The beginnings of its growth, however, had started earlier. In 1870, Benjamin F. Goodrich moved from New York and established a rubber factory in Akron. It was successful and one or two other small concerns located in the vicinity. Around 1900, the Goodyear Tire and Rubber Company and the Firestone Tire and Rubber Company also located at Akron, presumably because the region was already established as a rubber center. Then came the rapid development of the nearby automobile industry, which provided Akron with a rapidly expanding nearby market.

Few industries have had a more sudden and spectacular rise since 1900 than the manufacture of cement. Moreover, its location has also notably changed. In 1900, about 70 per cent of the cement was produced in the Lehigh Valley of Pennsylvania. Forty years later, that region produced less than 20 per cent, although in actual amount it had grown. The relative decline of Lehigh cement is explained chiefly by technical developments permitting the use of lower-grade raw materials, the application of other fuels than coal, and the rise of markets in the South and West, which could be served more cheaply from nearby manufacturing centers.[32]

THE MINING INDUSTRY

Although the mining industry has already been mentioned with reference to improving technique or shifting location, no effort has been made to deal with it as a whole. The industry furnished practically all of the nation's fuels, its principal metals, and much of its building materials. By value more than one half of the mineral industries consists of fuels and most of the remainder of metals. Significant as has been the mining industry in the development of modern civilization, its importance in certain respects has been minor. It has employed only from 2 to 3 per cent of the working population and has produced somewhat less than 2 per cent of the national wealth.[33]

Using the year 1899 to equal 100, the index figure for the physical output of metals in 1917 was 259, for fuels, 276, and for other nonmetals, 281, giving a total index figure for all mining of 268. The

[32] Alderfer and Michl, *Economics of American Industry*, p. 177.
[33] Harold Barger and Sam H. Schurr, *The Mining Industries, 1899–1939* (New York: National Bureau of Economics Research, 1944), p. 5.

corresponding figure for manufacturing was 257 and that for agriculture 124. Because of the First World War, production indexes were high in 1917, but the same was true of manufacturing and agriculture. The fact that the index for physical output of mining continued higher during the four decades after 1897 than for manufacturing and agriculture was not caused by increased output of metals; the figure achieved by metals in 1917 was not reached again until the Second World War. The great advance in mining came from the developing exploitation of petroleum and natural gas and from such nonmetals as building stone and crushed stone for highway construction. The latter, of course, like the production of petroleum, resulted chiefly from the development of the automobile. Production of anthracite and bituminous coal reached its high point during the First World War, only to decline during the next two decades.[34]

Of the total labor force in the nation's mining, those engaged in the separation of minerals from the earth and the simpler processing operations carried on at the mine or quarry comprised 2.7 per cent in 1900 and 3.0 per cent in 1920. The last figure marked the highest percentage ever reached. The number of persons engaged did not change greatly (from a little over 800,000 in 1900 to somewhat over 1,000,000 in 1919), nor did the number in the various types of mining industries. After the First World War, however, there was a relative decline in metal and coal workers and an increase in petroleum workers. Working hours in mining declined from 9.1 per shift in 1902 to 8.3 in 1919. Most of this decline was from 1909 to 1919, a result apparently of increased unionization during wartime.[35] If oil wells are excluded, the man-day output for mining (coal and metal) increased for the decade 1902 to 1912 about 10 per cent. After that, the man-day output increased more rapidly, with twice the speed in metal mining as in coal mining.[36]

Up to 1897 the production of minerals came largely from comparatively new underground mines. Certain processes such as shaft sinking, underground tunneling, and roof support were efficiently done with compressed-air drills used for tunneling. Otherwise, technical progress was small. Hand drilling and hand picking were still the common methods. Mining was largely a specialized hand process of individual miners who operated on highly selected first-class ores. The real mechanization of mining came after 1897 in the

[34] *Ibid.*, pp. 13–58.
[35] *Ibid.*, pp. 59–76.
[36] *Ibid.*, p. 89.

willingness or need to exploit lower-grade ore and in the development of techniques to do this both in extraction from the ground and in preparation for use.

It is difficult to select particular events to mark this change in mining technique, but the decision to use the crude steam shovel in the latter years of the nineteenth century on the Mesabi iron range and a few years later the development of opencut copper mining at Bingham, Utah, are significant. The speed of developing low-grade ores by a nonselective process depended on the quality of the ore obtainable and a similar refinement of the techniques of ore concentration. In any event, "nonselective mining appears to have been the mining industry's version of the process of specialization of functions which was occurring simultaneously in other industries. Ever since the introduction of opencut copper mining, nonselective mining methods have come to dominate the American mining industry." [37]

The development of nonselective underground mining had brought new techniques of breaking the ore, loading the broken ore and transporting the ore from the working face to the surface. Only the first and last of these processes showed any important growth before 1917. Breaking the ore brought new methods of sublevel and block caving, a transition from block blasting powder to dynamite, new cutting machines, and the substitution of drills of the hammer type for the earlier piston drills. Along with this was the substitution of electric for steam power. It was this new power which found use in locomotives and in various devices for hoisting that revolutionized the transportation of minerals. With the exception of loading machinery, most of these devices were in use before 1917.[38]

[37] *Ibid.*, p. 109.
[38] *Ibid.*, pp. 117–145.

CHAPTER VIII

Consolidation of Business

SIZE OF THE INDUSTRIAL ESTABLISHMENT

PROBABLY no aspect of American economic life during the years 1897–1917 has received more attention than the rapid development in the size and power of business organization. This expansion was fostered by an economic environment and technological considerations which encouraged large-scale operations and also by an artificial development through mergers and consolidation. The rapidity of this development and its significance captured the interest of economists, aroused legislatures to action, and struck fear into the heart of the common man. "The mere size of the consolidations which have recently appeared," said two economists, "is enough to startle those who saw them in the making. If the carboniferous age had returned and the earth had repeopled itself with dinosaurs, the change made in animal life would have scarcely seemed greater than that which has been made in the business world by these monster-like corporations." [1]

Although the consolidation movement was extremely rapid in the years after 1897, the factors which made large-scale industry possible had been developing for many decades. Essentially they were technological progress, an expansion of the marketing area, and the development of a technique in financing corporations and operating large concerns. [2] Most important of the technical developments were the improvements in power-generating machinery. The shift from water power to steam, the replacement of the older steam engine by the

---

[1] John Bates Clark and John Maurice Clark, *The Control of Trusts* (New York: The Macmillan Company, 1912), pp. 14–15.

[2] *Mergers in Industry* (New York: National Industrial Conference Board, 1929), pp. 17–24.

high-speed compound turbine, and the addition of electric power released manufacturing from the uncertainties and restrictions of old-fashioned water power and allowed unlimited expansion. Innumerable inventions freed important operations from hand production and made possible rapid and large-scale manufacturing. Development of machine tools which might speed up one process in manufacturing would force an entire industry, for the sake of economy, to accelerate all stages and increase the size of the output. Since the effect of mechanical inventions is cumulative, one improvement suggests the possibility of another. As an industry became mechanized, its equipment became more costly and large-scale production more necessary to cover the overhead. In brief, mechanical improvements made big business not only possible but imperative.

Important also was the expanding market. Large-scale production can exist only with a large-scale market, which in turn usually means distribution over a wide area. For this, quick and inexpensive means of transportation and communication are necessary both to collect the raw material and to distribute the finished product. By the end of the century such means were at hand—railroads reaching into every important population section of the country, an efficient postal service, the telegraph and the telephone. To these were added by the end of the First World War both the automobile and the radio. It should also be noted that office machinery, such as the typewriter, the adding machine, and other equipment necessary for large-scale business, developed along with the techniques of plant production.

One other factor should be emphasized in the evolution of large-scale industry—the development of the corporation. The large funds needed for buildings, machinery, and stocks of large-scale industry, to say nothing of the risks involved, had got beyond the capacity of single individuals or partnerships. Large-scale industry needed the financial backing and cooperation of many people. The corporate form made this possible. It was even more necessary for the mergers and consolidations which characterized the period after 1897. "Although the corporate form," says Willard Thorp, "is not the cause of the increased scale of production there can be no doubt that it is a *sine qua non*." [3] It should be added, of course, that there were many other advantages beyond the ease of raising capital which promoted the corporation form. Such factors as limited liability of stockholders, flexibility of management, release of stockholders from responsibility of management, blanket charters which allowed almost any type of

[3] Willard L. Thorp, *The Integration of Industrial Operation* (U.S. Bureau of the Census, *Census Monograph* III, Washington: Government Printing Office, 1924), p. 9.

development, and the opportunity afforded businessmen to command minority capital interests and retain control of the business—all help to account for the popularity of the corporate form.

In 1919, corporations represented only 31.5 per cent of the manufacturing establishments but they employed 86 per cent of the wage earners and produced 87.7 per cent of the products. Their importance grew significantly after 1900.[4] A glance at the following table will show that the value of the average product of each establishment increased over sixteenfold between 1859 and 1919 and that the average number of workers more than trebled. Between 1899 and 1919 the value of the product of each establishment increased fourfold and the number of workers increased 53 per cent. Concerning the last period two facts should be noted: first, the increase in workers in each establishment was negligible from 1904 to the opening of the First World War, after which it was substantial; second, the value of products in 1919 would be considerably reduced if adjusted to the purchasing value of the dollar of 1899 or 1914.[5] The trend, nevertheless, over the longer period is clear.

GROWTH OF MANUFACTURING ESTABLISHMENTS

	1859	1899	1904	1909	1914	1919
Average product ...	$13,429	$54,969	$68,433	$76,993	$87,916	$215,157
Average wage earners	9.34	20.49	25.30	24.64	25.51	31.36

Source: Computed from figures in Statistical Abstract of the United States, 1921, Table 482, p. 868.

Even more striking are the statistics which show the relative lessening in the importance of the small plant and the increasing importance of the large ones. Establishments with an annual output of less than $20,000 declined in their percentage of the total with respect to number of establishments, wage earners, and value of products. Those with an annual output of $20,000 to $100,000 declined in their percentage of the total with respect to wage earners and the value of product. On the other hand, establishments with products of $1,000,000 or over increased notably in each category. The 10,414 such establishments in 1919 numbered only 3.6 per cent of the total number but employed 56.9 per cent of the wage earners and manufactured 67.8 per cent of the products according to value.[6]

[4] Abstract of the Census of Manufactures, 1919 (U.S. Department of Commerce, Bureau of the Census, Washington: Government Printing Office, 1923), Table 195, p. 340.

[5] Thorp, The Integration of Industrial Operation, pp. 39–43, has adjusted these values to a 1914 basis.

[6] Statistical Abstract of the United States, 1922, Table 156, p. 198; Appendix, p. 418.

Although these statistics make clear a general over-all increase in size and output of establishments, the trend was not universal. Thorp's study of eighteen industries indicated wide differences in the nature of industrial development. Certain industries showed a notable increase in the average size of establishments based on wage earners and physical product: salt, beet sugar, leather, woolen goods, automobiles, iron and steel, and coke. Others, such as slaughtering and meat packing, artificial ice, cotton goods, and boot and shoe manufacturing, changed scarcely at all. A few, including silk, lumber, carriage and wagon manufacturing, and shipbuilding, showed tendencies to decrease in average size.[7]

CAUSES FOR CONSOLIDATION

So far the discussion has been largely concerned with the normal tendency of growth in a developing industrial system. Even without consolidations the United States was becoming a land of large manufacturing establishments. The golden age of the small industry passed with the old century. The tendency toward large-scale industry, however, was speeded by the movement toward consolidation. The latter appeared in industry in the late seventies, gained momentum in the eighties and early nineties, and reached a climax in the period 1897–1904. After that it slowed down, to appear again in revived strength in the 1920's. Consolidation up to 1904 was largely in railroads or in the manufacturing and mining industries. But it had begun to shift to public utilities, particularly the electric power industry. The revival in the 1920's included such new industries as automobile manufacturing, motion-picture production, and radio broadcasting, and extended into retailing and banking.

The development of large industrial plants was a continuous process and so obviously in line with the needs of the economic environment that it created little interest and less concern on the part of the general public. The movement toward consolidation and mergers as it developed in the 1880's and again in the late 1890's, however, was a different matter. Consolidation, as the country had discovered in its experience with the Standard Oil Company and the American Sugar Refining Company, might result in monopolies and as such was dangerous to the nation. Large industrialists might believe that laissez faire meant the right to consolidate and monopolize, but the average citizen dissented. "We have said to all the world," asserted

[7] Thorp, *The Integration of Industrial Operation*, p. 74.

Woodrow Wilson, "America was created to break every kind of monopoly and to set men free upon a footing of equality, upon a footing of opportunity to match their brains and their energies." [8] Nevertheless, it was evident to all that certain of the newly formed consolidations were often monopolies or potential monopolies.

There had been much criticism of consolidations in the 1880's and early 1890's which resulted in 1890 in the Sherman Antitrust Act and in 1894 in Henry Demarest Lloyd's great blast against monopolies in *Wealth against Commonwealth*. The uprising of those years was hardly comparable to that of a decade later. Economists turned their attentions to the problem of monopoly, produced learned monographs, and began to teach courses on the "Trust Movement." The federal government, through its Industrial Commission, investigated the causes and results of combinations, "muckrakers" directed their artillery against the abuses of monopolies, and the public press was full of clamor that sometimes produced as much heat as light. This intense interest lasted for more than a decade. It was asserted as late as 1912 that "of the practical problems which the American people have now to solve, the greatest is that of the control of vast corporations." [9]

The study of consolidation and monopoly was directed toward discovering the causes for this trend, its effects upon the nation, and remedies to overcome the dangers, if such existed. The causes were easier to determine than either the effects or the remedies. The Industrial Commission, after a thorough investigation, believed that competition was the chief cause, stating that "most of the witnesses were of the opinion that competition, so vigorous that profits of nearly all competing establishments were destroyed, is to be given first place." [10] Commenting on the same influence, a Wall Street editor insisted that "the suppression of competition or at least its regulation is one of the chief objects aimed at in consolidation is so obvious as to require no argument." [11]

There is much evidence in the decline of prices where severe competition existed to bear out this contention. As manufacturing plants grew in size, they were driving smaller and less efficient establishments out of business. Competition was intensified with the growth

[8] Woodrow Wilson, *The New Freedom* (New York: Doubleday, Page & Company, 1913), p. 54.

[9] Clark and Clark, *The Control of Trusts*, p. 1.

[10] Industrial Commission, *Report* (Washington: Government Printing Office, 19 vols., 1900–1902), I, 9.

[11] Luther Conant, "Industrial Consolidations in the United States," *Publications of the American Statistical Association*, VII, No. 53 (March, 1901), p. 220.

of the railroad system, which brought the larger firms into competition for the national market. Some of them in the process of expansion had erected facilities capable of producing a surplus, which had led to price cutting and other destructive devices. Competition, which had been severe enough in the 1880's, became more bitter after the panic of 1893. Industrialists, noting the fact that such existing monopolies as the Standard Oil Company, the American Sugar Refining Company, and the American Tobacco Company had paid dividends even during the depression, grasped at consolidation as an economic lifeline. Many were now convinced that competition was no longer the life but the death of trade.

Many witnesses appearing before the Industrial Commission stated that their organizations were formed "to make economies, to lessen competition and to get higher profits." [12] Large-scale production, vertical integration, and a more simplified system of selling and marketing may well, and often did, lower costs and increase profits. Greater economies and higher efficiency had the effect of driving smaller or less efficient competitors out of business or discouraged new competition from entering. Most of the causes, as far as they were explained by leading industrialists, can be summed up in the hope for survival or obtaining higher profits through the elimination of competition. What they aimed at primarily, however, was control of prices and markets without the need of reducing costs.

One well-known industrialist, Henry O. Havemeyer, president of the American Sugar Refining Company, approached the problem from a different angle. "The mother of all trusts," he said, "is the customs tariff bill. . . . Economic advantages incident to the consolidation of large interests in the same line of business are a great incentive to their formation, but these bear a very insignificant proportion to the advantages granted in the way of protection under the customs tariff." [13] In his own industry, sugar, this may well have been true, and many agreed that "inordinate" protection encouraged the formation of monopolies. Few, however, believed it as important as Havemeyer did. His contention, however, that the tariff laws were important opens up the influence of the American legal system and federal policy upon the consolidation movement.[14]

There can be no doubt that the American patent system, which confers upon inventors the exclusive right for seventeen years to

[12] Industrial Commission, *Report*, I, 9.
[13] *Ibid.*, I, 101.
[14] Joe S. Bain, "Industrial Concentration and Government Anti-Trust Policy," in H. F. Williamson, ed., *The Growth of American Economy* (New York: Prentice-Hall, 1944), p. 712.

make, sell, lease or withhold from use any invention, has had great influence on the growth of monopolies and upon prices, and it has made difficult the reconciling of the patent system with the antitrust laws. Since a patent is a monopoly, the ordinary results of a monopoly must be expected. When the Industrial Commission asked John W. Gates, chairman of the American Steel and Wire Company, why the price of barbed wire had advanced 50 per cent more than smooth wire, he frankly attributed it to patents. "We practically own every patent on barbed fence wire and machinery in existence in the United States," said he, "and we claim that no one can manufacture barbed wire without infringing our right. . . . In the barbed wire business if any concern sees fit to infringe our right we shall begin litigation against them. We have done that probably in almost every circuit court in the United States." [15] Along with patent rights was the fantastic system of disposal of the public land seemingly designed to promote the monopoly of minerals, lumber, and other natural resources in the hands of large-scale operators.[16] In practice the system made it possible for a small number of individuals to gain a virtual monopoly of valuable raw materials.[17]

Gates's comments on the significance of patents in his own concern give clear indication of their importance in the development of monopoly. The possible danger of the Sherman Act to various types of monopolistic practices stirred the corporations to quick action. "Almost at once," says Walton Hamilton, "they began to fortify the practices at which antitrust might thrust with sanctions derived from letters patent." [18] How it was done by one concern, the United Shoe Machinery Company, he describes as follows:

The basic inventions go back before the Civil War; they have been refreshed from time to time as needed. In an involved series of transactions almost all the patents which have to do with making the machines by which shoes are made—dominant and ancillary, sequential and competitive, along the horizontal and along the vertical line—were gathered under single ownership. United, continuing a practice of long standing, chose to lease rather than to sell outright its machines. Since a patentee it could dictate the terms upon which its technology could be used, it became overlord to the shoe industry.[19]

[15] Industrial Commission, *Report*, I, 1009–1010.

[16] See Fred A. Shannon, *The Farmer's Last Frontier*, in this series, Chap. III.

[17] For an excellent example see Fremont P. Wirth, *The Discovery and Exploitation of the Minnesota Iron Lands* (Grand Rapids, Ia.: The Torch Press, 1937).

[18] Walton Hamilton, *Patents and Free Enterprise* (Temporary National Economic Committee, *Monograph* No. 31, Senate Committee Print, 76 Cong., 3 Sess., Washington: Government Printing Office, 1941), p. 49.

[19] *Ibid.*, p. 47.

This corporation eventually collected six thousand patents to protect its manufacturing. Quite as important a technique as that of integrating patents was the constant threat of suit or use of legal action in discouraging alleged violations of patent rights. When the government instituted suit against the United Shoe Machinery Company, that organization had pending against its competitors more than one hundred actions for infringement. Moreover, the patent system allowed the accumulation of patents without an obligation to use them. The General Electric Company at one time had three hundred patents to protect its ordinary Mazda light, yet it used less than a score of them.

Undoubtedly, the division of control in the American legal system aided in the development of consolidation and monopoly. Although most of the states were passing antitrust acts or introducing constitutional provisions banning monopolies, other states, particularly New Jersey, Delaware, and West Virginia, were virtually encouraging them, or at least passing legislation making them possible. For all practical purposes, New Jersey's corporation laws had been worked out by 1889, when new legislation allowed corporations to hold and dispose of the stock of other companies. This was the year when the agitation for antitrust legislation began in many of the states and one year before the Sherman Act of 1890.[20] When corporation lawyers found the New Jersey law of 1889 too vague to allow them utter freedom, the state obliged in 1893 by making it lawful for any corporation in the state to "purchase, hold, and sell stock and bonds of any other corporation in the same manner that an individual could." This obviously gave carte blanche to the holding company.

The holding company might run afoul the Sherman Antitrust Act if it seemed to produce a monopoly, but the holding company at least made consolidations easier after the Sherman Act had been passed. That act outlawed "every contract, combination in the form of trust or otherwise, or conspiring in restraint of trade." This clause referred to pools, agreements, and trusts of the old type; it did not outlaw mergers, or consolidations in the form of holding companies, if such mergers or consolidations did not comprise a complete monopoly. Curiously enough, the Sherman Act seemed to encourage "firms to *combine* with competitors rather than to agree with them to limit competition" as had been true in earlier years.[21] After a decade of

---

[20] Jeremiah Whipple Jenks and Walter E. Clark, *The Trust Problem* (New York: Doubleday, Page & Company, 5th ed., 1920), pp. 209–243.
[21] Bain in Williamson, ed., *The Growth of American Economy*, p. 712.

the Sherman Act, lawyers had concluded that it was a sheep in wolf's clothing and were advising their clients that there were no legal barriers to large-scale consolidation.

Among numerous causes for the revival of business consolidations after 1897 was, of course, the return of prosperity and the buoyant optimism which suffused the nation at the opening of the new century. It is true that prosperity sometimes encouraged the businessman to resist the wiles of promoters and financiers who would seduce him into joining a great consolidation. In the long run, however, prosperity promoted such a move.[22] This accounts in part for the rise of consolidation after 1897 and its decline after 1914. It should be remembered that the methods of consolidation lend themselves to huge profits for promoters and underwriters. The cost of organization, including the pay of promoters and financiers, often amounted to from 20 to 40 per cent of the total amount of stock issued.[23] There were consolidations in which promoters' profits were small or entirely absent, but they were rare. Syndicate and promoters' profits in organizing the United States Steel Corporation have been estimated at $62,500,000; in organizing the American Can Company, $8,000,000; and in organizing the International Harvester Company, $2,957,000.[24] When economic conditions were favorable, shrewd and aggressive promoters seemed always ready to organize consolidations.

METHODS AND EFFECTS OF CONSOLIDATION

Whatever the causes for consolidation, they found full play in the economic environment after 1897. One enumeration of industrial combinations gives 86 as the number formed from 1887 to 1897 with a total capitalization of $1,414,293,000. During the next three years (1898–1900), 149 were organized. John Moody, writing in 1904, listed 46 combinations organized in 1901 (each with an outstanding capital of $1,000,000 or more), 63 in 1902, and 18 in 1903, making 127 in the three years.[25] Altogether, Moody gives 318 important and active trusts with an aggregate capitalization of $7,249,342,533 representing 5,288 distinct plants "covering practically every line of pro-

[22] Luther Conant, *Publications of the American Statistical Association*, VII, 220–221.
[23] Jenks and Clark, *The Trust Problem*, p. 190.
[24] Eliot Jones, *The Trust Problem in the United States* (New York: The Macmillan Company, 1924), pp. 288, 293–294.
[25] *Ibid.*, pp. 39–43. Also Conant, *Publications of the American Statistical Association*, VII, 207–226, and John Moody, *The Truth about the Trusts* (New York: The Moody Publishing Company, 1904), pp. 453–469.

ductive industry in the United States." Of these 318 consolidations or trusts, 236 were incorporated after January 1, 1898, and 170 under New Jersey laws. Says Moody, "Those incorporated to January 1, 1898 (the year in which the modern trust-forming period really dates its beginning) represent a total capitalization of but $1,196,724,310, while those formed since that date make an aggregate of $6,049,618,-223." [26]

Of the many consolidations, Moody lists seven as the "Greater Industrial Trusts," all but one organized after 1898:

| Company | Incorporation | | Plants | Capitalization |
	Date	State	Controlled	
Amalgamated Copper Co. . . .	1899	N.J.	11	$175,000,000
American Smelting and Refining Co.	1899	N.J.	121	201,550,400
American Sugar Refining Co.	1891	N.J.	55 (about)	145,000,000
Consolidated Tobacco Co. . . .	1901	N.J.	150 "	502,915,700
International Mercantile Marine Co.	1902	N.J.	6	170,786,000
Standard Oil Co.	1899	N.J.	400 (about)	97,500,000
United States Steel Co.	1901	N.J.	785 "	1,370,000,000
Totals	. . . .	. . . .	1,528	$2,662,752,100

Source: John Moody, The Truth about the Trusts (New York: The Moody Publishing Company, 1904), p. 453.

The discussion so far has been limited to industrial trusts. It should be remembered, however, that consolidation had been going on for half a century in the steam railroads and was well under way in such public services as the telephone, telegraph, gas, and electric power and light. About 1,336 original public service corporations had been drawn together by 1904 into consolidations with a capitalization of $3,735,456,091, one half that of the industrial trusts. According to Moody, 95 per cent of the nation's railway mileage had by 1904 been consolidated in the hands of six financial groups. They represented nearly 80 per cent of the $9,397,363,907 railroad capitalization of the country. The total capitalization of consolidations in various fields (steam railroads, other public utilities, and industrials) amounted to over $20,000,000,000.[27]

[26] Moody, The Truth about the Trusts, pp. 469, 486.
[27] Ibid., pp. 440–443, 470–477. Luther Conant, "Industrial Consolidations in the United States," Publications of the American Statistical Association, VII, 207–226, carries the statistics to the end of 1900. He differs from Moody only in detail. See also Jones, The Trust Problem in the United States, pp. 38–45.

The climax of the early consolidation movement was reached in 1901 with the organization by Elbert H. Gary and J. P. Morgan of the giant United States Steel Corporation. By the end of 1903 consolidation came to a halt in the industrial field. The stock market panic of that year shook public confidence, and the nation experienced an inevitable reaction after a period of speculation. Moreover, the market was loaded with "undigested securities" that had been offered to the public during six hectic years of consolidation. Although more new bonds were offered in 1903 than in 1902, the reverse was true in stocks, where new offerings declined from $784,032,000 in 1902 to $426,890,000 in 1903. At the same time, transactions in shares declined from 188,503,000 to 161,102,000. The market had begun to decline in 1902, but it slumped more radically in 1903, to reach a low in August. The losses in this panic appear to have gone chiefly to the original holders of securities in the new consolidations who still held them and to the syndicates organized to sell them. Speculators in these securities also lost with the slump.[28]

The problem had also become a political issue. It was clear to the public that many of these consolidations were organized to eliminate competition and had succeeded. Since 1896 the Democrats had criticized the trusts, and President Theodore Roosevelt joined in the attack in 1902. In 1903, Congress passed the Expediting Act giving preference in the federal courts to suits brought under the Interstate Commerce Act and the Sherman Antitrust Act. It also created a Department of Commerce and Labor with a subsidiary Bureau of Corporations to make "diligent investigation into the organization, conduct and management of corporations." The bureau immediately began an investigation of the Standard Oil Company, the American Tobacco Company, and other corporations which prepared the way for federal suits. It was in 1902 that the government began proceedings against the Northern Securities Company,[29] a holding company having a monopoly of transportation in the Northwest. The suit ended in the dissolution of that company in 1904 and at the same time made it clear that a monopoly could not disguise itself as a holding company or seek refuge in that form of organization.

[28] Henry Clews, *Fifty Years on Wall Street* (New York: Irving Publishing Company, 1915), pp. 771–773; Roger W. Babson, *Business Barometers Used in the Accumulation of Money* (Wellesley Hills, Mass.: Babson Institute, 13th ed., 1920), pp. 187–189, and table opposite p. 141.

[29] Balthasar Meyer, *A History of the Northern Securities Case* (University of Wisconsin, *Bulletin* No. 142, Madison: University of Wisconsin, 1906).

The consolidation movement halted for the time being in industry mainly because there was little left to combine. Industries adaptable to consolidation or offering a possibility of greater profits through some form of combination had already caught the eye of promoters and financiers. Between 1903 and the end of the First World War not more than a half-dozen important combinations were formed, and these were usually new industries that had hardly existed before 1903. They included General Motors, organized in 1908 and reorganized in 1916; Paramount-Famous-Lasky Corporation (1916) in the new motion-picture industry; Aluminum Company of America (1907); and the Union Carbide and Carbon Company (1917), the first of the great chemical combinations to appear in a rapidly growing industry. There was during this period a rapid consolidation in the electric light and power field which finally reached fantastic proportions in the 1920's.

Professor William Z. Ripley, writing in 1915, pointed out that a succession of devices had been utilized as a basis for promoting monopoly conditions since the Civil War—the pool, the trust, the simple corporation, and the finance company or holding corporation.[30] Other writers, influenced undoubtedly by John Moody's picture of the tremendous ramifications of the interlocking interests of the Morgan and Rockefeller groups,[31] have added "community of interest" to the various devices. Undoubtedly the favoritism shown to certain forms of consolidation followed roughly the chronology as pointed out by Ripley: pools in the 1870's and early 1880's, trusts in the late 1880's, and the merger or holding company during the period 1898–1904.

With the exception of trusts, which seemed so definitely outlawed by the Sherman Act and various legal decisions, all of these various methods existed in all of the periods. Pools, for example, are given little attention by historians after 1900, but one authority insisted in 1915 that the "number of pools has been, and still remains, far greater than the number of trusts [other forms of monopoly]. They probably affect a larger volume of business."[32] An excellent example of this period was the Atlantic Passenger Conference of 1908, in which

[30] William Z. Ripley, *Trusts, Pools and Corporations* (Boston: Ginn and Company, rev. ed., 1915), p. xiii.
[31] Moody, *The Truth about the Trusts*, pp. 490–493.
[32] Edward Dana Durand, *The Trust Problem* (Cambridge: Harvard University Press, 1915), p. 10, reprinted from the *Quarterly Journal of Economics;* William S. Stevens, ed., *Industrial Combinations and Trusts* (New York: The Macmillan Company, 1922), Chap. IX.

eight transatlantic steamship companies allotted the steerage business among themselves on an agreed ratio.[33]

Moreover, the fact that the United States Steel Corporation, the greatest single consolidation of these years and the largest ever organized at one time, was a holding company may have blinded observers to the fact that outright fusions were still being consummated and that "community of interests" also promoted monopoly. Of the eleven monopoly-seeking consolidations organized between 1887 and 1897, and mentioned by Jones as among the most important, only one was definitely a holding company.[34] Even during the active merger years of 1898 and 1899 there were more fusions formed—that is, organizations where the constituent companies were brought under direct ownership of a single corporation—than holding companies. The picture changed somewhat from 1900 to 1903, when the holding company appeared to predominate, but important fusions, such as the American Can Company (1901), Corn Products Company (1902), and the International Harvester Company (1902), were still being formed.

Delay in adopting the use of the holding company was undoubtedly due to the fear that it would share the same fate as the trust if it approximated monopoly conditions. After the Standard Oil Company reorganized as a holding company in 1899, promoters took heart. Organizers of United States Steel went the full length with the holding company pattern in 1901 when they piled one holding company on another to consolidate almost 800 plants and establish control of 60 per cent of the nation's basic manufacturing industry. Three years later, the federal courts in the Northern Securities case outlawed the holding company as a legal means of maintaining monopoly, but the United States Steel Corporation survived court attacks and remains today the largest of the industrial holding companies. In 1911 the American Tobacco Company, recently reorganized by merging the two major subsidiaries with the holding company, was declared a monopoly in restraint of trade. With the pool, the trust, the holding company, and the merger or fusion all illegal when they restrained trade, the only form of monopoly combination not positively ruled out by the courts was "community of interest." Congress, however, tried to deal with that in the Clayton Act of 1914.[35]

[33] William S. Stevens, "A Classification of Pools and Associations Based on American Experience," *American Economic Review*, III, No. 3 (September, 1913), 547–548.

[34] Jones, *The Trust Problem in the United States*, p. 40; James C. Bonbright and Gardiner C. Means, *The Holding Company* (New York: McGraw-Hill Book Company, 1932), pp. 68–70.

[35] Bonbright and Means, *The Holding Company*, p. 71.

The great day of the holding company came into reality during the consolidation movement of the 1920's. Of the twenty-one largest industrial holding companies at the end of that decade, only three, the Standard Oil Company of New Jersey, the United States Steel Corporation, and the Eastman Kodak Company, were formed before 1910.[36] Whether these various consolidations were outright mergers or holding companies, the method of establishing them was about the same. A promoter first of all secured options on the plants that were to be combined and then arranged through financiers or an underwriting syndicate to obtain the necessary funds. He then organized a corporation and arranged for the transfer of the plants to the new corporation.[37] The usual method was for each plant joining the merger to receive preferred stock of the new corporation equivalent to an agreed valuation on its own plant. On the theory that mergers meant a decline in competition and greater profits, each concern joining the merger expected a bonus of large blocks of common stock. The preferred stock usually represented the value of the plants and the common stock the hope of monopoly gains. It was through common stock, ordinarily representing little more than water, that the promoters, lawyers, financiers, and syndicates expected to profit by selling it to the public. Sometimes this type of organization did not need much actual cash, but a syndicate was required to guarantee such funds, if necessary. In other cases large amounts were raised to finance consolidations.

The classic example of consolidation is found in the United States Steel Corporation, organized in 1901. Here J. P. Morgan & Co. acted as promoter and syndicate with Judge Elbert H. Gary, later chairman of the board of the United States Steel Corporation, as the agent who directed the organization. The story of this giant corporation has been told many times and need not be repeated here in detail.[38] As founded, it comprised nine large corporations combining the Carnegie and Morgan interests as well as others. Its capital structure at the time of organization was as follows:

[36] *Ibid.*, p. 78.

[37] The activities of the promoter and the formation of a "trust" are developed in Edward S. Mead, *Trust Finance* (New York: D. Appleton and Company, 1914), Chaps. IV–VII; Lewis H. Haney, *Business Organization and Consolidation* (New York: The Macmillan Company, 1928), Chap. XVIII; Jenks and Clark, *The Trust Problem*, Chap. XII.

[38] U.S. Department of Commerce and Labor, Bureau of Corporations, *Report of the Commissioner of Corporations on the Steel Industry* (Washington: Government Printing Office, 3 pts., 1911–1913); Jones, *The Trust Problem in the United States*, Chap. IX; Henry R. Seager and Charles A. Gulick, Jr., *Trust and Corporation Problems* (New York: Harper & Brothers, 1929), Chaps. XIII–XIV.

Preferred stock	$510,205,743
Common stock	508,227,394
Steel Corporation bonds	303,450,000
Underlying bonds	59,091,657
Purchase money obligations and real-estate mortgages ..	21,872,023
Total	$1,402,846,817

After a detailed investigation the Commissioner of Corporations placed the physical valuation of the corporation's property, including ore property, when organized, at $682,000,000.[39] Assuming this to be a fair valuation, it is obvious that all of the common stock and more than one fourth of the preferred stock was water. About 50 per cent of the capitalization represented no tangible assets. So successful was the company, however, that it succeeded in absorbing the water and in paying dividends on its common stock, with the exception of two years, from 1901 until hit by the depression in 1929.

Whatever the causes for consolidations and the methods used to accomplish them, most Americans looked upon the results with suspicion and considered them dangerous. Years before trust promoters had frankly admitted to the Industrial Commission that they had organized consolidations to eliminate competition and to increase profits, the common man had understood this purpose. Experience with monopolies in the 1880's and 1890's had convinced him that the producer of raw materials and the consumer suffered. He had been acquainted with the railroad monopolies for a half century. He had watched the "Standard Oil Trust," the "Sugar Trust" (Sugar Refining Company, later the American Sugar Refining Company), and the "Whisky Trust" (Distilling and Cattle Feeding Company) repeatedly raise prices whenever the monopoly position of these organizations became stronger. He refused to take too seriously the arguments advanced by these companies that large-scale monopolies introduced savings that benefited the consumer by lowering the price of the finished article.

As far as the oil industry was concerned, his general impression was later reinforced by investigations of the Bureau of Corporations. In a report issued in 1907 the bureau insisted that price statistics up to 1897 demonstrated "the falsity of the historic claim of the Standard Oil Company that by reason of its extraordinary efficiency it has brought prices to a point lower than would have been reached had business remained under normal competitive conditions and in the

[39] *Report of the Commissioner of Corporations on the Steel Industry*, Pt. I, pp. 14–39.

hands of a number of comparatively smaller concerns." [40] After 1897, said the *Report*, "the Standard had consistently used its power to raise the price of oil . . . not only absolutely but also relatively to the cost of crude oil." [41]

Although it is not difficult to prove that monopolies often raised prices, at least temporarily, it has been difficult to get a clear over-all picture of the effect of monopolistic conditions on prices. In 1900, Professor Jeremiah H. Jenks came to the conclusion that "the fact that the power to increase the margin, temporarily at least, some-what arbitrarily, and the fact that this margin has been increased in specific cases, seem to be clearly established." [42] The Industrial Commission in 1902, after an exhaustive study, asserted that "in most cases the combination has exerted an appreciable power over prices, and in practically all cases it has increased the margin between raw materials and finished products. Since there is reason to believe that the cost of production over a period of years has lessened, the con-clusion is inevitable that the combinations have been able to increase their profits." [43] More than a quarter of a century later, however, Pro-fessor Jenks stated that a careful study of a series of price charts in-dicates that "the effect of these trusts, taking their history as a whole, has not been to increase prices to the consumers, although at certain times, especially before 1900, they have doubtless increased prices." [44]

Why great corporations, possessing virtual monopoly power, have sometimes increased prices to consumers beyond reason and at other times have reduced them, or why, when they had the power, have not charged all the traffic would bear, can be explained by a number of reasons. Seldom without patent protection has a complete private monopoly existed in the United States. Even when such a monopoly existed, there was always the fear of potential competition, the possi-bility that the consumer might use a substitute, the danger of arous-ing public opinion, the necessity at times of one trust selling to an-other, or ignorance of how much the traffic would bear. Whatever the reasons, many students of big business and monopolies have taken the view that the great business consolidations as a whole have not raised prices. The National Industrial Conference Board, a research organization supported by business, even insists that "it can only be

[40] *Report of the Commissioner of Corporations on the Petroleum Industry* (Wash-ington: Government Printing Office, 1907), Pt. 2, p. xxxiii.
[41] *Ibid.*, p. xxx.
[42] Jeremiah W. Jenks, *Trusts and Industrial Problems* (U.S. Department of Labor, *Bulletin* No. 29, Washington: Government Printing Office, 1900), p. 765.
[43] *Final Report of the Industrial Commission*, XIX, 621.
[44] Jenks and Clark, *The Trust Problem*, p. 136.

concluded that the consolidation movement has tended to keep prices from rising, that it has tended to stabilize prices as far as seasonal fluctuations are concerned, but that it has not tended to check the cyclical advances and declines of prices." [45] This study maintains that the rise in prices since 1900 of 26 lines of manufacture affected by combinations was only 28.8 per cent "as against a rise of 117.4 per cent during the same period in the 20 lines of manufacture . . . not affected by the consolidation movement." [46]

Prices on the whole and over a period of years may not have been increased by the consolidation movement. The question remained, however, whether the prices which did exist were higher than they should have been or would have been under more competitive conditions. If consolidations brought the many economies claimed by the trusts, if large aggregations of capital made it possible to maintain research organizations and take advantage of every technical advance, why did this not result in lower prices for the consumer? How could the price of Bessemer steel rails remain fixed from 1901 to 1916 when previous prices between 1867 and 1900 had never been the same for two consecutive years? What about the large profits which many of the trusts were making? And were these not at the expense of the consumers? The verdict here was more clear-cut. Consolidations were not immune from declining profits, losses, or even bankruptcy when hit by depressions or handicapped by unmanageable financial structure or incompetent management. Consolidation in itself was no royal road to profits. [47] Nevertheless, consolidations managed with reasonable ability, not only dictated prices for the nation but reaped enormous profits attributable largely to monopoly conditions. [48]

That inordinate monopoly profits existed could hardly be denied by such holders of patents as the American Steel and Wire Company and the United Shoe Machinery Company. It was also difficult for other monopolies to explain away their profits when their consolidations had started with a capitalization twice the value of their assets. In most consolidations the common stock, as noted earlier, represented little more than "water" and a hope of monopoly profits. As Judge William H. Moore, a well-known trust promoter, admitted

[45] *Mergers in Industry* (New York: National Industrial Conference Board, 1929), pp. 167–169.

[46] *Ibid.*, p. 173.

[47] *Mergers in Industry*, pp. 40–41.

[48] Jones, *The Trust Problems in the United States*, pp. 87–90, 119–121, 159–163, 184–185, 210–213, 265–268.

before the Industrial Commission in 1899, "Everybody knows what they are getting when they get common stock; they know they are not getting anything that represents assets." [49] Yet most successful consolidations were soon paying dividends on this watered stock. Judged in terms of monopoly profits, prices of many commodities were unreasonably high. Farmers were quick to notice one angle of this: while farm prices declined during depressions, prices of industrial commodities bolstered by monopoly conditions declined much less radically, if at all.

At least two statements can be made regarding combinations strong enough to dominate an industry: they had the power to fix prices and they generally earned profits so consistently high that only monopoly conditions made them possible. Prices could be set directly, as in the case of the aluminum corporation; indirectly, as in the sale of anthracite coal by the chief railroads of the area (the Philadelphia and Reading, the Lehigh Valley, the Delaware, Lackawanna and Western, the Central of New Jersey, the Delaware and Hudson, the Erie, and the Pennsylvania) which owned most of the coal and transported the rest; by agreement, as in the case of the United States Steel Corporation; or by sheer force of leadership, as with the Standard Oil and its successor companies. A study of these concerns and of such combinations as the American Tobacco Company and the International Harvester Company shows that prices quite out of line with costs were maintained for many years. Monopoly practices made them possible. [50]

PATTERNS OF THE NEW COMPETITION

With the development of combinations the pattern of competition changed. The ruthless competition of the older type, which represented the jungle warfare of business at its worst, declined. [51] New forms, however, sprang up to take their place. This change was by no means sudden; all of the worst methods of unfair competition continued to a more or less degree during the period under study. These included the well-known practices of cutting prices in one locality to meet local competition while recouping in another, the

[49] Industrial Commission, *Report*, I, 963.
[50] Harrison B. Summers in Roy E. Curtin, ed., *The Trust and Economic Control* (New York: McGraw-Hill Book Company, 1931), pp. 335–356.
[51] Arthur R. Burns, *The Decline of Competition* (New York: McGraw-Hill Book Company, 1936), and A. R. Burns, "The Process of Industrial Concentration," *Quarterly Journal of Economics*, XLVII (February, 1933), 277–311

operation of bogus "independent" concerns to maintain the fiction of competition, the pushing of special brands at a loss to drive out competitors, the insistence upon "tying clauses" or exclusive arrangements, the securing of rebates and preferential agreements, and the use of black lists, boycotts, espionage, coercion, and intimidation. In brief, all the shady and illegal practices and bullying methods were used which the big and strong can employ against the weaker competitor.[52]

These were the types of practices that often ruined small manufacturers, aroused widespread resentment, gave the "muckrakers" ammunition, and brought prohibitions in the Clayton Act. They were followed ruthlessly by such virtual monopolies as the Standard Oil Company, the American Tobacco Company, the American Sugar Refining Company, the Corn Products Refining Company, the American Can Company, the National Cash Register Company, and many others.[53] How one of these unfair practices persisted (and this one definitely illegal under the Interstate Commerce Act of 1887) was brought out by the Industrial Commission in 1900, when it reported "that the railroads still made discriminations between individuals and perhaps to as great an extent as ever before." [54]

Certain influences, however, operated to bring a decline of these methods. Since most important American industries were consolidated in a single large corporation or in a handful of large ones, these corporations became interested mainly in establishing and maintaining prices which would assure ample profits. Where several large concerns were in the same industry, it seemed wiser for all to survive in prosperity than to carry on a bitter competition on a price basis which might decrease profits for all. Moreover, as we shall see, certain unfair practices were definitely outlawed in new railroad legislation and in the Clayton Antitrust Act, while the Bureau of Corporations and later the Federal Trade Commission were established to investigate such practices. At the same time the federal courts had begun to differentiate between "good trusts" and "bad trusts"; that is, between those who tried to monopolize by unfair practices and those who by necessity or choice practiced toward their competitors

[52] Examples of all of these are given in William H. S. Stevens, *Unfair Competition* (Chicago: The University of Chicago Press, 1917). See also Myron W. Watkins, *Industrial Combinations and Public Policy* (Boston: Houghton Mifflin Company, 1927), Chap. V.

[53] Clair Wilcox, *Competition and Monopoly in American Industry* (Temporary National Economic Committee, *Monograph* No. 21 Senate Committee Print, 76 Cong., 3 Sess., Washington: Government Printing Office, 1940), pp. 65–98.

[54] Industrial Commission, *Report*, IV, 5.

the principle of "live and let live." The latter policy, it should be said, was granted to the weaker only on the terms of the stronger corporation.

The method followed was to establish relatively inflexible prices and then compete on a nonprice basis. Some of these practices appeared to be illegal under the antitrust acts; others clearly skirted the legal barriers. In the oil industry, where Standard Oil retained its premier position even under growing competition, it set the prices as the recognized leader. Rather than engage in bitter competition, others adopted the same prices as Standard.[55] In the steel business the United States Steel Corporation occupied the same position.[56] For a while it allowed its constituent companies to make pooling arrangements with competitors and, later, to hold trade meetings to reach agreements with respect to prices. Beginning in 1907, Elbert H. Gary, chairman of the board, held annual dinners for the leaders of the industry; his purpose, as he explained it, was "to prevent the demoralization of business, to maintain as far as practicable the stability of business and to prevent, if I could, not by agreement, but by exhortation, the wide and sudden fluctuation of prices which would be injurious to everyone interested in the business of the iron and steel manufacturers." [57]

The dominance of one great company or one financial interest in a field naturally brings to mind the interlocking financial interests of the great capitalists and the aggregation of wealth controlled by them. Moody in 1904 believed that two great rival financial interests—the Morgan and the Rockefeller—were rapidly and inevitably reaching out to dominate the business of the nation.[58] At the moment there might be gigantic battles between these financial dinosaurs, but gradually and also inevitably these rival interests tended to become interwoven. If such was the case, and the evidence seemed clear, the end result would be to soften competition.

One of the most significant developments illustrating the trend was the growth of the trade associations, or more particularly, that type known as "open price associations." Trade associations of various kinds had existed for many years, but those which favored open prices

[55] Burns, *The Decline of Competition*, pp. 95–109.

[56] *Ibid.*, pp. 77–93.

[57] United States *v.* United States Steel Corporation, *et al.* District Court of New Jersey, October term 1914 (No. 6,214), Pt. 21, p. 149. Quoted by Jones, *The Trust Problem in the United States*, pp. 225–226. See also Ida Tarbell, *Life of Elbert H. Gary* (New York: D. Appleton and Company, 1925), p. 205.

[58] Moody, *The Truth about the Trusts*, pp. 490–493.

and open competition did not appear until the second decade of the century. Their purpose, says one of the earliest studies of this development, was "to effect greater stability in business conditions, in order that profits may be made, if not greater, at least more steady, dependable, and calculable from year to year." [59] Along with this was the collection and dissemination of information relative to the industry, including statistics and prices, and the promotion of friendly relations between the members. This sometimes extended to cooperative control of output, types of product, and methods of selling.[60] They were in line with the growing tendency noticed earlier of establishing a conventional price and then competing for the market by other methods than price competition. They recognized the policy that absolute monopolies were no longer an objective in industry. An excellent and important example of the trade association was the American Iron and Steel Institute, which was organized after the "Gary dinners" were discontinued, to serve the same purpose in an enlarged manner. Gary himself was its founder and long-time president.

The background of the trade association was the desire to eliminate destructive cutthroat competition by some method which avoided the antitrust laws. In certain respects the trade associations stemmed from the pools and, says one student, marked "a reversion to the looser forms of combination." [61] The earliest of these trade associations of the open price variety appeared in 1911 in the iron and steel industry (Bridge Builders Society), in 1912 in the lumber industry (Yellow Pine Association), and in 1914 in textiles (National Association of Finishers of Cotton Fabrics). The organization of such associations was given great impetus by the propaganda of a Chicago lawyer, Arthur J. Eddy, whose book, The New Competition (1912), states the theory behind the associations. His slogan was "Competition is war, and war is hell," and he was convinced that the trade associations were legal under the antitrust laws.

Eddy himself organized many of the first trade associations and acted as their counsel.[62] The First World War gave a tremendous impetus to the spread of the association movement, since the govern-

[59] Milton N. Nelson, Open Price Associations (University of Illinois Studies in the Social Sciences, Vol. X, No. 2, Urbana: University of Illinois, 1922), p. 19.

[60] Burns, The Decline of Competition, pp. 64–75.

[61] I. L. Sharfman, "The Trade Association Movement," American Economic Review, XVI, No. 1, Supp. (March, 1926), 204.

[62] Arthur Jerome Eddy, The New Competition (New York: D. Appleton and Company, 1912); Nelson, Open Price Associations, pp. 24–28, 41–49.

ment preferred to deal with associations rather than with individuals. It was much easier in this way to get a complete picture of an industry as to raw materials, stocks on hand, and production capacity. By 1920 more than 1,000 associations were in existence, including over 100 of the open price variety. Few industries of any size were without trade associations of one kind or another.

Another evidence of the decline of certain types of competition may be seen in various devices for sharing the market, variations in most cases from the earlier methods of pooling. Efforts were made at one time or another in the direction of cooperative selling, perhaps the most notable example being the Continental Wall Paper Company (1898), which purchased the entire output of its membership (producing 98 per cent of the wall paper manufactured in the United States), determined the output of each member and the selling price of the paper, and regulated the activities of the jobbers.[63] Frequent and successful efforts were likewise made by producers in the same industry to share the market, but whether this was done by explicit agreement or tacit understanding is difficult to determine. Certainly the five great packers (Swift, Armour, Morris, Wilson, and Cudahy) at one time or another appeared to have shared the purchase of livestock and so eventually the market.[64] In a similar manner, the carriers of anthracite coal sought to distribute the coal tonnage on a stable basis, and similar efforts were made by other industries.[65]

It gradually became clear that to a considerable extent manufactured products no longer sold in markets where prices incessantly changed in response to actual changes in supply and demand. In their place came "administered prices," prices set in one way or another by administrative action. Prices often remained unchanged from day to day and even from year to year. This came, as has been suggested, in industries where one firm had a quasi monopoly, a firm strong enough to be a price leader, or where the number of firms dominating an industry was so small that agreements, understandings, and other methods could readily accomplish the objectives of monopoly organization. That such a condition rapidly developed after 1897 is clearly evident from the studies of Moody, Laidler, Burns, and many others. In brief, there is ample evidence to show that price stabilization followed concentration of industry.[66] But price stabilization did not necessarily mean an end of competition. Prices could be

[63] Burns, *The Decline of Competition*, p. 151.
[64] *Ibid.*, pp. 156–165.   [65] *Ibid.*, pp. 123, 166.
[66] Gardiner C. Means, "Industrial Prices and Their Relative Flexibility," *Senate Document* No. 13, 74 Cong., 1 Sess.

stabilized while nonprice competition continued aggressively. There might still be competition in quality, in service, and in style.[67]

REACTION TO CONSOLIDATION AND MONOPOLY

The opposition which followed the wave of business consolidation came primarily from two groups—the consumer and the small businessman. The consumer correctly believed that monopoly conditions accompanied by speculation and overcapitalization had increased the prices of commodities or maintained them at too high a level. The small businessman complained of unfair and illegal methods of competition which weakened his position, if they did not drive him out of business. Others could see wider economic or social implications in the development of monopolies.[68]

First of all there was the effect of consolidation upon labor. Since consolidation obviously increased the power of capital, a similar consolidation of labor seemed necessary to preserve what bargaining power it might already have achieved. It is not contented here that the failure of labor to make greater progress in the consolidated industries was caused alone by the size or effects of combination. Nevertheless, the effects of business consolidation on labor, organized or unorganized, were generally detrimental. Many of the consolidations, notably in the steel industry, were able to prevent the organization of labor in their industries until the middle 1930's. Except in railroad transportation, organized labor prospered better in the decentralized or smaller industries. In prosperous times there was less competition for labor among employers in the consolidated industries; in bad times the great consolidations could easily close up entire factories and maintain curtailed production in others. The savings and oftentimes greater efficiency from consolidation saved some duplication of labor and thus threw many out of work. There is little or no evidence that the consolidated industries generally paid higher wages than the smaller industries or that labor gained through wages any share in the greater profits of monopolies. Labor did, however, sometimes gain from certain welfare projects which large industries could better support than the smaller ones.[69]

Monopolies were also condemned because they discouraged competitors from coming into the field. This, it was believed, prevented

[67] Burns, The Decline of Competition, pp. 372–416.
[68] Industrial Commission, Report, I, 33–34.
[69] Jenks and Clark, The Trust Problem, pp. 138–156.

younger men from going into business independently. Thus the trusts were "sapping the courage and power of initiative of perhaps the most active and influential men in the community." [70] Heads of large corporations denied this charge, and to a large extent they were probably right, for the economy was still expanding rapidly, and with it economic opportunities. But the concentration of business had wider effects than merely the curtailment of free competition. As business grew in size, and consolidations were established under the corporate form, there was a widening separation between owners (stockholders) and their property. The older and more intimate relationship between the worker and the owner of the factory no longer existed; now the owners delegated their power to agents or managers. Thousands of stockholders never even saw the property they owned. Absentee ownership, with its concomitant evils, was, of course, not new in American economic life. With the growth of great corporations, however, it became the normal thing.

Not only was the typical stockholder quite out of touch with the business which he owned; he was rapidly losing control over his agents or, to be more exact, over the few larger stockholders and managers who ran the business. As a result the latter gradually stole away the rights of the masses of stockholders. As Professor W. Z. Ripley pointed out some years later, this tendency could be seen in the limitation upon the right of shareholders to participate in future issues of securities, in the arrogation by management of the sole responsibility to issue new securities, in the almost unrestrained authorization of management to dispose of new shares upon any terms they thought fit, and in the almost unrestrained power to sell the assets or enter into new corporate relationships without interference. It could also be seen in the successful attempts made by officers and directors to exempt themselves from liability to stockholders for corporation losses incurred in private deals in which the officers may have had a special interest. [71] The result was the gradual decline of the stockholder and the growth in the power of directors and officers. With this growth in power came a proportionately larger cut in the profits of the company. One result was the concentration of the industrial power and the nation's wealth in the hands of fewer people.

Although the implications of all this were clear enough to those who cared to see, it did not seem to arouse the average citizen as

[70] Industrial Commission, *Report,* I, 34.
[71] W. Z. Ripley, *Main Street and Wall Street* (Boston: Little, Brown & Company, 1929), pp. 37–38.

much as the charges of political corruption levied against the great corporations. Corporations like the United States Steel Corporation, the Pennsylvania Railroad, and later the American Telephone and Telegraph Company, owned wealth greater than the aggregate wealth of many American states, and employed more people than lived in some of them. As long as the people held assets which the corporations wanted or as long as there were politicians willing to trade with the corporations for personal gain, there was bound to be corruption. Political corruption was more blatant in the eighties and nineties than after 1900, but it flourished during the years of consolidations, and the trusts played a prominent part.

Each period which showed any growing tendency toward business consolidation has produced reaction. By 1888 all of the four leading American parties had placed antitrust planks in their platforms; by the end of 1898, six states had amended their constitutions to prohibit monopolies, and twenty-nine states had passed statutes against them. Henry George's *Progress and Poverty* (1879) had pointed to a solution of the problem of land monopoly, and Henry Demarest Lloyd's *Wealth against Commonwealth* (1894) had blasted the Standard Oil Company in the most powerful polemic ever launched against monopoly in America. Antagonism to private monopoly was deeply ingrained in Anglo-Saxon common law and by 1898 was widely expressed in the United States both in federal and in state statute law. The recrudescence of opposition to monopolies as a result of widespread consolidation after 1897 followed a normal pattern.

The new outburst of denunciation began with the "History of the Standard Oil Company," a scholarly series of articles written by Ida M. Tarbell, which appeared in *McClure's Magazine* in 1902–1904.[72] The idea had come from McClure himself, who believed that monopoly was one of the most serious problems facing the American people.[73] This series proved so successful that other magazines followed, and articles against "big business" took a prominent place in the literature of the "muckrake." Tarbell's study of the Standard Oil developed the thesis that the power of the trusts was based on "primary privileges." Thomas W. Lawson, in a series on "Frenzied Finance" for *Everybody's*, blasted the corruption of the monopolists, their crooked speculation on the securities exchanges, and the "sys-

[72] Ida M. Tarbell, *The History of the Standard Oil Company* (New York: McClure, Phillips & Co., 1904).

[73] Samuel S. McClure, *My Autobiography* (New York: Frederick A. Stokes Company, 1914), pp. 237–240.

tem" which made it impossible for any but the insiders to win. Before the Lawson articles were finished, Charles Edward Russell began a competent series in the same magazine on "The Greatest Trust in the World" ("Beef Trust"), but Upton Sinclair's novel, *The Jungle,* probably exerted more influence on the subsequent legislation to clean up the meat-packing business. Ray Stannard Baker exposed the continuing illegal abuses of the railroads in *McClure's* [74] and *Collier's,* and Burton J. Hendrick, basing his work on the exposures of the Armstrong investigation of the New York legislature, attacked the unsound and unethical practices into which the insurance companies had deteriorated.[75] These were but the most famous of many articles in which various writers opened to public view the illegal practices and abuses by which big business obtained wealth or achieved monopoly at the expense of the nation.[76]

This barrage of criticism, some of it sensational but most of it only too accurate, was particularly vocal from 1902 to 1907. The criticism, in fact, was so strong as to make it virtually impossible for politicians to ignore the problem, and Theodore Roosevelt was not one who closed his ears to popular demand. In the six years before Roosevelt became President the Sherman Act had been little used. The Supreme Court had apparently rendered it utterly ineffective in the Knight decision of 1895,[77] and state laws seemed equally futile. In an effort to strengthen the act, more than a hundred bills were proposed in Congress, but only one—the Wilson Tariff Act of 1894, which forbade importation of goods when the intention was to restrain trade or competition—had passed. None of the nation's presidents before Roosevelt had shown any particular interest in enforcing the Sherman Act.

Renewal of the attack on monopolies began with Roosevelt's message of 1901. In it he insisted that the great corporate fortunes were not due to the tariff or other governmental action, but to "natural causes in the business world." He realized, nevertheless, that "real and grave evils" had developed during the process of consolidation. Although he urged caution in dealing with the trust problem, he believed that Congress should insist on publicity for corporate affairs,

[74] "Railroads on Trial," *McClure's Magazine,* XXVI (1905–1906), 47–59, 179–194, 318–331, 398–411, 535–549.

[75] "The Story of Life Insurance," *McClure's Magazine,* XXVII (May–October, 1906), 36–49, and following issues; also, Burton J. Hendrick, *The Story of Life Insurance* (New York: McClure, Phillips & Co., 1907).

[76] Cornelius C. Regier, *The Era of the Muckrakers* (Chapel Hill: University of North Carolina Press, 1932), Chap. IX.

[77] United States *v.* E. C. Knight Co., 156 U.S. 1 (1895).

regulation of great combinations, the elimination of such abuses as overcapitalization, and a "proper" government supervision. If Congress lacked the power to do this, Roosevelt urged that a constitutional amendment be submitted to the states. He also urged the creation of a cabinet officer to be known as the Secretary of Commerce and Industries.

Roosevelt's recommendations were largely ignored by Congress, and in the summer of 1902 he elaborated his views to the country in a series of speeches in New England and the Middle West. Partly as a result of his efforts, Congress in February, 1903, established a Department of Commerce and Labor and a Bureau of Corporations within the department to investigate trusts and combinations (except common carriers) and advise the Department of Justice in cases involving antitrust laws. It also passed an Expediting Act giving preference in the courts to federal suits brought under the Sherman Antitrust Act and the Interstate Commerce Act. In another act it made $500,000 immediately available for the enforcement of the antitrust act.[78] The work of the Bureau of Corporations proved extremely valuable. Between 1905 and 1915 it published twenty-nine volumes giving detailed studies of various industries, notably oil and tobacco, studies which proved of great aid in the successful prosecution of these trusts. Although no further antitrust legislation of any importance passed Congress until 1914, the problem of the trusts remained paramount. The intervening years saw vigorous efforts by the Roosevelt and Taft administrations to enforce existing laws and a wide discussion of various methods to make the laws more effective.

Roosevelt believed that the chief weakness of the Sherman Act was lack of vigorous enforcement by the national government. During his administration the Department of Justice introduced eighteen bills in equity, obtained twenty-five indictments, and took part in one forfeiture proceeding. These included suits against the powerful oil, tobacco, and meat trusts as well as against important railroads. His greatest triumph was the dissolution in 1904 of the Northern Securities Company, a New Jersey holding company designed to create a transportation monopoly in the Northwest by controlling the stocks of the Great Northern, the Northern Pacific, and the Chicago, Burlington and Quincy. The decision was clear-cut. "If Congress has not," said the Court, "by the words used in this Act, described this

[78] The last three acts (32 *U.S. Statutes at Large*, p. 823; 32 *Statutes at Large*, p. 828, and 32 *Statutes at Large*, p. 903) are given in the Appendix to Jenks and Clark, *The Trust Problem*, pp. 451–456.

and like cases, it would, we apprehend, be impossible to find words that would describe them." [79] Roosevelt believed that the Northern Securities decision had restored to the federal government "the power to deal with industrial monopoly and suppress it and to control and regulate combinations of which the Knight case had deprived it." [80]

Roosevelt overrated the importance of the Northern Securities decision, for the Trans-Missouri Freight decision (1897) had already done much to restore vitality to the Sherman Act. The Northern Securities decision had little effect upon control or ownership, for the dissolution of the holding company left the majority of stocks of both the Northern Pacific and the Great Northern in the hands of the Hill-Morgan group, where they had rested before the consolidation. Although the decision showed that a holding company was not immune under the antitrust laws, it seemed to have had little or no effect in halting that type of consolidation. The great day of the holding company came after 1904. A more likely reason for the slowing up of consolidation was the fact that most of the great existing industries had already been consolidated.[81]

Prosecution of trusts continued with even greater vigor under Taft. As against Roosevelt's forty-four proceedings, Taft initiated ninety: forty-six bills in equity, forty-three indictments, and one contempt proceeding. Moreover, Taft was even more specific and more insistent upon new legislation than Roosevelt had been. He asked for the passage of a voluntary federal incorporation act, a body comparable to the Interstate Commerce Commission to supervise the granting of charters, and an end to stock watering and the erection of holding companies. While Congress did nothing, Taft continued his prosecutions. The best known were those involving the Standard Oil Company and the American Tobacco Company, both of which had originated under the Roosevelt administration and were finally decided in 1911. The Court found both concerns guilty of undue restraint of trade and ordered them broken up in a manner which presumably would restore competition.

Some students have tried to find encouragement in the decisions by pointing out that they reaffirmed the position taken in the Northern Securities case—that a holding company charter was no safeguard against prosecution under the Sherman Act—and that the decision reaffirmed the power of the courts to order any type of dis-

[79] Northern Securities Co. *et al. v.* United States, 193 U.S. 360 (1904).
[80] Theodore Roosevelt, *An Autobiography* (New York: The Macmillan Company, 1913), p. 469.
[81] Seager and Gulick, *Trust and Corporation Problems,* pp. 386–391.

solution that would break up the combination.[82] Actually the result of the decisions was to weaken and confuse the interpretation and execution of the act. In the Trans-Missouri Freight Association case of 1897 the majority of the Court had refused to differentiate between "reasonable" and "unreasonable" restraints of trade or between "good" and "bad" trusts. The law, the majority said, included "*every* control, combination in the form of trust, or otherwise, or conspiracy in restraint of trade or commerce . . . ." [83] In the Standard Oil and Tobacco cases, however, the Court reversed its position of 1897. It now asserted that the act of 1890, which many believed wrote common law into the federal statute book, did not prohibit at that time a "restraint of trade" which was reasonable and only partial in its operation. Said Chief Justice White:

> The statute under this view evidenced the intent not to restrain the right to make and enforce contracts, whether resulting from combinations or otherwise, which did not unduly restrain interstate or foreign commerce, but to protect the commerce from being restrained by methods, whether old or new, which would constitute an interference—that is, an undue restraint.[84]

To the so-called "rule of reason," highly satisfactory to big business, the Court soon added other interpretations equally helpful. In 1916, in the case of the American Can Company, a federal court refused to dissolve the company, though admitting that early methods of the company were intended to restrain competition and monopolize the product. It admitted that the company, because of its great power, was a potential instrument of monopoly, but that it was not attempting to use its powers at the time, and that the breaking up of the company would serve no useful purpose.[85] What apparently was happening during these years was that the Supreme Court had taken upon itself the responsibility of ignoring the intent of the Sherman Act even if the words of the act were not always clear, and deciding for itself in each case what seemed to it the wisest procedure for the general welfare. Since the existing economic system tended toward consolidation and monopoly, and a structure of legal practices regarding consolidation had developed, the attitude and procedure of the Supreme Court may have been realistic. But its obiter dicta and its arrogation of power did not solve the trust problem, if it could be solved. At least the Democrats felt that it did not. In their platform

[82] *Ibid.*, pp. 401–402.
[83] United States *v.* Trans-Missouri Freight Association, 166 U.S. 312 (1897).
[84] Standard Oil Company of New Jersey *et al. v.* United States, 221 U.S. 60 (1911).
[85] United States *v.* American Can Company *et al.*, 230 Fed. 859, 860 (1916).

of 1912 they regretted the "judicial construction" given in the Standard Oil and Tobacco cases and favored "enactment of legislation which will restore to the statute the strength of which it has been deprived by such interpretation." [86]

Although the Department of Justice often worked vigorously to enforce the Sherman Act, and the Supreme Court sometimes aided —according to its own lights—monopoly conditions persisted and control of the nation's economic life continued largely in the hands of big business. As this fact became increasingly evident, the demand for further legislation grew. Taft had urged amendments and the Republican party had admitted the need of them, but Congress had done little. The Democrats in their platform of 1908 blasted the Republican party as the partner of big monopolies, and urged criminal prosecution of "guilty trust magnates" and a law to end private monopolies. They advocated a federal license system requiring each corporation doing an interstate business to take out such a license if it controlled 25 per cent of its kind of business and a law prohibiting the existence of any concern controlling more than 50 per cent of the business. They urged a law forbidding interlocking directorates among competing concerns and one forcing all licensed corporations to sell to all purchasers on equal terms, making due allowances for cost of transportation.[87] These ideas were in part reiterated in the platform of 1912.[88]

REVISION OF ANTITRUST LEGISLATION

As for Woodrow Wilson, their presidential candidate in 1912, his attitude was generally known. While governor of New Jersey he had sponsored the stringent antitrust laws, familiarly known as the "Seven Sisters," [89] which temporarily ended the traditional welcome which that state had extended to monopolistic corporations. As a candidate, Wilson talked much of the "New Freedom." "American industry," he said, "is not free, as once it was free. American enterprise is not free; the man with only a little capital is finding it harder to get into the field, more and more impossible to compete with the big fellow. Why? Because the laws of this country do not prevent the strong from crushing the weak." [90] The purpose of the new adminis-

[86] Kirk H. Porter, *National Party Platforms* (New York: The Macmillan Company, 1924), p. 322.
[87] *Ibid.*, p. 277.   [88] *Ibid.*, p. 322.
[89] Jenks and Clark, *The Trust Problem*, Appendix E–2.
[90] Wilson, *The New Freedom*, p. 15

tration, it appeared, was to restore some of the older opportunities and competition. After years of criticism, the Democrats were committed to do something. If any added impetus was necessary, it came during the early months of the Wilson administration from the amazing revelations of the activities of the New York, New Haven and Hartford Railroad under the direction of J. P. Morgan in building up a monopoly of transportation in New England. Nothing could illustrate more clearly the utter contempt held by the monopoly makers for the public welfare.[91]

In 1914 the Democratic party fulfilled many of the antitrust pledges made in its platforms of 1908 and 1912. The first legislation was the Federal Trade Commission Act, approved September 26, 1914.[92] This established a Federal Trade Commission of five members to replace the earlier Bureau of Corporations, the purpose of which was to "prevent persons, partnerships, or corporations, excepting banks and common carriers subject to the acts to regulate commerce, from using unfair methods of competition in commerce." It had the power to make investigations of combinations, conduct hearings, issue cease and desist orders, and apply to the United States Circuit Court of Appeals for enforcement of its orders. The commission's powers included the enforcement of decrees under the antitrust acts and investigations of monopoly in foreign trade. This act was obviously intended as a means of prevention as well as punishment. It envisaged a government agent which would clarify the meaning of the legislation and aid business in obeying it.

Shortly thereafter Congress supplemented the existing antitrust legislation by passing the Clayton Act.[93] It forbade (1) discrimination in prices between purchasers when the effect was "to substantially lessen competition or tend to create a monopoly"; (2) exclusive selling or leasing contracts whether of patented or unpatented articles; and (3) interlocking directorates in concerns engaged in interstate commerce whose capital, surplus, and undivided profits aggregated more than $1,000,000 (if such concerns were competitors), and in banks when the deposits, capital, surplus, and undivided profits exceeded $5,000,000. Likewise, corporations were forbidden

[91] Interstate Commerce Commission, No. 6,569, *In Re Financial Transactions of the New York, New Haven and Hartford Railroad Company* (July 11, 1914), pp. 32–36.

[92] 38 *U.S. Statutes at Large*, p. 717. Reprinted in Jenks and Clark, *The Trust Problem*, Appendix F–9. Discussed in Seager and Gulick, *Trust and Corporation Problems*, pp. 516–551, and at length in Gerard C. Henderson, *The Federal Trade Commission* (New Haven: Yale University Press, 1925).

[93] Approved October 15, 1914. 38 *U.S. Statutes at Large*, p. 730. Reprinted in Jenks and Clark, Appendix, F–10.

to acquire stock in another concern when the effect would be to lessen competition or create a monopoly, but the holding of stock simply for investment was allowed. Other clauses in the act concerned the technical aspects of prosecution and penalties, and the limitations of common carriers in dealing or making contracts with other concerns, in which the director, officer, or agent of the common carrier might hold a position or have a substantial interest. Labor unions and farmers' organizations were specifically declared not to be conspiracies in restraint of trade.[94]

Both the Federal Trade Commission Act and the Clayton Antitrust Act were long overdue. They represented the firm belief that the Sherman Act had failed and that further federal legislation was necessary if monopoly was to be prevented. The desirability of some organization like the Interstate Commerce Commission to supervise, investigate, check, and prosecute illegal monopoly practices was recognized soon after the Sherman Act had been passed and had been partially provided for in the Bureau of Corporations. The Clayton Act was based on the belief that the Sherman Act was too general and that more specific legislation was necessary. Many held the optimistic view that if big business knew specifically what was legal and what was illegal, it would obey the law. In any event, a specific act would presumably be easier to enforce. The efforts of the Clayton Act to strengthen the previous legislation by making it more specific followed suggestions which twenty-five years of experience indicated as practical. Curiously enough, one method which had in it real possibilities of protecting the public welfare—the federal incorporation of concerns doing an interstate business—was ignored in the new legislation, although both Taft and Bryan had advocated it.[95]

FAILURE OF ANTITRUST LEGISLATION

From the foregoing discussion two facts seem evident: the great majority of the American people were committed to some type of antitrust legislation; and it seems equally certain that the legislation as a whole has failed appreciably to halt the tendency toward monopoly practices and the decline of competition. The reasons are many, and the forces which prevented success were in full play during the first decade of the century. The antitrust legislation, particularly the

[94] The latter was to end such actions as the Danbury Hatters' case and the Buck's Stove and Range case, which had been initiated under the Sherman Act. See below, Chap. XII.
[95] Discussed by Seager and Gulick, *Trust and Corporation Problems*, pp. 628–653.

earlier laws, was designed to maintain or restore competitive conditions of an economic order that was rapidly changing. "When the need was to shape the future," as Walton Hamilton put it, "it [Congress] looked toward the past. On the eve of the greatest of industrial revolutions, the National Government was fitted out with a weapon forged to meet the problems of petty trade . . . . A rule of the common law, emerging from petty trade, was thus evoked to control the affairs of industry." [96] Instead of recognizing increasing size and greater consolidation in a changing economic civilization and protecting the public welfare through federal licenses and supervision, it sought to hold on to the past. In an era when economic forces were obliterating state boundaries, legislators could find a constitutional means for the action only through restraint in interstate commerce. Inherently, the approach was inadequate.

Even if there was a possibility of success under the legislation, the administrative procedure virtually doomed it to failure. To dam back an inevitable tendency and to control American business, Congress simply turned over enforcement to the Department of Justice, already overloaded with work. No separate staff to enforce the act was set up for more than a decade. When in 1903 an Antitrust Division was established in the Department of Justice, it was given only $500,000 to be expended at the rate of $100,000 a year. From 1908 to 1935 the appropriation varied from $100,000 to $300,000. The staff was as fantastically inadequate as were the appropriations. The average number of attorneys in the division during the "trust-busting" period of Theodore Roosevelt was five. [97] The Federal Trade Commission fared much better. It started with an initial appropriation of $420,000. As a result it has probably accomplished more in its specific job than has the Antitrust Division; where the FTC has failed, the failure has been due to other causes.

In other ways the enforcement of the antitrust acts seemed doomed from the start. The difficulties of obtaining data and appraising it were often insuperable. The complainants or victims in the case can give only limited help, for they did not "sit in" on the conspiracy which injured them. The prosecuting officials had limited powers of obtaining records from the conspirators except through grand jury action, and it could hardly be expected that the defendants would willingly supply records which would incriminate themselves.

[96] Walton Hamilton, *Antitrust in Action* (Temporary National Economic Committee, *Monograph* No. 16, Senate Committee Print, 76 Cong., 3 Sess., Washington: Government Printing Office, 1941), pp. 11–12.
[97] *Ibid.*, pp. 23–26.

Even when such records were obtained, they might literally run into tons of paper, and neither government lawyers nor grand juries had the facilities to wade through them. Nor were the courts and juries adequate in many cases to deal with the technical aspects involved.

It was not alone the inadequacy of the courts to handle antitrust suits, but also the ignorance of government officials concerning matters pertaining to the type of business being sued. This is evident in the form of dissolution ordered in the Standard Oil and American Tobacco cases, as well as that for the Northern Securities Company. The decisions were moral victories rather than industrial correctives.[98] The small fines imposed had little, if any, significance in deterring monopoly practice. Imprisonment was almost unknown except in labor cases and business racketeering. Of six federal cases between 1897 and 1917 in which prison sentences were imposed, two involved labor unions, two business racketeering, and two war spies. Penalties were from four hours to one year. As the years went on, enforcement officers shifted to advisory opinions and consent decrees as in the cases of the Aluminum Corporation (1912), the American Telephone and Telegraph Company (1914), and the National Cash Register Company (1916). This form of approach was little more effective in the long run than court prosecutions.

Enforcement of the antitrust acts, so far as it could be done, depended largely on the interest and initiative of the executive branch. With the exception of the McKinley administration, which was too closely involved with big business to be concerned with this problem,[99] executive interest was present during this period. Roosevelt, Taft, and Wilson were all sincerely committed to enforce the laws. Even during wartime the Wilson administration maintained antitrust activity. Twelve antitrust cases were instituted in 1917 and eighteen in 1918. The Supreme Court was less consistent. Granting that it was interested in enforcing the antitrust laws, it shifted its point of view and its interpretation of the meaning of the acts so often that it confused the issues and weakened the possibility of doing much with existing legislation. So many influences, economic, political, and legal, operated against prevention of monopoly through antitrust legislation that the student is surprised that anything was accomplished through this medium.

[98] *Ibid.*, p. 86.
[99] Three cases were instituted in 1897, one was instituted in 1898, one in 1899, and none at all in 1900 and 1901.—*Ibid.*, p. 135.

CHAPTER IX

The Railroad Empire

FAILURE OF THE INTERSTATE COMMERCE ACT

TWO primary developments dominated American railway history between the Civil War and the end of the century. The first was the extension of railroads into every important area of the country; the second was the long battle to establish public control, both state and federal, over this rapidly expanding monopoly. By 1900 the first objective had been largely accomplished. Railroad mileage had increased from 30,625 in 1860 to 198,964 in 1900. In the Northeast and north of the Ohio all essential main line trackage had long since been laid; in the South the ravages of war had been repaired and thousands of miles of new tracks built. West of the Mississippi four major transcontinental railroads now reached the Pacific. Railroad construction continued after 1900, but the main task had been accomplished.

Skillful engineers and daring entrepreneurs had achieved the physical expansion. Public control, however, had failed. Handicapped by inept politicians, by apathetic, legalistic, or antagonistic judges, and by the unrelenting opposition of railroad management, the purpose of the Interstate Commerce Act of 1887 had been virtually nullified and the Interstate Commerce Commission rendered impotent. Failure was not caused by lack of interest on the part of Congress or the electorate. Congress on numerous occasions had passed legislation to clarify the act and strengthen the commission. The electorate continued firm in its belief in regulation. Even the railroads during the first three years of the act showed a desire to cooperate. Failure came from numerous causes. Federal regulation on such a large scale was new to the country; procedures had to be worked out and legal precedents developed. Railroad cases were likely to be technical and complicated; the commission had to blaze new trails in unmapped regions. More important was the strong opposition after 1890 of the railroads and the attitude of the courts, which appeared to have little sympathy with the purpose of the act. Of sixteen decisions on rate cases appealed to the Supreme Court for enforcement between 1887 and 1905, fifteen were decided in favor of the carriers and but one sustained in part for the commission.[1]

It was not failure to sustain rates, however, that was so significant as the curtailment of the powers of the commission in these decisions. Although it seems clear that the Interstate Commerce Act intended to give the commission the power to establish reasonable rates and to end pooling, rebates, and other types of discrimination, the commission found itself blocked at every turn. An appeal from a shipper was followed by a hearing and a decision establishing a reasonable rate. If the carrier refused to accept the decision, the commission was forced to appeal to the federal courts. All this involved time, but it was merely the beginning. Average duration of railroad cases carried through the courts during the period was close to four years; there were certain instances when litigation lasted nine years.[2] In such a situation the commission was speedily reduced to a position so subordinate to the courts that its role became merely that of instituting proceedings and appearing as complainant.

Inability to force witnesses to give material testimony, and the unwillingness of courts to accept as final findings of facts submitted by the commission, severely handicapped that body. It was not until 1896, nine years after the act was passed, that new legislation recognizing the power of the commission to compel testimony was upheld by the Supreme Court.[3] The Court's practice of ignoring the commission's facts and trying the case *de novo* was highly prejudicial to the prestige of the commission, for it became easy for the railroads to consider hearings before the ICC as merely preliminary skirmishes before the real battle began. So far had the practice gone that the Supreme Court itself finally denounced it in 1896 in the Social Circle case, asserting that it was the intention of the law to bring out the facts in the original proceedings before the commission.[4] Neverthe-

---

[1] William Z. Ripley, *Railroads: Rates and Regulation* (New York: Longmans, Green and Co., 1912), p. 463.

[2] Sidney L. Miller, *Railway Transportation* (Chicago: A. W. Shaw, 1924), p. 743.

[3] Brown *v.* Walker, 161 U.S. 591 (1896).

[4] Cincinnati, New Orleans and Texas Pacific Railway Company *et al. v.* Interstate Commerce Commission, 162 U.S. 196.

less, it took another decade before this problem was entirely clarified and the commission fully protected.

The long battle to overcome these handicaps gave hope that the commission might gradually win recognition and influence. Then suddenly, in 1897, the Court about-faced, and in two decisions rendered the commission virtually powerless. For ten years both the railroads and the courts apparently had taken it for granted that Congress had empowered the commission to establish reasonable rates. It was the judiciary and not the railroads that finally expressed doubts when the Supreme Court, in the Maximum Rate case, concluded that "Congress has not conferred upon the Commission the power of prescribing rates either maximum or minumum or absolute." [5] With this decision the chief purpose of the commission was nullified.

But there was more to come. No railroad abuse had aroused more opposition than the type of discrimination involved in charging more for a short haul than for a long one. This discrimination had apparently been outlawed by section 4 of the Interstate Commerce Act, which had declared it "unlawful . . . to charge or receive any greater compensation in the aggregate for the transportation of passengers or of like kind of property, under substantially similar circumstances and conditions, for a shorter than for a longer distance over the same line . . . ." [6] On the theory that Congress meant what it said and that there could be no question as to its power to end discrimination, the commission enforced the prohibition except where water competition or railroad competition not subject to the act existed at the distant point.

A decade of persistent effort on the part of the commission had virtually ended the abuse, when the Supreme Court in one crushing decision wiped out the hard-won gains. In the Alabama Midland case (1897) the Court held that the mere existence of railroad competition at the more distant point produced such a dissimilarity of circumstances and conditions as to justify departure from the principles laid down in the act.[7] Encouraged by lower-court decisions, the commission reopened the problem, but the Supreme Court in the Chattanooga decision of 1901 ended the possibility of enforcing section 4.[8] It was not until the Mann-Elkins Act of 1910 that the

[5] ICC v. Cincinnati, New Orleans and Texas Pacific Railway Company, 167 U.S. 511 (1897).
[6] 24 U.S. Statutes at Large, p. 380.
[7] ICC v. Alabama Midland Railway Co. et al., 168 U.S. 144.
[8] East Tennessee, Virginia and Georgia Railway Co. v. ICC, 181 U.S. 1.

long-and-short-haul prohibition was at least again made enforceable.[9]

With successive decisions robbing the commission of its power to determine reasonable future rates and end discriminations in long and short hauls, there was little left for that body to do but gather statistics. That the Supreme Court knew it had deliberately nullified a widespread desire on the part of the American people to regulate interstate traffic and eliminate long-standing abuses there can be no doubt. Justice Harlan, dissenting in the Alabama Midland case, made it perfectly clear. Said he:

> Taken in connection with other decisions defining the power of the Interstate Commerce Commission, the present decision, it seems to me, goes far to make that Commission a useless body for all practical purposes, and to defeat many of the important objects designed to be accomplished by the various enactments of Congress relating to interstate commerce. The Commission was established to protect the public against the improper practices of transportation companies engaged in commerce among the several states. It has been left, it is true, with power to make reports, and to issue protests. But it has been shorn, by judicial interpretation, of authority to do anything of an effective character.[10]

With the heart cut out of the law and the commission reduced to a "useless body," it was too much to expect that the law would be taken seriously. This was amply proved in the testimony taken by the Industrial Commission from 1898 to 1901. Every section of the act, it appeared, was being broken. Said the Industrial Commission:

> There is a general consensus of opinion among practically all witnesses, including members of the Interstate Commerce Commission, representatives of shippers, and railway officers, that the railways still make discriminations between individuals, and perhaps to as great an extent as ever before. In fact, it is stated by numerous witnesses that discriminations were probably worse during the year 1898 than at any previous time.[11]

Apparently no method was overlooked. There were both direct rebates and secret rates. Commissions were paid for securing freight; goods were billed at less than actual weight, goods were shipped under false classification, and allowances and advantages were granted in handling and storing—all these "discriminatory favors . . . granted generally to large shippers." Numerous examples were offered to show discriminations in favor of certain places through in-

[9] I. L. Sharfman, *The Interstate Commerce Commission* (New York: The Commonwealth Fund, 5 vols., 1931–1937), I, 28–32.

[10] 168 U.S. 176 (1897).

[11] Industrial Commission, *Report* (Washington: Government Printing Office, 19 vols., 1900–1902), IV, 5.

ability of the ICC to enforce the long-and-short-haul prohibition. These favorable discriminations were of great advantage to those receiving them, and disastrous to those who did not.[12] Pooling, it appeared, still existed,[13] but not to as great an extent as before. The same end was being accomplished by large-scale railroad consolidation and development of community of interest. Although testimony brought out few complaints against excessive freight and passenger charges, it elicited many with regard to discriminations. After a decade and a half of the Interstate Commerce Act the chief abuses of interstate railroad transportation seemed no nearer a solution.

RAILROAD CONSOLIDATION

Not only had the railroads, with the aid of the Supreme Court, escaped the intent of the Interstate Commerce Act; they also seemed destined to circumvent the Sherman Antitrust Act. Like other great industries, the railroads were being rapidly consolidated and at the same time were being drawn under banker domination. In 1895 the nation's railroads were separated into innumerable independent systems often competing against rival systems operating in the same region. Fifteen years later there were few independent roads; virtually all had been brought into one of seven or eight huge combinations. In the sixteen months alone from July 1, 1899, to November 1, 1900, some 25,000 miles of railroad—more than one eighth of the entire mileage of the country—were brought, in one way or another, under the control of other lines.

Although most of the consolidation, as with industry, took place after 1897, it was the severe panic of 1893 that cleared the way. The panic and the following depression threw 40,818 miles of railroads into the hands of receivers, representing about one fourth of the mileage and capitalization of the nation's railroads. It was, in the words of the ICC a "record of insolvency . . . without parallel in the previous history of American railways, except it be the period from 1838 to 1842."[14] Securities and sometimes entire railroads could be bought for a song, and banking houses, such as J. P. Morgan & Co. and Kuhn, Loeb & Co., already interested in railroads, now invested more heavily.

[12] *Ibid.*, IX, vi–vii.
[13] Personal and local discriminations are developed in detail in Ripley, *Railroads: Rates and Regulation*, pp. 185–263.
[14] ICC, *Seventh Annual Report of the Statistics of Railways in the United States for year ending June 30, 1894* (Washington: Government Printing Office, 1895), p. 10.

The other causes for the rapid consolidation of railroads were similar to the simultaneous movement in industry. The country was prosperous after 1898, banking interests were growing in strength, and it was possible to float large issues of securities for reorganization and consolidation. As with industrial consolidations, finance capital argued that consolidation was necessary for the salvation of the railroads. Francis L. Stetson, Morgan's chief lawyer in railroad consolidation, asserted before the Industrial Commission in 1900 that consolidation "had been rendered necessary by the inability of the corporations to meet their fixed charges, an inability which had been due largely to the ruinous reduction of railway rates, partly through legislation and partly through ruinous competition." [15]

Like the history of industrial combination the history of railroad consolidation was not without personal ambition and the unadulterated desire for easy profits whatever might be the fate of the particular enterprise. The Industrial Commission, however, seemed to be mainly impressed by the almost unanimous testimony of railroad men that the consolidations had been inspired by the desire to save the railroads through the elimination of competition. "Undoubtedly the most important of the objects sought in the recent wholesale consolidations," agreed the commission, "has been the elimination of competition; that is to say, to secure the maintenance of established rates by removal of the incentive to rate cutting which competition in the past has induced. In order to secure this end it has become practically necessary to dominate by one financial interest an entire geographical section of the country." [16]

Leadership in this process of reorganization and consolidation was taken in the 1890's by the elder Morgan, whose firm was responsible for the reorganization of the Erie, the Philadelphia and Reading, the Southern Railway and, along with Hill, the Northern Pacific and, to a lesser extent, the Baltimore and Ohio. Morgan's reorganizations followed the same general pattern: establishment of finances on a sound basis, retention of control in the succeeding years, and the use of the railroad to widen "a community of interest" with his other railroads.[17] It was not until 1897 that a new and more brilliant railroad operator, Edward H. Harriman, appeared on the scene as a rival of Morgan. Harriman, whose visions of consolidation encompassed not only a monopoly of a large share of American railroads but an exten-

[15] Industrial Commission, *Report*, IV, 37.
[16] Industrial Commission, *Final Report*, XIX (1902), 310.
[17] Edward G. Campbell, *The Reorganization of the American Railroad System, 1893–1900* (New York: Columbia University Press, 1938), p. 148.

sion of transportation in the Far East, tremendously stimulated the whole process of unification.

Only a man of the boldest imagination and supreme executive ability could have created in a little more than a decade a railroad empire of the proportions that Harriman achieved. Already a dominant figure in the Illinois Central, Harriman, in cooperation with Kuhn, Loeb & Co., picked up in 1897 under foreclosure proceedings the bankrupt and dilapidated Union Pacific. Under the impetus of his driving energy, the road was rehabilitated and put in a prosperous condition. The Oregon Short Line was reacquired; the Southern Pacific system was purchased in 1901 (after the death of Collis P. Huntington); heavy stock purchases were consummated in the Atchison, Topeka and Santa Fe; a half interest was acquired in a newly built road from Salt Lake City to Los Angeles; and even the Pacific Mail Steamship Company was purchased to control traffic from the East Coast to the West. Said the Interstate Commerce Commission in 1906: "The Union Pacific in the last six years has so grown in power and influence that at this time it controls every line of railroad reaching to the Pacific coast between Portland on the North and the Mexican border on the South—a distance as great as that from Maine to Florida—excepting alone the Santa Fe, in which it has a large stock interest." [18]

With its coffers bursting with funds, it was hardly to be expected that the Union Pacific would be content with trans-Mississippi traffic. Heavy purchases of Illinois Central stock (already closely tied to the Union Pacific through personal domination of Harriman) gave entry to Chicago and New Orleans. Similar purchases in the Baltimore and Ohio and the New York Central as well as in the Chicago and Northwestern, the New York Central's trans-Mississippi extension, secured an interest in trunk lines leading to the Atlantic seaport. When Harriman took over the Union Pacific in 1897 it had about 1,800 miles of poorly conditioned track. Ten years later that railroad absolutely controlled 25,000 miles of line; through stock ownership it powerfully influenced 30,000, and Harriman's alliances affected 16,000 more. Only Harriman's death in 1909 and Supreme Court decisions prevented this structure from rising to dizzier heights. [19]

Of all the events of these exciting railroad years none was more

[18] Interstate Commerce Commission, *Reports* (Washington: Government Printing Office, 1907), XII, 279; see also Interstate Commerce Commission, *Twenty-first Annual Report* (Washington: Government Printing Office, 1907), pp. 22–24.

[19] William Z. Ripley, *Railroads: Finance and Organization* (New York: Longmans, Green and Co., 1915), p. 461.

spectacular than the 1901 battle between Harriman and James J. Hill, dominating figure in the Great Northern and the Northern Pacific, for the control of the Chicago, Burlington and Quincy. Both were eager to control this road to provide entry into Chicago as well as to tap the rich territory served by the Burlington. Harriman, furthermore, had no desire to see his rival push into a region which he had picked for his own exploitation. When Hill and his Morgan bankers persuaded the directors of the Burlington to sell 97 per cent of its stock to the Northern Pacific and the Great Northern, it looked as if Harriman were beaten. Harriman, however, was not the type to admit defeat. Quietly he began to buy Northern Pacific stock. Then suddenly, while Morgan was in Europe and Hill on an inspection trip in the West, he intensified his drive. Hill, discovering from scanty reports in the papers that Northern Pacific was being heavily bought, suspected his rival, ordered the rails cleared, and dashed for the East. Morgan cabled his firm to buy 150,000 shares of Northern Pacific and the bitter battle developed in earnest.

Northern Pacific common, which had sold for $110 in April, was pushed to $1,000 by May 9. Brokers, hardly suspecting that this stock was being bought for actual delivery and not for speculation, discovered that they had sold 78,000 shares more than were in existence. It appeared that both interests had purchased more than a majority of the stock. Harriman, in fact, had a majority of the preferred, and the Hill-Morgan interests a majority of the common. With the market cornered, the shorts caught, and stock prices tumbling in every direction, the giants called off the battle to prevent a panic. Subsequently, an immense holding company, known as the Northern Securities Company, was organized with a capital of $400,000,000 to acquire the stock of the Great Northern and the Northern Pacific, thus indirectly controlling the Chicago, Burlington and Quincy. With Hill and Harriman now closely allied in the Northern Securities Company, competition in the vast region west of the Mississippi was virtually ended.[20] In brief, Hill, through control of the Northern Pacific and Great Northern, monopolized transcontinental traffic in the Northwest, while Harriman, through the Union Pacific and the Southern Pacific and interests in the Atchison, Topeka and Santa Fe, monopolized the central and southern routes.

[20] Balthasar H. Meyer, *A History of the Northern Securities Case* (University of Wisconsin, *Bulletin* No. 142, Madison: 1906), pp. 229–241; Joseph G. Pyle, *Life of James J. Hill* (New York: Doubleday & Company, 2 vols., 1927), Chaps. XXVII–XXIX; George Kennan, *E. H. Harriman* (Boston: Houghton Mifflin Company, 2 vols., 1922), Vol. I, Chaps. XI–XII.

The only other contender against the Harriman monopoly were the Gould railroads, which covered the region south of St. Louis and Kansas City through eastern and central Texas. The proposed basis of a transcontinental system was the Missouri Pacific, extending westward to Colorado. In 1901, the Gould system acquired the Denver and Rio Grande, thus extending its line as far west as Ogden, Utah. Refusal of the Union Pacific, however, to give it connection with the coast forced the building of a new railroad, the Western Pacific, from Ogden to San Francisco, completed in 1911. East of the Mississippi the Gould interests controlled the Wabash, extending as far as Buffalo. In an effort to get to the seacoast they acquired in 1901 the Wheeling and Lake Erie, which took the proposed transcontinental route to within sixty miles of Pittsburgh. Beyond Pittsburgh the Western Maryland was obtained the following year. To close the gap between the last two railroads meant costly building through difficult country and a terminal at Pittsburgh. To obtain the latter against the opposition of the Pennsylvania Railroad, which dominated Pittsburgh politics, was no easy matter. In the end the difficulties were overcome and the route was completed. But by that time the Gould system, milked dry by financial mismanagement and by the burden of supporting Gould's grandiose schemes, was caught in the panic of 1907 and partly disintegrated. The fatal blow was the bankruptcy of the Missouri Pacific in 1911.[21]

One other important consolidation west of the Appalachians—the Rock Island system—was built up in the years 1901–1911. It was maneuvered by a group of speculators, headed by William H. Moore, long famous as a trust promoter, and Daniel G. Reid. In comparison to their operations, "the manipulators of the old Fisk-Gould days were artless children."[22] The new system was based on the prosperous Chicago, Rock Island and Pacific Railway Company, to which were added the St. Louis and San Francisco lines, the Chicago and Alton, and others. At the height of expansion the system covered much of the Mississippi Valley extending as far west as Denver, as far southwest as El Paso, and controlling 15,000 miles.

The Moore-Reid group secured control of the stock of the Chicago, Rock Island and Pacific Railway Company by temporarily

21 Ripley, *Railroads: Finance and Organization*, pp. 516–524; Burton J. Hendrick, "The Passing of a Great Railroad Dynasty," *McClure's Magazine*, XXXVIII, No. 5 (March, 1912), 483–501.

22 Samuel Untermeyer, counsel of the stockholders' protective committee, in Max Lerner, "William Henry Moore" in *Dictionary of American Biography* (Allen Johnson and Dumas Malone, eds., New York: Charles Scribner's Sons, 21 vols., 1928–1937), XIII, 145.

pyramiding loans from New York banks. To pay these loans, two holding companies were set up, one of these exchanging collateral trust bonds for the Railway Company stock, most of which the Moore-Reid group owned. The bonds were then sold. During the years following, through the use of holding companies and the exchange of securities, the value of the preferred, upon which control rested, declined to reach 1 3/8 in 1914. In the end, $5,000,000 had secured control of 15,000 miles of railroad whose funded obligations and aggregate stock (including that of two holding companies) was at par $1,500,000,000. With no outlet on either the Atlantic or the Pacific coasts and under the direction of unscrupulous speculators whose only interest seemed to be personal gain, the Rock Island disintegrated in little more than a decade. Its operations are significant, says William Z. Ripley, merely as "illustrations of irregular financial methods attendant upon almost exclusively banker management, rather than as an elucidation of any principles, economic or operating, having to do with consolidation." [23]

Transportation from the Atlantic seacoast to the Mississippi Valley was largely dominated by the Vanderbilt and the Pennsylvania interests. Until 1898, the New York Central, major property of the Vanderbilts, was little more than a string of consolidated railroads leading westward from New York City to Buffalo. In that year it acquired the Lake Shore and the Michigan Southern, which gave it two routes from Buffalo to Chicago. Soon after, it took over the Michigan Central, a third route to the middle western metropolis. Control of the Big Four (Cleveland, Cincinnati, Chicago, and St. Louis Railway Company) and the Lake Erie and Western gave it facilities in Ohio, Indiana, and Illinois and entry to St. Louis, while heavy purchases in the Chicago and Northwestern extended it into the area west of Chicago. Like the New York Central, the Pennsylvania Railroad had its period of most rapid growth around the end of the century, when it acquired numerous roads, large and small, until it had a system of over 20,000 miles. Two other main routes to the west, the Baltimore and Ohio and the Chesapeake and Ohio, were jointly controlled by the New York Central and the Pennsylvania, but were usually included in the Pennsylvania system, as the latter road controlled the larger portion of the stock.

One other important group of railroads, those dominated by J. P. Morgan & Co., should be noted again. They included the shortest route between the seacoast and the Great Lakes, that followed by

[23] Ripley, *Railroads: Finance and Organization*, p. 525.

the Erie Railroad. The Erie, which had long been kicked around by Gould, Vanderbilt, and other speculators, was finally rescued by Morgan, who restored it after 1895 to the status of a well-run railroad. It was not until 1942, however, that it paid dividends on its common stock. Morgan also had holdings in the Lehigh Valley and other coal carriers, but his main interest was in the South, where in 1894 he reorganized a group of roads into the Southern Railroad system. By 1900, this system had extended its lines throughout the Southeast and by interlocking directorships and joint stockownership had working agreements with the Louisville and Nashville, the Atlantic Coast Line Railroad, and other important carriers so close as largely to weaken competition.[24]

By 1906 the great era of railroad consolidation had reached its climax and the division of ownership and territory had been marked out. Summarizing briefly, about two thirds of the 228,000 miles in existence at that time were in the hands of the seven groups mentioned above. The Vanderbilt roads (over 22,500 miles) controlled the northern routes from New York to Chicago; the Pennsylvania interests (over 20,000 miles) monopolized the central roads to the west originating in Pennsylvania and Maryland; the Morgan roads and other affiliates (18,000 miles) dominated the Southeast; the Gould roads (17,000 miles) and the Rock Island system were powerful in the Mississippi Valley. Beyond the Mississippi River, the Hill roads (over 21,000 miles) had a monopoly of the Northwest, and the Harriman roads dominated the central and southern transcontinental routes.

This situation does not convey the full significance of the extent of the consolidation. In the first place, these seven interests controlled 85 per cent of railroad earnings. Moreover, the seven interests were in practice only four: the Morgan-Hill-Vanderbilt-Pennsylvania, the Harriman, the Gould, and the Rock Island.[25] The New York Central (Vanderbilt) and the Pennsylvania, said the Interstate Commerce Commission, had created such "an extraordinary concentration of railway interests" along the Middle Atlantic seaboard as effectively to throttle competition.[26] So close were the Morgan-Vanderbilt-Pennsylvania interests that between them they virtually controlled

[24] *Ibid.*, pp. 486–490; Campbell, *The Reorganization of the American Railroad System, 1893–1900*, pp. 145–158.

[25] John Moody, *The Truth about the Trusts* (New York: Moody Publishing Co., 1904), pp. 132–139.

[26] ICC, *Intercorporate Relationships of Railways in the United States as of June 30, 1906* (Washington: Government Printing Office, 1906), p. 40.

the mining of anthracite coal, determined its price, and set the rates to the seaboard. It was a mining and transportation monopoly closely maintained.[27] Morgan was already attempting to create a transportation monopoly in New England, but without seriously antagonizing the Vanderbilt and Pennsylvania interests. It should again be recalled that Morgan was the banker for the Hill railroads of the Northwest. With monopoly practically existing on the Atlantic seaboard, in the Southeast, and on the transcontinental routes of the West, the only region where much competition existed was in the Midwest. Even here railroad magnates squelched rate wars to avoid risking their heavy investments.[28]

The situation just described was, of course, not static. Ownership and control of certain railroads were constantly shifting. Nevertheless, the picture of consolidation in 1906 remained much the same ten years later. The Vanderbilt, Morgan, Pennsylvania, Harriman, and Hill groups still dominated railway transportation. Even the Gould system, in the process of disintegrating, remained important.[29] Only the Rock Island consolidation had fallen to pieces. "The working out of the higher strategy in railroad consolidation," suggests a leading authority, "was the most significant feature of American transportation history in the decade of 1910. Within this brief period what now promises to become more or less permanent financial and operating groups, evolved out of the competitive chaos of the period of depression 1893–'97." [30]

BANKER CONTROL

Not only had great transportation monopolies developed, but railroad control had passed into the hands of bankers. To a large extent a railroad is a natural monopoly to start with. What happened during these years had been the erection of artificial monopolies in those few cases in which competition existed. The development of great railroad consolidations might well promote greater efficiency and economy, but such huge monopolies could hardly be contemplated unless they operated under wise and public-spirited ownership and under strict public control. Neither of these conditions

[27] Jules I. Bogen, *The Anthracite Railroads* (New York: The Ronald Press, 1927), pp. 206–251.
[28] Campbell, *The Reorganization of the American Railroad System, 1893–1900*, p. 331.
[29] Grover G. Huebner and Robert Riegel in Francis G. Wickware, ed., *American Yearbook, 1916* (New York: D. Appleton and Company, 1917), pp. 540–541.
[30] Ripley, *Railroads: Finance and Organization*, p. 459.

existed; the ICC, as we have seen, had no real power until after the Hepburn Act of 1906. Three years before the Hepburn Act was passed, Commissioner Prouty realized that the main business of the commission was changing:

Five years ago the crying evil in railway operations was discrimination, mainly discrimination between individual shippers. While many rates were too high, the general level was low; and in view of competitive conditions which had for some time and then existed, little apprehension was felt of any general unreasonable advance. Not so today. The vast consolidation of the past few years; the use of injunctions to prevent departures from the published tariff; the lessons which railroad operators themselves have learned, that competition in rates is always suicidal, since it does not increase traffic and does reduce revenues,—these have largely eliminated that competition. The discrimination is disappearing, but in its place comes that other danger which always attends monopoly, the exaction of an unreasonable charge.[31]

Consolidations often brought monopoly conditions and unreasonable rates; moreover, they were generally accompanied by banker control. The influence of the bankers was decidedly uneven. There were many examples where responsible reorganization and consolidation resulted in financial and physical rehabilitation. Such examples are to be found in the Southern, the Baltimore and Ohio, and the Union Pacific. On the other hand, the injection of banker control was often accompanied by unscrupulous financial manipulation which shattered the financial structure of the roads and impaired their physical property. Classic examples of this effect may be seen in the reorganization of the Chicago and Alton and a little later in the effort of Morgan to establish a monopoly of New England transportation. What Moore and Reid did to the Rock Island is in the same category. It is interesting to note that the same bankers who did a good job on one railroad were not above ruining another.

Prior to 1898 the Chicago and Alton was a conservatively financed and tremendously prosperous railroad. Its assets at the end of that year were over $39,900,000, representing $22,233,000 in common and preferred stocks and $11,500,000 in indebtedness outstanding. The rest was surplus. For years the road had paid 8 per cent on its stock, which sold in the market for from $150 to $200 a share. About this time Harriman, Mortimer L. Schiff (representing Jacob H. Schiff), George J. Gould, and James Stillman, president of the National City

[31] Charles A. Prouty, "National Regulation of Railroads," *Publications* of the American Economic Association, 3d Series, IV, No. 1 (New York: The Macmillan Company, 1903), 71.

Bank, formed a syndicate to buy the stock. Eventually they secured most of it and within seven years had expanded the capitalization from $33,950,000 to $114,600,000. Of this increase of over $80,000,-000, only $18,000,000 had gone into improvements and additions to property. The rest, approximately $62,600,000, had been added to the liabilities without a dollar in equipment, a sum amounting to over $66,000 for each mile of road. At the same time the members of the syndicate pocketed millions for themselves.

No sooner had the syndicate obtained control than it sold to the stockholders (that is, to itself) $40,000,000 of 3 per cent bonds at 65. These were then sold to the public including the New York Life Insurance Company, at an average of 90. The syndicate thus realized for its members a personal profit of $8,000,000, which, of course, would have gone to the railroad if sold in the first instance directly to the public. Having sold the bond issue, the stockholders (that is, the syndicate) voted themselves, as owners of the common and preferred stock, an extra cash dividend of 30 per cent, which was about one third of the receipts of the bond sale. Then the syndicate organized a holding company, the Chicago and Alton Railway Company, to which it transferred its preferred stock for $10,000,000 and exchanged its common stock for new common stock in the holding company. To obtain the $10,000,000 the syndicate sold to itself $22,000,000 of 3 1/2 per cent bonds at 60, which it quickly resold at 78 to 86 1/2. Its new stock in the holding company was then largely disposed of to the Union Pacific (controlled by Harriman, one of the Chicago and Alton syndicate) and to the Rock Island.[32]

These were only the outstanding operations in a series of deals which appear to have netted the insiders a profit of $23,600,000. The whole business, however, not only weakened the financial position of the railroad but took the control of the property from the hands of the original owners and transferred it to speculating bankers, who now owned its worthless common stock. Its full effect, as Ripley points out, was to enrich enormously "insiders at the expense of the investing public, and prejudice the interests of the shippers, both by crippling the road physically and by creating the need of high rates for service in order to support the fraudulent capitalization." [33]

[32] Briefly told in Ripley, *Railroads: Finance and Organization*, pp. 262–267; more fully described in ICC *Report* No. 340. Harriman is defended by George Kennan in *E. H. Harriman*, Vol. II, Chaps. XXVII–XXVIII and in *The Chicago and Alton Case* (Privately printed: 1916). Evidence on both sides is appraised by James G. Bonbright, *Railroad Capitalization* (New York: Longmans, Green and Co., 1920), Appendix C.
[33] Ripley, *Railroads: Finance and Organization*, p. 262.

The Chicago and Alton looting appeared to have been conceived for no other purpose than legal robbery by a syndicate including bankers whose front was highly respectable. The financial ruin of the New Haven, on the other hand, seems to have been the result of J. P. Morgan's ambitions to build up a transportation monopoly in New England and not merely a foray for immediate gain. Morgan's plan was to use the prosperous New York, New Haven and Hartford Railroad as the central link in his monopoly and to use its credit to absorb competing trolley systems and coastwise shipping lines and thus to pull into the network virtually all other New England railroads, including the Boston and Maine and the Maine Central. In temporarily achieving his project, Morgan financially ruined not only the New Haven but large parts of the whole transportation system of the area.

When Morgan began his program in 1903, the New Haven system had a capitalization of $93,000,000, of which $79,000,000 was in stock and $14,000,000 in bonds. Ten years later, the capitalization was $417,000,000 exclusive of stock premiums, or an increase of $324,-000,000. Of this increase approximately $20,000,000 was devoted to railroad betterment; the remaining $204,000,000 was used to build up a structure to monopolize freight and passenger traffic in five New England states. The cost of the "waste and mismanagement" to the New Haven railroad from "the unpardonable folly of the transaction," amounted, according to the ICC, to between $60,000,000 and $90,000,000. In addition would be the drain upon the railroad's resources for many a year.

Seldom has a government document been so pronounced in its criticism of a private industry as was the ICC in its report to the Senate on the New York, New Haven and Hartford Railroad. It spoke of the "loose, extravagant and improvident" administration of the finances; the "despoilment" of the Boston and Maine; the "iniquity" of the Westchester acquisition; [34] the "double price" paid for the Rhode Island trolleys; the "recklessness" in the purchase of the Connecticut and Massachusetts trolleys at prices exorbitantly in excess of market value; and the "unwarranted" expenditure of large amounts in "educating" the public. It condemned the "financial legerdemain," the "unlawful" diversion of corporate funds to political organizations; the "scattering of retainers" to lawyers in five states who

[34] This refers to the purchase of the New York, Westchester and Boston Railway Company, a tiny, 18.03-mile line from upper New York City to Mt. Vernon and White Plains. The New Haven paid over $36,434,000 for the road, which operated at an annual loss of $1,250,000.

rendered no itemized services; the "extensive use of a paid lobby"; the "profligate" issue of free passes; the "unwarranted increase" of the New Haven liabilities; and the "indefensible standard of business ethics and the absence of financial acumen displayed by eminent financiers in directing the destinies of this railroad in its attempt to establish a monopoly of the transportation of New England." The commission noted that the New Haven system had more than 300 subsidiary corporations "seemingly planned, created, and manipulated by lawyers expressly retained for the purpose of concealment or deception." [35]

Mismanagement of American railroads reached its low point in the first decade of the century. Morgan and Harriman, it appeared, had nothing to learn from Fiske or Gould. Only two railroads have been used here as examples of the reckless spoilation. What happened to the Chicago and Alton and the New Haven took place in a greater or less degree with other systems. Some years later it was charged by Glenn E. Plumb, a former railroad lawyer, that six western and southern railroads had given away between 1900 and 1910 more than $250,000,000 in stock bonuses and that the actual dividend disbursements on this excess capital for 1913 alone were more than $11,000,-000. During the same decade, he charged, eighteen representative railroads operating in all parts of the United States gave away stock bonuses aggregating $450,414,000. [36]

REVIVAL OF REGULATION

Long before the sordid details connected with the Rock Island reorganization and the New Haven monopoly were made known to the public, the demand for tighter federal regulation had borne fruit. It was not only clear by 1900 that the act of 1887 was a dead letter; it was also clear that the problem had been made more serious by the rapid consolidation of the railroads and the simultaneous development of banker domination. Whatever the ultimate gains of consolidation might be in the way of cheaper and more efficient service, there was little in the situation around 1900 to justify such expectations. The decline of freight rates, which had been the tendency since 1873, was sharply reversed after 1900. The continuous rise had a real basis in increased costs of operation, but to many it seemed

[35] ICC, No. 6,569, *In Re Financial Transactions of the New York, New Haven and Hartford Railroad Company* (July 11, 1914), pp. 32–35.
[36] House Committee on Interstate and Foreign Commerce, *Return of the Railroads to Private Ownership* (Washington: Government Printing Office, 3 vols., 1919), p. 823.

to have but one explanation—development of consolidation. At the same time it was clear that favorable discriminations were still being made for large shippers despite elimination of railroad competition by mergers.[37] Finally, it was evident that, except for a few insiders, investors rarely profited by the financial manipulations coincident to amalgamation.[38]

With the nation thoroughly aroused over the danger of monopoly both in industry and in transportation, some action was inevitable. In transportation it took the double form of an attempt to break up certain monopolies and an attempt to strengthen the legislation of 1887. Since the act of 1887 had forbidden railroads to pool their freight or earnings, the chief monopoly practice of railroads at the time, it was hoped that the worst effect of transportation monopoly had been taken care of. Whether the Sherman Antitrust Act of 1890 applied to railroads was at first uncertain. Eventually the Supreme Court decided, in the Trans-Missouri Freight Association case (1897) [39] and in the Joint Traffic Association case (1898),[40] that it did. Although rates set up by the Trans-Missouri Freight Association might be just and reasonable, and agreement among competing railroads, the Court held, was a restraint of trade, contrary to public policy, and illegal.

The decisions in these two cases made operations of the traffic association illegal. They did not, however, halt the movement toward consolidation. Rather they hastened it, for it was now necessary to accomplish the same object in other and sometimes less desirable ways. By purchase, by lease, by stock control, and by community of interest, the movement continued. The favorite method was the holding company, and it was the unscrupulous use of this device that brought the next famous antimonopoly railroad action in the Northern Securities case.[41] By the time the next important railroad case of this type, that of the Terminal Railroad Association of St. Louis, came before the Supreme Court in 1912, the Court had shifted to the possibility of "reasonable" restraint. The Terminal Railroad Association, composed of fifteen railroads converging in St. Louis, organized to make it possible for them to use the same bridges and approaches to the city. This seemed to be the only practical method of solving an otherwise unsurmountable problem. Other carriers

[37] Ripley, Railroads: Rates and Regulation, pp. 185–214.
[38] Industrial Commission, Final Report, XIX, 325–327.
[39] United States v. Trans-Missouri Freight Association, 166 U.S. 341–342 (1897).
[40] United States v. Joint Traffic Association, 171 U.S. 505 (1898).
[41] Above, pp. 179–180.

not in the association complained of discrimination and brought suit. The Supreme Court found the association guilty of violating the antitrust act, but, observing the economic need of the association, allowed it to operate on condition of certain modifications of organization and practice.[42]

During these years at least two other efforts were made under the Sherman Act to halt consolidation and restore competition. The first was to sever the Union Pacific and the Southern Pacific, properties joined by Harriman in 1901. This was accomplished in 1912 by an ingenious exchange of stockownership. It did something to restore competition between the East and California, but it was by no means an adequate solution of the difficulty.[43] The other effort was to break the monopoly built up by the New York, New Haven and Hartford Railroad Company. Suit was brought by the federal government, but was discontinued upon formal agreement that the company would obey the law. Failure to keep this promise brought another bill of complaint, which again was dropped upon agreement that the system would be separated into its various parts. Despite these efforts, the general situation changed little. The American railroads continued during the succeeding years to be dominated by a half-dozen great financial systems. After the experience of the First World War, Congress finally gave up the effort of attempting to maintain unlimited competition and instructed the ICC to draw up plans for greater consolidation.

While efforts were being made to curtail transportation monopolies, Congress turned to the problem of stiffer regulation of interstate commerce. The need was obvious and public pressure was increasing. Failure of the ICC to accomplish the ends for which it was established, persistence of long-standing abuses, fear of monopolies brought on by the wave of consolidation, and, finally, dissatisfaction over the advance in freight rates after 1900 were all contributing factors in the movement for new legislation. The first gun fired in the battle was the Expedition Act (1903).[44] It provided that any suit brought by the United States under the Interstate Commerce Act of 1887, the Sherman Antitrust Act of 1890, or like acts, when declared "of general public importance" must be given precedence over other cases and in "every way expedited and assigned for hear-

---

[42] United States v. Terminal Railroad Association of St. Louis, 224 U.S. 383 (1912).

[43] United States v. Union Pacific Railroad Company, 226 U.S. 61; Stuart Daggett, "The Decision on the Union Pacific Merger," Quarterly Journal of Economics, XXVII (February, 1913), 295–328.

[44] 32 U.S. Statutes at Large, p. 823.

ing at the earliest practical day." A few days later came the Elkins Amendment to the act of 1887.[45] It was designed to end the practice of rebates, which had often encouraged and fostered the growth of great corporations. By making deviation from published rates the sole test of discrimination, by making the corporations as well as their agents liable, and the receiver of a rebate guilty as well as the giver, and by other means, personal discriminations were largely ended.

The Elkins Act was sponsored by the railroads as well as by the public, but as far as the general problem of railroad regulation was concerned, it merely scratched the surface. "It was," as someone described it, "a truce of the principles to abolish piracy,"—at the most a preliminary skirmish.[46] The demand for strengthening federal regulation continued to grow. For years men like Shelby M. Cullom of Illinois and William B. Chandler of New Hampshire had presented legislation in the Senate to accomplish this purpose, but without success. Roosevelt's message of 1904, making railroad legislation "a paramount issue," and his repetition of this demand in 1905, accompanied as it was by numerous railroad scandals, changed the picture. Despite "the influence of one of the most powerful lobbies ever let loose upon a legislative body," [47] new legislation was achieved through the leadership of such men as Representative William P. Hepburn and Senators Robert M. La Follette and Jonathan Dolliver.

Briefly, the Hepburn Act of 1906 [48] enlarged the Interstate Commerce Commission from five to seven members (raised to nine in 1917) and extended its powers over other common carriers such as express, sleeping car, and pipeline companies, and switching and terminal facilities. It forbade the granting of most free passes and prohibited railroads from carrying in interstate commerce any materials, except timber and its products, manufactured or produced by companies owned or controlled by the carriers. It strengthened the law against rebates, granted the commission power to prescribe uniform systems of accounting, and empowered it to "determine and prescribe what will be the just and reasonable rate."

So strong was the demand for the Hepburn Act that but seven votes were cast against it in the House and three in the Senate. Nevertheless, the result was bound to be a compromise. La Follette, who believed that power to evaluate railroad property was essential to the determination of fair rates, was disappointed when the Senate

---

[45] 32 *U.S. Statutes at Large*, p. 847.
[46] Ripley, *Railroads: Rates and Regulation*, p. 494.   [47] *Ibid.*, p. 498.
[48] 34 *U.S. Statutes at Large*, p. 584.

turned down his amendment. Only six votes were cast for it.[49] Another weakness of the act was its failure to give the commission jurisdiction over coastwise and internal water-carrying trade, although it did grant jurisdiction over joint transportation by water and rail. Furthermore, no rate or regulation of a railroad company could be changed except on complaint. If the railroads appealed a decision, the old rates rather than those set by the commission remained, pending final decision by the courts. Even after the Hepburn Act the commission had power to prescribe only maximum rates, and the long-and-short-haul clause was still confused.

With all its weaknesses, the Hepburn Act was epoch-making in railroad history in that it established for the first time effective government control over interstate rail traffic. Under judicial interpretation of the act of 1887 the commission had been limited to determination of the reasonableness of past rates and fares. Under the new legislation it could "determine and prescribe" just and reasonable rates for the future. Furthermore, said the law, all orders of the commission, except those for the payment of money, "shall take effect within such reasonable time, not less than thirty days, and shall continue in force . . . unless the same shall be suspended or modified or set aside by the Commission or be suspended or set aside by a court of competent jurisdiction." Failure to comply was punishable by heavy fines.

Since the railroads could no longer ignore an order of the commission, the effect was to shift the initiative in testing the validity of an order from the commission to the carrier. This, as it proved, made all the difference in the world; the commission had become a powerful and responsible body. Its prestige was further increased by the decision of the Supreme Court that Congress intended to make the commission a competent and effective body, whose orders should have the same effect as those of a legislative body as long as they were confined to the field in which the commission was authorized to act.[50] In a later case the Court refused to "substitute its judgment for that of the Commission upon matters of fact within the Commission's province." [51]

Stunned by the Hepburn Act, the railroads for a time submitted to the new law with little opposition. To the middle of 1908 only one appeal was made to the courts. Having recovered somewhat by that

---

[49] R. M. La Follette, *Autobiography* (Madison, Wis.: The Robert M. La Follette Co., 1913), pp. 416–417.

[50] ICC *v.* Illinois Central Railroad, 215 U.S. 470 (1909).

[51] Los Angeles Switching Case, 234 U.S. 314 (1914).

time, the roads again began to hammer at the legislation, with the filing of thirty-eight suits before new legislation was passed. By 1910 certain weaknesses in the Hepburn Act were evident, and Congress, now under the control of a coalition of Democrats and insurgent Republicans,[52] pushed through the Mann-Elkins Act.[53] Its first important feature was grant of power to the commission to suspend up to ten months (120 days plus an extra 6 months) any new rates proposed by the carrier, and it forced upon the carrier, as it turned out, the burden of proof that the proposed rates were reasonable. In the second place, it ended any ambiguity regarding the long-and-short-haul clause of the 1887 legislation by deleting the words "under substantially similar circumstances and conditions"—words which had enabled the Supreme Court to make the provision useless. In the third place, the act provided for the establishment of a special Commerce Court to hear railroad cases. This move rested on the sound theory that railroad cases were usually of such a highly technical nature that only specially qualified jurists could handle them, and that a special court for railroad cases would speed their disposition. Minor features of the act gave the ICC jurisdiction over telegraph, telephone, and cable companies and power to institute inquiries upon its own initiative without waiting for complaints.[54]

It was evident by 1910 that Congress was determined to establish effective government regulation. When the new Commerce Court attempted to obstruct the commission in the exercise of powers granted by law and sustained by the Supreme Court, Congress abolished it by refusing to vote funds for its continuation. A number of factors entered into the demise of the Commerce Court: politics, alleged hostility of the Court to the commission and alleged favoritism toward the railroads, and its unwillingness to surrender to the ICC final authority in matters of fact. Fundamentally, however, it was the belief of Congress that its will was being thwarted. Not content with abolishing the Commerce Court, Congress proceeded to strengthen earlier legislation. By the Panama Canal Act (1912) [55] it forbade railroads to own, lease, operate, or control common carriers operating by water through the canal or elsewhere "with which said railroad or other carrier aforesaid does or may compete for traf-

[52] Kenneth W. Hechler, *Insurgency* (New York: Columbia University Press, 1940), pp. 163–177.

[53] 36 *U.S. Statutes at Large*, p. 539.

[54] Ripley, *Railroads: Rates and Regulation*, pp. 557–579; Frank H. Dixon, "The Mann-Elkins Act, Amending the Act to Regulate Commerce," *Quarterly Journal of Economics*, XXIV (August, 1910), 593–633.

[55] 37 *U.S. Statutes at Large*, p. 560.

fic." Questions of fact determined by the ICC were to be considered final. Other provisions sought to restrain the railroads from discrimination against water carriers.

Legislation directing the ICC to evaluate railroads finally came in 1913. The long agitation of La Follette had given the matter publicity. The ICC, bogged down by the decision of *Smyth* v. *Ames* ("fair return" on the "fair value"), had repeatedly urged it. The Democrats had pledged it in their platform of 1908 and the Republicans had intimated its necessity by favoring "legislation and supervision as will prevent the future over-issue of stocks and bonds by interstate carriers." Excesses of the railroads themselves made it inevitable even if the necessity of valuation in determining reasonable rates is discounted. The Senate, however, refused to legislate it in 1910, but did authorize the appointment by the President of a Railroad Securities Commission to investigate the subject.

This committee, headed by President Arthur Twining Hadley of Yale, recommended that the accounting provisions of the ICC be enlarged to cover fully all phases of railroad promotion and subsequent finance with the hope that full publicity would curtail some of the evils. It did not recommend federal regulation of the issuance of securities. In any event, the Hadley Commission played its part in preparing the way for the legislation. The ICC was directed to evaluate the railroads, taking into consideration such factors as original cost, cost of reproduction new, cost of reproduction less depreciation, and present value of all real property. It was instructed to determine the full financial history of the roads, along with the value of all grants and donations received by the railroads from whatever source they might have come.[56] The immensity and complexity of the task prevented notable results up to 1917, but I. L. Sharfman, writing in 1933, asserted that the "present status of the project constitutes in itself a monument to the Commission's genius for accomplishment."[57]

Before leaving the discussion of the transition from the chaotic laissez faire of the early eighties to the regulation accomplished by 1917, the fact should be recalled that the Clayton Antitrust Act dealt with railroads as well as with other industries. The prohibition of interlocking directorates and purchase of stock in competing companies applied to railroads, as did the prohibition of the purchase of

[56] 37 *U.S. Statutes at Large*, p. 701.
[57] Sharfman, *The Interstate Commerce Commission*, Pt. 3, Vol. A, p. 319. Sharfman's discussion of valuation is exhaustive. See Vol. I, pp. 117–132 and Pt. 3, Vol. A, pp. 97–319.

supplies and other articles from companies in which railroad directors or officials had a substantial interest.[58] It should also be remembered that Congress, beginning with the Safety Appliance Act of
1893, had entered the field of safety legislation to protect both the
public and labor. This protection had been extended to hour legislation in 1907 and to wages in 1916. At the same time the first feeble
efforts toward establishing better relations between capital and labor
in settlement of strikes had been made in the Erdman Act of 1898 as
amended in the Newlands Act of 1913.[59]

On the face of it, railroad regulation appeared by 1917 to have
gone far. By that year both federal and state commissions were of
the mandatory type, possessed of extensive power to enforce reasonable rates and prevent discriminatory practices. In fact, however,
regulation was inadequate and full of inconsistencies and confusion.[60]
Railroads, by their very nature, are generally monopolistic enterprises,
and commissions are set up to regulate them in the public interest.
Nevertheless, close cooperation between railroad systems is often
beneficial, but the policy of Congress and the Supreme Court during
most of these years was to maintain as complete competition as possible. This attitude, which forbade pooling and brought important
dissolutions of railroad combinations, was inconsistent with the policy
of public control. In the words of one expert, it was "practically sub-
versive of the normal functioning of railroad enterprise." [61]

Other weaknesses of railroad regulation were also evident. The
commission had not yet been able to do much in the supervision and
attainment of adequate service. The rate-making policy had grown
up in piecemeal fashion and lacked definite standards. In practice
it was a policy of protecting shippers and consumers from the abuses
of the carriers and had neglected the interests of the carriers, who
by 1914 were struggling with mounting costs. The commission itself
was handicapped by the conflicting jurisdiction between the federal
and state governments, which continued despite the efforts of the
Supreme Court, in the Minnesota Rate case [62] and the Shreveport
Rate case,[63] to curtail the power of state commissions. One of the
greatest difficulties faced by the commission until 1920 was its lack
of power to regulate the financial structure of the railroads. This complicated the whole problem of rate structure and left the railroads
free to engage in the same type of financial manipulation that has

[58] Above, p. 183.   [59] Below, p. 288.
[60] I. L. Sharfman, *The American Railroad Problem* (New York: The Century Company, 1921), pp. 53–64.
[61] *Ibid.*, p. 156.   [62] 230 U.S. 352 (1913).   [63] 234 U.S. 342 (1914).

ruined many of them. It took the nation over thirty years to discover that federal regulation of capital structure was the foundation stone upon which all else rested. By that time it was too late to undo much of the damage.

FULL TIDE AND RECESSION

It was shortly after 1900 that the railroads reached their highest position in the American economic system. Except on the Great Lakes, internal water transportation had declined; serious motor competition was almost two decades in the future. Despite heavy blows from the panic of 1893, the railroads had recovered sufficiently to embark on large-scale expansion. Construction, which had been somewhat less than 2,000 miles annually during the five years after the panic, moved forward rapidly after 1898 to reach a high point of 6,262 miles in 1906. This was not as great as in the 1880's, but it showed that American railroad expansion had not reached its limit. In addition to mileage increases, other statistics show an expanding prosperity. Between 1895 and 1905, ton mileage increased 118 per cent and passenger mileage 95 per cent as against an increase in track mileage of only 21 per cent. Financial statistics, as we shall see, reflected the prosperity. It was the golden day of the railroads.

In 1907, the halfway mark in the two decades under discussion, the situation began to change. After 1906, for example, railroad construction declined progressively until in 1917 more miles were abandoned than built. Railroad mileage in 1897 (June 30) was 183,284 and in 1916, at its highest point, was 259,705.[64] Of the 76,421 miles of railroad built between 1897 and 1917, 44,171, or an average of about 4,400 a year, were built during the first ten years, and 32,250, or an average of about 3,200 a year were built during the second of the two decades. The increase in ton mileage between 1906 and 1916 dropped to 60 per cent, about half the increase of the preceding decade. Expansion in passenger mileage, which had been 95 per cent for the preceding decade, dropped to 35; increase in miles constructed dropped from 21 per cent to 16. More serious than all this was the failure to keep rolling stock abreast of needs. In the four years 1904–1907, for example, 750,000 freight cars were built, but in the next four years, 1908–1911, only 423,000. The latter figure was far below the needs. Between 1908 and 1918 the increase of freight cars in service

[64] *Statistical Abstract of the United States,* 1923, p. 387.

was only 284,493, or 13.5 per cent, whereas the freight handled increased 90 per cent.

A better standard than the expansion in mileage or business upon which to judge the financial condition would be the "operating ratio," that is, the ratio of operating expenditure to operating revenue.[65] According to this standard, the lower the operating ratio, the more favorable the situation. Experience had shown that when operating expenses were approximately two thirds of operating revenue, the railroads were in a relatively prosperous condition. Such was the situation from 1890 to 1910. From 1911 until 1927, however, the operating ratio fluctuated around a level 4 or 5 points higher than during the preceding years, except in 1916, when heavy traffic made possible a better showing. It was in 1908 that the operating ratio passed 70 per cent, a percentage which reappeared many times in the succeeding years.

Possibly a still more accurate index is the ratio of income to expense. The latter would include not only operating expenses but taxes and interest on funded debt, and would give some indication of a railroad's success in retaining something for its stockholders. According to the most careful survey of the railroad problem in recent years, the proportion of receipts "left for stockholders, to be used either for dividends or reinvestment, increased steadily from the early nineties to 1906, then decreased steadily to 1920 when expenses surpassed revenue." [66] The same survey notes a somewhat similar trend in the ratio of income to investment in road and equipment. In general there was a steady improvement from 1900 to 1910, followed by a downward trend, interrupted by the recoveries of 1912 and 1916, until lows were reached in 1920 and 1921. A similar weakening in the position of railroad bonds after 1909 likewise indicates a weakened financial position.[67]

While operating ratio of expenses to income increased, the railroads suffered a marked decline in average receipts a ton-mile, a decline from 0.754 cents in 1908 to 0.715 in 1916. Stockholders saw the average rate of dividends on all railroad stock drop from 5.30 per cent in 1908 to 4.19 in 1916, while dividends of paying stock declined from 8.07 to 6.75. Between the high year of 1911 and 1916

[65] Harold G. Moulton and Others, *The American Transportation Problem* (Washington: The Brookings Institution, 1933), pp. 26–27. Operating expenditure, as used by Moulton, excludes taxes, bond interest, and other disbursements of a strictly financial character, and operating revenue does not include income derived from investments.
[66] *Ibid.*, p. 30.   [67] *Ibid.*, p. 39.

the aggregate amount paid in dividends fell off about $100,000,000.[68] Decline in income was reflected in the decline of railroad credit. At the opening of the century, railroads, with the possible exception of agriculture, represented the primary investment field of the nation. In the great security markets their position was regal. The rapid development and greater speculative possibilities of "industrials," however, had pushed the "rails" into a secondary position. It is true that at least $4,625,000,000 was invested in railroads between 1908 and 1916, but this amount was far from adequate to meet the necessary expansion program.

One fundamental weakness in the financial structure was the large amount of debt carried by the railroads. Railway capital as of July 30, 1897, included $4,301,687,000 of stock and $4,135,933,000 of bonds. This situation had deteriorated by the end of 1917, when the capital stock outstanding and not owned by the companies was $6,582,809,000 and the unmatured funded debt was $9,818,977,000.[69] Indebtedness had grown from slightly less than half to almost two thirds of the capital outstanding. The railroads may not have been overcapitalized in 1917 in relation to their value, but the amount of borrowed money in the capital structure endangered the railroads during periods of depression and was largely responsible for the numerous bankruptcies. Moreover, it discouraged new investments necessary for the proper maintenance of the roads.

The fact that a tightening of federal regulation came simultaneously with a decline in the position of American railroads gave railroad executives an opportunity to blame their situation on government control. This undoubtedly was one cause. The purpose of the railroad legislation had been to protect the shipper and the consumer and had perhaps neglected the interests of the railroad. Moreover, the whole problem of what was a "fair and reasonable return" had by no means been solved. When the Hepburn Act transferred the burden of proof in rate cases to the railroads, it slowed up advances in freight rates and passenger fares. At the same time, however, there is reason to believe that tightening government control made investors more confident about purchasing railroad securities.

Other factors also explain the declining financial position of the

[68] Interstate Commerce Commission, *Thirty Second Annual Report on the Statistics of Railroads in the United States, 1918* (Washington: Government Printing Office, 1920), pp. 35, 37.
[69] Interstate Commerce Commission, *Tenth Annual Report on the Statistics of Railroads in the United States* (Washington: Government Printing Office, 1898), pp. 48–50 and the *Thirty-first Annual Report,* 1917, p. 25.

railroads. Primarily the deterioration was caused by increased costs of capital, labor, and materials while the rate structure remained virtually the same. Not only had these costs increased, but taxes had mounted, and the government was imposing new responsibilities in the way of safety devices and physical plant. There was also a well-founded belief that, despite remarkable progress, the whole railroad business was conducted with astonishing waste and inefficiency.[70] In any event, the railroads for decades had been building ill will, and their struggle against rising costs brought little sympathy.

To the railroads, at least, there was no question after 1908 that rate increases were necessary. Coincident with a demand of railroad labor for higher wages, the eastern trunk lines, followed by the western railroads, filed new tariff schedules in 1910 with increases ranging from 8 to 20 per cent. Wide protest from the country induced Congress to confer upon the ICC, in the Mann-Elkins Act, power to suspend rate adjustments until investigation could be made. After investigation the commission early in 1911 unanimously disallowed the rate advances both in the East and in the West, asserting that the railroads had failed to prove their case at every point and that growth of their business had more than absorbed additional outlays. The fact that 1910 turned out to be a fairly prosperous year for the railroads weakened the latter's case.[71]

Decline in traffic in 1911,[72] demands by workers for increased pay, involvement of the railroads themselves in heavy expenditures, and a general rise in prices led the eastern roads in 1913 again to file with the commission an increase in freight rates. The commission immediately suspended them. In its decision handed down in July, 1914, it stated, however, that it was "of opinion that the net operating income of the railroads in official classification territory, taken as a whole, is smaller than is demanded in the interests of both the general public and the railroads; and it is our duty and our purpose to aid, as far as we legally may, in the solution as to the course that the carriers may pursue to meet the situation." [73] Nevertheless, the commission refused to grant all the charges which the carriers demanded. It rejected any rate increase in trunk line and New England railroads, but did allow a 5 per cent advance of class commodity rates

[70] Below, Chap. XI.
[71] 20 ICC, *Reports,* pp. 243 and 307; Ripley, *Railroads: Rates and Regulation,* pp. 594–600.
[72] In the five-year period 1910–1914, net operating revenue fell from $3,895 to $3,443 a mile, while operating expenses rose from $7,658 to $8,944 a mile of line, and taxes increased from $436 to $572.
[73] 31 ICC, *Reports,* p. 351.

to the roads in the United Freight Association territory (Middle West).

The roads again were unfortunate in submitting their rates in a year of improved business. The situation turned for the worse again in 1914 and the railroads petitioned for a reopening of their case. This was granted, and in the same year the commission allowed, with certain exceptions, a 5 per cent increase where such increases had been omitted in its earlier decision.[74] The results of the "Five Per Cent Cases" were of but temporary benefit to the railroads. The First World War increased tremendously the business of the roads, but it also pushed up costs to such an extent that the gains were soon nullified.

INDIAN SUMMER

Despite the relative decline of steam railroads in the years after 1907, railroad transportation was still a mighty enterprise at the opening of the First World War. Steam railroads may not have kept abreast of the nation's needs in every respect, but they had tremendously increased their facilities. The slowing down of new mileage construction was not entirely the result of a weakened credit position; it was caused in part by competition from interurban electric lines and in part by the fact that a saturation point had been reached. In New England, the Middle Atlantic, the East North Central, and other sections of the country, the nation had long since been well equipped with railroads—in fact, overbuilt in some areas. What was generally needed were more second or additional main tracks and more miles of yard track and siding. Such an effort was made to fill this need that the period might be described as one of improvement of facilities rather than one of main-line extension. It is interesting to note that main track mileage in 1908 was 233,468 and that second or additional main tracks numbered only 23,699. By 1914 the latter figure had been raised to 32,376. At the same time the miles of yard track and siding had been increased from 79,000 to 98,000.

Despite a declining credit position, railroads were still able to command support to push forward first track mileage where it was badly needed. The great era of railroad building was over, but extensions were continuous up to 1916, particularly in the Gulf states and the Far West. One of the most important of the new railroads built during these years was the San Pedro, Los Angeles and Salt Lake

[74] 33 ICC, *Reports,* p. 324 (December 16, 1914).

Railroad, a line 778 miles long which followed the old Mormon trail to connect Salt Lake City with Los Angeles and its harbor, San Pedro. This project, which had fired the imagination of farseeing Westerners, had been blocked by Collis P. Huntington, who had hoped in the interests of the Southern Pacific Railroad to develop the rival port of Santa Monica. Harriman, after his acquisition of the Southern Pacific, likewise had little interest in the project. But his hand was forced in 1902 by the copper magnate, Senator William A. Clark, who had obtained control of franchise and trackage around Los Angeles. Harriman quickly made terms, and the project was completed in 1905. The road not only opened new mineral regions to the outside world, but brought the fruit of southern California twenty-four hours nearer the eastern market. In subsequent years it was to provide the streamliners of the Union Pacific a route for the fastest passenger service between Chicago and Los Angeles.[75]

The San Pedro, Los Angeles and Salt Lake Railroad was not the only new route opened up to the Pacific. When the Gould system found its transcontinental project blocked by Harriman's refusal to cooperate through rates and shipment west of Ogden, Utah, the Gould lines built the 925-mile Western Pacific from Salt Lake City to San Francisco. Completed in 1911, the road crossed the Sierra Nevada through Beckwith Pass and found its way to San Francisco through Oroville, Marysville, Sacramento, Stockton, and Oakland. Its long and sparsely inhabited route, with less favorable eastern connections, has prevented the road's development as a serious rival to other California transcontinentals. It was also during this period that the Chicago, Milwaukee and St. Paul reached the Pacific at Tacoma, when it completed (1909) its subsidiary, the Chicago, Milwaukee and Puget Sound.

Florida as well as California had its empire builders. Henry M. Flagler, whose interests in Florida real estate and railroads went back to the 1880's, finally pushed his Florida East Coast Railroad south to Key West in 1911. The road from Miami south was largely through the swampy Everglades or along the coast, where continuous viaducts were necessary. Of its type it was one of the most remarkable pieces of railroad construction of the early years of the century.

Improvement of facilities took many forms. The rapid increase in electric street railways in the years 1890–1910 had been followed

[75] French Strother, "Swinging the March of Empire Southwestward," *World's Work,* XI, No. 3 (January, 1916), 7073–7081; Montgomery Schuyler, *Westward the Course of Empire* (New York: G. P. Putnam's Sons, 1906).

by a development of interurban electric rail service, which had clearly demonstrated the superiority in most cases of electric over steam power. Aroused by the competition of interurban electrics, many railroad companies attempted at first to solve the competition by gaining control over these competing lines. The New Haven, for example, finally got control of 1,500 miles of electric railways in New England, and the New York Central secured about half that amount in the Mohawk Valley. Having convinced themselves of the superiority of electric power, particularly for congested suburban passenger traffic, a number of the more prosperous railroads began to substitute electricity for steam. Operation by electricity out of the Grand Central Terminal was begun by the New York Central in 1906, and two years later the New York, New Haven and Hartford inaugurated complete electric passenger service between New York and Stamford, Connecticut.

Although a few of the railroads speeded suburban traffic by substituting electric power, others improved their facilities in various ways. One notable engineering achievement of these years was the Detroit River Tubular Tunnel, opened for regular service in October, 1910. It was built seventy-four feet under the river at the lowest point, and was a pioneer project of its type. Other roads, such as the Delaware, Lackawanna and Western, built cutoffs to shorten mileage and new or more adequate bridges. For the average passenger, however, perhaps the most impressive advance made by the railroads during this period was the construction of new and, for that time, luxurious stations. The era of the building of great stations began with the completion of the St. Louis Union Station in 1894 and the new South Station in Boston in 1898. But the most elaborate were yet to come. Encouraged by an act of Congress in 1901, the railroads entering the capital city pooled their resources to erect in 1907 the beautiful Washington Terminal. In 1911, the Chicago and Northwestern completed the first modern passenger station in Chicago, and, in 1914, the twelve systems serving Kansas City completed the Union Station there. An occasional railroad, such as the Delaware, Lackawanna and Western, whose prosperity overflowed, built new stations all along their routes.

These examples, however, pale into insignificance in comparison with the two great terminals in New York City. The Pennsylvania Station, built during the presidency of Alexander J. Cassatt, involved not merely the erection of a terminal but the extension of the railroad from New Jersey to New York City. It meant acquiring eighteen acres of land in the heart of the metropolis for station and yards and the tunneling under both the North River and the East River. When opened in 1910 at an approximate cost of $113,000,000, it was the finest station the world had yet seen. Nowhere had American architects more effectively combined beauty with functional utility. Its only competitor was the Grand Central Terminal in New York, completed in 1913.[76]

The building of monumental terminals while other facilities were starved seemed foolhardy to many. Other needs, however, were not entirely neglected. The number of steam locomotives was increased from 56,867 in 1908 to 66,406 in 1914, and passenger cars from 45,292 to 54,492. Tons of freight carried grew from 869,797,000 to 1,129,-992,000, and number of passengers from 890,000,000 to 1,063,000,000. The reported property investments increased approximately from $13,214,000,000 in 1908 to $17,154,000,000 in 1914. Certainly the railroads in 1914 could be conservatively valued at about $18,000,-000,000. As employers of over 1,700,000 persons (1917), the railroads occupied an important position in the American labor market. The number of railroad empolyees had not increased substantially since 1907, but that was a measure of increased efficiency rather than an indication of less business. Wasteful and inefficient as the railroads might often be, they, along with other industries, advanced in efficiency during these years. Train service became faster and more punctual. Equipment was improved. Average tonnage for each loaded freight car increased from 34 in 1908 to 41 in 1918, and average tonnage for each freight train from 357 to 655.[77]

Mention should be made of the notable work done by railroads at times of crises, as in California after the San Francisco earthquake in 1906. The Southern Pacific in the same year came to the rescue of the Imperial Valley when it assumed leadership in the battle against the flood waters of the Colorado to save that area from inundation and destruction. The disaster sustained by the railroads in the Ohio flood of 1913 necessitated reconstruction on a scale approaching the building of a major railroad system.[78] American railroads, built as they are along the river courses and often but a few feet above normal high water, are an easy prey to floods and washouts. The sort of en-

[76] Slason Thompson, A Short History of American Railroads (New York: D. Appleton and Company, 1925), pp. 276–283, 331–352.

Slason Thompson, ed., The Railway Library (Annually 1905–1915; Chicago: The Gunthrop-Warren Printing Company, 1906–1916), vol. for 1910, pp. 305–308; for 1912, pp. 151–157.

[77] Thompson, A Short History of American Railroads, p. 315.

[78] Ibid., pp. 298–311.

gineering required in the reconstruction after the Ohio floods may not have called forth the bold imagination of great railroad builders and entrepreneurs, but it did require persistence and high technical skill.

Fortunately the management of American railroads gradually shifted to a new type of leader. The first generation of men famous in railroad history, personalities of the type of Cornelius Vanderbilt, Daniel Drew, and Jay Gould, were essentially financial speculators rather than railroad builders. Their successors also included many speculators whose interest was personal power and fortune, but there were also many whose constructive ability and organizing genius contributed much to the development of American railroads. Stanford, Crocker, Hopkins, and Huntington may have bribed legislators, looted the public, and been guilty of all the financial sins, but they did lay the foundations of great railroads. The elder Morgan may have done much to ruin financially the New England railroad system, but his contributions in reorganizing the southern railroads and the Erie in the 1890's were important. Harriman, in similar fashion, helped to wreck the Chicago and Alton but he rebuilt the Union Pacific. More essentially a builder than any of these, James J. Hill was responsible for the construction or rehabilitation of the two great northwestern railroads, the Great Northern and the Northern Pacific.

By 1917 all of these men had passed from the scene. Huntington, the last of the great California builders, died in 1900; Harriman in 1909; the elder Morgan in 1913; and Hill in 1916. There remained, unfortunately, numerous speculators who used railroads as their medium, but as a whole the railroads were shifting into the hands of more responsible bankers, managers, and engineers. Railroad presidents of the second decade of the century were more likely to have started as telegraph operators, rodmen, or shopmen than as brokers' boys.[79]

Railroad men may have become the recognized leaders in railroad operation, but unfortunately they by no means held control, one explanation for the relative decline of the system. Of the $6,377,-531,082 of railroad stock of Class I and Class II railroads at the end of 1917, there were 636,208 distinct holdings of stock with an average holding of $10,024. Since many of these shares were held by corporations (including railroads), trustees and estates, actual ownership

[79] *Ibid.*, pp. 352–357, 415–441.

was far more widely divided.[80] At first glance this might seem to indicate widely distributed ownership and possibly democratic control. The assumption would be incorrect. When the ICC listed the twenty largest security holders in each of the Class I railroads (operating 95.6 per cent of the nation's mileage), it was found that these groups owned more than half of all the stock in point of value. It was also discovered that 8,301 of the 627,930 stockholders of Class I railroads held about one half of the number of outstanding shares. This meant close concentration of both ownership and control.[81]

American railroads experienced during the years 1914–1917 one of the most difficult periods in their history. It was a plethora of prosperity, not depression, that caused their difficulty. Increased demands resulting from the European war, and later the entry of the United States into the conflict, stretched their resources to a breaking point and accentuated all of the weaknesses that had grown over the preceding years. Gradually developing government control had done much to stabilize the railroad system, but it could not wipe out years of financial wreckage, failure to provide equipment sufficient for expanded needs, or lack of efficient coordination necessary in a war emergency. Railroad trackage was sufficient for the needs of the country, but lack of unity, of adequate equipment, of cooperation, and of efficiency resulted in the virtual breakdown of the system in the autumn and early winter of 1917. Government supervision in the prewar years was by no means faultless, and railroad management blamed the condition of the railroads on the slowness of the ICC in granting increased rates. The blame in varying degrees had to be shared: neither federal legislators nor railroad management had handled the railroad problem wisely for the benefit of the nation. Whatever the causes of the difficulty, there was little dispute over the necessity of government wartime control when Wilson's proclamation brought it about late in December of 1917.[82]

[80] Bureau of Railway Economics, *Railway Stockholders, December 31, 1917,* Consecutive No. 140, Miscellaneous Series No. 33 (Washington: 1919).

[81] For the earlier period, see Solomon Huebner, "The Distribution of Stockholdings in American Railways," American Academy of Political and Social Science, *Annals,* XXII (December, 1903), 475–490.

[82] Sharfman, *The American Railroad Problem,* pp. 65–73.

Revolution in Transportation

URBAN TRANSPORTATION

REGAL as was the position of steam railroads in the American transportation system, their power was by no means unchallenged. Nor did they bear the complete burden of freight and passenger traffic. Traffic on the rivers had indeed almost disappeared, but that on the Great Lakes was increasing rapidly, and coastwise shipping flourished. City transportation was undergoing a major transformation, and the automobile had already begun to play its role of revolutionizing rural transportation. The dominant position of railroads in long-distance traffic was unchallenged, but even here the invention of the airplane presaged eventual competition. It was in the improvement of short-distance traffic that the first two decades of the new century made their greatest contribution.

Americans of the present generation think of organized city transportation in terms of street railways, elevated railways, subways, and motor busses. Two of these methods were in operation in 1896, and a third began in Boston in the following year with the opening of the first subway in the Western Hemisphere. Horse-drawn stages or omnibuses were put on tracks in the 1850's and for half a century carried the chief burden of city passenger traffic. At the height of their usefulness in the early 1880's, the American Street Railway Association (organized 1882) estimated that the 415 street railways then in existence employed 35,000 men and used 18,000 cars and 100,-000 horses daily.[1] But the horsecars were small, their speed was slow, and they had long since become quite inadequate for urban needs.

[1] *Proceedings of the Federal Electric Railways Commission* (Washington: Government Printing Office, 3 vols., 1920), III, 2164.

Nor did cars propelled by moving cables as those used in San Francisco solve the problem except on steep hills.

New York City had pioneered with "elevateds" in the 1870's, the cars drawn by small steam locomotives, but when Chicago and Boston built their elevated lines in the 1890's they adopted electric power. Electric power, in fact, marked the first great revolution in city transportation. Experiments over a long period had made it clear that electricity could be utilized to propel railway cars, but it was not until 1886 that Charles J. Van Depoele constructed a practical electric street railway system in Montgomery, Alabama. In 1888, Frank J. Sprague finished a more difficult job at Richmond, Virginia.[2] Innumerable engineering problems remained to be solved, but the demonstration at Richmond was so convincing that within a decade horse-drawn cars had virtually disappeared.

STREET RAILWAY TRACKAGE IN THE UNITED STATES, CLASSIFIED ACCORDING TO POWER USED

Miles of Track Operated by	1890	1902	1907	1912	1917	1922
Electricity	1,262	21,902	34,038	40,808	44,677	43,789
Animal	5,661	259	136	58	11	4
Cable	488	241	61	56	45	46
Steam	711	170	105	76	41	1
Other	....	6	41	66	61	92

Source: U.S. Bureau of the Census, Street and Electric Railways, 1902, p. 8, and for 1922, p. 18.

It is clear from the preceding table that the transition from horse to electric power occurred between 1890 and 1902. In the former year, 69.7 per cent of trackage was operated by horses; in 1902, this type of power had declined to only 1.1 per cent, while electricity was used on 97 per cent. The shift was almost complete. The table also shows that the great period of electric street railways was in the twenty-seven years after 1890. Actually, 1918 was the year of greatest mileage (44,949) with a decline thereafter. Rail extensions were made after 1918, but they failed to balance the abandonment of unprofitable lines. The peak year of passenger traffic was 1923, when the number carried on electric railways reached 14,000,000,000. The number of employees increased from 70,764 in 1890 to 294,826 in 1917.

[2] John Anderson Miller, Fares, Please! (New York: D. Appleton–Century Company, 1941), pp. 60–62 says that the inventors Edward M. Bentley and Walter H. Knight electrified the East Cleveland Street Railway in 1884, using a third rail in an underground conduit to supply current to cars. "This," says Miller, "was the first commercial electric railway in the United States," but it was discontinued at the end of a year.

This brief period of electric street railway expansion is reminiscent of the early days of the railroads. Inventors interested in electricity and transportation, such as Charles J. Van Depoele, Frank J. Sprague, Elihu Thomson, and Charles Birney (designer of one-man cars), quickly turned their attention to this new form of transportation power and within a few years had solved most of the major technical problems. One of the most important was the method of supplying power. Since the third rail was not practical on open streets and since underground conduits were never widely used in the early years, engineers came to rely upon overhead wires.[3] Electric power was so superior to that furnished by horses, and the need for improved transportation was so great, that there was no lack of entrepreneurial interest or available funds. Moreover, innumerable small cities and towns were convinced that their hopes of future growth and power rested upon a "trolley line," just as a half century earlier the prospects of future greatness seemed dependent upon railroad connection with the outside world. At the head of these entrepreneurs were Thomas Fortune Ryan and August Belmont, who struggled for control of the New York City transit lines; Charles Tyson Yerkes, who controlled the Chicago system; Henry M. Whitney, who shifted the Boston streetcars from horse to electric power; and Henry Huntington, who created a 1,000-mile system radiating out of Los Angeles.[4] Scores of lesser magnates followed their methods, including Tom Loftin Johnson of Cleveland, who later became an advocate of strict government control and lower fares.[5]

As with steam railroads, entrepreneurs, capitalists, and speculators entered blithely upon the policy of reorganization, recapitalization, and consolidation, that is, as soon as there was enough property to warrant speculation and the creation of fictitious values through overcapitalization. Newton D. Baker, testifying before the Federal Electric Railways Commission, gave a typical example with Tom Johnson as his source:

> Mr. Johnson had been, I think, one of the formers, one of the organizers, of the group known as the Big Consolidated. He had owned a number of

[3] Apparently these were first used by Leo Daft at Orange, N.J., who "employed a system of two overhead wires and a little four-wheeled carriage connected to the car by a flexible cable. This carriage was called a 'troller' on account of the way it was pulled along the wires, and from this, by corruption, the word 'trolley' developed as a general term for electric streetcars obtaining power from overhead wires."—Miller, *Fares, Please!* p. 62.

[4] *Ibid.*, pp. 105–109.

[5] Newton D. Baker tells the story of the Cleveland system and Tom Johnson's ten year battle in *Proceedings of the Federal Electric Railways Commission*, II, 995–1037.

street railroads in Cleveland, had built a number there, a good many years prior to his having become mayor, and was, I am inclined to think, president of the Big Consolidated, Cleveland Electric Railroad Co., when it was formed. He used to tell me that the way that corporation was formed was that all of the roads which were consolidated met together by representatives from their boards of directors, turned in their stock, the aggregation assumed the bonded indebtedness of all of the constituent companies, and issued consolidated stock for each share of constituent stocks, in the ratio of one share of constituent stock for five shares of Consolidated stock. In other words, a man who put in a $100 share of stock in a constituent railroad took out $500 worth of stock in the Consolidated railroad.[6]

The markup may not always have been on a ratio of five to one but it was large, as later testimony on the history of transportation in New York, Pittsburgh, Chicago, San Francisco and many other cities revealed. Said one expert, testifying before the same commission on the basis of a study of eighteen or twenty cities:

A study of the financial history of many representative companies discloses an amazing story of financial manipulation clear through the life of the properties, the results of which have been to load them down with a staggering burden of overcapitalization to constitute a permanent charge against operating revenue. The ingenuity of the financial management in creating new sources of capitalization has been without limit. Nothing has been overlooked upon which to hang new issues of securities.[7]

It may be added that high finance was often accompanied by political bribery and corruption, particularly in obtaining city and state franchises.[8] Nor were opportunities for speculation limited only to holders of franchises and owners of street railway stocks. As with steam railroads, land values were also influenced by street railways. By speeding transportation, street railways opened up new suburban areas and widened the commuting range. Furthermore, by 1902, the long-distance transmission of electric power had reached a development which made possible the building of interurban railways.

Unlike the street railway, which serves only a single city and carries only passengers and their hand luggage, the interurban railways were designed to connect two or more independent communities and to carry baggage, mail, express, and even freight. The problems of interurban electric railway transportation were less understood than

[6] *Ibid.*, II, 996.

[7] Stiles P. Jones, *ibid.*, II, 1843. Quoted in Delos F. Wilcox, *Analysis of the Electric Railway Problem* (New York: The Author, 1921), p. 592. For New York City, see Burton J. Hendrick, "Great American Fortunes in the Making," *McClure's Magazine*, XXX (November, 1907—January, 1908), 33–48, 236–250, 323, 338.

[8] Delos F. Wilcox, *Municipal Franchises* (Rochester, N.Y.: The Gervaise Press, 2 vols., 1910), I, 1–132.

those of urban but they were quickly solved, and interurban business grew rapidly in many sections.[9] Electric interurbans had certain advantages over steam-operated railroads in the greater frequency of service and a higher average speed, the latter due chiefly to the higher rate of acceleration. They also had the advantage of more frequent terminals.

Although the interurban electrics rendered a real service in the transportation of passengers and freight, they never became a major transportation agency. Even while this service was expanding, the challenge of the automobile was felt, and its effect was far more detrimental upon them than upon the urban street railways. Nevertheless, it was possible by 1914 to travel from New York to Chicago or from New York to Portland, Maine, on a combination of streetcars and interurbans. In fact, during the heyday of the trolley, one could travel, if he had the patience, from Boston to New York entirely on street or interurban electric railways at a cost of $2.40 in fares. The time was twenty hours. Such a trip was made in March, 1912, by a group of electric railway officials in a private car owned by the Worcester Consolidated Street Railway.[10]

During the period of the rapid rise of the trolleys, marvels were accomplished by scientists, engineers, and traffic managers in improving and enlarging equipment and in solving many of the problems of traffic movement. Peak loads during one quarter of the day produced devices which would speed loading and unloading, while the reduction of stops hastened travel without increasing maximum speed. Traffic managers became experts in furnishing and withdrawing equipment during the rush hours and slack periods, and in encouraging traffic during the dull hours. For example, scores of amusement parks in the outskirts of American cities were built or inspired by the trolley companies in efforts to stimulate business on Sundays and holidays. With a rapidly growing population and a steady increase in business, the future of the trolleys seemed bright. Moreover, as a business, they had other advantages. Except for the rush hours and slack periods, their traffic was comparatively free of fluctuation —and the business was a monopoly. Since their revenues were collected in advance and at the time service was rendered, they had no bad debts and they needed little working capital.[11]

Despite their apparently favorable position, however, many of

[9] *Proceedings of the Federal Electric Railways Commission,* I, 696–699.

[10] Miller, *Fares, Please!* p. 109.

[11] Stuart Daggett, *Principles of Inland Transportation* (New York: Harper & Brothers, 2d ed., 1934), pp. 99–104.

the electric street railways were soon in financial difficulties. Some twenty-seven companies operating 1,152 miles of single track were in receivership in 1915, the first year that brankrupt mileage had passed 1,000 miles. The years 1917–1919 were particularly bad; receivers took over 1,177 miles in 1917; 2,018 in 1918; and 3,781 in 1919.[12] After that, conditions improved for several years. The causes for this situation are clear. In the first place, street railway companies ruined their credit by the same financial policies which had thrown hundreds of steam railways into bankruptcy. If possible, they exceeded the railroads at their worst. They were often handicapped from the start by the curse of overcapitalization, soon accentuated by the assumption of excessive fixed charges. They accomplished the latter by converting stock into guaranteed securities or by assuming fixed rental charges in connection with the consolidation of properties. Having done this, they subsequently refused or neglected to write off excessive capitalization or build up depreciation reserves.

Following the iniquitous example of steam railroads, the streetcar companies often artificially attempted to maintain credit by paying dividends while they neglected ordinary repairs and replacements. Also, like many railroads, they often overbuilt into territory too thin to sustain the investment. The latter was the result of the usual causes: competition, overoptimism, and speculation, often spurred on by municipal governments and outside speculators.[13] Again, as with the steam railroads, these practices often led to the control of street railways by investment bankers "whose profits were dependent upon the volume of securities turned out and frequent turnover in the companies' financial arrangements." [14] "The inevitable result," as one asserted in 1919, "is seen in the present undermining of the financial structure of street-railway investments in this country. The credit of the industry is so impaired that it can no longer finance its own enterprises on possible terms. It is facing collapse through its own devices." [15]

But financial mismanagement was not the only handicap which ruined the credit and darkened the prospects of the street railways. Most of their charters guaranteed them a five-cent fare, which meant big profits in the early years, but which was not enough to meet costs as wages and the price of raw materials increased. During the days

---

[12] *Ibid.*, p. 109.
[13] Wilcox, *Analysis of the Electric Railway Problem*, pp. 645–646.
[14] *Ibid.*, p. 646.
[15] Stiles P. Jones in *Proceedings of the Federal Electric Railways Commission*, II, 1843; quoted in Wilcox, *Analysis of the Electric Railway Problem*, p. 592.

of prosperity, the public tried to regain some of the profits by taxation, but later, when the five-cent fare failed to produce profits and the companies attempted to save by curtailing services, the public exerted the police power of the state and refused to permit these economies. By that time, new and more efficient public-utility commissions had been established to keep a closer eye on the companies. Although the street railways were guilty of almost every financial practice that could have harmed them, their greatest difficulties came from two causes over which they had little control: the increased cost of maintenance and operation, and the competition from the automobile.

Few industries were hit harder by increased costs. Street railways had profited excessively by exploiting labor through low wages, long hours, and generally unsatisfactory conditions. As time went on, these conditions improved as a result of public sympathy and union organization. The swing run was abolished, the twelve-hour day was reduced, and wages were increased. Average annual wages of operators rose from $655 in 1907 to $934 in 1917 and to $1,571 in 1921.[16] The increase for other wage earners of these companies was even greater. Cost of equipment went up more rapidly than labor; the prices of railway motors and car equipment, for example, increased 87 per cent between the middle of 1915 and June, 1919.[17] The *Electric Railway Journal* showed that the cost of electric-railway operating equipment valued at $100 in 1913, was $126 in 1916, was $172.2 in 1919 and $224.6 in 1920.[18] Street railways, of course, tried to break the five-cent fare restriction and convince municipalities and utility commissions that fares should be increased. This propaganda, however, made little headway up to 1917. It took the war inflation and widespread bankruptcy to break the sanctity of the five-cent fare. The problem was acute, and at least one experiment was started in Cleveland, Ohio, on a service-at-cost franchise.[19]

While the street railways struggled with higher costs, the ownership of automobiles expanded. The possibility of real competition was clear even before the First World War. It came suddenly in 1914 when scores of "jitneys" appeared in the streets of Los Angeles, automobiles of various types and conditions of decrepitude which would

[16] U.S. Department of Commerce, *Census of Electric Industries, 1922: Electric Railways* (Washington: Government Printing Office, 1925), p. 219.

[17] *Proceedings of the Federal Electric Railways Commission*, I, 393.

[18] *Electric Railway Journal*, January 1, 1927, p. 29. Cited by Daggett, *Principles of Inland Transportation*, p. 114.

[19] *Proceedings of the Federal Electric Railways Commission*, I, 590, and II, 1001–1007.

carry passengers almost anywhere for five cents. They soon spread
to other cities, often skimming the cream of business away from the
trolleys and causing consternation to the companies. While the companies demanded control of the jitneys and protection from the city,
the Los Angeles *Record* declared, "If the City Council or Board of
Public Utilities can't or won't tame the Trolley Trust there is something else that can and will. And that is the 5-cent fare autos." [20] To
demands for regulation of the jitneys the Public Utilities Committee
of the City Council retorted, "We hold as a sound economic principle that every mode of transportation in operation prior to the advent
of the motor bus should sustain its appeal to popular favor and profit
making upon its intrinsic merit and not upon protective legislation." [21] Fortunately for the street railways, they were generally
supplying a better, safer, and more economical service, and the
jitneys eventually disappeared from the streets.

The jitneys, however, was soon to be succeeded by the larger and
more dignified motorbus, which was destined largely to replace the
electric street railways. As early as 1905 the Fifth Avenue Coach
Company had imported a single 24-passenger double-decked motorbus. Within three years the company discarded horse-drawn vehicles
and operated only motorbuses. The chassis were built by De Bion-
Bouton in France and the bodies by the J. C. Brill Company of Philadelphia. In 1912 the Cleveland Railway purchased three motorbuses
for service in an outlying section of the city. However, few electric
railways were willing to follow these two companies. As late as 1920
there were only about sixty motorbuses operated by ten electric railways in the entire country.[22] Gasoline-powered busses, however, had
already spread widely in suburban and rural areas.

One characteristic of transportation in the rapidly growing cities
was its chronic inability to keep pace with the demand. This failing
was not due to the fact that engineers or entrepreneurs were unaware
of the problem; they made repeated efforts to solve it. New York City,
cramped into a narrow island, found the problem particularly acute
and generally took the leadership in experimenting with new devices.
The chief objective was to provide a faster transportation than that
offered by either the horse-drawn streetcar or the trolley. New
Yorkers experimented with elevated railroads in the late 1860's and
built practical lines in the 1870's. Chicago followed in the 1890's, and
Boston opened her first overhead railway in 1901. Chicago preceded

[20] Quoted by Miller, *Fares, Please!* p. 147.   [21] *Ibid.*, p. 152.
[22] *Ibid.*, pp. 153–164.

New York in the shift from steam to electricity (1895), but New York soon followed.

At the end of the nineties, both Boston and New York determined to follow the example of London and attack the problem by building subways. Boston completed the first unit of her system in 1897. New York began hers in 1900 and completed the first portion in 1904, when she opened the line running from City Hall on the south to 145th Street on the north. A year later, trains were running under the East River to Brooklyn and by 1908 under the North River to New Jersey. Where introduced, the elevated and subways did much to solve the problem of rapid city transportation and allow greater urban expansion.

THE HORSELESS CARRIAGE

To the railroads, approaching in 1900 the height of their power, any idea that the few self-propelled contraptions puttering through the streets would ever constitute a rival worth considering was too fantastic for serious consideration. In the year 1895 but four automobiles were made in the United States. Possibly three hundred were built by 1898, the product largely of tinkering mechanics working on their own, rather than cars manufactured in a factory. Formal manufacturing hardly existed in 1898, and the industry seemed not sufficiently important even in 1899 to be listed in the census under a separate heading.

But the groundwork for a rapid development had been laid. Basic inventions had been made, mostly in Europe, and the problem by the 1890's was to put them together into a practical automobile. In America the pioneers experimented chiefly with steam, electric, and internal-combustion engines, and many of them had actually constructed cars by 1897.[23] Undoubtedly the mechanics who built these early cars believed they had a future, but few outsiders dreamed of the tremendous possibilities. Certainly few capitalists, with the exception of the bicycle manufacturer Albert A. Pope, who paid for the experiments of Hiram P. Maxim, had enough faith in the future to invest large sums. In retrospect the rapid development seems logical enough. The problem of long-distance traffic, as exemplified in the railroads, had been solved, but facilities for local transportation had

[23] When the National Automobile Chamber of Commerce honored the pioneers in 1925 it presented medals to John B. Maxwell, Edgar L. Apperson, Andrew L. Riker, John S. Clarke, Rollin H. White, H. H. Franklin, Charles Duryea, Charles B. King, Elwood Haynes, Ransom E. Olds, and Alexander Winton.

lagged behind. Despite the rapidly developing electric trolleys, the nation desperately needed a speedier and more convenient form of short-distance transportation, and it was rich enough to afford it. Opportunities for inventors and entrepreneurs were wide open.

Although Charles Duryea had built his first car in 1892, Henry Ford in 1893, and Elwood Haynes in 1894, automobiles until 1900 were almost entirely built on order. Electric cars, easier to make, first achieved factory production. Until 1900, as many electrics were produced as gasoline and steam cars together. The great spurt which allowed factory production came after 1898. Ray Stannard Baker, writing with some exaggeration in July, 1899, asserted:

> Five years ago there were not thirty self-propelled carriages in practical use in the world. A year ago there were not thirty in America. And yet between the 1st of January and the 1st of May 1899 companies with the enormous aggregate capitalization of more than $388,000,000 had been organized in New York, Boston, Chicago and Philadelphia for the sole purpose of manufacturing and operating these vehicles. At least eighty establishments are now actually engaged in building . . . no fewer than 200 types of vehicles, with nearly half as many methods of propulsion. . . . A hundred electric cars are plying familiarly on the streets of New York and 200 more are being rushed to completion.[24]

Whether there were actually 80 establishments building motor cars in 1899 is doubtful. However, the manufacture of automobiles, like most new industries, particularly those of rapid growth, was characterized by the rise and fall of many establishments. The magazine *Motor*, in its issue of March, 1909, contains a list of 639 firms that "engaged" in the automobile business up to that year. As for those which actually manufactured motor cars, Epstein's records give a truer picture. He found a total of 181 companies in production between 1903 and 1926, including the 24 in existence in 1903, but admits that there might have been more. Of the 181 companies in passenger car production over this twenty-four-year period, 137 had retired by 1926. The average length of life for all 181 companies had been 9.4 years, the median length 7.0 years.[25] The hazards of a new industry, the necessity of frequent innovations and alterations in the product, the difficulty of predicting the market, the relatively high unit cost of the product, and the terrific competition help to explain the high mortality.

---

[24] Ray Stannard Baker, "The Automobile in Common Use," *McClure's Magazine*, XIII, No. 3 (July, 1899), 195–208.

[25] Ralph C. Epstein, *The Automobile Industry* (Chicago: A. W. Shaw Company, 1928), pp. 162–212, 299.

Another cause may have been the failure of the new industry to attract large aggregates of capital from the leading money centers of the nation. The industry, which was destined within thirty years to be the greatest in the country in the value of its products, had little lure for the financial giants who were playing with railroads and industrial trusts. Automobiles, if they were given any attention, seemed dubious. It was not until two years after William C. Durant had organized the General Motors Company that he was able in 1910 to obtain eastern capital. The Du Ponts came in about 1915, and after the war Wall Street was eager to participate in the great automobile profits.

Since industrial combination was in the air, it might be supposed that the chaotic competition of the early years would have turned producers toward combinations. This did not happen, in part because no great banks or bond houses were interested in the idea, and in part because of the nature of the product. Capitalists, according to one manufacturer, were skeptical of the industry because they believed that it was already overexpanded as early as 1904.[26] Automobile manufacturers themselves could not combine for they needed their own profits for the expansion of their own plants. Moreover, automobiles in the early years were a specialty product. A new type or a new design, if it caught the market, was in itself a monopoly, and the difficulties of developing a combination big enough to exclude competition were obvious. As long as there was room for innovations, it was difficult to create a monopoly.[27]

Only two efforts of importance were made before 1917 to achieve large-scale combinations. The first was accomplished by Durant, who purchased a wagon factory, turned it into the Buick Company, and on the basis of the success and profits of Buick gathered in the Cadillac, the Oldsmobile, and the Oakland in 1908, and almost obtained the Ford and the Maxwell. Durant was easily the most spectacular figure in the motorcar business. Entrepreneur and supersalesman rather than engineer or manufacturer, he had an abiding faith in the future of the automobile which nothing could discourage. His rapid expansion, however, almost ruined General Motors in 1910. It was saved by eastern capital headed by James J. Storrow of Lee, Higginson & Co. and Frederick Strauss of J. and W. Seligman & Co. General Motors got the money on condition that Durant be eliminated from the management, but six years later he was back again as president with the backing of Du Pont money. The other effort at combination

[26] *Ibid.*, pp. 224–225.   [27] *Ibid.*, p. 222.

was made in 1910 through the leadership of Benjamin Briscoe of the Maxwell-Briscoe concern under the name of the United States Motor Company. Briscoe picked up eight concerns for his merger, but except for his own company they were mostly "cats and dogs." The combination failed in 1912.[28]

A monopoly of a sort, although it never prevented vigorous competition, was almost consummated through the Association of Licensed Automobile Manufacturers. In 1879, George B. Selden, a patent attorney of Rochester, New York, applied for a patent on a pressure hydrocarbon engine. The patent was not finally granted until 1895, but in the meantime Selden had assigned it in 1889 to Pope and it later came under the control of the Electric Vehicle Company, headed by a group of New York financiers. No machine using the Selden patent, however, was ever built, and Selden's contribution to the automobile industry was slight. The industry was growing up quite independently of the patent, and when the Electric Vehicle Company in 1900 brought suit against the Winton Vehicle Company, the latter contended that the component parts of the Selden patent were merely a combination of known and existing elements and not patentable. The court, however, held for the patent holders and most of the makers organized the Association of Licensed Automobile Manufacturers in 1903 to protect the patent. The patent was again approved in 1909. Ford and Thomas P. Jeffery (manufacturer of the Rambler, eventually the Nash) fought the license until 1911, when a circuit court of appeals upheld the patent but ruled that Ford had not violated it. This ended any possibility of monopoly through patents.[29]

From an engineering and technical point of view two aspects of the automobile industry are especially interesting. In the first place, the early factories which turned out automobiles were, strictly speaking, not manufacturing plants as much as assembly centers. Most of the parts were manufactured elsewhere, gathered at the assembly factory, and then put together—a fact which helps to explain the ease with which so many new companies could enter the field. This characteristic of the industry has to some extent persisted as the large companies have purchased or set up subsidiaries to specialize in the

[28] Edward D. Kennedy, *The Automobile Industry* (New York: Reynal & Hitchcock, 1941), pp. 48–58; Epstein, *The Automobile Industry*, pp. 218–225; Lawrence H. Seltzer, *A Financial History of the American Automobile Industry* (Boston: Houghton Mifflin Company, 1928), pp. 160–172.

[29] Epstein, *The Automobile Industry*, pp. 227–235; Kennedy, *The Automobile Industry*, pp. 42–48.

manufacture of certain parts. A second outstanding characteristic of automobile history is, of course, the leadership taken by the industry in developing the assembly line and other techniques of mass production, a story which has been told in an earlier chapter.[30]

Beyond all else the most spectacular feature of the industry was its rapid development. The four automobiles registered in 1895 had grown to 4,983,340 in 1917, and the capital invested from $5,760,000 to $1,015,443,000 in 1919.[31] Census reports put the number of motor vehicles produced in 1899 at 3,700 (probably an overestimate) with a value of $4,750,000; the War Industries Board put the number in 1917 at 1,868,947 with a value of $1,274,438,449. Quantity production, measured in terms of those days, appeared early. Ransom E. Olds, known as the "pioneer exponent of quantity production," turned out 4,000 cars in 1903 when his "curved-dash" Oldsmobile was at the height of its popularity. The Ford Motor Company alone in 1917 produced 808,590 by methods which then marked the acme of efficiency.

The reasons for this tremendous advance were many: the economic need for more rapid short-distance transportation both for passengers and for freight, the appeal of this new-found convenience and pleasure to the average person, and, above all, the ability of the industry to widen the market by a continuous reduction of price. Although the basic inventions had been made, automobiles improved steadily from the "one-lung" motors of Ford, Olds, and Winton to the smooth-running "sixes" and "eights" of a decade later. Perhaps the improvement of greatest convenience was the invention of the self-starter in 1912 by Charles F. Kettering, one device which undoubtedly helped to account for a fivefold increase in production during the next five years. Better lighting, demountable rims, cord tires, and other improvements played their part. Many of these later advances, unlike the earlier basic inventions, were developed in the United States. But America's greatest contribution was standardization and mass production, which reduced prices and widened the market. For years the automobile was largely a plaything of the rich; by 1914, it reached down at least to the upper middle classes. It was soon to include every class.

[30] Above, pp. 121–124.
[31] Epstein, *The Automobile Industry*, pp. 316–317. The last figure does not include parts, accessories, body, or tire manufacturers.

MODERNIZATION OF HIGHWAYS

Of the innumerable economic and social effects of the automobile, none was more immediate and obvious than its influence upon the highway system. The coming of the motorcar did not inaugurate the "good roads movement" or the modernization of road administration. It did, however, speed both, and it greatly influenced the type of road construction. Nothing could have been more antiquated than road administration in the days before the automobile, characterized as it was by local supervision and the system of working out road taxes by personal labor. Little could be said of the two million miles of rural roads existing at the end of the century, not a mile of which had a first-class surface. "Commissioners of highways" were amateurs; especially trained highway engineers were almost unknown.

Nor did the demand for good roads arise fundamentally from the pecuniary interests of bicycle or automobile manufacturers or of railroads eager to develop improved roads as feeders for their lines. The primary objective, as one expert insists, "was to bring the standards of rural road transportation up to those already achieved through railroad development for urban areas and for the nation as a whole." It became a part of the whole movement for rural improvement and found support in political parties, government agencies on all levels, business interests, and citizens' groups.[32] Although numerous organizations had begun to agitate for better roads as early as the 1890's, the American Association for Highway Improvement was not organized until 1910.

The reform of American highway financing and administration was carried out in five ways. The first was the replacement of the statute labor system by money taxes. New York made a beginning in 1898, and by 1916 the labor tax system had been virtually eliminated. The second was the expansion in size of the taxing and administrative unit. It became clear, particularly after the advent of the automobile, that neither the road district nor the township unit was competent to support a program of major highway improvement. A fee for the registration of automobiles began with New York in 1904, but a motor fuel tax waited until Oregon imposed one in 1919. The third was the development, beginning with New Jersey in 1891, of state aid; the fourth was the assumption by the state of supervision

[32] Charles L. Dearing, *American Highway Policy* (Washington: The Brookings Institution, 1941), pp. 46–47, 222–229.

over designated road systems; and the fifth was the development of federal participation.[33] Since the early nineties, observed the Public Roads Administration, "there has been a continuous trend toward State and Federal administration and toward paying the cost of main highways through imposts on highway users." [34] It calls the period from 1900 to the end of the First World War a period of "preparation, promotion and organization." By 1917 some type of state highway agency existed in all of the states.

This trend, as it developed in most of the states, may be conveniently illustrated by its history in Connecticut. Realizing the need of better roads, the legislators created in 1895 a highway commission with a budget of $75,000 a year to administer state aid on the basis that the town, the county, and the state would contribute one third each. This was changed in 1897 to eliminate the counties, with the state and towns each contributing one half. A single commissioner was substituted for the former commission, and the state contribution was raised to $100,000. After 1899, the large towns were to pay one third and the smaller towns one fourth. In 1906, the state recognized the need of joining the detached state-aid roads into a trunk line system and appropriated money for it. The next year, the legislature gave to the highway commissioner the final selection of the highways to be improved, increased his powers in construction, and reduced the proportion paid by the towns. In 1911, the state assumed the full cost of repairs and, in 1913, definitely established "a system of trunk line highways." Other roads besides those in the trunk system were provided for in 1923, when the commissioner was directed to maintain and keep in repair all state-aid roads.[35]

Two decades of agitation for better roads and experimentation with improved administration logically resulted in federal participation. Undertaken after long consideration and careful investigation, federal aid came with the act of 1916.[36] Its motives and constitutional justification rested on a desire to improve post roads, administer national forest reserves, and promote general commerce. The latter, which was the primary motive, meant in practice the interconnection of the larger cities of the country with a system of two-lane surfaced roads. The act appropriated $75,000,000 to be spent over five

[33] *Ibid.*, pp. 50–59.

[34] Public Roads Administration, Federal Works Agency Bulletin, *Highways in the United States*, 1945, p. 3.

[35] Bureau of Public Roads, U.S. Department of Agriculture and Connecticut State Highway Department, *Report of a Survey of Transportation in the State Highway System of Connecticut* (Washington: Government Printing Office, 1926), pp. 9–13.

[36] 39 *U.S. Statutes at Large*, p. 355.

years, beginning with $5,000,000 for 1017 and increasing by that amount each year. The Secretary of Agriculture, through the Bureau of Public Roads, was to determine with the highway department of each state what roads were to be improved. The consent of the state legislature had to be obtained, and the states were committed to maintain the roads. The appropriations were apportioned to the states on the basis of area, population and mileage of rural post roads; generally the federal payments were limited to half the cost of construction.

The act not only revived federal participation in road building but speeded the development of state highway commissions and the establishment of definite highway systems.[37] The essential question—whether the appropriations were to be spent for secondary roads leading to market centers or for interstate connecting highways—was left uncertain in the act of 1916. Farmers and railroads favored the former. The long-distance viewpoint, however, won in an act of 1921, when the Secretary of Agriculture was instructed to "give preference to such projects as will expedite the completion of an adequate and connected system of highways, interstate in character." [38]

The nation, of course, did not wait for federal help in road expansion. The mileage of rural roads increased in the decade 1904–1914 from 2,151,379 to 2,445,761. During the same decade 100,000 miles of road were surfaced and over 3,000 more were given a surface of a high type.[39] The speed and weight of automobiles, particularly after trucks appeared, brought a revolution in road building. The old dirt, gravel, and waterbound macadam were unequal to the strain of motor traffic, and engineers experimented with various types of bituminous macadam and bitulithic pavement. It is asserted that concrete pavement was first used in Bellefontaine, Ohio, as early as 1893, but it did not appear in rural road construction until 1909 in Wayne County, Michigan.[40] After that, concrete expanded rapidly until it became the leading material in the 1930's. The declining cost of the ingredients of concrete undoubtedly helped to promote its wider use.

Expansion of mileage and strengthening of surfaces were by no

[37] Dearing, American Highway Policy, pp. 78–86; Thomas R. Agg and John E. Brindley, Highway Administration and Finance (New York: McGraw-Hill Book Company, 1927), pp. 139–150.
[38] 42 U.S. Statutes at Large, p. 213.
[39] Dearing, American Highway Policy, Appendix B.
[40] Arthur H. Blanchard and Henry B. Drowne, Textbook on Highway Engineering (New York: John Wiley & Sons, 1914), p. 583; and Arthur G. Bruce, Highway Design and Construction (Scranton, Pa.; International Textbooks Company, 1937), p. 8.

means the only engineering problems in this renaissance of road build-ing. Increased automobile traffic forced the widening of roads, and the increased speed of motor cars necessitated the straightening of curves. Road reconstruction also meant thousands of new bridges, wider and stronger than those of earlier years. For bridge construc-tion, engineers increasingly turned their backs on steel in favor of reinforced concrete, which was more easily shaped and more perma-nent. The period 1897–1917 was one of agitation, revival, and experi-mentation. Notable improvements and experiments were made, but the great era of improvement came in the two following decades.

AVIATION

Up to 1917 the thrilling story of the birth of modern aviation as represented in heavier-than-air machines is largely a technical ac-count of invention and experimentation. Not until the middle 1920's did the airplane enter significantly into the economic life of the na-tion. Its importance up to that time was chiefly military. By 1914 the airplane had reached a technical development which made possi-ble its combat use in the First World War, but its chief value was in the field of reconnaissance and combat control. The government dur-ing the war undertook a large-scale program of construction for mili-tary purposes and actually obtained over 3,000 planes, but the effort was essentially a failure. Airplanes used in combat service were al-most entirely built abroad. For all practical purposes, commercial aviation, or nonmilitary use of airplanes, began in the United States when the government inaugurated an air-mail service between New York and Washington (May 15, 1918) and extended it to Chicago in the next year. Supported by various types of subsidies, as well as by popular demand, commercial aviation developed in the postwar years.

INTERNAL WATERWAYS: CANALS AND RIVERS

Equipped with an unrivaled system of internal waterways, the United States made relatively little use of them after the railroads were well established. For this there were two main reasons. First, the internal waterways—except on the Great Lakes—ran generally in a northerly-southerly direction, whereas the main current of traffic was east-west. In the second place, the 4,000 miles of canals built before 1860 to connect the Atlantic coast with the western rivers were unable to meet the competition and hostility of the railroads. Railroads had advantages in costs of construction and in flexibility and speed, to say nothing of the fact that they could more easily follow the normal routes of traffic. All this, with other reasons, make them superior to the canal in ability to meet American conditions.

Railroads profited from other advantages which were temporary rather than inherent. Except for the annual Rivers and Harbors bill, the government had ended before 1850 large-scale aid to rivers and canals, but it lavishly subsidized the Illinois Central and various transcontinental railroads. Moreover, the railroad companies themselves had acquired by 1909 almost one third of the canal mileage of the country, that is, 632.2 miles of the 1,991.1 then in existence. Of these privately owned canals, the Baltimore and Ohio and the Western Maryland railroads controlled the Chesapeake and Ohio Canal (185 miles); the Lehigh Valley Railroad had leased in perpetuity the Morris Canal (106.7 miles); the Pennsylvania Railroad had a 999-year lease on the Delaware and Raritan canal (44 miles); and the Philadelphia and Reading controlled various Pennsylvania canals.[41]

As a whole these railroads showed little if any interest in maintaining the canals and sometimes deliberately stopped using them. In cases of canals such as the Erie, owned by the state, the railroads often sabotaged them by gaining control of terminals and establishing their own lines of canal boats. Then they refused to exchange freight with independent lines, thus forcing the latter to depend entirely on local business. At the same time they maintained a rate war to ruin the canals. A report of the Bureau of Corporations submitted in 1912 stated the situation tersely and accurately when it asserted that "in nearly every case where a canal had passed under the influence of a railroad the volume of canal traffic has decreased. In some cases it is apparent that railroads deliberately endeavored to kill off traffic by water route. In other cases, however, the disappearances or decrease in canal traffic is very largely due as much to the general change in transportation conditions as to any deliberate effort on the part of railroads to destroy the usefulness of canals." [42]

Although the railroads could not buy the rivers and discontinue traffic on them, they could—and did—establish steamship lines to drive independents out of business, and they lowered the rates on railroads running parallel to the rivers to destroy steamboat competi-

[41] *Report of the Commissioner of Corporations on Transportation by Water in the United States* (Washington: Government Printing Office, 4 pts., 1909–1913), Pt. I, pp. 39–43; Pt. 4, pp. 56–65.
[42] *Ibid.*, Pt. 4, p. 64.

tion. Unfortunately for the river traffic, the Supreme Court interpreted section 4 of the Interstate Commerce Act in such a manner as to countenance this practice (Alabama Midland case).[43] Said the Report of the National Waterways Commission:

> The words "under substantially similar circumstances and conditions" found in this section have been interpreted to mean that the existence of actual water competition constitutes a circumstance sufficiently dissimilar to relieve the carrier from the operation of the law. Under this interpretation the cutting of rates, where water competition exists, has been carried to an almost unlimited extent. It is now a question whether the right to lower competitive rates has not been exercised to an extent much in excess of what was intended when the act was passed, and, it may be added, to a degree quite inconsistent with the most salutary policy for the commercial and industrial interests of the country.[44]

Whatever the causes, traffic on the waterways, except for the Great Lakes, had declined. The Erie Canal, for example, carried 4,608,651 tons between New York and Buffalo in 1880, or 18 per cent of the total traffic; in 1906 the tonnage had declined to 2,385,491 or 3 per cent of the entire traffic as against 78,703,315 tons transported by the New York Central and the Erie railroads. The decrease on other canals was usually greater. Quite as spectacular was the decline on the Mississippi and its tributaries. Between 1889 and 1906, traffic on the upper Mississippi fell off 85 per cent, on the Illinois River 41 per cent, on the Missouri and other tributaries above St. Louis, 49 per cent.[45] During the period 1880–1910, total receipts and shipments at St. Louis decreased almost 90 per cent.[46] In 1880, at least 63.4 per cent of the cotton received at New Orleans came by river; this had dropped to 10 per cent in 1910. Only the Ohio River, which had lost but 3 per cent of its traffic between 1889 and 1906, had stood up against the general collapse. Between 1802 and 1911, the nation had appropriated over $650,000,000 for rivers and internal waterways, only to see a declining use of its water facilities.[47]

With the picture of decline clear to anyone, the great revival of interest in inland waterways seems surprising. It is also astonishing that this tremendous interest developed at a time when the railroad system was in its last great period of expansion, when electric street

[43] Above, pp. 189–190.
[44] National Waterways Commission, *Final Report, Senate Document* No. 469, 62 Cong., 2 Sess. (Washington: Government Printing Office, 1912), p. 70.
[45] *Ibid.*, p. 67.   [46] *Ibid.*, p. 511.
[47] Appropriations included $366,000,000 for rivers; $240,000,000 for harbors; $40,-000,000 for canals; $10,000,000 for examinations, surveys, and other items.—*Final Report*, pp. 510–511

railways were being rapidly constructed, when automobiles were developing, and when the nation was embarking on a new era of highway building. Even the age of air traffic was on the near horizon. The eagerness of that generation for wider transportation facilities seemed insatiable. Interest in waterways derived from a number of sources. For one thing, it was part of the general movement for conservation of national resources. Many argued that improvement of waterways for transportation would purify the water supply, develop new and large sources of water power, provide cheaper transportation between many points, break railroad monopolies, encourage a salutary competition, and provide more adequate transportation facilities during periods of great economic activity. The successful use of waterways in Europe was pointed to as an example of how America might better use its own facilities. At the same time the Panama Canal, then in the process of building, dramatized the possibilities of new waterways. Behind all this were the hopes and ambitions of businessmen, speculators, and millions of people who lived along the lakes and rivers, areas which might be stimulated by greater river transportation.[48]

The excitement about internal waterways arose in part from artificial stimulation. This began in earnest in 1895 with the holding of an International Waterways Convention in Cleveland and a meeting in 1901 of the first National Rivers and Harbors Congress in Baltimore. During the next decade commercial associations promoted various waterway projects and held a succession of conventions. The two most important were the St. Louis Convention in 1906, out of which grew the Lakes-to-the-Gulf Deep Waterway Association, and the Washington Session of the Rivers and Harbors Congress of the same year, which led directly to the appointment by President Roosevelt in 1907 of the Inland Waterways Commission.[49] As a climax of a summer of intensive study of the possibilities of inland waterways the commission, accompanied by Roosevelt, floated down the Mississippi from Keokuk to Memphis amid the acclaims of the populace, the shrieking of whistles, and the rattle of fireworks. Enthusiasm

[48] Harold G. Moulton, *Waterways Versus Railways* (Boston: Houghton Mifflin Company, 1912), pp. 1–17, for a discussion and analysis of the arguments for revival of inland water transportation. See also Harold G. Moulton and Associates, *The American Transportation Problem* (Washington: The Brookings Institution, 1933), pp. 434–438.

[49] The commission was composed of Theodore E. Burton, chairman; Brig. Gen. Alexander McKenzie; Senators William Warner and Francis G. Newlands; Congressman John H. Bankhead; and Gifford Pinchot, Frederick H. Newell, Herbert Knox Smith, and William J. McGee.

showed no letup, and two years later President Taft was guest of honor on another holiday junket which floated down the Mississippi.[50] Like Roosevelt, he also appointed a commission—the National Waterways Commission, headed by Senator Theodore E. Burton—which studied European waterways as well as American, and made its final report in 1912.

What came from this widespread agitation and the numerous projects it fostered? It cannot be credited with the two most important waterway accomplishments of the period, the Panama Canal and the New York Barge Canal. Both of these were born and authorized before the agitation reached its height. These projects stimulated the agitation rather than resulted from it. The revival of interest did, however, bring concrete results. One was the canalization of the Ohio authorized by Congress in 1911. The completion of this project at a cost, exclusive of maintenance charges and terminals, of a little less than $100,000,000 was finally celebrated in 1929.[51] The improvement of the Missouri River, which finally got under way in 1912, also resulted from this agitation. Unlike the Ohio, where the canalization of the rivers helped to preserve and encourage traffic, the Missouri River improvement seems to have done nothing but waste the taxpayers' money.[52] Propaganda for a Lakes-to-the-Gulf Deep Waterway was persistent after 1906 and during the next thirty years was virtually achieved. It might have come earlier if the project had not become entangled in a battle between two factions of Illinois politicians, who differed on the role which the state should play in financing the costs of the Chicago Drainage Canal and the necessary improvement of the Illinois River. In the end, large sums of federal money administered by a permanent Mississippi River Commission were granted both for flood control and for improvement of river navigation. Fortunately both types of projects were correlated, and the so-called Lakes-to-the-Gulf Deep Waterway was gradually built.

Interest also revived in the century-old proposal of Albert Gallatin for an intercoastal waterway along the Atlantic, and Congress in 1909 authorized the War Department to make a preliminary survey. Before this survey was well under way, a private corporation, headed by the capitalist August Belmont, Jr., and the engineer Barclay Parsons, undertook to build the first unit of the system by cutting a canal

[50] Moulton, *Waterways Versus Railways*, pp. 1–5.
[51] Moulton and Associates, *The American Transportation Problem*, pp. 476–486.
[52] *Ibid.*, pp. 486–491.

across Cape Cod. The Cape Cod Canal, which connects Buzzard's Bay and Barnstable Bay, shortened the route around the Cape by seventy miles. It was achieved by cutting eight miles through the land at a depth of twenty-five feet in low water and deepening the channels and approaches. After five years of labor and a cost of $12,000,-000, it was opened in 1914. A contemporary prophecy that the Cape Cod Canal would be "one of the most important waterways in the world" [53] fell far short of fulfillment, and the disappointed entrepreneurs managed to unload the canal on the federal government in 1928. The remaining intercoastal waterways project was even less successful than the Cape Cod Canal. The federal government pushed it haphazardly during the next quarter century, but it proved of little economic value.

Of the various artificial waterways constructed in the United States, the Erie Canal has occupied a unique position. Built in the days before railroads, it opened the first practical transportation route between the Atlantic and the Middle West. For a half century it played an important role in fixing rates between the Atlantic seacoast and the interior.[54] Tonnage carried on the Erie and its subsidiary canals reached its high point in 1872, when 6,673,570 tons were moved. After the early 1880's, decline was persistent until by 1900 the tonnage carried by the canal was but a small fraction of that moved by competing railroads.[55] There was, of course, nothing mysterious about the causes of this decline. Competition of rival ports and the bitter rate wars of competing railroads were the most important. To this must be added decreased production of iron ore from the Lake Champlain mines, of lumber from the forests of New York, and of other local products which normally moved over the canal. Railroads were hauling the grain and other long-distance commodities from the West. In later years motor trucks also cut heavily into local traffic. Above all else was the fact that the railroads could offer superior traffic advantages at comparable rates.

Despite these obvious causes of the decline in canal traffic, many believed that the waterway should be improved and every effort made to revive its traffic. Tolls were cut and then finally abolished in 1883 by a constitutional amendment. Abolition of tolls, however, seemed to have no effect in staying the decline, nor did a halfhearted

---

[53] A. Barton Hepburn, *Artificial Waterways of the World* (New York: The Macmillan Company, 1914), p. 122.

[54] Moulton, *Waterways Versus Railways*, p. 417.

[55] Daggett, *Principles of Inland Transportation*, p. 27. In 1903 the New York Central carried 38,081,380 tons; the Erie, 30,586,743; and the canals, 3,616,385.

effort in 1895 to improve the canal by deepening it.[56] It was clear by
the end of the century that only a complete overhauling of the New
York State canal system could make it functional for future transportation. Governor Theodore Roosevelt appointed a state commission in 1899 to study the problem. It reported in favor of a barge
canal rather than a ship canal, and in 1903 the legislature appropriated $101,000,000 to carry out the project and submitted the plans to
a referendum vote. Except for the terminal ports of Buffalo and New
York, the state showed little enthusiasm; the majority vote of 673,-
010 to 427,698 was largely accumulated in the terminal cities.[57] The
new Erie Barge Canal, which followed approximately the old route
of the Erie Canal, with four side canals to Oswego on Lake Ontario,
and to lakes Champlain, Cayuga, and Seneca, had a length of approximately 450 miles. Where possible the engineers preferred to
canalize the Mohawk and other rivers and the lakes of central New
York rather than enlarge the old canal bed. Work was begun in 1905
and the enlarged canal opened to traffic in 1918. Originally estimated
in 1903 at $101,000,000, the cost of improvement up to and including
1924 was $230,881,000.[58]

GREAT LAKES TRANSPORTATION

Although river and canal transportation had declined in the years
after 1880, commerce on the Great Lakes steadily increased. Unlike
the major rivers, this incomparable system of waterways was located
on the east-west trade route and easily became a normal part of the
American transportation system.[59] Moreover, the Great Lakes enjoyed the major advantages of water transportation and, in particular,
special advantages over rivers and canals—long-distance conveyance
for deep-draft vessels and lower maintenance costs. Their favorable
position can be illustrated by freights on wheat, which were 4.42 cents
a bushel in 1900 from Chicago to New York by lake and canal, and
9.98 by railroad. In 1920 they were 14.60 and 16.68 cents, respectively.

This long-distance traffic, of course, was made possible by canals
or canalized rivers which connected Lake Superior with Lake Huron
and the latter with Lake Erie. Between Superior and Huron were
the Sault Ste. Marie Canals; between Huron and Erie, the channel

---

[56] Hepburn, *Artificial Waterways of the World*, pp. 77–79.
[57] Moulton, *Waterways Versus Railways*, pp. 419–422.
[58] *Ibid.*, pp. 422–438.
[59] *Report of the Commissioner of Corporations on Transportation by Water in the United States*, Pt. 1, pp. 25–26.

through the St. Clair River, the St. Clair Flats Canal, Lake St. Clair, and the Detroit River. The Welland Canal connected Lake Erie and Lake Ontario, but only a small proportion of the commerce moved beyond Buffalo into Lake Ontario. The commodities carried on the Great Lakes were particularly suitable to water transportation, for they consisted almost entirely of bulky raw materials. The eastward movement was made up largely of iron ore and grain, and the westward of anthracite and bituminous coal. The period of greatest development came with the development of the Mesabi iron range west of Lake Superior, and with the exploitation of Canadian wheat areas in Saskatchewan, Alberta, and Manitoba. Most of the Canadian wheat was shipped from Fort William or Port Arthur on Lake Superior and reached eastern ports through Superior, Huron, and Erie. A much smaller amount of American wheat, chiefly from the Northwest, also used the Great Lakes, either from Duluth-Superior on Lake Superior, or from Milwaukee, Chicago, and Calumet on Lake Michigan.[60]

By far the largest traffic on the lakes was the transportation of iron ore from the head of Lake Superior (chiefly from Duluth-Superior, Agate Bay, and Ashland) to Calumet, Indiana Harbor, and Gary on Lake Michigan and to Cleveland, Ashtabula, Conneaut, Lorain, Buffalo, and Fairport on Lake Erie. Here the ore was smelted or was sent inland by rail to Pittsburgh, Youngstown, or other steel areas. Bituminous and anthracite coal provided freight for the return voyage and was shipped from the lower to the upper lake ports either for local manufacturing or heating, or for shipment into Canada or to the West North Central states.[61] The pattern of this trade was well established before 1900, but its great development came in succeeding years.

One reason for cheaper transportation costs on the Great Lakes, and thus for the development of lake transportation, was the active competition. Ownership of the vessels in the early years of the century fell into three groups. The first was the trunk line railroads serving the Great Lakes which went into shipping to maintain further control of the business. The largest of this group were the Western Transit Company, owned by the New York Central, and the Erie and Western Transportation Company (Anchor Line), owned by the Pennsylvania Railroad; but at least eight other railroads operated

[60] Daggett, *Principles of Inland Transportation,* pp. 231–246.
[61] James C. Mills, *Our Inland Seas* (Chicago: A. C. McClurg & Co., 1910), Chap. XXV.

lines on the lakes. A second group included large mining, producing, and manufacturing companies such as the United States Steel Corporation and the Standard Oil Company, which carried their own commodities. As early as 1904, United States Steel owned seventy lake steamers and forty-two barges. Lake transportation was also provided by many ships of individual owners and small companies. Such a situation was conducive to bitter competition, but the battle was softened by associations of carriers which attempted to regulate rates, and by the marked tendency toward the consolidation of ownership.[62] By 1910, the Great Lakes fleet was larger than that of any foreign nation except Great Britain and Germany.

OCEAN TRANSPORTATION

Favored by federal discriminatory legislation, American coastwise shipping had become "a well-developed and reasonably prosperous business, a trade of vigorous competition, dominated by no trust or monopoly and steadily growing." So said a report of the Boston Chamber of Commerce in 1916, and added, "It needs no more national encouragement and it asks none." [63] Reserved to American vessels since the founding of the federal government, coastwise trade handled 3,897,000 tons in 1897 and 6,393,000 in 1917. It was incomparably the greatest coastwise shipping in the world.

In contrast to the prosperity of coastwise shipping, that employed in foreign commerce reached its low point about the end of the century. Tonnage registered for foreign trade dropped to 726,213 in 1898, the lowest point in the history of the American merchant marine. The proportion of imports and exports (by value) carried in American vessels declined to a low of 8.2 per cent in 1901; a century earlier, American vessels had carried over nine tenths of the nation's foreign trade. Many causes had contributed to this decline: delay in shifting to iron ships and to steam power, the greater cost of building and operating American vessels, the heavy subsidies granted to foreign ships, and the failure of the United States government to adopt the same policy. Above all was the fact that domestic capital found

---

[62] Report of the Commissioner of Corporations on Transportation by Water in the United States, Pt. 4, pp. 85–87; E. R. Johnson, Ocean and Inland Water Transportation (New York: D. Appleton and Company, 1906), pp. 353–358.

[63] "Report of the Special Committee on Merchant Marine of the Boston Chamber of Commerce," reprinted in Edith M. Phelps, Selected Articles on the American Merchant Marine (New York: H. W. Wilson Company, 1916), p. 7. Coastwise traffic is discussed in John G. B. Hutchins, The American Maritime Industries and Public Policy, 1789–1914 (Cambridge: Harvard University Press, 1941), pp. 542–581.

greater profits in industry, internal improvements, and the development of the West. Just as the United States in its early national period presented the unusual picture of a young nation supporting a large merchant marine, so in maturity it revealed another quite as unusual —a great nation fronting two oceans with an insignificant overseas fleet.[64]

Although most Americans were satisfied to allow the subsidized ships of other nations to carry their foreign trade at a lower cost, a minority believed that the nation should re-establish herself on the high seas. Propaganda was continuous during the 1890's and thereafter, with the usual arguments presented. An American merchant marine, it was asserted, would channel freight profits into American hands and a large fleet would increase foreign commerce. Many insisted that such a fleet was needed to carry American commodities during wars abroad and was essential to national defense in supplying sailors and auxiliary ships in case the United States should be involved in war.[65] The force of the latter argument was demonstrated during the Spanish-American War of 1898. The few available ships of the merchant marine were invaluable in that conflict, but they were quite inadequate for a naval reserve needed in war.[66] Despite these arguments and a certain nostalgia for the glorious days of the past, little was done between 1891 and 1916. Economic arguments of shipowners were ignored by the more powerful industrial and agricultural interests, and the military needs of a merchant marine were soon forgotten after the brief war with Spain.

An earlier policy of aid to the merchant marine through mail subsidies had been renewed by the Ocean Mail Act of 1891. As originally passed by the Senate, the bill provided both for mail subsidies and for bounties for cargoes. Middle western representatives, however, eliminated the bounty feature and radically reduced the mail subsidies. Nevertheless, the aid was sufficient to induce the International Navigation Company to start a weekly service from New York to England (1895–1896) and to build two new ships in the Cramp yards in Philadelphia, ships which did valiant service as auxiliary cruisers in the war with Spain. The act was the basis of the absurdly small and insufficient subsidies granted to American ships until it was sup-

---

[64] See George Rogers Taylor, *The Transportation Revolution, 1815–1860*, Vol. IV, in this series.

[65] Walter T. Dunmore, *Ship Subsidies* (Boston: Houghton Mifflin Company, 1907), pp. 58–70; John G. B. Hutchins, "The Declining American Maritime Industries, 1860–1940," *The Tasks of Economic History*, Supp. VI, 1946, pp. 103–122.

[66] Winthrop L. Marvin, *The American Merchant Marine* (New York: Charles Scribner's Sons, 1902), pp. 424–434.

plemented by the Merchant Marine Act of 1920.[67] Inadequate as these subsidies were in comparison to the large subventions granted by the British, French, and German governments, they helped to maintain the Ward Line of American steamers from New York to Cuba and Mexico, the Red D Line from New York to Venezuela, and the Oceanic Steamship Company from San Francisco to Australia, as well as the boats on the Euopean run mentioned above.[68]

Agitation during these years was persistent even if unsuccessful. With senatorial leaders of the stature of William P. Frye and Mark Hanna, it could not be ignored. It was sufficiently strong in 1903 for Roosevelt to recommend in his annual message a Congressional commission to investigate and report "what legislation is desirable or necessary for the development of the American merchant marine and American commerce, and incidentally of a national ocean mail service of adequate auxiliary naval cruisers and naval reserves." Such a commission was appointed in 1904 under the chairmanship of Senator Jacob H. Gallenger of New Hampshire. Its report, submitted 1904–1905, recommended encouragement of regular steamship services to the West Indies, South America, South Africa, Australia, and the Orient by mail and cargo subsidies.[69] The bill carrying these provisions was eventually defeated, chiefly through the opposition of the South and Middle West.

Although Roosevelt again urged action in his message of 1907, virtually nothing was done to revive the American merchant marine through federal aid until the First World War forced such action. Congress did, however, as part of the Panama Canal Act of 1912, change a traditional policy by offering free registry for the overseas trade to American-owned, foreign-built vessels not more than five years old. The gesture was fruitless; not a single foreign-built ship was registered under its provisions. With the coming of war, however, the situation changed rapidly. Congress immediately passed an amendment to the previous act in August, 1914, admitting to American registry for purposes of foreign commerce American-owned,

[67] William S. Benson, *The Merchant Marine* (New York: The Macmillan Company, 1923), pp. 98–101.

[68] Committee on Commerce, "Development of the American Merchant Marine and American Commerce," *Senate Report* No. 10, 59 Cong., 1 Sess., pp. 48–55; Royal Meeker, "History of Shipping Subsidies," *Publications of the American Economic Association*, 3d Series, Vol. VI, No. 3 (New York: The Macmillan Company, 1905), pp. 166–171.

[69] *Report of the Merchant Marine Commission, Senate Document* No. 2, 755, 58 Cong., 3 Sess. (3 vols., 1904–1905), I, xlvi–li; Paul Maxwell Zeis, *American Shipping Policy* (Princeton: Princeton University Press, 1938), pp. 29–53.

foreign-built vessels without regard to age. Also, the President was authorized to suspend the requirement that the officers of foreign-built ships be American citizens, and to exempt such ships from compliance with American inspection and measurement regulations.

This act was not as successful as anticipated, but it did bring under American registry during the first year of its operation over 170 ships with a total tonnage of over 580,000. American owners of foreign-built ships, such as the United Fruit Company, the Standard Oil Company, and the United States Steel Corporation, hastened to neutralize their ships under this act, but there were few new purchases of foreign-built ships, and a large proportion of vessels controlled by American capital continued under foreign colors. In the same year another act created a Bureau of War Risk Insurance in the Treasury Department to insure American vessels and cargoes, if insurance could not otherwise be obtained on reasonable terms. This would free American ships from the necessity of accepting the rating and insurance of Lloyd's, the English marine insurance agency, believed to be discriminating against American ships.

One of the earliest difficulties faced by the United States as a neutral during the First World War was her lack of an adequate merchant marine. With the German ships driven from the ocean and much Allied tonnage withdrawn for war purposes or destroyed by German submarines, the situation became increasingly acute. Having but a tiny merchant marine of her own, the United States largely depended on foreign shipping at a time when the latter was becoming scarcer. Congress was now forced into action which looked toward the creation of a permanent American merchant marine. In September, 1916, it established a United States Shipping Board with authority to form one or more corporations for the purchase, construction, equipment, lease, charter, maintenance, and operation of merchant vessels in the commerce of the United States. The board was not formally organized until late January, 1917, and in less than three months the nation was at war. The history of the board and its subsidiary body, the Emergency Fleet Corporation, is described in the next volume of this series.[70]

The story of the decline and rise of the American merchant marine was by no means the only interesting aspect of its history during these years. Like other industries, that of ocean transportation did not escape the mania for consolidation which spread so widely during the early years of the century. Through the manipulations of

[70] George Soule, *Prosperity Decade*, pp. 29–32.

J. P. Morgan, the International Navigation Company (successor to the old Inman Line and the only important American line in the North Atlantic traffic) changed its name in 1902 to the International Mercantile Marine Company and increased its capital from $15,000,-000 to $170,600,000. Into the trust were drawn the White Star Line, the Dominion Line, the Atlantic Transport Line, the Leyland Line, the Red Star Line, and others.[71] Morgan tried to bring in the Cunard Line, but this organization was bought off by increased subsidies from the British government. His efforts to bring in the Hamburg-American and the North German Lloyd were prevented by contracts with the German government not to sell. The German lines, however, entered into an agreement for a territorial division of traffic so that the main objectives of the consolidation seemed to be secured.

Morgan's grandiose steamship trust proved to be one of the least successful of his major operations. It soon collapsed, but not before it had strengthened the system of "conferences" or agreements and other methods used by the ocean carriers to soften competition. It also aroused the fear of monopoly conditions on ocean carriers. So concerned was the nation that Congress in 1912 authorized an investigation of steamship conferences as they related to the foreign and domestic commerce of the United States.[72] The investigation, covering several years, influenced the position taken in the Shipping Act of 1916. The Congressional committee opposed steamship agreements and conferences, unless brought under some form of government supervision. Such supervision on foreign trade routes was widely established in the act of 1916.

[71] Frank C. Bowen, A Century of Atlantic Travel, 1830–1930 (Boston: Little, Brown & Company, 1930), pp. 266–267; Edward S. Meade, "The Capitalization of the International Mercantile Marine Company," Political Science Quarterly, XIX, No. 1 (March, 1904), 50–65; Hutchins, American Maritime Industries and Public Policy, pp. 537–539.
[72] House Committee on the Merchant Marine and Fisheries, Proceedings in the Investigation of Shipping Combinations, House Resolution No. 587, 62 Cong., 4 vols., 1913–1914.

CHAPTER XI

Status of the Workers

THE NATION'S WORKERS

ALTHOUGH the estimates made of American workers for the period after 1897 differ slightly in methods of classification and in the derivation of statistics, the conclusions show no major differences.[1] The estimates indicate very clearly both the increasing industrialization of the nation and the relative decline of agriculture. In 1900 the number of farmers and farm laborers and the number of industrial wage earners were about the same; in 1920 the first two groups accounted for 25.5 per cent of the working force, and the industrial wage earners 42.4. Farm proprietors had increased in number, but declined in relation to other important groups. The number of farm laborers remained about the same. The decline in the percentage of both farm proprietors and farm laborers came despite a large increase in agricultural production, and was caused chiefly by the mechanization of agriculture, particularly after 1910.

As part of the picture of increasing industrialization came a relative and actual increase in proprietors and officials, in professions, and in the lower-salaried workers. The decline of servants, actually and relatively, was in a sense more apparent than real. Much personal service had become industrialized; much work done in the home in 1900 had moved outside by 1920. Despite the relative and actual increase in proprietors and officials and the decline of servants, it is significant to note that the combined groups of farm laborers

[1] Appendix, p. 415. Here the estimates of Alvin H. Hansen are given rather than those of Alba M. Edwards, W. S. Woytinsky, or the Bureau of Labor Statistics of the Department of Labor chiefly because they cover the census material for all decades of the period under discussion. They also serve the purpose at this point better than those of Pascal K. Whelpton. See bibliography for this chapter.

and industrial wage earners increased from 45.6 per cent of the total working force in 1890 to 52.4 per cent in 1920.

Among the potent influences upon American labor during these years was the large-scale immigration, particularly between 1900 and 1914. This made it possible for the employable part of the population to increase more rapidly than the total population. Heavy immigration filled many manual and unskilled occupations largely with immigrant labor. A government study made in 1908–1909 found that only one fifth of the total number of wage earners in twenty-one principal branches of industry were native white Americans, while almost three fifths were of foreign birth.[2] The foreign born, however, made up but one fifth of the total working population of the nation. Another notable feature of labor history during these years was the acceleration of the movement of women from the home to

GAINFULLY EMPLOYED PERSONS, TEN YEARS AND OLDER, 1890–1920

Year	Total Persons 10 Years of Age and Over	Total Number of Those Gainfully Employed	Per Cent of Population 10 Years of Age and Over	Males Gainfully Employed	Females Gainfully Employed
1890	47,413,559	23,318,183	49.2	19,312,651	4,005,532
1900	57,949,824	29,073,233	50.3	23,753,836	5,319,397
1910	71,580,270	38,167,336	53.3	30,091,564	8,075,772
1920	82,739,047	41,614,248	50.3	33,064,737	8,549,511

Sources: Fifteenth Census: Population, V, 37, Table 1. Also Don D. Lescohier and Elizabeth Brandeis, History of Labor in the United States, 1896–1932 (New York: The Macmillan Company, 1935), pp. 35–37.

outside occupations. Between 1890 and 1920 the gainfully employed females increased over 200 per cent. In 1890 about one fifth (18.9 per cent) of the women in the United States were gainfully employed whereas in 1910 the percentage was over one fourth (25.4). During these same years the proportion of married women in the group of women workers increased from 13.9 per cent to 24.7.[3]

The increase in the number of working women was due to new opportunities provided by urbanization and expanding industry, as well as to the changing mores which preceded and followed this movement of women from the home to the office or the factory. Urbanization made an increasing proportion of women available for office and light factory work. While the men carried on the lumbering, mining, transportation, road construction, and agriculture outside the cities, women tended to migrate to urban centers and into the working force.

[2] Jeremiah W. Jenks and W. Jett Lauck, The Immigration Problem (New York: Funk & Wagnalls, 6th ed., 1926), p. 148. Above, p. 107.

[3] Fifteenth Census: Population, V, 272, Table 1.

While women moved from the home to factory and office, the battle against child labor made notable progress. The number of children aged ten to fifteen years gainfully employed rose from 1,750,178 in 1900 to about 1,990,000 in 1910, but dropped to 1,060,858 in 1920. An even better picture can be seen from the drop in the percentage of working children of this age group—a drop from 18.4 in 1910 to 8.5 in 1920. In 1900 children in the 10–15 age group represented 6 per cent of all those gainfully employed; by 1920 this percentage had declined to 2.6.[4]

Considerable redistribution of labor, as suggested in Chapter V, took place during the first two decades of the century. It involved not only increased employment of women and a declining use of children, but the findings of new sources of industrial labor among the Negroes and mountain whites of the South.[5] The redistribution was also occupational. According to the census of 1920 there were eight occupations in which the number of females ten years of age and over had increased by more than 50,000: clerks in offices; operatives or laborers in manufacturing; stenographers; bookkeepers and cashiers; teachers; saleswomen and clerks in stores; telephone operators; and trained nurses. On the other hand, decreases of 50,000 or more occurred among women farm laborers, cooks, general servants, laundresses (not in laundries), dressmakers and seamstresses (not in factories), and milliners and millinery dealers. The great increase came in office workers, the great decrease in agricultural workers and servants. The occupational shift in male occupation largely followed the rise of new industries and the relative decline of older ones, but the most unusual increase was among those engaged in various aspects of buying and selling.[6] The shift of Negroes from agriculture has been noted.[7]

INCOME OF LABOR

Economists are agreed at least upon two points with regard to labor in the period after 1897. First, the real income of most wage earners increased little during the twenty years after 1897. Second, this income was inadequate to support decently the vast majority of wage earners. Although labor had suffered bitterly during the early

---

[4] Lescohier and Brandeis, *History of Labor in the United States, 1896–1932*, p. 40.
[5] *Ibid.*, pp. 42–45.
[6] *Fourteenth Census: Occupations IV*, pp. 35–43; Joseph A. Hill, *Women in Occupations 1870 to 1920* (U.S. Bureau of the Census, *Census Monograph IX*, Washington: Government Printing Office, 1929), pp. 32–35.
[7] Above, pp. 100–101.

1890's from unemployment, wage scales had remained fairly stable. This period of stability ended with 1899 and was followed by three decades of changing wage levels. Living costs rose 7 per cent between 1898 and 1901 and another 17 per cent from 1902 to 1907. With the panic of 1907 the cost of living dropped temporarily, but resumed its upward trend in the latter part of 1909. By 1914 it was at least 16 per cent above the period 1906–1909,[8] and it continued to rise even more rapidly during the war years 1914–1918.[9] Paul H. Douglas, who has made perhaps the most comprehensive study of real wages during the period, believes that the index for the total cost of living for workingmen rose from 100 in 1897 (1890–1899 = 100) to 139 in 1914.[10]

Wages from 1897 to 1914 as a whole lagged behind the rising cost of living, but in most cases eventually caught up with it. There was, of course, much difference in the various groups. Wages of unionized workers rose more quickly and to a higher level than those of the unorganized, and those of skilled workers responded more quickly than those of the unskilled. Among the classes of workers who experienced a rise in real earnings between 1901 and 1913 were teachers, railroad employees, and coal miners; those who felt a decline were postal employees, clerical and low-salaried workers, manufacturing wage earners, ministers, and government employees. Among manufacturing wage earners, those engaged in producing land vehicles, clothing, paper and printing, and leather and leather goods enjoyed a rise. Workers in iron and steel, tobacco products, and lumber products experienced a decline. The real income of textile workers remained the same.[11]

The Douglas index figure gives the average annual real earnings of all industries (excluding farm labor) as 98 in 1897 and 104 in 1914, and for all industry (including farm labor) as 97 in 1897 and 107 in 1914.[12] He points out, however, that real *hourly* wages in manufactures remained almost stationary between 1900 and 1914.[13] As for

[8] Lescohier and Brandeis, *History of Labor in the United States, 1896–1932*, pp. 55–61.

[9] Paul H. Douglas, *Real Wages in the United States, 1890–1926* (Boston: Houghton Mifflin Company, 1930), pp. 43–46.

[10] *Ibid.*, p. 41.

[11] Frederick C. Mills, *Economic Tendencies in the United States* (New York: National Bureau of Economic Research, Inc., 1932), pp. 132–135; Paul F. Brissenden, *Earnings of Factory Workers, 1897–1927* (U.S. Bureau of the Census, *Census Monograph X*, Washington: Government Printing Office, 1929), pp. 56–76.

[12] Douglas, *Real Wages in the United States, 1890–1926*, Table 147, opposite p. 392.

[13] *Ibid.*, Table 25, p. 111.

unskilled labor in manufacturing, these years saw a decline in real wages,[14] but by 1917 they had almost recovered to the level of 1897. Summarizing the data of Douglas and other students of this problem, Mills estimates that the gain in real wages for all workers during the years 1896–1913 "was at the rate of one half of 1 per cent each year, representing a slow but sustained improvement in well being. The corresponding figure for employees of manufacturing plants is one tenth of 1 per cent a year. The earnings of these workers barely kept ahead of living costs during this period." [15]

Less technically, Don D. Lescohier pictures the labor situation between 1900 and 1914 as one "in which the cost of living was rising almost steadily, wage earners struggling, in some cases successfully, in others vainly, to keep their wages rising with the cost of living, a steady and large inflow of immigrants tending to retard wage increases, but a rapidly expanding industrial system and the easy profit margins of a period of expansion making increases in money wages attainable. Such improvement in welfare as labor was able to attain after 1900 came from more plentiful employment rather than from wage rates." [16] It would appear that the increased industrial productivity of those years resulted in no substantial addition to the real income of employed workers in general.[17] The federal Commission on Industrial Relations, for example, noted that while the nation's wealth increased between 1890 and 1912 from $65,000,000,000 to approximately $187,000,000,000 or 188 per cent, the aggregate income of wage earners in manufacturing, mining, and transportation had risen between 1889 and 1909 only 95 per cent. It also pointed out that the wage earners' share of the net product of manufactures had declined from 44.9 per cent in 1889 to 40.2 per cent in 1909.[18]

Although it is exceedingly significant to know that real wages increased but slightly from 1897 to 1914, it is even more important to discover whether the income of the typical wage earner was adequate to maintain a decent standard of living. What sort of monetary income did wage earners receive during these years? Carefully tabulated returns of the census of 1900 show that two thirds of the male

[14] *Ibid.*, pp. 174–184; Whitney Coombs, *The Wages of Unskilled Labor in Manufacturing Industries in the United States, 1890–1924* (New York: Columbia University Press, 1926), p. 119.

[15] Frederick C. Mills in *Recent Economic Changes* (New York: McGraw-Hill Book Company, 1929), II, 623–626.

[16] Lescohier and Brandeis, *History of Labor in the United States, 1896–1932*, p. 61.

[17] Mills, *Economic Tendencies in the United States*, p. 133.

[18] Commission on Industrial Relations, *Final Report and Testimony, Senate Document* No. 415, 64 Cong., 1 Sess., I, 21.

workers over sixteen received less than $12.50 a week, with only occasional groups paid as much as $18 a week.[19] The Interstate Commerce Commission reporting in 1900 showed that 82 per cent of the million persons, exclusive of executives, employed on railroads in 1899 received less than $2.50 a day.[20] The average wage throughout the nation was less than $2.00 a day and only the most highly skilled worker was able to obtain $3.00.[21]

Annual incomes, of course, give a truer picture of a standard of living than do hourly, daily, or even weekly incomes. This is particularly true of such seasonal work as building construction in cold climates. The United States Commissioner of Labor, reporting in 1903, put the average income of 11,156 normal families (a wage earning father, a mother, and not more than five children, all under fourteen) at $650.98 a year.[22] Specialists studying wage sales in 1904 and 1905 believed that at least two thirds of adult male workers received less than $600 a year.[23] Their findings were in part verified by the Census of Manufacturers in 1905.[24] Douglas put the average earnings in all industries (excluding farm labor) in 1900 at $490 and in 1914 at $682; the comparative figures (including farm labor) were $438 in 1900 and $627 in 1914.[25] Paul Brissenden put $449 as the "actual money earnings" a year for industrial workers in 1900 and $576 in 1914.[26] The Immigration Commission estimated the average annual earnings of male immigrants eighteen years and over at $455 in 1908–1909, the earnings of immigrant male heads of families at somewhat more, and the average annual family income of both natives and immigrants at $721.[27]

Prices were, of course, much lower in the first decade of the cen-

[19] U.S. Bureau of Census, *Employees and Wages* (Special Report for 1900), pp. ci–civ.

[20] Interstate Commerce Commission, *Thirteenth Annual Report of the Statistics of Railways in the United States, 1900* (Washington: Government Printing Office, 1901), pp. 39–40.

[21] For example, Coombs, *The Wages of Unskilled Labor in Manufacturing Industries in the United States, 1890–1924*, lists only one group of unskilled workers between 1900 and 1904, those in blast furnace establishments, as earning more than $12 a week. Their average weekly wage was $12.24 in 1900 and $12.76 in 1904.

[22] Commissioner of Labor, *Eighteenth Annual Report, 1903* (Washington: Government Printing Office, 1904), pp. 20, 90, 581.

[23] John A. Ryan, *A Living Wage* (New York: The Macmillan Company, 1906), p. 162.

[24] *Census of Manufactures: 1905*, IV, 645.

[25] Douglas, *Real Wages in the United States, 1890–1926*, Table 147, opposite p. 392. His estimates for 1914 are $682 and $627, respectively.

[26] Brissenden, *Earnings of Factory Workers, 1899 to 1927*, p. 53, Table 20.

[27] Immigration Commission, *Reports, Senate Document* No. 633, 61 Cong., 2 Sess., XX, 389–390, 413.

tury than in later years.[28] They were, however, increasing. Complaints of the high cost of living were frequent, and the fact that real wages for many groups increased slightly if at all at a time when industry and production greatly expanded led to various studies of the cost of living in relation to income.[29] These studies, made between 1906 and 1910, place the minimum for living wages for a workingman's family in the city at from $650 to $800. When compared with other estimates of income, these studies help to make clear the inadequate income of a majority of wage earning families to maintain decent living standards. From one half to two thirds of the wage earners received less than enough to meet such standards.

WORKING STANDARDS

The discouraging lack of progress in real wages between 1897 and 1914 does not mean that the condition of the wage earner did not improve in some respects during these years. In particular this was evident in the length of the working day, reduced as it was by technological changes, humanitarian legislation, and the efforts of organized labor. Agitation covering almost three quarters of a century had finally won the ten-hour day in most industries by the 1890's.[30] Using material first gathered by the United States Bureau of Labor and later by the Bureau of Labor Statistics of the Department of Labor, Douglas estimates the average hours worked in manufacturing industries at 59.1 in 1897 and 55.2 in 1914.[31] A notable difference existed, however, in the data collected in six unionized industries and in eight groups of "payroll" industries largely unorganized. The unionized group showed a decline from 53.4 hours in 1897 to 48.8 in 1914; the largely unorganized group from 61.9 hours to 58.2.[32]

[28] Massachusetts Commission on the Cost of Living, Report (Boston: 1900), p. 64; U.S. Commissioner of Labor, Eighteenth Annual Report, 1903, pp. 664–853.

[29] Louis B. More, Wage Earners' Budgets (New York: Henry Holt and Company, 1907), p. 269; Robert C. Chapin, The Standard of Life in New York City (New York: Russell Sage Foundation, 1909), p. 246; Ryan, A Living Wage, p. 145; Frank H. Straightoff, The Standard of Living among the Industrial People of America (Boston: Houghton Mifflin Company, 1911), p. 162; J. C. Kennedy and Others, Wage and Family Budgets in the Chicago Stockyards District (Chicago: The University of Chicago Press 1914), p. 79.

[30] Summarized in Lescohier and Brandeis, History of Labor in the United States, 1896–1932, pp. 97–106.

[31] Douglas, Real Wages in the United States, 1890–1926, p. 116.

[32] Ibid., pp. 112, 114. The author worked on the trolleys at a New Jersey seacoast summer resort in 1911 a 12-hour, 20-minute day for 7 days a week (84 hours, 20 minutes). The day was split into two working periods ("swing runs") of about 6 hours each, with 6 hours off between—the whole covering 18 hours, 20 minutes. The force was not unionized.

Generally speaking, the workday was longest in the baking industry and among the unorganized textile workers; shortest in the granite and stone industries and among newspaper printers. As a whole, hours were longer in the unorganized South, in the unorganized industries manned by Negroes and immigrants, and in rural rather than urban regions.

The movement for shorter hours, however, which began in the building trades and other highly skilled, unionized groups, spread rapidly to all types of workers and to all sections, and was speeded by the war. The following table shows that in 1909 the largest group of workers (69.4 per cent) were in establishments where the prevailing hours were 55 or over. In 1919, the largest single group (48.6 per cent) worked 48 hours a week or less, while 65 per cent worked less than 54 hours a week. By that year the eight-hour day (on the basis of six full days' labor) had been achieved by almost half of labor in manufacturing industries.

Prevailing Hours Per Week	Percentage of Employees in Establishments with Prevailing Hours		
	1909	1914	1919
48 or less	7.9	11.9	48.6
49–53	7.3	13.4	16.4
54	15.4	25.8	9.1
55–59	30.2	21.9	13.7
60	30.5	21.1	9.1
Over 60	8.7	5.8	3.0

Sources: U.S. Bureau of the Census, *Abstract of the Census of Manufactures, 1914* (Washington: Government Printing Office, 1917), p. 482; U.S. Bureau of the Census, *Abstract of the Census of Manufactures, 1919* (Washington: Government Printing Office, 1923), p. 444.

The decline in working hours, as well as the improvement of labor standards generally, was the result not only of the increased strength of labor organizations but also of the wave of humanitarian reform which swept the nation during the first two decades of the century. Both helped to bring the greatest bulk of labor legislation ever passed up to that time in a similar period in American history. Most of it was the result of state action. And it had to stand against state and federal courts manned by a judiciary grounded in eighteenth-century legal theory, unacquainted with modern industrial conditions, and conservative by nature. It was a judiciary which at one time or another held practically every type of labor legislation unconstitutional on the ground that it was "class legislation" or that it took away property without due process of law.[33]

Women and children probably gained the most from this legislation, but men also received great benefits. Efforts to reduce hours by legislation had begun in government work, the history of these efforts going back to the ten-hour movement of the 1830's. By the 1890's states and cities were attempting to reduce the working day to eight hours. Despite the fact that the right of a state to determine the conditions of a contract which it made seems clear enough, it was not until 1903 that the Supreme Court upheld the constitutionality of such labor legislation.[34] Except on public works, the constitutionality of hour laws and other labor legislation rested largely on the police power of the state as against property rights guaranteed in the Fifth and Fourteenth Amendments. As far as regulating hours of work on public conveyances was concerned, few questioned the police power of the state. If proof was necessary of the close relation between excessive hours of work and number of accidents, the Interstate Commerce Commission had supplied it.[35] Beginning in 1890 various states had sought to curtail hours, and in 1907 Congress passed a law applying to territories, the District of Columbia, and trains moving between states. It required ten hours' rest after sixteen hours of work for trainmen, and a nine-hour day for train dispatchers.[36] This law (upheld in 1914) made further state legislation unnecessary. The Adamson Act of 1916, although it made eight hours the basic day on interstate carriers, was fundamentally concerned with wages and was so interpreted by the courts.[37]

It should be noted that in transportation the police power of the state was used primarily to protect the traveling public rather than the workmen. When such power was used in other industries, notably mining, to protect the health and safety of the workers, it was challenged by the courts. The Supreme Court did uphold a Utah mining act in the famous case of *Holden v. Hardy*,[38] but a Colorado court ignored the decision a year later when it declared a miners' act unconstitutional. Nevertheless, at least seventeen states passed hour laws covering miners between 1896 and 1920. After the *Holden v.*

[33] Commission on Industrial Relations, *Final Report and Testimony*, I, 38–80.
[34] Atkins v. Kansas, 191 U.S. 207 (1903).
[35] Lescohier and Brandeis, *History of Labor in the United States, 1896–1932*, pp. 548–550.
[36] 34 *U.S. Statutes at Large*, p. 415.
[37] Wilson v. New, 243 U.S. 332 (1917).   [38] 169 U.S. 366 (1898).

Hardy approval of mining legislation, various states attempted to limit hours in other occupations where workers seemed to need protection. New York's effort, however, to limit bakers to ten hours was declared unconstitutional by the Supreme Court on the ground that it had "reached and passed the limit of police power." [39] The Lochner decision appeared greatly to restrict the field in which hour legislation might be applied, but subsequent decisions soon broadened the possibilities.

Limitation of work hours for women by legislation was more easily accomplished and made greater progress than that for men. Backed by labor organizations and by humanitarians outside labor's ranks, it seemed more clearly to fall under the police power of the state. This was true despite the fact that an Illinois eight-hour act for women had been declared unconstitutional by that state's supreme court in the Ritchie case of 1895.[40] It was not until 1908 that the United States Supreme Court, in a unanimous decision in *Muller v. Oregon,* established beyond question the constitutionality of women's hour legislation.[41] Up to 1896 some thirteen women's hour laws had been placed on the statute books, but all except three were virtually dead, and the Ritchie decision had questioned the constitutionality of all of them.[42] Nevertheless, eight states during the years 1896 to 1908 added hour legislation, including the great industrial states of Pennsylvania and New York. It was in the period from 1909 to 1917, however, that greatest progress was made when nineteen states and the District of Columbia enacted women's hour laws for the first time and twenty more improved existing laws. These improvements reduced working hours, restricted night work, and widened the scope to include larger groups of women.

Nothing was more indicative of the reform era than the mass of legislation to protect working children. Child labor legislation, of course, was not limited to the new century. In 1899 at least twenty-eight states had some kind of protection for children. Nine of them placed the minimum age for factory workers at fourteen years, but as a whole the laws were utterly inadequate. One student says that the typical child labor law before 1900 "remained limited in scope to children employed in manufacturing; set a minimum age of 12 years; fixed maximum hours at 10 per day; contained some sketchy

[39] Lochner *v.* New York, 198 U.S. 45 (1905).
[40] Ritchie *v.* People, 155, Ill. 98 (1895).
[41] 208 U.S. 412 (1908).
[42] Lescohier and Brandeis, *History of Labor in the United States, 1896–1932,* pp. 466–481.

requirements as to school attendance and literacy; and accepted the affidavit of the parent as proof that the child had reached the legal minimum age." [43] The objective during the following years was to strengthen the acts and extend them to cover the entire country.

More specifically the movement sought to improve standards which would prevent parents and employers from circumventing the age limits set in the laws, raise the age limits to bear a better relationship to the type of work done, exclude the child from work which might be injurious to health or morals, and ensure at least some reasonable provisions for education. The movement was helped by the rising consciousness of the evils of child labor, particularly in the South, where 25,000 children under sixteen were working in cotton mills by 1900, and by the active work of many organizations. Of these the National Child Labor Committee, organized in 1904, was the most effective. Vigorous and idealistic, it immediately drew up a model plan, which, with some revision, was published in 1911 as a "Uniform Child Labor Law." It included a minimum age of fourteen in manufacturing and sixteen in mining, a maximum workday of eight hours, a prohibition of night work between 7 P.M. and 6 A.M., and documentary proof of age.

When the Child Labor Committee was organized in 1904 not a single state in the union met these requirements. Despite the mass of legislation during the next decade and the great improvement in the situation which had curtailed by 1920 the work of children in industry by several hundred thousand, only nine states had met the standards by 1914.[44] Convinced that progress was too slow, particularly in the South, and that only federal legislation would accomplish the purpose, the National Child Labor Committee and other organizations backed the Palmer-Owen bill, passed overwhelmingly in both houses of Congress in 1916. It forbade the interstate shipment of products of mines or quarries produced in whole or in part by children under sixteen and of products of manufacturing establishments produced in whole or in part by children under fourteen who worked more than eight hours in one day or more than six days a week. The only persons who opposed the bill at the hearings were the representatives of Southern cotton mills and the counsel of the National Association of Manufacturers. Two years later the Supreme Court killed the act in a five-to-four decision holding that the power of Congress

[43] Elizabeth S. Johnson in Lescohier and Brandeis, *History of Labor in the United States, 1896–1932*, p. 405.
[44] *Ibid.*, p. 438.

over interstate commerce could not "control the exercise of the police power over local trade and manufacture." [45] Congress tried again in 1919 with an amendment to the Revenue Act that placed a 10 per cent tax on the net profits of any concern employing children in violation of the standards set up in the previous act. The Supreme Court declared this provision unconstitutional as a misuse of the taxing power.[46]

One notable effort to improve working standards during these years, namely minimum-wage legislation, had little effect at the time, but it did constitute "a great innovation in American thought and practice" [47] and prepared the way for such New Deal legislation as the Fair Labor Standards Act. The inspiration came from experiments in Australia and Great Britain, and started in America with the appointment of a Massachusetts commission to investigate the condition of women wage earners in 1911. The next year Massachusetts passed a minimum-wage law, nonmandatory and to be enforced only by publicity. In 1913 eight other states—California, Colorado, Minnesota, Nebraska, Oregon, Utah, Washington, and Wisconsin— enacted minimum-wage legislation. Two more, Arkansas and Kansas, were added in 1915, Arizona following in 1917. After that the movement declined. Only three more states, in addition to the District of Columbia and Puerto Rico, passed such laws before the Supreme Court temporarily ended the experiment in 1923 by declaring a District of Columbia law unconstitutional.[48] Massachusetts and Wisconsin struggled along with their minimum-wage laws and helped to keep the idea alive until the public and the courts could catch up.

In many ways the La Follette Seamen's Act of 1915 symbolized as well as any other piece of legislation the tremendous movement for improved conditions of labor. It was a federal law that affected radically the status of an entire group of workers, and it covered many aspects of labor legislation. Although laws governing this group of workers were incredibly antiquated and barbaric, efforts to improve them had been foiled by presidential veto and judicial interpretation. It took years of agitation by the International Seamen's Union and its leader, Andrew Furuseth, as well as a more progressive and humane era, to bring a radical change. Most important of the features of the seamen's act were those which abolished imprisonment for desertion. The act allowed seamen to demand one half of their wages

[45] Hammer v. Dagenhart, 247 U.S. 251 (1918).
[46] Bailey v. Drexel Furniture Co., 259 U.S. 20 (1922).
[47] Lescohier and Brandeis, *History of Labor in the United States, 1896–1932*, p. 502.
[48] Atkins v. Children's Hospital, 261 U.S. 525 (1923).

earned and unpaid in ports of loading and discharging cargoes and it abolished the system of allotments to original creditors. Work hours were reduced to at least two watches at sea (twelve hours) for seamen and to three watches (eight hours) for firemen. Nine hours was to constitute a day's work in port, with ordinarily no work on Sundays and holidays. Working and living conditions were improved by raising the minimum daily food allowance and by providing larger forecastles, hospital space, washrooms, men's rooms, and other facilities. Safety and job protective devices were put into the law by requiring that 65 per cent of the deck department must be able bodied seamen and that 75 per cent of the members of each department must be able to understand any order given by the officers.[49]

Shipowners asserted that the extra costs involved would drive an American merchant marine from the sea. To the seamen, however, it introduced a new era. Said the secretary of the Seamen's Union a year later:

It is impossible . . . to describe all the improvements that have taken place. The change has been not alone in improved safety, in the working conditions, and to some extent in the wages of the men, but the whole life on shipboard has been improved, and instead of the old spirit of bitterness and hatred . . . there is an air of freedom and a growing recognition of rights and responsibilities on the part of everybody connected with the ship.[50]

THE PROBLEM OF UNEMPLOYMENT

There can be no doubt that the decade of the 1890's was a bitter one for labor. Unemployment after the panic of 1893 was widespread and the suffering severe. With the end of the decade, however, the situation greatly improved. During the twenty years after 1899 the problem of unemployment became really serious only in the depression years 1904, 1908, 1914, and 1915. Otherwise these twenty years were years of rapid expansion of industry, national prosperity, and active employment. This relatively full employment was maintained despite tremendous immigration until 1914.

Data regarding unemployment during these years are quite in-

[49] 38 U.S. Statutes at Large, p. 1164; Selig Perlman and Philip Taft, History of Labor in the United States, 1896–1932 (New York: The Macmillan Company, 1935), pp. 160–163; Arthur F. Albrecht, International Seamen's Union of America: A Study of Its History and Problems (U.S. Department of Labor, Bureau of Labor Statistics, Bulletin No. 342, Washington: Government Printing Office, 1923), pp. 33–44.

[50] Albrecht, International Seamen's Union of America, p. 39; Proceedings of the Twentieth Annual Convention of the International Seamen's Union of America, 1916 (New York: Faehse and Dienhart Co., 1916), p. 32.

adequate and for agricultural labor virtually nonexistent. Paul H. Douglas and Aaron Director, however, have made two estimates, one for unemployment in manufacturing and transportation, and one for manufacturing, transportation, the building trades, and mining. The latter estimate for the four industries, two of which are seasonal, shows 18 per cent unemployment in 1897, 16.9 in 1898, 10.1 in 1904, 16.4 in 1908, 16.4 in 1914, and 15.5 in 1915. The lowest years were 6 per cent in 1917 and 6.3 in 1916. In summarizing their study of the four industries for the period 1897 to 1926, these authors estimate the average percentage of unemployment for this span of years at 10 per cent. If other occupations, such as public utilities, trade, domestic and professional services, and government employment are added, the average is slightly lower. The minimum percentage of employment in the four sets of industry was about 6 per cent, the maximum in periods of depression being as high as 20 per cent. Although these students admit a higher relative volume of unemployment in the 1890's, they perceived in the years following "no observable or pronounced tendency for the volume of unemployment either to diminish or increase." [51]

Unemployment in the 1890's was large, but it evoked little constructive thinking. The final report of the Industrial Commission, which ended the decade, gave less than 17 of its 1,134 pages to the unemployment problem.[52] Increased interest, however, was evinced during the early years of the new century, particularly in a partial solution through public employment offices. A report issued by New York State in 1911 showed that many had begun to realize that the problem was essentially industrial and economic rather than personal.[53] In February, 1914, the First National Conference on Unemployment was held under the joint auspices of the American section of the International Association on Unemployment and of the Association for Labor Legislation. In this same depression year a Second National Conference convened ten months later in Philadelphia. As a result of these two conferences appeared a "Practical Program"

[51] Paul H. Douglas and Aaron Director, *The Problem of Unemployment* (New York: The Macmillan Company, 1934), pp. 26–33. Hornell Hart, *Fluctuations in Unemployment in Cities of the United States, 1902–1917* (Cincinnati: Helen S. Troustine Foundation Studies, Vol. I, No. 2, 1918), pp. 48, 51–53, uses a more comprehensive group than do Douglas and Director, but reaches the same conclusion of about 10 per cent as the average number of unemployed.

[52] U.S. Industrial Commission, *Final Report*, XIX, 746–763.

[53] Lescohier and Brandeis, *History of Labor in the United States, 1896–1932*, pp. 129–132.

under the title *The Prevention of Unemployment*.[54] Besides offering a plan for a system of federal-state-local public employment offices, the program urged regular and emergency public works to relieve unemployment and recommended regularization of industry and unemployment insurance. As supplementary measures it urged industrial training, a constructive immigration program, an improvement of agricultural life to encourage people to remain on the land, reduction of excessively long working hours, and limitation of the working hours of children under eighteen. This program "sounded the keynote for the American attack upon unemployment from 1914 to 1933." [55]

Work relief of various kinds and the use of public works to relieve unemployment did not, of course, begin with the New Deal. Experiments of one kind or another were made in earlier depressions, notably in the 1890's, in 1914, and in 1921. In New York City, for example, the Mayor's Committee on Unemployment established during 1914–1915 a total of twenty-two workrooms for the unemployed which gave work to as many as five thousand daily from funds raised and administered by the committee.[56] Work relief provided from private funds, however, never was large. More important, although still inadequate, was work provided on public projects. Ninety-one cities in twenty-two states reported that they had provided special work of this type during the winter of 1914–1915 for the unemployed.[57] Although the relief work provided by private funds or by government appropriations during 1914–1915 was inadequate for the need, the experience was sufficient to make clear the problems involved. One result was the increased emphasis after 1914 on public works.[58] In December of that year the Second National Conference on Unemployment declared that "a careful arrangement of public works to be increased in slack seasons and lean years of private industry would help equalize the varying demand for labor. *Public works must be systematically distributed.*" [59]

Another important development from the depression of 1914 was the increased interest in the need for public employment offices. Private commercial employment agencies of one kind or another had existed for many years. Those dealing with unskilled manual labor

[54] *American Labor Legislation Review*, V, No. 2 (June, 1915), 176–192.
[55] Lescohier and Brandeis, *History of Labor in the United States, 1896–1932*, p. 132.
[56] *Ibid.*, p. 167.
[57] John B. Andrews, "American Cities and the Prevention of Unemployment," *American City*, XIV, No. 2 (February, 1916), 117–121.
[58] Lescohier and Brandeis, *History of Labor in the United States, 1896–1932*, p. 169.
[59] *American Labor Legislation Review*, V, No. 2 (June, 1915), 174.

had often been characterized by serious abuses, those providing aid in the placement of teachers and other professional and office workers had generally been conducted on a higher level. State legislative efforts to reform the former were nullified by the Supreme Court,[60] while the federal government did nothing either to remedy abuses or to provide a substitute system. The first public employment agencies of a permanent nature appeared in 1890 when Ohio established them in five of its cities. The number throughout the country grew gradually to reach ninety-six by 1914.[61] Interest in public employment offices rose with depressions and declined with better times. These offices, because of politics, public indifference, and small appropriations, fell far short of their possibilities, but they proved their worth and laid the foundation for further expansion both by the states and by the federal government. This expansion was speeded, at least temporarily, by the necessity of organizing the labor market during the First World War.[62]

Attention had been called in the 1890's and later to the possibilities of unemployment insurance as developed in Europe,[63] but little popular interest appeared in America until the 1920's.[64] The first unemployment benefit plans in the United States are found in the trade unions as early as 1831. In 1908, however, the United States Commissioner of Labor discovered only 10 out of 530 local unions paying unemployment benefits and little growth occurred in the next twenty years. The same may be said of company plans. The first employer voluntarily to establish unemployment insurance was the Dennison Manufacturing Company of Framingham, Massachusetts, in 1916, but the first benefits were not paid until 1920. The Columbia Conserve Company of Indianapolis began a plan in 1917 of guaranteeing a full salary of fifty-two weeks to a selected group of employees. Only one joint agreement plan between a union and an employer devel-

[60] Joe Adams, et al., v. W. V. Tanner, 244 U.S. 590 (1917), and Rubnik v. McBride, 277 U.S. 350 (1928).

[61] For map, see American Labor Legislation Review, IV, No. 2 (May, 1914), 208, and 359–371. See also Don D. Lescohier, The Labor Market (New York: The Macmillan Company, 1919), pp. 164–176.

[62] Darrell H. Smith, The United States Employment Service (Baltimore: The Johns Hopkins Press, 1923).

[63] John Graham Brooks, "Insurance of the Unemployed," Quarterly Journal of Economics, X (April, 1896), 341–348; William F. Willoughby, "Insurance against Unemployment," Political Science Quarterly, XII, No. 3 (September, 1897), 477–489; "Present Status of Unemployment Insurance," American Labor Legislation Review, IV, No. 2 (May, 1914), 375–387.

[64] Lescohier and Brandeis, History of Labor in the United States, 1896–1932, pp. 616–620. A bill was introduced into the Massachusetts legislature in 1916 but not passed.

oped before 1917. This was in the wallpaper industry, where a series of agreements beginning in 1894 sought to guarantee continuous work over most of the year.[65]

On the other hand, some progress was made through education in the transition of the worker from home to factory. Contrary to the belief of many, the Industrial Revolution by no means eliminated the skilled and the semiskilled. Their proportion might be smaller in the old industries, but their number often increased. Development of machinery might eliminate certain old skills and reduce the value of others, but it also created new trades and new skills. In any event, the old-fashioned system of apprenticeship was breaking down in America. Employers, who particularly disliked any control of apprenticeship by labor unions, came to depend upon a continuous supply of skilled labor from Europe and to search for new methods of supplying skilled native labor. In the development of new methods of industrial education various types of schools were started, some supported and supervised by governments, some by industry, some by labor unions, and others by a combination of two or more of them.[66]

The interest in industrial education was speeded by the annual report of the Commissioner of Labor on *Trade and Technical Education* in 1902. Between that date and a second report in 1911, seven states appointed commissions to study plans of industrial education, while eight states and many cities made provision for industrial training in the public school system.[67] In the meantime the American Federation of Labor began in 1903 to appoint committees to study the problem, and the National Association of Manufacturers established (1905) a standing committee on industrial education. Eventually both agreed that trade schools should be provided at public expense where both a general education and specialized shop training might be obtained. It was soon discovered, however, that such schools encountered great difficulty in providing adequate training for industry, and as a result, other types of training were developed after 1910.

Many large corporations, such as the General Electric Company in Schenectady and Lynn, set up their own schools to provide apprenticeship training and improve the efficiency of individual and

[65] Bryce M. Stewart, *Unemployment Benefits in the United States* (New York: Industrial Relations Counsellors, 1930), pp. 82–97, 227–361.

[66] Lescohier and Brandeis, *History of Labor in the United States, 1896–1932*, pp. 270–292.

[67] U.S. Commissioner of Labor, Twenty-fifth Annual Report, *Industrial Education,* 1910 (Washington: Government Printing Office, 1911).

factory. By 1918 the National Association of Corporation Schools had a membership of 146. At the same time many cities in cooperation with industry established "cooperative schools" where an attempt was made to combine privately administered shop training with public school education in general science. Lescohier describes these schools as a combination of instruction on the job, under true working conditions, with the continuation of general school training in such a way that the child was "educated simultaneously both as a productive worker and an intelligent citizen." [68]

Quite distinct from the corporation apprentice schools and the cooperative schools were the continuation schools designed for children who had received no formal education after they had left the elementary grade schools to go to work. Although much trade-improvement education had been offered, the emphasis had usually been on cultural education. The movement for continuation schools began with laws in Ohio in 1910 and Wisconsin in 1911. Other states soon followed, and in 1917 the federal government lent a hand in the Smith-Hughes Vocational Education Act of 1917.[69] The federal act distinctly emphasized vocational training, providing that federal aid was

to be paid to the respective states [on the basis of a dollar by the federal government for each dollar appropriated by state or locality] for the purpose of cooperating with the states in paying the salaries of teachers, supervisors, and directors of agricultural subjects, and teachers of trade, home economics, and industrial subjects, and in the preparation of teachers of agricultural, trade, industrial, and home economics subjects; and for the administration of the Act and for the purpose of making studies, investigations and reports to aid in the organization and conduct of vocational education.

There can be no doubt that vocational education increased rapidly in the years after the Smith-Hughes Act was passed.[70] It also seems fair to say that the end result of the various developments of apprenticeship and employee training just described was of substantial benefit to labor, particularly skilled workers. It also made an important contribution to the unemployment problem by educating young people for jobs and preparing them for better and more secure positions.

[68] Lescohier and Brandeis, *History of Labor in the United States, 1896–1932*, pp. 278–279.

[69] 39 *U.S. Statutes at Large*, p. 929.

[70] Paul H. Douglas, *American Apprenticeship and Industrial Education* (New York: Columbia University Press, 1921), pp. 293–314. See also Stewart Scrimshaw, *Apprenticeship* (New York: McGraw-Hill Book Company, 1932), pp. 136–185.

"SCIENTIFIC MANAGEMENT"

In 1897 the relations between employer and labor were still in the primitive age of the early factory system. Factories and industries had grown in size with no similar development in human relations. "Functional management," "personnel management," scientific time and operational studies, and intelligent wage systems were as yet in the future. The typical factory at that time was characterized by high accident rates, incredibly heavy labor turnover, and, judged by present standards, widespread inefficiency. A few employers were beginning to play with ideas of welfare projects, health and safety programs in factories, and profit sharing to promote greater efficiency, loyalty, and profits. A few were trying out plans of "employee representation" to promote efficiency and profits and to counteract the influence of unions. In general, however, the employer ignored the problems of human relations. He rarely considered that the answer to maximum production would be solved by considering the worker first as a human being.

Probably no influence was greater in changing the actual routine of factory work during the second decade of the century than "scientific management" as preached by Frederick W. Taylor and his disciples.[71] Taylor was convinced that careful studies of time and methods of work would reveal the quickest and best manner of doing the job, after which it could be pitched to the standard of the most efficient. By eliminating the incompetent and stimulating the best workers through wage systems believed to be psychologically sound, greater production might be obtained and higher wages paid. This was the core of a system which envisaged a more scientific approach to the whole process of factory production.[72] Remedies for existing inefficiency, Taylor believed, lay with management.

Taylor began the propagation of his ideas in a paper, "A Piece Rate System,"[73] presented to the American Society of Mechanical

[71] Such men as Henry L. Gantt, Carl G. Barth, Sanford E. Thompson, Henry R. Towne, Frank B. Gilbreth, and Harrington Emerson.

[72] The best bibliography on scientific management is Clarence B. Thompson, "The Literature of Scientific Management," *Quarterly Journal of Economics*, XXVIII (May, 1914), 506–557. It is reprinted in Clarence B. Thompson, ed., *Scientific Management* (Cambridge: Harvard University Press, 1914), pp. 3–48. See also Horace R. Drury, *Scientific Management*. (New York: Columbia University Press, 3d ed., 1922).

[73] Frederick W. Taylor, "A Piece-Rate System: Being a Step toward Partial Solution of the Labor Question," *Transactions of the American Society of Mechanical Engineers*, XVI (1895), 856–903; reprinted in American Economic Association, *Economic Studies*, I, No. 2 (June, 1896), 89–129.

Engineers in 1895, followed by another on "Shop Management" in 1903.[74] His theories took hold slowly, but after he became president of the American Society of Mechanical Engineers (1905–1906), wide-awake engineers and executives began to give them close attention. The Harvard Graduate School of Business Administration, founded in 1908, and the Amos Tuck School of Dartmouth, founded in 1910, both accepted Taylor's ideas as fundamental in factory production.[75] It was Louis D. Brandeis, however, who first brought them to wide public attention and popularized the term "scientific management." Retained by a manufacturer to oppose the application of the north-eastern railroads for an increase in freight rates, Brandeis rested his opposition (1910–1911) on the contention that greater efficiency would obviate the necessity of higher rates.[76] Brandeis called before the Interstate Commerce Commission engineers associated with Taylor and managers of companies which had installed the "Taylor system." One of the engineers, Harrington Emerson, startled the na-tion by asserting that the railroads of the country would save $1,000,-000 a day by greater efficiency.

Since 1916 the ideas and procedures of scientific management have been "so widely accepted and applied by so many thousands of engineers and managers that they have become commonplace in American industrial practice." [77] They contributed to make Ameri-can factories the most efficient in the world and to speed the devel-opment of mass production and the assembly line. This was true despite the increasing opposition of labor, which resented the stop-watch and time-measuring techniques of "scientific managers" which seemed inevitably to lead to the speed-up. When the War Depart-ment attempted to introduce scientific management into several government arsenals, the protests of labor were so great that Congress appointed a committee in 1911 to investigate. The committee made no recommendation for legislation, but opponents of scientific man-agement succeeded in 1916 in attaching riders to the army and navy appropriation bills withholding pay from officers, managers, or other supervisors engaged in stop-watch or other time-measuring studies.[78]

[74] *Transactions of the American Society of Mechanical Engineers,* Vol. XXIV; also Frederick W. Taylor, *Shop Management* (New York: Harper & Brothers, 1911).
[75] Frank B. Copley, *Frederick W. Taylor* (New York: Harper & Brothers, 2 vols., 1923), II, 288, 298, 353.
[76] Drury, *Scientific Management,* pp. 35–39; and Louis D. Brandeis, *Business—A Profession* (Boston: Small, Maynard & Company, 1914), pp. 306–312, reprinted from *Engineering Magazine,* October, 1911.
[77] Lescohier and Brandeis, *History of Labor in the United States, 1896–1932,* p. 315.
[78] 39 *U.S. Statutes at Large,* pp. 351, 619.

MANAGEMENT AND WELFARE PROJECTS

It might be supposed that "personnel management" would have developed inevitably as a counterpart of "scientific management." This was not the case; personnel management was largely an outgrowth of the labor scarcity of the First World War and a realization of the terrific waste resulting from large labor turnover.[79] Scientific management did, however, give some impetus to industrial welfare projects which were inaugurated to sugar-coat the introduction of time studies and speed-up.[80] The motive behind welfare projects varied widely. In some cases it was the humanitarian impulse of an influential member of a firm; in other cases an effort to discourage unionization. Sometimes it was the desire to obtain favorable publicity. More usually it was the hope of developing loyalty and obtaining greater steadiness of employment by reducing absence from illness, labor turnover, and strikes. Primarily it was the hope of "greater production at less cost." [81] Welfare work was "good business."

Welfare work, that is, service rendered by the employer to his workers over and above the payment of wages, was by no means new. Its first great development, however, came in the two decades after 1897, and it took a multiplicity of forms. One study of labor conditions published in 1917 mentions rest and recreation rooms, cloakrooms and locker rooms, lunchrooms and restaurants, clubrooms and clubhouses, first-aid rooms, bath- and washrooms, and hospital arrangements. It notes libraries and reading rooms, gymnasiums, recreation grounds, social gatherings, outings, music and lectures, kindergartens and playgrounds for employees' children, clinic and visiting-nurse service, vocational education and classes for instruction of foreigners in English, benefit associations for the relief of persons injured in accidents or incapacitated by sickness, pension funds for the disabled and aged, and group insurance. It declared that "of late there had been developed a system of physical examination of employees to ascertain their fitness for any occupation for which they apply"; and noted "considerable development in granting vacation and sick leave; particularly . . . in office and clerical work." [82]

[79] Lescohier and Brandeis, *History of Labor in the United States, 1896–1932*, pp. 323–335.

[80] *Ibid.*, p. 316.

[81] W. Jett Lauck and Edgar Sydenstricker, *Conditions of Labor in American Industries* (New York: Funk & Wagnalls Company, 1917), p. 227.

[82] *Ibid.*, pp. 228–230.

Even this list could be expanded, but it covers the most important fields into which welfare work was extended. Administration varied: in certain cases the company managed the welfare program; in some all or part of it was turned over to employees' organizations; in others the company cooperated with such outside organizations as the YMCA. The extent such welfare projects reached before 1917 cannot be exactly determined. One study believed that by 1909 welfare projects covered 1,500,000 employees.[83] The Bureau of Labor Statistics in 1913 described the welfare work of fifty-one larger employers,[84] but probably from fifteen hundred to two thousand firms at that time carried on some form of welfare activity. This rapid development appears more imposing than it actually was. It is doubtful, however, if more than 10 per cent of industrial workers benefited from such projects before 1910. Moreover, two important types of welfare management—medical treatment and safety and accident prevention work—were but little known before that date. At no time, even during the lush expansion of the First World War period, was welfare activity adopted by the majority of employers.

Among the types of welfare work mentioned, special note should be made of old-age pensions because of their subsequent history. Industrial old-age pensions began in America with a contributory plan of the Grand Trunk Railway of Canada in 1874, and was followed in the next year by a noncontributory plan of the American Express Company, and by a similar plan of the Baltimore and Ohio Railroad in 1884. By 1908 seventy-two rail systems, employing almost 955,000 persons, over two thirds of the total number of railroad employees in the United States, reported expenditures for pensions.[85] A few years later over eight tenths of railroad employees worked on roads maintaining formal pension systems. The Consolidated Gas Company set up an informal plan in 1892 and four banks had done so by 1900. Pension plans in manufacturing were hardly known before the twentieth century. The first enduring one was that of the Carnegie Steel Company in 1901, followed by an even more important plan in the Standard Oil Company in 1903. The first pension plans in mining and mercantile establishments were also set up from 1901 to 1905.

[83] William H. Tolman, *Social Engineering: A Record of Things Done by American Industrialists Employing Upwards of One and One-Half Million People* (New York: McGraw-Hill Publishing Company, 1909).

[84] Elizabeth L. Otey, *Employers' Welfare Work* (U.S. Department of Labor, Bureau of Labor Statistics, *Bulletin* No. 123, Washington: Government Printing Office, May, 1913).

[85] Murray W. Latimer, *Industrial Pension Systems in the United States and Canada* (New York: Industrial Relations Counsellors, 2 vols., 1932), pp. 20–26.

"So far as the non-railroad section of American industry is concerned," says Lescohier, "1910 represents for practical purposes the beginning of the pension movement." [86] In fact, 85 per cent of the 421 pension schemes started in the United States and Canada between 1874 and 1929 were established after 1910. Most of the plans in existence, even at the latter date, were in railroads and in the public-utility, iron and steel, and the oil industries where pension plans had originally started.

If pension schemes had made but little progress in the years previous to 1917, the development of profit sharing was even less notable. The idea had received early attention, but only fifty profit-sharing plans had been established before 1896 and of these thirty-three had been abandoned.[87] When the Bureau of Labor Statistics twenty years later surveyed the situation, it found only sixty "true profit-sharing" plans in operation (that is, profit sharing which benefited the wage earners), and more than two thirds of these were less than ten years old.[88] Of the sixty, four were organized in the 1880's, fifteen from 1897 to 1907, and forty-one in the period 1910–1916.

It should be remembered that there were many other "limited" profit-sharing schemes benefiting only a small group of workers in a concern, besides the sixty "true" schemes already mentioned. Nevertheless, this was a meager result to show for a half century of experimentation. The general opinion in 1916 was none too optimistic. The National Civic Federation, after an investigation and analysis of more than two hundred plans in the United States, reported that "many of these experiments have been abandoned as acknowledged failures." It did insist, however, that "many of them, from the standpoint of special local conditions or by contrast with some previous order of things, no doubt show a net improvement in the welfare of the employees affected and the morale of the plants." [89] Like other types of welfare work, profit sharing was motivated either by humanitarian employers or by those who believed that it was "good business." The movement did not make greater progress chiefly because the hopes of employers were not fulfilled. They came to the conclusion that profit sharing was not worth the cost. Opposition of

[86] Lescohier and Brandeis, *History of Labor in the United States, 1896–1932*, p. 388.
[87] Paul Monroe, "Profit Sharing in the United States," *American Journal of Sociology*, I, No. 6 (May, 1896), 685–709.
[88] Boris Emmet, *Profit Sharing in the United States* (U.S. Department of Labor, Bureau of Labor Statistics, *Bulletin* No. 208, Washington: Government Printing Office, 1917).
[89] Welfare Department, National Civic Federation, *Profit Sharing by American Employers* (New York: 1916), pp. 5–6.

organized labor, which considered it a substitute for adequate wages, was another important cause.[90]

Profit sharing received tremendous publicity,[91] but in the end, stockownership, particularly in the 1920's, was to exert more influence. Employee stockownership seems to have begun with the Illinois Central Railroad in 1893, but only three plans were started before 1900, fourteen between 1901 and 1905, and forty-three more between 1906 and 1915. The great development came in the next ten years.[92] The motives behind the promotion of stockownership by employees were much the same as those behind profit sharing, except that stockownership made the employee a part owner (even if a small one) in the firm for which he worked.

Without entering into the discussion of the interesting aspects of the dual position of capitalist employer and worker assumed by stockownership, of the investment value of the securities bought, or of the fact that the relationship between employer and worker was not essentially changed, it will suffice here to note some of the earliest plans. In the period before 1917 the sale of securities on the installment plan was limited chiefly to public utilities and large manufacturing plants. Later the movement spread into all types of industry. In 1900 the Pittsburgh Coal Company and in 1901 the National Biscuit Company established plans, followed by the Firestone Tire and Rubber Company in 1902, and the United States Steel Corporation and Proctor and Gamble in 1903. In 1909 the E. I. du Pont de Nemours & Company, the International Harvester Company, and the Commonwealth Edison of Chicago provided for stock sales to employees. The Brooklyn Edison adopted a plan in 1910, the Dennison Manufacturing Company in 1911, the Consolidated Gas and Electric Light and Power Company of Baltimore in 1913, and the American Tobacco Company and others in 1917.[93] Stockownership by wage earners, however, was too trivial during these years to have any appreciable effect on any aspect of industry.

[90] Lescohier and Brandeis, *History of Labor in the United States, 1896–1932*, pp. 371–380; National Industrial Conference Board, *Practical Experience with Profit Sharing in Industrial Establishments*, Research Report No. 29 (Boston: 1920).

[91] Emmet, *Profit Sharing in the United States*, pp. 173–188; "Profit Sharing and Labor Copartnership: A List of Recent References," *Monthly Labor Review*, XVI, No. 4 (April, 1923), 167–179.

[92] *Employee Stock Purchase Plans in the United States* (New York: National Industrial Conference Board, 1928) pp. 1–6; and Robert F. Foerster and Else H. Dietel, *Employee Stock Ownership in the United States* (Princeton: Princeton University Press, 1926), pp. 6–8.

[93] Foerster and Dietel, *Employee Stock Ownership in the United States*, pp. 6–7 and Appendix B.

It is hardly necessary to emphasize the fact that organized labor almost without exception opposed welfare work of every kind. Labor recognized that it was often introduced to counteract unionism, that it developed autocracy and paternalism on the part of the employer, and in turn suppressed initiative on the part of the employee. Labor insisted that welfare work including profit sharing was a substitute for higher wages and better working conditions. The National Civic Federation could find no labor leaders in favor of profit sharing, but quotes twenty-two leaders opposing it.[94] "To attain the greatest possible development of civilization, it is essential, among other things, that the people should never delegate to others those activities and responsibilities which they are capable of assuming for themselves," said the Reconstruction Program of the American Federation of Labor in 1918. These words, although directed against government control, are equally indicative of labor's attitude toward employers' welfare schemes.[95]

COMPANY UNIONS

Although organized labor was quick to see the dangers of welfare projects, it found the earliest forms of "company unions" somewhat confusing. In the early years they were called "employee representation plans," "works councils," or "shop committees," which sometimes graduated into complex systems of employee participation to which employers attached the grandiose term of "industrial democracy." As a matter of fact, relatively few had appeared before 1917. The great era of "employee representation plans," or "company unions," as organized labor called them, was in the 1920's. By the early 1930's some 2,000,000 wage earners were in organizations "initiated, nursed, protected and financed by the employers." [96]

The movement toward such plans or organizations began in the progressively conducted Filene store in Boston in 1898 where, as the years went by, employees were more and more called in to assist and were given wide jurisdiction over their own problems. Developments during the next few years, such as those in the Nernst Lamp Company of Pittsburgh and the American Rolling Mill Company in

[94] National Civic Federation, *Profit Sharing by American Employers* (New York: National Civic Federation, 1920), pp. 234–254.

[95] Hayes Robbins, ed., *Samuel Gompers, Labor and the Employer* (New York: E. P. Dutton & Co., 1920), p. 294.

[96] Lescohier and Brandeis, *History of Labor in the United States, 1896–1932*, p. 336.

1904, were largely in the form of establishing "factory committees" to confer with the management on matters on mutual interest. More elaborate were the Cooperative Welfare Association of the Philadelphia Rapid Transit Company (1911) and the Employees' Mutual Benefit Association of the Milwaukee Electric Railway and Light Company (1912), which began to look more like the company unions of later days.

Perhaps the most elaborate of all was the Leitch plan for "Industrial Democracy" first installed in the Packard Piano Company after a strike in 1912. This plan called for a house of representatives, composed of employees, a senate composed of foremen and union executives, and a cabinet composed of executive officials. In nomenclature it resembled the United States government; in actuality it did not, for the senate and cabinet were chosen by the management and the "little Democratic state," as Leitch called it, was really controlled from the top.[97] The "employee representation plan," however, which received the greatest publicity was that introduced by John D. Rockefeller, Jr., in the Colorado Fuel and Iron Company after the bitter strike of 1915.[98] A substitute for collective bargaining and by no means an unqualified success, it seemed to many people at the time an important step forward. Said one statement, "For a corporation whose traditional policy had so long ignored the slightest claims of labor to recognition and had insisted upon individual bargaining, the change to a policy of collective dealing through joint committees of its own men was a big step forward." [99]

Shop committees and various employee representation plans were given a tremendous impetus during the war, when the National War Labor Board virtually forced the election by workers of representatives to present, mediate, and adjust difficulties. Other government agencies added their pressure. By the end of the war local shop committees had become firmly planted in many industries.[100] During these

[97] John Leitch, *Man to Man, The Story of Industrial Democracy* (New York: B. C. Forbes Co., 1919), p. 140.

[98] Below, pp. 311–312.

[99] Carroll E. French, *The Shop Committee in the United States* (Baltimore: The Johns Hopkins Press, 1923), p. 18. The Rockefeller plan (originated in part by Mackenzie King, later Prime Minister of Canada) is described briefly in Paul F. Gemmill, *Present-Day Labor Relations* (New York: John Wiley & Sons, 1929), pp. 123–140, and more fully in B. M. Selekman and Mary Van Kleek, *Employees' Representation in Coal Mines* (New York: Russell Sage Foundation, 1924). Descriptions of many types of plans are given in Gemmill and in W. Jett Lauck, *Political and Industrial Democracy, 1776–1926* (New York: Funk & Wagnalls Company, 1926).

[100] Louis B. Wehle, "War Labor Policies and Their Outcome in Peace," *Quarterly Journal of Economics*, XXXIII (February, 1919), 321–343; *Collective Bargaining through Employee Representation* (New York: National Industrial Conference Board, 1933), pp. 6–11.

(*Above*) An open trolley car for summer transportation in Syracuse, New York, 1906. (*Below*) An early Rambler showing the chain drive. The horses seem interested but not greatly concerned. (*Both pictures Culver Service*)

(*Above*) Orville Wright flying one of the early airplanes in 1908. (*Bettmann Archive*) (*Below*) Building the Cape Cod canal. It was constructed in five years and opened in 1914. (*Brown Brothers*)

(*Above*) Child labor in a Northern factory. (*Below*) Child workers in a Southern cotton mill. (*Both pictures Brown Brothers*)

(*Above*) The Anthracite Coal Commission which mediated the coal strike of 1902. *Left to right:* Carroll D. Wright (Commissioner of Labor), Thomas H. Watkins, John M. Wilson, George Gray, Edward W. Parker, Edgar E. Clark, Bishop John L. Spalding. (*Courtesy The Scranton Times*) (*Below left*) John Mitchell, President of the United Mine Workers and leader of the strike. (*Courtesy The Scranton Times*) (*Below right*) Samuel Gompers, a founder and long a leader of the American Federation of Labor. (*Culver Service*)

(*Above*) A scene in the shirtwaist-makers strike of 1909 and (*below*) the clothing strike of 1912, both in New York. They represent the early activities of what later became the two strong clothing unions—the International Ladies' Garment Workers' Union and the Amalgamated Clothing Workers. (*Both pictures Culver Service*)

Scene from the famous Lawrence strike of 1912, led by the I.W.W. (*Brown Brothers*)

Children of strikers during the Lawrence strike, who were sent outside of the city to stay in the homes of strike sympathizers. (*Brown Brothers*)

A Sunday labor meeting held at Haledon, New Jersey, near Paterson during the Paterson strike of 1913. (*Brown Brothers*)

(*Above*) Threshing by hand, horse, and machine power about 1900. (*Below*) Harvesting on a small farm in Pennsylvania. (*Both pictures Culver Service*)

Thirty horses pulling a combine and harvesting wheat in the Northwest. This represents the final development of horse power agriculture before the coming of the tractor. (*Culver Service*)

years leaders of the American Federation of Labor seemed to hope that the shop committees would be steppingstones to unionism.[101] By 1919 they were quite disillusioned. An editorial in the *American Federationist* for September of that year (p. 829) asserts: "There is present in every case subtle efforts to delude the workers into the belief that they are exercising a voice in industry when as a matter of fact the employer holds the veto and deciding power. It is quite apparent that the underlying motive in all these schemes is to prevent the workers from organizing or joining a trade union or to weaken the trade union where it may exist and thereby disable the workers from entering into an effective strike to force the employer beyond his veto and deciding power." [102]

HEALTH AND SAFETY

However labor may have felt about welfare work in general, it distinctly excepted efforts made to safeguard the health of factory workers and to prevent accidents. By 1900 some of the most dangerous occupation poisons and dusts, particularly phosphorous, lead, and arsenic poisoning, had become known to a small group of medical men. This knowledge expanded slowly during the next ten years through private studies and government reports, and by 1911 there was actually in existence a considerable body of state legislation covering welfare and health in industry.[103] In the meantime the American Association for Labor Legislation had taken the leadership in the campaign against occupational diseases and had called the First National Conference on Industrial Diseases in June, 1910. At that time, said its secretary, John B. Andrews, "it was possible only to mention the appointment of the first state commission on occupational diseases and to note the completion of an investigation of one industrial poison. That practically marked the extent of serious public interest in diseases of occupation, and the first conference attracted attention to this as a new problem. Since then there has been a remarkable development of interest in the subject." [104]

[101] Lescohier and Brandeis, *History of Labor in the United States, 1896–1932*, pp. 345–348.

[102] Reprinted in Gompers, *Labor and the Employer*, p. 308.

[103] "Comparative Analysis of Existing Laws—Comfort and Health," *American Labor Legislation Review*, I, No. 2 (June, 1911), 6–59.

[104] *American Labor Legislation Review*, II, No. 2 (June, 1912), Introduction, 181. The commission referred to was that in Illinois and the investigation was that by John B. Andrews, *Phosphorus Poisoning in the Match Industry in the United States*, U.S. Department of Commerce and Labor, Bureau of Labor, *Bulletin* No. 86, Washington: Government Printing Office, January, 1910), pp. 31–44.

This "remarkable development" included federal legislation which virtually ended the manufacture of phosphorous articles. It included a vigorous attack led by the American Association for Labor Legislation and the United States Bureau of Labor Statistics on lead poisoning, and it marked the real beginning of improved sanitary conditions in the clothing industry. When a Second National Conference on Industrial Diseases was held in 1912 under the joint auspices of the American Association of Labor Legislation and the American Medical Association, it was the first time in its history that the latter organization had given a place on its program to industrial diseases. By that time numerous physicians throughout the country were employed by industry to treat occupational diseases, and many factories supported medical departments. A group of physicians heading these medical departments organized in 1914 the Conference Board of Physicians in Industry. When the United States Bureau of Labor Statistics surveyed in 1916–1917 the welfare work in 431 establishments covering over 1,000,000 workers it discovered a picture far different from that at the beginning of the century. It found medical service in 375 of these concerns, with hospital or emergency rooms in over 70 per cent, doctors in 45 per cent, and nurses in over 50 per cent. Nearly 197,000 cases were being treated a month in 261 medical departments.[105] Although the battle against occupational diseases continued and health work in factories expanded in later years, the period 1900 to 1920 was the significant era in the history of occupational health.

Massachusetts had passed an act requiring the safeguarding of machinery and elevators as early as 1877, and certain other states had passed similar laws and established inspection services, but the American safety movement did not start in an important way until about 1907. Lucian W. Chaney and Hugh S. Hanna, writing in 1917 on *The Safety Movement in the Iron and Steel Industry, 1907–1917*, assert that the period covered in their report "embraces practically the entire history of the safety movement, not only in the manufacture of iron and steel but in the whole field of American industry. Prior to that time efforts toward accident prevention had been made, but they were isolated, were individual in character and were not productive of any general results." The result was a frightful disregard of human life and "a condition not paralleled at any other time

[105] *Welfare Work for Employees in Industrial Establishments in the United States* (U.S. Department of Labor, Bureau of Labor Statistics, *Bulletin* No. 250, Washington: Government Printing Office, February, 1919), pp. 7–36.

or place." [106] In 1907, for example, the number of employees killed on steam railroads reached a record number of 4,534, an average of over 12 a day. The number of employees injured was 87,644, a number which was to increase to a record of 176,923 in 1916.[107] The number of fatal accidents in manufacturing industries in 1917 was 11,338, and of nonfatal, 1,363,080.[108]

The chief causes for the unprecedented frequency and severity of accidents during the years between 1903 and 1907 were the tremendous degree of business activity, the proportion of inexperienced immigrant labor larger than at any time before or since, and, of course, the absence of any organized safety effort as the term is understood today.[109] The rapid change after 1907 came, first of all, because of the merciless exposé and criticism by journalists of the needless bloodshed in industry.[110] Much ammunition was provided for this by the famous Pittsburgh Survey, which revealed the situation in one great industrial community.[111] In the second place, there was a realization by industrialists of the need and opportunity for safety prevention work. The leadership in this was taken by the United States Steel Corporation and the Chicago and Northwestern Railroad, and the remarkable results achieved were unanswerable proof of the possibilities of accident prevention work. [112] The enactment of workmen's compensation laws after 1911, which placed on the employer a large share of the cost of accidents, was another strong incentive to the development of safety work. The whole movement was aided by the establishment of the American Museum of Safety in New York City in 1907 (maintained since 1919 by the Safety Institute of America); by the founding in 1907 of the Association of Iron and Steel Engineers, which from the beginning had ardently promoted safety and from whose activities came in 1913 the formation of the National Council

[106] Lucian W. Chaney and Hugh S. Hanna, *The Safety Movement in the Iron and Steel Industry, 1907–1917* (U.S. Department of Labor, Bureau of Labor Statistics, *Bulletin* No. 234, Washington: Government Printing Office, 1918), p. 13.

[107] *Statistics of Industrial Accidents in the United States to the End of 1927* (U.S. Department of Labor, Bureau of Labor Statistics, *Bulletin* No. 490, Washington: Government Printing Office, 1929), p. 173.

[108] *Ibid.*, p. 14. Figures for "fatal accidents" do not include those in Kentucky and Connecticut which are included in "nonfatal accidents."

[109] Chaney and Hanna, *The Safety Movement in the Iron and Steel Industry, 1907–1917*, p. 13.

[110] Lescohier and Brandeis, *History of Labor in the United States, 1896–1932*, p. 376.

[111] Crystal Eastman, *Work Accidents and the Law; The Pittsburgh Survey* (New York: Russell Sage Foundation, 1910).

[112] *Statistics of Industrial Accidents in the United States to the End of 1927*, pp. 4, 127.

for Industrial Safety (National Safety Council). By 1917 the National Safety Council had 3,300 members and was promoting safety work both inside and outside industry.

One of the results of the great interest in accident prevention was the development in the United States of workmen's compensation laws, perhaps the most important tangible outcome of the wave of labor legislation which characterized these years. "No other kind of labor legislation," says one student, "gained such general accept- ance in so brief a period in this country." [113] Such legislation was pos- sible only after a fundamental change in the public attitude toward the whole problem of industrial accidents. First of all, the public had to see the injustice and inadequacy of the common-law approach to the problem. In the second place, it was necessary to understand clearly that the cost of an accident must be borne as far as possible by the industry (ultimately by the consumer of the product) rather than by the workmen, who had already paid the price of physical in- jury. Lawsuits brought by injured persons to determine whether an accident was due to the negligence of the employer, the workman himself, or a "fellow servant" made little sense in a highly mechanical age, particularly when the law seemed designed largely to protect the employer.[114]

Europe had taken the leadership in shifting the basic conception of handling industrial accidents from employers' liability to work- men's compensation. Following the lead of Germany, most European nations had adopted some type of workmen's compensation by 1897. It was a study of these experiments that first aroused interest in the United States. Between 1903 and 1909 forty commissions were set up either through legislative or gubernatorial action to study the prob- lem.[115] Unanimously they recommended abolition of employers' lia- bility. Under the old system they found recovery inadequate, uncer- tain, and slow. The system, moreover, was wasteful, with only a small percentage of the awards ever getting to the workers or their de- pendents, and it fostered misunderstanding and antagonism between worker and employer.

In the meantime legislatures had begun to experiment. Maryland (1902) and Montana (1909) had passed laws limited to certain in-

---

[113] Harry Weiss in Lescohier and Brandeis, *History of Labor in the United States, 1896–1932,* p. 575.

[114] *Ibid.,* pp. 564–569.

[115] *Workmen's Compensation Laws in the United States and Foreign Countries* (U.S. Department of Labor, Bureau of Labor Statistics, *Bulletin* No. 203, Washington: Government Printing Office, 1917).

dustries, but the courts held them invalid in whole or in part. A similar fate awaited New York's legislation, a more modern and comprehensive law passed in 1910.[116] Despite this adverse decision of the courts of New York State, a veritable deluge of compensation laws followed. At least ten states passed such laws in 1911 and three more in 1912. Wisconsin's law was the first actually in operation. By 1917 some forty states and territories had enacted workmen's compensation. Only in the ten southern states, North Dakota, and the District of Columbia had the legislatures failed to act.[117] Many of these laws were far from satisfactory. They were full of compromises, restrictions, exclusions. Some were compulsory, some elective or voluntary. None up to 1914 specifically covered industrial diseases. This hedging and timidity on the part of legislators was undoubtedly due in part to their uncertainty as to the constitutionality of the laws. Fortunately this barrier was largely cleared away when the Supreme Court on March 6, 1917, upheld three acts which covered most of the existing types of workmen's compensation laws.[118] In many ways workmen's compensation laws were the greatest contribution to labor legislation in the period 1897–1917.

[116] Ives v. South Buffalo Railroad Co., 201 N.Y. 271 (1911).

[117] Carl Hookstadt, Comparison of Workmen's Compensation Laws in the United States up to December 31, 1917 (U.S. Department of Labor, Bureau of Labor Statistics, Bulletin No. 240, Washington: Government Printing Office, 1918), pp. 9–13.

[118] New York Central Railroad Co. v. White, 243 U.S. 188 (1917); Hawkins v. Blakley, 243 U.S. 210 (1917); Mountain Timber Co. v. State of Washington, 243 U.S. 219 (1917).

CHAPTER XII

Advance of Organized Labor

POLICY AND PHILOSOPHY

ORGANIZED labor in America first won significant political and economic recognition in the two decades after 1897, and achieved strength beyond anything hitherto attained. The best estimates put total union membership at about 447,000 in 1897 and at 3,104,000 in 1917, a figure which was to increase to over 5,111,000 in 1920.[1] This growth, as will be noted in later sections, was by no means progressively regular. Membership was less in 1908 than in 1904, and there was a decline in 1914 and 1915 over that of 1913. Nor was the advance equally distributed. More than one fifth of the workers in transportation, mining, and quarrying were organized in 1920, but only one eighth in manufacturing, in the mechanical industries, and in the building trades. In agriculture the extent of organization was negligible. Moreover, it varied from industry to industry and from locality to locality. By the opening of the First World War it was strongest in transportation, coal mining, the building trades, and printing, with increasing membership in the metal industries and the needle trades. It was weakest in the South and in manufacturing.

Membership, it is clear, represented but a small proportion of American labor. Exclusive of agricultural workers, less than 4 per cent were organized in 1900, about 11 per cent in 1910, and only about 21 per cent as late as 1920.[2] But membership statistics tell only part of the story. There was an expansion in the area of workers included in the American Federation of Labor, an increase in affiliates (national and international) from 55 in 1899 to 110 in 1914. More-

[1] Leo Wolman, *The Growth of American Trade Unions* (New York: National Bureau of Economic Research, 1924), pp. 110–119 and Appendix.

[2] *Ibid.*, p. 85.

over, there was a consolidation of strength. In 1897 the Federation included about 59 per cent of 447,000 members of organized labor; in the succeeding years it drew to itself from 75 to 80 per cent. Outside its ranks in 1897 were the four railroad brotherhoods with a membership of about 100,000, and a few unaffiliated national or local unions. The latter included such unions as the Western Federation of Miners and the Bricklayers' and Masons' Union.

The growing development of organized labor rested on other factors as well as increasing membership. In general it included the most skillful, active, and capable workers. Moreover, it had attained by 1897 a certain maturity evident in greater financial stability, a willingness to embark on collective action, and a willingness to submit to a modicum of discipline.[3] In brief, a foundation had been laid for a strong structure of unionism which grew during the first two decades of the new century. Two other factors also aided labor. One was the spirit of reform which dominated the "muckraking era" and from which labor profited. The other was the prosperity which encompassed most of this period. The demand for labor gave the unions greater power. At the same time the increase in the cost of living spurred them to drives for higher wages and shorter hours, as did unfavorable government action and adverse decisions of the Supreme Court. The result was a sizable increase in membership.

Between 1886, when the AFL was founded as an amalgamation of the Federation of Organized Trades and Labor Unions of the United States and Canada with various other unions, and 1897, the AFL had experienced difficult times, but it had developed capable leaders, and a structure and philosophy which endured in the epochal years of the new century. The dominant personality was Samuel Gompers, president, with the exception of one year (1895), from the birth of the organization until his death in 1924. He stamped his philosophy, program, and personality so deeply upon the Federation that the story of his forty years of leadership is to a large extent the history of the American labor movement.[4] Others who shared his philosophy and made important contributions to the advancement of labor were Adolph Strasser, long-time president of the Cigarmakers' International Union; James Duncan of the Granite Cutters' Inter-

---

[3] Lewis L. Lorwin, *The American Federation of Labor* (Washington: The Brookings Institution, 1933), pp. 57–58.

[4] Gompers told this story in his autobiography, *Seventy Years of Life and Labor* (New York: E. P. Dutton & Co., 2 vols., 1925). See also Rowland H. Harvey, *Samuel Gompers, Champion of the Toiling Masses* (Stanford University: Stanford University Press, 1935).

national and first vice-president of the AFL for twenty-eight years; P. J. McGuire, president of the United Brotherhood of Carpenters and Joiners; John McBride and John Mitchell, leaders of the miners; and Frank Morrison, long-time secretary-treasurer of the Federation.

During the formative years organized labor had seen its energies dissipated in greenback, free silver, and "anti-monopoly" campaigns, had fought bitterly with socialists over control of the unions, had suffered the disastrous effects of the Homestead and Pullman strikes and the depression of 1893. Too many workers had dallied along by-paths to the millennium only to weaken the labor movement, or so it seemed to many labor leaders. Too often workers had seen state and federal legislation used against unions. From these experiences developed the philosophy and policy which dominated the movement after 1897.

In brief, this philosophy included what Gompers called "voluntarism," an opposition to socialism, a nonpartisan political activity, and an aggressive battle to win trade agreements and immediate improvements. "Voluntarism" was in a sense labor's way of meeting a laissez-faire philosophy and operating in a capitalist society. Reluctantly, for many early American labor leaders were sympathetic to socialism, did the leadership forgo a class-conscious socialism for "pure and simple" unionism. It had come to realize that labor could win public sympathy and approval necessary for further progress only by avoiding radical policies.[5] The leaders had seen the power of the government exerted too often against labor to welcome more of it, and they feared any plan which might deny the right to strike through compulsory arbitration. Moreover, labor as a whole did not consider itself a proletariat, and it was not opposed to capitalism or the wage system. What it wanted was an opportunity to work freely to obtain better conditions in the existing society. In the words of two labor experts, "The 'voluntarism' or anti-governmentalism of the Gompers group was not the result of an assiduous study of Herbert Spencer but of Attorney General Olney's invoking the Sherman Anti-Trust Law and the Interstate Commerce Act against striking railway men." [6]

What Gompers called the policy of "voluntarism" he made perfectly clear:

---

[5] The philosophy of the AFL is discussed in Selig Perlman and Philip Taft, *History of Labor in the United States, 1896–1932* (New York: The Macmillan Company, 1935), pp. 3–12; in Lorwin, *The American Federation of Labor*, pp. 41–54; and in Selig Perlman, *A Theory of the Labor Movement* (New York: The Macmillan Company, 1928), Chap. V.

[6] Perlman and Taft, *History of Labor in the United States, 1896–1932*, p. 6.

Several times [said he] the plain question has been put to me by members of the Senate Committee on Judiciary: "Mr. Gompers, what can we do to allay the causes of strikes that bring discomfort and financial suffering to all alike?" I have had to answer "Nothing." . . . Foremost in my mind is to tell the politicians to keep their hands off and thus to preserve voluntary institutions and opportunity for individual and group initiative and leave the way open to deal with problems as the experience and facts of industry shall indicate. . . . the most important human justice comes through other agencies than the political. Economic justice will come through the organization of economic agencies, the increasing adjustment of economic relationships in accord with principles evolved by experience, the formulation of material scientific standards, and the development of the principles and co-ordinating functions of management, based upon understanding and human welfare.[7]

As far as government was concerned this meant in practice that labor asked no favors, but it did insist that there should be no discrimination against it.

Although a nonpartisan political policy was an aspect of "voluntarism," its background was somewhat different. Labor was disillusioned with its unsuccessful contacts with early third parties. It understood the difficulties of organizing a new party in the American federal and constitutional systems. It knew further that it lacked sufficient strength and solidarity to warrant such a move. Labor was also suspicious of politicians, reformers, and intellectuals who would swarm into such a party to further their pet schemes. Convinced that the organization of a labor party was an unrealistic approach, labor refused to countenance such a move nor did the Executive Committee of the AFL ever, except in the La Follette campaign of 1924, endorse officially a presidential candidate.

But a nonpartisan approach did not mean that labor was nonpolitical. It continually endorsed candidates friendly to labor and followed a policy of "rewarding friends and punishing enemies." It used its power, when such power existed, in nominating candidates, securing results at elections, and lobbying on local, state, and federal levels. Its political action became particularly active after 1906. In that year it presented a Bill of Grievances to the President, the Senate, and the Speaker of the House, protesting against the failure of the government to enforce the eight-hour day, to restrict the manufacture and sale of the products of convict labor, to limit immigration, and to correct the misuse of the injunction and the Sherman Anti-

---

[7] Gompers, *Seventy Years of Life and Labor*, II, 26–27. Reprinted by permission of E. P. Dutton & Co., publishers.

trust Act. The grievances were followed by a program of economic and political demands.[8]

Failure to heed the Bill of Grievances led to active participation in the campaign of 1906 under a Labor Representations Committee and to a wide publicity of labor's program. Two years later the AFL, aroused over the use of the injunction, presented a moderate list of demands to both political parties. The Republicans not only ignored them but nominated William Howard Taft, known in labor circles as the "father of injunctions." The Democrats, on the other hand, inserted an anti-injunction plank approved by their candidate, William Jennings Bryan.[9] After that, Gompers and other leaders worked unofficially but openly for Bryan in 1908 and Wilson in 1912. The Democrats reciprocated by attempting in the Clayton Antitrust Act of 1914 to exempt labor unions from the antitrust acts and to soften the use of the injunction. After 1908 the majority of labor leaders tended to support the Democratic party from which it had secured most of the labor legislation.[10]

Whether nonpartisan politics was the wisest policy cannot be determined. But political activity undoubtedly aided in the mass of labor legislation enacted after 1906 both on the state and on the federal levels. Much of this was described in the last chapter. Among the gains in federal legislation should be noted the eight-hour day for government employees and workmen on government contracts; safety and hour legislation covering railroad workers; child labor laws in the District of Columbia, Puerto Rico, and the country as a whole; the establishment of a Department of Labor with a Children's Bureau; and the Lloyd–La Follette Act of 1912, which secured to government employees the right to lobby and affiliate with organized labor. This was climaxed, as already noted, by the anti-injunction clauses in the Clayton Antitrust Act (1914), by the La Follette Seamen's Act (1915), and by the Adamson Act (1916). As Gompers succinctly said, "I have always sought to use political situations for labor's advantage." [11]

[8] Report of the Proceedings of the Twenty-sixth Annual Convention of the American Federation of Labor, 1906 (Washington: The Graphic Arts Printing Company, 1906), pp. 32, 78–82; Lorwin, The American Federation of Labor, pp. 88–95; Gompers, Seventy Years of Life and Labor, II, 367–375.

[9] Lorwin, The American Federation of Labor, p. 92; Selig Perlman, A History of Trade Unionism in the United States (New York: The Macmillan Company, 1922), pp. 198–207.

[10] It was, however, under Republican President Herbert Hoover that the Norris-La Guardia Act (1932) was signed, the first effective anti-injunction act.

[11] Gompers, Seventy Years of Life and Labor, II, 77.

Refusal to stake its future upon a political party or to depend primarily upon political action threw labor back upon itself and its own resources. It strengthened its determination to fight its own battles by old-line trade-union methods and it became a philosophy built upon "economism" rather than upon large and sometimes distant humanitarian objectives. The policy had little to do with "ultimate ends"; it was an immediate struggle for higher wages, better working conditions, greater comforts, more education, and more of anything that might raise the workers' standard of living and position in the community. What labor really wanted, in the words of Gompers, was "more, and more, here and now."

This program was to be achieved through national and international unions closely integrated in themselves, but bound loosely together in a great federation. At the opening of the century the AFL was composed almost entirely of craft unions, but this method of organization was questioned as early as 1901. At the Scranton convention of that year the Federation insisted that it was "neither necessary nor expedient to make any radical departure from this fundamental principle," but it did "hold that the interests of the trade union movement will be promoted by closely allying the subdivided crafts, giving consideration to amalgamation and to the organization of District and National Trade Councils to which should be referred questions in dispute, and which should be adjusted within allied crafts' lines." [12] It was the latter statement that predicted the development of labor practice.

One writer in 1915 estimated that of the 133 national unions, most of which were in the AFL, 5 were true industrial unions, 28 were strictly craft unions, and about 100 were various intermediate types, most of which represented amalgamations of many groups. Of the industrial unions, those in the AFL at that time were the United Brewery Workers, the Western Federation of Miners, the United Mine Workers, and the Quarry Workers' International Union. Actually by 1914 the AFL had become in fact mainly a group of "amalgamated craft organizations." They maintained a craft psychology while they continually reached out to amalgamate workers in new processes and interrelated trades.[13]

Cursed by factionalism, dual unionism, and outlaw strikes, the

12 *Report of the Proceedings of the Twenty-first Annual Convention of the American Federation of Labor* (Washington: Globe Printing Company, 1901), p. 240.
13 Theodore W. Glocker, "Amalgamation of Related Trades in American Unions," *American Economic Review*, V, No. 3 (September, 1915), 554–575 and Lorwin, *The American Federation of Labor*, pp. 305–306, 489–491.

Federation encouraged the amalgamation of various craft unions and also the organization of state federations and city central bodies. Moreover, this policy was continued through the chartering of a Building Trades Department and a Metal Trades Department in 1908. In the following year a Railroad Employees' Department and a Union Label Department were added. The first three groups were to settle jurisdictional disputes and promote united action in their trades; the Union Label Department was to promote the use of goods marked by a union label or services covered by a union sign.[14] Efforts at amalgamation and unified action strengthened labor in the industries affected and brought more favorable trade agreements, higher wages, and better conditions. But even with a development of amalgamation and unified effort, the Federation faced the continual criticism of weakness through lack of unity.

Better conditions were to be won through recognition of the union, collective bargaining, and then a trade agreement to clinch the decisions reached. The trade agreement became one of the accepted principles and main objectives of the American labor movement. John Mitchell asserted that "the hope of future peace in the industrial world lies in the trade agreement," and here he echoed the belief of other labor leaders.[15] This technique meant careful preparation for labor conflicts by high dues, large strike funds, and systems of benefits, and it meant the cautious use of strikes, boycotts, and sympathetic strikes. It meant organization, restraint, compromise, conciliation, sometimes voluntary arbitration, and discipline on the part of labor in carrying out the terms of agreements.[16] This technique was essentially a peaceful one and looked in the end toward a dual responsibility of employer and labor union regarding work and wages. Labor was eager to gain its ends peacefully, but it was prepared to use the strike, the boycott, or any other weapon in the arsenal of labor conflict.

Lorwin describes the unionism of the Federation in 1898 as "craft, job conscious, business, and wage conscious." Except for some decline in the emphasis on craft organization this description remained true in 1917. So also does his further comment: "Wage consciousness was combined with the idea of a gradual elevation in the social posi-

[14] Lorwin, *The American Federation of Labor,* pp. 93–95; *Report of the Proceedings of the Thirty-second Annual Convention of the American Federation of Labor,* 1912 (Washington: The Law Reporter Printing Company, 1912), p. 29.

[15] John Mitchell, *Organized Labor* (Philadelphia: American Book and Bible House, 1903), p. 347.

[16] Lorwin, *The American Federation of Labor,* pp. 47–48.

tion of the workers. Gompers coined the vague phrase 'pure and simple unionism,' to describe the mixed elements of craft unionism, inchoate syndicalism, social meliorism, vague humanitarianism, and practical opportunism which entered into the make-up of the Federation." [17] These elements had persisted and even been strengthened by the development of the Socialist party, the reform movement of the first decade of the century, and the growing participation of labor in politics and in its demands for social legislation.

THE RAILROAD BROTHERHOODS

What has been said regarding the philosophy, structure, and technique of the AFL applies largely to the railroad brotherhoods, the most important of the independent unions during these years.[18] All four were founded before the AFL, and all four have refused to throw in their lot with the larger movement. Unlike the typical labor organizer, the founders of the brotherhoods were more interested in mutual insurance and benefit societies than in starting labor unions as such. Since railroading is a particularly dangerous occupation, the ordinary insurance company would not sell policies to railroad men. This forced the new railroad unions to organize their own insurance companies, and as the years went by, these companies became relatively large and wealthy concerns. Anxious to conserve this wealth and safeguard their resources, the brotherhoods tended to avoid the strike, the most costly of labor's weapons.[19]

A second conservative influence was the fortunate situation in which the brotherhoods were able to obtain their demands without striking. The severe railroad strikes in the 1870's and 1880's between the "robber barons" and the young railroad unions became rare by the 1890's. The brotherhoods had grown stronger with the years, for most of the operating men had found it advantageous to join them. Since railroading requires skill, the brotherhoods did not have to face the competition of low-paid, unskilled labor. Their strategic position was strong, and when they began in the late eighties to press for recognition, higher wages, and seniority rights, they were generally successful.

Eventually this favorable position changed. The rising cost of living after 1900 brought repeated demands for higher wages. Until

[17] *Ibid.*, pp. 50–51.
[18] The Locomotive Engineers (founded 1863), Railroad Conductors (1868), Locomotive Firemen and Engineers (1873), and Railroad Trainmen (1883).
[19] Perlman, *History of Trade Unionism in the United States*, pp. 180–186.

the Hepburn Act of 1906 the railroads had been able to pass on the cost of increased wages to the consumer; with rates and fares under government control after 1906, it was no longer possible. In such a situation both employers and workers were amenable to mediation. During the Cleveland administration Congress had passed an act providing for voluntary railroad mediation. This was superseded by the Erdman Act of 1898, which provided that either management or employees' organizations could ask the Commissioner of Labor and the Chairman of the Interstate Commerce Commission to act as mediators. Mediation failing, resort could be made to a board of arbitration, one representative from each side, and a third chosen by the other two. An award had to come within thirty days after the appointment of this board and was binding for a year. This act was improved in detail and strengthened by the Newlands Act of 1913.

Repeatedly after 1907, resort was made to arbitration and mediation, with results unsatisfactory to labor. Particularly disconcerting was a recommendation of the arbitration board in 1912 that arbitration on railroads be compulsory. Failure to obtain satisfactory results from arbitration gradually changed the mild, cautious, and conservative brotherhoods into fighting unions. When in 1916 they demanded a basic eight-hour day in determining wage scales and negotiation failed, the brotherhoods emphatically rejected arbitration, even when urged by President Wilson. They called a strike for September 4, and preparations were well under way when Wilson appeared before Congress on August 30 and asked, among other things, for an eight-hour day in train service, an enlargement of the Interstate Commerce Commission, and compulsory arbitration. Congress replied by the Adamson Act making eight hours the legal day, the men to be paid the same wage as on their old schedule, usually ten hours. Work in excess of the legal day was to be paid pro rata, and a commission was created to watch the workings of the shorter day and report to Congress within ten months after the law went into effect.[20]

The railroads refused to obey the law until it had been tested by the courts and the brotherhoods made preparation in March to strike again. However, the Supreme Court upheld the act on March 19, 1917, by a five-to-four decision.[21] The brotherhoods had picked the psychological moment for their battle: business was good, railroad revenues were high, traffic in the months before American entry into the war glutted the railroads, and skilled labor was scarce. Moreover

[20] 39 U.S. *Statutes at Large*, p. 721.
[21] Wilson v. New, 243 U.S. 332 (1917).

the argument for the eight-hour day in a highly dangerous occupation was valid. Says Edwin A. Robbins: "Never before in the history of industrial warfare have 400,000 employees received an eight-hour day without reduction of wages, the loss of one hour of work, or the expenditure of a cent of strike money." [22] Nevertheless, the brotherhoods were subjected to severe criticism for picking this particular time and Congress and the President were assailed for bowing to the unions.

THE FIRST GREAT ADVANCE

Organized labor in America has had three great periods of growth and prosperity: the first from 1897 to 1904, the second during the period of the First World War, and the third in the years of the New Deal administration and the Second World War. Between 1897 and 1904, the AFL increased from 264,825 to 1,676,200, and the total trade-union membership from 447,000 to 2,072,700.[23] Although this growth was largely a swelling of craft internationals already in existence, it represented much geographical spread and a movement into the smaller cities.[24] The greatest progress was in the building trades, in the metal trades, in mining, in personal service, and among the longshoremen and teamsters. The reasons are not difficult to find. The hard school of experience and the bitter industrial struggles of the 1880's and 1890's had developed a discipline, cohesion, confidence, and steadiness of purpose. The AFL had established its leadership in the labor world and was becoming a national force. Like business and capital, which had grown tremendously and consolidated their resources in the wave of prosperity after the Spanish-American War, organized labor took advantage of the upswing of the economic cycle. The need for activity was particularly urgent since the strength of capital was growing more rapidly than that of labor.

Gompers himself attributed the rapid advance to preparation. "It was," he said, "the harvest of the years of organizing work which were

[22] Edwin A. Robins, "The Trainmen's Eight Hour Day," *Political Science Quarterly*, XXXI, No. 4 (December, 1916), 541–557 and XXXII, No. 3 (September, 1917), 412–428; also Perlman and Taft, *History of Labor in the United States, 1896–1932*, pp. 374–385; Edward Berman, *Labor Disputes and the President of the United States* (New York: Columbia University Press, 1924), pp. 73–76, 106–124.

[23] Appendix, p. 421. In 1904 the AFL had 114 international unions, 828 directly affiliated locals, 549 city locals, and 29 state federations. Receipts on a 4 cent per capita tax rose from $18,639 in 1898 to $220,995 in 1904. It had increased its paid organizers from 20 in 1900 to 99 in 1904.

[24] Perlman and Taft, *History of Labor in the United States, 1896–1932*, pp. 13–19.

beginning to bear fruit." [25] But it was much more than that; these were the "heroic" days of unionism, a period of high idealism, self-sacrifice, and aggressive action. Moreover, aid came from outside the ranks of labor, notably from the National Civic Federation. This organization was an outgrowth of the Chicago Civic Federation, founded in 1893 to study civic problems and promote better relations between capital and labor.[26] It proved sufficiently successful to extend its operations on a wider scale in 1900, when a national organization was founded with Mark Hanna as president and Samuel Gompers as vice-president. According to its preamble of 1900 its purpose was "to show that organized labor cannot be destroyed without debasement of the masses . . . that organized labor can correct its errors . . . that capital can be taught the practicability of securing industrial peace in accordance with business methods." [27]

Translated into action, this statement meant that the National Civic Foundation attempted to bring together capitalists, employers, workers, and representatives of the public to avoid strikes and lockouts, promote trade agreements, and provide machinery for mediation and conciliation. It entered specific strike situations and in some cases brought settlements, and it vigorously opposed the "open-shop" propaganda of the National Association of Manufacturers.[28] To socialist trade unionists, the affiliation of labor leaders with such an organization was little short of treason, while "open-shop" employers were equally opposed. Gompers, on the other hand, felt that the organization provided contacts which "contributed to the making of a new concept of human relations in industry and to laying the foundation for the rule of reason." [29] At the same time many manufacturers with their eyes on expanding markets and engaged in large projects of consolidation were not averse to the propaganda of the National Civic Federation, if it provided security against strikes.[30] So far had the rapprochement progressed that one labor historian has called these years "a honeymoon period of capital and labor." [31]

Although growth of organization was undoubtedly the greatest single factor in the advancing status of labor, it should not be for-

[25] Gompers, *Seventy Years of Life and Labor*, II, 104–105.
[26] Herbert Croly, *Marcus Alonzo Hanna* (New York: The Macmillan Company, 1912), p. 388.
[27] Elsie Gluck, *John Mitchell* (New York: The John Day Company, 1929), p. 85.
[28] Perlman and Taft, *History of Labor in the United States, 1896–1932*, pp. 48–49.
[29] Gompers, *Seventy Years of Life and Labor*, II, 106.
[30] Lorwin, *The American Federation of Labor*, p. 62.
[31] Selig Perlman in Commons and Others, *History of Labor in the United States*, II, 524.

gotten that the sympathy of the public or the lack of it was often the determining influence in victory or defeat. Whether the National Civic Federation greatly helped labor's advance is difficult to determine. Many labor leaders believed that it had made a contribution. Help also came from other outside organizations—the National Consumers' League, organized in 1898 to combat the sweatshop evil; the National Child Labor Committee, formed in 1904 to agitate for the abolition of child labor; and the American Association of Labor Legislation, founded in 1906 to promote better labor legislation and the stricter enforcement of existing laws. Such aid was welcomed, for it was given by organizations which asked nothing in return.

A glance at the records, however, is clear proof that labor's progress was due to an aggressive fighting spirit as well as to preparation, outside sympathy, and other factors. An exhaustive study of strikes from 1881 to 1905 made by the Commissioner of Labor reveals the fact that the total number of strikes in the six years 1893–1898 was 7,029 and that this number more than doubled to 15,463 in the next six years, 1899–1904. The average number of strikes a year during the two periods increased from 1,171 to 2,577, and the number of workers involved from 1,684,249 during the first period to 2,564,782 in the second. These, of course, are raw figures of strikes lasting twenty-four hours or longer and do not include estimates of shorter strikes or the number of days lost by nonstrikers as a result of strikes. Nor do they cover lockouts, which numbered 922 from 1893 to 1895 with almost 500,000 thrown out of work.[32]

After 1905 no adequate strike statistics are available until 1916. When the causes of these strikes were examined, students of labor history saw a distinct improvement in the status of labor. Three fifths of the strikes called in 1881 were for increased wages and but one sixteenth for recognition of the union, whereas in 1905 less than one third were for higher pay and about an equal proportion for recognition. Moreover, although the unions were responsible for less than half the strikes in 1881, they instigated directly or indirectly three fourths of those in 1905. During the whole period, workers won all of their demands in 48 per cent of the establishments, lost in 37 per cent, and partly succeeded in 15 per cent.[33]

[32] United States Commissioner of Labor, *Twenty-first Annual Report*, 1906 (Washington: Government Printing Office, 1907), p. 15; Lorwin, *The American Federation of Labor*, p. 61.

[33] The strikes are analyzed in George G. Groat, *Organized Labor in America* (New York: The Macmillan Company, 1916), pp. 159–187, and Paul H. Douglas, "An Analysis of Strike Statistics, 1881–1921," *Journal of the American Statistical Association*, XVIII, U.S., No. 143 (September, 1923), 866–877.

The increase in strikes was not the result of any noticeable change in the philosophy of the AFL regarding this type of action. Excerpts from the annual proceedings of the AFL and its predecessor, going back to 1884 and reprinted in the *History, Encyclopedia and Reference Book* for 1919, show a consistent position. Strikes were to be avoided when possible, and used only as a last resort. The strike, however, was a legitimate weapon which often accomplished much even when apparently it had failed. The position was stated clearly as far back as 1884:

> While conscious of the fact that the strike is an industrial war, whose precipitation is to be avoided if possible, and whose consequences are often lamentable, we are yet convinced this war is sometimes a necessity, as affording the only alternative against outrageous injustice and intolerable oppression. . . . We contend that the strike, when based on justice, conducted with discretion, and used as a last resort, is a perfectly legitimate weapon, whose force is moral as well as physical, and whose results are often more beneficial than its apparent ending would indicate.[34]

Aggressive labor action combined with a more sympathetic understanding of the aims of labor by employer groups brought numerous "trade agreements" and improvements in labor conditions. Trade agreements on a large scale began in the machinery and metal trades when the National Founders Association (organized in 1898) created machinery for arbitration in 1899 with the International Molders' Union of North America. In the following year a similar pact (Murray Hill Agreement) was signed between the National Metal Trades Association and the International Association of Machinists. Unfortunately, neither agreement lasted long, and the metal trades soon returned to a condition of warfare and chaos.[35] More successful was the ten-year battle between the International Typographical Union and the United Typothetae, which finally won both a trade agreement and the eight-hour day. This long battle illustrated labor tactics and statesmanship at their highest level. Nor were the printing trades the only group of workers to win the eight-hour day. By 1900 the building trades, the granite workers, and many of the bituminous coal miners had achieved that fortunate position.

During these years of expansion, labor improved its position and

---

[34] *Report of the Fourth Annual Session of the Federation of Organized Trades and Labor Unions of the United States and Canada,* 1884 (published by direction of the Federation, n.d.), p. 10.

[35] Perlman and Taft, *History of Labor in the United States, 1896–1932,* pp. 110–116; Perlman, *A History of Trade Unionism,* pp. 186–190.

won important victories on many fronts. The building trades particularly increased their strength in the prosperous years after 1897.[36] Along with other unions they became so strong in San Francisco as to virtually take over the city government.[37] Perhaps the most spectacular successes were in the mining industry. As late as 1897 only a mere handful of bituminous miners, perhaps 10,000, mostly in Ohio, were organized. Nevertheless, the time seemed ripe for action, and when the leaders called a strike in that year, at least 100,000 dropped their tools. Unqualified victory followed a twelve weeks' struggle, including a 20 per cent wage increase, an eight-hour day, the abolition of company stores, recognition of the union, and a provision for annual joint conferences with the operators. This success did much to stabilize the chaotic conditions in the central bituminous region; on the other hand, the United Mine Workers made little headway among the Negroes and the mountain whites in West Virginia.

More difficult were the problems of organization and improvement of conditions in the anthracite regions of northeastern Pennsylvania. Here the miners were chiefly immigrants; moreover, the operators were so closely joined in a community of interest that anthracite mining was virtually a monopoly. The industry was largely controlled by the eight railroads which tapped the region, and these railroads in turn were dominated by Morgan and the most powerful capitalists of the day. The United Mine Workers had about 8,000 members in the region. Nevertheless, when John Mitchell, able leader of the miners, called a strike in 1900 for higher wages and recognition of the union, over 100,000 responded. Under the influence of Mark Hanna, who feared the effect of the strike on McKinley's prospects in the impending presidential campaign, the operators compromised.

But 1900 was merely a curtain raiser to the more important strike of 1902. This time the hard-coal miners demanded an eight-hour day, a 20 per cent increase in wages, payment according to weight of coal mined, and recognition of the union. Under Mitchell's skillful leadership, and aided by large contributions from his soft-coal miners, the strikers held their ranks firm from May to October. Repeatedly the

[36] Perlman and Taft, *History of Labor in the United States, 1896–1932,* pp. 82–96.
[37] *Ibid.,* pp. 71–81; Harold U. Faulkner, *The Quest for Social Justice* (New York: The Macmillan Company, 1931), pp. 96–98; Franklin Hichborn, *The System as Uncovered by the San Francisco Graft Prosecution* (San Francisco: J. H. Berry, 1915); Frederick L. Ryan, *Industrial Relations in the San Francisco Building Trades* (Norman: University of Oklahoma Press, 1934).

miners offered to arbitrate and as often the operators refused. Brushing aside all arguments for improved working conditions or decent standards of living, George F. Baer, spokesman of the operators, insisted that "anthracite mining is a business, and not a religious, sentimental or academic proposition." [38] He also asserted that the "rights and interests of the laboring man will be protected and cared for not by labor agitators but by the Christian men to whom God has given control of the property rights of the country." [39]

As winter approached with a threatening coal famine, President Theodore Roosevelt sent his Commissioner of Labor, Carroll D. Wright, to investigate the Pennsylvania coal situation and called a conference of operators and miners at the White House on October 3. Again the miners agreed to submit their claims to a tribunal if the operators would accept the decisions, but the operators again refused. This intransigence aroused Roosevelt and alienated the public. The President threatened to take over the mines, but his Secretary of War, Elihu Root, persuaded Morgan to accept mediation. The President then appointed an Anthracite Coal Strike Commission of seven and the miners returned to work on October 23.

Between October and March 18, when its report was submitted, the commission listened to 558 witnesses. It heard operators and an imposing array of lawyers denounce unionism, assert that conditions were satisfactory, and insist upon a continuation of laissez faire. It also listened to Clarence Darrow, Henry Demarest Lloyd, and others bring out testimony on the high accident rates (one death to 117,000 tons of coal mined), the long hours, the low pay, and the unsatisfactory living conditions. It was a major economic battle in an important natural resource industry between a virtual monopoly of owners and workers seeking union rights and better conditions. The commission awarded a 10 per cent increase in pay to contract miners, a nine-hour day to "day men" with the same pay, equivalent to a 10 per cent increase, and the right of miners to elect and pay their own checkweighman. The commission directed that the distribution of cars be equitable, that contract miners' helpers be paid directly by the owners, and that there be no discrimination by miners or employers in the hiring of union or nonunion men. It fixed the price of anthracite at $4.50 a ton at tidewater and directed that a 5 cent increase in

[38] *Report of the Anthracite Coal Commission* (U.S. Department of Labor, *Bulletin* No. 46, Washington: Government Printing Office, May, 1903), p. 461.

[39] Quoted in Ray Allen Billington, Bert James Loewenberg, and Samuel Hugh Brockunier, eds., *The Making of American Democracy* (New York: Rinehart & Company, Inc., 1950), II, 300.

price called for a 1 per cent increase in wages. The awards were for three years with an arbitration board to adjust disputes.[40]

Although the gains were tangible, the total awards were a compromise. It will be noted that the commission did not grant union recognition. It took two more strikes in 1912 and 1916 to win that recognition and an eight-hour day. What made the strike of 1902 the "most important single event in the history of American trade unionism until that time," says Perlman, was "that for the first time a labor organization tied up for months a strategic industry and caused wide suffering and discomfort to the public without being condemned as a revolutionary menace to the existing social order calling for suppression by the government . . . ."[41] On the contrary, it won wide public sympathy as a legitimate struggle against a powerful and dangerous monopoly.

EMPLOYERS' COUNTEROFFENSIVE

The success of labor and the increasing industrial strife brought inevitable opposition. Local employers' associations and Citizens' Alliances began to spring up after 1900 dedicated to fighting unionism, particularly the closed shop. Leadership was supplied in 1903 when the National Association of Manufacturers, under the leadership of President David M. Parry, declared strongly against union recognition. Although the NAM insisted that it did not oppose organized labor as such, it maintained a persistent fight against all important methods used by unions in their struggle. Under the leadership of the NAM, local employers' associations were integrated in 1903 into the Citizens' Industrial Association under the chairmanship of Parry. Another bitter foe of organized labor was the American Anti-Boycott Association (later the League for Industrial Rights), founded in 1902 largely through the energy of Daniel Davenport, a Bridgeport lawyer, to oppose labor in the courts. It financed the Danbury Hatters' case and the Buck's Stove and Range case, the two important boycott cases of the period. In 1907 the NAM organized

[40] *Report on the Anthracite Coal Strike of May–October, 1902, Senate Document* No. 6, 58 Cong., Spec. Sess., 1903, reprinted as *Report of the Anthracite Coal Commission* (U.S. Department of Labor, *Bulletin* No. 46, Washington: Government Printing Office, May, 1903); Berman, *Labor Disputes and the President of the United States,* pp. 46–48; Perlman, *A History of Trade Unionism,* pp. 167–180; Perlman and Taft, *History of Labor in the United States, 1896–1932,* pp. 38–47; Gluck, *John Mitchell,* pp. 102–156; Arthur E. Suffern, *Conciliation and Arbitration in the Coal Industry of America* (Boston: Houghton Mifflin Company, 1915), pp. 244–255.
[41] Perlman, *A History of Trade Unionism,* p. 177.

another subsidiary, the National Council for Industrial Defense, for political and lobbying purposes. At the same time various employers' associations, such as the National Metal Trades Association and the National Founders Association, broke with the unions.[42]

For organized labor the period 1904–1909 was one of discouragement. Trade-union membership as a whole, including that of the AFL, declined.[43] This failure to advance was not caused alone by the mass offensive of organized capital;[44] other factors included the depression of 1907, internal friction, and outside rivalry. The organized opposition of the employer, nevertheless, was extremely potent, and the results could be seen in many communities. It not only smashed unionism in many places, particularly in the smaller communities, but spread the usual propaganda that the closed shop was "un-American" and that the strikebreaker was an "American hero." Their most influential ally was Charles W. Eliot, President of Harvard University, who insisted that nothing "is more essential to the preservation of individual liberty" than protecting the "independent workman," that is, the strikebreaker.[45] Jubilantly, although with exaggeration, employers recorded their success. Said the president of the National Association of Manufacturers in 1906: "Only a few years ago trades unionism unrestrained and militant was rapidly forcing the industries of the country to a closed shop basis. It was almost a crime to criticize the unions. . . . But a change has come and the Association is largely responsible for it. . . . What has brought these changes? The question can be answered in one word—Organization."[46]

Labor lost prestige during these years not only because of the persistent propaganda of the NAM and its subsidiaries, but also because of certain activities on the part of labor itself. Two incidents in particular hurt the labor movement—the murder of Steunenburg, which was never proved against labor leaders, and the dynamiting of the Los Angeles Times, which was. On December 30, 1905, Frank Steunenburg, whose ruthless and extralegal activities as governor of Idaho during the Coeur d'Alene strike in 1899 had won him the hatred

[42] Lorwin, The American Federation of Labor, pp. 76–80; Perlman and Taft, History of Labor in the United States, 1896–1932, pp. 129–137.
[43] Wolman, Growth of American Trade Unions, p. 33. Appendix, p. 421.
[44] Ray Stannard Baker, "Organized Capital Challenges Organized Labor," McClure's Magazine, XXIII, No. 3 (July, 1904), 269–292.
[45] Charles W. Eliot, "Employers' Policies in the Industrial Strife," Harper's Monthly Magazine, CX (March, 1905), 529–532.
[46] Proceedings of the Eleventh Annual Convention of the National Association of Manufacturers of the United States of America (New York: National Association of Manufacturers, 1906), p. 15.

of labor, was assassinated by a bomb which exploded as he opened the gate at his home in Caldwell, Idaho. A certain Harry Orchard confessed to placing the bomb but implicated the leadership of the Western Federation of Miners. Thereupon a county attorney secretly swore that Charles H. Moyer, president, and William D. Haywood, secretary-treasurer of the Western Federation of Miners, and George Pettibone, a businessman of Denver, Colorado, were present in Caldwell on December 30, and had assisted in the murder of Steunenburg. The governor of Colorado secretly signed extradition papers and the accused men were whisked away to Idaho and indicted for murder. In the press the accused were widely denounced as criminals, even President Roosevelt blasting them as "undesirable citizens" on the eve of their trial.[47] Labor and socialist organizations, aroused over the kidnapping, provided able legal defense.[48] Edmund F. Richardson of Denver, a leading attorney of the West, and Clarence Darrow, famous labor attorney, acted for the accused, and William E. Borah (later Senator) for the prosecution. In the end, Haywood and Pettibone were acquitted and the charges against Moyer dropped.[49]

The unfortunate publicity of the Steunenburg case was as nothing to that which came from the dynamiting of the *Los Angeles Times* on October 1, 1910, with the loss of twenty-one lives. It was the climax of a long battle between the National Erectors' Association, backed by the antiunion steel companies, and the International Association of Bridge and Structural Iron Workers. The latter, defeated all along the line, turned to terrorism and violence. In Los Angeles the Merchants and Manufacturers Association, led by General Harrison Gray Otis of the *Times,* were at the same time locked in a battle with the printers and metal workers over the open shop, a battle in which the structural iron workers joined. The local authorities hired William J. Burns, the well-known detective, to probe the dynamite mystery. As a result of his work, John J. McNamara, secretary-treasurer of the International Association of Bridge and Structural Iron Workers, his brother, J. B. McNamara, and Ortie McManigal, were arrested for the dynamiting.

[47] Theodore Roosevelt, *Autobiography* (New York: The Macmillan Company, 1913), pp. 528–533.
[48] AFL, *Proceedings,* 1906, pp. 37–38; Gompers, *Seventy Years of Life and Labor,* II, 182.
[49] Perlman and Taft, *History of Labor in the United States, 1896–1932,* pp. 208–213; Clarence Darrow, *The Story of My Life* (New York: Charles Scribner's Sons, 1932), pp. 127–171; Irving Stone, *Darrow for the Defense* (New York: Doubleday, Doran & Company, 1941), pp. 185–247.

McManigal made a confession involving the others, but the McNamaras so vehemently protested their innocence that labor leaders hastened to their defense and again secured Darrow to defend the accused dynamiters. In the end the McNamara brothers pleaded guilty, and later other officers of the union were tried and imprisoned for conspiracy to transport explosives. Burns accused the men "higher up" of implication and asserted that Gompers had known for some time of the guilt of the McNamaras, but he produced no evidence to prove it.[50] The McNamara case came at the end of five years of stiff opposition to labor, and was one of the most trying ordeals which organized labor had faced, but the turn for the better during the next few years proved that it was not an irreparable blow.[51]

While the reputation of organized labor declined, its legal position was also weakened. In 1902 the United Hatters of North America called a strike against D. E. Loewe and Company of Danbury, Connecticut, in an effort to obtain a closed shop. According to the courts the union had also attempted a nation-wide boycott of the products of the company. Backed by the American Anti-Boycott Association, Loewe sued the officers and members of the union for violation of the Sherman Antitrust Act and won in both the state and the federal courts. Awarded triple damages of $240,000 under the Sherman Act, the company attached the homes and bank accounts of 197 defendants. Settlement was eventually made for $234,000, of which the AFL raised $216,000.[52] The decision was a severe blow since it made individual members liable for the actions of union officers and other members, and also because the Supreme Court ruled that an interstate boycott by labor clearly fell under the Sherman Act.[53] From that time

[50] "Gompers and Burns on Unionism and Dynamite," McClure's Magazine, XXXVIII, No. 4 (February, 1912), 363–376.

[51] Perlman and Taft, History of Labor in the United States, 1896–1932, pp. 318–325; Lorwin, The American Federation of Labor, pp. 102–105; Gompers, Seventy Years of Life and Labor, II, 183 ff.; Report of the Proceedings of the Thirtieth Annual Convention of the American Federation of Labor, 1911 (Washington: The Law Reporter Printing Company, 1911), pp. 41–45; Charles L. Gettemy in Francis G. Wickware, ed., American Yearbook, 1911 (New York: D. Appleton and Company, 1912), pp. 252–254; Clarence Darrow, The Story of My Life (New York: Charles Scribner's Sons, 1932), pp. 177–178; Lincoln Steffens, Autobiography (New York: Harcourt, Brace and Company, 1931), pp. 659–689.

[52] E. E. Witte, The Government in Labor Disputes (New York: McGraw-Hill Book Company, 1932), pp. 134–136.

[53] Edward Berman, Labor and the Sherman Act (New York: Harper & Brothers, 1930), pp. 77–87; Harry W. Laidler, Boycotts and the Labor Struggle (New York: John Lane, Ltd., 1913), pp. 151–156, 454–456; Leo Wolman, The Boycott in American Trade Unions (Baltimore: The Johns Hopkins Press, 1916), pp. 131–133; Report of the Proceedings of the Thirty-fifth Annual Convention of the American Federation of Labor, 1915 (Washington: The Law Reporter Printing Company, 1915), pp. 73–77. The AFL did not endorse the boycott.

on, organized labor made the exemption of labor unions from the operation of the antitrust acts a major objective.

While the Danbury Hatters' case was before the courts the AFL became involved in another boycott suit, one with even wider implications because it also concerned the use of the injunction. Charging that the Buck's Stove and Range Company of St. Louis had refused to continue the nine-hour day and had violated an agreement, the International Brotherhood of Foundry Employees called a strike in 1906 and appealed to the Federation. After due investigation the Federation placed the company on the "We Don't Patronize" list in the *American Federationist* (May, 1907) and urged its members to boycott the concern. So effective was the boycott that J. W. Van Cleave, president of the company,[54] and bitter foe of labor, obtained an injunction in the federal court of the District of Columbia, forbidding the AFL and its affiliated bodies to prosecute the boycott, to include the plaintiff's name on the "unfair list," or even to refer to the dispute "in writing or orally." This injunction, written by the complainants' lawyers and signed by the judge with scarcely a change in its wording, has been accurately described as "one of the most sweeping orders given in American jurisprudence."[55]

This almost unbelievable injunction was obeyed as far as the unfair list was concerned but otherwise ignored. As a result, Gompers, Mitchell, and Morrison were sentenced to prison for contempt of court. New complications developed, the sentences were never served, and the case dragged through the courts until it was finally dismissed in 1914 and outlawed under the statute of limitations. Throughout the dispute the AFL attempted to use the Buck's Stove injunction to test the power of a court to restrain citizens in an industrial dispute from exercising their constitutional rights of free speech, free press, and peaceable assemblage. The United States Supreme Court, however, avoided a discussion of the fundamental issues.[56] One result was to strengthen the hatred of unions for the labor injunction.

In general, organized labor looked upon the courts as their unre-

[54] Also president of the National Association of Manufacturers and vice-president of the Citizens' Industrial Association.

[55] Laidler, *Boycotts and the Labor Struggle*, p. 143.

[56] *Ibid.*, pp. 134–150, 450–454; Harold U. Faulkner, *The Quest for Social Justice, 1898–1914* (Vol. XI of *A History of American Life*, A. M. Schlesinger and D. R. Fox, eds., New York: The Macmillan Company, 1931), pp. 62–64; Gompers, *Seventy Years of Life and Labor*, Vol. II, Chap. XXXIII; *American Federationist*, XV (1908), 1072–1076 and XIX (1921), 601–611; *Report of the Proceedings of the Twenty-eighth Annual Convention of the American Federation of Labor*, 1908 (Washington: The National Tribune Company, 1908), pp. 16–17.

lenting enemy, an attitude developed from long experience. The same was true of the state national guards, whose chief duty seemed to be that of breaking strikes. A new enemy, or so it seemed to labor, now suddenly appeared on the scene with the development of the state police. Massachusetts had supported a small state constabulary since 1865, but the state police did not actually appear until after 1900. The Arizona rangers were established in 1901, the Connecticut state police in 1903, the New Mexico mounted police in 1905, an emergency force in Nevada in 1908, the Pennsylvania state police in 1905, and similar systems in New York, Colorado, and Michigan in 1917.[57] Proponents of the state police insisted that their main purpose was to counteract rural crime, but the inevitable appearance of the constabulary on the scene of important industrial disputes, as well as the frequently alleged incidents of brutality, won for the new system the enmity of labor. Labor denounced them as the "American Cossacks."[58] Time, however, was to prove that the private police hired by industrialists, such as the coal and iron police in Pennsylvania, were far more dangerous than the state police, and that often the local police, controlled by local industrialists, were less fair and objective in labor disputes than the state constabulary. Labor opposition, nevertheless, prevented for some time the extention of the system and kept its advocates on the defensive.

The growing force of this counteroffensive eventually contributed to one failure of labor after another. Typical was the sympathetic strike of the Chicago teamsters (1905–1908) against Montgomery, Ward and Company in behalf of a garment workers' strike which resulted in a major struggle between the Chicago Employers' Association and the Chicago labor movement, and a crushing defeat of the International Brotherhood of Teamsters.[59] A similar defeat was experienced by the Amalgamated Meat Cutters and Butchers Workmen of North America with their center in Chicago, when, in the summer of 1904, they called out their 50,000 members to support higher wages for the unskilled workers. This unusual interest of the skilled in the unskilled workers resulted in the virtual destruction of organized labor in the western meat packing establishments until revived by the First World War. Insubordination in calling a wildcat strike on the New York City transit system in 1905 wiped out years of patient

[57] The Arizona, New Mexico, and Colorado systems were later disbanded. West Virginia established a state police in 1918; New Jersey, in 1921. The Nevada constabulary was established as a direct result of the Goldfield strike.—Bruce Smith, The State Police (New York: The Macmillan Company, 1925), pp. 36–44, 54–65.

[58] Pennsylvania State Federation of Labor, The American Cossack (Philadelphia, 1915).

[59] Perlman and Taft, History of Labor in the United States, 1896–1932, pp. 61–70.

work of organization and virtually destroyed for years the power of organized labor in New York City transportation.[60] Extension of control over traffic on the Great Lakes by the strongly antiunion steel trust also eventually smashed organized labor on internal water transportation.[61]

Discouraging as were these setbacks, labor's most significant defeat was in steel. Here organization was represented by the Amalgamated Association of Iron, Steel and Tin Workers, a tiny group of skilled workers with a membership of between 10,000 and 14,000 out of 160,000 wage earners in the industry. What strength it had was challenged by the rapid consolidation of the industry climaxed by the formation of the United States Steel Corporation in 1901. Business consolidation endangered the unions, for in time of labor trouble, work could be shifted from union to nonunion mills. The controversy, therefore, was not concerned primarily with wages or conditions of work, but with the recognition and extension of unionism. It also involved the problem as to whether the newly formed United States Steel Corporation would accept or reject unionism. The corporation, still busy with the details of consolidation and security flotations and concerned with public reaction to the merger, had no desire for an immediate clash with labor. When the union, therefore, in 1901 called a strike against the American Sheet Steel, the American Steel Hoop, and the American Tin Plate Companies for higher wages and the right to organize all the mills in these companies, the United States Steel was willing to compromise. The union, convinced that time was on the side of the corporation and that the issue would have to be fought out immediately, refused.

The Amalgamated understood the issue clearly, but the weakness of its own structure made victory impossible without the full support of the entire labor movement. This was apparently promised, but never fulfilled. Before the strike collapsed, Morgan and other leaders of the steel industry made clear their antiunion policy. At the same time Gompers and Mitchell, as well as the labor movement as a whole, showed a lack of understanding of the significance of the struggle. The victory of the United States Steel Corporation smashed unionism in the steel industry for thirty-five years. More than that, it established an antiunion pattern among the great corporations, particularly the heavy industries, just as the consolidation movement reached its height.[62]

[60] *Ibid.*, pp. 124–128. [61] *Ibid.*, pp. 145–149.
[62] *Ibid.*, pp. 97–109; Lorwin, *The American Federation of Labor*, pp. 63–65; Jesse S. Robinson, *The Amalgamated Association of Iron, Steel, and Tin Workers* (Baltimore: The Johns Hopkins Press, 1920), pp. 19–21, 94.

INTERNAL DISSENSION

Organized labor was weakened not only by attacks from without but also by dissensions and differences of policy within. Some of these dissensions were largely the result of rapid growth; others involved fundamental differences in strategy and policy. Jurisdictional disputes, as already noted, were one cause of friction. The problem of organizing the unskilled was another. In theory, the AFL maintained an interest in the unskilled worker and as early as 1896 the convention instructed the Executive Council to organize this group. In the following year, the convention pointed out that new inventions and the division and subdivision of labor had thrown many skilled workers out of jobs and that "the artisan of yesterday" was the "unskilled laborer of today." [63] The Federation, in fact, had organized many unskilled workers into federal unions from which they were later usually drawn into existing national unions. In certain cases unions of skilled workers took in the unskilled as helpers. Also in these early years a few unions such as the International Hod-Carriers, Building, and Common Laborers' Union of America and the Brotherhood of Maintenance of Way Employees were organized for the unskilled. Generally speaking, however, the Federation gave a modicum of attention to the unskilled and carefully restricted the power of the federal unions of the unskilled when the latter were organized.[64]

During much of its history American labor faced a distinct division in its ranks between those who favored a labor party and those who adhered to a nonpartisan policy of rewarding friends and punishing enemies. Although advocates of a labor party were widely scattered in the various unions, the leading proponents, as in Europe, were the left-wing groups. The Socialist Labor party, which came under the leadership of Daniel De Leon in the 1890's, believed that labor should develop a "class consciousness," endorse Socialist candidates, and work for the overthrow of the capitalist system. Endorsement of socialist principles should be a condition of union membership. Having failed to capture either the Knights of Labor or the AFL, De Leon started in 1895 a short-lived rival organization, the Socialist Trade and Labor Alliance in New York City. This attempt at dual unionism precipitated a split in the Socialist Labor

---

[63] *Report of the Proceedings of the Seventeenth Annual Convention of the American Federation of Labor*, 1897 (Published by the direction of the AFL: n. d.), p. 15.
[64] Lorwin, *The American Federation of Labor*, pp. 70–72.

party and the organization of the Social Democratic party (later the Socialist party) in 1898. The leaders of the new party—Victor Berger, newspaper editor of Milwaukee, Morris Hillquit, a New York lawyer, and Eugene V. Debs, leader of the Pullman strike of 1894— were opposed to dualism and believed that labor could be won to the Socialist party. Even if this could not be done, they were convinced that labor should play a more active political role than that countenanced by many of the dominant leaders of the AFL.

Not only were the Socialists eager for more aggressive political action, but they led the fight in the unions for eighteen years against Gompers and conservative old-line unionism. It was a battle for socialist principles, industrial unionism, and political action. By 1912 the Socialists controlled unions of the miners and machinists; they had carried elections in Milwaukee, Schenectady, Berkeley, and elsewhere; they published scores of daily and weekly papers, and polled a vote of 897,000 in 1912.[65] Whatever their political victories might be, Gompers skillfully fought their influence within the unions. His battle was personal as well as founded on principles. He never forgave the Socialists for their part in ousting him from the presidency in 1894 and for their effort at dual unionism in 1895. Gompers may not have been too well acquainted with Socialist theory, but he understood well enough that it differed in principle and practice from his own policies.[66] "I declare it to you," he said to the Socialists in 1903, "I am not only at variance with your doctrines, but with your philosophy. Economically, you are unsound; socially, you are wrong; industrially, you are an impossibility." [67]

Probably the most vigorous challenge directed at the philosophy and technique of the AFL during these years came from the Industrial Workers of the World. Ideological origins of the revolutionary industrial unionism advocated and practiced by the IWW may have originated largely in European socialism and syndicalism, but conditions of the frontier mining camps produced the movement. Daring, aggressive, and imbued with the true spirit of the pioneer, the miners of the West fought back against the exploitation of absentee owners

[65] Perlman, *A Theory of the Labor Movement*, pp. 219–221.

[66] Gompers, *Seventy Years of Life and Labor*, I, 355–427; William C. Roberts, comp., *American Federation of Labor, History, Encyclopedia, Reference Book* (published by authority of the 1916 and 1917 conventions, Washington: 1919), pp. 352–359; Louis S. Reed, *The Labor Philosophy of Samuel Gompers*, (New York: Columbia University Press, 1930), pp. 75–96; Harvey, *Samuel Gompers, Champion of the Toiling Masses*, pp. 101–118.

[67] *Report of the Proceedings of the Twenty-third Annual Convention of the American Federation of Labor*, 1903 (no place or date), p. 198.

and powerful corporations in strikes which "came nearer to real warfare than did any other contests in the history of the American labor movement." [68] Strikes at Coeur d'Alene (1892 and 1899), Cripple Creek (1894 and 1903–1904), Leadville (1896–1897), Telluride (1901), and Idaho Springs (1903) had all the characteristics of the most bitter labor warfare—armed strikers battling company guards, strikebreakers, state militia, even federal troops; barricades, dead and wounded, "bull pens" (concentration camps), and local and state governments acting at the behest of mine owners.

This kind of experience made it clear very early that only by including in the same organization every worker employed in or about the mine could the miners hope for success. The result was the founding in 1893 of an industrial organization, the Western Federation of Miners. The Western Federation of Miners immediately joined the AFL, but withdrew in 1897 in resentment over the failure of the Federation to aid it in the Leadville strike. The Federation at this time hardly operated west of the Mississippi. In the following year the miners helped to organize the Western Labor Union designed to include migratory workers of various categories, often used as strikebreakers by mining corporations. In 1902 these two organizations launched the American Labor Union as a rival of the AFL in the West. The new organization emphasized industrial organization, favored independent political action, and endorsed the platform of the Socialist party. This development in the West was a challenge not only to the craft unionism of the AFL, but also to the conciliatory policy of cooperation with employers through the National Civic Federation.

Feeling that the time was ripe for a new labor movement of national scope based upon ideals of industrial organization, the Western Federation of Miners, the American Labor Union, the Socialist Trade and Labor Alliance, the Socialist Labor party, and a few members of the Socialist party issued a call for a convention to meet in Chicago in June, 1905. There some two hundred delegates, representing perhaps fifty thousand workers in forty distinct occupations, launched the Industrial Workers of the World.[69] Among those in attendance were Daniel De Leon, founder of the Socialist Labor party; Eugene V. Debs, leader of the Socialist party, and William D. (Big

[68] Louis Levine, "The Development of Syndicalism in America," *Political Science Quarterly*, XXVIII, No. 3 (September, 1903), 457–458.

[69] Paul F. Brissenden, *The I.W.W.* (New York: Columbia University Press, 1919), pp. 67–77.

Bill) Haywood, soon to emerge as the real leader of the new organization.[70] The Western Federation of Miners was the most powerful
group represented at the conference and the most influential. Utterly
repudiating the AFL belief that the worker might improve his lot
within the framework of capitalism, the preamble to the IWW constitution asserted: "The working class and the employing class have
nothing in common. . . . Between these two classes a struggle must
go on until the toilers come together . . . and take hold of that
which they produce by their labor through an economic organization
of the working class." [71] A later revision, after the more moderate
Socialists were ousted, was even more radical.

The syndicalist organization of the IWW was to begin with all
workers in a single plant. These local unions were to be joined into
national industrial unions and the national unions of related industries into thirteen departments. These large plans, which were to
form "the structure of the new society within the shell of the old,"
were never fulfilled. Overloaded with strong leaders, the IWW was
cursed by factional quarrels from the start. It split between the more
conservative group, led by the Western Federation of Miners, who
gave lip service to a radical program but were chiefly concerned with
effective organization, and the revolutionary group led by De Leon,
Trautman, and Vincent St. John. Wearied of the quarrel, the Western
Federation of Miners seceded in 1907 and rejoined the AFL in 1911.
The remnant split into two groups in 1908—a revolutionary-political
faction led by De Leon and a nonpolitical and direct-actionist faction.
The latter became the real IWW. With the ousting of De Leon, the
organization was in a position to become the mouthpiece of the unskilled and migratory workers and take the leadership among labor
unions in the class struggle.[72]

Paid-up membership of the IWW was never large. Although
2,000 locals were probably chartered and 200,000 membership cards
issued in the period 1905–1916, it is improbable that the membership
at any time exceeded 60,000 or 70,000. At the beginning of its great

[70] Other important leaders included William E. Trautman, editor of the official
organ of the United Brewery Workers; Charles O. Sherman, General Secretary of
the United Metal Workers International Union; and Algie M. Simons, editor of the
International Socialist Review.

[71] Brissenden, *The I.W.W.*, pp. 349–350.

[72] Perlman and Taft, *History of Labor in the United States, 1896–1932*, pp.
230–247; Perlman, *History of Trade Unionism*, pp. 213–219; Brissenden, *The I.W.W.*,
pp. 136–154, 213–241. The De Leon group kept the name I.W.W. until 1915, when
it took the name Workers' International Industrial Union.

activity in 1912, membership was less than 5,000.[73] Nevertheless, able leadership and the revolutionary ardor of its membership gave the organization an influence far beyond its numerical strength. It made its greatest appeal to the migratory "wobblies" of the West who cut the timber and followed the harvest—the wandering, casual laborers, exploited, persecuted, and homeless. Some temporary successes were also won among unskilled factory workers of the East. The IWW first attracted attention in the unsuccessful Goldfield, Nevada, strike of the Western Federation of Miners in 1907. Two years later it entered the strike against the Pressed Steel Car Company at McKees Rocks, Pennsylvania, to give aid and direction to the unorganized workers when no other established labor organization would step in. Their aid helped to strengthen the workers and to win a strike unusual in the extent of its violence and bloodshed.[74]

During the next three years the energies of the IWW were largely absorbed in their battles over the right to free speech fights at Spokane, Fresno, San Diego, and other cities on the Pacific Coast. The tactics of the IWW, when a member was arrested, was to descend upon a town in large numbers and force the authorities to arrest them until the expense to the town was so great that the authorities gave up. Over 500 were arrested in Spokane. The largest battle was in San Diego in 1912, when the extralegal violence of vigilantes and city authorities created a reign of terror that brought a coalition of decent-minded Californians, pressure upon Governor Hiram Johnson to investigate the conditions, and eventually a temporary cessation of this type of persecution. These battles, as far as the IWW was concerned, were not merely to vindicate the constitutional right of free speech; the right to use city streets for purposes of agitation was necessary to the migratory workers of the IWW.[75]

By 1912 the IWW was again participating actively in strikes, notably in the unsuccessful efforts of the timber workers in Louisiana, and in the textile workers' strike at Lawrence, Massachusetts. When the 20,000 strikers at Lawrence received no cooperation from the craft unions, the unskilled workers, mostly recent immigrants, turned to the IWW. Under the skillful leadership of Haywood and Joseph J. Ettor, the strike was finally won. Not, however, before Massachusetts

[73] Brissenden, *The I.W.W.*, pp. 341–348, 357; Robert F. Hoxie, "The Truth about the I.W.W.," *The Journal of Political Economy*, XXI, No. 9 (November, 1913), 785–797.

[74] Perlman and Taft, *History of Labor in the United States, 1896–1932*, pp. 234–235, 263–265.

[75] *Ibid.*, pp. 236–243.

gave an exhibition of employer tactics almost as ruthless as the IWW encountered in California and Louisiana. In clashes with the authorities, women and children were clubbed and dragged off to jail, an Italian woman was shot, and a young Armenian was bayoneted to death. In an effort to discredit the strikers, a Lawrence businessman "planted" dynamite in several places. As a last resort, Ettor and Arturo Giovanitti were thrown into prison. By the time the strike ended, there were almost as many militiamen in the company-owned city of Lawrence as there were strikers. Despite all provocations, the strike leaders did much to keep their followers in order and combat the employers' propaganda. One method which helped to win publicity and widespread sympathy was the sending of strikers' children out of the city to spend "vacations" at the homes of strike sympathizers.[76]

Lawrence marked the crest of power and influence of the IWW. The Paterson strike of 1913 was the beginning of its decline. Starting on February 25 with the broad-silk weavers, the strike quickly spread to dye shops and ribbon factories until every branch of the industry and over 25,000 workers were affected. The demands were the re-establishment of the two-loom system, the eight-hour day, higher wages, and better sanitary conditions in the mills. Haywood, Ettor, Carlo Tresca, and Elizabeth Gurley Flynn, the ablest of the IWW leaders, and Patrick Quinlan, a Socialist organizer, directed the fight. Despite police brutality, infringement of constitutional liberties by the judiciary, and imprisonment of many of their leaders, the IWW held the ranks intact for twenty-two weeks. During the strike, 2,338 were arrested, 300 held for the grand jury, and over 100 sentenced to imprisonment. Lack of funds and loss of morale finally brought the collapse of the long strike.[77]

The Paterson strike had barely ended before the IWW was lead-

[76] Frederick C. Croxton, "Report on Strike of Textile Workers in Lawrence, Mass., in 1912," *Senate Document* No. 870, 62 Cong., 2 Sess.; "Hearings on Strike at Lawrence, Massachusetts," *House Document* No. 671, 62 Cong., 2 Sess.; Walter E. Weyl and Others, "The Lawrence Strike from Various Angles," *Survey*, XXVIII, No. 1 (April, 1912), 65–80; James P. Heaton, "The Legal Aftermath of the Lawrence Strike," *Survey*, XXVIII, No. 14 (June, 1912), 503–510; *Bill Haywood's Book: The Autobiography of William D. Haywood* (New York: International Publishers, 1929), pp. 239–260.

[77] Perlman and Taft, *History of Labor in the United States, 1896–1932*, pp. 274–277; *American Yearbook*, 1913, pp. 411–413; *Survey*, XXX, No. 3 (April 19, 1913), 81–83, No. 9 (May 31), 300, 315–316, No. 11 (June 14), p. 368, No. 13 (June 28), 428; John A. Fitch, "The I.W.W., An Outlaw Organization," *Survey*, No. 10 (June 7, 1913), 355–364; Commission on Industrial Relations, *Final Report and Testimony, Senate Document* No. 415, 66 Cong., III, 2411–2645; *Bill Haywood's Book*, pp. 261–277.

ing the hop-field harvest hands at Wheatland, California, in a protest against low wages and the intolerable housing and unsanitary conditions forced upon 2,800 migratory workers. This group was composed of men, women, and children, about half of whom were immigrants and who were subjected to much the same type of deliberate injustice and exploitation pictured a quarter of a century later in Steinbeck's *Grapes of Wrath*. When a deputy sheriff fired into a meeting of workers, wounding one of the pickets, general firing broke out resulting in the death of the district attorney, a deputy sheriff, and two workers. Four strike leaders were selected for prosecution, two being convicted of second-degree murder and sentenced to life imprisonment. Defense was provided by the International Workers' Defense League, founded for the purpose. Although the Wheatland strike was only partially successful, the publicity given by the IWW and other groups led to the appointment of Carleton H. Parker to investigate the abuses of labor camps, and to some remedial legislation. The latter, however, appears to have done little good, for the treatment of migratory agricultural labor in California continued to be a public scandal.[78]

That America needed aggressive labor leadership was amply proved by conditions at Lawrence, Paterson, and Wheatland. The IWW, however, was bitterly denounced by capital and conservative labor alike. Its antagonism toward the existing economic order, its willingness to employ sabotage, and its success among the unskilled and unorganized workers account for this hostility. Gompers saw in the IWW a dangerous rival which must be crushed and the Executive Committee of the Federation issued orders to the unions to fight it. Employers' propaganda helped to prejudice the middle class against it. Opposition to the IWW, in fact, was so strong that the organization was welcomed only when conditions were particularly hopeless. Said an IWW leader, speaking of the Wheatland strike, "We can't agitate in the country unless things are rotten enough to bring the crowd along." [79] And that statement applied also to the city. Opposition of the IWW to American entry into the First World War provided its many enemies with an opportunity to attack it for treason, and it was largely destroyed at that time.[80]

[78] Perlman and Taft, *History of Labor in the United States, 1896–1932*, pp. 243–245; Commission on Industrial Relations, *Final Report and Testimony*, V, 4913–5026; Carleton H. Parker, "The Wheatland Riot and What Lay Behind It," *Survey*, XXXI, No. 25 (March 21, 1914), 768–770.
[79] Quoted by Parker, "The Wheatland Riot and What Lay Behind It," p. 770.
[80] Perlman, *Theory of the Labor Movement*, pp. 159–162.

Its influence upon American labor, however, was important. Although it strengthened the antagonism of the AFL toward dual unionism, it also made clear the need for more aggressive leadership and the importance of doing something for the unskilled worker. It was the inability, if not the unwillingness, of the United Textile Workers to take the leadership at Lawrence and Paterson that opened the way for the IWW.[81] Undoubtedly, the IWW strengthened the tendency toward industrial unionism at a time when the new mass industries were creating millions of unskilled workers. It was also interested in the organization of Negro workers and prepared the way for their larger participation in trade-union activity. The IWW undoubtedly improved the conditions among various groups of workers, particularly those in the lumber camps of the West. Its interest in the Negro, in the unskilled worker, and in industrial organization presaged a similar interest a quarter of a century later by the Congress of Industrial Organizations.

THE SECOND ADVANCE, 1910–1916

Membership in American trade unions, which had remained almost stationary from 1905 to 1909, moved ahead again in the years 1910 to 1913. Total union membership and membership in the AFL increased by slightly more than one third. This advance was by no means distributed evenly over the labor movement. Over three fourths of the AFL increase went to four industries: 157,000 in mining; 94,000 in building; 16,000 in clothing; 77,000 in transportation. Of the individual industries the most spectacular advances (1910–1913) were in clothing (68 per cent) and mining (60 per cent). In building (21 per cent) and transportation (16 per cent) the unions were largely holding their own in expanding industries.[82] One of the most significant features of this advance was the fact that women for the first time began to take an important place in the American labor movement. Exact statistics of female membership for these years are uncertain, but it appears that the number increased from about 76,700 in 1910 to 386,900 in 1920. Since the membership in the

[81] Perlman, A History of Trade Unionism, pp. 302–306.
[82] Wolman, Growth of American Trade Unions, pp. 33–34, 45–55, and Appendix. Perlman and Taft, History of Labor in the United States, 1896–1932, p. 289. Income in 1913 from the 1,996,004 members and from other sources was $244,292.04. Benefits paid by Internationals to members amounted to $2,939,663.28—Report of the Proceedings of the Thirty-third Annual Convention of the American Federation of Labor, 1913 (Washington: The Law Reporter Printing Company, 1913), pp. 14, 24, 41.

women's clothing unions was the dominating item in both years and since the great advance of the women's clothing unions came in the early years of the decade, the part played by women during this second great advance was obviously important.[83]

Although the advance of labor from 1910 to 1913 was relatively neither as rapid nor as important as the growth from 1899 to 1904, it was, nevertheless, significant. The resumption of the forward movement was made possible, in the first place, by the ability of organized labor to survive the depression of 1907 and the aggressive attacks of organized capital to crush it. Attacks of Socialists and industrial unionists both within and without upon the philosophy, structure, and tactics of the AFL probably widened its horizon, liberalized its point of view, and improved its resiliency. Labor gained much political knowledge after 1906 and was in a position to cash in on it. The years 1905–1907 had been a period of storm and stress, but adversity had provided valuable experience.[84]

As labor shifted from a defensive to an offensive position, it was helped by a distinct improvement in middle-class attitude. Led by the "muckrakers," America during these years was engaged in a reappraisal of her economic and social system.[85] Oppression of monopolies, political corruption of "big business," glaring inequalities of wealth, and the rising cost of living conditioned a larger element of the American public to a sympathetic attitude toward labor unions. Moreover, labor profited, whatever its own contribution may have been, in the increased interest in, demand for, and progress of social legislation. Labor was able to hold onto this good will and continue the offensive despite the embarrassments of the McNamara incident, the traditional American opposition to the radicalism of the IWW, and the costly defeats in specific labor struggles. Since the most notable gains made during these years were in the mining industry and the garment trades, a word is in order regarding them.

The great advance in the membership of the United Mine Workers was due to a partial victory in the West Virginia strike of 1912–1913 and to an improved union position in the anthracite region. Finding it extremely difficult to maintain union wages and conditions in the Central Competitive Field because the rapidly expanding bituminous mining in West Virginia was unorganized, the

[83] Leo Wolman, "The Extent of Labor Organization in the United States in 1910," *Quarterly Journal of Economics*, XXX (May, 1916), 501, 602–605; *Wolman, Growth of Trade Unions*, pp. 97–108.
[84] Lorwin, *The American Federation of Labor*, pp. 96–124.
[85] Told in detail in Faulkner, *The Quest for Social Justice*.

United Mine Workers determined to organize that state. A year's strike, characterized by violation of civil liberties, martial law, and virtual warfare, won the right to organize, a nine-hour day, the right to trade in noncompany stores, and semimonthly paydays, but it failed to win important wage advances or the right to elect check-weighmen.[86] In the anthracite regions there had been but little change in wages or conditions of work since the famous strike of 1902, despite the increased cost of living. Expiring agreements were usually renewed for three-year terms. In 1912, however, a full-length strike brought a larger degree of union recognition and a wage increase of approximately 10 per cent. After this strike the union entered seriously on the work of organization and within two years had quadrupled its membership in the anthracite region.[87]

Although the United Mine Workers was making progress in the East, it failed to organize the southern Colorado coal fields in one of the bitterest and most publicized strikes in American history (September, 1913–December, 1914). The conditions in southern Colorado were not unlike those of many mining towns, both in the East and in the West, and the history of the strike is similar to those of earlier mining strikes in the West. Most of the Colorado mining towns were isolated, devoid of decent living accommodations, without elementary sanitation, and deprived of opportunities for recreation or medical attention; moreover, they were controlled politically, socially, and economically by mine officials representing absentee stockholders. The miners lived, said one observer, "under a despotism so absolute that the radical press is not far wrong in calling them slaves." [88]

The strikers in 1913 called for the usual coal miners' demands— 10 per cent increase in wages, union recognition, observance of the Colorado mining laws, discharge of armed guards, the right to choose one's boardinghouse and doctor.[89] Operators immediately imported several hundred armed guards, who were deputized by the sheriff. Miners and their families, ousted from company-owned houses, established themselves in tent colonies. After armed clashes between the workers and the imported guards and deputy sheriffs, in which several miners were killed, the entire state militia was called out. Friction and violence continued, reaching a climax on April 20 when

[86] Perlman and Taft, *History of Labor in the United States, 1896–1932*, pp. 330–335.
[87] *Ibid.*, pp. 341–342.
[88] W. T. Davis, "The Strike War in Colorado," *Outlook*, CVII (May 9, 1914), 73.
[89] Perlman and Taft, *History of Labor in the United States, 1896–1932*, pp. 336–341.

a pitched battle at Ludlow ended in the burning of the tent colony, the death of several men, two women, and eleven children. Nine days later President Wilson ordered federal troops into Colorado to restore order. In the meantime, government pressure was brought to bear upon John D. Rockefeller, Jr., chief stockholder of the Colorado Fuel and Iron Company, one of the largest companies involved, to intervene, but he refused. Twice in the autumn of 1914 President Wilson suggested terms upon which the strike could be settled. The miners accepted both times but the operators refused. After more than a year of the bitterest economic warfare, the strike collapsed. As well as any other, this strike represented the climax during these years of the private warfare between capital and labor.[90]

One of the great milestones of union progress was the organization of the clothing workers, a group composed chiefly of immigrants and women, exploited by low wages, long hours, and unsanitary conditions of work. Small unions had existed for some time, but the turning point came in the fall of 1909, when the Ladies' Waist Makers' Union, Local 25 of the International Ladies' Garment Workers' Union, called a general strike. Some twenty thousand women participated, and New York was treated to the sight of women picketers subjected to the brutality of police and hired guards as dozens of them were dragged daily to the magistrates to be fined. Public aid and sympathy helped to win the strike, and in a series of conferences where the strikers were represented by John Mitchell and Morris Hillquit, the workers won all their demands but the closed shop.[91] This "uprising of the twenty thousand," as Gompers pointed out, showed "the extent to which women are taking up with industrial life; their consequent tendency to stand together in the struggle to protect their common interests as wage earners, . . . and the capacity of women as strikers to suffer, to do, and to dare in support of their rights."[92]

[90] Faulkner, *The Quest for Social Justice*, pp. 73–75; John A. Fitch, "Law and Order, the Issue in Colorado," *Survey*, XXXIII, No. 10 (December, 1914), 241–258; Commission on Industrial Relations, *Final Report and Testimony*, VII, 6347–6990; VIII, 6993–7425, 7761–8013; IX, 8017–8948; House Committee on Mines, *Condition in the Coal Mines of Colorado*, 63 Cong., 2 Sess. (Washington: Government Printing Office, 2 vols., 1914), II, Pt. 10; Berman, *Labor Disputes and the President of the United States*, pp. 76–99.

[91] Mabel H. Willett, *The Employment of Women in the Clothing Trade* (New York: Columbia University Press, 1902), pp. 11–93; Perlman and Taft, *History of Labor in the United States, 1896–1932*, pp. 293–296; Faulkner, *The Quest for Social Justice*, pp. 58–59; Constance D. Leupp, "The Shirtwaist Makers' Strike," *Survey*, XXIII, No. 12 (December 18, 1909), 383–386, No. 17, 535–536, 541–558; Pearl Goodman and Elsa Ueland, "The Shirtwaist Trade," *Journal of Political Economy*, XVIII, No. 10 (December, 1910), 816–828; Joel Seidman, *The Needle Trades* (New York: Farrar & Rinehart, 1942), pp. 95–114.

[92] *Report of the Proceedings of the Thirtieth Annual Convention of the American*

The strike of the waist makers' union was also significant as a preliminary to a strike of the New York cloak and suit makers called in July to secure the abolition of subcontracting, to obtain higher wages and better working conditions, and to win the closed shop. In a series of conferences between representatives of employers and the union, the prime mover of which was Louis Brandeis, the strikers won all of their demands but the closed shop. More than that, machinery of arbitration was set up to take care of future disputes, and a Joint Board of Sanitary Control was established to maintain legal standards in the shops.[93] In this same notable year of 1910 the workers in men's clothing, then part of the United Garment Workers, struck under the leadership of Sidney Hillman against Hart, Shaffner and Marx in Chicago. This developed into a general strike and a partial victory, at least in the Hart, Shaffner and Marx firm. The main results were to give an impetus to organization of the workers in men's clothing,[94] and to the "beginning of the most highly elaborated industrial government in America based on the equal participation of employer and union."[95]

The second advance of organized labor was first of all characterized, as already noted, by the emergence of large numbers of women in the American labor movement. In the second place, it was a period in which organized labor for the first time established strong unions in the clothing industry. In the third place, the organization of the clothing trade put the immigrant workers for the first time in the forefront of the American labor movement. In earlier years the exploited immigrant was often responsible for low wage scales and open shops. Now the Jewish and Italian wage earners in the clothing industry had become "America's staunchest fighters for industrial government based on union recognition."[96] Finally, the advance of unionism into the clothing trade had reinvigorated the American

Federation of Labor, 1910 (Washington: The Law Reporter Printing Company, 1910), p. 23.

[93] Perlman and Taft, History of Labor in the United States, 1896–1932, pp. 296–304; John Bruce McPherson, "The New York Cloakmakers' Strike," Journal of Political Economy, XIX, No. 3 (March, 1911), 153–187; Mary B. Sumner, "Settlement of the Cloakmakers' Strike," Survey, XXIV, No. 25 (September 17, 1910), 847–850; Chicago Joint Board, Amalgamated Clothing Workers of America, The Clothing Workers of Chicago, 1910–1922 (Chicago: 1922), pp. 17–108.

[94] Most of the workers in men's clothing broke away from the United Garment Workers in 1914 and organized the Amalgamated Clothing Workers of America under the leadership of Joseph Schlossberg and Sidney Hillman. In 1924 the Amalgamated joined the AFL, but was suspended in 1936 as one of the original organizers of the Committee for Industrial Organization.

[95] Perlman and Taft, History of Labor in the United States, 1896–1932, pp. 304–317.

[96] Ibid., p. 300.

labor movement with a left-wing ideology. The constituency of both the International Ladies' Garment Workers and the Amalgamated Clothing Workers had carried to America many of the ideals of international socialism.

Repeatedly these unions showed a readiness to help other unions as well as their own, and they were interested in general social reform as well as strengthening the labor movement. Moreover they had no antipathy to industrial unionism. In fact, the clothing workers skillfully superimposed industrial unionism on the variations of craft skills, notably in the integration of the various locals of the ILGWU. And this, interestingly enough, was accompanied by an intensive use of the trade agreement, the keystone of the "old unionism" of Gompers and the AFL. The philosophy and program of the clothing workers was called the "new unionism." Its chief contribution, says Perlman, was first "that it has rationalized and developed industrial government by collective bargaining and trade agreements as no other unionism, and second, . . . that it has applied a spirit of broad-minded all-inclusiveness to all workers in the industry." [97]

Labor's second great advance as revealed by the membership of the AFL was temporarily halted by the economic recession of 1914–1915. Advance was resumed, however, in 1916, and American labor entered the war in a position of unprecedented strength. Victories during 1915–1916 in important strikes increased union power while the Federation won the good will of the railroad brotherhoods by supporting their movement for the eight-hour day. The AFL widened its activities to include professional workers when it chartered in 1916 the American Federation of Teachers and the Actors' Equity Association. Labor's increased influence in the federal government was evident in the La Follette Seaman's Act and a federal child labor bill, both in 1916. Its new national prestige was, in a sense, officially demonstrated when President Wilson officiated at the dedication of the Federation's office building in July of that year. That organized labor had won a significant place in American economic life was made clear in the months preceding the entrance of the United States into the war as both pacifists and interventionists trained their propaganda on Gompers and other leaders to win the support of labor.[98]

[97] Perlman, *History of Trade Unionism*, p. 220.
[98] Lorwin, *The American Federation of Labor*, pp. 131–145.

CHAPTER XIII

The New Agriculture

THE CHANGING SCENE

AS a whole the last third of the nineteenth century was a difficult period for the American farmer. Brief spans of relative prosperity had alternated with long years of discouragement and hard times.[1] Of the latter the three years following the panic of 1893 had been particularly disastrous. With the year 1899, however, the situation changed for the better, and for the next two decades American agriculture enjoyed one of its rare periods of prosperity. Between 1900 and 1920 the value of farm lands and crops increased almost fourfold and the prices of farm products nearly threefold, although the mass of crop production during the same period increased less than 50 per cent.[2] Although the content of agricultural exports changed radically in the years before the First World War, the exportation of farm products remained large and continued to be an important item in the farmer's well-being. Along with these tangible evidences of prosperity was the increasing interest of the federal government in the financial and marketing problems of the farmer.

Despite this prosperity the period was not one of unqualified or unbounded optimism. It was clear to farmers as well as to census enumerators that the frontier of good usable land was approaching an end and that the material resources of the nation were not inexhaustible. For the thirty years previous to 1900 the farm area had expanded almost 15,000,000 acres a year; the increase from 1900 to 1910 was only 4,000,000 acres annually or 4.8 per cent for the decade.

[1] Fred A. Shannon, *The Farmer's Last Frontier,* Vol. V in this series, particularly Chap. XIII.
[2] These value figures must be discounted by the inflation caused largely by the First World War.

From 1910 to 1920 the farm acreage increased 8.8 per cent and improved land on farms 5.1 per cent, but it was an expansion artificially stimulated by the war. The slowing up of the farmers' frontier presaged important changes in American agriculture, for one thing a trend toward more intensive farming and toward the use of scientific methods.

Another aspect of the situation was also obvious. Compared to industry, agriculture was falling behind in the economic life of the nation.[3] The same was true of rural population. As late as 1910 the urban population (those living in towns of over 2,500) numbered 42,166,000, only 45.8 per cent of the total population. By 1920 the percentage was 51.4 (54,304,603). Between 1900 and 1910 rural population increased 11.2 per cent and the urban 34.8; between 1910 and 1920 the rural increase was 5.4 per cent, the urban 25.7. More significant at this point than the fact that urban population was increasing far more rapidly than rural are the statistics on that part of the rural population living on farms, and the statistics on the workers engaged in agriculture. Although farm population was not enumerated until 1920, it appears that in 1900 about 28,000,000 of the 45,600,000 rural population actually lived on farms. In 1920 this was true of about 31,614,000 of a rural population of 51,406,000. Thus, of the rural population about three fifths actually lived on farms in both years. Of the total population of the nation, this group represented 37 per cent in 1900 and 29.9 in 1920.[4] It is also significant that the number of people over ten years of age engaged in agriculture increased but slightly between 1900 and 1920 (from 10,699,000 to 10,923,000, according to P. K. Whelpton), while the percentage of those engaged in agriculture to the total working force of the nation declined from 36.8 per cent to 26.1.[5]

The fact that city population was growing more rapidly than rural and that industry was advancing faster than agriculture in itself might have no deleterious effect upon the farmer or the nation as a whole. On the contrary, the fact that the farms could support this more rapidly growing industry and population was an evidence of more efficient farming and the growth of a larger domestic market. What wor-

[3] Harold Barger and Hans H. Landsberg, *American Agriculture, 1899–1939* (New York: National Bureau of Economic Research, 1942), pp. 291–316.
[4] Shannon, *The Farmer's Last Frontier*, pp. 350–351; *Statistical Abstract of the United States*, 1931, pp. 8–9, 637.
[5] Pascal K. Whelpton, "Occupational Groups in the United States, 1820–1920," *Journal of the American Statistical Association*, XXI, No. 155 (September, 1926), 335–343. These estimates are slightly, but not significantly, higher than those of Hanson given in the Appendix.

ried students of rural life was a feeling that the rural areas were deteriorating in relation to other sections, that farmers were not taking advantage of new opportunities nor insisting upon adequate facilities for a better life.

This paradox of a general prosperity accompanied by a relative decline aroused a new and wider interest in the sociological, economic, and technical problems of the farmer. Universities and theological seminaries began to take an interest in rural sociology; courses and books on agricultural economic problems increased in number, and the work of the agricultural colleges expanded. Books on the "new day," the "new earth," and the "new agriculture" began to appear.[6] Many, hoping to direct these changes into beneficial channels or to improve some of the aspects of rural living, suggested programs of one type or another.[7] At the same time various bureaus of the Department of Agriculture did what they could to develop these suggestions and plans.[8] Still others tried to write optimistically but at the same time objectively, showing the advantages as well as the disadvantages of agriculture as a way of life, and so hold a proportion of ambitious young men to the farm.

Perhaps all this can be symbolized by two acts of Theodore Roosevelt, whose ear was never deaf to popular discussion. Although the interests of agriculture were not specifically represented in the Conference of Governors, called by the President in 1908 "to consider the question of the conservation and use of the great fundamental sources of wealth," or in the National Conservation Commission appointed in 1908, the significance for agriculture of these conservation efforts was clear. The commission was organized in four sections to consider the four great classes of water, forest, land, and mineral resources.[9] In the same year Roosevelt also appointed a five-man Commission on Country Life "to secure from it such information and advice" as would enable him to recommend legislation to

[6] For example, T. Bayard Collins, *The New Agriculture* (New York: Munn & Co., 1909); Kenyon L. Butterfield, *The Farmer and the New Day* (New York: The Macmillan Company, 1919); William S. Harwood, *The New Earth* (New York: The Macmillan Company, 1907).

[7] Frank A. Waugh, *Rural Improvement* (New York: Orange Judd Company, 1917); Butterfield, *The Farmer and the New Day*, pp. 84–210; Thomas Nixon Carver, "The Organization of Rural Interests," *Yearbook of the Department of Agriculture*, 1913, pp. 239–258, and "The Organization of a Rural Community," *Yearbook of the Department of Agriculture*, 1914, pp. 89–138.

[8] Carl W. Thompson, "How the Department of Agriculture Promotes Organization of Rural Life," *Yearbook of the Department of Agriculture*, 1915, pp. 272A–278P.

[9] Liberty Hyde Bailey, ed., *Cyclopedia of American Agriculture* (New York: The Macmillan Company, 3d ed., 1910), Introduction to Chap. VII, Vol. IV, pp. 276–280.

Congress. While pointing out that Americans were making great progress in the development of agricultural resources, the President asserted that "it is equally true that the social and economic institutions of the open country are not keeping pace with the development of the nation as a whole. The farmer is, as a rule, better off than his forebears; but his increase in well-being has not kept pace with the country as a whole."

The commission, consisting for the most part of experts on country life,[10] had no difficulty in getting at the heart of the problem. Reporting in 1909, it asserted that "agriculture is not commercially as profitable as it is entitled to be for the labor and energy that the farmer expends and the risks he assumes" and that "the social conditions in the open country are far short of their possibilities." It pointed out the lack of good roads and of adequate and properly directed schools. It also noted the lack of labor and of adequate credit facilities, and of sufficient incentives to keep the rising generation on the farm. It viewed with concern the "lessening of soil fertility . . . in every part of the United States," the result of wasteful pioneering farming, and a serious agricultural unrest in all parts of the country.

Remedies were suggested and the commission urged that three "great movements of the utmost consequence . . . should be set under way at the earliest possible time, because they are fundamental to the whole problem of ultimate permanent reconstruction." They were (1) to take inventory of country life by means of "an exhaustive study or survey of all the conditions that surround the business of farming," (2) to organize a nationalized extension work, and (3) to inaugurate a general campaign of rural progress. At the time, Congress did little to follow the suggestions of the commission, but, eventually, much was done.[11]

Although agricultural leaders and intelligent farmers realized that important changes were taking place, few even as late as 1917 understood their full significance. They could not, of course, know that farm production as a whole was still increasing relatively more rapidly than it would subsequently, except during wartime, or that agricultural exports as a whole had achieved an importance greater than

[10] The commission consisted of Dean Liberty Hyde Bailey of Cornell University; Henry Wallace, editor of *Wallace's Farmer;* President Kenyon L. Butterfield of the Massachusetts Agricultural College; Gifford Pinchot of the National Forest Service; and Walter H. Page, editor of *World's Work.* Later Charles S. Barrett of Georgia and William A. Beard of California were added.

[11] *Senate Document* No. 705, 60 Cong., 2 Sess. The President's letter in submitting the Report is in *Congressional Record,* 60 Cong., 2 Sess., Vol. XLIII, Pt. 3, pp. 2080–2082.

they would have again in normal times.[12] No farmer could know that most of the basic potentialities of horse-drawn agricultural machinery had been achieved by 1900 nor could he know that within a few years gasoline-driven tractors would provide the chief energy on the farm. He could see trends which showed the declining importance of grains and meats and the growing significance of poultry, eggs, milk, sugar, and citrus fruit, but the extent of this shift was impossible to predict. He could also see a growing interest in scientific agriculture, but he could hardly appreciate the fact that the scientific farming and agricultural education which existed in 1900 was but a mere beginning to what it would be two decades later.

One Iowa farm boy, who later rose high in government service, pictured with a fair degree of accuracy the status of scientific farming in the great agricultural areas of the Middle West:

In the last twenty years before America's entrance into the [First] World War, the horse and buggy pattern of commercial farming culture was for the first time directly or widely changed by the advance of science. . . . until the turn of the century only a few cranks farmed scientifically. Most farmers did indeed use some new machinery that was obviously labor-saving, grew a bit more clover perhaps, and perhaps also were more interested than before in cutting out runts from breeding stock. But the rest was "book-farming" which was a contemptuous way of saying high brow and impractical.

But shortly after the twentieth century began, science began to work a revolution among the mass of farmers. When I went to Ames to study agriculture in 1902, I was not the first boy in my Iowa neighborhood to go to college, but I was the first boy from that neighborhood to go to an *agricultural* college. Ten or fifteen years later it was becoming an accepted thing for all who could afford it. A few farmers began to keep books, count costs, and calculate where profit came and loss occurred. Still more farmers began to feed their stock scientifically, following the advice from "Feeders' Hints" columns in farm journals. Alfalfa came in, and farmers became aware of nitrogen needs of the soil. Dairymen began building up new herds of high-producing Holsteins. Hardy and rust-resistant strains of wheat were accepted eagerly by more and more farmers. Hog men improved their stock, and innoculated against cholera. And finally came the popular demand for county agents—for thoroughly trained men to bring to farmers the advantages of scientific training.[13]

[12] Barger and Landsberg, *American Agriculture, 1899–1939*, pp. 34–37; Everett E. Edwards, "American Agriculture—The First 300 Years," *Yearbook of the Department of Agriculture*, 1940, p. 241.
[13] Milburn L. Wilson in Oliver E. Baker, Ralph Borsodi, and M. L. Wilson, *Agriculture in Modern Life* (New York: Harper & Brothers, 1939), pp. 223–224. Reprinted by permission of Harper & Brothers, publishers.

EXPANSION AND PROSPERITY

Although the relative position of agriculture in American life declined during the thirty years from 1890 to 1920 and rural growth
lagged behind that of total population growth, there was an absolute
expansion in rural population and farm production. The same was
true of the total number of farms and of farm acreage, despite the
fact that the number of farms increased but slightly after 1910. A
glance at the production figures of corn, wheat, and meat animals
as given in the Appendix or in the index figures in the next section
will also make clear that the increase in the production of certain
agricultural commodities was slower than that of farm acreage. Moreover, the growth in crop production was also slower than that for
other types of productive activity. It has been estimated that for the
years 1870 to 1930 the average annual rates of growth were 1.9 per
cent for population, 2.3–2.5 for crops, 4.2 for construction, 4.3 for
manufacturing, 4.7 for railway freight, 5.7 for mining, and 3.7–3.8
for total production.[14]

Agricultural output may have lagged behind other areas of economic production, but the increase in its value in terms of current
dollars was large. Estimates put the value of crops and livestock products grown on farms in 1899 at $4,717,000,000 and in 1917 at $19,331,-
000,000,[15] with the great centers in the North Central states. By
value the most important crops in 1899 were cattle, milk and milk
products, hogs, wheat, and cotton; in 1919 they were hogs, milk and
milk products, cotton, wheat, cattle, and eggs. This great agricultural
production, which surpassed that of any other nation in the world,
was accomplished by less than 11,000,000 workers both in 1900 and
in 1920.

Of farm laborers, that is, members of the family working on the
home farm or hired laborers working out, there were about 4,411,000
in 1900 (15.2 per cent of those gainfully employed) and 4,179,000
in 1920 (10 per cent). Of the total farm labor group, hired labor working out appears to have been slightly more than a third both in 1900
and in 1920.[16] The laborers varied from the hired man employed on
the old-fashioned farm to the heterogeneous group of migratory work-

---

[14] Arthur F. Burns, *Production Trends in the United States since 1870* (New
York: National Bureau of Economic Research, 1934), p. 263.

[15] *Statistical Abstract of the United States*, 1922, p. 133.

[16] Appendix, p. 415; Barger and Landsberg, *American Agriculture, 1899–1939*, p.
231; H. Dewey Anderson and Percy E. Davidson, *Occupational Trends in the
United States* (Stanford University: Stanford University Press, 1940), p. 98.

ers recruited for seasonal jobs on large, single-crop commercial farms. In general they were unskilled, casual laborers, whose wages were low but whose members grew with the development of the mechanized wheat farms of the Middle West and the great fruit and vegetable farms of the Pacific Coast. Sporadic, weak, and short-lived organizations appeared among these groups during the first two decades of the century, generally promoted by organizers of the Socialist party or the Industrial Workers of the World. They often included tenant farmers as well as migratory laborers and were a protest against intolerable conditions. A Sheep Shearers Union was chartered in 1912, but union organization did not appear to any considerable extent until the 1930's.[17]

The rise in prices of agricultural commodities after 1899 was more regular than the previous decline and was the result of a number of influences. The period 1897 to 1914 was one of general prosperity accompanied by a rising price structure for most commodities. The discovery of new sources of gold and new methods of extracting it tended to inflate the currency established officially in 1900 on a basis of gold. To gold inflation and the increasing demands of a prosperous nation must be added the fact that toward the end of the century the demand for foodstuffs was beginning to overtake the supply. A glance at the next table will show that in the years immediately before the First World War the prices received for crops and livestock were not in line with what the farmer paid for labor or for the articles which he needed to buy. After 1914 the insatiable war demands created an artificial situation which sent the prices of agricultural products skyrocketing. During the years 1917 to 1919, in fact, prices for crops and livestock moved ahead sufficiently over the cost of labor or the articles which the farmer bought to put him in a distinctly favorable position. But this lush period was brief. By 1920 the situation was reversed. By that year the cost of farm labor and of the articles needed for farm living and production had moved upward and the prices of farm commodities had dropped. The chief improvement in the status of the farmer had come from 1899 to 1914.

During the deflationary period after the First World War and particularly after the depression beginning in 1929, agricultural experts looked upon the prewar years as a golden age of American agriculture. Much of the New Deal agricultural legislation of the

---

[17] Stuart Jamieson, *Labor Unionism in American Agriculture* (U.S. Department of Agriculture, Bureau of Labor Statistics, *Bulletin* No. 836, Washington: Government Printing Office, 1945), p. 222.

1930's was specifically drawn to restore this level, and the years 1909–1914 were chosen as the criterion upon which to base "parity prices." The following index figures (100 = the average, 1909–1913) give clear indication that the farmer was relatively well off at that time.

TREND IN AGRICULTURAL STATISTICAL DATA

Year	Land Values	Farm Wages	Crop Prices	Live-stock Prices	Crop and Livestock	Crops Value per Acre	Articles Farmer Buys
1899	45	68				57	86
1909	93	98	101	95	98	101	97
1911	99	99	101	90	96	97	100
1914	111	104	101	112	107	103	103
1915	123	105	101	104	102	108	112
1916	136	114	124	122	123	142	125
1917	153	142	198	181	189	209	153
1918	167	176	212	211	211	212	188
1919	202	207	221	212	217	323	212
1920	184	230	208	183	189	148	231

Source: Yearbook of the Department of Agriculture, 1921, p. 787. These index figures check roughly with those of the Bureau of Agricultural Economics. See Frederick Straus and Louis H. Bean, Gross Farm Income and Indices of Farm Production and Prices in the United States, 1869–1937 (U.S. Department of Agriculture, Technical Bulletin No. 703, Washington: Government Printing Office, 1940), p. 125.

AGRICULTURAL OUTPUT

Note has already been made of the fact that the increase in agricultural production in the early decades of the present century was not as rapid as that in industry or mining. The fact should not be forgotten, however, that the agricultural advance was notable, total production increasing over 30 per cent for the two decades 1897–1917. An index of the National Bureau of Economic Research, based on a study of eighty-eight commodities (1899 = 100), shows an increase in the index figures from 95 in 1897 to 120 in 1914, and 124 in 1917.[18] These index figures show an almost uninterrupted rise between 1897 and 1914 except for a major decline in 1907 and minor declines in 1901 and 1913. Several causes may be advanced to explain the lag in agricultural output as against the advance of industry: the slowing up of growth in farm acreage, the tardy acceptance of improved agricultural methods, and the increased cost of farm

[18] Barger and Landsberg, American Agriculture, 1899–1939, p. 21; Frederick Straus and Louis H. Bean, Gross Farm Income and Indices of Farm Production and Prices in the United States, 1869–1937 (U.S. Department of Agriculture, Technical Bulletin No. 703, Washington: Government Printing Office, 1940), pp. 124–139, is more conservative than the NBER index.

operation. Two other factors may have played a part: the decline in the importance of foodstuffs in the export trade and changing dietary habits combined with a tendency to eat less.

One characteristic of agricultural output was the relatively narrow year-by-year fluctuations. Although the rule in agriculture was generally a 2- or 3-point shift, with 7 or 8 points the exception, manufacturing activity ordinarily changed from 5 to 10 points a year. Sometimes the shift was as high as 30 points.[19] Demand for agricultural products is less elastic than that for manufactured products; moreover, the farmer, in any event, is unable to respond as quickly as other producers to changes in demand. Although agricultural output is largely determined by weather, the size of the United States makes the weather seldom uniformly good or bad. High yields in one area offset low yields in another, thus minimizing exaggerated year-by-year fluctuations.

The following index figures from the National Bureau of Economic Research will help to break down the production statistics for the years 1897–1914.

GROUP INDEXES OF OUTPUT

(Average annual percentage change, by groups, 1897–1914)

Grains	+0.6
Potatoes and related crops	+2.8
Tobacco	+1.5
Cotton	+2.6
Wool	+0.6
Sugar crops	+5.0
Meat animals	+0.7
Poultry and eggs	+3.1
Milk and milk products	+1.5
Noncitrus fruit	+1.5
Citrus fruit	+8.9
Oil crops	+3.8
Total	+1.5

Source: Harold Barger and Hans H. Landsberg, *American Agriculture, 1899–1939* (New York: National Bureau of Economic Research, 1942), p. 36. The data for tree nuts and truck crops, which grew tremendously in the years after 1914, were not available for this period, nor were they for hay.

A glance at this table makes clear the fact that citrus fruits, sugar, oil crops (cottonseed, flaxseed, peanuts), and poultry and eggs moved ahead most rapidly. On the other hand, hay, grains, wool, and meat animals showed the slowest advance. In other words, grains, hay,

[19] Solomon Fabricant, *The Output of Manufacturing Industries, 1897–1937* (New York: National Bureau of Economic Research, 1940), p. 44.

and meat were losing ground, while poultry, eggs, milk, sugar, and citrus fruits were developing a growing share in the total output. Despite this fact, a comparison of the net output of all crops and of all livestock products shows that after 1915 the growth of live-stock products was more rapid than the growth of crops.[20] Concerning the trends in the groups listed in the last table more specific information is needed. Of the grains (wheat, corn, oats, rye, barley, rice, buckwheat, and flaxseed), which altogether registered a .6 per cent increase, rice showed the largest increase with 6.6 per cent and wheat the lowest with .3 per cent. Production of buckwheat and flaxseed declined. With the exception of the last two, the output of grains was still advancing up to 1914, but the influences which were to retard them, particularly wheat, were already in evidence—the decline in the per capita consumption of wheat flour and the slackening of foreign demand.[21]

The output of tobacco showed a sudden jump in 1898, a year which marked a permanent transition to a million-acre level and the first 800-pound-an-acre yield since 1875. Little change in the output occurred again until 1909, when a second substantial advance took place. A third upward swing came during the First World War. The United States had long been the largest tobacco exporting nation, but the chief cause for the increased output was the rising domestic consumption, which by 1917 had reached about 8 pounds per capita.[22] The year 1917, according to the NBER index, marked the highest per capita consumption up to 1939, the end of the bureau's computations. Between 1900 and 1939 the consumption of cigars reached the high point in 1920, chewing tobacco in 1900, smoking tobacco in 1916, and snuff in 1918, whereas cigarettes showed a steady increase in each year. A great spurt in cigarette smoking came during the First World War. Less than one tenth of all tobacco consumed went into cigarettes in 1915; three years later, cigarettes took one sixth. The wider use of cigarettes goes far to explain the increase by about 50 per cent in the acreage planted to tobacco between 1900 and 1917 and the shift to the production of flue-cured tobacco.[23]

Cotton, the most valuable of all American exports, experienced

[20] Barger and Landsberg, *American Agriculture, 1899–1939*, pp. 30–31.

[21] *Ibid.*, p. 59; Carleton R. Ball, C. E. Leighton, Oscar C. Stine, and Oliver E. Baker, "Wheat Production and Marketing," *Yearbook of the Department of Agriculture*, 1921, pp. 77–160.

[22] Barger and Landsberg, *American Agriculture, 1899–1939*, pp. 71–72; Wightman W. Gardner, Eugene G. Moss, and Others, "History and Status of Tobacco Culture," *Yearbook of the Department of Agriculture*, 1922, pp. 451–453.

[23] *Yearbook of the Department of Agriculture*, 1922, Table 246, p. 725.

between 1897 and 1914 a great period of expansion. During these years acreage increased from 24,320,000 to 36,832,000 and production from 10,898,000 bales to 16,135,000, most of the acreage increase occurring in Oklahoma and western Texas. Although acreage expanded considerably in the mid-1920's, the production an acre never again surpassed that of 1914 and the total production surpassed it only twice up to 1937. Despite the demands of the First World War, cotton production decreased between 1916 and 1922. The causes were destruction from the boll weevil, decline in exports, and greater competition from abroad.[24]

Increase in wool production, as disclosed in the preceding index table, was slight between 1897 and 1917. The best years were from 1908 to 1911; domestic production in 1909 reached a prewar record of somewhat over 328,000,000 pounds. Beginning in 1910 there was a prolonged decline not reversed until 1922. Both production and consumption of wool were affected somewhat by the tariff. The period of free wool from 1894 to 1897 brought greatly increased imports and the highest per capita consumption since 1874. It also brought the highest consumption relative to other fibers suitable for clothing. The reimposition of tariffs in 1897 probably helped to increase domestic production but held back domestic consumption. It is impossible to determine the effect of the return of free wool in the tariff of 1913 because of the abnormal demands of the war. Despite this urgent demand, there was a slight decline in domestic production, but a great increase in imports.[25]

During the years 1897–1901 the proportion of domestically produced sugar consumed in the United States was 14.3 per cent. This expanded during the years 1912–1916 to 23.2 per cent. Of the 14.3 per cent from 1897 to 1901, the figure for cane sugar was 11.1 and that for beet 3.2. Of the 23.2 per cent from 1912 to 1916, the amount of cane was 5.7 and that of beet 17.5. It is clear that the proportion of home-grown sugar was increasing and that beet sugar was growing at the expense of cane. Actually, the production of both advanced until 1911, after which came a period of stagnation for both. Expansion of beet sugar began when the McKinley Tariff of 1890 put sugar on the free list but granted to domestic growers a cash bounty, sometimes augmented by state bounties. Later tariffs were high enough

[24] *Yearbook of the Department of Agriculture,* 1931, p. 672; Alexander M. Agelasto, C. B. Doyle, and Others, "The Cotton Situation," *Yearbook of the Department of Agriculture,* 1921, p. 334; Barger and Landsberg, *American Agriculture, 1899–1939,* pp. 76–84.
[25] Barger and Landsberg, *American Agriculture, 1899–1939,* pp. 84–88.

to continue its promotion. The period of most spectacular growth was from 1899 to 1906. In the latter year more domestic sugar was obtained from beets than from cane. From 50 to 60 per cent of this new industry was centered in the Rocky Mountain states and western Nebraska.[26]

By far the most important branch of farm economy in 1897 was the production of meat animals; this continued to be true during the next twenty years. It amounted in 1899 to 32.5 per cent of all agricultural output. Of the various meat animals, hogs and cattle were the most important, with hog raising maintaining throughout these years a slight lead. Although the center of meat animal production was in the North Central states, Iowa taking the lead, livestock raising remained the least concentrated type of agricultural activity. Livestock increased steadily to the end of the First World War, but by no means as fast as farm output as a whole. Production of calves expanded rapidly from 1897 to 1917; sheep and lamb production moved ahead to about 1910 and then declined. Cattle and hog production increased slowly. The failure to expand more rapidly, or even keep up in relation to the growth of population, was caused chiefly by the changing dietary habits of the nation, by the decline in the export trade of both commodities, by the inability of beef raising to compete successfully with other farm enterprises, and by the end of the frontier. Aggregate beef production and per capita consumption rose until 1909 and then declined.[27]

Except for meat animals combined, milk and its products represented the most important farm product in value in 1897 and never dropped below second place throughout the period. Growth was continuous, but most rapid during the war and postwar period. From 1897 to about 1918 more milk left the farms as butter or butter fat than as milk; after that the situation was reversed. Although the center of dairying was in the North Central states, the distribution of milk cows in 1920 was as wide as that of farming. New York State, for example, had more milk cows than any state except Wisconsin. Like dairying, the distribution of poultry and eggs was also wide and also expanded rapidly. Between 1897 and 1914 poultry and egg production increased more rapidly than that of agricultural products as

[26] *Ibid.*, pp. 89–95; Elmer W. Brandeis, Charles O. Townsend, and Others, "Sugar," *Yearbook of the Department of Agriculture*, 1923, pp. 151–228.
[27] Barger and Landsberg, *American Agriculture, 1899–1939*, pp. 27, 36, 97, 100–106; Earl W. Sheets, Oliver E. Baker, and Others, "Our Beef Industry," *Yearbook of the Department of Agriculture*, 1921, pp. 227–322.

a whole and was exceeded in rapidity of growth only by citrus fruits, sugar, and oil crops.[28]

Despite the dietary shifts in the habits of the American people, the place of noncitrus fruits in domestic agriculture changed but little between 1897 and 1914. Their growth was about the same as the growth of agriculture as a whole. Statistics on fruit production prior to 1917 are not reliable, but it appears that between 1897 and 1914 apples and peaches approximately held their own, whereas pears, apricots, dried prunes, and grapes moved ahead. Unlike the noncitrus, the citrus fruits grew tremendously, profiting from improvements in transportation and the demand for nonfattening foods and vitamins. During the forty years from 1897 to 1937 production of citrus fruits led all other farm products in rapidity of growth, the most accelerated period being from 1897 to 1914. From the beginning California and Florida were the chief citrus-producing states. California produced all the lemons, Florida and California most of the oranges and, until recent years, most of the grapefruit. The first shipment of oranges left California as early as 1877, but it was not until 1899 that she achieved the leading position. By 1905 her output surpassed the ten-million-box level; ten years later the figure was twenty million. Florida took the lead in grapefruit in the 1890's and retained it, but her yield did not reach a million boxes until 1909. Production in California did not develop on a large scale until after 1910 nor that of Texas until the 1920's. California reached a million-box output of lemons in 1900 and doubled it by 1914. Growth was particularly rapid in the next decade.[29]

GEOGRAPHIC SHIFT

Although the frontier had officially ended in 1890, the movement of agriculture continued westward. Production of wheat, it is true, began to decline in California in the 1890's, but there was increased production in the Red River Valley, in the Kansas-Nebraska belt, and in Idaho, Washington, and Oregon. Oklahoma, but recently opened to settlement, was already producing a large crop. During the first decade of the new century the California crop continued

[28] Barger and Landsberg, *American Agriculture, 1899–1939*, pp. 27, 36, 106–113, 372–373; Edmund E. Vial, *Production and Consumption of Manufactured Dairy Products* (U.S. Department of Agriculture, *Technical Bulletin* No. 722, Washington: Government Printing Office, April, 1940), pp. 1–20.

[29] Barger and Landsberg, *American Agriculture, 1899–1939*, pp. 36, 119–128.

to decline, but the great wheat belt of the Midwest shifted a little farther west on the Great Plains. During this decade the crops of Kansas, Nebraska, and the Dakotas more than doubled and there was a large increase in Montana, Idaho, and the eastern Oregon-Washington district.

The shifting westward of wheat production in the early years of the twentieth century into the West North Central states was caused chiefly by two factors. The first was the development of the technique of dry farming. This included not only the methods of conserving moisture but also the invention or adaptation of machinery for use on level land—a manageable tractor, a disk plow, and a disk drill. The second was the realization that the best bread wheats were not the soft wheats favored by Eastern farmers but hard wheat of high gluten content produced in regions of limited rainfall. Such hard winter wheats were discovered and introduced, particularly "turkey red," a variety of Russian hard winter wheat. To these stimuli came a great artificial impetus after 1914 with the First World War. Production of wheat reached new heights, particularly in Kansas (where 15 per cent of the 1919 crop was grown) and in other areas of this region.[30]

As with wheat, the corn belt also moved westward and northward in the 1890's, particularly in the Missouri Valley. The most important development in corn during the decade 1899–1909 was the increase of three million acres in Oklahoma. This advance was not permanent; by 1919 the acreage of corn in that state was about the same and the production less than in 1899. The land relinquished there by corn had been taken over by wheat. Nevertheless, production maps for 1919 show a definite westward shift of corn over earlier decades, particularly in the area west of the ninetieth meridian.[31]

The history of the lesser grains shows a somewhat similar pattern. Production of oats increased in relative importance in the southern part of the Great Plains and westward to California, while it decreased in the cotton states east of Texas and in the belt of states just north of them. The history of barley was largely dominated by the production of stock feed and by the malt business. When the New York crop proved inadequate, the malt houses shifted to Wisconsin

[30] John D. Hicks, "The Western Middle West, 1900–1914," *Agricultural History*, XX, No. 2 (April, 1946), 65–77; C. Warren Thornthwaite, "Climate and Settlement in the Great Plains," *Yearbook of the Department of Agriculture*, 1941, pp. 184–185; Carleton R. Ball and Others, "Wheat Production and Marketing," *Yearbook of the Department of Agriculture*, 1921, pp. 94–96.

[31] Clyde E. Leighty, Clyde W. Warburton, and Others, "The Corn Crop," *Yearbook of the Department of Agriculture*, 1921, pp. 173–175.

and Minnesota, and the crops then expanded in Minnesota, California, and in eastern Washington and Oregon. In the decade ending in 1909 there was a rapid development in the Dakotas and Kansas. Minnesota by 1909 was the leading barley state with California second, but almost half the national crop was raised in Minnesota and the Dakotas.[32] In these areas barley was grown more often for stock feed than for the brewing industry. The pertinent aspects of the story of rye between 1899 and 1919 may be briefly stated by noting that production almost disappeared from New England and New York but increased in the North Central dairy states of Michigan, Wisconsin, Minnesota, and particularly in North Dakota.

Turning from the food crops to cotton and tobacco, the outstanding geographic fact regarding cotton was the tripling of production in Texas between 1879 and 1899. This development of cotton in the Southwest, particularly in western Texas and in Oklahoma, continued during the decade 1899–1909. These years were also marked by the introduction of cotton into the irrigated districts of southern California. Indeed, this decade saw a total cotton acreage increase for the country of 32 per cent, and the expansion continued until 1914. By that year, however, the ravages of the boll weevil had begun to affect the cotton crop seriously as the pest spread northeastward from Texas. Texas remained the leading state, but the relative positions of Georgia, South Carolina, Oklahoma, Arkansas, and North Carolina improved.[33] The old centers of tobacco culture remained, but the increased demand, particularly for the bright flue-cured product, led to the development of the so called "new belt" section of eastern North Carolina and South Carolina. During the period 1899 to 1919 the production of North Carolina more than doubled and that of South Carolina more than trebled. Production in Virginia, Ohio, and Maryland declined.[34]

In the two decades 1880–1900 beef cattle had declined in the northeastern states because of the growth of the dairy industry. On the other hand, the number of beef cattle on the prairies and the Great Plains expanded greatly, particularly in Iowa and Kansas and in the western part of the corn belt. After 1900 there was a consider-

[32] Carleton R. Ball, Thomas R. Stanton, and Others, "Oats, Barley, Rye, Rice, Grain Sorghums, Feed, Flax and Buckwheat," *Yearbook of the Department of Agriculture*, 1922, pp. 476, 480–481, 488–496, 506–508, 563–566.

[33] Agelasto and Others, "The Cotton Situation," *Yearbook of the Department of Agriculture*, 1921, pp. 332–334, 350; Barger and Landsberg, *American Agriculture, 1899–1939*, pp. 76–82.

[34] Garner and Others, "History and Status of Tobacco Culture," *Yearbook of the Department of Agriculture*, 1922, pp. 406–408.

able increase of beef cattle in Minnesota, South Dakota, and Nebraska, where wheat growing in some regions gave way to livestock. Beef cattle increased on the Pacific Coast, on the coastal plains of the cotton belt, and in the western range region. In this area there was also a rapid development of purebred beef cattle after 1900.[35]

By 1890 Chicago had become the market center of the greatest dairy system in the United States. During the 1890's Wisconsin showed the greatest increase of dairy cows in the nation. Between 1900 and 1910, however, Wisconsin dropped to second place (Iowa was first), pushing New York into third. Marked increases were also evident in Minnesota and on the Pacific Coast, with a decline in New England. By this time a distinct dairy belt had developed, extending from the Atlantic Coast north of Maryland and north of the corn belt west to the semiarid plains. By 1920 Wisconsin had resumed first rank among the dairy states, with New York second and Minnesota third. City markets in all sections had built up and maintained a milk industry within an accessible radius. The production of butter and cheese, however, tended toward the Middle West, where feed was more abundant and cheaper.[36]

Although the growing of hogs is widely dispersed throughout the nation, commercial production is largely centered in the area of greatest corn production. However, some movement is discernible, largely westward into the Great Plains or northward into Wisconsin and Minnesota. As early as 1900 almost three fifths of the sheep were in the western range country; the number in the eastern seaboard or Middle West had long been declining. By 1900 sheep had largely disappeared from the Atlantic Coast. There still remained large numbers in Ohio's wool region; in fact, about as many as in Montana or Wyoming. Sheep were also to be found in the Appalachian mountains and southern Michigan, but west of the Mississippi sheepherding had already moved out of the Great Plains and into the more mountainous areas.[37]

MECHANIZATION

The relatively high degree of mechanization in American agriculture is the result primarily of three factors: the importance of

[35] Sheets and Others, "Our Beef Supply," *Yearbook of the Department of Agriculture,* 1921, pp. 236–239.

[36] Carl W. Larson, L. M. Davis, and Others, "The Dairy Industry," *Yearbook of the Department of Agriculture,* 1922, pp. 300–301.

[37] Damon A. Spencer, Maurice C. Hall, and Others, "The Sheep Industry," *Yearbook of the Department of Agriculture,* 1923, pp. 234–251.

commercial agriculture, the size of the American farm, and the scarcity of farm labor. All of these influences continued to operate in the period 1897–1917. By the earlier date they had produced much of the machinery basic to the technique of modern farming—steel plows, seed drills, cultivators, mowers, harvesters, threshers, cream separators and testers, and other more specialized machinery. Before 1900 self-binders, headers, and, on the Pacific Coast, combines were also used. In fact, most of these machines had already experienced decades of testing and improvement.[38] By the end of the century horse-age agriculture had reached its highest development. Horse (or mule) power had been adapted to almost all types of farm machinery where it was at all feasible and had reached its climax in the combines in the western wheat fields drawn by twenty to forty horses.

Steam power had been used successfully since 1850 for stationary threshing, but experiments with steam traction had achieved only limited success. The expensive, clumsy, and heavy steam engines were used with combines on the Pacific Coast as early as the 1880's, but not east of the Rocky Mountains until about 1910, and then in smaller sizes. The headers and barges used on the prairies and the Great Plains in the early years of the present century were still drawn by horses.[39] Clearly, a new source of power was needed. Many agricultural engineers at the opening of the century saw possibilities in electric power, but its use hitherto had been limited to stationary engines, particularly for dairying and pumping water. As for hauling machinery for plowing, cultivating, and harvesting, electricity offered even less than steam, although it came to be used for plowing in a few localities in Europe.[40]

The most important development in farm machinery after 1900 was the introduction of the internal-combustion engine, first as a source of stationary power, then in the tractor, and finally in the truck. This introduction came slowly and it made headway first in the great wheat-producing regions of California, Montana, the Dakotas, Nebraska, and Kansas, the same regions where steam power had first been used. As with steam power, the early tractors could be used for plowing, harvesting, and threshing, but not for cultivating row

[38] C. L. Holmes and Maurice R. Cooper, "Farm Mechanization," *Yearbook of the Department of Agriculture*, 1932; Barger and Landsberg, *American Agriculture, 1899–1939*, pp. 194–201.

[39] Shannon, *The Farmer's Last Frontier*, pp. 133–137.

[40] Lynn W. Ellis and Edward A. Rumley, *Power and the Plow* (Garden City: Doubleday, Page & Company, 1911), p. 11.

crops.[41] It was not until 1924 that an all-purpose tractor was developed. As late as 1921 an Illinois study of power operations believed that the chief use of farm tractors was for plowing, disking, and harrowing. Other operations, it believed, were not suitable for the gasoline tractor.[42]

Although gasoline as a source of power in agriculture was not unknown at the opening of the century, it made little impression for some years. Its real development as a source of agricultural power appears to date from the Winnipeg Exposition of 1908, where gasoline and steam tractors were pitted against one another for the first time in a series of plowing contests. Two influences were mainly responsible for the subsequent adoption of gasoline power on the farm. The first was the constant improvement of the gasoline tractor as a mobile power unit and the development of the combined harvester-thresher. Reduction of weight, simplification of design, and greater ease in operation were all important factors. The second great influence was the pressure for greater production and the scarcity of labor during the First World War. The following table illustrates the growth of gasoline-combustion power units on the farm during the early years.

Year	Tractors	Trucks	Automobiles
1910	1,000	0	50,000
1914	17,000	15,000	343,000
1917	51,000	60,000	966,000
1919	158,000	111,000	1,760,000

Adapted from Harold Barger and Hans H. Landsberg, *American Agriculture, 1899–1939* (New York: National Bureau of Economic Research, 1942), p. 204. By permission of National Bureau of Economic Research.

Introduction of the tractor not only substituted mechanical power for animal power, and the gasoline for the steam engine, but it also stimulated the redesigning of many farm implements. Above all, it made possible the pulling of gangs of more plows at one time. The influence of mechanical power upon seeding, drilling, harrowing, and fertilizing has been less spectacular, but eventually these operations have also been done mechanically. Since harvesting machinery is heavier and more complicated than machinery for planting and seeding, the gasoline tractor was more quickly adapted to harvesting.

[41] *Yearbook of the Department of Agriculture,* 1932, pp. 414–423; Barger and Landsberg, *American Agriculture, 1899–1939,* p. 202.

[42] Walter F. Handschin, J. B. Andrews, and Emil Rauchenstein, "The Horse and the Tractor," University of Illinois Agricultural Experiment Station, *Bulletin* No. 231 (Urbana: University of Illinois Press, 1921), pp. 202–205.

It is true, nevertheless, that steam-powered combines were being built in California as late as 1905, and that the internal-combustion engine was not seriously applied to the combine until after 1910. As late as 1911 more steam engines were used for plowing than were gasoline tractors. Nevertheless, by 1917 Ford had already started building gasoline tractors on the assembly line.

The transition from the era of animal power to that of mechanical power marked a real agricultural revolution. As already noted, its major effects were not evident until the 1920's, and the process is not even yet wholly completed. Moreover, the revolution was by no means equally distributed over the various sections of the country. Chiefly responsible for the adoption of mechanical power was the fact that it cost less than manual labor. Certainly the reduction of labor requirements, or to state it another way, the increase in the physical efficiency of human labor, was the most important effect of mechanical development. According to one study the approximate labor requirements for major operations in the production of one acre of wheat (20 bushels) declined from 8.8 hours in 1896 to 3.3 hours in 1930; similar requirements for the production of one acre of corn (40 bushels) dropped from 15.1 hours in 1894 to 6.9 in 1930; and for cotton, from 102.4 hours in 1895 to 71.8 in 1930.[43] Man-hours required in the production of some crops were reduced as much as 50 per cent in some localities during the first thirty years of the century. Other statistics help to illustrate this increased efficiency of labor. The number of acres harvested by a worker increased from 25.6 in 1890 to 33.2 in 1920. By 1929 the number of acres harvested by a worker in North and South Dakota, Nebraska, and Kansas was over 100. While total agricultural production increased, the ratio of agricultural workers to all workers declined from 36.8 per cent in 1900 to 26.1 in 1920. It is not surprising that the number of farms above 174 acres increased more rapidly between 1900 and 1920 than did those with a lower acreage.[44]

In summarizing this section it should be noted that although the number of horses on farms increased until 1918 and the number of mules until 1926, mechanical power made relatively greater gains, at least after 1914. The stationary gas engine came into use between 1890 and 1900, whereas electricity, the gasoline-powered tractor, and the truck began to be used on farms between 1900 and 1910. Since

[43] Wilbur M. Hurst and Lillian M. Church, *Power and Machinery in Agriculture* (U.S. Department of Agriculture, *Miscellaneous Publications* No. 157, Washington: Government Printing Office, April, 1933), pp. 13–21.
[44] *Ibid.*, pp. 8–13.

then the use of all of these, including electric motor power, has expanded with new devices. The value of machinery on an average farm increased in current dollars from $378 in 1890 to $981 in 1920 and the value for each worker from $189 to $577. In certain ways the coming of the truck and the automobile was more significant to farmers up to 1917 than was the gasoline tractor. The truck lessened the time consumed in production and widened the immediate marketing area for vegetable, fruit, and poultry farms. The influence of the automobile in enlarging the business and social opportunities of the farmer and his family did much to improve many aspects of farm life. Both the truck and the automobile contributed greatly to the movement for better rural roads.

AGRICULTURE IN FOREIGN TRADE

Agriculture played an important role not only in American economic life but in that of western Europe as well. This reached a climax between 1870 and 1900, when a large and mounting volume of agricultural exports moved into Great Britain, Germany, France, and other nearby nations. These exports included all of the principal cereals, livestock products, cotton, and tobacco. The chief causes for the tremendous flow were the industrialization of western Europe, the rapid growth of its urban population, and, at least in England and Germany, the partial neglect of agriculture, as these nations turned definitely to industry. This flow of trade was perfectly normal from the point of view of international trade balances. The United States had long been a debtor to western Europe, and she paid her interest and principal largely with agricultural products.[45]

In brief, American agricultural products had made possible the rapid industrialization and urbanization of western Europe and incidentally had provided a means for payment to Europe of money that had helped to build American railroads and industries. The insatiable European market was likewise an important factor in rapidly developing the agricultural production of the United States. It should be noted, however, that this expansion was not all gain. The European market encouraged a too rapid extension of the frontier and a production of agricultural commodities so large as to force sales at prices often ruinously low to the farmer. "The European markets absorbed the quantities of American farm exports that they did,"

[45] Arthur P. Chew, "The Meaning of Foreign Trade for Agriculture," *Yearbook of the Department of Agriculture*, 1940, pp. 566–584.

says one expert, "largely because we were conducting the most stupendous bargain counter in the history of agriculture." [46]

But this bargain counter based on the rapid and ruinous exploitation of America's virgin land could not go on indefinitely. Various influences changed the picture of American foreign trade during the early years of the new century. First of all, the nations of continental Europe began again to emphasize the policy of economic self-sufficiency in a new mercantilism which sought to strengthen agriculture through bounties, tariffs, and special transportation rates. Their reasons were economic and political, and the results, particularly in Germany, were remarkably successful. Aided by the most advanced scientific agriculture and the shifting of crops, Germany stemmed the tide of agricultural decline and greatly increased such important crops as potatoes and sugar beets. She also tripled pork production between 1873 and 1912. One result was that American exports of corn, bacon, hams, and shoulders to Germany almost disappeared by 1914. Likewise the efforts of France to strengthen her agriculture cut her net import of wheat from one seventh of her home production to one thirteenth. [47]

Europe, moreover, was by no means entirely dependent upon the American bargain counter. As Germany pushed her manufactured exports into Russia, the Danubian countries, and South America, she increasingly took agricultural products in exchange. Great Britain in similar manner found large markets in Latin America and in her own colonies of Canada, Australia, and India, and in return bought large amounts of agricultural products from them, particularly beef and pork. Viewing the picture from another angle, it should be noted that the United States was becoming increasingly an industrial nation, in fact, by 1900 the greatest in the world. In theory, her position as a place where manufactured commodities could be sold should have declined. Nevertheless, the value of imports both from Great Britain and from Germany almost tripled between 1898 and 1914.

Exportation of agricultural commodities also declined because of a developing domestic market. Industrial development and a rapidly increasing urban population had "caught up with the overstimulated agricultural development of the free-land period." [48] This increased demand at home was accompanied by rising prices and enough inflation to make the United States a less desirable region from which to

[46] Edwin G. Nourse, *American Agriculture and the European Market* (New York: McGraw-Hill Book Company, 1924), p. 28.
[47] *Ibid.*, pp. 33–36.   [48] *Ibid.*, p. 38.

buy for those nations desiring to exchange manufactured goods for agricultural products. It is true that the price rise during these years was world-wide, but the important fact was that prices rose more rapidly in the United States than in Great Britain, the principal market for American farm products.[49]

It is impossible to determine with exactness the effect of the American high tariff policy on domestic agriculture during the pre-war years. Clearly the high tariffs retarded imports, but since the United States was a debtor nation, she needed a favorable balance of trade. As it happened, this created no great difficulties in foreign trade, for under the conditions existing before the First World War the western European nations had an adequate supply of dollar exchange to buy from America more than they sold. The long-run effect upon American agriculture, however, seems to have been detrimental. By protecting American "infant" industries, the tariff kept the prices of manufactured goods which farmers bought higher than they would otherwise have been, and by helping to develop American manufacturing it often reduced the market in the United States for foreign-manufactured commodities used to pay for American agricultural products. It was also clear that the high tariffs as a rule gave but slight protection to the American farmer. He produced a surplus of most commodities for export, and the prices he obtained were set by the world market and not by the tariff. The few commodities, such as sugar and wool, which were not produced in surplus, and the prices of which in the domestic market might be set by the tariff, affected directly but relatively few domestic producers.[50]

A combination of these influences changed fundamentally the picture of American agricultural exports. Domestic agricultural exports as a whole did not decline in value; they rose, in fact, from $951,628,000 in 1901 to $1,113,974,000 in the first war year of 1914. Nevertheless, two important developments took place: first, the percentage of agricultural products in total exports dropped during these years from 65.2 per cent to 47.8; and, second, the importance of foodstuffs in the American export trade declined. Exports of fresh beef, for example, dropped from 352,000,000 pounds in 1901 to 6,000,000 in 1914; bacon from a 1898 maximum of 650,000,000 pounds to a low point of 152,000,000 in 1910 and 194,000,000 in 1914. Exports of lard stood up better, but even here the drop from 711,000,000

[49] *Ibid.*, pp. 274–303.
[50] L. A. Wheeler, "Reciprocal Trade Agreements—A New Method of Tariff Making," *Yearbook of the Department of Agriculture*, 1940, pp. 587–588.

pounds in 1899 to about half of that in 1910, and 481,000,000 in 1914 was astonishing. Wheat and flour exports reached their prewar peak (in terms of grain) with 235,000,000 bushels in 1902. This figure dropped as low as 44,000,000 bushels in 1905 and averaged less than 79,000,000 in 1910–1912, but recovered to 146,000,000 in 1914. The biggest prewar year for corn and corn meal (in terms of grain) was 213,000,000 bushels in 1900; the smallest was less than 11,000,000 in 1914, although the latter figure was far less than the average for the preceding decade.[51]

Although the export of coarser and bulkier foods fell off, that of other foods, such as rice, cottonseed oil, and fresh, dried, and canned fruits maintained or increased its volume. Moreover, cotton and tobacco exports continued to increase at a fairly steady rate. The shift in the relative importance of various exports in value may be illustrated by the fact that cotton in 1900 (fiscal year) comprised less than 30 per cent of all agricultural exports, but in 1914 it reached 55 per cent; grain products in the same year decreased from 31 per cent to 15 per cent; packing house products from slightly over 21 per cent to less than 14 per cent. Tobacco, on the other hand, showed an increase from 3.4 per cent to 4.8, and the remaining agricultural exports lumped together showed a slight decrease. As far as the dependence of the four principal export crops on the foreign market was concerned, cotton exhibited the greatest stability. In 1900 the percentage of the cotton crop exported was 66.30; in 1913 it was 62.56, averaging about two thirds of domestic production throughout the period. The proportion of the wheat crop exported declined from 35.84 per cent to 19.07, and the corn crop from 7.24 to 0.44. Tobacco showed an increase from 38.78 per cent to 47.16, but actually the average for the period was less than that of the 1890's.[52] Except for cotton, tobacco, and fruit, the volume of agricultural exports by 1910 was down nearly to the level of the 1880's.

The principal destination of American agricultural exports, as already noted, was western Europe. During the years 1895–1899 that area purchased on the average 88.20 per cent of all American agricultural exports; the average from 1910–1914 dropped to 83.29. The chief purchasers were Great Britain and Germany. For the years 1895–1899 Britain purchased 53.40 per cent of American agricultural exports, but for 1910–1914 about 37.47. Germany, on the other hand,

---

[51] These figures are largely taken from the *Yearbook of the Department of Agriculture*, 1919, pp. 698–702.
[52] Nourse, *Agriculture and the European Market*, pp. 277–285.

increased her purchases from an average of 13.60 per cent to 20.34.[53] Although the British market declined, the markets in Canada, and in Mexico, Cuba, and other Latin American nations increased, as did those in Asia. Since the principal change in destination occurred in the trade with Great Britain, it should be recalled that the decline was caused primarily by a falling off in purchases of wheat, wheat flour, corn, beef, and bacon. On the other hand, cotton exports to Great Britain declined but little and the exports of tobacco increased.

Although the export of basic American foodstuffs fell off, these years saw an accelerated rate of growth in agricultural imports. Such imports were valued in 1900 at $420,139,000; in 1914, at $924,247,000. From the preceding discussion of exports it is evident that the growth in the value of agricultural exports was caused in part by a rising level of prices as well as an increase in their physical quantity. On the other hand, the physical quantity of certain important agricultural imports did increase strikingly during the period 1900–1914. The value of agricultural imports during the years 1897–1901 averaged 45 per cent of the value of agricultural exports; in the year ending June 30, 1914, they amounted to 83 per cent.[54]

The most important of the agricultural imports in dollar value during these years were sugar, coffee, hides and skins, silk, and vegetable fibers. Except for coffee and silk, all of these groups were in some competition with domestic production. With the exception of sugar, all of these imports grew strikingly in value whereas sugar grew in physical volume. From 1900 on, sugar, coffee, and hides and skins contended for first place. Measured in value, sugar averaged between 1902 and 1914 about 14.7 per cent of total agricultural imports; coffee, 13.5, and the hides group, 12.9. Throughout the period 1870–1940 fruits comprised between 4 and 5 per cent of the total value of imports and wool about 4 per cent. In 1914 the vegetable fibers (cotton, manila, sisal, jute, and flax) comprised 8 per cent, and tobacco 3.8.

AGRICULTURE AND THE FIRST WORLD WAR

Undoubtedly the slump in the export trade of foodstuffs was the most discouraging aspect of American agriculture in the years previous to the First World War. Nevertheless, the years 1909–1914 have

---

[53] "Distribution of Agricultural Exports from the United States," *Trade of Information Bulletin* No. 177 (Washington: Government Printing Office, 1924), p. 9.
[54] Nourse, *Agriculture and the European Market*, pp. 312–322.

come to be regarded as the nearest to an ideal situation that the American farmer has enjoyed during periods of peace, at least up to 1946. Says an agricultural economist, "Farming had emerged finally as a comparatively stable business, with gradually advancing land values, an improving physical plant, fairly tolerable conditions of tenure and debt, and a strengthened voice in national affairs." [55] Exportation of food crops declined, it is true, but the production of an exportable surplus remained an important part of the American agricultural system. To make up for a declining foreign market was the increasing domestic outlet.

Although the Wilson administration had begun to tackle the problems of credit and distribution, the major problem of that period was considered to be production. The research and educational facilities of the government were rapidly expanding and were at the service of the farmer. By 1914 the exploitation of virgin land had leveled off into a more intensive agricultural system with some attention to conservation. Into this "relatively tranquil period" came the First World War to upset some tendencies, intensify others, and in general to force America, at least for the time being, to fit itself to an altered pattern of trade and consumption. One of the war's first and most obvious effects was to reverse the downward trend of food-crop exports and send them skyrocketing.

Shortages of food in the Allied countries (Great Britain, France, Italy, and Belgium) developed early and were particularly acute in breadstuffs, fats, and sugars. Before the war the Allies had produced about 1,500,000 bushels of wheat, corn, oats, barley, and rye, but consumed nearly 2,250,000,000. The United States, Russia, Canada, and other nations had made up the difference. Similarly the Allies in 1913 imported 1,500,000,000 pounds of animal fats mainly from Denmark, the Netherlands, Switzerland, Scandinavia, and Russia. Sugar was largely obtained from their own beet sugar farms. Shortages developed primarily from three causes: the shutting off of normal imports, the lack of manpower, and the destruction of crops. The German navy cut off imports from Russia and the Baltic nations while the destruction of Allied shipping by submarines and mines made the long haul from Australia and the Argentine a risky affair. Typical of the effect of the war upon certain crops was the almost complete destruction of the European beet sugar industry.[56]

[55] Albert B. Genung, "Agriculture in the World War Period," *Yearbook of the Department of Agriculture*, 1940, pp. 277–278.
[56] *Ibid.*, pp. 279–280; Frank M. Surface, *American Pork Production in the World War* (Chicago: A. W. Shaw Company, 1926), pp. 11–23.

The first effect of the war on American agriculture was the closing of the commodity exchanges and a brief depression. With the arrival of official buying representatives from Great Britain and France, the situation quickly changed. It was clear that the United States would be called on to supply the major portion of the foodstuffs needed which western Europe had previously obtained elsewhere. Of the various crops stimulated by the war, wheat received the first and greatest impulse. In the ten years before the war the United States had harvested annually about 48,000,000 acres and exported 107,000,-000 bushels. In 1915 the wheat acreage expanded to 60,000,000, and the crop, the largest up to that time in American history, ran to over 1,000,000,000 bushels, 243,000,000 bushels of which were exported. Falling prices and a black-rust epidemic reduced the planting in 1916 to 52,000,000 acres and the crop to 636,000,000 bushels. This short crop sent the price of wheat up to $2.40 a bushel by the spring of 1917, when the United States entered the war.[57]

Corn, on the other hand, did not expand substantially either in acreage or in production. Acreage average from 1909 to 1913 was 104,-229,000 and average production 2,708,334,000 bushels. The best war year was 1917, when acreage climbed to 116,730,000 and production to 3,055,000,000 bushels. This relatively small expansion is curious because the demand for pork and lard (into which most corn goes) was great. In the five prewar years the United States export of pork and lard to Great Britain averaged 450,000,000 pounds; by 1918 this had climbed to over 1,000,000,000. The increase in exports was made possible by a decrease in domestic consumption of pork, but prices more than doubled. Beef as well as pork was greatly stimulated by the war. The number of cattle other than milk cows increased by 25 per cent. Prices received by farmers for beef cattle jumped from $6.24 in 1914 to $9.56 in 1919; exports of beef from 150,000,000 pounds in 1914 to 957,000,000 in 1918. At the same time domestic per capita consumption increased. Despite large-scale beef exports, dairy products also showed considerable advance in production and in exports.[58]

The World War history of cotton and tobacco is interesting. The production of cotton in 1914 was the largest up to that time in American history—16,000,000 bales from 36,000,000 acres. War closed American cotton exchanges, cut off the German market, and demoralized the cotton trade. Cotton exports, which had averaged about 8,500,000 bales in the prewar years, dropped to a little over 6,000,000

[57] Genung, "Agriculture in the World War Period," pp. 280–284.
[58] Ibid., pp. 284, 286–288.

during the war. Increased domestic demand, however, stimulated prices and that, with moderately small crops, pushed prices up to an average of over 25 cents a pound from 1917 to 1919. Acreage in tobacco increased from about 1,250,000 to nearly 2,000,000, but exports fell off. Tobacco tripled above the prewar price of 10 cents a pound.[59]

America's contribution to victory through food production was important, and the Department of Agriculture deserves no small credit for the accomplishment. Even before the United States entered the war, the department conducted campaigns to promote conservation and greater production. Two days before war was declared, Secretary of Agriculture David F. Houston called a conference of state commissioners of agriculture and presidents of land-grant colleges to meet at St. Louis on April 9. There they conferred with editors of farm journals, surveyed the major problems, and drew up a program to meet them. A few days later a similar conference was held for the states west of the Rocky Mountains. The chief problems, as these conferences saw them, were the production of sufficient foods and foodstuffs to provide for the domestic market and for exports, the conservation of farm products, the mobilization of farm labor, the regulation of storage and distributing agencies, and the further organization of all the nation's agricultural instrumentalities.[60] Shortly after these conferences Secretary Houston called representatives of the farm organizations to Washington to discuss the same problem. Within four months after war had been declared Congress had passed the Food Control Act and the Food Production Act (both approved August 10, 1917). The first was administered through the United States Food Administration under the chairmanship of Herbert Hoover. The second gave to the Department of Agriculture the responsibility of speeding production in the existing emergency.[61]

[59] Ibid., 285–286; Yearbook of the Department of Agriculture, 1919, pp. 11–15.
[60] Yearbook of the Department of Agriculture, 1917, pp. 12–16.
[61] The story of agriculture during the war is developed in George Soule, Prosperity Decade, Vol. VIII of this series, pp. 20–29, 53–54. 56–57.

CHAPTER XIV

Expanding Agriculture:
Problems and Policies

THE DEPARTMENT OF AGRICULTURE UNDER WILSON AND HOUSTON

PROBABLY no nation in history has promoted the interests of agriculture as has the United States. When James Wilson of Iowa became Secretary of Agriculture in 1897, the department functioned through two bureaus and eighteen divisions, offices, or sections.[1] The budget for the year was $2,448,532 plus $720,000 paid directly to the agricultural experiment stations connected with the state colleges of agriculture, but supervised by the department.[2] The number of employees was 2,444.[3] The department had already become an important research organization to which scientists gravitated from the agricultural colleges and experiment stations, and to which students came to continue research under conditions approximating graduate-school education. Under the stimulus of Congressional appropriations and the demands of farmers, the research of the department was of a decidedly practical type, and it was being continually extended through the creation of new divisions and subdivisions and the assumption of new duties placed upon it by Congressional legislation. By consolidations and new groupings of subject matter, the bureaus

---

[1] The Weather Bureau and the Bureau of Animal Industry; the divisions of Statistics, Foreign Markets, Chemistry, Entomology, Biological Survey, Forestry, Botany, Vegetable Physiology and Pathology, Agrostology, Pomology, Agricultural Soils, Publications, Gardens and Grounds, Accounts and Disbursements, and Seeds; the offices of Experiment Stations, Fiber Investigations, and Public Road Inquiries. The department also maintained a library and museum.

[2] *Yearbook of the Department of Agriculture*, 1897, p. 622.

[3] The number of employees on July 1, 1912, was 13,858; appropriations for the fiscal year 1913 were $24,752,044.

of Chemistry, Forestry, Plant Industry, and Soils were established in 1901 on a level with the older Bureau of Animal Industry. The Division of Statistics and the Division of Foreign Markets (created in 1898) were merged in 1902 into the Bureau of Statistics. The Division of Entomology became a bureau in 1902 and the Division of Biological Survey in 1904.[4]

Under the secretaryship of Wilson, who served under McKinley, Roosevelt, and Taft, the department emphasized the idea of increased production. Agriculture was prosperous, rapidly spreading over the Great Plains and the areas farther west, and it was easy to dwell on the glories of expansion. At the same time that prosperity was being challenged by an increasing number of virulent plant and animal pests. Both the desire for increased production and the challenge of plant and animal diseases stimulated research of a high quality. Important advances were made, and the morale of the expanding service was high. As the years went on, the department also widened its interests to include social and economic studies and to increase its regulatory, educational, and conservational services.

Alfred Charles True, noted historian of the Department of Agriculture, has described its work during the years 1897 to 1913:

The experimental and research work . . . very greatly increased in variety and extent during Secretary Wilson's administration. In its general range it extended from search for plants and animals suitable for use in this country, and simple tests of varieties of plants, fertilizers, and methods of cultivation, to elaborate studies of problems in plant and animal biology and physiology, the laws of human nutrition, the relations of insects, fungi, and bacteria to plant and animal diseases, and the chemistry, physics and bacteriology of soils. Most of this work related to agricultural production, but studies in the field of agricultural economics, including marketing and farm management, were begun, particularly in the later years of this period. The experimental operations of the Department dealt not only with the agricultural problems of the 48 states but during this period also extended into Alaska and the island possessions of the United States and thus reached from near the Arctic Circle to the tropical regions of Puerto Rico, Hawaii, and Guam.[5]

[4] John N. Gaus and Leon O. Wolcott, *Public Administration and the United States Department of Agriculture* (Chicago: Public Administration Service, 1940), pp. 19–20; T. Swann Harding, *Some Landmarks in the History of the Department of Agriculture* (U.S. Department of Agriculture, *History Series*, No. 2, Washington: Government Printing Office, 1942), pp. 57–58.

[5] Alfred C. True, *A History of Agricultural Experimentation and Research in the United States 1607–1925 including a History of the United States Department of Agriculture* (U.S. Department of Agriculture, *Miscellaneous Publications* No. 251, Washington: Government Printing Office, 1937), p. 194.

Even to list the accomplishments of the thousands of scientists in what was then undoubtedly the world's greatest research organization would be almost impossible. And it would be invidious as well to attempt to sort out the most important work of these men. A few examples, however, may be suggested to show the nature and influence of their work.[6] The Weather Bureau not only issued daily forecasts based on observations from 131 stations in 1897 and from 193 in 1912, but also made studies, through kites and through captive and free balloons, of meteorological conditions in the upper air. The observatory at Mount Weather also made measurements of the amount and intensity of solar radiation, the degree of absorption of the earth's atmosphere, and the polarization of blue skylight.[7]

Some of the most notable work during these years was done by the Bureau of Animal Industry in combating diseases. Although Theobold Smith, a member of the bureau, had discovered in the 1890's that the tick was the carrier of Texas fever, no systematic effort to eradicate the disease was made until a special Congressional appropriation was voted in 1906. Between then and 1912 the bureau cleared 165,000 square miles from the tick and developed much new information on the best methods of eradication.[8] It was from the pioneer work of Smith and his collaborators that it was fully proved that diseases could be transmitted by insect carriers. It checked with the later work of Walter Reed on the mosquito as a carrier of yellow fever and made possible the basic information furnished by Dr. Leland O. Howard, another bureau scientist, for the eradication of mosquitoes.[9] Much of the foundation work on bovine and avian tuberculosis was done at this time, and in 1917 the bureau first undertook to cooperate with individual herd owners and with city and state officials for the eradication of tuberculosis from dairy herds.[10]

Investigations into hog cholera by Marion Dorset and others culminated in 1903 with the discovery that it is caused by a microorganism so small that it could not be identified through the most powerful microscope. These same workers, however, produced a protective serum from immune hogs. Other scientists developed tests

[6] Such examples are given by E. G. Moore, "Men Who Went Before," *Yearbook of the Department of Agriculture*, 1943–1947, pp. 1–16, and more fully in T. Swann Harding, *Two Blades of Grass* (Norman: University of Oklahoma Press, 1947).
[7] The description here of the work of the department and the bureaus is taken largely from True's study cited above, pp. 195–205.
[8] *Yearbook of the Department of Agriculture*, 1912, pp. 163–164.
[9] Moore, "Men Who Went Before," p. 3; Leland O. Howard, *Fighting the Insects* (New York: The Macmillan Company, 1933).
[10] *Yearbook of the Department of Agriculture*, 1912, p. 166.

to recognize and identify glanders, Malta fever, dourine, infectious abortion, and other diseases. Much work was also done on animal parasites and parasitic diseases. Beginning in 1902 the Dairy Division of the Bureau of Animal Industry carried on laboratory work in connection with the agricultural stations in Wisconsin, Connecticut, and Missouri on the production and pasteurization of milk, and on the fungi and bacteria concerned in the production and ripening of various kinds of cheeses.[11] Lest it might be thought that this digression into science has little to do with economic history, it should be noted that the research cost to the government in discovering the causes for tick fever and how it was carried was $65,000. The Department of Agriculture estimated the value of the discovery at $40,000,-000 a year.[12]

The economic value of the work of the Bureau of Plant Industry was possibly even greater than that of the Bureau of Animal Industry. It was concerned with the study and eradication of plant diseases and with the testing, adaptation, and breeding of fruits, vegetables, and other plants. Perhaps its most spectacular work was the introduction of foreign plants. Secretary Wilson was greatly interested in this phase of the bureau's work and in 1898 set up a new unit as the Section of Seed and Plant Introduction and appointed David G. Fairchild at its head.[13] Interest in plant introduction was by no means limited to Wilson and Fairchild. The organization of the new unit, says one commentator, "occurred when the shade of Malthus was haunting economic graveyards and there was widespread worry over food supplies for the immediate future." [14] In any event, Fairchild and other explorers such as Niels E. Hansen (cold-resistant cereals from Russia) and Mark A. Carlton (durum wheat) introduced through the Department of Agriculture approximately 34,000 varieties of plants.[15]

The most important of these plants included the Japanese varieties of short-kernel rice, brought in from 1898 to 1901, important factors in the spread of rice culture in Louisiana and Texas; drought-resistant durum wheat introduced about the same time, eventually the great crop in the dry lands of Nebraska and the Dakotas; and

[11] Ibid., pp. 155–169.   [12] Moore, "Men Who Went Before," p. 3.

[13] Fairchild has told the story of his interesting and scientifically productive life in Exploring for Plants (New York: The Macmillan Company, 1930) and The World Was My Garden (New York: Charles Scribner's Sons, 1938).

[14] Knowles A. Ryerson, "History and Significance of Foreign Plant Introduction Work of the United States Department of Agriculture," Agricultural History, VII, No. 2 (April, 1933), 122.

[15] Ibid., p. 125, Ryerson speaks of 103,500 numbered introductions; True, A History of Agricultural Experimentation and Research, p. 197.

alfalfa from Liberia, Turkestan, and Peru, which helped to produce hybrid strains that prospered in the Southwest. Sudan grass was introduced into the southern portion of the Great Plains, and Rhodes grass from Africa improved the hay in Florida and the Gulf Coast region. California received seedless grapes from Italy and Greece as well as dates and other tropical fruits. In the meantime native plants were improved and significant field experiments conducted both on the problem of agriculture under irrigation and on the technique of dry farming. While the Bureau of Plant Industry carried on work of this type, the Forest Service under Gifford Pinchot (1898–1910) and his successor conducted scientific and practical experiments in forest management, utilization of forest products, and the whole area of silvaculture. Pinchot and the Forest Service, in fact, were leaders in the conservation movement then getting under way.

Although emphasis has been laid here on the activities of the Bureau of Animal and Plant Industries, other bureaus and offices in the Department of Agriculture also accomplished work of vast importance. The Bureau of Chemistry not only aided other bureaus but did much original research on its own, and under its enthusiastic chief, Harvey W. Wiley, carried on an aggressive campaign for pure food and drugs. The Bureau of Entomology, almost entirely a research organization, did much original work in economic entomology, particularly in the field of injurious insects and methods of combating them. In 1897 it carried on its work almost entirely in a single laboratory in Washington; by 1913 it had thirty-five field laboratories in various parts of the country well equipped for research. The Bureau of Biological Survey continued its studies not only in the distribution, habits, and life history of mammals and birds, but also in methods of destroying injurious animals and preserving others of value which seemed likely to disappear. Engaged in studies of rural economics, the Bureau of Statistics covered such subjects as land tenure, transportation, production and use of agricultural commodities in foreign countries, and the costs and methods of marketing and of cooperatives. The Office of Public Roads and the studies it made in road materials were of particular importance in these years of the rapid expansion of the automobile and the rebuilding of many miles of the nation's rural roads.

Throughout these years, as well as before and after, important research work was also carried on by the agricultural experiment stations connected with the state agricultural colleges. Federal subsidies for this work, begun with the Hatch Act of 1887, were extended in

1906 by the Adams Act,[16] which doubled the earlier annual appropriation of $15,000 to each state. The experiment stations had long since proved their value, but the concurrent success of the agricultural colleges had so drained the energies of the experiment stations that larger appropriations were necessary. Work carried on through the Hatch and Adams Acts was supervised by the Office of Experimental Stations, at this time under the direction of Alfred C. True. Its policy of carefully restricting the Adams funds to research was rigidly applied. As a result, says True, the Adams Act "has been a large factor in strengthening the scientific work of the stations and its influence has gone far beyond the use of the funds it has furnished." [17]

With the advent of the Democrats under Woodrow Wilson in 1913, the department came under the leadership of David F. Houston (1913–1920). All of the existing activities continued with increased intensity, but the period of Houston's incumbency marked in a sense a new era. Under Secretary Wilson the chief attention had been given to production; Houston ushered in a period when the department turned its attention to marketing, distribution, farm living standards, and rural sociology; in brief, to a consideration of broad social and economic issues. Said Houston: "I was aware, too, that the farmers' more acute problems were in the field of economics, and in this field I was particularly interested." [18] It should be added that interest in the economic problems of the farmer did not originate with Houston. As early as 1902 Secretary Wilson recognized farm management as a separate and distinct field of research. Work was started by William J. Spillman in the Bureau of Plant Industry and in 1905 was concentrated in the newly set up Office of Farm Management in that bureau. Through various evolutions it finally became part of the Bureau of Agricultural Economics. Besides Spillman, pioneers in this work were Professors Willett M. Hays of Minnesota, Thomas F. Hunt and George F. Warren of Cornell, and Henry C. Taylor of Wisconsin.

The administration of Houston was inevitably influenced greatly by the World War. Houston gives his own impression of the most important achievements of his term: a considerable increase in agricultural appropriations; development of information work and the

[16] 34 U.S. Statutes at Large, Chap. 951. It was fathered by Representative Henry Cullen Adams of Wisconsin, formerly president of the Wisconsin State Dairymen's Association.

[17] True, A History of Agricultural Experimentation and Research, p. 172.

[18] David F. Houston and Helen Basil, Eight Years with Wilson's Cabinet (New York: Doubleday, Doran & Company, 1926), I, 16.

creation of the Office of Information; the establishment of the Extension Service and the Office of Markets and Rural Organization; reorganization of the department with the attachment of the Office of Farm Management and the States Relation Service to the office of the Secretary; passage of the Cotton Futures Act, the Grain Standards Act, and the Warehouse Act; improvement of farm credit through the Federal Reserve and Farm Loan Acts; the passage of the Federal-Aid Road Act.[19] Old lines of research and investigation were also continued during his administration, though often hampered by the war. The new research was mainly economic.[20] Houston's theories, policies, and accomplishments fitted in closely with Wilson's doctrine of the "New Freedom."

EDUCATIONAL AND REGULATORY ACTIVITIES OF THE DEPARTMENT OF AGRICULTURE

The chief burden of agricultural education has rested primarily with the states through the agricultural colleges, but the Department of Agriculture contributed significantly. The Morrill Act of 1862, which gave the initial impetus to the founding of the land-grant colleges, was strengthened through subsidies in a second Morrill Act of 1890 and in the Nelson Amendment of 1907. By 1911 this subsidy amounted to $50,000 annually for each state and territory. The Hatch Act of 1887, supplemented by the Adams Act of 1906, encouraged research, the results of which were soon made known to the farmers by state and federal agencies. The publications of the department, almost entirely of an educational nature, were growing constantly. By the early 1920's the department was issuing annually from 400 to 500 new publications and 600 reprints, and distributing annually 30,000,000 copies, of which about 12,000,000 were farmers' bulletins.

One of the most important of the educational activities of the department was the development of farm-demonstration experiments to show the value of scientific methods to farmers in various localities. This work is first mentioned by the Secretary in 1902 in connection with the fight against the ravages of the boll weevil.[21] Seaman A.

[19] Harding, *Two Blades of Grass*, pp. 288–289; Houston and Basil, *Eight Years with Wilson's Cabinet*, I, 199–210.

[20] True, *A History of Agricultural Experimentation and Research*, p. 197.

[21] *Yearbook of the Department of Agriculture*, 1902, p. 84. Extension work of this kind had been done by the state agricultural colleges long before this. Alfred C. True, *History of Agricultural Education in the United States* (U.S. Department of Agriculture, *Miscellaneous Publications* No. 36, Washington: Government Printing

Knapp of the Bureau of Plant Industry had set up a demonstration farm in Texas to show southern farmers how to combat the evil. Special agents acting under Knapp's guidance extended the work to Arkansas and Louisiana and then into noninfected areas, and the General Education Board of New York City, interested in promoting better economic conditions in the South, supplemented the government funds for the employment of field agents. Later the movement for demonstration work spread to other parts of the country, where it was organized on a county basis and in part supported by local farmers and businessmen. It was directed by the Office of Farm Management in cooperation with the state agricultural stations.

This work of taking education directly to the farmers also grew through farmers' "institutes," meetings organized by the agricultural colleges, where members of the staff outlined to farmers the latest discoveries and the best methods known to agricultural science. These institutes later declined, but at least 8,861 were held in 1914 and were attended by over 3,000,000 farmers.[22] This work seemed so valuable that in 1914 Congress passed the Smith-Lever Act to aid in "giving education and practical demonstrations in agriculture and home economics to persons not attending or resident in" the land-grant colleges. It provided $10,000 for each state annually, with additional amounts on the basis of rural population from a fund of $600,000, increasing by $500,000 annually for seven years and then continuing at a total of $4,100,000.[23] The additional amounts were to be matched by state appropriations. Secretary Houston in 1915 grouped the various agencies dealing directly with the farmers into a States Relation Service (Office of Home Economics, Office of Experiment Stations, and Office of Cooperative Demonstration Work). This was reorganized in 1923 as the Extension Service.[24]

No history of agricultural education during these years would be complete without noting the agitation for the extension of vocational agricultural education into the secondary schools and the passage of

Office, 1929), pp. 126 passim; Joseph C. Bailey, Seaman A. Knapp (New York: Columbia University Press, 1945), pp. 187–243.

[22] Alfred C. True, A History of Agricultural Extension Work in the United States, 1785–1923 (U.S. Department of Agriculture, Miscellaneous Publications No. 15, Washington: Government Printing Office, 1928), pp. 32–41.

[23] Ibid., pp. 100–127; Clarence B. Smith and Meredith C. Wilson, The Agricultural Extension System in the United States (New York: John Wiley & Sons, Inc., 1930), pp. 36–42.

[24] Milton E. Eisenhower and Arthur P. Chew, The United States Department of Agriculture (U.S. Department of Agriculture, Miscellaneous Publications No. 88, Washington: Government Printing Office, 1930), pp. 78–82.

the Smith-Hughes Vocational Education Act (1917). This act, already noted in Chapter XI, was a result of widespread agitation for greater vocational education in the secondary schools. Originated largely to promote industrial, commercial, and mechanical education, the program was widened to include agriculture through the agitation of the Association of American Agricultural Colleges and Experiment Stations and other agricultural interests. By this legislation the federal government offered financial aid to those states willing to expand their secondary school work to include vocational education in agriculture, trade, industries, and home economics. A Federal Board of Vocational Education was established to cooperate with similar state boards to assist in this project.[25] If the type of vocational work proposed by the school and ratified by the state authorities met the requirements of the board, and if local and state funds were provided equal to the proposed federal subsidy, such a program could be introduced into the school curriculum. Up to 1917 this seems to represent the farthest extent to which the federal government had moved toward aid to local education.[26]

As with other branches of government, both federal and state, the regulatory functions of the Department of Agriculture increased rapidly after 1905. It was in that year that Theodore Roosevelt transferred from the Department of the Interior to the Department of Agriculture the custody and administration of the national forest. This brought to the department extensive responsibilities over grazing on the ranges within the national forests and the more important problems of planning the policies and administration of the national forests. Largely because of the interest of Chief Forester Gifford Pinchot, it also placed the Bureau of Forestry at the forefront of the conservation movement.

Although the Bureau of Animal Industry had been authorized from the beginning of its existence (1884) to regulate the shipment of cattle in the interest of more humane treatment and to inspect meats and "live cattle, hogs, and the carcasses and products thereof which are subjects of interstate commerce," the laws were inadequate, and the bureau lacked the personnel and other resources for proper enforcement. Further legislation culminating in the Meat Inspection Act of 1906 made this an important regulatory task of this bureau. In 1908 it was also given the work of inspection and certifica-

[25] True, *History of Agricultural Education*, pp. 358–382.
[26] Whitney H. Shepardson, *Agricultural Education in the United States* (New York: The Macmillan Company, 1929), pp. 44–48.

tion of dairy products in the export trade. In the meantime the inadequate Pure Food and Drug Act of 1906 was passed and its enforcement placed in the Bureau of Chemistry.[27] The two acts just mentioned were doubtless intended to create a feeling of security against unwholesome, injurious, and poisonous food and drugs among both foreign and domestic buyers. But Congress had little serious intention of granting a protection that might diminish the profits of producers. To some extent the acts were a sop to the muckrakers and to Harvey Wiley, head of the Bureau of Chemistry, who had long agitated for pure food and drugs.

In addition to this legislation a new type of regulation had long been demanded—the establishment of grades and standards of quality. The demands came from foreign and domestic buyers for uniform and honest measures of quality and from farmers for prices in accordance with quality. Such standardization became necessary as crops were marketed at great distances from the farm on which they had been grown, with the product handled by many agents and involving sales for future deliveries. This problem had been recognized as a serious one for many years and research had been done on it. Finally Congress passed the Grain Standards Act (1916) providing for the establishment and promulgation of "standards of quality and condition for corn (maize), wheat, rye, oats, barley, flaxseed, and such other grains as in his [the Secretary of Agriculture] judgment the usages of trade may warrant or permit." [28] It forbade interstate and foreign commerce in grain for which standards were established unless the grain had been inspected and graded by a licensee under the act. The federal government itself did not employ grain inspectors but it licensed those employed by state and private agencies.

In the meantime the Cotton Futures Act of 1914 (revised in 1916) had imposed a tax upon all sales of cotton for future delivery unless the contract for sale met certain conditions, one of which was that the grade of cotton involved in the transaction be specified.[29] The Secretary of Agriculture was to set up the standards. The Warehouse Act of 1916 empowered the Secretary of Agriculture to issue licenses to warehouses, authorized the establishment of standards of agricultural products, required inspection and grading of fungible products stored for interstate or foreign commerce, provided grading and other inspection services on a free basis, and required that inspectors be

[27] Harding, *Two Blades of Grass*, pp. 45–48, 312–318; *Harvey W. Wiley: An Autobiography* (Indianapolis: The Bobbs-Merrill Company, 1930), pp. 198–273.
[28] 39 *U.S. Statutes at Large*, p. 482.   [29] 39 *U.S. Statutes at Large*, p. 476.

licensed by the Secretary.[30] The act sought to encourage farmers to store and market their products in a more orderly way and provide warehouse receipts which would have real loan value. The enforcement of these three acts, the first important efforts by Congress to establish and inspect standards and grades of agricultural products, was given to the recently organized Office of Markets (1913), itself set up to study the problems of marketing and distribution of farm products.[31]

DEVELOPMENT OF COOPERATIVES

The emphasis placed in this chapter upon the scientific, educational, and regulatory work of both the federal and the state departments of agriculture does not mean that all improvements in agricultural conditions were initiated by government agencies. The development of farmers' organizations and the growth of cooperatives are examples of initiative taken largely by the farmers themselves. Farmers' cooperatives go back to the 1850's, but as a whole the early efforts were unsuccessful. Strong organizations, such as the Patrons of Husbandry, had encouraged them; the Grange had, in fact, participated enthusiastically in their formation. Nevertheless, the cooperative movement seems to have practically come to a standstill in the early 1880's. The situation, however, began to change in the later years of that decade with a new cooperative movement of slower growth and greater permanence.[32] Data on the late 1880's and the 1890's are meager, but it appears that 438 dairy marketing associations out of 1,551 reporting in 1923 (28 per cent) were organized between 1883 and 1903, and that 48 fruit and vegetable associations out of 616 (8 per cent) appeared during those years. Most of the cooperatives originating in the 1890's were cooperative creameries and cheese factories in Wisconsin, Minnesota, and other North Central states. There was, however, a definite development in cooperative grain elevators in the North Central states and of fruit marketing projects in California.[33]

A new impetus developed after 1903. As in earlier periods of co-

[30] 39 U.S. Statutes at Large, p. 486.

[31] Later developing into the Bureau of Marketing; much of its work was incorporated into the Bureau of Agricultural Economics in 1921.

[32] Henry C. Taylor, Outlines of Agricultural Economics (New York: The Macmillan Company, rev. ed., 1931), p. 519.

[33] Fred A. Shannon, The Farmer's Last Frontier (New York: Farrar & Rinehart, 1945), V, 329–348, in this series, discusses farmers' cooperative movements from 1865 to 1907.

operative activity, this later effort seems to have come largely from the educational influences of various organizations. In this case it was the American Society of Equity, the Right Relationship League (organized in Chicago in 1898), and the Farmers' Educational and Cooperative Union of America, strong in the Southwest.[34] Agricultural cooperatives generally developed more rapidly during periods of economic distress, but the movement after 1903 came in a period of prosperity. When the Department of Agriculture conducted its first nation-wide survey of cooperatives from 1912 to 1915 it found in the latter year from 11,000 to 12,000 associations. Only 5,424, however, responded to the questionnaire. These 5,424 associations had 661,728 members doing an estimated business of $625,940,448 annually. The great centers were in the West North Central states, particularly Minnesota, Iowa, and Kansas, which included 47.5 per cent of the cooperatives, and the East North Central, with 17.9. The Pacific states had 7.7 per cent and the South Atlantic, 6.1; the remaining five sections had less than 6 per cent each. Most of these cooperatives engaged primarily in selling. Of the total number reporting, the percentage of distribution according to business was dairy products, 31.5; grain, 32.2; fruit and vegetables, 16.0; merchandise (farmers' stores), 5.1; cotton and cotton products, 3.9; livestock, 1.8; tobacco, 0.8 and all others, 10.7. In value of business, over 45 per cent was credited to grain elevators and warehouses, about 32 per cent to fruit and produce associations, and 14 per cent to creameries and cheese factories.[35]

It was now clear that farmers' cooperatives were firmly established and growing. New state laws had facilitated their organization and the Clayton Antitrust Act had exempted them from the trust prosecution. Moreover, farmers were becoming better acquainted with the differences between ordinary joint-stock companies and the "true Rochdale principles" of cooperatives, including the conduct of business on a cash basis with annual division of profits and the method of one-man-one-vote and no proxy voting. State-wide and regional

[34] Gordon S. Watkins, "Cooperation," University of Illinois *Bulletin*, XVIII, No. 28 (March 14, 1921), p. 40; Edwin G. Nourse and Joseph G. Knapp, *The Co-operative Marketing of Livestock* (Washington: The Brookings Institution, 1931), pp. 12–14.

[35] Oscar B. Jesness and William H. Kerr, *Cooperative Purchasing and Marketing Organizations among Farmers in the United States* (U.S. Department of Agriculture, *Department Bulletin* No. 547, Washington: Government Printing Office, September 19, 1917), pp. 12–27; Ralph H. Elsworth, *Development and Present Status of Farmers' Cooperative Business Organizations* (U.S. Department of Agriculture, *Department Bulletin* No. 1,302, Washington: Government Printing Office, December 29, 1924), pp. 5–12.

associations also developed. Data collected by the census of 1919 revealed that 9.7 per cent of all the farms reported cooperative buying and selling, with total sales and purchases amounting to $806,599,000. Another survey published by the Department of Agriculture in 1924 estimated that the business done by cooperatives had almost tripled since 1919.

Among the landmarks of cooperative history during the first two decades of the present century was the development of grain cooperatives, with their ownership of farmers' elevators. This development had been hampered in earlier years by opposition from railroads and commission men, but as the cooperatives grew stronger they organized state associations and finally a National Council of Farmers Cooperative Associations. As the grain cooperatives established themselves more securely they widened their activities to handle such commodities as coal, lumber, brick, flour, and feed. Cooperatives in dairy products (creameries and cheese factories) were operated from the beginning according to cooperative principles to a greater extent than were the grain elevators, and they were fortunate in not encountering the well-organized opposition met by the farmers' elevators. During these years farmers' creameries and cheese factories were for the most part local in character. Fruit and produce cooperatives made progress, but the most notable development was among the fruit growers of California and other Pacific states. Here the great necessity of marketing highly perishable commodities, much of them at a distance, induced many fruit growers, large and small, to organize efficient sales organizations big enough to move the fruit rapidly and to conduct large-scale advertising. Cotton cooperatives grew more slowly than those of the fruit, grain, and dairy farmers, and they were less well organized and less successful. Their chief difficulty was the fact that much of the crop was grown by tenant farmers who, under the existing credit system, had no control over marketing their own crops.

Although most of these cooperatives were selling associations, farmers did engage in some cooperative purchasing. However, most of it was through informal arrangement and without a definite association. Frequently farmers used their selling cooperatives as mediums for cooperative purchasing of supplies, but their cooperative stores were generally not successful during these years. Mismanagement, the fact that farmers did not understand this type of business as well as that of conducting elevators or creameries, and failure to follow Rochdale principles are among the reasons offered by observers for the failures.[36] It may be added that the development of mail-order houses and the introduction of the parcel-post system in 1913 may have played a part in delaying cooperative buying.

THE GROWTH OF TENANCY

Some emphasis has been given to the relative agricultural prosperity during the two decades after 1897 and to the contributions made by the Department of Agriculture. One disturbing aspect of an otherwise reasonably cheerful picture nevertheless remained—the continual growth of tenancy. Most government economists of the time found some comfort in the so-called "ladder theory," taking the position that tenancy was merely a stage in the upward progress of the landless proletariat to farm ownership.[37] This route may often have been followed, but the fact that tenancy was increasing in the nation as a whole involved factors that weakened the optimism of many. However, even those who looked upon growing tenancy as a national disaster found some comfort in the slackening growth. The statistics below are taken back to 1880 to show this decline.

PERCENTAGE OF FARMS OPERATED BY TENANTS

Area	1880	1890	1900	1910	1920
United States	25.6	28.4	35.3	37.0	38.1
New England	8.5	9.3	9.4	8.0	7.4
Middle Atlantic	19.2	22.1	25.3	22.3	20.7
East North Central	20.5	22.8	26.3	27.0	28.1
West North Central	20.5	24.0	29.6	30.9	34.2
South Atlantic	36.1	38.5	44.2	45.9	46.8
East South Central	36.8	38.3	48.1	50.7	49.7
West South Central	35.2	38.6	49.1	52.8	52.9
Mountain	7.4	7.1	12.2	10.7	15.4
Pacific	16.8	14.7	19.7	17.2	20.1

Source: *Fourteenth Census: Agriculture*, V, 133–134.

Although the percentage of farms operated by tenants (cash tenants, sharecroppers, cash-share tenants, and other types) grew from 28.4 in 1890 to 35.3 in 1900, an increase of 6.9 per cent, the rise from 1900 to 1910 was only 1.7 and from 1910 to 1920 but 1.1 per

---

[36] Jesness and Kerr, *Cooperative Purchasing and Marketing Organizations in the United States*, pp. 5–10.

[37] Fred A. Shannon, *The Farmer's Last Frontier*, Vol. V of this series, discusses tenancy in Chap. V and elsewhere.

cent.[38] A glance at the table reveals the fact that tenancy became increasingly high in the West North Central and West South Central states, that the increase was slight in the remainder of the South, that it declined in the New England and Middle Atlantic states but increased in the Mountain states. Slightly over three fifths of the farm operators in 1920 were owners and almost two fifths were tenants of various types. These two fifths were centered chiefly in the corn and cotton belts. In the South, tenancy had assumed alarming proportions, that is, if one is willing to concede that a situation in which almost 50 per cent of the land was worked by tenants was an amount too high for either individual or national good.

One student suggests that the "most outstanding correlation between tenancy and other phenomena is found in connection with the selling value of land, the type of farming and the qualities of the farmers themselves," and then insists that the emphasis must be placed on the first two criteria.[39] Certainly these two would help to explain the increase of tenancy in the corn belt. Various studies have tended to show that the percentage of tenancy is high where land is expensive, and low where it is cheap.[40] More important than that, however, "is the relation of the tenants' rate of saving to the value of the land alone," which determines the chance of the tenant becoming a farm owner.[41] The relation of income to the value of the land is the important factor. The fact that land was costlier, and in many parts of the corn belt was increasing more rapidly than yield, helps to account for the high prevalence of tenancy in that section. It is also an area adapted to the tenant who is distinctly a transient. Tenants tend to deal primarily with animals and crops that can be made to yield their increase in twelve months. Such agriculture is typical of the cotton, corn, and wheat districts.[42] Tenant farmers are generally not interested in dairying or in the type of farming that must be built up over several years.

The fact that land is generally cheaper in the South (where

[38] Fred R. Yoder, *Introduction to Agricultural Economics* (New York: Thomas Y. Crowell Company, 1929), p. 138, explains the different types of tenants, as does Shannon, *The Farmer's Last Frontier*, pp. 88–89.

[39] Benjamin H. Hibbard, "Farm Tenancy in 1920," *Journal of Farm Economics*, III (October, 1921), 168.

[40] *Ibid.*, pp. 169–170; William J. Spillman and Emanuel A. Goldenweiser, "Farm Tenantry in the United States," *Yearbook of the Department of Agriculture*, 1916, pp. 334–344.

[41] Henry C. Taylor, *Outlines of Agricultural Economics* (New York: The Macmillan Company, rev. ed., 1931), pp. 314–320.

[42] Benjamin H. Hibbard, "Farm Tenancy in the United States," *International Review of Agricultural Economics*, LXXVI (April, 1917), 94–95.

tenancy is highest) than in the North would appear to discount the theory that tenancy is high where land is expensive. But even here it can be shown that tenancy is higher on the richer land. It is clear that in the cotton belt other factors conspired to divorce the ownership from the tillage of the soil.[43] The crop required little capital on the part of the tenant and few improvements in the way of buildings or fences; moreover, the process of production and sale could be accomplished within the year. Negro tenancy in the cotton belt, which often represented a movement from the status of wage earner to that of sharecropper, originated largely from new arrangements on the old cotton plantations formerly operated by slave labor. It grew rapidly up to 1900 and but slightly after that. The percentage of tenants among colored farmers rose from 74.6 in 1900 to 76.2 in 1920, and location synchronized closely, even as late as 1910, with the old area where slaves were abundant in 1860.[44]

The southern Negro farmers were generally sharecroppers. White tenants in the South, on the other hand, were generally cash-share tenants, and their number increased more rapidly than the number of Negro tenants. The percentage of white tenant farmers in the South grew from 36.1 in 1900 to 39.2 in 1910, but declined to 38.9 in 1920. They were located chiefly in the Black Land Prairie of Texas [45] and in the northern areas of the older cotton states. Just as the division of the large slave plantations into sharecropper or tenant holdings laid the background of Negro tenant farming in the Old South, so in the Black Lands of Texas it was the shift from stock raising to cotton growing that opened the way for white tenancy in that area. Increase of tenancy in the Far West was attributed chiefly to the passing of the land from the first generation of settlers, who generally owned it in fee simple through purchases or homestead claims, to a new generation of farmers. The reason which seems to throw the most light on the decline of tenancy in the East after 1900 is the fact that the income an acre increased more rapidly than the value of the land, and the tenant was able to move into a landowning status in fewer years.

Summing up the history of farm tenancy since 1880, one authority concludes that "beginning with pioneer conditions, the proportion of tenants increases, at first rapidly and then more and more slowly as the forces making for an increase of tenants and a decrease in owners,

[43] *Ibid.*, p. 95.
[44] See maps in Taylor, *Outlines of Agricultural Economics*, pp. 310–311.
[45] Jesse T. Sanders, *Farm Ownership and Tenancy in the Black Prairie of Texas* (U.S. Department of Agriculture, *Bulletin* No. 1,068, Washington: Government Printing Office, May 18, 1822), pp. 1–9.

and those making for a decrease of tenants and increase of owners, tend to come into balance. Thereafter, aside from gradual changes due to such factors as changes in methods of handling plantations, changes in the age of retirement, or changes in the customary initial payment in purchasing, the proportion of tenants will tend to remain constant." [46] To those who noted the stabilization of tenancy in some areas and the slowing up of the increase in the country as a whole, these comments seemed valid and comforting. And it was strengthened by the almost universal belief in the "ladder theory" held by agricultural economists in the second and third decades of the century.[47]

But it was also true that American statesmen of earlier years, including the framers of the Homestead Acts, had hardly envisaged the future of agricultural land as one of landlords and tenants. Rather it was the picture of the family farm owned and operated by those who lived on it. And if the statistics of tenancy were accurate, the owner-operator farm was declining. That tens of thousands laboriously climbed the ladder to ownership, there can be no doubt.[48] But it is also true that more descended the ladder than climbed it. Large-scale and rapid descent was accentuated during depressions just as ascent was a characteristic of prosperity, at least when the prices of land and commodities were in some equilibrium. In any event, it was obvious that tenancy continued to increase and it had become clear to the most optimistic that the increasing cost of land and farm equipment was making the climb to ownership more difficult.[49]

PROBLEM OF FARM CREDIT

One of the evidences of increased interest in farm economics which developed rapidly under Secretary Houston was an attack on the problem of rural credits. For decades American farmers had faced the difficulty of securing adequate credit at reasonable rates, and they

[46] Taylor, *Outlines of Agricultural Economics*, p. 320.

[47] Examples are Spillman and Goldenweiser, "Farm Tenantry in the United States," pp. 321–346; Louis C. Gray, Charles L. Stewart, Howard A. Turner, Jesse T. Sanders, and William J. Spillman, "Farm Ownership and Tenancy," *Yearbook of the Department of Agriculture*, 1923, pp. 507–600; William J. Spillman, "The Agricultural Ladder," *American Economic Review*, IX, No. 1, Supp. (March, 1919), 170–179.

[48] Emanuel A. Goldenweiser and Leon E. Truesdell, *Farm Tenancy in the United States* (U.S. Bureau of the Census, *Census Monograph* IV, Washington: Government Printing Office, 1924), pp. 83–116.

[49] Lawanda F. Cox, "Tenancy in the United States, 1865–1900," *Agricultural History*, XVIII, No. 3 (July, 1944), 97–105.

had themselves at one time or another suggested remedies.[50] This difficulty had continued into the new century despite the extension of state and national banks into rural areas,[51] the wide use of life insurance funds for rural credit, the existence of farm mortgage companies, and the loans of private individuals. It continued in spite of the fact that the prices of land and products were increasing and presumably the risk of banks and other loan agencies had declined. Undoubtedly the increased interest in farm credits was in part inspired by the shift of emphasis in the Department of Agriculture from production to marketing and other problems of farm economics. The continuing increase in tenancy, as well as the mounting burden of farm mortgages, also directed attention to credit facilities, particularly to the high interest rates. It should be added that interest in rural credits was stimulated by and was part of the whole movement for banking reform which produced the National Monetary Commission of 1908 and the Federal Reserve Act of 1913.

Probably the greatest difficulty was not the inability to obtain credit of some sort but the excessively high costs it entailed. As late as 1916 average short-time interest rates paid by farmers on personal security, including such costs as discounts, bonuses, commissions, and other extra charges, ran from 6.2 per cent in Connecticut and Delaware to 12.4 in Alabama, 13.8 in New Mexico, and 15.6 in Oklahoma. Even in the rich agricultural state of Iowa the average was 7.9.[52] In general the costs were lowest in New England and in the Middle Atlantic states and highest in the South and in the Rocky Mountain section. The conditions surrounding longer-term farm mortgages were not quite so onerous, but were bad enough. On these, interest rates including costs ran from 5.3 per cent in New Hampshire to over 10 per cent in Montana, Wyoming, and New Mexico. There was considerable variation sometimes between districts in the same states, the result of differences in rainfall, climate, or soil fertility.[53] Among other difficulties encountered in obtaining rural credit were the lack of sufficient rural banks and the inability of the national banks under

[50] Solon J. Buck, *The Granger Movement* (Cambridge: Harvard University Press, 1913), pp. 238–278; and John Hicks, *The Populist Revolt* (Minneapolis: The University of Minnesota Press, 1931), pp. 186–204.

[51] Ivan Wright, *Bank Credit and Agriculture* (New York: McGraw-Hill Book Company, 1922), pp. 60–63.

[52] *Hearings before the Subcommittee of the Joint Committee on Rural Credits*, 64 Cong., 1 Sess., Pt. 3, pp. 86–108. Reprinted in part in Edwin G. Nourse, *Agricultural Economics* (Chicago: The University of Chicago Press, 1916), pp. 700–705.

[53] Carl W. Thompson, *Costs and Sources of Farm-Mortgage Loans in the United States* (U.S. Department of Agriculture, *Department Bulletin* No. 384, Washington: Government Printing Office, July 31, 1916), pp. 13–14.

the law to take real estate, directly or indirectly, as original security for a loan. This virtually eliminated the national banks from the long-term mortgage field, and left such business in the hands of state banks and various other agencies.

Although the national banking system was never intended to discriminate against agriculture, it was clearly not designed to take care of the long-term or intermediate credit needs of farmers. Nor, indeed, was the American currency system, based as it was largely on inelastic bonds, adequate at times of harvest to provide sufficient funds. In fact, the very nature of the operations of the national banking system tended to concentrate the surplus of the nation's banks in New York, leaving the South and the West insufficiently supplied for either agriculture or commerce. Existing funds were more likely to be employed in commerce than in agricultural enterprises because of a more rapid turnover and greater earnings. Neither state nor national bankers in rural areas were equipped psychologically or financially to meet the needs of agriculture. Both preferred to lend short-term credits for the usual commercial ninety-day period rather than for the six-, nine-, or twelve-month spans needed by farmers.[54]

Contrary to the belief of many farmers, the existence of high in·terest rates and inadequate credit facilities was not the result of a deep-dyed plot of bankers to gouge the long-suffering farmer. It was the normal functioning of an economy seeking to obtain the highest rates for services rendered, and the result of a banking system inadequate to meet the needs of the nation. The high interest rates are easily explained: high risks involved in climatic conditions and the possibility of destruction from animal and plant diseases; frequent overproduction in terms of the buying market, a characteristic of the years after the Civil War; inadequate managerial ability among farmers as a group, particularly tenants and share croppers. Distance from financial centers and the consequent relative scarcity of credit also help to explain the high interest rates.[55] All of these factors except large-scale overproduction were operative in this period as in earlier ones.

To what extent credit difficulties influenced the amount of farm debt and tenancy it is impossible to say. The increase in tenancy up to 1920 has already been discussed. Tenancy continued to grow even

[54] Wright, *Bank Credit and Agriculture*, pp. 46–59.
[55] Yoder, *Introduction to Agricultural Economics*, pp. 221–222; Carl W. Thompson, *Factors Affecting Interest Rates and Other Charges on Short-Term Farm Loans* (U.S. Department of Agriculture, *Department Bulletin* No. 409, Washington: Government Printing Office, August 26, 1916), pp. 2–6.

after credit conditions had improved. Certain factors, such as the long depression in agriculture after 1920, probably largely nullified any salutary results from an improvement in credit conditions. The same may also have been true of the mounting mortgage load revealed in the following table.

GROWTH OF MORTGAGE DEBT

Year	Mortgage Debt on Farms Occupied by Owners (in millions)	Ratio of Debt to Value of Land Mortgages (per cent)	Ratio of Number of Mortgaged Farms to All Reporting Farms (per cent)
1890	$1,086	35.5	27.8
1900	.....	...	30.0
1910	1,726	27.3	33.2
1920	4,004	29.1	37.2

Sources: Fourteenth Census: Agriculture, V, 486–489, and Clara Eliot, The Farmer's Campaign for Credit (New York: D. Appleton and Company, 1927), pp. 31–34.

These figures cover only mortgages on farms occupied by owners who rented no additional land. From these known figures the total farm mortgage indebtedness in 1910 has been estimated at approximately $3,600,000,000 or 10.3 per cent of the total value of the land and buildings; the total indebtedness for 1920 has been estimated at nearly $7,860,000,000 or 11.9 per cent. It seems clear from the statistics just given and those which follow that the increase in indebtedness, particularly from 1910 to 1920, was outstripping the increase in farm value. The average value of farm land and buildings increased 83.6 per cent during the decade, but the average farm mortgage debt increased 95.7. It will also be noticed that in the second period, 1910–1920, half the length of the first, the average mortgage debt increased more than twice that of the first period.

CHANGE IN AVERAGE MORTGAGE DEBT PER FARM

Year	Average Mortgage Debt Per Farm	Average Value of Land and Buildings Per Farm	Average Equity Per Farm
1890	$1,224	$3,444	$2,220
1910	1,715	6,289	4,574
1920	3,356	11,546	8,191
		Per Cent of Increase	
1890–1910 ...	40.1	82.6	106.0
1910–1920 ...	95.7	83.6	79.1

Sources: Fifteenth Census: Agriculture, V, 490, and Eliot, The Farmer's Campaign for Credit, p. 33.

It is impossible to learn with exactness the sources from which the credit for these mortgages came. One study in 1916 estimated that 20.6 per cent came from banks, 19.3 from life insurance companies, and the remaining 60.1 from mortgage companies, private individuals, and from certain states which had school or land-grant funds to loan.[56] A later study for 1920 shows about 40 per cent distributed as follows: banks, 17 per cent; insurance companies, 14; federal and joint-stock land banks, 5; mortgage bankers, 3; state financial agencies, 1. The breakdown of the remaining 60 per cent was not known, but it was recognized that former owners and private investors in farm lands were important groups.[57] Before closing this discussion of farmers' debts and the general position of the farmer it should be noted that personal indebtedness was almost two thirds that of real-estate indebtedness and presumably growing. One estimate by George K. Holmes, agricultural statistician, puts this debt in 1910 as follows: chattel mortgages, $700,000,000; liens on cotton crops, $390,000,000; liens on crops other than cotton, $450,000,000; unsecured debts to local merchants, $250,000,000; other unsecured debts, $410,000,000.[58]

Except for the fact that there were more rural banks at the opening of Wilson's administration, conditions of farm credit had not notably changed since the advent of William McKinley. Share-croppers and tenants in the South, for example, were still dependent upon "store credit" and the landlord to carry on from year to year.[59] Interest rates remained as high and facilities as inadequate. It is understandable that agitation for reform developed. Roosevelt's Country Life Commission urged the need of better credit facilities. Myron T. Herrick, American ambassador to France, 1912–1914, and a leader in this agitation, notes the "valuable information on land-banks and coöperative credit systems of Europe" provided by the National Monetary Commission, and states that "the question was beginning to be widely discussed in 1910." [60] Herrick himself began

[56] Thompson, *Costs and Sources of Farm-Mortgage Loans in the United States*, pp. 9–13.

[57] Victor N. Valgren and Elmer N. Engelbert, *Farm Mortgage Loans by Banks, Insurance Companies, and Other Agencies* (U.S. Department of Agriculture, *Department Bulletin* No. 1047, Washington: Government Printing Office, December 28, 1921), pp. 1–6.

[58] Jesse E. Pope, "Agricultural Credit in the United States," *Quarterly Journal of Economics*, XXVIII (August, 1914), 722; Clara Eliot, *The Farmer's Campaign for Credit* (New York: D. Appleton and Company, 1927), pp. 98–101.

[59] Compare the picture given by Shannon in *The Farmer's Last Frontier*, Vol. V of this series, Chap. IV, with Lewis H. Haney, "Farm Credit Conditions in a Cotton State," *American Economic Review*, IV, No. 1 (March, 1914), 47–67.

[60] Myron T. Herrick and R. Ingalls, *Rural Credits, Land and Coöperative* (New York: D. Appleton and Company, 1915), pp. vi–vii.

in that year a thorough investigation of rural credit in Europe and brought the subject before the American Bankers Association at its annual meeting in 1911 in New Orleans. The association set up a Committee on Agricultural and Financial Education and Development with instructions to investigate the general subject of rural finances. The following year the Southern Commercial Congress held a conference on rural cooperative credit.

In the meantime President Taft instructed State Department representatives in Europe to gather information on the subject of land credit and to submit it to the Paris embassy for preparation of a general report. This was published by the State Department in 1912.[61] Conventions of the three major parties of 1912 (Democratic, Republican, and Progressive) all endorsed planks or resolutions favoring improved rural credit, and President Wilson backed the demand in his inaugural address. In March, 1913, Congress passed an act for the appointment by the President of a United States Commission on Rural Credits to cooperate with the American Commission appointed by the Southern Commercial Congress and to investigate and report. The reports of these commissions were presented to Congress in 1913 and 1914.[62] From this background came revisions of the National Banking Act to help the farmers, the Federal Farm Loan Act of 1916, and later legislation.

THE FEDERAL RESERVE ACT AND THE FEDERAL FARM LOAN ACT

Very definite efforts were made in the Federal Reserve Act of 1913 to meet the needs of the farmer. It had long been seen that the national banking system had two weaknesses from the point of view of the farmer: the inelasticity of its funds and its inability to make agricultural loans either for long or for short terms. How greater elasticity was obtained has been described in Chapter II. The new act allowed the extension of agricultural credits in two ways. First of all, any national bank not situated in a central reserve city might now make loans on improved farm land, not to exceed 50 per cent of the actual value of the property offered as security, for a period not exceeding five years. Such loans could be made in an aggregate sum up to 25 per cent of its capital and surplus, or to one third of its time deposits. As for short-term loans, the act allowed the central federal

---

[61] U.S. State Department, Information Division, *Preliminary Report on Land and Agricultural Credit in Europe* (Washington: Government Printing Office, 1912).
[62] Herrick and Ingalls, *Rural Credits*, pp. vii–ix.

reserve banks to rediscount notes, drafts, and bills of exchange drawn for agricultural purposes or based on livestock having a maturity of not more than six months. As interpreted by the Federal Reserve Board, these loans might be made for practically any purpose except permanent or fixed investments.[63] The features of the Federal Reserve Act just described were undoubtedly of real benefit to farmers. They did not, however, entirely solve the problem of the length of credit desired, nor did they overcome the lack of national banks in many rural areas.

To help these defects an effort was made with the Federal Farm Loan Act of 1916. It provided for the creation of a federal farm land bank in each of the twelve federal reserve districts. Each bank was to have a capitalization of $750,000 in shares of $5 each to be subscribed by the public or by the government. Farmers desiring to borrow from the land bank were required to organize national farm loan associations. Each member of the association had to take stock in it equivalent to 5 per cent of the amount he wished to borrow, and each association had to take stock in the land bank equivalent to 5 per cent of the amount it wished to borrow for its members. Loans were to be made only on first mortgages up to 50 per cent of the appraised value of land and 20 per cent of the appraised value of insured improvements, to be not less than five years in length and the interest no more than 6 per cent. Upon the basis of the mortgages taken for loans, the banks were to secure money by selling tax-exempt bonds. The act also provided for joint-stock land banks which might be organized by private corporations. They might issue bonds on the security of their mortgages up to fifteen times the capital stock of the bank, but they were a liability simply on the corporation which issued them. Both types were supervised by a Federal Farm Loan Board.[64]

Borrowing through the federal farm loan banks seemed somewhat complicated, but the new system helped to solve the problem of long-term credits and soon became an important source of farm credit. Within a decade after this act was passed, the farm loan banks had unmatured mortgage loans of over $1,000,000,000. Regulations governing the joint-stock land banks were less tight; they were less conservatively managed, and many failed. The federal government began to liquidate them in 1933 and to substitute other methods of providing credit. Despite their not very successful career, the Federal

[63] 38 *U.S. Statutes at Large*, p. 273.

[64] 39 *U.S. Statutes at Large*, p. 360. For a history of the legislation see Robert J. Bulkley, "The Federal Farm Loan Act," *Journal of Political Economy*, XXV, No. 2 (February, 1917), 129–147.

Farm Loan Board had chartered 83 joint-stock land banks by 1927, of which 50 were in active operation with outstanding unmatured principal of mortgage loans of almost $670,000,000. It was quickly apparent that the farmers used both types of banks chiefly to refinance existing mortgages. Up to the end of 1929 about 62 per cent of the loans of the land banks and 77 per cent of those of the joint-stock land banks had been for this purpose.[65] The creation of the Federal Farm Loan System was somewhat overshadowed by the revamping of the National Banking System two years earlier, but it was a far more important step in the breakdown of laissez faire. By the act of 1916 the federal government definitely assumed some responsibility in providing credit facilities for a particular economic group, one which had hitherto received aid in many other ways.

[65] The acts are described in Wright, *Bank Credit and Agriculture*, pp. 285–291; and in Earl S. Sparks, *History and Theory of Agricultural Credit in the United States* (New York: Thomas Y. Crowell Company, 1932), pp. 114–166.

CHAPTER XV

The Era of Reform

INTERNAL COLLAPSE OF LAISSEZ FAIRE

MANY phrases have been used to describe the period 1897–1917: "the age of big business," "the quest for social justice," "the era of reform," "the decline of laissez faire." Whatever the phrase, the period was one of revolt against an older order and a demand for reform. But it should be remembered that the decline of laissez faire did not begin with the development of government controls in such legislation as the Interstate Commerce Act or the Sherman Antitrust Act. Nor did it originally come because the nation demanded protection from the policies of some economic group. The first and foremost advocates were those who wanted government aid for their own benefit. Whatever the main business of representative government may have been in the United States, it has generally responded to the demands of the most powerful economic groups. Those groups never followed laissez faire when anything could be gained by government action; they extolled the theory only when they wanted to be let alone. In the early years of the Republic, Jefferson was the theoretical follower of laissez faire; Hamilton, the advocate of legislation designed to help the industrialist, the capitalist, and incidentally the speculator. His followers have been legion.

Generally speaking, the masses brought no pressure on government to restrict or supervise the operation of private business until the conduct of such business became obviously disastrous or dangerous to the public welfare. The type of conduct which aroused resentment was usually characterized by the development of power which curtailed enterprise. Such development meant the accumulation in some form or other of monopolistic power in private hands.

366

When the government finally stepped in, it was to control or break up monopolies already formed. It was essentially the decline of laissez faire in the economic system itself that brought government action. Absolute economic laissez faire, of course, never existed in the United States. To the extent that it did, it was a system that carried within itself the seeds of its own destruction. After 1900 it declined rapidly both internally and externally. Internally, it deteriorated with the development of industrial and financial monopolies which weakened the position of producer and consumer. Externally, laissez faire declined through a mass of federal and state legislation evident in every aspect of economic life.

Although the early years of the century have been accurately described as a period in which laissez faire declined through the extension of government controls, much of the legislation which accomplished this was passed, interestingly enough, with the specific intention of restoring it. This was true, at least, insofar as the theory and policy of laissez faire meant the preservation of economic opportunity and "free enterprise." Behind much of the new legislation was the definite conviction that monopolies had curtailed an earlier freedom and opportunity that must be restored. Woodrow Wilson gave the clearest expression of this philosophy in his talk of the "new freedom." In reality the "new freedom" was a restoration of what Wilson believed had been an old freedom. It was a nostalgic approach to a previous era which could hardly be restored under capitalism or any other economic system. Certainly the legislation of this period, and that which followed in later years, did not accomplish it.

A difference in the theories of Theodore Roosevelt and Wilson existed although the purport of their domestic policies was much the same. Both believed that the power of big business in government should be broken and both believed that it should be accomplished by the federal government. Both were convinced that the strengthening of American political life could be accomplished by the widening of democratic processes and that of economic life by the curtailment of older rights and methods. Roosevelt talked eventually of the "new nationalism" and a greater America integrated by economic and social reforms on a national basis. This, he believed, would not only prepare the way for a stronger nation at home, but would allow greater activity in foreign relations. Unlike Roosevelt, Wilson had no imperialist conceptions; his domestic policy he would accomplish by emphasizing the "new freedom" of the individual rather than by a full-fledged national integration. He believed that laws could accomplish much and the fact that his presidency came at the climax of the reform period brought a greater amount of legislation than did that of Roosevelt. This dealt with banking, monopoly, and the tariff in his first administration and with railroads in the second. In the end, the "new freedom" and the "new nationalism" served much the same purpose.

Neither Wilson nor Roosevelt was an economist who had much fundamental understanding of the economic system. Each was convinced that it was fundamentally sound if abuses could be eradicated. Neither was opposed to "big business" as such, as long as it achieved its position honestly, behaved itself, and obeyed the laws. Both presumably believed that great private aggregation of business wealth could exist and, if they operated within the law, would not be dangerous to the nation. The legislation which both men sponsored had no intention of changing fundamentally the economic system or fundamentally ending laissez-faire capitalism. Its essential purpose was to remedy abuses, and restore what they believed to be the freedom in a "free enterprise" system.

Despite long isolation in the academic groves of Princeton, Wilson by 1912 understood that the nation was ready for reform. "Society," said he, "is looking itself over, in our day, from top to bottom; is making fresh and critical analysis of its very elements; is questioning its oldest practices as freely as its newest, scrutinizing every arrangement and motive of its life; and it stands ready to attempt nothing less than a radical reconstruction, which only frank and honest counsels and the forces of generous cooperation can hold back from becoming a revolution." He doubted "if any age was ever more conscious of its task or more continuously desirous of radical and extended changes in its economic and political practices." [1] A political scientist rather than an economist, Wilson, nevertheless, both as Governor and as President, did what he could to remedy economic abuses as well as promote political democracy.

THE MUCKRAKERS

The decline of political democracy and the rise of monopolies were not the only dark aspects of American civilization. Among those which called for remedy were the gross inequality of wealth, wide

[1] Woodrow Wilson, *The New Freedom* (New York: Doubleday, Page & Company, 1914), pp. 29–30, 180–181.

existence of poverty, racial inequality, the domination by big business of politics, religion, education, and the courts, the selfish and stupid waste of natural resources, carelessness of human life, exploitation of women and children. The crusading idealism of the age of Jackson had largely disappeared in the years of rampant individualism and chaotic laissez faire after the Civil War. The result had been an incredibly rapid economic expansion achieved at a sacrifice of other aspects of American civilization. America's new rulers were the "robber barons" and her new God, Financial Success.

Why the wave of criticism and resentment against the old order became suddenly so strong and the demand for reform so insistent seem reasonably clear. Undoubtedly the long and bitter conflicts of the eighties and nineties over railroad abuses, industrial monopolies, tariffs, and currency had shaken the naïve faith of the masses in the beneficence of unrestrained individualism and their admiration of the rulers of big business. Particularly had the rapid business consolidation at the turn of the century brought home to the nation the great power of a conscious capitalism and the increasing helplessness of laborer and consumer. Perhaps the end of the frontier also had an influence. If the frontier had exerted, as claimed, a psychological effect upon the eastern wage earner by holding before him an opportunity of escape from old conditions, that influence was declining. In any event, the disappearing frontier slowed expansion and gave the nation a chance to take stock of its resources.

Above all, the uprising came through a fortuitous combination of brilliant "muckraking" journalists, reforming politicians, and a people ready for change. But, like all historical movements, the rise of progressivism and the demand for reform did not burst suddenly upon the country. Its origins reach back into the economic discontent which gave birth to the Greenback, Populist, Socialist, and other third parties which appeared after 1870. Moreover, there was always the voice of protest even in the darkest days of reaction, just as conservatism is always vocal in the eras of greatest reform.[2] This voice of protest as expressed in Henry George's *Progress and Poverty* (1879), Edward Bellamy's *Looking Backward* (1888), and Henry Demarest Lloyd's *Wealth against Commonwealth* (1894) was listened to widely.

The decade of the nineties was a notably restless one. It began with the efforts to control monopolies in the Sherman Antitrust Act

[2] Harc.d U. Faulkner, "Antecedents of New Deal Liberalism," *Social Education*, III, No. 3 (March, 1939), 153–160.

(1890) and to lower tariffs (1894). It was dominated by the depres-sion and the feeling that reform legislation had failed. It was the decade of the Homestead and Pullman strikes, the march of Coxey's army, and the agrarian revolt of 1896. The decade was full of agita-tion, of "movements," and of demands for reform. This restlessness found wide expression, but it was consistently expressed by only one high-class magazine, the *Arena*, founded by Benjamin O. Flower.[3] At the same time a realistic tone began to appear in literature in the work of William Dean Howells, Hamlin Garland, and others, men who were willing to write realistically not only of the social scene, but also of the economic and political problems of the nation.[4]

If a date could be picked as a beginning of the "era of the muck-rakers," it could be logically that of Lloyd's *Wealth against Common-wealth*. From then on, articles of protest appeared until the sudden outburst of 1902. In that year Lincoln Steffens published his first ex-posé of municipal corruption in *McClure's* and Ida Tarbell began her series on the *History of the Standard Oil Company*. It was largely a coincidence that Steffens, Miss Tarbell, and Ray Stannard Baker happened to be on *McClure's* to commence their famous articles at the same time. The tremendous success of these articles and the mounting circulation of *McClure's* soon brought into the field other widely read magazines such as *Everybody's, Pearson's, Hampton's*, and the *Cosmopolitan*. Steffens, Baker, and Miss Tarbell took over the *American* in 1906 and made it also a leader in the movement of exposure.

It would be a long task to list even the most important contribu-tions to the literature of exposure, for the muckrakers probed into almost every phase of American civilization of the period—corrup-tion in state and national politics, big business, child labor, vice, reli-gion, the press, fake advertising, impure food and drugs, to name but the most outstanding.[5] Most of the work was ephemeral and much of it sensational, but it was unusually accurate. Filled as the articles were with apparently libelous material, no major suit was ever sus-tained against author or publisher. To those who read the popular magazines of the day, the following studies probably made the great-

[3] Editor, 1889–1896 and 1904–1909.
[4] Cornelius C. Regier, *The Era of the Muckrakers* (Chapel Hill: University of North Carolina Press, 1932), pp. 22–48; Louis Filler, *Crusaders for American Liberalism* (New York: Harcourt, Brace and Company, 1939), pp. 19–36; John Chamberlain, *Farewell to Reform* (New York: Liveright Publishing Corp., 1932), pp. 3–37.
[5] The most detailed listing is in Regier, *The Era of the Muckrakers*, pp. 220–241.

est impression: Ida Tarbell's scholarly work on the Standard Oil Company, Burton J. Hendrick's exposure of the life insurance scandals, Lincoln Steffens's meticulously accurate articles on municipal corruption, Ray Stannard Baker's contributions to the railroad and Negro problems, Charles Edward Russell's article on the beef trust, George Kibbe Turner's on vice in Chicago and New York, and Samuel Hopkins Adams's on patent medicines and fraudulent advertising. Perhaps the most sensational were David Graham Phillips's scathing attacks on the United States Senate ("The Treason of the Senate") and Thomas W. Larson's on the ways of big business ("Frenzied Finance").

Many of these series were later given wider circulation in book form. At the same time many writers of popular fiction took the cue, and the historical novels so popular at the turn of the century were in part displaced by the new fiction which dealt with social problems. Of the latter Upton Sinclair's *The Jungle*, which was concerned with the Chicago stockyards, was the most powerful in its immediate effects. This attack on existing abuses, which began on a large scale in 1902, became militant in 1903 and sensational in 1904. It began to decline in 1908 but revived in part as a result of the Republican failure to reform the tariff and aggressively push conservation. Then it merged into the Progressive movement that culminated in 1912. Its virtual disappearance after that year seems to have been largely caused by a natural conservative reaction, by the belief that many conditions had been improved, by the destruction or purchase of some of the liberal magazines by big business, by the fact that Congressional investigating committees had taken over the role of muckraking, and by the absorption of the nation in the First World War. Just as the earlier reform period had finally concentrated on slavery and then burned itself out in the Civil War, so the progressive spirit of the Roosevelt and Wilson era ended in a crusade for world democracy and a war to end wars. Almost the only muckraker who stuck to his earlier work was Upton Sinclair.[6] Most of the others turned to what had become a more popular type of writing or wrote their biographies.[7]

While muckraking was at its height in 1906, Roosevelt likened some of the more sensational writers to the man with the muckrake in Bunyan's *Pilgrim's Progress*, "that could look no way but down-

---

[6] Sinclair's later muckraking novels included *The Profits of Religion* (1918), *The Goose Step* (1923), and *The Goslings* (1924), all published by the Author at Pasadena, California.

[7] A list is given in the bibliography at the end of this book.

wards with a muck-rake in his hand." Such men who saw only the evil things, he asserted, were bound to be a force for evil. Then in typical Rooseveltian fashion, he turned around and hailed "as a benefactor every writer or speaker, every man who, on the platform, or in a book, magazine, or newspaper with merciless severity makes such attack, provided always that he in turn remembers that the attack is of use only if it is absolutely truthful." The term "muckrakers," which Roosevelt may have aptly applied to a few, was now popularly applied to all. Roosevelt's vague distinction between the sensational and the more conventional type of exposure led some of the more distinguished journalists to protest. Roosevelt assured them that they were not the ones he meant. Nevertheless, the term used by Roosevelt as a term of opprobrium has long since come to describe without distinction the good and the bad.[8]

More important than the name is the extent of the influence of the muckrakers. Like that of any such problem in history the answer can be only approximate. The muckrakers seem to have been quite definitely responsible for certain reforms—the pure food and drug acts, the meat inspection act, the improvement in advertising, the reforms in life insurance.[9] The "era of the muckrakers" was a period of reform, and the literature of exposure was merely a part of it. The contribution of the muckrakers was to deepen and strengthen the entire movement. Definite proof of such influence is hard to pin down, but there can be no doubt that it existed. The muckrakers wrote for the popular low-priced magazines which circulated among the middle class, the bulwark of reform movements. For a decade, magazines with a total circulation of over three million hammered at existing abuses, and at times at least a fifth of their space was given to muckraking articles. Collections of these articles in book form, as well as the muckraking fiction and the few liberal newspapers, reached many others.

EXPANSION OF GOVERNMENT CONTROL

The muckrakers were primarily interested in exposing abuses and suggesting causes rather than in offering particular programs for remedy. That was the business of others. They did, however, by publicizing reforms then being tried, particularly the new mechanisms of political democracy and the experience of other nations, make

8 Regier, *The Era of the Muckrakers*, pp. 1–2.
9 See *ibid.*, pp. 194–216, for others.

definite contributions. Just as the literature of exposure covered almost every important aspect of the American scene, so the movement for reform was widely extended.[10] If there was an emphasis to all of this reform, it was undoubtedly in the economic area. It was business that bore the brunt of the muckraking attack. "The muckrakers," says Regier, "discovered that the great corporations were behind the corruption . . ." It was the opinion of most of them that "almost all of the evils of American life were directly traceable to the aims and methods of industrialists and financiers, and it was in the hope of arousing public opinion and thus changing these aims and methods that they did their work." [11]

Surely a glance backward over the purely economic efforts at reform would support this contention. The attack on industrial monopolies antedated the muckrakers, as Lloyd's famous blast against the Standard Oil Company amply proves, and the burst of consolidation between 1899 and 1902 might have brought efforts to control monopolies without help from the muckrakers. Nevertheless the antitrust suits during the Roosevelt and Taft administrations were strongly approved, in fact, demanded, as was the Clayton Antitrust Act under Wilson. The latter was considered as an appropriate, logical, and necessary addition to earlier legislation. The establishment of the Federal Trade Commission was approved as a step forward in the program of limiting monopoly abuses.

As in industry, government interference in railroad transportation did not come until developing monopoly practices had curtailed what little competition remained. The transformation of the American railroad systems from a conglomeration of hundreds of independent lines to seven or eight huge combinations took place largely after 1897. Where such consolidations did not achieve an area monopoly, the railroads, as in New England, often reached out to control other types of transportation. Despite the fact that the railroads were admittedly consolidating to eliminate competition that endangered efficiency and profits, the Hepburn Act showed little interest in the strictly monopolistic aspects of the problem. An exception to this statement was the clause forbidding the railroads to carry commodities in interstate commerce (with some exceptions) produced or manufactured by companies owned or controlled by the carriers. The emphasis in the act was on the extension of government controls,

[10] Told in some detail in Harold U. Faulkner, *The Quest for Social Justice* (New York: The Macmillan Company, 1931).
[11] Regier, *The Era of the Muckrakers*, p. 201.

perhaps on the theory that the Sherman Act, as interpreted by the courts, had taken care of the monopoly problem. Consolidation, of course, could and often did promote economy and efficiency in railroad transportation and much of it was for public as well as private benefit. It was not, however, until the Transportation Act of 1920 that Congress realized this fact sufficiently to encourage consolidation by federal legislation. Whether through internal consolidation or the increase of external supervision, the decline of laissez faire had been rapid.

The revival of old forms of transportation, such as river and canal transportation and the construction of a new American merchant marine, seemed to point to a renewal of competition and free enterprise in the field of transportation. The appearance of the automobile promoted this tendency. But the results were to strengthen the pattern of government control as well as to revive competition. Rebuilding of canals and canalizing of rivers was done almost entirely by state and federal funds. Few projects were the result of private initiative. The new merchant marine which appeared as a result of the First World War was created by the federal government and was at first owned and operated by it. Motor vehicles impinged too closely upon the interests of all to be allowed to operate uncontrolled. Before many had appeared on the roads, the states required licenses and the long history of automobile legislation began. Nor was it long before the integration and control of local and state highways shifted to higher and more central authority. By 1916 the federal government was back in the business of subsidizing roads. Probably no single influence in the present century did more to strengthen the waning power of the state governments than the automobile.

If there is one phase of economic life in which close government connection would seem to be implicit, it is banking. Banks in America originated through state or federal charters and operated under state or federal laws. But supervision and control were weak, and the business of providing credit and money, the economic lifeblood of the nation, continued to remain largely in the hands of private individuals. Of these private bankers the dominating personality and the respected leader was J. Pierpont Morgan, whose philosophy was summed up in the statement, "I owe the public nothing." [12] The fantastic situation in which the nation's financial welfare was controlled by some of the more unscrupulous of the "robber barons" called for

[12] Lewis Corey, *House of Morgan* (New York: G. Howard Watt, 1930), pp. 282, 301; New York *World*, May 12, 1901, p. 1.

legislation as loudly as the uncontrolled power of the Second Bank of the United States in the days of Andrew Jackson. Conditions were improved by the establishment of the Federal Reserve System, and the farmers were aided by the federal farm loan banks. In the meantime the small depositor was offered safety by the creation of postal savings banks.

Since the farmers had been the largest single economic group throughout the nineteenth century and always politically powerful, there was never on the part of the government any fundamental question of a laissez-faire attitude toward them. Responsibility for their welfare was taken for granted. This tender solicitude for agriculture, which the farmer insisted upon, is evident after the Civil War in many ways. Four may be noted. First, the farmers demanded protection from industrial and transportation monopolies, and they got it in the antitrust acts and those passed to control railroads. Second, they demanded aid in the protection of farm commodities. An expanding market toward the end of the century both at home and abroad combined with the rapid expansion of farm land on the western prairies naturally turned the minds of farmers and the Department of Agriculture to greater production. The cumulative effect of scientific development, agricultural education, and an expanding frontier was reflected in mounting production as the nation basked in the glory of a mighty agricultural effort. In all this the work of government scientists, Congressional subsidies to agricultural education, and other aids were important factors.

By the opening of the First World War the problem of production in normal times had been solved. Government aid then entered a third phase, solving the problem of marketing and distribution. It is seen in the increased attention given by the Department of Agriculture during the Wilson administration to the economic problems on the farm, when better credit facilities were provided in the federal farm land banks and in joint-stock land banks. Not until after the war did the federal government have to wrestle with a fourth problem, that of overproduction and marketing of surpluses. In the meantime, the farmers had been experimenting on their own with one method of protecting themselves—various types of cooperatives.

To Americans of today the social legislation of the early years of the century may seem meager. It was, however, substantial in any comparison with previous decades. In fact, it was notable when the handicaps are considered: indifference or opposition of labor to government interference; conservatism of the judiciary; and the bulwarks of the Fifth and Fourteenth Amendments, which had to be overcome. Most of the labor legislation was accomplished on the state level and under the police power, and it was concerned chiefly with wages, hours, and working conditions. The greatest step forward, however, was the firm establishment in many of the states of workmen's compensation, an outstanding milepost in the progress toward improved labor conditions. To attain this goal socially minded reformers faced problems typical of so much legislation: the convincing of the legislatures of individual states, and then the proving to state and federal courts the constitutionality of their legislation.

The federal government, as well as those of the states, found it impossible longer to evade the problem of labor legislation. By 1915 it was deeply concerned with maritime shipping and found it necessary to humanize the antiquated codes regarding the sailor's rights. In the following year its responsibility over interstate traffic widened in the Adamson Act to include the hours and indirectly the wages of railroad workers. Labor unions played the major role in achieving the La Follette and Adamson Acts, but much of the agitation and pressure for labor legislation, particularly on the state level, came from various middle-class organizations devoted to reform.

To the employer, "laissez faire" meant the unmolested right to determine labor policy and conditions of work. Among other things it meant the "open shop." To labor, "laissez faire" meant the right to organize and to force agreements from employers regarding wages and conditions of work without interference from local, state, or federal authorities. In reality this meant the pitting of one monopoly against another. With virtual monopoly already achieved by employers in certain industries, this was perhaps the only way to maintain competition or free bargaining between the two groups. Unfortunately for labor, such monopolies in its own ranks were by no means extensive by 1917. Strong unions existed among the railroad brotherhoods, the anthracite coal miners, and the northern bituminous miners, among the typographical workers, and among the building and metal trades in many areas. But the mass industries had been largely neglected, and for most workers equality of bargaining power did not exist. Like industry, labor wanted no government interference unless it was one of practical aid. In general it preferred to work out its own destiny. Nevertheless, like industry, which desired a protective tariff and other help, labor gladly welcomed and strongly advocated many kinds of social legislation. Just as industry wanted protection from foreign commodities, so labor wanted protection from foreign workers and consistently urged raising the bars to immigration. As to over-all economic theories, there was little consistency in either group.

Two aspects of advancing government regulation, not yet discussed but symbolic of the trend, were the adoption of a federal income tax and the conservation movement. The adoption of the Sixteenth Amendment, which made possible a federal income tax, was significant as marking the first time in forty-three years that the nation had been sufficiently aroused to add an amendment to the Constitution. A federal income tax had been advocated by political scientists and economists, by progressive Republican and Democratic politicians eager to find a substitute for the high protective tariff, and by Theodore Roosevelt. By 1909 sixteen states and three territories had considered an income tax by commission reports, legislative action, or constitutional amendment, and five states were using it, although with little success. Wisconsin introduced the tax in 1911 with full intent of substituting it for the former state property tax; its success was spectacular.[13] But the movement for this type of taxation, as one expert put it, was "not due to the success of the tax in any state, but rather to the spirit of reform now sweeping the country. This movement would scarcely leave untouched the subject of taxation, where injustice is so common." [14] The adoption of the federal amendment in 1913 overthrew the Supreme Court decision of 1894, shifted the basis of federal finance, and went far to revolutionize in America the whole concept of the function of taxation.

Perhaps the conservation movement epitomizes more inclusively the changing attitude of the nation than any other aspect of declining laissez faire. Yet interestingly enough it did not represent at the beginning an upsurge of discontent or a wholesale and spontaneous demand for reform. The prodigality of resources had ill conditioned Americans to an interest in conservation. Only a few prophets, among them John Wesley Powell, Frederick H. Newell, and Gifford Pinchot, saw the need, while a few scientific associations called attention to the necessity of legislation. It was only after Theodore Roosevelt committed himself to the movement that widespread interest developed and important action was taken. In the face of opposition from lumbermen, sheepmen, cattle ranchers, and owners of water sites, progress was difficult, although many whose farms were injured

[13] Edwin R. A. Seligman, *The Income Tax* (New York: The Macmillan Company, rev. ed., 1914), pp. 388–429.
[14] Delos O. Kinsman, "The Present Period of Income Tax Activity in the United States," *Quarterly Journal of Economics,* XXXIII (February, 1909), 296–306.

by floods or who sought a revival of American waterways did approve of conservation. As a whole, conservation of natural resources was achieved in spite of the opposition of the West.

Federal action on conservation began, for all practical purposes, with the withdrawal by Harrison, Cleveland, and McKinley of 46,-828,449 acres from public entry to control water supply, an area raised by Theodore Roosevelt to over 172,000,000 acres. It was followed in 1902 by the Newlands Act (a substitute for the unsuccessful Carey Act of 1894), which started the federal construction of irrigation projects in the arid West. Later, by a somewhat dubious interpretation of existing laws, Roosevelt withdrew through Chief Forester Pinchot 2,565 water sites (1,500,000 acres) and took similar action on all the known coal lands in the public domain (about 68,-000,000 acres) and on 4,700,000 acres of phosphate beds. Interest in conservation was widened by Roosevelt's appointment of an Inland Waterways Commission in 1907 and by his sponsorship of a conference of governors in 1908 to discuss the conservation problem. Within two years, forty-one states had established conservation commissions. In 1908 the President also appointed a National Conservation Commission whose report contained "the only authoritative statement as to the amounts of natural resources, the amounts which have been exhausted and their probable future life." [15] Although President Taft's more cautious policy brought him into conflict with the more ardent conservationists, he obtained by the end of his administration Congressional legislation making the presidential powers for withdrawal virtually all-inclusive. Methods of opening, leasing, and administering withdrawn lands remained for further legislation.[16]

It has been repeatedly noted, but perhaps not sufficiently emphasized, that the decline of laissez faire, as evidenced in government regulation, was prevalent on the state as well as on the national level. National legislation usually came, in fact, when state laws prove ineffective. This was true of the antitrust acts and the laws to control railroads, reforms which were impossible on a state basis alone. State legislation, however, remained on the statute books even after the federal government had taken over the major responsibility. For years labor legislation remained largely in the province of the states, in part because initial efforts of the federal government to ban child labor were blocked by the Supreme Court. Early motor vehicle con-

[15] Charles R. Van Hise, *The Conservation of Natural Resources in the United States* (New York: The Macmillan Company, 1910), p. 11.
[16] The story is sketched by Roy M. Robbins, *Our Landed Heritage* (Princeton: Princeton University Press, 1942), pp. 301–397.

trol was entirely state; it was not until 1935 that Congress gave the Interstate Commerce Commission power over commercial interstate motor traffic. For the common man, no reform of the era was more helpful than the tightening of the regulations concerning insurance companies. This control was entirely on a state level.

To this brief résumé of the expansion of government control one more comment may be added. By 1917 a change appeared evident in the entrepreneurial spirit and conduct of private business. The flush days of the "robber barons" had passed; leaders of business and of the larger institutions had begun to show some of the characteristics which distinguish them today. Risk and profit had become less important than security and power. This may have been the result simply of a maturing economic system or it may have been caused in part by the extension of government regulations, in themselves a product of the demand for reform. More likely it was caused by the domination of most industries by a few great corporations that controlled a large part of the business. It is also possible that this new attitude in itself may have eased slightly the opposition to the extension of government regulation.

OBSERVATIONS IN CONCLUSION

An effort has been made in this final chapter to integrate certain aspects of the period and to emphasize the spirit of reform and its accomplishments. That such a spirit existed must have been obvious to any reader who has followed the extensive state and federal legislation already described. The proliferation of the reform spirit was wide and deep; only the necessity of holding this account to the most important economic aspects has prevented the inclusion of many political and social reforms. It has prevented, for example, a description of such political experiments as the commission form of government, the city manager, the initiative, the referendum, the recall, the primaries, direct election of senators, and the adoption of woman suffrage. It has prevented an account of the fight for prohibition and the Eighteenth Amendment and the story of significant advances in American education. Those who study the thought and spirit of these years with its incessant criticism and demand for change, and note the development of radical thought as evidenced in the growth of socialism, might come to the conclusion that it was a period of disillusion, restlessness, and bitterness.

To some extent this was true. On the other hand, the wide range of reform legislation gave to the generation a feeling of accomplishment and satisfaction. The belief that it was righting many wrongs and setting the nation's house in order inspired pride and confidence in the future. The fight for reform was an exhilarating experience. That this reform wave, unlike the next wave of the 1930's, occurred during a period of prosperity undoubtedly strengthened the morale. Despite the incessant demand for change, the era in a sense had a stability that has not been experienced since. There was real foundation for the nostalgic yearning with which the postwar generation looked back on what it called "normalcy," and which the agrarian reformers of the 1930's recalled as the golden age of agricultural prosperity. The reformers of prewar years had, in fact, done much for their country.

It is not difficult in retrospect to see the defects and the shortcomings of this era of reform. It has been charged with being an age of crusaders, not of scientific reformers, and with being a period of halfway measures when only fundamental changes could solve the problems. Many believed that it came too late and it did too little. The movement only proved, they insisted, that reform had failed and that revolution could be the only cure.[17] The first criticism has little validity. The reform movement had its scientists as well as its crusaders, and it needed both. Most of the reforms had a background in other countries which had been studied and were well known to specialists. Moreover, certain states, such as Wisconsin, had acted as laboratories for other states and the federal government. There were always some reformers who knew the most approved scientific thought on the subject, though they always had to meet ignorance, conservative inertia, and the opposition of intrenched interests. Despite opposition, America attacked her problems in her own environment and was herself groping in an experimental stage.

That much of the reform came too late is obvious enough, but that fault is inherent in problems of change. A nation must be convinced of the need for reform before the demand is sufficiently great to achieve it. No more striking example of action too long delayed can be found than in that of the conservation of natural resources. The conservation movement protected what was left of the national domain from the looting of private interests, but what was left was largely marginal except for water sites. The door was locked after the horse had been stolen. The conservation movement, however,

[17] Chamberlain, *Farewell to Reform*, pp. 306–324.

did save what was left, and it inspired other attempts at conservation outside the realm of federal lands.

Probably no legislation received more publicity or wider approval than the Hepburn Act. Nevertheless, the nation, after two decades of experience in dealing with railroads, failed to incorporate the most essential control necessary—that over railroad capitalization. It may have been too late by that time to prevent certain of the railroads from destroying themselves; certainly it was too late fourteen years later, when Congress got around to do something about it. The Hepburn Act, however, was by no means fruitless. It finally established effective government control over rates and fares and, with the support of other legislation, brought some real protection to those dependent on interstate traffic.

Least successful, perhaps, of all the reform legislation was the Clayton Act and other laws to prevent monopolies. Along with the Federal Trade Commission Act, the antitrust legislation mitigated some evils and was a club held over the heads of those who would use monopoly practices to the detriment of consumers. The failure of antitrust legislation was lack of realism. If great monopolies could not be prevented, the alternative, if government ownership is eliminated—and such a solution was hardly contemplated by the vast majority at that time—was government control. Roosevelt, Taft, and Bryan saw this, but Congress preferred to follow an earlier pattern. The banking legislation improved the currency and credit situation. Reformers understood the main objective to be attained, but they did not go far enough. As with banking, the agricultural legislation moved in the right direction. The idea that the government should supply credit was radical enough at the time, and the Federal Farm Loan Act went as far as could be expected. It failed in time of crisis to meet the need, but at the time it was passed the farmer was prosperous and the deep agricultural depression of the next decade was hardly envisaged.

Despite the hurdles of legal interpretations and strong opposition, labor legislation made significant advances. As for the income tax, its success may be measured in part by the objectives of its advocates. For those who hoped that it would destroy the tariff, it failed. For those who would use it as a means of preventing concentration of great wealth, it failed at least for the moment. It was, in fact, never used with that as the primary objective. It was the rising cost of government rather than an attack on wealth which has made it pre-eminent in federal tax structure. Those who hoped that an income tax would be the basic support of the federal government were soon gratified; the costs of the First World War were too great for a tariff to support. An income tax would probably have been inevitable without the aid of reformers.

In the reaction of the 1920's and the disillusionment of the great depression, it was easy to view the reform efforts of the previous years with pessimism and cynicism. They were obviously inadequate, in many cases merely a beginning. They brought no millennium. Some of the gains, in fact, were wiped out in the postwar reaction of the twenties. Reform seemed to have failed. But the pessimism was as exaggerated as perhaps the optimism had been during the days of reform. The reaction of the twenties notwithstanding, the age of the muckrakers changed the intellectual climate of America. The mass of reform legislation accustomed the nation to a decline of laissez faire, and after the brief reaction of the twenties the reform movement revived.

CHAPTER XVI

The Literature of the Subject

GENERAL WORKS

THE most useful general discussion of American economic life during these years is Frederick C. Mills, *Economic Tendencies in the United States: Aspects of Pre-War and Post-War Changes* (New York: National Bureau of Economic Research, 1932). The National Bureau of Economic Research, founded in 1920 and largely supported by grants from various foundations, has produced numerous studies of a highly statistical and quantitative nature characterized by a high degree of objectivity. Specialization has been on the period since 1919, but where studies go back to an earlier period they will be noted. Also useful is Willard Long Thorp, *Business Annals* (New York: National Bureau of Economic Research, 1926) with a long introductory chapter by Wesley C. Mitchell. It itemizes by years the leading economic developments in the United States and sixteen other countries.

Harold U. Faulkner, *The Quest for Social Justice, 1898–1914* (Vol. XI in Arthur Meier Schlesinger and Dixon Ryan Fox, eds., *A History of American Life*, 13 vols., New York: The Macmillan Company, 1927–1948), deals with certain phases of economic as well as social history. The same is true of Mark Sullivan, *Our Times: The United States, 1900–1925* (6 vols., New York: Charles Scribner's Sons, 1926–1935). An excellent general history of the last five years of this period is Frederick L. Paxon, *Pre-War Years, 1913–1917* (Boston: Houghton Mifflin Company, 1936). Two books of sufficiently general nature to be listed here are John Chamberlain, *Farewell to Reform* (New York: Liveright Publishing Corp., 1932), an interpretation of the reform efforts of the prewar years, and George W. Edwards, *The Evolution of*

Finance Capitalism (New York: Longmans, Green and Co., 1938). Introductions to the economic history of this period are given in the economic history textbooks of Ernest L. Bogart and Donald D. Kemmerer, Arthur C. Bining, Edward C. Kirkland, Reginald C. McGrane, Broadus and L. M. Mitchell, Fred A. Shannon, Chester W. Wright, and Harold U. Faulkner.

PERIODICAL LITERATURE

The *Commercial and Financial Chronicle*, published weekly under that name in New York since 1896, is essential for a detailed economic history of the period. At least three publications are or have been devoted entirely to economic history: *Agricultural History,* published since 1927 by the Agricultural History Society; *Journal of Economic History,* published twice a year with *Supplements* since 1941 by the Economic History Association; and the *Journal of Economic and Business History,* 1928–1932, published by the Harvard Graduate School of Business Administration. The same group has published the *Harvard Business Review* since 1922, largely devoted to economic history.

Other economic journals published quarterly contain many articles on economic history. They include the *American Economic Review* since 1911 (superseding the *Economic Bulletin* and the *Economic Association Quarterly*), a publication of the American Economic Association; the *Quarterly Journal of Economics,* Harvard University, 1887—; *Journal of Political Economy,* University of Chicago, 1892—; and the *Political Science Quarterly,* Columbia University, 1886—. Economic history will also be found in the *Journal of the American Statistical Association,* 1889—, published before 1922 under the titles *Publications of the American Statistical Association* or *Quarterly Publications of the American Statistical Association.* Labor legislation may be followed in the *American Labor Legislation Review,* New York, 1911—, a journal of the American Association for Labor Legislation. Many numbers of the *Annals* of the American Academy of Political and Social Science, Philadelphia, 1890—, will be found useful.

The "muckraking" articles, largely on economic problems, can be found mainly in *McClure's,* New York, 1893–1928, directed by Samuel G. McClure; in *Cosmopolitan,* New York, 1886—, edited by John Brisbane Walker; *Collier's,* New York, 1877—, and the *American* New York, 1906—, edited by seceders from the McClure staff.

FOREIGN TRADE AND THE DEVELOPMENT OF ECONOMIC IMPERIALISM

Of great importance in the history of commerce are the *Foreign Commerce and Navigation of the United States* published annually since 1820 (under the direction of the Bureau of Statistics of the Treasury Department 1867–1903 and then published by the Department of Commerce and Labor 1903–1912) and the *Monthly Summary of Commerce and Finance,* published since 1896 by the Bureau of Statistics, first with the Treasury Department and then with the Department of Commerce and Labor. Both publications came in 1913 under the control of the Bureau of Foreign and Domestic Commerce of the Department of Commerce. The *Statistical Abstract of the United States,* an annual since 1878, had a similar history up to 1913. Another short cut to statistical material is the *Historical Statistics of the United States 1789–1945, a Supplement to the Statistical Abstract of the United States* (1949), prepared by the Bureau of Census with the cooperation of the Social Science Research Council. Also useful are *Commercial Relations* (1855–1911), prepared by the Bureau of Foreign Commerce, Department of State until 1902 and thereafter by the Bureau of Statistics, Department of Commerce and Labor; the *Daily Consular and Trade Reports,* January 1, 1898—February 28, 1910, and July 5, 1910—, prepared by the Department of State and then by the Department of Commerce; and the *Monthly Consular and Trade Reports* (1880–1910), prepared by the Bureau of Foreign Commerce, Department of State to 1903, and then transferred to the Department of Commerce and Labor. The Tariff Board (1909–1912), headed by Henry C. Emory and created under authorization of the Payne-Aldrich Tariff Act, published three useful reports on the *Pulp and Newsprint Industry* (1911), on *Wool and the Manufactures of Wool* (4 vols., 1912), and on *Cotton Manufacture* (2 vols., 1912).

Various aspects of commerce are covered in Emory R. Johnson, Thurman W. Van Metre, Grover G. Huebner, and David S. Hanchett, *History of Domestic and Foreign Commerce of the United States* (2 vols., Washington: Carnegie Institution of Washington, 1915). Frank W. Taussig, the leading tariff expert of this period, has four volumes on this problem: *Tariff History of the United States* (New York: G. P. Putnam's Sons, 7th ed., 1923), a series of essays on various tariffs; *Some Aspects of the Tariff Question* (Cambridge: Harvard University Press, 1915); *Free Trade, the Tariff and Recriprocity*

(New York: The Macmillan Company, 1920); and *International Trade* (New York: The Macmillan Company, 1927). Percy W. L. Ashley, *Modern Tariff History* (London: John Murray, Ltd. 3d ed., 1920), includes the American aspect. Both Chester W. Wright, *Wool Growing and the Tariff: A Study in the Economic History of the United States* (Harvard Economic Studies, Vol. V, 1910), and Arthur H. Cole, *The American Wool Industry* (2 vols., Cambridge: Harvard University Press, 1926), deal with an important protected commodity. The same is true of Abraham Berglund and Philip G. Wright, *The Tariff on Iron and Steel* (Washington: The Brookings Institution, 1929). Sidney Ratner, *American Taxation* (New York: W. W. Norton & Company, 1942), deals with the tariff in connection with other forms of taxation; Kenneth W. Hechler, *Insurgency* (New York: Columbia University Press, 1940), discusses the tariff battles of the Taft administration; and Benjamin H. Williams, *Economic Foreign Policy of the United States* (New York: McGraw-Hill Book Company, 1929), gives a wider picture of American economic interests in foreign commerce. The battle over Canadian reciprocity is fully told in Lewis E. Ellis, *Reciprocity 1911* (New Haven: Yale University Press, 1939).

Two articles of value are John Bell Osborne, "The Work of the Reciprocity Commission," *Forum*, XXX (December, 1900), 394–411, and George B. Cortelyou, "Some Agencies for Extension of Our Domestic and Foreign Trade," American Academy of Political and Social Science, *Annals*, Vol. XXIV (July, 1904).

On the development of economic imperialism many important documents are contained in the State Department's official *Papers Relating to the Foreign Relations of the United States*, now brought down to the early 1930's, and in *Treaties, Conventions, International Acts, Protocols and Agreements between the United States and Other Powers* (4 vols., Washington: Government Printing Office, 1910–1938).

Essential in understanding the making of foreign policy are Charles S. Olcott, *William McKinley* (2 vols., Boston: Houghton Mifflin Company, 1916); Tyler Dennett, *John Hay* (New York: Dodd, Mead & Company, 1933); Theodore Roosevelt, *Autobiography* (The Macmillan Company, 1913); Henry F. Pringle, *Theodore Roosevelt, a Biography* (New York: Harcourt, Brace and Company, 1931); Henry F. Pringle, *The Life and Times of William Howard Taft* (2 vols., New York: Farrar & Rinehart, 1939); Harley Notter, *The Origins of the Foreign Policy of Woodrow Wilson* (Baltimore:

The Johns Hopkins Press, 1937); and Merle Curti, "Bryan and World Peace," *Smith College Studies in History*, Vol. XVI, Nos. 3–4 (Northampton, Mass.: April–July, 1931). An important influence was examined by Alfred T. Mahan in *The Interest of America in Sea Power, Present and Future* (Boston: Little, Brown & Company, 1897), and in his other books.

Significant interpretations of this policy are in Samuel F. Bemis, *The Latin American Policy of the United States* (New Haven: Yale University Press, 1943); W. H. Callcott, *The Caribbean Policy of the United States* (Baltimore: The Johns Hopkins Press, 1942); Julius W. Pratt, *Expansionists of 1898* (Baltimore: The Johns Hopkins Press, 1930), and his "The Large Policy of 1898," *Mississippi Valley Historical Review*, XIX, No. 2 (September, 1932), 219–242; Howard C. Hill, *Roosevelt and the Caribbean* (Chicago: The University of Chicago Press, 1927); A. Whitney Griswold, *The Far Eastern Policy of the United States* (New York: Harcourt, Brace and Company, 1938); and Albert K. Weinberg, *Manifest Destiny* (Baltimore: The Johns Hopkins Press, 1930). Whitelaw Reid, *Problems of Expansion* (New York: The Century Company, 1900), is a contemporary plea for expansion.

Interpretations of the background and results of the Spanish-American War are also in Walter Millis, *The Martial Spirit* (Boston: Houghton Mifflin Company, 1931); Marcus M. Wilkerson, *Public Opinion and the Spanish-American War, a Study in War Propaganda* (Baton Rouge: University of Louisiana Press, 1932); Joseph E. Wisan, *The Cuban Crises as Reported in the New York Press, 1895–1898* (New York: Columbia University Press, 1934); George W. Auxier, "Middle Western Newspapers and the Spanish-American War," *Mississippi Valley Historical Review*, XXVII, No. 4 (March, 1940), 523–534; Fred W. Harrington, "The Anti-Imperialist Movement in the United States," *Mississippi Valley Historical Review*, XXII, No. 2 (September, 1935), 211–230 and "Literary Aspects of American Anti-Imperialism, 1898–1902," *New England Quarterly*, X, No. 4 (December, 1937), 650–667; Erving Winslow, "The Anti-Imperialist League," *The Independent*, LI, No. 2,633 (May 18, 1899), 1347–1350; and Thomas A. Bailey, "Was the Presidential Election of 1900 a Mandate on Imperialism?" *Mississippi Valley Historical Review*, XXIV, No. 1 (June, 1937), 43–52.

Adequate information on American foreign investments before the First World War is sketchy. The best work is that of Cleona Lewis, *America's Stake in International Investments* (Washington: The

Brookings Institution, 1938). Robert W. Dunn, *American Foreign Investments* (New York: B. W. Huebsch and The Viking Press, 1926), has material on the prewar years. Frequently quoted estimates are in Nathaniel T. Bacon, "American International Indebtedness," *Yale Review*, IX (November, 1900), 265–285; Charles F. Speare, "Foreign Investments of the Nations," *North American Review*, CXC, No. 649 (July, 1909), 82–92; John Ball Osborne, "Protection of American Commerce and Capital Abroad," *North American Review*, CXCV, No. 678 (May, 1912), 686–700; and Charles T. Bullock, John H. Williams, and Rufus S. Tucker, "The Balance of Trade of the United States," *The Review of Economic Statistics*, I (1919), 245–246. Scott Nearing and Joseph Freeman, *Dollar Diplomacy* (New York: The Viking Press, 1925), is a highly critical account of American imperialism.

Among the volumes which emphasize the economic aspects of imperialism are Herbert Marshall, Frank A. Southard, Jr., and Kenneth W. Taylor, *Canadian American Industry* (New Haven: Yale University Press, 1936); Edgar Turlington, *Mexico and Her Foreign Creditors* (New York: Columbia University Press, 1930); Leland H. Jenks, *Our Cuban Colony* (New York: The Vanguard Press, 1928); Melvin M. Knight, *The Americans in Santo Domingo* (New York: The Vanguard Press, 1928); Bailey W. and Justine W. Diffie, *Porto Rico, a Broken Pledge* (New York: The Vanguard Press, 1931); Margaret A. Marsh, *The Bankers in Bolivia* (New York: The Vanguard Press, 1928); J. Fred Rippy, *The Capitalists and Colombia* (New York: The Vanguard Press, 1931); Charles D. Kepner and Jay H. Soothill, *The Banana Empire* (New York: The Vanguard Press, 1935); and Charles F. Remer, *Foreign Investments in China* (New York: The Macmillan Company, 1933). Also important on China is Herbert Croly, *Willard Straight* (New York: The Macmillan Company, 1925). See also *American Journal of International Law*, VII, No. 2 (April, 1913), 335–341; and George A. Finch, "American Diplomacy and the Financing of China," *American Journal of International Law*, XVI (January, 1922), 25–42.

On the economic causes of American entry into the First World War, the chief source is the report of the Special Committee Investigating the Munitions Industry, *Senate Resolution* No. 286, 73 Cong., 2 Sess. (40 pts., 1934–1943). The best secondary discussions are Charles C. Tansill, *America Goes to War* (Boston: Little, Brown and Company, 1938); George G. Edwards, *The Evolution of Finance Capitalism* (New York: Longmans, Green and Co., 1938); Newton

D. Baker, "Why We Went to War," *Foreign Affairs*, XV, No. 1 (October, 1936), 1–86; and Harold C. Syrett, "The Business Press and American Neutrality, 1914–1917," *Mississippi Valley Historical Review*, XXXII, No. 2 (September, 1945), 215–230.

THE BUSINESS CYCLE AND THE RISE OF FINANCE CAPITALISM

The most notable federal publications on banking and currency produced during these years were the studies of experts employed by the National Monetary Commission established by the Aldrich-Vreeland Act of 1908. Approximately forty studies were published in 1910, covering many phases of the financial history of Europe and the United States. Their work was reviewed by Wesley C. Mitchell, "The Publications of the National Monetary Commission," *Quarterly Journal of Economics*, XXV (May, 1911), 563–593. See particularly the *Report of the National Monetary Commission* (Washington: Government Printing Office, 1912). Significant also is the "Money Trust Investigation," *Report of the Committee Pursuant to House Resolutions 429 and 504 to Investigate the Concentration of Control of Money and Credit* (3 vols., Washington: Government Printing Office, 1912–1913). Of interest to students of finance capitalism is the State of New York, *Report of the Joint Committee of the State and Assembly of the State of New York Appointed to Investigate the Affairs of Life Insurance Companies* (Albany, 1907).

The most adequate studies of income during these years are by Willford I. King, *The Wealth and Income of the People of the United States* (New York: The Macmillan Company, 1915), and *The National Income and Its Purchasing Power* (New York: National Bureau of Economic Research, 1930); and by the Staff of the National Bureau of Economic Research, *Income in the United States: Its Amount and Distribution, 1909–1919* (Vol. I, New York: Harcourt, Brace and Company, 1921; Vol. II, New York: National Bureau of Economic Research, 1922). On the business cycles of this period the following are helpful: Wesley C. Mitchell, *Business Cycles and Their Causes* (Berkeley: University of California Press, new ed., 1941); O. M. W. Sprague, *History of Crises under the National Banking System* (National Monetary Commission, Washington: Government Printing Office, 1910); and William C. Schluter, "The Pre-War Business Cycle, 1907 to 1914," *Columbia University Studies in History, Economics and Public Law*, Vol. CVIII, No. 1 (1923).

On the financial history of these years the most available secondary material includes Alexander D. Noyes, *Forty Years of American Finance, 1865–1907* (New York: G. P. Putnam's Sons, 1909), and his *War Period of American Finance, 1908–1925* (New York: G. P. Putnam's Sons, 1926); Henry Clews, *Fifty Years in Wall Street* (New York: Irving Publishing Co., 1908), reminiscences of a Wall Street broker; Margaret G. Myers and others, *The New York Money Market* (4 vols., New York: Columbia University Press, 1931–1932; Vol. I by Miss Myers); Harold G. Moulton, George W. Edwards, James D. Magee, and Cleona Lewis, *Capital Expansion, Employment and Economic Stability* (Washington: The Brookings Institution, 1940); George W. Edwards, *The Evolution of Finance Capitalism* (New York: Longmans, Green and Co., 1938); and Louis D. Brandeis, *Other People's Money and How the Bankers Use It* (New York: Frederick A. Stokes Company, 1913), largely from data obtained by the Pujo Committee.

For a more personal approach see John Moody, *Masters of Capital* (Vol. XLI of *Chronicles of America Series,* New Haven: Yale University Press, 1921); Frederick L. Allen, *The Lords of Creation* (New York: Harper & Brothers, 1935), and *The Great Pierpont Morgan* (New York: Harper & Brothers, 1949); Lewis Corey, *The House of Morgan* (New York: G. Howard Watt, 1930); Carl Hovey, *Life Story of J. Pierpont Morgan* (New York: Sturgis & Walton Co., 1911); and Harvey O'Connor, *Mellon's Millions* (New York: The John Day Company, 1933).

On the background, legislation, and the early period of the new banking system, Henry Parker Willis, *The Federal Reserve System* (New York: The Ronald Press, 1923), is most useful. Willis was an expert for the House Banking and Currency Committee, which wrote the legislation. Paul M. Warburg, *The Federal Reserve System* (2 vols., New York: The Macmillan Company, 1930), records the reflections and recollections of one of the first members of the Federal Reserve Board. J. Laurence Laughlin, *The Federal Reserve Act: Its Origins and Problems* (New York: The Macmillan Company, 1933), is excellent on the origin and history of the act, and Seymour E. Harris, *Twenty Years of the Federal Reserve Act* (2 vols., Cambridge: Harvard University Press, 1933), is the most intensive study of the early years.

Articles of interest on this chapter include Serano S. Pratt, "Who Owns the United States," *World's Work,* Vol. VII, No. 2 (December, 1903); Burton J. Hendrick, "The Story of Life Insurance," *McClure's Magazine,* Vol. XXVII, No. 1 (May, 1906), and following numbers (also later as a book); Abram P. Andrew, "Substitutes for Cash in the Panic of 1907," *Quarterly Journal of Economics*, XXII (August, 1908), 497–516, and his "Hoarding in the Panic of 1907," *ibid.*, (February, 1908), pp. 290–299. One item of banking history not discussed in this chapter is handled in two articles by Edwin W. Kemmerer, "The United States Postal Bank," *Political Science Quarterly*, XXVI, No. 3 (September, 1911), 462–499, and "Six Years of Postal Savings in the United States," *American Economic Review*, VII, No. 1 (March, 1917), 46–90.

MOVEMENT OF POPULATION

The primary source material is obviously in the volumes on *Population* in the Twelfth, Thirteenth, and Fourteenth Census reports. The statistics are interpreted in various special reports, among which may be mentioned William S. Rossiter, *Increase of Population in the United States, 1910–1920* (U.S. Bureau of the Census, *Census Monograph* I, Washington: Government Printing Office, 1922); in Charles J. Galpin and Theodore B. Manny, *Interstate Migration among the Native White Population as Indicated by Differences between the State of Birth and State of Residence* (U.S. Department of Agriculture, Bureau of Agriculture Economics, Washington: Government Printing Office, 1934); in Walter F. Willcox, *A Discussion of Increase of Population* (Census Office, *Bulletin* 4, Washington: Government Printing Office, 1903); and in Leon E. Truesdale, *Farm Population of the United States* (U.S. Bureau of Census, Washington: Government Printing Office, 1926). Maps of internal migration will be found in the Galpin and Manny study just mentioned, and in the *Statistical Atlas* for 1903, 1914, and 1924.

Useful also are the studies by C. Warren Thornthwaite and Helen I. Slentz, *Internal Migration in the United States* (Philadelphia: University of Pennsylvania Press, 1934) and in Carter L. Goodrich and Others, *Migration and Economic Opportunity* (Philadelphia: University of Pennsylvania Press, 1936), both volumes equipped with excellent graphic maps. Excellent interpretations are in Warren S. Thompson and P. K. Whelpton, *Population Trends in the United States*, New York: McGraw-Hill Book Company, 1933). More general in their treatment are Corrado Gini, Shiroshi Nasu, Robert R. Kuczynski, and Oliver E. Baker, *Population* (Chicago: The University of Chicago Press, 1930); Walter F. Willcox, *Studies in American Demography* (Ithaca, N.Y.: Cornell University Press, 1940); and

Louis I. Dublin, ed., *Population Problems in the United States and Canada* (Boston: Houghton Mifflin Company, 1926). Also of interest are Oliver E. Baker, "Rural-Urban Migration and the National Welfare," *Annals of the Association of American Geographers,* XXIII, No. 2 (June, 1933), 59–126; Edgar M. Hoover, Jr., "Interstate Redistribution of Population, 1850–1940," *Journal of Economic History,* I, No. 2 (November, 1941), 199–205; John M. Gillette and George R. Davies, "Measure of Rural Migration and Other Factors of Urban Increase in the United States," *Publications of the American Statistical Association,* XIV, No. 111 (September, 1915), 642–653; and Earle Clark, "Contributions to Urban Growth," *Publications of the American Statistical Association,* XIV, No. 111 (September, 1915), 654–670.

The northward movement of Negroes during the war turned the interest of students to this aspect of Negro life, and is covered in Frank A. Ross and Louise V. Kennedy, *A Bibliography of Negro Migration* (New York: Columbia University Press, 1934). The studies included R. H. Leavell and Others, *Negro Migration in 1916–1917* (U.S. Department of Labor, Negro Economics Division, Washington: Government Printing Office, 1919); Louise V. Kennedy, *The Negro Peasant Turns Cityward* (New York: Columbia University Press, 1930); Emmet J. Scott, *Negro Migration during the War* (New York: Carnegie Endowment for International Peace, Oxford University Press, 1920); Carter G. Woodson, *A Century of Negro Migration* (Washington: Association for the Study of Negro Life and History, 1918); Charles H. Wesley, *Negro Labor in the United States* (New York: The Vanguard Press, 1927); Lorenzo J. Greene and Carter G. Woodson, *The Negro Wage Earner* (Washington: Association for the Study of Negro Life and History, 1930); Sterling D. Spero and Abram L. Harris, *The Black Worker* (New York: Columbia University Press, 1913); and William O. Scroggs, "Interstate Migration of Negro Population," *Journal of Political Economy,* XXV, No. 10 (December, 1917), 1034–1043.

The most valuable work done on immigration during these years will be found in *Reports of the Immigration Commission* (42 vols., Washington: Government Printing Office, 1911). This joint committee of the House and Senate and three persons appointed by the President was created by the Immigration Act of 1907. Senator William P. Dillingham of Vermont acted as chairman; the President's appointments were Charles P. Neill, United States Commissioner of Labor, Professor Jeremiah W. Jenks of New York University and William R. Wheeler of California. The many studies were made by experts. The conclusions of the commission with its recommendations are in Vol. I. Jeremiah W. Jenks and W. Jett Lauck, *The Immigrant Problem* (New York: Funk & Wagnalls, 6th ed., 1926) is largely based on the commission's reports and is a short cut to important material. Another statistical study of value is Niles Carpenter, *Immigrants and Their Children* (U.S. Bureau of the Census, *Census Monograph VII*, Washington: Government Printing Office, 1927). Of considerable economic interest is Harry Jerome, *Migration and Business Cycles* (New York: National Bureau of Economic Research, 1926). Of the state documents, the most useful is the Massachusetts Commission on Immigration, *Report on the Problem of Immigration* (Boston: 1914).

Among the more useful books produced by the long controversy over immigration restriction are George M. Stephenson, *A History of American Immigration, 1820–1924* (Boston: Ginn and Company, 1926); Roy L. Garis, *Immigration Restriction* (New York: The Macmillan Company, 1927); Frank J. Warne, *The Immigrant Invasion* (New York: Dodd, Mead & Company, 1913), and his *The Tide of Immigration* (New York: D. Appleton and Company, 1916); William M. Leiserson, *Adjusting Immigrant and Industry* (New York: Harper & Brothers, 1924); Henry P. Fairchild, *Immigration* (New York: The Macmillan Company, 1914) and his *The Melting Pot Mistake* (Boston: Little, Brown & Company, 1926); Isaac A. Hourwich, *Immigration and Labor* (New York: G. P. Putnam's Sons, 1912); Thomas J. Woofter, Jr., *Races and Ethnic Groups in American Life* (New York: McGraw-Hill Book Company, 1933); Walter F. Willcox, "The Distribution of Immigrants in the United States," *Quarterly Journal of Economics,* XX (August, 1906), 523–546; and Henry P. Fairchild, "The Literacy Test and Its Making," *Quarterly Journal of Economics,* XXXI (May, 1917), 447–460.

Included in the studies of particular nationalities are Stanley C. Johnson, *A History of Immigration from the United Kingdom to North America, 1763–1912* (New York: E. P. Dutton & Co., 1914); Marcus L. Hansen, *The Mingling of the Canadian and American Peoples,* completed by John B. Brebner (New Haven: Yale University Press, 1940); Kendric C. Babcock, *The Scandinavian Element in the United States* (Vol. III, No. 3, of University of Illinois *Studies in the Social Sciences,* Urbana: University of Illinois Press, 1914); Henry P. Fairchild, *Greek Immigration to the United States* (New Haven: Yale University Press, 1911); Robert F. Foerster, *The Italian Immigration in Our Times* (Vol. XX in Harvard University *Economic*

Studies, Cambridge: Harvard University Press, 1919); and Emily J. Balch, *Our Slavic Fellow Citizens* (New York: Charities Publication Committee, 1910).

The problem of Japanese immigration may be studied through Sidney L. Gulick, *The American-Japanese Problem* (New York: Charles Scribner's Sons, 1914); Harry A. Millis, *The Japanese Problem in the United States* (New York: The Macmillan Company, 1915), a thorough study; Yamato Ichihashi, *The Japanese in the United States* (Stanford University: Stanford University Press, 1932); and Thomas A. Bailey, "California, Japan and the Alien Land Legislation of 1913," *Pacific Historical Review,* I (1932), 36–59.

MANUFACTURING

An essential source for this period is the *Report of the Industrial Commission* (19 vols., Washington: Government Printing Office, 1900–1902), prepared under an act of Congress approved June 18, 1898. This was a joint commission of the House and Senate with nine others appointed by the President. It investigated many aspects of American economic life including immigration, labor, agriculture, and transportation, as well as manufacturing and consolidation. It employed the leading available economists of the time. In addition to the census of manufactures taken with the regular censuses of 1900, 1910, and 1920, Congress provided for a census of manufacturing in 1905 and 1914. The following are important on the growth of manufacturing: Edmund E. Day and Woodlief Thomas, *The Growth of Manufactures, 1899–1923* (U.S. Bureau of the Census, *Census Monograph* VIII, Washington: Government Printing Office, 1928); Frederick C. Mills, *Economic Tendencies in the United States* (New York; National Bureau of Economic Research, 1932); Solomon Fabricant, *The Output of Manufacturing Industries* (New York: National Bureau of Economic Research, 1940); Henry Jerome, *Mechanization in Industry* (New York: National Bureau of Economic Research, 1934); and Lewis L. Lorwin and John M. Blair, *Technology in Our Economy,* Temporary National Economic Committee, *Monograph* No. 22 (Washington: Government Printing Office, 1941).

On the movement and location of industry consult Harold D. Kube and Ralph H. Danhof, *Changes in Distribution of Manufacturing Wage Earners, 1899–1939* (U.S. Bureau of the Census and Bureau of Agricultural Economics, Washington: Government Printing Office, 1942); Frederic B. Garner, Francis M. Boddy, and Alvor J.

Nixon, *The Location of Manufactures in the United States* (Bulletin of the Employment Stabilization Institute, Minneapolis: University of Minnesota Press, 1933); Frederick S. Hall, "The Localization of Industries," *Twelfth Census*, Vol. VII, *Manufactures*, Pt. 1, 1902, pp. cxc–ccxvii; Tracy E. Thompson, *Location of Manufactures, 1899–1929* (U.S. Bureau of the Census, Washington: Government Printing Office, 1933); Glenn E. McLaughlin, *Growth of American Manufacturing Areas* (Pittsburgh: Bureau of Business Research, University of Pittsburgh, 1938); Daniel B. Creamer, *Is Industry Decentralizing?* (Philadelphia: University of Pennsylvania Press, 1935); and Harold H. McCarty, *The Geographic Basis of American Economic Life* (New York: Harper & Brothers, 1940).

A shift in the location of particular industries is often described in specialized treatments of those industries. Examples are Victor G. Pickett and Roland S. Vaile, *The Decline of Northwestern Flour Milling* (Minneapolis: University of Minnesota Press, 1933); Herbert J. Lahne, *The Cotton Mill Workers* (New York: Farrar & Rinehart, 1944); Edgar M. Hoover, Jr., "The Location of the Shoe Industry in the United States," *Quarterly Journal of Economics*, Vol. XLVII (February, 1933), and his *Location Theory and the Shoe and Leather Industries* (Cambridge: Harvard University Press, 1937).

The bibliography on American industry remains unsatisfactory. Victor Clark, *History of Manufactures* (3 vols., New York: McGraw-Hill Book Company, 1929), covers the period to 1914, but is skimpy on the more recent years. Malcolm Keir, *Manufacturing* (New York: The Ronald Press, 1928), like the Clark book, is better on the earlier years. In Herman T. Warshow, ed., *Representative Industries in the United States* (New York: Henry Holt and Company, 1928), twenty-nine industries are described by those presumed to be experts. The contributions vary greatly in their excellence. Less descriptive but more interested in the economic problems of American industry are Evon B. Alderfer and Herman E. Michl in *Economics of American Industry* (New York: McGraw-Hill Book Company, 1942), an extremely helpful volume. Useful also are three chapters in Harold F. Williamson, *The Growth of the American Economy* (New York: Prentice-Hall, 1944), those by Charles B. Kuhlmann, "The Processing of Agricultural Products after 1860"; by Louis C. Hunter, "The Heavy Industries Since 1860"; and by Samuel Rezneck, "Mass Production Since the War between the States."

Among the most useful studies of individual industries are Melvin T. Copeland, *The Cotton Manufacturing Industry in the United*

States (Cambridge: Harvard University Press, 1912); Arthur H. Cole, *The American Wool Manufacture* (2 vols., Cambridge: Harvard University Press, 1926); Charles B. Kuhlmann, *The Development of the Flour Milling Industry in the United States* (Boston: Houghton Mifflin Company, 1929); A. O. Backert, ed., *The A B C of Iron and Steel* (4th ed., Cleveland: Penton Printing Company, 1921); Rudolf A. Clemen, *The American Livestock and Meat Industry* (New York: The Ronald Press, 1923); Harold Barger and Sam H. Schurr, *The Mining Industries: A Study of Output, Employment and Production* (New York: National Bureau of Economic Research, 1944); Howard and Ralph Wolf, *Rubber: A Story of Glory and Greed* (New York: Covici, Friede, 1936); and Joel Seidman, *The Needle Trades* (New York: Farrar & Rinehart, 1942). Three excellent books on the automobile industry are Lawrence H. Seltzer, *A Financial History of the American Automobile Industry* (Boston: Houghton Mifflin Company, 1928), a Hart, Schaffner and Marx prize essay; Ralph C. Epstein, *The Automobile Industry* (Chicago: A. W. Shaw Company, 1928), also emphasizing the commercial and financial aspects; and Edward E. Kennedy, *The Automobile Industry* (New York: Reynal & Hitchcock, 1941), more inclusive and with greater human interest.

On research during these years see John W. Hammond, *Men and Volts: The Story of General Electric* (Philadelphia: J. B. Lippincott Company, 1941); Frank B. Jewett, *Industrial Research* (Washington: National Research Council, 1918); Alfred D. Flinn, *Research Laboratories in Industrial Establishments of the United States of America* (Washington: National Research Council, 1920); and Ralph C. Epstein, "Industrial Invention: Heroic or Systematic?" *Quarterly Journal of Economics,* Vol. VL (February, 1926).

CONSOLIDATION OF BUSINESS

The *Report of the Industrial Commission* (cited under "Manufacturing") gives an excellent picture of many aspects of the trust problem at the turn of the century. After the organization of the Department of Commerce and Labor in 1903, the Bureau of Corporations published important studies of various industries. These included the *Report of the Commissioner of Corporations on the Beef Industry, March 3, 1905* (Washington: Government Printing Office, 1905); . . . *on Freight Rates in Connection with the Oil Industry* (1906); . . . *on the Petroleum Industry* (2 vols., 1907); . . . *on*

Prices of Tobacco (1909); . . . *on the Tobacco Industry* (3 vols., 1911–1913); . . . *on the Steel Industry* (3 vols., 1911–1913; . . . *on the International Harvester Company, March 3, 1913* (1913); . . . *on Trust Laws and Unfair Competition, March 15, 1915* (1916). Later the Federal Trade Commission published by the end of 1917 studies on *Trust Laws and Unfair Competition* (Washington: Government Printing Office, 1915); *Pipe Line Transportation of Petroleum* (1916); *Newsprint Paper Industry* (1917); *High Cost of Living* (1917); *Book Paper Industry* (1917); and *Coal—Anthracite and Bituminous* (1917). Other government material includes the hearings and committee reports of various Congressional committees, the court papers, and the principal decisions in cases involving the antitrust laws. Citations for these are given in Henry R. Seager and Charles A. Gulick, Jr., *Trust and Corporation Problems* (New York: Harper & Brothers, 1929), pp. 673–684, 694–698.

Four government studies of great value are Willard L. Thorp, *The Integration of Industrial Operation* (U.S. Bureau of the Census, *Census Monograph* III, Washington: Government Printing Office, 1924); Walton Hamilton, *Patents and Free Enterprise*, Temporary National Economic Committee Investigations of the Concentration of Economic Power, *Monograph* No. 31 (Washington: Government Printing Office, 1941), and his *Antitrust in Action*, Temporary National Economic Committee, *Monograph* No. 16 (Washington: Government Printing Office, 1941); and Clair Wilcox, *Competition and Monopoly in American Industry*, Temporary National Economic Committee, *Monograph* No. 21 (Washington: Government Printing Office, 1940).

Of the textbooks, the Seager and Gulick, cited above, is the most satisfactory general summary of the legal aspects. Jeremiah W. Jenks and Walter E. Clark, *The Trust Problem* (New York: Doubleday, Page & Company, 5th ed., 1920), excels in its price studies; Eliot Jones, *The Trust Problem in the United States* (New York: The Macmillan Company, 1924), gives an excellent historical account; and Myron W. Watkins, *Industrial Combinations and Public Policy* (Boston: Houghton Mifflin Company, 1927), has unusually good analyses of the causes for consolidation and its legal aspects.

Two efforts to deal with the trusts statistically in the early years of the century are Luther Conant, "Industrial Consolidation in the United States," *Publications of the American Statistical Association*, VII, n.s., No. 53 (March, 1901), 208–227, and John Moody, *The Truth about the Trusts* (New York: The Moody Publishing Company, 1904), long a highly regarded source. John Bates Clark and John Maurice Clark, *The Control of Trusts* (New York: The Macmillan Company, 1912), is an intelligent discussion of the problem. The National Industrial Conference Board, *Mergers in Industry* (New York: 1929) is an effort by a research organization supported by manufacturers to minimize the evils of consolidation. Edward Dana Durand, *The Trust Problem* (Cambridge: Harvard University Press, 1915), emphasizes the persistence of pools, as does William S. Stevens, "A Classification of Pools and Associations Based on American Experience," *American Economic Review*, III, No. 3 (September, 1913), 547–548. James C. Bonbright and Gardiner C. Means, *The Holding Company* (New York: McGraw-Hill Book Company, 1932), is the standard volume on this subject. Of equal value in their respective fields is Arthur S. Dewing, *Corporate Promotions and Reorganizations* (No. 10 in Harvard University *Economic Studies*, Cambridge: Harvard University Press, 1914), and his *The Financial Policy of Corporations* (New York: The Ronald Press, 1934).

Edward S. Mead, *Trust Finance* (New York: D. Appleton and Company, 1914), describes the activities of the promoter; William H. S. Stevens, *Unfair Competition* (Chicago: The University of Chicago Press, 1917), has the best discussion of unfair practices; Harry W. Laidler, *Concentration of American Industry* (New York: Thomas Y. Crowell Company, 1931), gives a picture of the situation at the end of the 1920's; and William Z. Ripley, *Main Street and Wall Street* (Boston: Little, Brown & Company, 1929), of the separation between those who run the industry and the stockholders who own it. Charles R. Flint and Others, *The Trust: Its Book* (New York: Doubleday Page & Company, 1912), defends the trusts. Oswald W. Knauth, *The Policy of the United States towards Industrial Monopoly* (Vol. LVI in Columbia University *Studies in History, Economics, and Public Law*, New York: Columbia University Press, 1914), describes the government's attitude toward monopoly.

On the decline of competition, see Arthur R. Burns, *The Decline of Competition* (New York: McGraw-Hill Book Company, 1936), and his "The Process of Industrial Concentration," *Quarterly Journal of Economics*, XLVII (February, 1933), 277–311; National Industrial Conference Board, *Trade Associations: Their Economic Significance and Legal Status* (New York: 1925); Milton N. Nelson, *Open Price Associations* (Vol. X, No. 2, in University of Illinois *Studies in the Social Sciences*, Urbana: University Illinois Press, 1922); I. L. Sharfman, "The Trade Association Movement," *American Economic*

Review, Supp. Vol. XVI, No. 1 (March, 1926); Arthur Jerome Eddy, *The New Competition* (New York: D. Appleton and Company, 1912); Joseph H. Foth, *Trade Associations* (New York: The Ronald Press, 1930); and Benjamin S. Kirsh, *Trade Associations; The Legal Aspects* (New York: Central Book Co., 1928).

On the early years of the Federal Trade Commission, consult Thomas C. Blaisdell, Jr., *Federal Trade Commission: An Experiment in the Control of Business* (New York: Columbia University Press, 1932), and particularly Gerard C. Henderson, *The Federal Trade Commission* (New Haven: Yale University Press, 1925).

TRANSPORTATION

The most valuable accessible material on railroads is found in the publications of the Interstate Commerce Commission. Of these the most useful are the *Annual Reports* and *Statistics of Railways in the United States,* annually since 1888. The *Annual Reports* not only note the most important problems faced yearly by the ICC, but summarize the transportation cases in the Supreme Court and in the district courts and digest the federal court decisions and the points decided by the commission in reported cases. See also Industrial Commission, *Report,* Vol. IV. Of the private sources, Henry V. Poor, *Manual of the Railroads of the United States,* annually since 1868, gives the financial history and structure of the individual railroad companies. *The Railway Library,* edited by Slason Thompson and published annually from 1906 to 1916, gives material favorable to the railroads.

On the history of railroads, Slason Thompson, *A Short History of American Railroads* (New York: D. Appleton and Company, 1925), gives the railroad point of view. The two volumes by William Z. Ripley, *Railroads: Rates and Regulation* (New York: Longmans, Green and Co., 1912) and *Railroads: Finance and Organization* (New York: Longmans, Green and Co., 1915), are objective, scholarly, and rich in illustrative material. John Moody, *Railroad Builders* (Vol. XXXVIII in *Chronicles of America Series,* New Haven: Yale University Press, 1921), deals largely with the period before 1897 but provides valuable background. The following deal with special phases: Edward G. Campbell, *The Reorganization of the American Railroad System, 1893-1900* (New York: Columbia University Press, 1938); Balthasar H. Meyer, *A History of the Northern Securities Case,* University of Wisconsin, *Bulletin* No. 142 (Madison: 1906); Jules I. Bogen, *The Anthracite Railroads* (New York: The Ronald

Press, 1927); and Henry Lee Staples and Alpheus Thomas Mason, *The Fall of a Railroad Empire* (Syracuse: Syracuse University Press, 1947), a story of Brandeis and the New Haven merger battle. Of interest also are Joseph G. Pyle, *Life of James J. Hill* (2 vols., New York: Doubleday, Page & Company, 1917); George Kennan, *E. H. Harriman* (2 vols., Boston: Houghton Mifflin Company, 1922), and his *The Chicago and Alton Case* (New York: Privately printed, 1916).

Exhaustive both on the history and on the problems confronting the ICC is I. L. Sharfman, *The Interstate Commerce Commission* (4 vols. in 5, New York: The Commonwealth Fund, 1931–1937), but the Bureau of Statistics of the Interstate Commerce Commission, *Interstate Commerce Commission Activities,* 1887–1937 (Washington: Government Printing Office, 1937), should also be consulted. Besides the Sharfman volume and the two by Ripley mentioned above, various aspects of the railroad transportation problem are ably handled in D. Philip Locklin, *Economics of Transportation* (Chicago: Business Publications, Inc., 1938), with excellent footnotes and bibliographies; Harold G. Moulton and Others, *The American Transportation Problem* (Washington: The Brookings Institution, 1933), which dips back into these years and covers other transportation facilities than railroads; in I. L. Sharfman, *The American Railroad Problem* (New York: The Century Company, 1921); in Sidney L. Miller, *Railway Transportation* (Chicago: A. W. Shaw Company, 1924); in James C. Bonbright, *Railroad Capitalization* (Vol. XCV, No. 1, in Columbia University *Studies in History, Economics, and Public Law,* New York: Columbia University Press, 1920); in Frank Haigh Dixon, *Railroads and Government* (New York: Charles Scribner's Sons, 1922); and in the following articles: F. H. Dixon, "The Interstate Commerce Act as Amended," *Quarterly Journal of Economics,* XXI (November, 1906), 22–51, his "The Mann-Elkins Act, Amending the Act to Regulate Commerce," *ibid.,* XXIV (August, 1910), 593–633; Charles A. Prouty, "National Regulations of Railroads," *American Economic Association Publications* 3d Series, Vol. IV, No. 1 (February, 1903); Stuart Daggett, "The Decision on the Union Pacific Merger," *Quarterly Journal of Economics,* XXVII (February, 1913), 295–328; and Solomon Huebner, "The Distribution of Stockholdings in American Railways," American Academy of Political and Social Science, *Annals,* XXII (December, 1903), 479–490.

Statistics on street railways were collected by the U.S. Bureau of the Census, *Street and Electric Railways*, 1902 (Washington: Government Printing Office, 1905), for 1917 (Washington: Government Printing Office, 1920), and for 1922 (Washington: Government Printing Office, 1925). The difficulties faced by the electric railways were thoroughly explored in *Proceedings of the Federal Electric Railways Commission* (3 vols., Washington: Government Printing Office, 1920), and summarized by Delos F. Wilcox in *Analysis of the Electric Railway Problem* (New York: The author, 1921). The only adequate textbook is Stuart Daggett, *Principles of Inland Transportation* (New York: Harper & Brothers, 2d ed., 1934). Delos F. Wilcox, *Municipal Franchises* (2 vols., Rochester, N.Y.: The Gervaise Press, 1910), is standard on this subject. Edward S. Mason, *The Street Railway in Massachusetts* (Cambridge: Harvard University Press, 1932), is an excellent study of the rise and decline of this industry in a single state. John Anderson Miller, *Fares, Please!* (New York: D. Appleton–Century Company, 1941), is a well-written popular history; and Burton J. Hendrick's three articles in *McClure's Magazine XXX* (November, 1907—January, 1908), 33–48, 236–250, 323–338, on "Great American Fortunes in the Making," throw much light on the financing of the street railroads. The entire issue of the *Annals* of the American Academy of Political and Social Science, Vol. XXXVII, No. 1 (January, 1911), is devoted to problems of urban and interurban transportation.

Besides the publications of the National Automobile Chamber of Commerce, the automobile industry has been the subject of three excellent books by Ralph C. Epstein, Lawrence H. Seltzer, and Edward D. Kennedy, already cited under "Manufacturing." The best study of Ford is by the psychologist Keith T. Sward, *The Legend of Henry Ford* (New York: Rinehart & Company, 1948). Material on federal aid to roads will be found in the publications of the Office of Public Roads and Rural Engineering and in those of the Bureau of Public Roads of the Department of Agriculture (1916–1939), after the latter date published by the Public Road Administration of the Federal Works Agency. The most helpful study of the development of centralized highway control is the Bureau of Public Roads, United States Department of Agriculture and Connecticut State Highway Department, *Report of a Survey of Transportation in the State Highway System of Connecticut* (Washington: Government Printing Office, 1926). The best general book is Charles L. Dearing, *American*

Highway Policy (Washington: The Brookings Institution, 1941). See also John E. Brindley, *Highway Administration and Finance* (New York: McGraw-Hill Book Company, 1927).

The most useful federal studies of inland waterways are the *Report of the Commissioner of Corporations on Transportation by Water in the United States* (4 pts., Washington: Government Printing Office, 1909–1913); *Preliminary Report of the Inland Waterways Commission*, 60 Con., 1 Sess., *Senate Document* No. 325; and the *Final Report of the National Waterways Commission, Senate Document* No. 469, 62 Cong., 2 Sess. Also important is Noble E. Whitford, *History of the Barge Canal of New York State* (Albany: Supplement to the Annual Report of the State Engineer and Surveyor for the Year Ended June 30, 1921). Harold G. Moulton, *Waterways Versus Railways* (Boston: Houghton Mifflin Company, 1912), is a comparison favorable to railways, and Harold G. Moulton and Others, *The American Transportation Problem* (Washington: The Brookings Institution, 1932), carries the study into more recent years, Daggett, *Principles of Inland Transportation,* cited above, gives the textbook discussion.

An unusually full bibliography on the whole problem of the American merchant marine up to 1919 has been provided by the Library of Congress in Herman H. B. Meyer, *List of References on Shipping and Shipbuilding* (Washington: Government Printing Office, 1919). Two of the most important documents are *Report of the Merchant Marine Commission, Senate Document* No. 2,755, 58 Cong., 3 Sess. (3 vols., 1904–1905), and "Development of the American Merchant Marine and American Commerce," *Senate Report* No. 10, 59 Cong., 1 Sess. Early studies of the problem of subsidies include Walter T. Dunmore, *Ship Subsidies* (Boston: Houghton Mifflin Company, 1907), and Royal Meeker, *History of Shipping Subsidies,* American Economic Association, 3 Series, *Publications,* Vol. VI, No. 3 (August, 1905). Two recent volumes of value are Paul M. Zeis, *American Shipping Policy* (Princeton: Princeton University Press, 1938), and John G. B. Hutchins, *The American Maritime Industries and Public Policy, 1789–1914* (Cambridge: Harvard University Press, 1941).

LABOR

Primary sources on labor are in the *Annual Reports* of the Bureau of Labor beginning 1886, of the Department of Labor, 1888–1903, along with *Special Reports* and bimonthly *Bulletins,* and the more frequent publications of the Department of Commerce and Labor, 1903–1913, and the Department of Labor thereafter. The *Report of the Anthracite Coal Commission* is printed in *Bulletin* No. 46 (May, 1903). The *Hearings on Strike at Lawrence, Massachusetts* will be found in *House Document* No. 671, 62 Cong., 2 Sess., and *A Report on the Lawrence, Massachusetts Strike* in *Senate Document* No. 870, 62 Cong., 2 Sess. Congress in 1912 created a Commission on Industrial Relations of nine persons to be appointed by the President. Its chairman was Frank P. Walsh and its director of research Basil M. Manly. Its *Final Report and Testimony of United States Commission on Industrial Relations* (12 vols., Washington: Government Printing Office, 1916) was the most comprehensive study of the problem made during these years. Although the commission gave much attention to the Colorado mine strike in Vols. VII–IX, it also published as a supplement to its final report a study by George P. West, *Report on the Colorado Strike* (Washington: 1915).

Lack of space forbids the citation of the publications of the various state bureaus of labor statistics or of the numerous unions in the American Federation of Labor. Two items, however, should be noted: the reports of the annual sessions of the Federation of Organized Trades and Labor Unions of the United States and Canada (1881–1886) and of the American Federation of Labor (1886—) and the *American Federationist* (1894—), the monthly paper of the AFL. Both are essential for the policies of the organization.

Among the most valuable items in the historical material of these years are Selig Perlman and Philip Taft, *A History of Labor in the United States, 1896–1932* (New York: The Macmillan Company, 1935, Vol. IV in a continuation of John R. Commons and Others, *History of Labour in the United States,* 2 vols., New York: The Macmillan Company, 1918); Lewis L. Lorwin, *The American Federation of Labor* (Washington: The Brookings Institution, 1933); Selig Perlman, *A History of Trade Unionism in the United States* (New York: The Macmillan Company, 1922), and his *A Theory of the Labor Movement* (New York: The Macmillan Company, 1928); Leo Wolman, *The Growth of American Trade Unions* (New York: National Bureau of Economic Research, 1924); George G. Groat, *Organized Labor in America* (New York: The Macmillan Company, 1916); Samuel Gompers, *Seventy Years of Life and Labor* (2 vols., New York: E. P. Dutton & Co., 1925), a history of labor as well as an autobiography; Rowland H. Harvey, *Samuel Gompers, Champion of the Toiling Masses* (Stanford University: Stanford University Press,

1935), a biography with human interest; John Mitchell, *Organized Labor* (Philadelphia: American Book and Bible House, 1903); Elsie Glück, *John Mitchell* (New York: The John Day Company, 1929); Paul F. Brissenden, *The I.W.W.* (New York: Columbia University Press, 1919); John S. Gambs, *The Decline of the I.W.W.* (New York; Columbia University Press, 1932); *Bill Haywood's Book: The Autobiography of William Haywood* (New York: International Publishers, 1929); Charles H. Wesley, *Negro Labor in the United States* (New York: The Viking Press, 1927); Lorenzo J. Greene and Carter G. Woodson, *The Negro Wage Earner* (Washington: Association for the Study of Negro Life and History, 1930); and Sterling D. Spero and Abram L. Harris, *The Black Worker* (New York: Columbia University Press, 1931).

On the government and labor disputes, see Edward Berman, *Labor Disputes and the President of the United States* (New York: Columbia University Press, 1924); Arthur E. Suffern, *Conciliation and Arbitration in the Coal Industry of America* (Boston: Houghton Mifflin Company, 1915); Edwin E. Witte, *The Government in Labor Disputes* (New York: McGraw-Hill Book Company, 1932); Harry W. Laidler, *Boycotts and the Labor Struggle* (New York: John Lane, Ltd., 1913); and Leo Wolman, *The Boycott in American Trade Unions* (Baltimore: The Johns Hopkins Press, 1916). Clarence Darrow, *The Story of My Life* (New York: Charles Scribner's Sons, 1932), and Irving Stone, *Darrow for the Defense* (New York: Doubleday, Doran & Company, 1941), as well as Lincoln Steffens, *Autobiography* (New York: Harcourt, Brace and Company, 1931), contain material on various legal cases. Louis I. Reed, *The Labor Philosophy of Samuel Gompers* (New York: Columbia University Press, 1930), discusses the ideas of the great labor leader.

The most useful volume on the general condition of labor, as distinguished from the history of trade unionism, is Don D. Lescohier and Elizabeth Brandeis, *History of Labor in the United States, 1896–1932* (New York: The Macmillan Company, 1935, Vol. III in a continuation of John R. Commons and Others, *History of Labour in the United States*, 2 vols., New York: The Macmillan Company, 1918). Also useful is W. Jett Lauck and Edgar Sydenstricker, *Condition of Labor in American Industries* (New York: Funk & Wagnalls Company, 1917). Estimates on the number and distribution of labor will be found in Alba M. Edwards, *A Social-Economic Grouping of the Gainful Workers of the United States* (U.S. Department of Commerce, Bureau of the Census, Washington: Government Printing

Office, 1938); in Wladimir S. Woytinsky, *Labor in the United States* (Washington: Social Science Research Council, 1938); in Pascal K. Whelpton, "Occupational Groups in the United States," *Journal of the American Statistical Association*, XXI, n.s. No. 155 (September, 1926), 335–343; in H. Dewey Anderson and Percy E. Davidson, *Occupational Trends* (Stanford University: Stanford University Press, 1940); and in two articles by Alvin H. Hansen, "Industrial Class Alignments in the United States," *Quarterly Publication of the American Statistical Association*, XVII, No. 132 (December, 1920), 417–422, and "Industrial Classes in the United States in 1920," *Journal of the American Statistical Association*, XVIII, No. 140 (December, 1922), 503–506. See also Joseph A. Hill, *Women in Gainful Occupations, 1870–1920* (U.S. Bureau of the Census, *Census Monograph* IX, Washington: Government Printing Office, 1929).

Basic to any study of wages, money or real, during this period is Paul H. Douglas, *Real Wages in the United States, 1890–1926* (Boston: Houghton Mifflin Company, 1930). Other significant studies include Paul F. Brissenden, *Earnings of Factory Workers, 1899–1927* (U.S. Bureau of the Census, *Census Monograph* X, Washington: Government Printing Office, 1929); Whitney Coombs, *The Wages of Unskilled Labor in Manufacturing Industries in the United States, 1890–1924* (New York: Columbia University Press, 1926); and Massachusetts Commission on the Cost of Living, *Report* (Boston: 1900). More specific in their study of the budgets of wage earners are Louise B. More, *Wage Earners' Budgets* (New York: Henry Holt and Company, 1907); Robert C. Chapin, *The Standard of Life in New York City* (New York: Russell Sage Foundation, 1909); John A. Ryan, *A Living Wage* (New York: The Macmillan Company, 1906); Frank H. Straightoff, *The Standard of Living among the Industrial People of America* (Boston: Houghton Mifflin Company, 1911); and J. C. Kennedy and Others, *Wage and Family Budgets in the Chicago Stockyards District* (Chicago: The University of Chicago Press, 1914).

Unemployment has been ably studied by Paul H. Douglas and Aaron Director, *The Problem of Unemployment* (New York: The Macmillan Company, 1934). Other important contributions include Hornell Hart, *Fluctuations in Unemployment in Cities of the United States, 1902–1917*, Helen S. Troustine Foundation Studies, Vol. I, No. 2 (Cincinnati, 1918); Don D. Lescohier, *The Labor Market* (New York: The Macmillan Company, 1919); Darrell H. Smith, *The United States Employment Service* (Baltimore: The Johns Hopkins Press, 1932); Bryce M. Stewart, *Unemployment Benefits in the United*

States (New York: Industrial Relations Counsellors, 1930); U.S. Commissioner of Labor, *Twenty-fifth Annual Report: Industrial Education, 1910* (Washington: Government Printing Office, 1911); and Paul H. Douglas, *American Apprenticeship and Industrial Education* (New York: McGraw-Hill Book Company, 1932).

The best bibliography on "scientific management" is by Clarence B. Thompson, "The Literature of Scientific Management," *Quarterly Journal of Economics*, XXVIII (May, 1914), 506–557, reprinted in Clarence B. Thompson, ed., *Scientific Management* (Cambridge: Harvard University Press, 1914). See also Horace R. Drury, *Scientific Management* (New York: Columbia University Press, 3d ed., 1922); Frederick W. Taylor, *Shop Management* (New York: Harper & Brothers, 1912); and Frank B. Copley, *Frederick W. Taylor* (2 vols., New York: Harper & Brothers, 1923).

On employee welfare projects the following are useful: William H. Tolman, *Social Engineering: A Record of Things Done by American Industrialists Employing Upwards of One and One-Half Million People* (New York: McGraw-Hill Publishing Company, 1909); Elizabeth L. Otey, *Employers' Welfare Work* (U.S. Department of Labor, Bureau of Labor Statistics, *Bulletin* No. 123, Washington: Government Printing Office, 1913); Murray W. Latimer, *Industrial Pensions Systems in the United States* (New York: 2 vols., Industrial Relations Counsellors, 1932); Boris Emmet, *Profit Sharing in the United States* (U.S. Bureau of Labor, Bureau of Labor Statistics, *Bulletin* No. 208, Washington: Government Printing Office, 1917); Welfare Department, National Civic Federation, *Profit Sharing by American Employers* (New York: 1916); *Practical Experience with Profit Sharing in Industrial Establishments* (Boston: National Conference Board, 1920); *Employee Stock Purchase Plans in the United States* (New York: National Industrial Conference Board, 1928); and Robert E. Foerster and Else H. Dietel, *Employee Stock Ownership in the United States* (Princeton: Princeton University Press, 1926).

The rise of "company unions" can be followed in such books as John Leitch, *Man to Man, the Story of Industrial Democracy* (New York: B. C. Forbes Co., 1919); Carroll E. French, *The Shop Committee in the United States* (Baltimore: The Johns Hopkins Press, 1923); Paul F. Gemmill, *Present-day Labor Relations* (New York: John Wiley & Sons, 1929); Ben M. Selekman and Mary Van Kleeck, *Employees' Representation in Coal Mines* (New York: Russell Sage Foundation, 1924); W. Jett Lauck, *Political and Industrial Democracy, 1776–1926* (New York: Funk & Wagnalls Company, 1926); and

Collective Bargaining through Employee Representation (New York: National Industrial Conference Board, 1933).

The health and safety movement is described in John B. Andrews, *Phosphorus Poisoning in the Match Industry in the United States* (U.S. Department of Labor, Bureau of Labor, *Bulletin* No. 86, Washington: Government Printing Office, 1910); *Welfare Work for Employees in Industrial Establishments in the United States* (U.S. Department of Labor, Bureau of Labor Statistics, *Bulletin* No. 250, Washington: Government Printing Office, 1919); Lucian W. Chaney. and Hugh S. Hanna, *The Safety Movement in the Iron and Steel Industry in the United States* (U.S. Department of Labor, Bureau of Labor Statistics, *Bulletin* No. 234, Washington: Government Printing Office, 1918); *Statistics of Industrial Accidents in the United States to the End of 1927* (U.S. Department of Labor, Bureau of Labor Statistics, *Bulletin* No. 490, Washington: Government Printing Office, 1929); Crystal Eastman, *Work Accidents and the Law: The Pittsburgh Survey* (New York: Russell Sage Foundation, 1910); *Workmen's Compensation Laws in the United States and Foreign Countries* (U.S. Department of Labor, Bureau of Labor Statistics, *Bulletin* No. 203, Washington: Government Printing Office, 1917); and Carl Hookstadt, *Comparison of Workmen's Compensation Laws in the United States up to December 31, 1917* (U.S. Department of Labor, Bureau of Labor Statistics, *Bulletin* No. 240, Washington: Government Printing Office, 1918).

Many valuable articles in professional journals and a number of historics of specific unions are cited in the footnotes of Chap. XI and XII.

AGRICULTURE

An exhaustive guide to the bibliography of agricultural history is in Fred A. Shannon, *The Farmer's Last Frontier* (New York: Farrar & Rinehart, 1945, Vol. V of this series), pp. 379–384. The chief sources used in this volume are various publications of the Department of Agriculture, particularly the annual *Reports* since 1894, and various items in the *Department Bulletins,* the *Technical Bulletins,* the *Miscellaneous Publications,* and the *History Series,* cited in the footnotes, but omitted in most instances from this bibliography. Certain of these are outstanding: Alfred C. True, *A History of Agricultural Experimentation and Research in the United States, 1607–1925, including a History of the United States Department of Agriculture*

(U.S. Department of Agriculture, *Miscellaneous Publication* No. 251, Washington: Government Printing Office, 1937); Alfred C. True, *History of Agricultural Education in the United States* (U.S. Department of Agriculture, *Miscellaneous Publication* No. 36, Washington: Government Printing Office, 1929); and the *Yearbook of the Department of Agriculture* (Washington: Government Printing Office, 1940), *Farmers in a Changing World,* devoted particularly to history and containing Everett E. Edwards, "American Agriculture—The First 300 Years," the best brief history of agriculture. The work of the department is described in Arthur P. Chew, *The United States Department of Agriculture, Its Structure and Functions* (U.S. Department of Agriculture, *Miscellaneous Publication* No. 88, Washington: Government Printing Office, 1940); and in John M. Gaus and Leon O. Wolcott, *Public Administration and the United States Department of Agriculture* (Chicago: Public Administration Service, 1940). Liberty Hyde Bailey, ed., *Cyclopedia of American Agriculture* (4 vols., New York: The Macmillan Company, 3d ed., 1910) contains much history. The report of the Commission on Country Life is in *Senate Document* No. 705, 60 Cong., 2 Sess.

No full-length history of American agriculture has been attempted covering the period since 1897. However, Harold Barger and Hans H. Landsberg, *American Agriculture, 1899–1939* (New York: National Bureau of Economic Research, 1942), largely a quantitative and statistical study, is extremely useful. Arthur F. Burns, *Production Trends in the United States Since 1870* (New York: National Bureau of Economic Research, 1939), also gives some attention to agriculture. Statistical studies on rural population are cited in the bibliography on "Movement of Population" and the scanty efforts to organize unions in agriculture are described in Stuart Jamieson, *Labor Unionism in American Agriculture* (U.S. Department of Labor, Bureau of Labor Statistics *Bulletin* No. 836, Washington: Government Printing Office, 1945). Material on mechanization covering the early years of the century is meager, but Lynn W. Ellis and Edward A. Rumely, *Power and the Plow* (Garden City: Doubleday, Page & Company, 1911), and Walter F. Handschin, J. B. Andrews, and Emil Rauchenstein, "The Horse and the Tractor," *University of Illinois Agricultural Experiment Station, Bulletin* No. 231, 1921, are useful. Edwin G. Nourse, *American Agriculture and the European Market* (New York: The Macmillan Company, 1924), is adequate for the prewar years.

Besides the studies of True, already cited, the following will be useful on the history of agriculture, particularly the research and experimentation: T. Swann Harding, *Two Blades of Grass* (Norman: University of Oklahoma Press, 1947); Leland O. Howard, *Fighting the Insects* (New York: The Macmillan Company, 1933); David G. Fairchild, *Exploring for Plants* (New York: The Macmillan Company, 1930) and *The World Was My Garden* (New York: Charles Scribner's Sons, 1938); Joseph C. Bailey, *Seaman A. Knapp* (New York: Columbia University Press, 1945); and Harvey W. Wiley, *An Autobiography* (Indianapolis: The Bobbs-Merrill Company, 1930). The work of David F. Houston, Secretary of Agriculture, 1913–1920, is told in David F. Houston and Helen Basil, *Eight Years with Wilson's Cabinet* (2 vols., New York: Doubleday, Doran & Company, 1926). On education see Clarence B. Smith and Meredith C. Wilson, *The Agricultural Extension System in the United States* (New York: John Wiley & Sons, 1930), and Whitney H. Shepardson, *Agricultural Education in the United States* (New York: The Macmillan Company, 1929).

On farm cooperatives, besides the two Department of Agriculture studies by Jesness and Kerr, and by Ellsworth, cited in footnotes, information is available in Horace C. Taylor, *Outline of Agricultural Economics* (New York: The Macmillan Company, rev. ed., 1931); Fred A. Shannon, *The Farmer's Last Frontier;* Gordon S. Watkins, *Cooperation,* University of Illinois *Bulletin,* Vol. XVIII, No. 28 (Urbana: University of Illinois Press, March, 1921); and Edwin G. Nourse and Joseph G. Knapp, *The Cooperative Marketing of Livestock* (Washington: The Brookings Institution, 1931).

Farm tenancy has been ably discussed in Department of Agriculture studies, cited in the footnotes. Besides these the following should be noted: Emanuel A. Goldenweiser and Leon E. Truesdell, *Farm Tenancy in the United States* (U.S. Bureau of the Census, *Census Monograph* IV, Washington: Government Printing Office, 1924); Benjamin H. Hubbard, "Farm Tenancy in 1920," *Journal of Farm Economics,* Vol. III (October, 1921); William J. Spillman, "The Agricultural Ladder," *American Economic Review,* Vol. IX, No. 1, Supp. (March, 1919); Lawanda F. Cox, "Tenancy in the United States, 1865–1900," *Agricultural History,* Vol. XVIII, No. 3 (July, 1944); and Fred A. Shannon, *The Farmer's Last Frontier.*

Two studies of farm credit by Carl W. Thompson and by Victor N. Valgren and Elmer N. Englebert, cited in footnotes, are essential in this problem. Also useful are Clara Eliot, *The Farmer's Campaign for Credit* (New York: D. Appleton and Company, 1927); Ivan

Wright, *Bank Credit and Agriculture* (New York: McGraw-Hill Book Company, 1922); Myron T. Herrick and R. Ingalls, *Rural Credit, Land and Cooperatives* (New York: D. Appleton and Company, 1915), an early agitator for improved farm credit; and Earl S. Sparks, *History and Theory of Agricultural Credit in the United States* (New York: Thomas Y. Crowell Company, 1932). The following articles should be noted: Jesse E. Pope, "Agricultural Credit in the United States," *Quarterly Journal of Economics*, Vol. XXVIII (August, 1914); Lewis H. Haney, "Farm Credit Conditions in a Cotton State," *American Economic Review*, Vol. IV, No. 1 (March, 1914); and Robert J. Bulkley, "The Federal Farm Loan Act," *Journal of Political Economy*, Vol. XXV, No. 2 (February, 1917).

THE ERA OF REFORM

Efforts to interpret America toward the close of the muckraking period include Herbert D. Croly, *Promise of American Life* (New York: The Macmillan Company, 1909); Walter E. Weyl, *The New Democracy* (New York: The Macmillan Company, 1912); Walter Lippmann, *A Preface to Politics* (New York: M. Kennerley, 1913) and *Drift and Mastery* (New York: M. Kennerley, 1914); and Benjamin P. De Witt, *The Progressive Movement: A Non-Partisan Comprehensive Discussion of Current Tendencies in American Politics* (New York: The Macmillan Company, 1915). See also Lewis Corey, *The Decline of American Capitalism* (New York: Covici, Friede, 1934).

The only full-length history of the muckrakers is Cornelius C. Regier, *The Era of the Muckrakers* (Chapel Hill: University of North Carolina Press, 1932), containing the most complete bibliography of the work of the muckrakers. Louis Filler, *Crusaders for American Liberalism* (New York: Harcourt, Brace and Company, 1939) is the most complete picture of the reform movement as it functioned in the literature of exposure; John Chamberlain, *Farewell to Reform* (New York: Liveright Publishing Corp., 1932), is a pessimistic interpretation of the reforming efforts. How the work of the muckrakers reacted on two reforming political leaders may be seen in Theodore Roosevelt, *Autobiography* (New York: The Macmillan Company, 1913), and Woodrow Wilson, *The New Freedom* (New York: Doubleday, Page & Company, 1914). Harold U. Faulkner, *The Quest for Social Justice* (New York: The Macmillan Company, 1931), is a social history of those years.

The autobiographies or reminiscences of many of the muckrakers and reformers of these years are invaluable: Lincoln Steffens, *Autobiography of Lincoln Steffens* (New York: Harcourt, Brace and Company, 1931); Frederic C. Howe, *Confessions of a Reformer* (New York: Charles Scribner's Sons, 1925); Charles Edward Russell, *Bare Hands and Stone Walls* (New York: Charles Scribner's Sons, 1933); Ida Tarbell, *All in the Day's Work* (New York: The Macmillan Company, 1939); Morris Hillquit, *Loose Leaves from a Busy Life* (New York: The Macmillan Company, 1934); Fremont Older, *My Own Story* (San Francisco: Call Publishing Co., 1919); Brand Whitlock, *Forty Years of It* (New York: D. Appleton and Company, 1914); Tom Loftin Johnson, *My Story* (New York: B. W. Huebsch, 1911); Robert M. La Follette, *La Follette's Autobiography* (Madison, Wis.: Robert M. La Follette Co., 1913); Arthur Henry Young, *Art Young, His Life and Times* (New York: Sheridan House, 1939); Harvey W. Wiley, *An Autobiography* (Indianapolis: The Bobbs-Merrill Company, 1930); William Allen White, *The Autobiography of William Allen White* (New York: The Macmillan Company, 1946); and Gifford Pinchot, *Breaking New Ground* (Harcourt, Brace and Company, 1947).

The background of the income tax agitation is in Sidney Ratner, *American Taxation* (New York: W. W. Norton & Company, 1942) and contemporary history and discussion are in Edwin R. A. Seligman, *The Income Tax* (New York: The Macmillan Company, 1911, rev. ed., 1914), and Delos O. Kinsman, "The Present Period of Income Tax Activity in the United States," *Quarterly Journal of Economics,* Vol. XXXIII (February, 1909). Important on conservation are Charles R. Van Hise, *The Conservation of Natural Resources in the United States* (New York: The Macmillan Company, 1910); *Report of the National Conservation Commission, Senate Document* No. 676, 60 Cong., 2 Sess.; Gifford Pinchot, *The Fight for Conservation* (New York: Doubleday, Page & Company, 1910) and his *Breaking New Ground,* cited above; Roy M. Robbins, *Our Landed Heritage* (Princeton: Princeton University Press, 1942); John Ise, *The United States Forest Policy* (New Haven: Yale University Press, 1924); and Rose M. Stahl, "The Ballinger-Pinchot Controversy," *Smith College Studies in History.* Vol. XI, No. 2 (Northampton, Mass.: January, 1926).

Appendix

BALANCE OF PAYMENTS OF THE UNITED STATES, 1896–1914
(*Units of $1,000*)

	Credit	Debit
Credit Items		
Exports of merchandise and silver	$32,128,126	
Exports of gold	1,219,005	
New capital borrowings from abroad	2,000,000	
Interest payments on American capital invested abroad	760,000	
Freight charges receivable	86,000	
Debit Items		
Imports of merchandise and silver		$22,866,028
Imports of gold		1,392,907
New capital loans by United States		1,000,000
Interest payments on total foreign capital invested in the United States		3,800,000
Tourists' expenditures		3,230,000
Immigrants' remittances		2,850,000 [a]
Freight charges payable		727,000
Insurance premiums, commissions, etc.		570,000
Totals	$36,193,131	$36,435,935

[a] As before, the net money brought by immigrants cannot be reckoned. The sums shown to the officials average about $25, which for 14,493,000 immigrants makes about $300,000,000.

Source: Charles J. Bullock, John H. Williams and Rufus S. Tucker, "The Balance of Trade in the United States," *Review of Economic Statistics,* Prelim. Vol. I (July, 1919), 231–232.

INCREASE OF POPULATION BY SECTIONS

Sections	Population				Per Cent Increase		
	1890	1900	1910	1920	1890–1900	1900–1910	1910–1920
New England	4,700,749	5,592,017	6,552,681	7,400,909	19.0	17.2	12.9
Middle Atlantic	12,706,220	15,454,678	19,315,892	22,261,144	21.6	25	15.2
East North Central	13,478,305	15,985,581	18,250,621	21,475,543	18.6	14.2	17.7
West North Central	8,932,112	10,347,423	11,194,895	12,544,249	15.8	12.5	7.8
South Atlantic	8,857,922	10,443,480	12,194,895	13,990,272	17.9	16.8	14.7
East South Central	6,429,154	7,547,757	8,409,901	8,893,307	17.4	11.4	5.7
West South Central	4,740,983	6,532,290	8,784,534	10,242,224	37.8	34.5	16.6
Mountain	1,213,935	1,674,657	2,633,517	3,336,101	38.0	57.3	26.7
Pacific	1,888,334	2,416,692	4,192,304	5,566,871	28.0	73.5	32.8

Source: U.S. Bureau of the Census, Abstract of the Fifteenth Census of the United States, 1920 (Washington: Government Printing Office, 1923), pp. 10–12.

OCCUPATIONS OF AMERICAN WORKERS

Groups	1890	Per Cent	1900	Per Cent	1910	Per Cent	1920	Per Cent
Farm laborers a	3,004,061	13.2	4,410,877	15.2	6,143,998	16.1	4,178,673	10.0
Farmers b	5,370,181	23.6	5,770,738	19.8	6,229,161	16.3	6,463,708	15.5
Proprietors and officials c	1,347,329	5.9	1,811,715	6.2	2,879,023	7.5	3,168,418	7.6
Professional d	1,114,507	4.9	1,565,686	5.4	2,074,992	5.4	2,760,190	6.6
Lower salaried e	965,852	4.3	1,329,928	4.6	2,393,620	6.3	3,985,306	9.6
Servants	1,454,791	6.4	1,453,677	5.0	1,572,225	4.1	1,270,946	3.1
Industrial wage earners	7,360,442	32.4	10,263,569	35.3	14,556,979	38.2	17,648,072	42.4
Unclassified f	2,118,498	9.3	2,467,043	8.5	2,317,538	6.0	2,138,971	5.1
Total	22,735,661	...	29,073,233	...	38,167,336	...	41,614,971	...

a Members of the family working on the home farm and laborers working out.

b Farm owners and tenants.

c Managers, proprietors, officials, bankers and brokers, real-estate and insurance agents, commercial travelers, hucksters and peddlers, restaurant, hotel, and saloon keepers, etc.

d Not only the groups regularly referred to as professional but public-service workers of local, state, and federal governments.

e Foremen, overseers, bookkeepers, stenographers, agents and collectors, sales agents, ticket and express agents, mail carriers, chauffeurs and other groups.

f Largely occupations for which the census designation does not distinguish between proprietor and workman.

Sources: Alvin H. Hansen, "Industrial Class Alignments in the United States," *Quarterly Publication of the American Statistical Association*, XVII, No. 132 (December, 1920), 417–422 and "Industrial Classes in the United States in 1920," *Journal of the American Statistical Association*, XVIII, No. 140 (December, 1922), 503–506.

RANK OF LEADING INDUSTRIES, 1900, 1914, AND 1919

Rank	Industry (1900)	Value of Products (in thousands)	Industry (1914)	Value of Products (in thousands)
1	Iron and steel, steel works and rolling mills	$803,968	Slaughtering and meat packing	$1,651,965
2	Slaughtering and meat packing	790,253	Iron and steel, steel works and rolling mills	918,665
3	Foundry and machine-shop products	644,991	Flour mill and gristmill products	877,680
4	Lumber and timber products	566,622	Foundry and machine-shop products	866,545
5	Flour mill and gristmill products	560,719	Lumber and timber products	715,310
6	Clothing, men's	415,256	Cotton goods	676,569
7	Printing and publishing, newspapers and periodicals	347,055	Cars and general shop construction and repairs by steam railroad companies	510,041
8	Cotton manufactures	339,200	Automobiles	503,230
9	Carpentering	316,102	Boots and shoes	501,760
10	Woolen manufactures	296,990	Printing and publishing, newspapers and periodicals	405,906
11	Boots and shoes	261,029	Bread and other bakery products	491,893
12	Sugar and molasses refining	240,970	Clothing, women's	437,888
13	Liquors, malt	237,270	Clothing, men's	458,211
14	Cars and general shop construction and repairs by steam railroad companies	218,114	Smelting and refining copper	444,022
15	Leather, tanned and finished	204,038	Liquors, malt	442,149

Sources: Figures for 1900 from U.S. Bureau of the Census, *Abstract of the Twelfth Census of the United States* (Washington: Government Printing Office, 1904), p. 322; for 1914 from Bureau of the Census, *Abstract of the Census of Manufactures,* 1914

Industry (*1919*)	Value of Products (*in thousands*)
Slaughtering and meat packing	$4,246,291
Iron and steel, steel works and rolling mills	2,828,902
Automobiles	2,387,903
Foundry and machine-shop products	2,289,251
Cotton goods	2,125,272
Flour mill and gristmill products	2,052,434
Petroleum	1,632,533
Ship building	1,456,490
Lumber and timber products	1,387,471
Cars and general shop construction and repairs by steam railroad companies	1,279,235
Clothing, women's	1,208,543
Clothing, men's	1,162,986
Boots and shoes	1,155,041
Bread and other bakery products	1,151,896
Woolen and worsted goods	1,065,434

(Washington: Government Printing Office, 1917), Table 220, pp. 516 ff.; for 1919 from Bureau of the Census, *Abstract of the Census of Manufactures,* 1919 (Washington: Government Printing Office, 1923), Table 9, pp. 19–20.

MANUFACTURES: Classified According to Size of Establishment, as Measured by the Value of Products, Calendar Years 1904, 1909, 1914, and 1919

Value of Product and Year	Establishments		Wage Earners		Products		Added by Manufacture	
	Number	Per cent of total	Average Number	Per cent of total	Value	Per cent of total	Value	Per cent of total
Less than $5,000								
1904	71,147	32.9	106,353	1.9	$176,128,212	1.2	$114,781,124	1.8
1909	93,349	34.8	142,430	2.2	222,463,847	1.1	144,246,008	1.7
1914	97,061	35.2	129,623	1.8	233,381,081	1.0	151,739,764	1.5
1919	65,485	22.6	45,813	0.5	167,085,044	0.3	106,653,362	0.4
$5,000 and less than $20,000								
1904	72,791	33.7	419,466	7.7	$751,047,759	5.1	$424,129,643	6.7
1909	86,988	32.4	470,006	7.1	904,645,664	4.4	509,907,934	6.0
1914	87,931	31.9	429,037	6.1	905,693,168	3.7	507,430,875	5.1
1919	87,440	30.1	249,722	2.7	945,602,857	1.5	539,698,109	2.2
$20,000 and less than $100,000								
1904	48,096	22.2	1,027,047	18.8	$2,129,257,883	14.4	$1,090,271,887	17.3
1909	57,270	21.3	1,090,449	16.5	2,544,426,711	12.3	1,258,347,991	14.8
1914	56,814	20.6	999,510	14.2	2,550,229,411	10.5	1,238,879,430	12.5
1919	77,911	26.9	793,528	8.7	3,571,283,301	5.7	1,474,729,538	7.0

$100,000 and less than $1,000,000							
1904	22,246	10.3	2,515,064	46.0	$6,109,012,538	41.3	$2,782,641,883	44.2
1909	27,824	10.4	2,896,532	43.8	7,946,935,255	38.4	3,572,746,038	41.9
1914	30,166	11.0	3,002,071	42.7	8,763,070,135	36.2	3,888,094,982	39.4
1919	48,856	16.9	2,834,776	31.2	15,443,227,140	24.8	7,035,589,748	28.1
$1,000,000 and over							
1904	1,900	0.9	1,400,453	25.6	$5,628,456,171	38.9	$1,881,870,216	29.3
1909	3,060	1.1	2,015,629	30.5	9,053,580,393	43.8	3,044,043,021	35.7
1914	3,819	1.4	2,476,006	35.2	11,794,060,929	48.6	4,092,200,842	41.4
1919	10,413	3.6	5,172,533	56.9	42,290,880,431	67.8	15,612,027,733	62.3
Total							
1904	216,180	100.0	5,468,383	100.0	$14,793,902,563	100.0	$6,293,694,753	100.0
1909	268,491	100.0	6,615,046	100.0	20,672,051,870	100.0	8,529,260,992	100.0
1914	275,791	100.0	7,036,247	100.0	24,246,434,724	100.0	9,878,345,893	100.0
1919	290,105	100.0	9,096,372	100.0	62,418,078,773	100.0	25,041,698,490	100.0

Source: Statistical Abstract of the United States, 1922, p. 198.

UNEMPLOYMENT

Year	Estimated Percentage of Unemployment in Manufacturing and Transportation	Estimated Percentage of Unemployment in Manufacturing, Transportation, Building Trades, and Mining
1897	14.5	18.0
1898	13.9	16.9
1899	7.7	10.5
1900	6.3	10.0
1901	4.5	7.5
1902	3.5	6.8
1903	3.5	7.0
1904	7.1	10.1
1905	4.0	6.7
1906	3.5	5.9
1907	3.5	6.9
1908	12.0	16.4
1909	5.1	8.9
1910	3.7	7.2
1911	5.6	9.4
1912	4.0	7.0
1913	5.4	8.2
1914	12.9	16.4
1915	12.4	15.5
1916	3.5	6.3
1917	3.5	6.0

Sources: Paul H. Douglas and Aaron Director, *The Problem of Unemployment* (New York: The Macmillan Company, 1934), pp. 25–28, and Paul H. Douglas, *Real Wages in the United States* (Boston: Houghton Mifflin Company, 1930), p. 445.

AMERICAN UNIONS, 1897–1917

Year	Membership of AFL	Estimated Membership of All Unions
1897	264,825	447,000
1898	278,016	500,700
1899	349,422	611,000
1900	548,321	868,500
1901	787,537	1,124,700
1902	1,024,399	1,375,900
1903	1,465,800	1,913,900
1904	1,676,200	2,072,700
1905	1,494,300	2,022,300
1906	1,454,200	1,958,700
1907	1,538,970	2,122,800
1908	1,586,885	2,130,600
1909	1,482,872	2,047,400
1910	1,562,112	2,184,200
1911	1,761,835	2,382,800
1912	1,770,145	2,483,500
1913	1,996,004	2,753,400
1914	2,020,671	2,716,900
1915	1,946,347	2,607,700
1916	2,072,702	2,808,000
1917	2,371,434	3,104,600

Sources: The membership figures of the AFL are from the *Report of the Fifty-third Annual Convention of the American Federation of Labor,* 1933 (Washington: Judd & Detweiler, 1933), p. 33; the estimates of all unions are from Leo Wolman, *The Growth of American Trade Unions, 1880–1923* (New York: National Bureau of Economic Research, 1924), p. 33.

RURAL POPULATION

Year	Total Population (*in millions*)	Rural Population	Rural Population (*per cent of total*)	Increase in Percentage	
				Total	Rural
1890	62.9	40.8	64.9	25.5	13.4
1900	76.0	45.8	60.3	20.7	12.2
1910	92.0	50.0	54.3	21.0	9.0
1920	105.7	51.6	48.8	14.9	3.2

Source: Sixteenth Census: Agriculture, 1940, III, p. 33. The figures on rural population in the third column of this table are revisions of those in previous census reports and do not agree in detail with those on page 96.

FARMS AND ACREAGE

Year	Total Number of Farms (*in millions*)	Per Cent of Increase	Acres (*in millions*)	Per Cent of Total Area in Farms
1890	4.6	13.9	623.2	32.7
1900	5.7	25.7	838.6	44.1
1910	6.36	10.9	878.8	46.2
1920	6.4	1.4	955.9	50.2

Sources: Sixteenth Census: Agriculture, 1940, III, 33 and A. W. Zelomek and Irving Mark, "Historical Prospectus for Post-War Agricultural Forecasts: 1870–1940," *Rural Sociology* X, No. 1 (March, 1945), 51.

AVERAGE ANNUAL FARM PRODUCTION
(*In millions of bushels, bales, or dollars*)

Year	Corn		Wheat		Cotton	
	Bushels	Value	Bushels	Value	Bales	Value
1901–1905 ...	2,529.1	$1,113.7	647.8	$483.1	10,801	$485.6
1906–1910 ...	2,735.5	1,451.3	664.3	580.0	11,847	658.9
1911–1915 ...	2,609.6	1,724.7	801.1	712.0	14,167	729.2
1916–1920 ...	2,704.8	3,347.8	790.8	1,526.2	11,918	1,468.0

Sources: Statistical Abstract of the United States, 1941, pp. 739–741.

FARM PROPERTIES

Year	Total (*millions of dollars*)	Per Cent Increase	Land and Buildings (*millions of dollars*)	Per Cent Increase	Implements and Machinery (*millions of dollars*)	Per Cent Increase
1890	$16,082	32	$13,279	30.2	$494	21.6
1900	20,228	25.8	16,615	25.1	750	51.7
1910	40,838	101.9	34,801	109.5	1,265	68.7
1920	77,924	90.8	66,316	90.6	3,594	184.1

Sources: Sixteenth Census: Agriculture, 1940, III, 35.

Index

BETHANY
COLLEGE
LIBRARY

DISCARD